EYEWITNESS TRAVEL

THAILAND

D0253785

DK

LONDON, NEW YORK,
MELBOURNE, MUNICH AND DELHI
www.dk.com

PROJECT EDITOR Rosalyn Thiro
ART EDITORS Ian Midson, David Rowley
EDITORS Jonathan Cox, Marcus Hardy, Tim Hollis,
Lesley McCave, Sean O'Connor
US EDITORS Mary Sutherland, Michael Wise
DESIGNERS Susan Blackburn, Des Hemsley,
Tim Mann, Malcolm Parchment, Adrian Waite
MAP CO-ORDINATORS Emily Green, David Pugh
RESEARCHER Warangkana Nibhatsukit

CONTRIBUTORS
Philip Cornwel-Smith, Andrew Forbes, Tim Forsyth, Rachel Harrison, David
Henley, John Hoskin, Gavin Pattison, Jonathan Rigg, Sarah Rooney, Ken Scott

PHOTOGRAPHERS
Philip Blenkinsop, Stuart Isett, Kim Sayer, Michael Spencer

ILLUSTRATORS
Stephen Conlin, Gary Cross, Richard Draper,
Roger Hutchins, Chris Orr & Assocs, John Woodcock

Printed and bound by South China Printing Co. Ltd., China

First American Edition, 1997
**Reprinted with revisions 1999, 2000, 2001, 2002, 2004, 2006,
2008, 2010, 2012**

12 13 14 15 10 9 8 7 6 5 4 3 2 1

Published in the United States by:
Dorling Kindersley Limited, 80 Strand,
London, WC2R 0RL, UK

Copyright © 1997, 2012 Dorling Kindersley Limited, London

A catalog record for this book is available from the Library of Congress.

ISSN 1542-1554
ISBN 978-0-7566-85621

Transliteration of Thai words in this book mostly follows the General System
recommended by the Thai Royal Institute, but visitors will
encounter many variant spellings in Thailand.

THROUGHOUT THIS BOOK, FLOORS ARE REFERRED TO IN ACCORDANCE
WITH EUROPEAN USAGE, I.E. THE "FIRST FLOOR" IS ONE FLOOR UP.

Front cover main image: Wat Mahathat Sukhothai Historical Park

MIX
Paper from
responsible sources
FSC
www.fsc.org   FSC™ C018179

**The information in every
DK Eyewitness Travel Guide is checked regularly.**
Every effort has been made to ensure that this book is as up-to-date
as possible at the time of going to press. Some details, however,
such as telephone numbers, opening hours, prices, gallery hanging
arrangements and travel information are liable to change. The
publishers cannot accept responsibility for any consequences arising
from the use of this book, nor for any material on third party websites,
and cannot guarantee that any website address in this book will be
a suitable source of travel information. We value the views and
suggestions of our readers very highly. Please write to: Publisher,
DK Eyewitness Travel Guides, Dorling Kindersley, 80 Strand,
London WC2R 0RL, UK, or email: travelguides@dk.com.

CONTENTS

HOW TO USE
THIS GUIDE 6

Lakshman and Sita, characters
from the Ramakien

INTRODUCING
THAILAND

DISCOVERING
THAILAND 10

PUTTING THAILAND
ON THE MAP 14

A PORTRAIT OF
THAILAND 20

THAILAND
THROUGH THE YEAR 48

THE HISTORY OF
THAILAND 52

BANGKOK

INTRODUCING
BANGKOK 72

OLD CITY 76

CHINATOWN 94

Cho fas, Wat Pan Tao in Chiang Mai

◁ The *chedis* of Wat Chong Klang reflected in the tranquil waters of Chong Kham Lake, Mae Hong Son

Hat Maenam, a beach on Ko Samui in the Gulf of Thailand

DUSIT **100**

DOWNTOWN **110**

THON BURI **122**

FARTHER AFIELD **130**

SHOPPING IN
BANGKOK **138**

ENTERTAINMENT IN
BANGKOK **142**

STREET FINDER **144**

THE CENTRAL PLAINS

INTRODUCING THE
CENTRAL PLAINS
158

SOUTH CENTRAL
PLAINS **164**

NORTH CENTRAL
PLAINS **186**

NORTHERN THAILAND

INTRODUCING
NORTHERN THAILAND
204

NORTHWEST
HEARTLAND **212**

FAR NORTH **238**

NORTHEAST THAILAND

INTRODUCING
NORTHEAST THAILAND
262

KHORAT PLATEAU **268**

MEKONG RIVER
VALLEY **282**

THE GULF OF THAILAND

INTRODUCING THE
GULF OF THAILAND **306**

EASTERN SEABOARD **312**

WESTERN SEABOARD **324**

SOUTHERN THAILAND

INTRODUCING
SOUTHERN THAILAND
344

UPPER ANDAMAN
COAST **352**

DEEP SOUTH
374

TRAVELERS' NEEDS

WHERE TO STAY **392**

WHERE TO EAT **422**

SHOPPING IN
THAILAND **450**

ENTERTAINMENT IN
THAILAND **458**

OUTDOOR ACTIVITIES
& SPECIAL INTERESTS
462

SURVIVAL GUIDE

PRACTICAL
INFORMATION **474**

TRAVEL INFORMATION
490

GENERAL INDEX **498**

ACKNOWLEDGMENTS
522

PHRASE BOOK
524

The Khmer
shrine at
Phimai

HOW TO USE THIS GUIDE

This guide helps you get the most from your vacation in Thailand. It provides detailed practical information and expert recommendations. *Introducing Thailand* maps the country and sets it in its historical and cultural context. The five regional chapters, plus *Bangkok*, describe important sights, using maps, pictures, and illustrations. Features cover topics from architecture and crafts to wildlife and sports. Hotel and restaurant recommendations are found in *Travelers' Needs*. The *Survival Guide* has information on everything from transportation to personal safety.

BANGKOK

The center of Bangkok has been divided into five sight-seeing areas. Each has its own chapter, which opens with a list of the sights described. The *Farther Afield* section covers the best sights outside the center. All sights are numbered and plotted on an area map. The information for each sight follows the map's numerical order, making sights easy to locate within the chapter.

All pages relating to Bangkok have red thumb tabs.

Sights at a Glance lists the chapter's sights by category: *Wats and Palaces*; Museums and Monuments; Parks and Districts; Markets and Notable Roads.

1 Area Map
For easy reference, the sights are numbered and located on a map. Sights in the city center are also marked on the Street Finder on pages 148–55.

A locator map shows where you are in relation to other areas of the city center.

2 Street-by-Street Map
This gives a bird's-eye view of the key areas in each chapter.

Stars indicate the sights that no visitor should miss.

A suggested route for a walk is shown in red.

3 Detailed Information
The sights in Bangkok are described individually. Addresses, telephone numbers, opening hours, and other practical information are also provided. The key to the symbols used is on the back flap of the book.

1 Introduction
The landscape and character of each region is outlined here, showing how the area has developed and what it has to offer the visitor today.

THAILAND AREA BY AREA

Apart from Bangkok, Thailand has been divided into ten regions, each of which has a separate chapter. The most interesting towns and places to visit have been numbered on a *Regional Map*.

Each area of Thailand can be identified quickly by its color coding, shown on the inside front cover.

2 Regional Map
This shows the main road network and gives an illustrated overview of the whole region. All entries are numbered, and there are also useful tips on getting around the region by car, train, and other forms of transportation.

3 Detailed Information
All the important towns and other places to visit are described individually. They are listed in order, following the numbering on the Regional Map. Within each entry, there is detailed information on important buildings and other sights.

Story boxes explore related topics.

For all the top sights, a Visitors' Checklist provides the practical information you need to plan your visit.

4 Thailand's Top Sights
These are given one or more full pages. Three-dimensional illustrations reveal the layouts and interiors of historic monuments. Interesting town and city centers are given street-by-street maps, featuring individual sights.

INTRODUCING THAILAND

DISCOVERING THAILAND 10–13
PUTTING THAILAND ON THE MAP 14–19
A PORTRAIT OF THAILAND 20–47
THAILAND THROUGH THE YEAR 48–51
THE HISTORY OF THAILAND 52–69

DISCOVERING THAILAND

Thailand's wide range of activities and attractions makes it the premier tourist destination in Southeast Asia. From sun-soaked beaches in the south, to hill-tribe villages in the mountains of the north, the country has an astounding number of beautiful locations, many protected as national monuments. Its main destinations, such as Bangkok,

A lotus flower, symbol of purity

Chiang Mai, and Phuket, offer a heady mix of temples, markets, shops, and restaurants. Energetic visitors are also well catered for, with diving, kayaking, rock climbing, elephant riding, and trekking just a few of the exciting activities on offer. The following four pages are designed to help visitors pinpoint the highlights of each fascinating region.

Praying at the Erawan Shrine *(see p118)* under the tracks of the Skytrain

BANGKOK

- Glittering temples
- Canals and floating markets
- Upscale shopping malls
- Sizzling nightlife

Bangkok is a city of contrasts, with soaring skyscrapers next to tin-roofed shacks, and temples decorated with colored-glass mosaics snuggled up beside state-of-the-art boutiques. The city's most unmissable sight is the **Grand Palace and Wat Phra Kaeo**, or Emerald Buddha Temple *(see pp80–5)*, full of beautiful art and architecture.

A good way to get a feel for the way the city used to be is to take a boat tour of the canals that fan off from the west bank of the Chao Phraya River *(see pp74–5)*. A trip to a floating market is an essential part of any visit to Bangkok and shows how virtually all commerce in the kingdom was once waterborne.

However, many visitors are more interested in Bangkok's modern side, spending hours in the city's shopping malls or sprawling markets in search of a bargain *(see pp138–9)*. After dark, the city comes into its own, with sensational cuisine served up in exotic settings, and music, cabaret, and the latest international sounds playing in dimly lit discos.

SOUTH CENTRAL PLAINS

- The ruins of Ayutthaya
- Khao Yai and Erawan national parks
- The "Death Railway" at Kanchanaburi
- Crossing into Myanmar (Burma) via the Three Pagodas Pass

Forming part of Thailand's "rice bowl," the South Central Plains are largely agricultural, with rice paddies as far as the eye can see. The main cultural attraction is the ancient city

of **Ayutthaya** *(see pp176–81)*, which was the capital of Siam for about 400 years. The remains of temples like Wat Phra Si Sanphet and Wat Phra Mahathat give an idea of the splendor of the site in the 16th century. Many people visit the city on a day trip from Bangkok, but history buffs should stay a little longer to explore some of the outlying temples. A little farther north, the town of **Lop Buri** *(see pp174–5)* offers several attractive monuments, including King Narai's Palace.

Hilly areas on the western and eastern fringes of the region feature national parks. To the east lies **Khao Yai National Park** *(see pp184–5)* and, to the west, **Erawan National Park** *(see p169)*, with the turquoise waters of the Erewan falls.

The laid-back town of **Kanchanaburi** *(see pp170–71)*, famous as home of the bridge over the Khwae Yai River, is popular for its museums and war cemeteries, as well as for

The glistening Erawan falls at Erawan National Park

A monk praying at Wat Si Chum, part of Sukhothai Historical Park

its proximity to several national parks. Adventurous travelers can continue on from here to the **Three Pagodas Pass** *(see p168)* and into Myanmar.

NORTH CENTRAL PLAINS

- **Splendidly restored temples at Sukhothai Historical Park**
- **Kamphaeng Phet and Si Satchanalai-Chalieng**
- **Burmese influences at Mae Sot**
- **Birdwatching at Umphang Wildlife Sanctuary**

The main attraction of this region is the ancient city of **Sukhothai** *(see pp194–5)*, which pre-dated Ayutthaya as the capital of Siam. The well-preserved ruins, which include more than 40 temple complexes, are set over a wide historical park and are worth exploring, since the art and architecture of this period are considered the pinnacle of Thai creative expression.

The nearby towns of **Kamphaeng Phet** *(see pp192–3)* to the southwest and **Si Satchanalai** *(see pp198–9)* to the north are rich in ancient monuments and huge stone Buddhas.

Phitsanulok *(see p201)* is the region's largest town, and its main attraction is the famous Buddha image in Wat Phra Si Rattana Mahathat. Smaller but more interesting is the town of **Mae Sot**

(see p190), near the Myanmar border, where both the temples and the food have strong Burmese influences.

Also near the Myanmar border is the wildlife sanctuary of **Umphang** *(see p191)*, which is rich in bird life and features Thi Lo Su, Thailand's highest and most dramatic waterfall.

NORTHWEST HEARTLAND

- **Vibrant Chiang Mai**
- **Beautiful Wat Phra That Lampang Luang**
- **Trekking to hill-tribe villages**
- **Doi Inthanon, Thailand's highest mountain**

The Northwest Heartland of Thailand is popular with visitors because of its wealth of attractions and activities. The ancient city of **Chiang Mai** *(see pp224–7)* captivates with its crumbling walls and moat around the old city; its fledgling modernity; countless temples, including **Wat Phra That Doi Suthep** *(see pp222–3)* on the mountain behind the city; and local crafts.

Perhaps the most famous temple in the region is **Wat Phra That Lampang Luang** *(see pp234–5)*, near Lampang. Some parts of this graceful *wat* date back to the 1400s.

The Northwest Heartland is ideal for trekking to hill-tribe villages or participating in one of many adventure sports: rock climbing, white-water rafting and kayaking, mountain biking, caving, and elephant riding. Cookery,

massage, and meditation courses are also popular.

Several national parks in the region offer log-cabin accommodations and forest-walk trails. **Doi Inthanon National Park** *(see pp230–31)*, centered around Thailand's highest mountain, attracts many unusual species of birds in the cool winter months.

FAR NORTH

- **The Golden Triangle**
- **The ancient city of Chiang Saen**
- **Wat Phumin's 19th-century murals**

Chiang Rai *(see pp250–51)*, the biggest town in the region, is the starting point for adventures in the once renowned **Golden Triangle** *(see pp246–7)*. A good road network makes it easy to take in several of the main sights. The village of **Sop Ruak** *(see p248)* is always busy with tour buses pausing to take pictures where the borders of three countries (Thailand, Myanmar, and Laos) converge; and the bustling border town of **Mae Sai** *(see p246)* marks the country's northernmost point.

To the east are **Chiang Saen** *(see pp248–9)*, home to evocative temple ruins dating back more than 700 years, and **Nan** *(see pp254–5)*, which features a fascinating museum and the lovely **Wat Phumin** *(see pp256–7)*, with its well-preserved murals.

A hiking trail in the forests of Doi Inthanon National Park

KHORAT PLATEAU

- Khmer temples at Phimai and Phnom Rung
- Ancient artifacts at Ban Chiang
- Surin Elephant Roundup
- Yasothon Rocket Festival

This remote area in the northeast offers an appealing mix of Khmer temples, colorful festivals, and silk-weaving villages. The main town of **Khorat** *(see pp274–5)* is the best base from which to visit the Khmer temples at **Phimai** *(see pp276–7)* and **Phnom Rung** *(see pp280–81)*. Both of these temples have been carefully restored.

At the northern edge of the plateau, tiny **Ban Chiang** *(see p272)* is home to one of Southeast Asia's major archaeological sites; the National Museum here has a collection of precious bronze-ware and ceramics dating from 2100 BC to AD 200.

Surin *(see p279)* is famous as a center of silk production but also as the home of the **Elephant Roundup** *(see p50)*. This festival takes place each November and gives the local Suay tribesmen the chance to show off their elephant-handling skills. Another colorful event is the **Rocket Festival** *(see p48)* in **Yasothon** *(see p274)*. Each May, home-made rockets are launched to try to guarantee a good rainy season.

Colorful masks at the festival of Phi Ta Khon in Dan Sai

Skilfully decorated ceramic pots typical of the Ban Chiang area

MEKONG RIVER VALLEY

- Crossing the border to Laos
- Climbing Phu Kradung
- Wat Phra That Phanom
- Exciting Phi Ta Khon Festival

The fertile valley that borders the Mekong River as it skirts northeast Thailand is the perfect place to get a taste of rural Thai life – and of Laos: from **Nong Khai** *(see pp292–3)*, it is just a short trip across the river to the Lao capital **Vientiane** *(see pp294–5)*.

Several national parks in this region offer excellent trekking territory, especially **Phu Kradung** *(see pp286–7)*, a magical plateau dotted with waterfalls in the northwest of the region.

The Mekong River Valley's religious monuments show a strong influence from nearby Laos, in particular **Wat Phra That Phanom** *(see p297)*, where the gold decoration on the stupa is an especially striking feature.

As with the Khorat Plateau, unusual festivals show the locals' love of fun, none more so than the **Phi Ta Khon Festival** *(see p49)* in Dan Sai, near **Loei** *(see p289)*. Each June, young men dress up as spirits, complete with colorful scary masks, and go around taunting onlookers in a playful manner.

EASTERN SEABOARD

- Pattaya's dual identity
- Chanthaburi's gems
- Koh Samet's sandy beaches
- Diving off Ko Chang

Pattaya *(see p317)* is famed for its buzzing nightlife: it must have more bars than any other similarly-sized Thai town. However, it also attracts families and offers a number of activities such as water sports, not to mention a great choice of restaurants.

Chanthaburi *(see pp320–21)* is a gem-mining town with a rich ethnic mix, including a large Vietnamese community. At weekends, its Gem Quarter is busy with people from all over the world. Within easy reach of the town are three rarely visited national parks *(see pp319–321)* that offer the chance to spot wildlife along the forest trails.

The islands of **Ko Samet** *(see pp318–19)* and **Ko Chang** *(see pp322–3)* offer plenty of opportunities for sun-bathing and swimming. Ko Samet is tiny and has some great beaches on the east coast but, being just a few hours' drive from Bangkok, tends to get crowded at weekends. Ko Chang, Thailand's second-largest island, is an excellent base for divers and has several idyllic, sunset-facing beaches, as well as inland trails to waterfalls.

WESTERN SEABOARD

- White, sandy beaches of Ko Samui
- Pristine Angthong National Marine Park
- Phetchaburi's sights
- National parks for nature lovers

Beaches are the main attraction of this region, with the silky sands of **Ko Samui** (see pp336–8) providing the top draw. Samui's neighbouring islands, **Ko Pha Ngan** (see p339) and **Ko Tao** (see p341), have both achieved fame: the former for its full-moon parties and the latter for its superb dive sites. Another cluster of nearby islands makes up the **Angthong National Marine Park** (see pp340–41).

On the mainland, **Hua Hin** (see p331) enjoys the honour of being Thailand's first-ever beach resort, popularized by the royal family in the 1920s. Just north of Hua Hin, **Cha Am** (see pp330–31) also attracts plenty of weekenders from Bangkok, though the beaches fronting both these towns cannot compare to those on the offshore islands.

Phetchaburi (see pp328–30), at the northern end of the peninsula, is one of the country's longest-inhabited towns and has several beautifully preserved temples and monuments.

Nature enthusiasts might like to check out the region's two national parks: **Kaeng Krachan** (see p330), the largest in the country and little visited, and **Khao Sam Roi Yot** (see p332), literally "Three Hundred Peaks Park," a reference to its distinctive limestone pinnacles.

UPPER ANDAMAN COAST

- Phuket's varied offerings
- Diving off Ko Surin and Ko Similan
- Rock climbing in Krabi
- Trekking in the parks

Visitors flock to the island of **Phuket** (see pp358–63), which is geared up to answer their every need, with luxurious resorts, international restaurants, well-stocked boutiques, and excellent beaches, the latter mostly located on the west coast. From here, few can resist a day trip to **Phangnga Bay** (see pp364–7), where limestone stacks rise sheer from the sea. Phuket is also a good base for divers heading to **Ko Similan** and **Ko Surin** (see p357), which have the country's best dive sites.

This region offers many other idyllic options for sun-seekers. **Ko Phi Phi** (see pp372–3) is famed for its back-to-back horseshoe bays, though it can get crowded.

Krabi (see p371) attracts a younger crowd, particularly rock climbers who find a challenge in the sheer walls of limestone stacks around Railay (see p466).

Limestone stack rising from the sea in Phangnga Bay

At the nearby **Khao Phanom Bencha National Park** (see p370), visitors can trek to two impressive waterfalls; however, the most popular national park in the region is **Khao Sok** (see p356), where trails wind through dramatic scenery and boats can be hired for trips on the reservoir behind the Rachabrapha Dam.

DEEP SOUTH

- Wat Phra Mahathat in Nakhon Si Thammarat
- Historic Songkhla
- Trang's Andaman Islands
- Tarutao's deserted beaches

The Deep South is culturally distinct from the rest of the country, with the majority of the population practicing Islam. Sadly, the actions of separatists have made it a dangerous area, though tourists have not yet been targeted. The towns of **Nakhon Si Thammarat** (see pp378–9) and **Songkhla** (see pp384–5) attract visitors with their interesting museums and ancient temples, especially **Wat Phra Mahathat** (see p378), one of the most sacred temples in the country.

Within easy reach of **Trang** (see pp380–81) is a cluster of islands, including **Ko Muk** and **Ko Kradan** (see p380), where a visitor might find perfect solitude. Farther south, the **Tarutao National Marine Park** (see p386) offers some of the best diving sites in the world and the chance to leave civilization far behind.

One of the golden beaches on the island of Ko Samui

Putting Thailand on the Map

Thailand is located at the heart of Southeast Asia, between the Indian Ocean and the South China Sea. The country covers 513,000 sq km (198,000 sq miles) and has a population of 67 million, the majority of whom are concentrated in the fertile Central Plains and in the capital, Bangkok. The verdant North is mainly mountainous, and towering ranges run along the long western border with Myanmar (Burma). In contrast, the Northeast is a flat, poor, arid region. Much of the eastern border with Laos is defined by the Mekong River. Further south are the hills of northern Cambodia. Thailand's Southern peninsula offers many of the best beaches and islands.

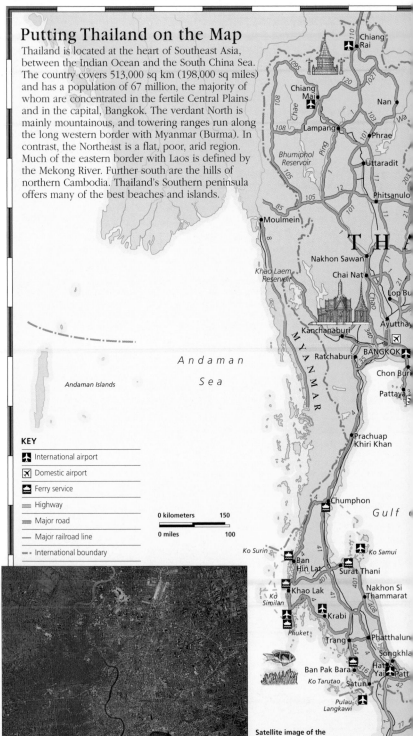

Chiang Rai

Chiang Mai

Nan

Lampang

Phrae

Bhumiphol Reservoir

Uttaradit

Phitsanulo

Moulmein

T H A

Nakhon Sawan

Khao Laem Reservoir

Chai Nat

Lop Bu

Andaman Sea

Kanchanaburi

Ayutthay

BANGKOK

Andaman Islands

Ratchaburi

Chon Bur

Pattaya

MYANMAR

Prachuap Khiri Khan

KEY

✈	International airport
✕	Domestic airport
⛴	Ferry service
▬	Highway
▬	Major road
—	Major railroad line
–·–	International boundary

Chumphon

Gulf

0 kilometers   150

0 miles   100

Ko Surin

Ban Hin Lat

Ko Samui

Surat Thani

Khao Lak

Nakhon Si Thammarat

Ko Similan

Krabi

Phuket

Trang

Phatthalun

Songkhla

Ban Pak Bara

Hat Yai   Patt

Ko Tarutao

Satun

42

Pulau Langkawi

Satellite image of the Greater Bangkok area

Georgetown

Luang
Phabang

LAOS

Mekhong

Vinh

VIENTIANE
Nong Khai

Udon
Thani
Nakhon Phanom

Khon
Kaen

Mukdahan

Banghiang

LAND
Yasothon
Ubon
Ratchathani

Khorat
Surin

Sirindhorn
Reservoir

Dá Nẵng

achin Buri

Siĕmréab

Tônlè
Sab

CAMBODIA

Srêpôk

Qui Nho'n

Chanthaburi

Laem Ngop

Ko Chang

PHNOM
PENH

VIETNAM

Da Ráng

Nha Trang

Hô Chí
Minh

Mekhong

hailand

Satellite image of Southeast Asia

South

China

Sea

Narathiwat

MALAYSIA

SOUTHEAST ASIA

CHINA

SOUTH
KOREA

JAPAN

NEPAL BHUTAN

BANGLA-
DESH

INDIA

MYANMAR

LAOS

THAILAND
Bangkok

VIETNAM

CAMBODIA

PHILIPPINES

SRI
LANKA

MALAYSIA

BRUNEI

SINGAPORE

INDONESIA

PAPUA
NEW
GUINEA

AUSTRALIA

Northern Thailand

An extensive road network covers most of the North, Northeast, and Central Plains of Thailand. Air-conditioned buses run between many of the major towns, and local buses are plentiful. Only in isolated border areas are road links unreliable. The railroad system connects Bangkok to the Central Plains and Chiang Mai. Bangkok, Chiang Mai, and Chiang Rai have international airports, and many major towns are served by domestic flights.

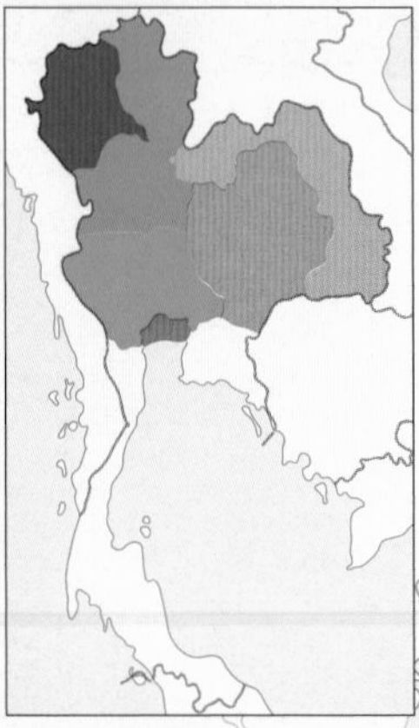

KEY TO AREAS

- Northwest Heartland
- Far North
- North Central Plains
- South Central Plains
- Khorat Plateau
- Mekong River Valley
- Bangkok

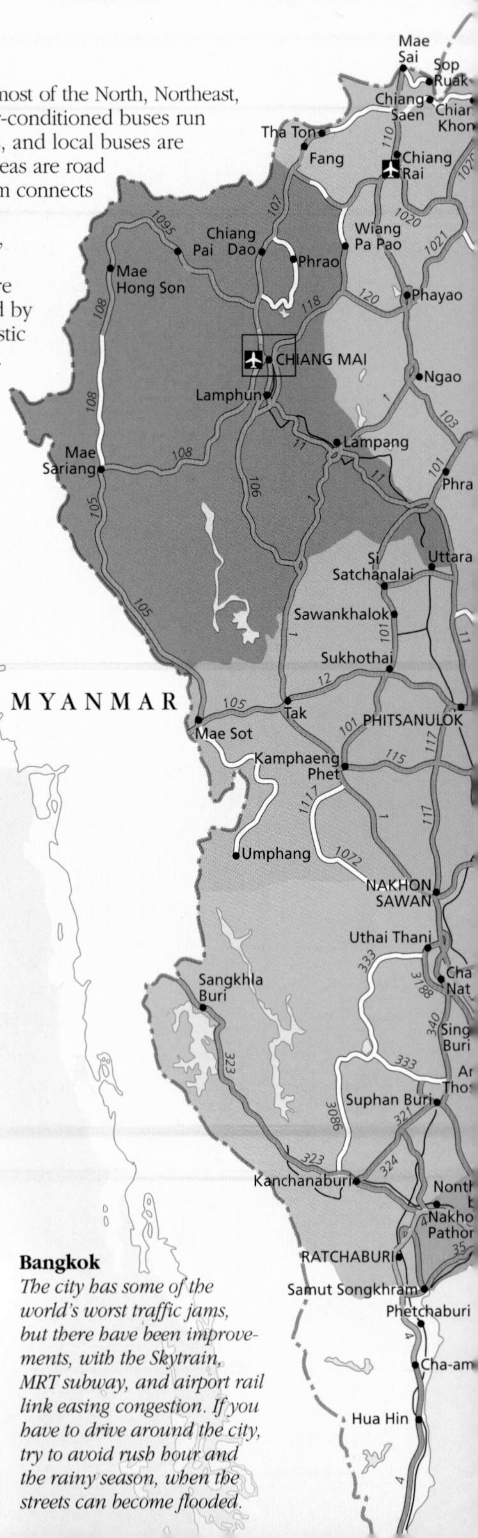

MYANMAR

Mae Sai
Sop Ruak
Chiang Saen
Chiang Khon
Chiar
Tha Ton
Fang
Chiang Rai
Chiang Pai
Dao
Phrao
Wiang Pa Pao
Mae Hong Son
Phayao
CHIANG MAI
Lamphun
Ngao
Mae Sariang
Lampang
Phra
Si Satchanalai
Uttara
Sawankhalok
Sukhothai
Tak
PHITSANULOK
Mae Sot
Kamphaeng Phet
Umphang
NAKHON SAWAN
Uthai Thani
Cha Nat
Sing Buri
Sangkhla Buri
Ar Tho
Suphan Buri
Kanchanaburi
North
Nakho Pathor
RATCHABURI
Samut Songkhram
Phetchaburi
Cha-am
Hua Hin

Bangkok

The city has some of the world's worst traffic jams, but there have been improvements, with the Skytrain, MRT subway, and airport rail link easing congestion. If you have to drive around the city, try to avoid rush hour and the rainy season, when the streets can become flooded.

BANGKOK AND ENVIRONS

Ayutthaya
Don Muang
Nonthaburi
Min Buri
Nakhon Pathom
Suvarnabhumi
Chanthaburi
Samut Prakan

0 kilometers   20

0 miles   10

Chiang Mai

*Chiang Mai has good
road and rail links
with Bangkok and
the rest of Thailand.
The "Super Highway"
connects to the
airport and main
routes into the city.
City roads can
be very congested
at rush hour.*

CHIANG MAI AND ENVIRONS

Doi Saket

*Chiang
Rai*

San
Sai

118

1001

1001

Nam Mae Taeng

107

DOI SUTHEP

1004

1014

1006

Chiang Mai ✈

106

108

11

1147

San
Kamphaeng

Saraphi

1030

*Mae
Sariang*

*Lamphun,
Lampang*

0 kilometers   10

0 miles   5

Nong
Bua

Nan

LAOS

VIENTIANE

212

Chiang
Khan

211

Nong Khai

222

212

Ban
Chiang

Nakhon
Phanom

201

Loei

Udon
Thani ✕

22

22

Renu
Nakhon

103

210

Sakhon
Nakhon

That
Phanom

213

Mukdahan

Phetchabun

KHON
KAEN

209

Kalasin

12

201

Maha
Sarakham

214

Roi Et

Khemmarat

214

Selaphum

202

13

Chaiyaphum

202

Yasothon

225

Bua Yai

23

212

21

205

Suwannaphum

UBON
RATCHATHAN ✕

Khong
Chiam

201

Phimai

Buri
Ram

219

214

226

217

*Sirindhorn
Dam*

KHORAT
(Nakhon Ratchasima)

226

218

219

Surin

24

ri

2

24

214

Phra
Phutthabat

304

Saraburi

CAMBODIA

UTTHAYA

Prachin Buri

Bang Pa-in

319

304

NGKOK ✈

304

33

Aranyaprathet

Chachoengsao

317

o
ang

CHON BURI

344

Si Racha

36

ttaya

Rayong ✕

2

Ban Phe

3

tahip

Chanthaburi

Ko Samet

318

0 kilometers   100

0 miles   50

Laem Ngop

Trat

*Ko
Chang*

KEY

✈ International airport

✕ Domestic airport

⛴ Ferry service

Highway

Major road

Minor road

Railroad line

International border

Southern Thailand

Thailand's long coastline, fine beaches, and idyllic offshore islands are a major attraction for visitors to the Gulf of Thailand and the South. Good-quality roads stretch from the Cambodian border in the east to the Malaysian border in the south and along the western Andaman Sea coast. Air-conditioned buses operate regularly between the main towns. There is one north–south railroad line from Bangkok that passes through, or has connections with, most of the towns on the Gulf of Thailand. The Eastern Seaboard has good road connections with Bangkok, but the railroad line terminates at Sattahip. Ferry services from ports to the main islands are frequent, and it is possible to buy tickets in Bangkok that combine train, bus, and ferry trips. Many towns have regional airports, and Ko Samui, Phuket, Hat Yai, and Krabi are also served by international flights.

KEY TO AREAS

- Eastern Seaboard
- Bangkok
- Western Seaboard
- Upper Andaman Coast
- Deep South

KEY

- ✈ International airport
- ☒ Domestic airport
- ⛴ Ferry service
- Highway
- Major road
- Minor road
- Railroad line
- International border

0 kilometers 100
0 miles 50

CAMBODIA

GULF OF THAILAND

VIETNAM

MALAYSIA

MILEAGE CHART

10 = Distance in miles
10 = Distance in kilometers

BANGKOK										
432 **695**	CHIANG MAI									
487 **785**	112 **180**	CHIANG RAI								
161 **260**	481 **775**	540 **870**	KHORAT							
484 **780**	916 **1475**	972 **1565**	646 **1040**	NAKHON SI THAMMARAT						
233 **375**	208 **335**	258 **415**	283 **455**	717 **1155**	PHITSANULOK					
534 **860**	969 **1560**	1022 **1645**	696 **1120**	209 **336**	770 **1240**	PHUKET				
590 **950**	1022 **1645**	1077 **1735**	751 **1210**	100 **161**	823 **1325**	307 **495**	SONGKHLA			
196 **315**	627 **1010**	683 **1100**	206 **330**	680 **1095**	428 **690**	730 **1175**	786 **1265**	TRAT		
368 **590**	581 **935**	630 **1015**	207 **335**	852 **1375**	373 **600**	903 **1455**	958 **1540**	563 **905**	UBON RATCHATHANI	
351 **565**	476 **770**	526 **850**	189 **305**	835 **1345**	270 **435**	885 **1425**	941 **1515**	546 **880**	248 **400**	UDON THANI

A PORTRAIT OF THAILAND

*S*et within a lush, tropical landscape, Thailand is a theater of cultural and sensual contrasts for the visitor. The long, rich heritage and abundant natural resources of this proud Buddhist nation jostle for space within the dynamism of a country undergoing economic boom and bust. In turns zestful and tranquil, resplendent and subtle, Thailand is always compelling.

Thailand is located in a fertile monsoon belt midway between India and China, the two civilizations that have molded Southeast Asia. But the Thais have long delighted in their distinctive culture. For instance, though the Tai (rather than Thai) ethnic group probably originated in Southern China sometime in the first millennium AD, their tonal language is quite unlike any form of Chinese. Moreover, the elegant Thai script, though derived from that of ancient Southern India, is distinct.

Tuk-tuk

Today, Thailand is a member of the Association of Southeast Asian Nations (ASEAN), though Thais still take pride in a long tradition of independence. Unlike all its immediate neighbors, Myanmar (Burma), Laos, Cambodia, and Malaysia, the country never fell to a European colonial power.

More fundamentally, though, the Thai sense of identity is allied with Theravada Buddhism and the monarchy. Both have been dignified institutions since the Sukhothai period (13th–14th century), an era when the first real Thai kingdom flourished. Indeed, the colors of the modern Thai flag *(thong trai rong)* symbolize the nation (red), the three forces of Buddhism (white), and the monarchy (blue).

Colorful *korlae* fishing boats in the clear waters of Southern Thailand

◁ Young men parading in Old Sukhothai for the annual Loy Krathong Festival

Today, the great majority of Thailand's 63 million inhabitants regard themselves as Thai. Hill tribes are the most obvious ethnic minority groups, but it is the Chinese who form the largest (and most integrated) group. The various peoples live relatively peaceably nowadays, though in 1939, in a wave of nationalism encouraged by Prime Minister Phibun Songkram, the country's name was changed from Siam to Prathet Thai (Thailand), or "land of the Thai people."

Bangkok is a sprawling modern metropolis with a continually evolving skyline

The country is divided into four main regions, and there are many subtle differences between the peoples and dialects of the Central Plains, North, Northeast, and South. Each region also has its own topographical identity. The North is an area of forested mountains, where hill-tribe minorities coexist with mainstream society. In the South, the narrow Kra Peninsula presents a 2,500-km (1,500-mile) coastline with a hilly interior of rainforests and rubber plantations. Malay-Muslim culture is a major influence here.

Between these two extremes are the Central Plains, the cradle of Thai civilization and a fertile, rice-growing region. Near the mouth of the Chao Phraya River, the capital, Bangkok, sprawls ever farther each year. Its palatial splendor can still be discerned, but the city is among the world's most congested and polluted, despite great efforts to clean the air and local rivers. Different again is Northeast Thailand (also widely known as Isan), the poorest part of the country occupying the Khorat Plateau, its eastern border with Laos defined by the Mekong River. In this semiarid region traditional farming communities, many of them Thai-Lao, eke out a subsistence living.

ECONOMIC DEVELOPMENT

Rice and other agricultural crops were long the mainstays of the Thai economy, and farming is still highly respected. From the mid-1980s, however, a concerted export drive triggered an unprecedented economic boom. For several years, Thailand enjoyed double-digit growth and was known as one of Asia's "tiger" economies. Economic growth came to an abrupt halt, however, in a chain of events that began in May 1997 with financial speculation against the Thai *baht*. Flotation

Fisherman on the Mekong, the river defining Northeast Thailand's border

Noodle vendor at Damnoen Saduak Floating Market, a colorful and popular sight near Bangkok

of the *baht* in July pushed the economies of various Asian countries, including Thailand, Indonesia, and South Korea, into crisis.

While Thai politicians blamed everyone from bankers to city-dwellers, the people of Thailand immediately suffered, with large-scale redundancies, pay cuts, and repossessions.

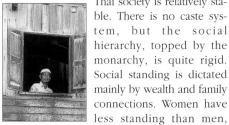

Muslim Thai in Southern Thailand

Thailand has since recovered fully, and Bangkok's skyline is seeing much construction work. Tourism is still the single largest foreign exchange earner. The Tourism Authority of Thailand (TAT) revived the "Amazing Thailand Year," which was a great success in 1998. In 2006 Thailand recorded 13.8 million visitors, and though this figure dropped in 2008, 2010 saw it rise to 16 million. Bangkok and the beach resorts attract most of the visitors, followed by Chiang Mai and the North. Thailand's deluxe hotels and luxurious spa resorts are some of the finest in the world.

Transport infrastructure remains a weak point, resulting in Bangkok's notorious traffic chaos. Commerce and communications are concentrated in Bangkok, with a population of 9.5 million and rising, while the rest of the country remains largely rural.

Raw materials top the country's list of imports, and the leading exports include garments, electrical goods, mechanical equipment, seafood products, rice, rubber, gems, and jewelry.

The environment has taken many blows in the last 50 years, and forest cover has declined from 70 percent of the land to less than 20 percent. Many animal species have lost their habitats and been hunted almost to extinction. However, conservation awareness is increasing, and measures are being taken to preserve what remains of the nation's rich natural bounty.

SOCIETY AND POLITICS

In spite of the pressures of change, Thai society is relatively stable. There is no caste system, but the social hierarchy, topped by the monarchy, is quite rigid. Social standing is dictated mainly by wealth and family connections. Women have less standing than men, despite playing a major role in the economy, mainly as laborers and white-collar workers. However, in 2011, Thailand elected

Elephant in Bangkok, surprisingly not a rare sight

its first female prime minister, Yingluck Shinawatra, sister of deposed PM Thaksin Shinawatra. Elders are always accorded respect within families and in society.

Hierarchy permeates daily life in many ways. The traditional greeting, the *wai*, in which the hands are brought together near the chin, is always initiated by the inferior, and the

Seated Buddha image, one of thousands in Thailand

height of the *wai* reflects the social gap between the parties. If the gap is extreme, inferiors may approach their superiors on their knees. Other rules of etiquette, such as never raising the voice, transcend class. Despite such rules for themselves, Thais are renowned for their tolerance of other cultures and friendliness to visitors. Offense is taken only if there is any perceived disrespect to the king or Buddhism.

There is no criticism of the king in Thailand's press. Constitutional since 1932, the monarchy is revered almost as much as when kings were *chakravatin*, or "king of kings." Kingship and religion are inextricably linked in Thailand. The present monarch, King Bhumibol Adulyadej (Rama IX),

Garland of jasmine, a ubiquitous sight

served as a monk in his youth and presides over some major religious ceremonies. He is the longest-reigning living monarch in the world, having ascended to the throne in 1946, and has won widespread respect for his devotion to Thai welfare and environmental projects.

The monkhood (*sangha*), some 250,000 strong, plays a crucial social role. Most teenage boys become novice monks for a while, which is seen as fortuitous for their families, especially their mothers, as well as a rite of passage. Some enter the monkhood properly later in life and may choose its austere precepts for life. Monks conduct numerous Buddhist rites, ranging from festivals to everyday blessings and other social events. In rural areas, they traditionally play an important role as teachers, a profession that in Thailand is perhaps held higher in regard than anywhere else in the world.

In contrast, politicians are held in far less respect, and the Thai press openly criticizes the running of the country. The economic boom and bust of the 1980s and 1990s exerted considerable pressure on Thai society. The extended family remains important, but it has become an idealized concept espoused by conservative groups. As soon as they are old

Lisu hill-tribe women and children in their colorful traditional clothing

Monks chanting in Pali, the language of Theravada Buddhism

enough, many young people move away from their towns and villages to find work in the city, sending money back to their parents each month.

THAI CULTURE AND ARTS

Thailand's classical arts have developed almost exclusively (and anonymously) in the service of Theravada Buddhism. Accordingly, the best showcase is the *wat*, where traditional architecture, typified by sweeping, multitiered roofs, countless Buddha images and murals, and decorative arts, such as woodcarving, stucco, gilt,

lacquer, colored glass mosaic, and mother-of-pearl inlay, are all used to striking effect.

The literary tradition of Thailand is confined mostly to classic tales, the most important of which is the Ramakien, an ancient moral epic with its origins in the Indian Ramayana. Such sagas provided the narrative content for the once-thriving performing arts, best preserved today in highly stylized classical dance-drama called *khon* and *lakhon*. Thailand's most notable literary figure is the 19th-century poet Sunthorn Phu.

Thai cinema continues to go from strength to strength. In 2002, *Sut Sanaeha* ("Blissfully Yours"), the story of a romance between a Thai woman and an illegal Burmese immigrant, was selected for special consideration at

Lakhon dancers at a Buddhist shrine

the Cannes Film Festival, and the 2008 film *Ploy* was premiered there during Director's Fortnight. The Bangkok International Film Festival was launched in 2002.

On the sports front, Thailand's unique style of kick boxing draws big crowds, while other traditional pastimes range from *takraw,* a game not unlike volleyball, but using the feet, to kite-flying. Numerous colorful festivals, many linked to both Buddhism and the changing seasons, are celebrated with exuberance. Whatever the activity, Thais believe that life should be *sanuk* – "fun." *Sanuk* can be found in all things, from eating – something for which Thais have a passion – to simply going for a stroll with friends.

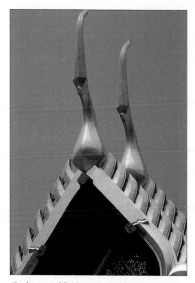
Cho fas, or roof finials, at the Grand Palace, Bangkok

Monsoon Country

The rice cycle, upon which the Thais have long believed their health, wealth, and happiness depends, is governed by the advance and retreat of the monsoon rains. As most people in the kingdom define themselves as *chao na*, rice farmers, the monsoon could be said to govern the cycle of life. This analogy is seen clearly in many Thai beliefs and practices. The rice goddess must be honored before cultivation if the crop is to be bountiful. The rice grain contains a spirit *(kwan)* and is planted in the rainy season to become "pregnant." The Thai word for irrigation *(chon prathan)* translates as "gift of water."

Thailand's pre-eminent crop

The Central Plains *of Thailand enjoy good conditions for wet rice cultivation. The flat paddies become flooded in the rainy season.*

Bundles of rice seedlings ready for transplanting

A "calling for rains" Buddha *image – a standing posture with both arms pointing to the earth – is found in some Northern wats. The rice crop depends on rain.*

Transplanting takes place in the rainy season, when the heavy clay soil is saturated.

Songkran, *or Thai New Year, in April, is a water festival marking the imminent end of the cool, dry season. People celebrate by pouring or throwing water over each other.*

MONSOON SEASONS

"Monsoon" comes from the Arabic *mawsim* (season). It refers to South Asia's seasonal winds (not heavy rain). In Thailand, the southwest monsoon is the rainy season; the northeast monsoon is dry, called the cool season; and between these periods is the hot season.

The southwest monsoon *comes from the Indian Ocean with rain-laden clouds, from about June to October. Most days there are downpours, though Thailand's east coast is fairly dry.*

Flooding in Bangkok at the end of the rainy season

Seedlings transplanted in rows

RAINY SEASON

Flooded paddies

Machinery *has replaced animals on many farms, reflecting the increasing mechanization of the Thai farming industry. However, plowing and cultivating the land is still hard work.*

The main harvest *for lowland wet rice cultivation takes place in the middle of the cool season. Entire families and villages labor in the fields at this busy time, cutting off the golden stalks with sickles.*

Water channel between fields

Seedlings need to be semisubmerged

Threshing *is usually undertaken in the rice fields by the same laborers who have harvested the crop. The stalks are beaten to separate the grain from the chaff. The grain is then dried in the sun.*

TRANSPLANTING

Since most varieties of rice can only propagate in flood conditions, rice seedlings may initially be nurtured in nursery fields, where irrigation can be carefully managed and monitored. Later these seedlings will be transplanted into flooded paddies.

The northeast monsoon *from central Asia usually blows from November to March, bringing relatively cool, dry conditions to Thailand, though rains often affect the east coast.*

Between the two monsoons *the land heats up, creating an area of low pressure above it. Eventually the high pressure over the Indian Ocean moves inland, and the monsoon cycle begins again.*

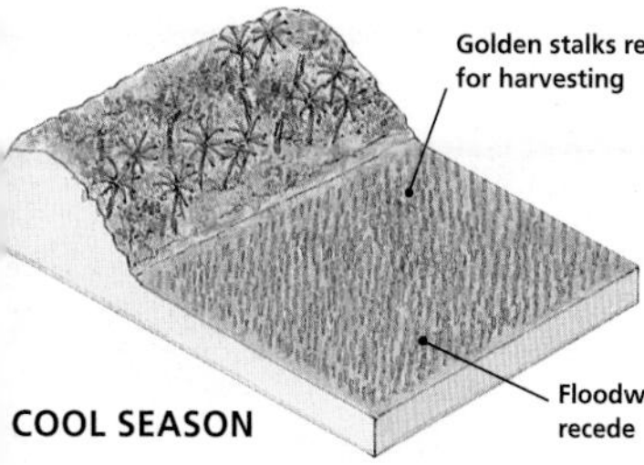

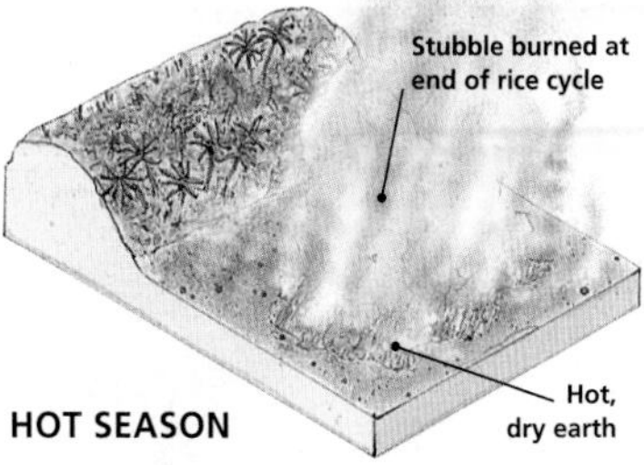

Golden stalks ready for harvesting

Stubble burned at end of rice cycle

COOL SEASON

Floodwaters recede

HOT SEASON

Hot, dry earth

The Landscape and Wildlife of Thailand

Thailand stretches from south of the tropic of Cancer to about 1,000 km (620 miles) north of the equator; its tropical climate is affected by two monsoons *(see pp26–7)*. Varied topography and a gentle climate have led to a rich diversity of flora and fauna. Limestone hills in the North are clad in dense tropical forest. Open forest is more usual in the Northeast and Central Plains while the South and Gulf have superb coastlines and pockets of rainforest. Many habitats are threatened by industry and tourism; deforestation is rife, and some animal species face extinction *(see p219)*. As a result, many national parks have been established. The first, Khao Yai *(see pp184–5)*, opened in 1962.

Green parakeet

Coconut palms on the island of
Ko Samui in the Gulf of Thailand

MONTANE TROPICAL FOREST

This type of forest is made up mostly of broadleaf evergreens and some deciduous trees such as laurel, oak, and chestnut. Mosses, ferns, and epiphytic orchids, growing on o ther plants, are common.

Atlas moths *are the world's largest species. The female is larger than the male.*

Serow, *a type of antelope, are becoming increasingly rare in the hills of Northern Thailand.*

Palm civets *are nocturnal. They are found in tropical forests, but may also live near humans and eat cultivated fruit.*

OPEN FOREST

The most common trees in the open forest, also called savanna forest, are dipterocarps, a family of trees native to Southeast Asia. The ground around them is often carpeted by coarse scrub.

Sambar, *Thailand's largest deer, can be seen on the Central Plains and in the Northeast.*

Capped gibbons *are found mainly on the southern edge of Northeast Thailand. They are extremely agile.*

Wild boars *have been heavily hunted in the past. They feed mainly on grass.*

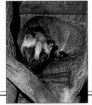

THAI FLOWERS

The diversity of Thailand's flowers reflects its range of natural habitats. Most famous of all are its orchids; there are some 1,300 different varieties. Unfortunately, illegal collection has led to their growing rarity in the wild. Other flowers are used as spices and for medicinal purposes.

The mallow flower, *a relative of the hibiscus, is common throughout Southeast Asia.*

Mountain pitcher plants *are insectivorous. Their prey falls into the "pitcher" where the plant's juices slowly dissolve it.*

Lotus lilies' *seed pods and stems are edible. Other lilies are grown for ornament only.*

Orchids (see p220) *come mainly from Northern Thailand; they are prized for their beauty.*

WETLANDS

Freshwater swamp forests have been decimated by farming, though some survive in the South. River basins and man-made lakes and ponds can be found all over Thailand.

Dusky leaf-monkeys *are found in the Thai-Malay peninsula. Three other species of leaf-monkey also live in Thailand.*

Painted storks *migrate to Thailand's swamps to breed. During this time the pigment in their faces turns pink.*

Purple swamp hens *are common. Longtoed feet allow them to walk on floating vegetation.*

COASTAL FOREST

The seeds of trees such as pines and Indian almond are transported on sea currents; thus ribbons of coastal forest are found all over Southeast Asia. Thailand's coastal forests are now threatened by farming and tourism.

Green turtles *are the only herbivorous sea turtles; they feed on sea grass and algae and are nocturnal.*

Lizards *are common in island forests. Most eat insects, though some species eat mice and small birds.*

Crested wood partridges *are found in the South, in areas of coastal, lowland forest.*

Thai Buddhism

At least 90 percent of Thais practice Theravada Buddhism. This was first brought to the region from India around the 3rd century BC and is based on the ancient Pali canon of the Buddha's teachings (Tripitaka). However, Thai practice incorporates many Hindu, Tantric, and Mahayana Buddhist influences. The worship of Buddha images, for instance, is a Mahayana Buddhist practice. Animist beliefs in spirits and the magical and in astrology are also widespread. Thais believe that Buddhism is one of three forces that give their kingdom its strength, the other two being the monarchy and nationhood. Religious rituals color daily life, especially in the form of merit-making *(see p129)*.

Monk with Thai flags

King Bhumibol, *like many kings before him, spent time as a monk. For Thais, this act reinforces the notion that Buddhism and the monarchy are unified powers.*

Siddhartha sets out to attain Enlightenment.

Most Thai males *are ordained as monks at adolescence – a major rite of passage. They usually spend at least a few months as monks, earning merit for themselves and their families. Few Thai women become nuns.*

Applying gold leaf *to Buddha images is a popular act of merit-making. Books of gold leaf can be readily purchased at temples, and the thin leaves are applied in profusion on Buddha images, wat decoration, and murals.*

STORY OF THE BUDDHA

The Buddha was born Prince Siddhartha Gautama in India in the 6th century BC. He gave up his riches to seek Enlightenment, and later taught the way to *nirvana*. Statues of the Buddha *(see p173)* and murals depicting his previous ten lives *(jatakas)* abound in Thailand.

The family *is held in high regard in Thailand. A senior monk will be asked by the family for his blessing at child-naming ceremonies, weddings, to bless a new house or car, or simply after a donation to the wat has been made. Children are taught the simple moral codes of Buddhism from an early age.*

Walking meditation *is practiced by most monks. Here, the most senior monk leads the line walking around the temple clockwise. Meditation on the nature of existence is a major way in which Buddhists progress toward Enlightenment – "Buddha" literally means "One who is Enlightened."*

Vishnu, with four arms, is one of the three principal Hindu gods.

Thai folding book painting, c.1900

Heavenly beings *(devas)* bear the Prince through the air.

A ring of jasmine *symbolizes the beauty of the Buddha's teachings and, as it perishes, the impermanence of all life. Vendors offer wreaths of jasmine to be hung in cars and shrines.*

Cremation ceremonies *are sober but not morbid; they are a rite of passage from this life to the next. The scale of the pyre reflects the status of the deceased. Chulalongkorn's funeral (see pp66–7) was one of the grandest.*

Incantations in the ancient Pali script

Ritualistic tattooing *is an ancient Hindu-Buddhist custom. Such tattoos are believed to act as powerful talismans against bad forces.*

THE BASIC TENETS OF BUDDHISM

Buddhist cosmology encompasses many states of being and heavenly realms. Buddhists believe in perpetual reincarnation, whereby each life is influenced by the actions and deeds of the previous one. This underlying philosophy of cause and effect, known as *karma*, is symbolized by the "wheel of law." Enlightenment *(nirvana)* is the only state that will end the cycle of rebirth. To reach this, Buddhists try to develop morality, meditation, and then wisdom (the "three pillars"). Following certain codes of behavior in each life, including the basic principles of tolerance and nonviolence, assists in this aim.

The "wheel of law" on the Thai flag of Buddhism

The Wat Complex

A *wat* is a collection of buildings within an enclosure serving dual purposes: Buddhist monastery, temple, and community center. There are about 30,000 *wats* in Thailand. Their construction is often funded by wealthy patrons – contributing to a *wat* is a good way to make merit *(see p129)*. Each period of Thai history has seen modifications to *wat* architecture, and the exact layout and style of buildings vary considerably. However, the basic layout of most *wats* follows set principles, as do the functions of different buildings.

A mondop *is a square-based structure topped with either a spire, as pictured here with the mondop at Wat Phra Kaeo (see pp80–83), or a cruciform roof. The edifice contains an object of worship or sacred texts.*

A Bodhi tree is found in many *wats*. According to Buddhist lore, the Buddha sat beneath one as he attempted to attain enlightenment *(see pp30–31)*.

A wall or cloister *may enclose the main part of the temple (known as the* phutthawat*). A cloister sometimes houses a row of Buddha images, and murals may be painted on its walls.*

Monks' living quarters and dormitories are in a separate compound known as the *sanghawat*.

The *sala kanparien* is a small meeting hall, sometimes the venue for lectures on the holy scriptures.

Minor *salas* (halls) act as meeting places for pilgrims.

The *ho trai*, *or library, is used to house holy scriptures. A comparatively rare feature of wat complexes, they come in an assortment of shapes and sizes; this one at Wat Paknam in Bangkok is typical of a ho trai in a city wat. A ho trai in the countryside may have a high base, or be surrounded by water to minimize damage from insects.*

Ornamental pond

IMPORTANT WATS

Wats whose names begin with Rat-, Racha- or Maha- have been founded by royalty, or contain highly revered objects (with names often prefaced by "Phra"). There are about 180 important *wats* in Thailand, and this imagined *wat* is typical. The *bot* and *wihan* are grand affairs, and there are a number of minor *salas*, as well as extensive monks' quarters. Lesser *wats* have fewer buildings and sometimes no *wihan*.

A *chedi* is a solid structure encasing a relic of the Buddha, such as a hair or fragment of bone, or the ashes of a king. Wat *complexes are often built expressly to surround a sacred* chedi.

The wihan, an assembly hall, is very similar to but usually larger than a bot and not demarcated by bai semas. There may be several wihans. This one at Wat Rachabophit (see p91) is, like several in Bangkok, an eclectic mix of architectural styles.

Buddha images in the cloister help mark the divide between the profane, outer world and the inner, sacred *wat.*

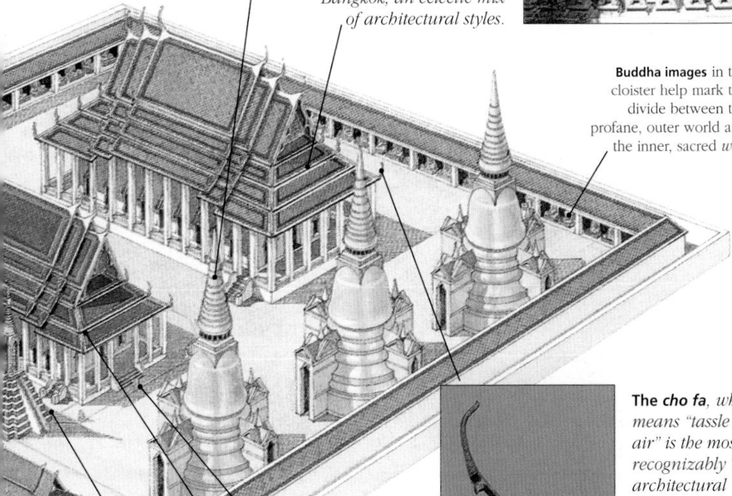

The cho fa, which means "tassle of air" is the most recognizably Thai architectural detail. Its shape is thought to derive from a highly stylized garuda, *a fierce bird featured in Hindu mythology.*

Bai semas, sacred boundary stones, are used to demarcate the consecrated ground of the *bot.*

Entrance to wat

The bot (or ubosot) is the ordination hall reserved mainly for monks. It looks like a wihan but is surrounded by bai semas. The bot usually faces east and often houses the wat's main Buddha, as seen here at Wat Suthat (see pp90–91), Bangkok.

Ho rakangs or bell towers are used to toll the hour and summon monks to prayer. This one at Wat Rakhang (see p125) is a comparatively large, ornate structure.

Religious Architecture

Thailand's religious sites span more than 11 centuries. The materials used to build them invariably determine how much of each site can be seen today. Hindu-Buddhist Khmer temples were built of stone and, where restored, are fairly complete. Generally, all that is left of the *wihans* and *bots (see pp32–3)* of the Buddhist temples at Sukhothai and Ayutthaya are foundations and stone pillars, though some stone structures such as *chedis* and *mondops* are still standing. There are many fine examples of later Lanna and Rattanakosin Buddhist temples.

Gilded pediment of *wihan*, Wat Saket *(see p87)*

KHMER (9TH TO 13TH CENTURIES)

Stone temple complexes, or *prasats*, in Northeast Thailand were built by the Khmers *(see pp264–5)*. Most have staircases or bridges lined with stone *nagas* (serpents) leading to a central sanctuary which is usually decorated with carved stone reliefs depicting Hindu myths and topped by a *prang* (tower). The two most important Khmer sites in Thailand are Prasat Hin Khao Phnom Rung *(pp280–81)* and Prasat Hin Phimai *(see pp276–7)*.

Khmer prangs symbolized Mount Meru, the mythical abode of the gods.

Lintels and pediments over the entrances depict Hindu and Buddhist deities.

The inner chamber of the *prang* housed either a *lingam (see p265)* or a Buddha image.

Naga antefix on the *prang* of Prasat Hin Khao Phnom Rung

Central sanctuary of Prasat Hin Khao Phnom Rung

SUKHOTHAI (MID-13TH TO 15TH CENTURIES)

The cities of Sukhothai *(see pp194–7)* and Si Satchanalai *(see pp198–200)* witnessed the most radical architectural leap in Thai history. Amid sacred Khmer ruins, King Si Intharathit *(see p58)* and his successors built *wihans* and *bots* to house Buddha images. *Chedis*, modeled on Sri Lankan bell-shaped reliquary towers *(see p198)*, were added. Vast new temple complexes, such as Wat Mahathat *(see pp196–7)*, sometimes incorporated a unique development, the lotus-bud *chedi*.

Central lotus-bud chedi

Small chedis surround the main one.

Niches (foreground) once housed stucco Buddhas.

Some chedis (background) show Khmer influence.

A frieze of walking monks is carved around the base.

Mondop housing a Buddha image at Wat Si Chum *(see p195)*

Six (illustrated) of the nine *chedis* at the heart of Wat Mahathat

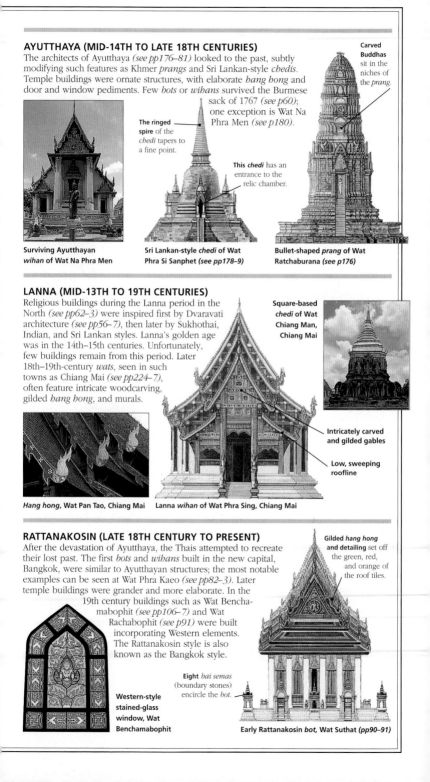

AYUTTHAYA (MID-14TH TO LATE 18TH CENTURIES)

The architects of Ayutthaya *(see pp176–81)* looked to the past, subtly modifying such features as Khmer *prangs* and Sri Lankan-style *chedis*. Temple buildings were ornate structures, with elaborate *hang hong* and door and window pediments. Few *bots* or *wihans* survived the Burmese sack of 1767 *(see p60)*; one exception is Wat Na Phra Men *(see p180)*.

Carved Buddhas sit in the niches of the *prang*.

The ringed spire of the *chedi* tapers to a fine point.

This *chedi* has an entrance to the relic chamber.

Surviving Ayutthayan *wihan* of Wat Na Phra Men

Sri Lankan-style *chedi* of Wat Phra Si Sanphet *(see pp178–9)*

Bullet-shaped *prang* of Wat Ratchaburana *(see p176)*

LANNA (MID-13TH TO 19TH CENTURIES)

Religious buildings during the Lanna period in the North *(see pp62–3)* were inspired first by Dvaravati architecture *(see pp56–7)*, then later by Sukhothai, Indian, and Sri Lankan styles. Lanna's golden age was in the 14th–15th centuries. Unfortunately, few buildings remain from this period. Later 18th–19th-century *wats*, seen in such towns as Chiang Mai *(see pp224–7)*, often feature intricate woodcarving, gilded *hang hong*, and murals.

Square-based *chedi* of Wat Chiang Man, Chiang Mai

Intricately carved and gilded gables

Low, sweeping roofline

Hang hong, **Wat Pan Tao, Chiang Mai**

Lanna *wihan* of Wat Phra Sing, Chiang Mai

RATTANAKOSIN (LATE 18TH CENTURY TO PRESENT)

After the devastation of Ayutthaya, the Thais attempted to recreate their lost past. The first *bots* and *wihans* built in the new capital, Bangkok, were similar to Ayutthayan structures; the most notable examples can be seen at Wat Phra Kaeo *(see pp82–3)*. Later temple buildings were grander and more elaborate. In the 19th century buildings such as Wat Benchamabophit *(see pp106–7)* and Wat Rachabophit *(see p91)* were built incorporating Western elements. The Rattanakosin style is also known as the Bangkok style.

Gilded *hang hong* and detailing set off the green, red, and orange of the roof tiles.

Eight *bai semas* (boundary stones) encircle the *bot*.

Western-style stained-glass window, Wat Benchamabophit

Early Rattanakosin *bot*, Wat Suthat *(pp90–91)*

Traditional Thai Houses

Traditional Thai houses are well adapted to the tropical climate. Many are raised on stilts to protect from flooding. A steeply slanting roof helps to channel rainwater off the house, and natural materials such as hardwoods, bamboo, and dried leaves help keep the building cool. The design also reflects spiritual beliefs. The innermost room is believed to be the abode of the spirits of family ancestors, and this is usually used as the sleeping quarters. Traditional Thai houses are most often seen in rural areas, though grand versions may be found in cities.

Plantation house, Northern Thailand

NORTHERN HOUSES

Northern Thailand can be relatively cool. As a result, the windows of Northern houses are smaller than those in the rest of the country. The kitchen and living areas are often joined together, which makes good use of the available heat. Outer walls are commonly built to slope outward, toward the roof, for strength. In more rural areas of Northern Thailand some houses have thatched roofs.

Decorative *kalae*, a traditional feature of Northern houses

Traditional Northern houses, constructed from teak

Plain *kalae*

Slanted walls

Typically *the whole structure of a Northern house is raised on pillars. An open balcony running along the front of the house is common, as are plain or decorative* kalae.

Front veranda

CENTRAL PLAINS HOUSES

In the hot Central Plains, a large, centrally situated veranda is the dominant feature of many traditional houses and acts for much of the year as an outside living area. Some houses in the Central Plains have covered verandas running along the sides of the main structure. Sometimes, a communal veranda will have several houses clustered around it. Houses found in the Central Plains tend to have wood-paneled walls.

Wood-paneled gable

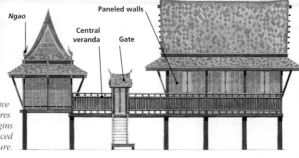

Ngao

Paneled walls

Central veranda

Gate

The gables *often have decorative features called* ngaos, *the origins of which can be traced to Khmer architecture.*

HOUSES ON WATER

River houses can be found in the Central Plains. The *khlongs* of early Bangkok *(see p125)* had many floating shop-houses. Such houses are very practical in areas prone to seasonal flooding. Houses can either be anchored to posts above the water line, or built on bamboo rafts so that during flood conditions they are able to float on the rising waters.

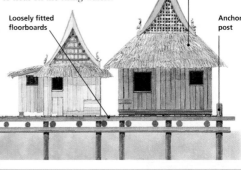

Thatched roof

Loosely fitted floorboards

Anchor post

Floating houses, Sangkhla Buri *(see p168)*

Houses *close to the river's edge are often anchored on posts. Floorboards are loosely fitted so that they move with the water beneath them.*

ROYAL HOUSES

Royal houses and mansions are typically a mixture of Thai temple and house styles and Western architecture. The main structural material of such buildings is usually teak, which gives them their distinctive rich, red color. Windows and doors usually have ornate frames and pediments, which are themselves sometimes decorated in gilt bronze.

Window pediment, Prince of Lampang's Palace *(see p137)*

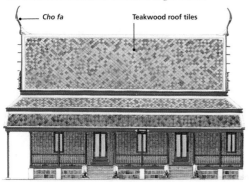

Cho fa   **Teakwood roof tiles**

The Red House *at the National Museum* (see pp88–9) *is a typical royal house. As its name reflects, it is built entirely of teak and, like a temple, has cho fas.*

SPIRIT HOUSES

Spirit houses can be found on the grounds of many Thai homes. They are small structures, usually elevated on a pole, and house the spiritual guardian of the property. Resembling both dolls' houses and bird-tables, they come in a wide collection of styles: sometimes simple replicas of the houses to which they belong, at other times elaborate models of religious buildings. Spirit houses are erected to placate the spirits of the land, traditionally before the construction of the main building begins. They are then adorned daily with incense, flowers, and food to further mollify the spirits. Spirit worship predates Theravada Buddhism *(see pp30–31)*, but the flexibility of Thai religion means that worship of the Buddha and spirits is a normal part of daily life.

Decorated spirit house

The Art of Thai Food

Thai food is justifiably renowned for its quality and diversity – and for being as much a feast for the eyes as for the stomach. The simplest of dishes is often served with a carved carrot flower or a scallion tassel; a full-blown Royal Thai meal in a high-class restaurant may be accompanied by spectacular virtuoso fruit and vegetable carvings. The cooking and presentation techniques of Thai cuisine are so respected that Bangkok's celebrated cooking schools attract pupils from all over the world. For the majority of Thais, eating is an informal, social activity. Whether it is an important family occasion, such as a wedding, an impromptu outdoor garden party, or a colorful festival, food will play a central role. Many restaurants serving Northern *khantoke* dinners may be aimed at tourists, but the principle of communal sharing of food is genuinely Thai.

Elaborately carved melon

The pre-rice planting festival *in Northern Thailand, like many Thai festivals, involves the preparation and consumption of a wide variety of food.*

White radish petals around a papaya heart

Royal Thai cuisine is based on the dishes that at one time were served only at the Thai court. It is characterized by complex cooking methods and elaborate decoration. Royal Thai cooking also often uses ingredients that are (or were) expensive, such as ice for chilled dishes.

Papaya has a firm texture and is a popular fruit to carve.

Cucumber carved into leaves

Radish

***Khantoke** is a traditional way of eating in Northern Thailand. Guests sit on raised platforms around a circular table and share a selection of typical Northern dishes served with sticky rice.*

FRUIT AND VEGETABLE CARVING

Few visitors to Thailand fail to be impressed by the exquisitely carved fruit and vegetables that accompany many dishes in restaurants. Scallions are transformed into tassels and chrysanthemums; carrots and chilies become flowers; and tomatoes are magically turned into roses. The practice was once the preserve of the women of the royal court. Today, most Thai chefs know the basic carving skills, but few have the dexterity and application needed to master the more advanced techniques. Skilled practitioners, capable of producing astonishingly elaborate creations, are highly esteemed.

Demonstrating the art of vegetable carving

Cooking schools *provide trainee chefs and interested amateurs with a grounding in Thai cooking techniques, although most chefs learn their trade over a period of years in a restaurant kitchen. The most famous schools are in Bangkok (see p464).*

Thai pumpkin

Carrot

Pumpkin

Beets, expensive in Thailand, are sometimes replaced by dyed carrots.

Miang kham, *a snack dish of ginger, coconut, lemons, red onions, dried shrimps, peanuts, and a syrup sauce, is presented here with a typical Thai attention to detail. The idea that food should look as good as it tastes applies to simple as well as elaborate dishes.*

Rice *is endowed with spiritual significance in Thailand (see pp26–7) as well as being the central pillar of the country's cuisine. Here, Brahmins present offerings of rice in a Bangkok temple.*

Luk chub *are utterly exquisite sweetmeats made to resemble tiny vegetables. Because few people possess the skills to make them, they are quite expensive, but well worth trying nonetheless.*

Cucumber petals

A communal meal *is the subject of this 19th-century temple mural. Although the Thais are inveterate snackers, sitting down for a full meal is still an important social event. Weddings and funerals are never without food and drink for all guests to enjoy. Eating out of doors, in a pavilion or a garden, is a popular way of dining in Thailand and is known as* suan ahan. *On Sundays many* wats *host a large communal meal.*

The Ramakien

The Ramakien, the Thai version of the Indian Ramayana, is an allegory of the triumph of good over evil. The hero, Rama, is a paragon of virtue – the ideal king. The villain, the demon king Tosakan, is a tragic character of great dignity. This epic tale is thought to have become established after the Thais occupied Angkor in the 15th century. It has been an inspiration for painting and classical drama. All the Chakri kings have taken Rama as one of their names, and the old capital of Ayutthaya *(see pp176–81)* was named after Ayodhya, a fictional kingdom in the story.

Hun krabok (rod puppets), in a scene from the Ramakien

Monkey armies accompany Rama to Longka.

Buildings and chariots are painted in Thai style even though the story is set in India and Sri Lanka.

Rama is a skilled archer, *as this bas-relief marble panel at Wat Pho (see pp92–3) shows. Rama wins Sita's hand by stringing a bow that no other suitor is even able to lift.*

THE STORY

Rama, the heir to the throne of Ayodhya, is sent into exile for 14 years, through the intrigues of his stepmother. His wife, Sita, and brother Lakshman go with him deep into the forest. Tosakan, the demon king of Longka (Sri Lanka), abducts Sita and carries her off to his island kingdom in the hope of marrying her. The brothers pursue him. Hanuman, the white monkey god, volunteers his services. Together they win the alliance of two monkey kings, Sukrip and Chompupan, each with a powerful army. They march south to the coast opposite Longka. The monkey armies build a road of stone through the sea and lay siege to Longka. Many victorious battles are waged against Tosakan's demon armies. Finally, when all his champions have been defeated, Tosakan fights Rama and is killed. Rama then crowns his ally, Piphek (Tosakan's banished brother), as King of Longka and returns with Sita to resume his reign in Ayodhya.

Mural at Wat Phra Kaeo: Hanuman using his tail as a bridge

Many demons were overcome *by Rama during his forest exile. Some recognized his divine nature. As they died, his blessings released them from the punishment of being reincarnated as demons in the next life.*

Nang yai shadow plays (see p383), *based on the Ramakien, were first documented in the 15th century. Today this art form is rarely performed in Thailand but can still be seen in Cambodia.*

In this view, the sea is narrowed to allow both countries in the tale to be seen.

Rama in the chariot rides high above his followers, as befits a king.

THE MAIN CHARACTERS

Hundreds of characters are featured in the many episodes of the epic Ramakien. However, the central thread of the drama is carried by the five most important figures, who are described below.

Rama, *often depicted with a deep green face, is an incarnation of the god Vishnu. Rama's purpose is to defeat the demon race whose power threatens the gods.*

Sita, *the daughter of Tosakan's consort and incarnation of the goddess Lakshmi, remains loyal to Rama while held captive by the evil Tosakan.*

Lakshman, *Rama's loyal younger brother, is often shown in gold. He accompanies Rama into exile in the forest.*

Hanuman, *the white monkey, son of the wind god, is totally devoted to Rama, but still finds time to seduce beautiful women.*

RAMAKIEN MURALS AT WAT PHRA KAEO

The Ramakien is beautifully depicted through a series of 178 colorful murals, dating from the late 18th century, at Wat Phra Kaeo (see pp80–83). In this scene Hanuman displays his supernatural powers to assist Rama in rescuing Sita by building a stone causeway across the sea.

Hanuman finds Sita *imprisoned by the wicked king of Longka, Tosakan. He gives her Rama's ring and tells her she will soon be rescued.*

Tosakan (*meaning "ten necks"), the demon king of Longka, has multiple heads and arms. In the Indian version of the Ramayana he is called Ravanna.*

Thai Theater and Music

The two principal forms of classical Thai drama are *khon* and *lakhon*. *Khon* was first performed in the royal court in the 15th century, with story lines taken from the Ramakien *(see pp40–41)*. The more graceful *lakhon*, which also features elements from the *jataka* tales *(see p30)*, was originally performed inside the palace, but moved outside at a later date. Both *khon* and *lakhon* involve slow, highly stylized, angular dance movements set to the music of a *piphat* ensemble.

Classical Thai dancer

Students learn *gestures by imitating their teacher. Training begins at an early age (when limbs are still supple) and includes a sequence of moves known as the Alphabet of Dancing* (mae bot).

Graceful gestures typify classical Thai drama. Here, weapons are raised to attack the enemy.

Lavish costumes, made of heavy brocade and adorned with jewelry, are modeled on traditional court garments.

White mask of Hanuman (see p41)

Ganesh, the elephant god

Khon masks, decorated with gold and jewelry, are treated as sacred objects with supernatural powers.

Khon and lakhon performances are often staged at outdoor shrines. Dancers are hired to perform to the resident god by supplicants whose wishes have been granted.

A KHON PERFORMANCE

In *khon* drama, demons and monkeys wear masks, while human heroes and celestial beings sport crowns. As the story is told mainly through gestures, *khon* can be enjoyed by non-Thais. Visitors today are most likely to see performances at restaurants catering to tourists.

INSTRUMENTS OF CLASSICAL THAI MUSIC

A *mahori* ensemble shown in a mural

Thailand's classical music originated in the Sukhothai era. The basic melody is set by the composer, but, as no notation is used, each musician varies the tune and adopts the character of the instrument, like actors in a play. A tuned percussion ensemble, or *piphat*, accompanies theater performances and boxing matches *(see p44)*. A *mahori* ensemble includes stringed instruments.

Ranat (xylophones)

The keys of a flat xylophone produce a different tone from those of a curved one.

Likay, *by far the most popular type of dance-drama, is a satirical form of* khon *and* lakhon. *The actors wear gaudy costumes and the plot derives from ancient tales laced with improvised jokes and puns.*

Khon and **lakhon** *troupes, employed by the royal palace until the early 20th century, are now based at Bangkok's Fine Arts Department.*

Finger extensions *emphasizing the graceful curves of a dancer's hands, are seen in* lakhon *perfomances and in "nail dances" of the North.*

This mural *at Wat Benchamabophit, Bangkok, depicts a scene from a* khon *performance. In it, Erawan, the elephant mount of Indra, descends from heaven.*

Natural-looking makeup enhances the features of characters who do not wear masks. This replaces a heavy white paint that was traditionally worn.

Hun krabok *puppets, rodded marionettes, are operated by hidden threads pulled from under the costume. Hun krabok perform-ances are very rare today.*

Khong wong lek **(small gong circle)**

Chake **("crocodile")**

The hollowed hardwood body is inlaid with ivory.

Small gongs are struck by the player to give the tune's basic melody.

The strings of a *chake* are plucked. It accompa-nies fiddles and flutes in a string ensemble.

A **piphat mon** *ensemble, including a vertical gong circle, plays at funerals.*

Thai Boxing

Nai Khanom Dtom

Thai boxing *(muay thai)*, Thailand's unique national sport, is gaining popularity worldwide. It was first documented in 1411, but probably evolved from an earlier form of armed combat, *krabi-krabong. Muay thai* is highly ritualistic – many techniques are inspired by battle stories from the Ramakien *(see pp40–41).* The country's first famous boxer was Nai Khanom Dtom, who in 1774 defeated ten Burmese fighters. Due to a high injury rate, the sport was banned in the 1920s. In 1937 it was revived with rules for protecting fighters.

In the stadium, *the audience becomes excited, shouting encouragement to the boxers. Thais bet furiously, often staking large sums on their favorite fighter. Bouts between famous boxers can be sold out well in advance.*

This manuscript, *which dates from the early 20th century, depicts a fight between two Thai boxers.*

Training gear varies in style from camp to camp.

Phone Kingphet *was the first world champion Thai boxer. He trained in the cool climate of Phu Kradung National Park (see pp286–7) in preparation for his numerous bouts abroad.*

Feet are kept bare in training sessions, though ankle covers may be worn for protection during a match.

A ringside *piphat* **band** *is an essential element of a Thai boxing match. During the opening ceremony, the music is soft in tone; when the fighting begins it switches to a more upbeat "fight melody." As the action becomes more frenzied, the music increases in tempo, adding tension to the match.*

TYPES OF MOVES

Points are awarded for each blow to the opponent. The groin is not a valid target, and biting and head-butting are not allowed. A match may end with a spectacular knockout.

The jumping downward strike elbow *is a physically demanding move. It gives the boxer an excellent vantage point over his opponent.*

Amulets (see p78), *worn around one or both biceps during the match, are believed to offer protection to the boxer while fighting. They consist of a piece of cord that usually contains a Buddha image or an herb that is thought to be lucky.*

WHERE TO SEE THAI BOXING

Matches are held at Ratchadamnoen Stadium *(p461)* every Mon, Wed, Thu & Sun. Lumphini Stadium *(p461)* has matches on Tue, Fri & Sat. For other towns, check sites. Several TV channels now televise Thai Boxing.

Fists are bound with cloth for protection during training. Before 1937, glass-impregnated hemp was often used, to injure the opponent.

The *wai kru*, *a ritual bow, is the first part of the* ram muay, *a gesture of respect to the trainer (kru) and the spirit of boxing. In honor of their training camp, boxers often take its name as their surname.*

Before the match, *the boxer performs a slow, solemn dance* (ram muay). *The exact movements differ according to the boxer's camp, but usually involve sweeping arm motions, which are said to draw the power of earth, air, fire, and water into the body.*

THAI BOXING VERSUS WESTERN BOXING

Thai boxing, or "kick boxing," exerts parts of the body not used in Western boxing, such as the feet and elbows. Thai boxing matches are also faster paced, and are thus limited to five rounds of three minutes, each separated by a short break. Professional boxers, who may start the rigorous training as young as six, often retire by 25. Several Thai boxers have won Western boxing titles.

Kicks are common *in Thai boxing. A high kick to the neck, as shown here, may knock out a rival. A push kick, in which one boxer pushes the sole of his foot into the face of the other, is regarded as a great insult to the opponent.*

Knee hooks *can be devastating. To perform a "rising knee," aimed at either the head or body, the boxer pushes down his rival's head, bringing his knee up to hit it.*

Elbows deliver *fierce blows to the face, and, like knee strikes, are often decisive in matches. An elbow strike is more powerful than a punch, the weakest blow.*

Festivals in Thailand

Thai festivals are rarely solemn occasions, and few countries celebrate them with so much fun and color. Annual rites and festivities, marking religious devotion or the passage of seasons, have long been an integral part of Thai life. A 13th-century inscription reads: "Whoever wants to make merry, does so; whoever wants to laugh, does so."

Phi Ta Khon, held in Dan Sai and Loei

This still applies today, with dozens of festivities taking place each month. The main festivals, such as Songkran, are celebrated nationwide, with the most exuberant activities taking place in Bangkok and other major cities. Each region has its own unique festivals, too. Many festival dates change each year, as they follow the lunar calendar.

Decorated oxen, paraded for Bangkok's Royal Plowing Ceremony

BANGKOK

Songkran, the Thai New Year, is celebrated nationally from April 12th–14th *(see p48)*. In Bangkok, festivities take place at Sanam Luang, where a revered Buddha image is bathed as part of the merit-making rituals. Over the years, the festival has become a boisterous affair involving water throwing when few people escape getting soaked.

Visakha Bucha *(see p49)*, in May, marks the birth, Enlightenment, and death of the Buddha, all said to have occurred on the same day of the year. It is celebrated with candlelight processions around important temples.

The Royal Plowing Ceremony is held at Sanam Luang at the start of the rice-planting season in May *(see p48)*. The display features oxen plowing and Brahmin priests sowing rice seeds. The oxen predict the coming year's harvest by selecting one of several types of food offered to them.

The Golden Mount Fair *(see p50)* is in November. With its carnival, performers, and candlelight processions, this is Thailand's best temple fair.

December's Trooping of the Colors in the Royal Plaza is the best of many nationwide celebrations marking King Bhumibol's birthday *(see p51)*.

CENTRAL PLAINS

Every March, pilgrims flock to the Temple of the Holy Footprint near Saraburi for the elaborate Phra Phutthabat Fair *(see p48)*, which has theater and folk music performances.

Full-moon night in November is the occasion for Loy Krathong. It is celebrated throughout the country, but magically amid the ruins of Old Sukhothai *(see p195)*, where it is said to have originated. The festival is held in honor of Mae Kongkha, the goddess of waterways, and takes place by rivers, lakes, and ponds. Small, lotus-shaped vessels carrying offerings for Mae Kongkha are floated to take away the sins of the past year and to bring good luck for the future.

Khwae River Bridge Week (late November/early December), held at Kanchanaburi, marks the building of the infamous bridge with historical displays and a dramatic sound and light show.

NORTHERN THAILAND

Bo Sang, which is famous for its hand-painted umbrellas, holds an Umbrella Fair every January. Umbrella painting competitions, umbrella exhibitions, parades, and a "Miss Bo Sang" beauty contest are part of the festival.

Northern Thailand shows off its beautiful blooms to full effect during Chiang Mai's Festival of Flowers in February, when parades of lavish floral floats fill the town with color. Events include floral exhibitions, handicraft sales, and a beauty pageant.

Mae Hong Son comes alive during its Poi Sang Long Festival, held in late March

Painting umbrellas for the Umbrella Festival in Bo Sang

Young Buddhist novices at the Poi Sang Long Festival in Mae Hong Son

or early April. The highlight of this Buddhist festival is a mass ordination ceremony for Shan boys. Wearing sumptuous costumes, the novices parade through the town before exchanging their finery for simple monks' robes in a symbolic gesture of renouncing worldly goods.

NORTHEAST THAILAND

Northeast Thailand is renowned for its unique festivals. In May, the town of Yasothon hosts the Bun Bang Fai (Rocket Festival), perhaps the most thrilling of Thailand's regional celebrations. This two-day event, accompanied by much high-spirited revelry, is staged to ensure plentiful rains during the coming rice-planting season. On the first day there is a parade of car-nival floats, as well as carni-vals, music, and folk dancing. The next day, huge, home-made rockets are set off.

Dan Sai and Loei, both in Loei province, are known for their Phi Ta Khon Festival *(see p289)*, held in June. Celebrations begin with a

parade, where locals dressed as ghosts follow a Buddha image through the streets of town to make Buddhist merit and call for rain.

Ubon Ratchathani has a Candle Festival in July, its own version of the nationally celebrated "beginning of the rains retreat," or Khao Phansa *(see p49)*. As part of the celebrations, huge, intricately carved beeswax candles are exhibited on floats in the town before being presented to temples, where they burn throughout the rainy season.

The national holiday of "end of the rains retreat," or Ok Phansa, is celebrated in particular style at Nakhon Phanom in October with the Illuminated Boat Procession. Intricately fashioned model boats carrying single candles are set adrift on the Mekong River at nightfall.

GULF OF THAILAND

Modern-style merrymaking is found at Pattaya, which hosts the week-long Pattaya Festival in April. Floral float parades, beauty contests, and fireworks displays feature amid a non-stop carnival atmosphere. One of Thai-land's most colorful water festivals is the Receiving of the Lotus Festi-val, which is celebrated in

Mud-covered revelers at Dan Sai, Northeast Thailand

late October at Bang Phli, just south of Bangkok. Here, Ok Phansa is marked by a ceremony in which a locally revered Buddha image is showered with thousands of lotus buds while it is paraded by barge along Khlong Sam-rong, the local canal. Lively crowds, thronging the canal banks, throw flowers until only the image's head re-mains visible above the mounting floral offerings. Other events include boat races, boxing matches fought on poles placed across the canal, and *likay* theater shows.

Displays of self-mortification, part of the Vegetarian Festival, Phuket

SOUTHERN THAILAND

Traditional Southern culture gets an airing at the week-long Narathiwat Fair (last week of September). This features races between brightly painted traditional *korlae* fishing boats *(see p388)*, as well as dove-cooing contests and performances of Southern music and dance.

For sheer spectacle, it is hard to beat Phuket's Vegetar-ian Festival (late September/early October, *see p360*). This nine-day festival, marking the start of Taoist Lent, is cel-ebrated by people of Chinese ancestry. During the festival followers eat only vegetarian food and take part in acts of self-mortification, such as piercing the body with skew-ers, with no apparent harm.

THAILAND THROUGH THE YEAR

The Thai year revolves around the monsoon seasons – which dictate the year's farming activities – and the religious calendar. Most religious festivals are Buddhist, and often observed on significant days of the lunar cycle, such as full moon. Festivals may also mark a seasonal change, such as the end of the rains, or a related agricultural event, such as the beginning of the planting season. The three seasons – wet, cool, and hot – are

Celebration of Loy Krathong, Sukhothai

produced by the Southwest and Northeast monsoons *(see pp26–7)*. At the start of the wet season farmers plant rice seedlings. The rice-growing period is the traditional time for boys to enter the monkhood for a few weeks. In the cool season the drier weather ripens the crop, which is gathered before the hot season. Village life then slows down. During most weeks a festival is held somewhere in the country, especially in the cool season.

HOT SEASON

High temperatures combined with high humidity make this an uncomfortable time, April being especially hot. With the fields empty and rivers running low, the landscape appears faded and spent in the bright sunshine. Considering the heat, it is not surprising that Thailand's traditional New Year, Songkran, is celebrated with water.

MARCH

ASEAN Barred Ground Dove Fair *(first week)*, Yala. Dove-singing contest that attracts bird lovers from as far away as Cambodia, Malaysia, Singapore, and Indonesia.
Phra Phutthabat Fair *(first or second week)*, Saraburi. Celebration of the annual pilgrimage to the Temple of the Holy Footprint *(see p172)*.

Temple of the Holy Footprint during the Phra Phutthabat Fair

Water throwing during Songkran celebrations in Chiang Mai

Phra That Chaw Hae Fair *(third week)*. A colorful procession of townspeople, all dressed in traditional Lanna attire, carry robes to cover the *chedi*.
Poi Sang Long Festival *(late Mar/early Apr)*, Mae Hong Son. Mass ordination of 15- and 16-year-old-boys, who dress up as princes in memory of the Buddha's origins.

APRIL

Chakri Day *(Apr 6)*. Commemorates Rama I founding the Chakri Dynasty. The Royal Pantheon – which displays statues of former kings – in Wat Phra Kaeo's grounds, Bangkok, is open to the public on this day only.
Songkran *(Apr 12–14/15)*. Traditional Thai New Year. Celebrated nationwide, but Chiang Mai has the reputation for the most fun *(see p236)*.

Pattaya Festival *(mid-Apr)*. Features a week of food and floral floats, beauty contests, and a huge fireworks display.
Phnom Rung Fair *(Apr full moon)*. Daytime procession and a nighttime sound and light show at Prasat Hin Khao Phnom Rung *(see pp280–81)*.

MAY

Coronation Day *(May 5)*. Ceremony to mark the crowning of King Bhumibol.
Royal Plowing Ceremony *(early May)*, Bangkok. Observes the official start of the rice-planting season with an elaborate royal rite at Bangkok's Sanam Luang.
Bun Bang Fai (Rocket) Festival *(second week)*, Northeast Thailand. Homemade rockets are fired to ensure plentiful rains amid a carnival atmosphere. Celebrated exuberantly at Yasothon *(see p274)*.

AVERAGE DAILY HOURS OF SUNSHINE

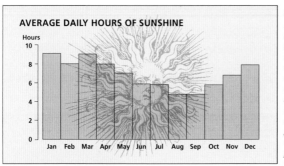

Sunshine Chart
Even during the rainy season, most days have some sunshine. The tropical sun can be very fierce, and adequate precautions against sunburn and sunstroke should be taken. Sun screen, a sun hat, and sunglasses are highly recommended. Drinking plenty of water reduces the risk of dehydration.

Visakha Bucha celebrations at Wat Benchamabophit, Bangkok

Visakha Bucha *(May full moon)*. Most important date on the Buddhist calendar. Celebrates the birth, Enlightenment, and death of the Buddha. Sermons and candlelit processions at temples.

RAINY SEASON

The rural scene comes alive with the advent of the annual rains, which soften the soil ready for plowing. Once the rice has been planted, there is a lull in farming activity. This coincides with the annual three-month Buddhist Rains Retreat, the period when young men traditionally enter the monkhood for a brief period. This is something that young Thai men should do at least once in their lives. The rainy season is a good time to observe the ordination ceremonies held throughout Thailand, which blend high-spirited festivities with deep religious feelings.

JUNE

Phi Ta Khon Festival
(mid/late Jun), Loei. An event unique to the Dan Sai district of Loei province, comprising masked players reenacting the legend of Prince Vessandon, the Buddha's penultimate incarnation *(see p289)*.

JULY

Asanha Bucha *(Jul full moon)*. Second of the year's three major Buddhist festivals. Commemorates the anniversary of the Lord Buddha's first sermon to his first five disciples.
Khao Phansa *(Jul full moon)*. Marks the start of the three-month Buddhist Rains Retreat (which is also referred to as Buddhist Lent), when monks remain in their temples to devote themselves to study and meditation. Young men are ordained for short periods.

Young man in ordination robes

Candle Festival *(Jul full moon)*, Ubon Ratchathani. Unique festival held in the Northeast to mark the beginning of Khao Phansa. Features parades of carved candles (made by villagers from all over the province) displayed on floats and later presented to temples throughout the city. Some candles are several meters tall *(see pp302–3)*.

AUGUST

Her Majesty the Queen's Birthday
(Aug 12). Buildings and streets are lavishly decorated in honor of Queen Sirikit's birthday. The most elaborate decorations can be seen in Bangkok, especially along Ratchadamnoen Avenue and around the Grand Palace, where the streets and government offices are exuberantly adorned with colored lights.

Parade of candles at the Ubon Ratchathani Candle Festival

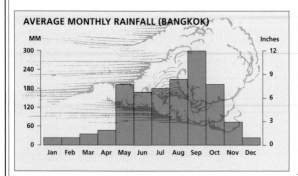

AVERAGE MONTHLY RAINFALL (BANGKOK)

Rainfall Chart
Thailand's rainfall is not evenly distributed. The southern peninsula has the highest, some 2,400 mm (95 inches) annually; the north and central regions receive 1,300 mm (51 inches). In many places, torrential rain falls almost daily during the rainy season, usually from June to October.

SEPTEMBER

Food and Fruits Fair *(first week)*, Nakhon Pathom. Held at Thailand's largest Buddhist temple, Phra Pathom Chedi. Cooking, folk theater, and floral floats.
Phichit Boat Races *(Sep)*, Nan. This annual regatta takes place on the Nan river as part of the Nan Provincial Fair and feature traditional low-slung boats.
Narathiwat Fair *(last week)*. A good opportunity to experience Southern culture.

Mangoes on display at Nakhon Pathom

OCTOBER

Vegetarian Festival *(early Oct)*. Trang and Phuket provinces *(see p360)*. Self-mortification rituals following abstinence from meat.
Chulalongkorn Day *(Oct 23)*, Bangkok. Commemorates the death of Rama V (King Chulalongkorn). Floral trib-

utes are placed by the King's equestrian statue by the Royal Plaza in Bangkok.
Receiving of the Lotus Festival *(late Oct)*, Bang Phli *(see p47)*. The end of the rains celebrated by pouring lotus buds over a locally revered Budda image.
Ok Phansa *(Oct full moon)*. Nationwide celebration of the Lord Buddha's reappearance on Earth after a season spent preaching in heaven. Marks the end of the Buddhist Rains Retreat.
Krathin *(begins Oct full moon)*. One-month period during which monks are presented with new robes.
Nan Boat Races *(late Oct)*. Festive regatta *(see p255)*.
Illuminated Boat Procession *(Oct full moon)*, Nakhon Phanom. Boats with candles and offerings set afloat down the Mekong River. Entertainments provided in the town *(see p296)*.

COOL SEASON

After the rains, the skies clear and the air cools to a comfortable warmth. The countryside looks its best, lush and green from the rains, with full rivers and waterfalls. In general this is the best time to visit Thailand, especially during the coolest months of December and January. Numerous festivals, to celebrate of the end of the rains, afford a period of relaxation before rural activity climaxes with the rice harvest in December and January.

NOVEMBER

Golden Mount Fair *(first week)*, Bangkok. Thailand's largest temple fair, held at the foot of the Golden Mount.
Elephant Roundup *(third week)*, Surin. Annual spectacle honoring the many and varied roles played by the elephant in Thailand's development *(see p278)*. More than 150 elephants take part in displays of forestry skills and a mock battle.
Khwae River Bridge Week *(late Nov/early Dec)*, Kanchanaburi. Commemorates the construction of the bridge by POWs and slave labor.
Loy Krathong *(Nov full moon)*. One of Thailand's best-loved national festivals. Pays homage to the goddess of rivers and waterways, Mae Khongkha. In the evening, people gather at rivers, lakes, and ponds to float *krathongs*. Sukhothai is the best place to watch this festival *(see p195)*.

Colorful spectacle of the boat races at Nan in Northern Thailand

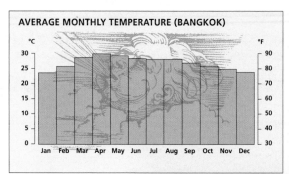

AVERAGE MONTHLY TEMPERATURE (BANGKOK)

°C   °F

Temperature Chart
For visitors from temperate climes, Thailand is hot and humid throughout the year, especially in the South. It is uncomfortably so during April and May, pleasantly so in November and December. Though it is less humid in Northern Thailand, it can be chilly at night during the coolest months.

DECEMBER

Trooping of the Colors
(Dec 3), Royal Plaza, Bangkok. A very impressive ceremony that offers a vivid picture of regal pageantry. It is presided over by the king and queen and features members of the elite Royal Guards, arrayed in bright dress uniform. The guardsmen swear allegiance to the king and march past members of the royal family.
His Majesty the King's Birthday *(Dec 5)*. Government and private buildings throughout the country are elaborately decorated, and the area around the Grand Palace is illuminated. In the evening, crowds gather around Sanam Luang for celebrations. This occasion shows the deep respect Thais have for their king.

Soldiers in dress uniform for the Trooping of the Colors in Bangkok

JANUARY

Chinese New Year *(Jan/Feb)*. Not an official holiday, but this three-day festival is widely observed by the large number of Thais of Chinese origin.
Umbrella Fair *(mid-Jan)*, Bo Sang, Chiang Mai province. Celebrates traditional paper and wood umbrella making *(see p228)*.
Don Chedi Memorial Fair *(late Jan)*, Suphan Buri province. Marks the victory of King Naresuan of Ayutthaya over the Burmese. The highlight of the events is an elephant-back duel.

FEBRUARY

Festival of Flowers *(first week)*, Chiang Mai. Beautiful blooms of the north displayed on floral float parades.
Kite Flying Season *(Feb–Apr)*, Sanam Luang, Bangkok. Colorful displays and kite flying contests.

Makha Bucha *(Feb full moon)*. Third of the year's major Buddhist festivals. Merit-making and candlelit processions at temples.

PUBLIC HOLIDAYS

Western New Year's Day (Jan 1)
Makha Bucha (Feb or Mar full moon)
Chakri Day (Apr 6)
Thai New Year – Song-kran (Apr 13-15)
Labour Day (May 1)
Coronation Day (May 5)
Royal Plowing Ceremony (early May)
Visakha Bucha Day (May full moon)
Asanha Bucha and Khao Phansa (Jul full moon)
Queen's Birthday (Aug 12)
Chulalongkorn Day (Oct 23)
King's Birthday (Dec 5)
Constitution Day (Dec 10)
Western New Year's Eve (Dec 31)

Wat Phra Kaeo on the King's Birthday

THE HISTORY OF THAILAND

The history of Thailand is that of an area of Southeast Asia, rather than of a single nation, and over the centuries numerous peoples have made their home in this region. The most recent were the Tai of Southern China, who migrated south in the first millennium AD, and from whom most Thais today are descended.

Prehistoric Thailand was once regarded as a cultural backwater. In the Northeast of the country, however, archaeologists uncovered the earliest evidence of agriculture and metallurgy

Votive tablet from Ayutthaya

in Southeast Asia. Also among the finds were ceramic pots, some dating as far back as 3000 BC, that display a high level of artistic skill.

The earliest known powers in the region were the Dvaravati Kingdom (6th–11th centuries AD), the Sumatran-based Srivijaya Empire (7th–13th centuries), and the Khmer Empire (9th–13th centuries) based at Angkor *(see p264)*, all of which were heavily influenced by Indian culture and religion.

The Lanna Kingdom in the North and the Sukhothai Kingdom, which imported Theravada Buddhism to Thailand, in the Central Plains grew in power from around the 12th century. Today, Thai schoolchildren are taught that Sukhothai marks the beginning of their history. Of all its kings, Ramkamhaeng (1279–98) stands out: part heroic myth, part historical figure.

Sukhothai was conquered by the Kingdom of Ayutthaya – also Tai – in the 14th century. At its height Ayutthaya ruled most of what is now Thailand, and the city of Ayutthaya saw the arrival of the first Europeans. The city was destroyed by the Burmese in 1767. A new city, Krung Thep (Bangkok), was then built farther south, on the Chao Phraya River, and the Chakri dynasty founded. In the 19th century Kings Mongkut and Chulalongkorn modernized Thailand. During this period, Thailand resisted colonization by France and Britain.

A revolution in 1932 ended absolute monarchy, and in 1939 Phibun Songkram, formerly a soldier in the Thai army, changed the country's name from Siam to Thailand. There have been a number of coups since then, and a cycle of economic boom and bust in the 1980s and '90s, but Thailand remains relatively stable in comparison to neighboring countries.

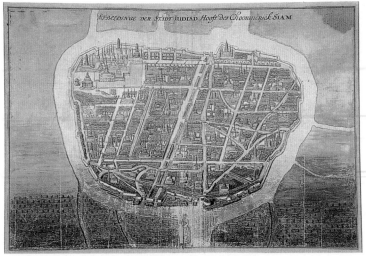

Dutch map of the city of Ayutthaya, probably drawn in the 17th century

◁ Chakri period painted screen, dating from the late 18th century

Prehistoric Thailand

Hunter-gatherers were already established in the area of modern-day Thailand by around 40,000 BC. They lived in semi-permanent settlements and made tools from wood and stone. Ancient seed husks found in caves in Northern Thailand have led to speculation that agriculture began to develop around 9000 BC. Rice was being cultivated around 3000 BC. Subsequently, in the area of Ban Chiang, elaborate pottery and bronze work began to be produced. This Bronze Age culture is believed by some historians to be the earliest in the world.

Jewelry from Ban Chiang

PREHISTORIC SITES

Ban Kao Tripod
This three-legged, terra-cotta pot was made by Neolithic artisans around 2100 BC. It was found at Ban Kao (see p170) in the Central Plains.

The flared rim and slightly more complex geometric pattern on this black and white, cord-incised pot were new stylistic features.

Molded shoulders

Bronze Axe Head
The earliest bronze artifacts found at Ban Chiang, such as this axe head, are thought to date from about 2100 BC.

A black and white pattern was created by incising the clay with cord.

Clay feet

2100 BC

c.1600

Clay Molds
Clay molds confirm that bronze objects were cast at Ban Chiang and not imported from elsewhere.

BAN CHIANG POTTERY

Pots found at Ban Chiang *(see p272)* date from 2100 BC to AD 200. Until their discovery in 1966, this area of Southeast Asia was thought to have produced little of cultural merit in prehistoric times. These, and other finds, show that the indigenous peoples were capable of producing sophisticated, beautiful works of art.

TIMELINE

40,000 BC Hunter-gatherers in area of modern-day Thailand	*Bronze spearhead*		**2100–1500 BC** Bronze artifacts and elaborate cord-marked pottery created at Ban Chiang	**1000 BC** Cave and cliff paintings at Pha Taem *(p298)*
6000 BC First pottery created by inhabitants of Spirit Cave		**3000 BC** Domestication of animals (pigs, dogs, chickens, and cattle)		
50,000 BC	**5000 BC**	**4000 BC**	**3000 BC**	**2000 BC**
	3500 BC Rice chaff left in Banyan Valley Cave – beginning of rice cultivation		**2000 BC** Clay and bronze pots created at Ban Kao	**1000 BC** Bronze animals cast at Don Tha Phet
	9000–7000 BC Seed and plant husks left in caves in Northern Thailand may indicate the beginnings of agriculture			

Iron Age Rooster
A find of bronze and iron artifacts at Don Tha Phet, near Kanchanaburi (see p170), includes this iron rooster from about 1000 BC.

WHERE TO SEE PREHISTORIC THAILAND

At Ban Chiang (see p272) visitors can see burial sites and artifacts housed in the Ban Chiang National Museum. More Ban Chiang artifacts can be seen in the Bangkok National Museum (pp88–9). At Ban Kao (p170) there are burial sites and a museum, and cave paintings can be seen at Pha Taem (p298) and Phu Phrabat Historical Park (p295).

Cave Painting
These paintings at Pha Taem date from around 1000 BC. The artists were probably descended from the early inhabitants of Ban Chiang.

Paint rather than cord is used to create a complex geometric pattern.

Burial sites *at Ban Chiang were filled with pots that were placed around the dead.*

Narrow stand

300 BC–AD 1

Rust-colored geometric designs were painted on a beige ground.

300 BC–AD 200

Bronze Bracelets
As well as practical objects, the craftsmen of Ban Chiang were skilled at making elaborate jewelry. These bracelets probably date from the height of Ban Chiang's Bronze Age, around 300–200 BC.

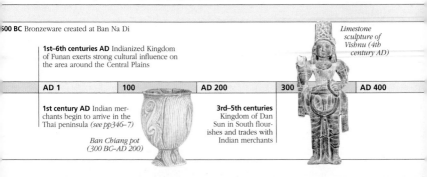

500 BC Bronzeware created at Ban Na Di

1st–6th centuries AD Indianized Kingdom of Funan exerts strong cultural influence on the area around the Central Plains

Limestone sculpture of Vishnu (4th century AD)

AD 1	100	AD 200	300	AD 400

1st century AD Indian merchants begin to arrive in the Thai peninsula (see pp346–7)

Ban Chiang pot (300 BC–AD 200)

3rd–5th centuries Kingdom of Dan Sun in South flourishes and trades with Indian merchants

The First States

Srivijayan votive tablet

From the first few centuries BC Hindu and Buddhist missionaries from India and Sri Lanka came to Southeast Asia. Over the next millennium distinctly Indianized kingdoms emerged. The Dvaravati Kingdom (6th–11th centuries) flourished in what is now the heart of Thailand; the Srivijaya Empire of Sumatra (7th–13th centuries) was strong in the peninsula (see pp346–7); while the Khmer Empire (9th–13th centuries) expanded from Cambodia (see pp264–5). The Tai, from southern China, migrated to the area from the 11th century onward.

KHMER EMPIRE IN AD 960

☐ Extent of Khmer Empire

Flying Buddha (8th–9th centuries)
This Dvaravati sculpture shows the Buddha on the back of Panaspati, a strange beast that comprises Nandin the bull, Shiva's mount, and a garuda (a mythical bird).

Vishnu, asleep on the back of the *naga*, dreams of a new universe.

Stone Relief
Dvaravati craftsmen were renowned for their stonework. They excelled at bas-reliefs such as this one, at Wat Suthat (see p90), which depicts Buddhist and Hindu figures.

Dvaravati Deities
Dvaravati bas-reliefs, found in a cave near Saraburi, central Thailand, depict Brahma, Vishnu, the Buddha, and flying figures.

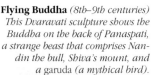

The **naga** (serpent) bearing Vishnu represents the Milky Sea of Eternity.

TIMELINE

Early 6th century Mon people establish Dvaravati culture. They have already inherited Buddhism from Indian missionaries	**7th century** Srivijaya civilization expands from Sumatra	**8th century** Tai people inhabit the upland valleys of Laos, northern Vietnam, and southern China

Dvaravati coin

500	600	700	800

Dvaravati stucco head

7th century Chamadevi of Lop Buri becomes Queen of the Dvaravati Kingdom

AD 661 Haripunchai said to be founded at Lamphun, Northern Thailand (see p229), by Buddhist holymen

9th century Khmer Empire founded at Angkor

Devaraja
This Khmer bas-relief, one of many found at Angkor Wat (see pp264–5), shows the god-king, or devaraja, *King Suryavarman II (1113–50).*

Terra-cotta Lion *(8th-century) Dvaravati figures, such as this lion from Phetchaburi (see pp328–9), were influenced by earlier Gupta art from India.*

The Creator, Brahma, sitting on a lotus blossom springing from Vishnu's stomach, has the task of realizing Vishnu's dream of creating a new universe.

WHERE TO SEE THE FIRST STATES

Dvaravati, Srivijayan, and Khmer artifacts can be seen at the Bangkok National Museum *(see pp88–9)* as well as at other regional national museums. Two Dvaravati-style *chedis* can be seen at Wat Chama Thewi in Lamphun *(p229)*. Phra Boromathat Chaiya *(p333)* is the best-surviving example of a Srivijayan temple. Khmer sites in Thailand include Prasat Hin Phimai *(pp276–7)* and Prasat Hin Khao Phnom Rung *(pp280–81)*.

Prasat Hin Phimai *was built mostly during the reign of Surya-varman I in the 11th century.*

Srivijayan Buddha
This Buddha image, one of the most notable of the Srivijaya period, was found in Chaiya (see p333), an ancient city in peninsular Thailand.

KHMER LINTEL
The Khmers built temples throughout their vast empire, many of which are in present-day Northeast Thailand. Intricate stone carvings are a striking feature of the monuments – the characters depicted *(see p41)* are mainly Hindu, though some are Mahayana Buddhist. This lintel, from Prasat Hin Khao Phnom Rung *(see pp280–81)*, depicts a Hindu creation myth.

11th–13th centuries Lop Buri incorporated into Khmer Empire as a significant provincial capital	**1001–1002** Reign of Udayadit-yavarman, who invades Haripunchai (Lamphun) following an assault on Lop Buri	**1229–43** Reign of Indravarman II	
		1115–55 Lop Buri tries to assert its independence from Khmer control	
900	**1000**	**1100**	**1200**
10th–12th centuries Srivijaya becomes involved in ruinous wars with Chola state in India	**11th–12th centuries** Population of Tai people increases in areas of present-day Thailand, then under Khmer control	**1113–50** Reign of Suryavarman II *Lop Buri Buddha*	**1181–1220** Reign of Jayavarman VII, the most powerful and innovative of the Khmer kings

The Kingdom of Sukhothai

Sukhothai coin

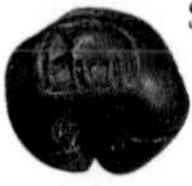

Sukhothai was the first notable kingdom of the Tai people, centered around the city of Sukhothai *(see pp194–7)* in the Central Plains. The Khmers referred to the Tai as *Siam*, a name that came to be used for this and subsequent Tai kingdoms. Theravada Buddhism achieved new expression during the Sukhothai period, in innovative architecture and images of the Buddha finely cast in bronze. Sukhothai was made powerful by its most illustrious ruler, Ramkamhaeng, but by 1320 was only a local power again.

SUKHOTHAI IN 1300

☐ *Sukhothai Kingdom*

Ramkamhaeng (c.1279–98)
This modern relief depicts Ramkamhaeng, Sukhothai's most illustrious ruler. He extended the kingdom and negotiated treaties with neighboring states.

Inscription No. 1 (1292)
Ramkamhaeng is credited with inventing the Thai alphabet and using it to record the history of Sukhothai on this stone.

Roof Decoration
Ceramics were used to adorn buildings. This one is from the 14th century.

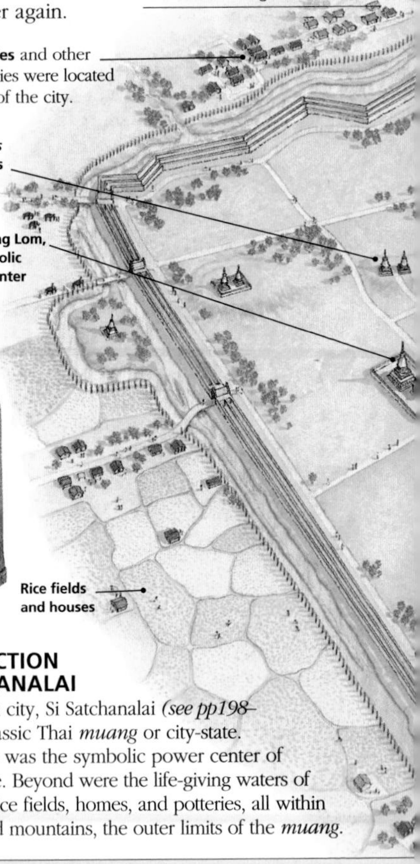

Potteries and other industries were located north of the city.

Minor *wats* on low hills

Wat Chang Lom, the symbolic power center

Rice fields and houses

RECONSTRUCTION OF SI SATCHANALAI

Sukhothai's twin city, Si Satchanalai *(see pp198–200)* was the classic Thai *muang* or city-state. Within the walls was the symbolic power center of the crown prince. Beyond were the life-giving waters of the Yom River, rice fields, homes, and potteries, all within a ring of forested mountains, the outer limits of the *muang*.

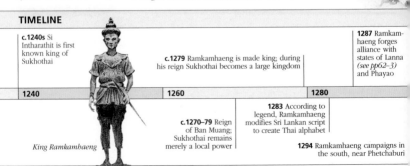

TIMELINE

c.1240s Si Intharathit is first known king of Sukhothai

c.1279 Ramkamhaeng is made king; during his reign Sukhothai becomes a large kingdom

1287 Ramkamhaeng forges alliance with states of Lanna *(see pp62–3)* and Phayao

1240 — **1260** — **1280**

King Ramkamhaeng

c.1270–79 Reign of Ban Muang; Sukhothai remains merely a local power

1283 According to legend, Ramkamhaeng modifies Sri Lankan script to create Thai alphabet

1294 Ramkamhaeng campaigns in the south, near Phetchaburi

Slate Engraving
This 14th-century engraving shows the Buddha being reincarnated as a horse. It is one of a series discovered at Wat Si Chum (see p195) at Sukhothai.

Minor *wat*

Rapids

Sangkhalok Pottery
Sawankhalok was the old name for Si Satchanalai, where many kilns (see pp160–61) were sited. From this derives the name Sangkhalok, given to 13th–15th-century pottery from the Sukhothai Kingdom.

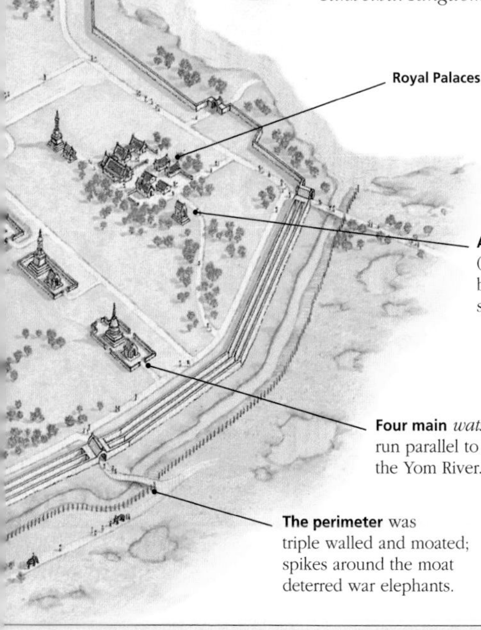

WHERE TO SEE THE SUKHOTHAI KINGDOM
The main sites are Sukhothai itself (see pp194–7), Si Satchanalai (pp198–200), and Kamphaeng Phet (pp192–3). Artifacts are housed in the Bangkok National Museum (pp88–9), the Ramkamhaeng National Museum (pp194–5), the Sawankha Woranayok National Museum (p200), and the Kamphaeng Phet National Museum (see p192).

Wat Sa Si *(see p195) is just one of dozens of wats at Sukhothai Historical Park.*

Royal Palaces

A Lak Muang
(city pillar) was built to appease the spirits of the land.

Walking Buddha
New, sophisticated techniques for casting bronze produced this classic 14th-century Walking Buddha image.

Four main *wats* run parallel to the Yom River.

The perimeter was triple walled and moated; spikes around the moat deterred war elephants.

1298 Ramkamhaeng dies

End of 13th century Sukhothai first called Siam by Chinese

14th–15th-century Sangkhalok bowl

1346–7 Reign of Ngua Nam Thom

1300 | **1320** | **1340**

1298–1346 Reign of Lo Thai, who succeeds Ramkamhaeng. Empire begins to unravel

14th–15th-century Sukhothai stoneware

1321 Tak, formerly part of Sukhothai, falls under Lanna control; Sukhothai is now a small kingdom, one of many competing states

1347–1368 Reign of Maha Thammaracha I

The Kingdom of Ayutthaya

Ayutthayan Buddha

Ayutthaya supplanted Sukhothai as the most powerful kingdom in Siam in the mid-14th century and by 1438 had incorporated it into its empire. By the mid-16th century Ayutthaya controlled the entire Central Plains area and at its height held sway over much of what is now Thailand. The Ayutthaya period saw military, legal, and administrative reforms and a flowering of the arts, as well as diplomatic and trade links with the West (see pp162–3). Its end came after years of conflict with Burma, when in 1767 the capital was sacked.

AYUTTHAYA IN 1540

☐ *Kingdom of Ayutthaya*

Ayutthayan Frescoes
Few frescoes have survived. These, from the 15th century, are from Wat Ratchaburana in Ayutthaya (see pp176–81).

Gold Elephant
The Ayutthayans were masters at working gold. This elephant, studded with gems and crafted to look as though it is paying homage, was discovered in Wat Ratchaburana.

Votive Tablets
Clay and terra-cotta tablets from the Ayutthaya period often show the Buddha resplendent beneath a naga (serpent).

Ornate, stylized carvings

A huge oar at the stern helped steer the boat.

Gold lacquer was used to decorate the barges.

RECONSTRUCTION OF A ROYAL BARGE

When foreigners (*farangs*) first came to Ayutthaya, they often met the sight of grand royal barges. This illustration is based on French engravings in some of the first accounts of the opulent city of Ayutthaya to reach the West.

TIMELINE OF THE AYUTTHAYA KINGDOM

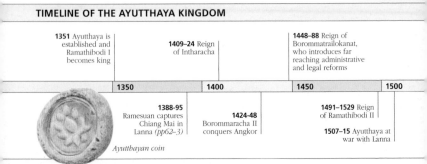

1351 Ayutthaya is established and Ramathibodi I becomes king

1409–24 Reign of Intharacha

1448–88 Reign of Borommatrailokanat, who introduces far reaching administrative and legal reforms

1350	1400	1450	1500

1388–95 Ramesuan captures Chiang Mai in Lanna (*pp62–3*)

1424–48 Borommaracha II conquers Angkor

1491–1529 Reign of Ramathibodi II

1507–15 Ayutthaya at war with Lanna

Ayutthayan coin

Gilded Lacquer Cabinet
The craftsmen of Ayutthaya were adept at working wood. The doors of this cabinet are inlaid with gold; the pattern is of trees. Other such cabinets depict scenes from the jataka *or Westerners.*

WHERE TO SEE AYUTTHAYA

The city of Ayutthaya in the South Central Plains has some of the most spectacular ruins in Thailand *(see pp176–81)*. Ayutthayan artifacts are housed in the Chao Sam Phraya National Museum *(p178)* and in the Bangkok National Museum *(pp88–9)*.

Wat Chai Watthanaram, *built by King Prasat Thong in 1630.*

Door Panel from Ayutthaya
This 17th–18th-century wood panel once formed part of the door of a temple. It was discovered in Wat Huntra in Ayutthaya.

Carving of the king

Royal insignia

The oarsmen would chant barge songs to keep paddling in time.

Deva Figure
Carved "angels," such as this 18th-century figure, were used in religious ceremonies.

1585–7 Naresuan defeats Burmese twice

1555 Naresuan is born

Ayutthayan soldier

1593 Naresuan defeats Burmese at Battle of Nong Sarai *(pp62–3)*

1660 Narai tries to take Chiang Mai and Lampang in Lanna from Burmese rule, but is repelled by a Burmese army

1685 First French mission in Ayutthaya

1766 Burmese forces, after taking Chiang Mai, besiege Ayutthaya

| 1550 | 1600 | 1650 | 1700 | 1750 |

1564 Burmese invade the kingdom of Ayutthaya

1608 Siam sends its first diplomatic mission to Europe

1569–90 Ayutthaya under Burmese rule

1662 Narai invades Burma

1688 Narai's death leads to "revolution" in Ayutthaya

King Narai

1767 Ayutthaya sacked, capital moves to Thon Buri

Lanna and Burmese Kingdoms

Lanna urn

The northern kingdom of Lanna was established at the same time as Sukhothai and endured for 600 years. Its first ruler, Mengrai, extended Lanna rule into Burma (now Myanmar), and the reigns of Ku Na and Tilok saw a golden age. Wars with Burma and Ayutthaya in the 16th and 17th centuries, however, led to decline. Ayutthaya had driven the Burmese out of Lanna once before, but in 1615 the Burmese took back the Lanna capital, Chiang Mai, for almost a century. In the late 1700s, newly allied

Siamese and Lanna forces drove the Burmese out. Lanna remained autonomous into the 19th century.

LANNA IN 1540

☐ *Lanna Kingdom*

Golden Door
Decorated with gold leaf, this temple door is at Wat Phra That Lampang Luang (see pp234–5), one of the oldest Lanna structures in Thailand.

Naresuan, on his elephant, engages the Burmese crown prince.

Ayutthayan soldiers, in traditional helmets, rally round Naresuan.

Lanna Elephant
This bronze elephant, from the 16th century, was used as a pedestal upon which Buddhist merit offerings were presented.

Bronze Buddha
Buddha images such as this one from the 14th–15th century are regarded as the pinnacle of classical Lanna art. After the Burmese took the north, this style of Lanna art declined.

BATTLE OF NONG SARAI (1593)

The Burmese attempted to control all of Siam, and, in 1564, invaded Ayutthaya. This 19th-century painting shows the Battle of Nong Sarai, when Naresuan (1590–1605) defeated the Burmese crown prince and Ayutthaya gained independence. In 1598 Ayutthaya drove Burma from the north, but in the 17th century the Burmese retook it.

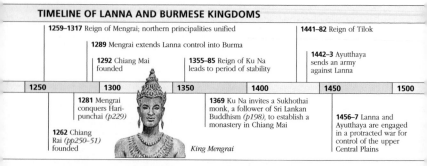

TIMELINE OF LANNA AND BURMESE KINGDOMS

1259–1317 Reign of Mengrai; northern principalities unified

1289 Mengrai extends Lanna control into Burma

1292 Chiang Mai founded

1355–85 Reign of Ku Na leads to period of stability

1441–82 Reign of Tilok

1442–3 Ayutthaya sends an army against Lanna

1250	1300	1350	1400	1450	1500

1281 Mengrai conquers Haripunchai (p229)

1262 Chiang Rai (pp250–51) founded

1369 Ku Na invites a Sukhothai monk, a follower of Sri Lankan Buddhism (p198), to establish a monastery in Chiang Mai

1456–7 Lanna and Ayutthaya are engaged in a protracted war for control of the upper Central Plains

King Mengrai

Model Wihan

Models of wihans *are common throughout Thailand. This Lanna one, from the 18th–19th century, cast in bronze, has a high base, an exaggerated version of the bases found on many Lanna temple buidings.*

WHERE TO SEE LANNA AND BURMESE THAILAND

Lanna artifacts can be seen in national museums at Chiang Mai, Lamphun *(see p229)*, and Bangkok. Chiang Mai *(pp224–7)*, Chiang Khong *(p249)*, Lamphun, and Lampang *(p236)* all have buildings that date from the Lanna period. Mae Hong Son *(pp216–17)* and Phrae *(pp258–9)* have buildings showing Burmese influence.

The ho trai *(scripture library) of Wat Phra Sing, Chiang Mai, is one of the most notable late Lanna structures in Thailand.*

Burmese Dancer

This temple mural of a Burmese dancing girl is from Chiang Mai (see pp224–7). A number of wats *in the North bear similar indications of Burmese occupation.*

Burmese soldiers wear simple bandanas around their heads.

Lanna Coin

During the 18th and 19th centuries, bronze rings were used as coinage in the Lanna Kingdom.

Lanna Wood Carvings

The pediment of the 19th-century wihan *at Wat Pan Tao (see p225) is typical of the elaborate work produced by Lanna wood carvers.*

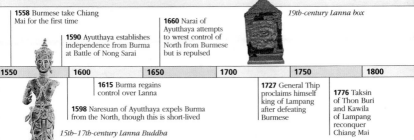

19th-century Lanna box

1558 Burmese take Chiang Mai for the first time

1590 Ayutthaya establishes independence from Burma at Battle of Nong Sarai

1660 Narai of Ayutthaya attempts to wrest control of North from Burmese but is repulsed

1615 Burma regains control over Lanna

1598 Naresuan of Ayutthaya expels Burma from the North, though this is short-lived

15th–17th-century Lanna Buddha

1727 General Thip proclaims himself king of Lampang after defeating Burmese

1776 Taksin of Thon Buri and Kawila of Lampang reconquer Chiang Mai

1550	1600	1650	1700	1750	1800

The Early Chakri Dynasty

Court dress, c.1850

After the sack of Ayutthaya, Taksin, an army general, established a new capital at Thon Buri, on the west bank of the Chao Phraya opposite what would later become Bangkok. He became king in 1768, and in ten years Siam was a regional power again. However, he became increasingly despotic and, in 1782, was ousted by the military commander Chao Phraya Chakri, who was later pronounced King Rama I. Chakri's descendant, King Mongkut (Rama IV), modernized Siam, opening it up to foreign trade and influence.

SIAM IN 1809

☐ *Siamese territories*

Chakri Kings
The reigns of Ramas I, II, and III signaled an era of stable monarchical rule. Rama II was a literary man, while Rama III was a great merchant.

Khlongs are an important means of transportation

Chakri Throne
The Busabok Mala Maha Piman Throne was built in the reign of Rama I for important occasions. It is in the Grand Palace (see pp80–85).

The Grand Palace
(see pp80–85) was founded in the late 18th century; by the mid-19th century it is already vast.

Sir John Bowring
The Bowring Treaty (1855) allowed the British free trade. Later, Siam forged similar treaties with other colonial powers, thus avoiding annexation.

TIMELINE

1768 Taksin begins to re-establish Siamese Empire

Ramakien mural

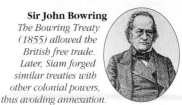

1800 Burmese finally expelled from Siam

1797 Rama I "writes" Ramakien *(see pp40–41)*

1813 Siam withdraws from Cambodia leaving Vietnam as dominant power

1770	1780	1790	1800	1810

1782 Rama I overthrows an increasingly despotic Taksin; relocates capital

1783 Wat Phra Kaeo begun

1785 Massive Burmese invasion repulsed

1805 Rama I appoints a committee of judges to reform Siamese law

1808–24 Reign of Rama II

Thai Etiquette *(1855)*
In mid-19th century Siam, prostrating oneself before a superior was common. It was officially abolished by Rama V (see pp66–7).

WHERE TO SEE EARLY CHAKRI THAILAND
Almost all the best examples of architecture from the early Chakri – or Rattanakosin *(see p35)* – period can be seen in Bangkok. The earliest Chakri building is the *bot* of Wat Phra Kaeo *(p80)*. Other examples include the *bot* of Wat Suthat *(pp90–91)*, the *wihan* of Wat Suthat, Wat Pho *(pp92–3)*, and Phra Nakhon Khiri *(see p330)*.

Mongkut *(1851–68)*
Before coming to the throne Mongkut, pictured here with his favorite wife, traveled widely, meeting many Westerners.

Thon Buri, on the western bank of the Chao Phraya, is still just a small town.

Wat Suthat, *built in the early 19th century by Rama I, is the site of Bangkok's tallest* wihan.

EARLY BANGKOK (KRUNG THEP)

The Siamese capital was moved from Thon Buri to the east of the river in 1782 as a defense against the Burmese. Its official 43-syllable name matches the majesterial plans that Rama I had for his new city: the first two words, "Krung Thep," mean "city of angels." This mural from 1864 shows the temples and river houses of early Bangkok.

King Mongkut Mural
In this mural King Mongkut is in his palace observing an eclipse through a telescope, his subjects below him.

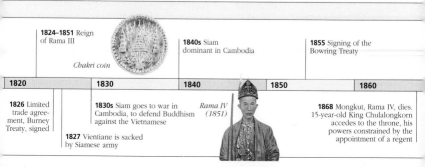

1824–1851 Reign of Rama III

Chakri coin

1840s Siam dominant in Cambodia

1855 Signing of the Bowring Treaty

| 1820 | 1830 | 1840 | 1850 | 1860 |

1826 Limited trade agreement, Burney Treaty, signed

1830s Siam goes to war in Cambodia, to defend Buddhism against the Vietnamese

Rama IV (1851)

1827 Vientiane is sacked by Siamese army

1868 Mongkut, Rama IV, dies. 15-year-old King Chulalongkorn accedes to the throne, his powers constrained by the appointment of a regent

Reign of King Chulalongkorn

Perhaps the greatest king of the Chakri dynasty, Chulalongkorn (1868–1910) carried on the modernization of Siam that his father, Mongkut, had started. Financial reforms were made, the government restructured, and slavery abolished. Reform angered older ministers, the "conservatives" *(hua boran)*, and led to the Front Palace Crisis of 1875. This was also a time when Britain and France were consolidating their positions in Southeast Asia.

Rama V in Western garb

Chulalongkorn's policies and diplomacy kept the colonial powers at bay, though parts of Burma, Laos, Cambodia, and the Malay states were ceded to them.

SIAM IN 1909

☐ *Siamese territories*

▨ *Ceded territories*

Rama V
Chulalongkorn (Rama V) came to the throne, under the guidance of a regent, at the age of 15. He had received an excellent Thai and Western education and was well qualified for the task of reforming Siam.

Soldiers attending the cremation wore colonial uniforms.

Drummers wore traditional Thai headdresses.

Life on the Khlongs
At the end of the 19th century, and into the 20th, Bangkok was known as the "Venice of the East" (see p125).

Classical Dancers at Court
Many Siamese traditions, among them classical dance, remained unchanged. Scenes such as this were often recorded with the aid of new technology – photography.

TIMELINE

1874 Chulalongkorn (Rama V) introduces a series of reforms that anger the "conservatives" or *hua boran*

1874 Thai High Commissioner sent to govern Lanna

1875 Front Palace Crisis – the "conservatives" demonstrate their anger. Chulalongkorn has to tone down some of his reforms

Tile detail, Wat Rachabophit

1885 Enlightened Prince Devawongse made Foreign Minister

1887 Prince Devawongse attends the celebrations, in London, of Queen Victoria's 50th year; the prince studies European government with a view to reform in Siam

1888 New administrative system, centralizing power, is introduced

| 1870 | 1875 | 1880 | 1885 |

Franco-Siamese Crisis

In an attempt to consolidate her hold over Indochina, in 1893 France asserted sovereignty over Siamese-controlled Laos. This cartoon shows a French "wolf" hungrily assessing a Siamese "lamb."

Chulalongkorn's body was cremated in this funeral tower.

WHERE TO SEE LATE CHAKRI THAILAND

During the latter part of the 19th century there was little change in the basic style of religious buildings. Chulalongkorn, however, left his mark on some buildings in Bangkok. Wat Benchamabophit *(see pp106–7)* employs an eclectic mixture of Chinese, Italian, and Khmer styles, while Wat Rachabophit *(p89)* displays traditional Thai and Western motifs.

At Wat Rachabopit, *Rama V had the interior decorated in Italianate-Thai style.*

CREMATION OF CHULALONGKORN

Chulalongkorn's cremation, held in Bangkok in 1910, was a grand state affair. As a great reformer, he was idealized by his subjects, and even today the people of Thailand commemorate his death on Chulalongkorn Day *(see p50).*

Modern Developments

Chulalongkorn promoted many new ideas; cars appeared in Bangkok at the beginning of the 20th century.

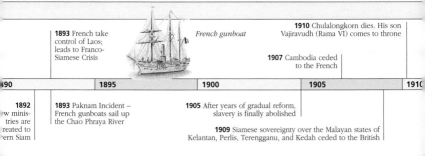

1893 French take control of Laos; leads to Franco-Siamese Crisis

French gunboat

1910 Chulalongkorn dies. His son Vajiravudh (Rama VI) comes to throne

1907 Cambodia ceded to the French

1890   **1895**   **1900**   **1905**   **1910**

1892 ew ministries are reated to ern Siam

1893 Paknam Incident – French gunboats sail up the Chao Phraya River

1905 After years of gradual reform, slavery is finally abolished

1909 Siamese sovereignty over the Malayan states of Kelantan, Perlis, Terengganu, and Kedah ceded to the British

Modern Thailand

Modern Thai flag

In 1932 Siam became a constitutional monarchy. Under Prime Minister Phibun Songkram, the 1930s saw rising nationalism: the country was renamed Prathet Thai (Thailand) and sided with Japan in World War II. However, during the Vietnam War, fear of Communism led Thailand to help the US. A number of military coups have since hindered democratization; in 2006 the ousting of Prime Minister Thaksin Shinawatra caused political division. Shinawatra's sister, Yingluck, was elected Prime Minister in 2011 and aims to reconcile the nation.

ASEAN IN 2008

☐ *Association of SE Asian Nations*

King Vajiravudh

Chulalongkorn's son Vajiravudh (1910–25) clashed with his father's senior advisors. To build a following of his own he created the elite corps, the Wild Tigers, in 1911.

Democracy Monument

A meeting place during prodemocracy rallies, this monument was built in 1939 to mark the revolution of 1932. The last major demonstration held here was in 1992.

Commercial buildings by the Waterfront

Wat Phra Kaeo

MODERN BANGKOK

With an official population of around 9.5 million (though unofficially it could be closer to 15 million), Bangkok is one of the most frenetic, congested, and polluted cities in the world. It is also a colorful city where old traditions are still important. The 1982 Bangkok Bicentennial and the celebrations of Bhumibol's 50th year as King in 1996 (shown here), featured splendid royal barges.

TIMELINE

1911 Wild Tigers, an elite paramilitary corps, formed

1932 Revolution; Siam made a constitutional monarchy

1935 Prajadhipok abdicates, Ananda Mahidol becomes king

1938 Phibun Songkram becomes Prime Minister

1939 Phibun renames Siam

1959 Sarit Thanarat becomes Prime Minister in coup

1946 Phibun resigns; Pridi Phanomyong forms government

1920	1930	1940	1950	1960

1917 Siam sends a small force of men to fight on the side of the Allies in WWI

Phibun Songkram

1925 Prajadhipok becomes king

1934–8 Increasing power struggle between Phibun Songkram and Pridi Phanomyong

1940 Thais invade Laos and Cambodia after fall of France to Germany

1941 Phibun capitulates to Japan; Pridi Phanomyong organizes underground resistance

1946 Mahidol killed; Bhumibol made king

1967 Thailand becomes founder member of Association of Southeast Asian Nations (ASEAN)

Traffic Congestion
Modern Bangkok has a reputation for severe traffic jams, but the Skytrain, airport rail link, and underground have eased traffic congestion.

King Bhumibol
Against a backdrop of unstable politics, the revered King Bhumibol (Rama IX) has represented virtue and stability. Through his authority, the military coup and bloody demonstrations of 1992 were ended.

WHERE TO SEE MODERN THAILAND

Apart from palaces and *wats*, most 20th-century architecture in Thailand, particularly in Bangkok, tends to be very dull and functional. However, some of the many edifices built in the 1980s and 1990s are worth a look if only for their sheer outrageousness *(see p121)*. Modern resort hotels sometimes incorporate traditional touches.

The Robot Building, *in downtown Bangkok, was designed by Sumet Jumsai in the mid-1980s.*

Ayutthaya Style barge

Stylish riverside apartments

Tourism
Despite the 2004 tsunami and the closure of Bangkok's main airport in late 2008 by anti-government protestors, Thailand remains popular with tourists.

1973–6 Turbulent democratic government; student demonstrations

1988 Fully democratic elections

2004 December 26, west coast of Southern Thailand hit by a tsunami – some 5,300 deaths

1997 Thai economy collapses

2008 Thailand returns to civilian rule

2011 Yingluck Shinawatra elected Prime Minister following anti-government protests

| 1970 | 1980 | 1990 | 2000 | 2010 | 2020 |

1976 Massacre of students at Thammasat University brings huge support for the CPT *(see p288)*

1980s CPT a spent force; Thailand enters a period of rapid economic growth

1992 Massacre of pro-democracy demonstrators in Bangkok followed by democratic elections

King Bhumibol

2006 Bloodless military coup deposes Prime Minister Thaksin Shinawatra

BANGKOK

INTRODUCING BANGKOK 72–75
OLD CITY 76–93
CHINATOWN 94–99
DUSIT 100–109
DOWNTOWN 110–121
THON BURI 122–129
FARTHER AFIELD 130–137
SHOPPING IN BANGKOK 138–141
ENTERTAINMENT IN BANGKOK 142–143
BANGKOK STREET FINDER 144–155

Introducing Bangkok

Guard statue at Wat Arun

Thailand's capital, straddling the great Chao Phraya River, 20 km (12 miles) upstream from the Gulf of Thailand, is an exuberant, exhilarating metropolis of seven and a half million people. Founded by Rama I in 1782, this relatively young city is known to Thais as Krung Thep ("city of angels"), a shortened form of a full name in excess of 150 letters. Bangkok may be a lesson in the dangers of uncontrolled urban expansion, but it is also one of the world's most exciting cities. It is highly regarded for its trendy nightclubs and cosmopolitan dining scene, and its markets, shops, magnificent *wats*, museums, palaces, and parks offer something for everyone.

The National Museum (see pp88–9) *contains a wealth of treasures, such as this 7th–8th-century head of the Buddha.*

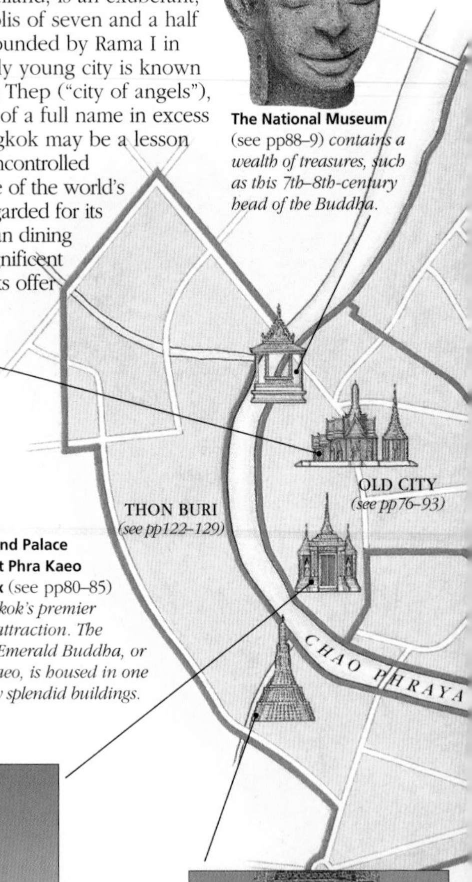

THON BURI *(see pp122–129)*

OLD CITY *(see pp76–93)*

CHAO PHRAYA

The Grand Palace and Wat Phra Kaeo complex (see pp80–85) *is Bangkok's premier tourist attraction. The sacred Emerald Buddha, or Phra Kaeo, is housed in one of many splendid buildings.*

Wat Pho (see pp92–3) *is one of the oldest temples in the capital, dating originally from the 16th century. It is also a famous center for traditional medicine and contains the much respected Institute of Massage.*

Wat Arun (see pp124–5), *otherwise known as the Temple of Dawn, is one of Bangkok's best known landmarks. Its Khmer-influenced prangs are encrusted with thousands of pieces of broken porcelain.*

◁ Intricately decorated *prangs* of the Grand Palace and Wat Phra Kaeo embellishing Bangkok's skyline

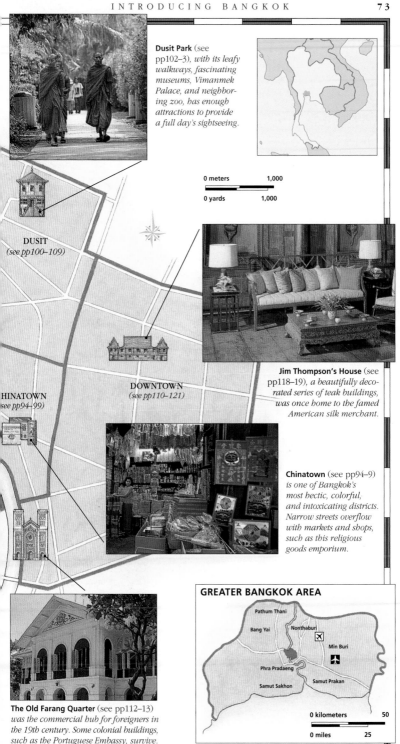

Dusit Park (see pp102–3), *with its leafy walkways, fascinating museums, Vimanmek Palace, and neighboring zoo, has enough attractions to provide a full day's sightseeing.*

| 0 meters | 1,000 |
| 0 yards | 1,000 |

DUSIT
(see pp100–109)

Jim Thompson's House (see pp118–19), *a beautifully decorated series of teak buildings, was once home to the famed American silk merchant.*

DOWNTOWN
(see pp110–121)

CHINATOWN
see pp94–99

Chinatown (see pp94–9) *is one of Bangkok's most hectic, colorful, and intoxicating districts. Narrow streets overflow with markets and shops, such as this religious goods emporium.*

GREATER BANGKOK AREA

Pathum Thani

Bang Yai   Nonthaburi

Min Buri

Phra Pradaeng

Samut Sakhon   Samut Prakan

| 0 kilometers | 50 |
| 0 miles | 25 |

The Old Farang Quarter (see pp112–13) *was the commercial hub for foreigners in the 19th century. Some colonial buildings, such as the Portuguese Embassy, survive.*

A River View of Bangkok

The two great rivers of the North, the Ping and the Nan, join at Nakhon Sawan in the Central Plains to form the Chao Phraya ("river of kings"), Thailand's most important waterway. This vital transportation link drains some of the country's most fertile rice-growing land. The stretch shown here is actually a canal, built in the 16th century as a shortcut at a point where the Chao Phraya took a huge meander along what is now Khlong Bangkok Noi and Khlong Bangkok Yai. Along this busy "royal mile" you can catch glimpses of the Grand Palace, temples, and colonial buildings, and experience a flavor of old Bangkok's colorful riverfront.

A typical Chao Phraya barge, transporting goods along the river

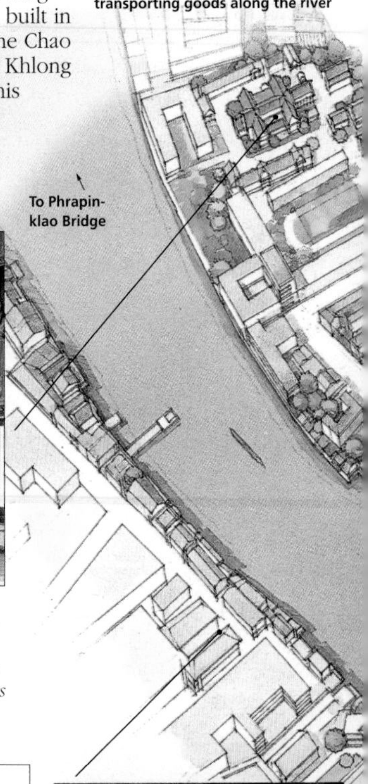

To Phrapin-klao Bridge

The Buddhaisawan Chapel in the National Museum (see pp88–9) *is home to the Phra Buddha Sing, one of the most venerated Buddha images in Thailand after the Emerald Buddha. Elsewhere in the museum is a fabulous collection of arts and crafts from every period of Thai history. Exhibits include Buddha images, weapons, and pottery.*

RIVERBOATS ON THE CHAO PHRAYA

The Chao Phraya is a major transportation artery, for both goods and people. Hefty rice barges, tiny boats laden with fruit and vegetables, and a variety of ferry services continually ply the river. No visitor to Bangkok should miss seeing the city from the water, and jumping on the Chao Phraya Express is one of the easiest and cheapest ways to do so. The stops are indicated on the Street Finder (maps 1–2, 5–6). There are also cross-river ferries from almost every river pier, as well as countless long-tail boats that operate as buses or can be specially chartered to explore the city's *khlongs*.

Wat Rakhang (see p125) *is a little visited but rewarding temple containing fine murals painted in the 1920s.*

Long-tail boat on the Chao Phraya

0 meters	200
0 yards	200

For hotels and restaurants in this region see pp398–402 and pp428–32

Wat Phra Kaeo (see pp80–83) *contains one of Thailand's most sacred Buddha images, the Emerald Buddha. The temple and palace complex is a superb collection of buildings with lavish decorative details.*

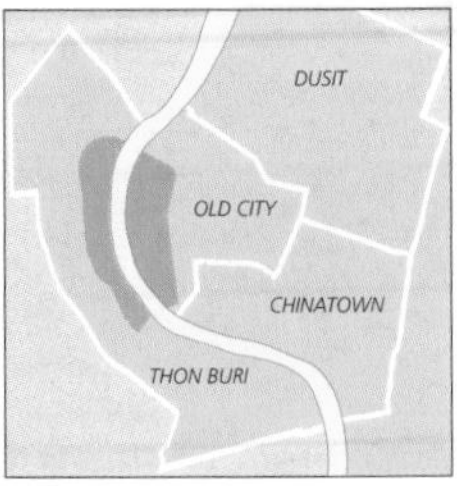

KEY

See Street Finder maps 1, 5

Sanam Luang, ("field of kings"), the venue for national ceremonies, is one of Bangkok's few open spaces.

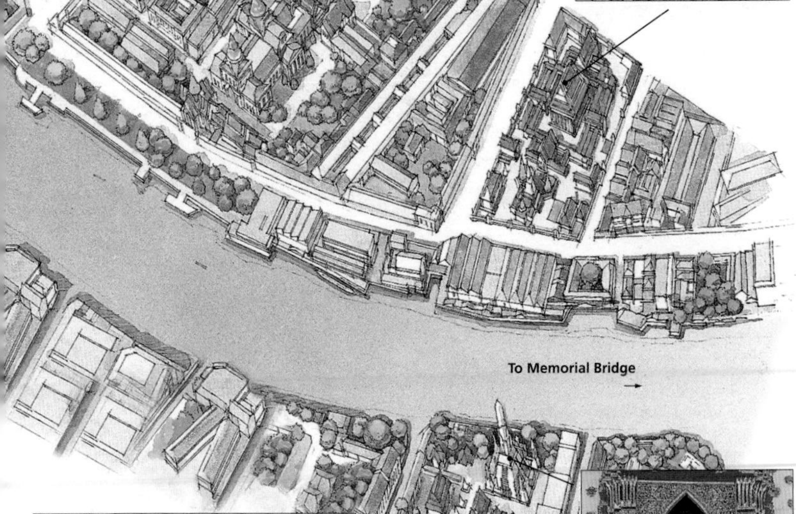

Wat Pho (see pp92–3), *the city's oldest temple, dates from the 17th century. It is famed for its school of massage, as well as for fine details such as this painting of a Chinese soldier.*

To Memorial Bridge →

The Memorial Bridge *spans the Chao Phraya River, connecting traditional Thon Buri to the modern Downtown area.*

Wat Arun (see pp126–7) *is covered in pieces of broken porcelain. This Buddha image is outside the main bot.*

OLD CITY

As the spiritual and historical heart of Bangkok, the Old City is dense with temples and shrines. Known as Rattanakosin, this was the center of the new capital Rama I founded in 1782 *(see pp64–5)*. Remnants of a defensive wall can be seen between the Golden Mount and Wat Rachanadda. Some of Thailand's finest Rattanakosin period architecture is within the Old City. The foremost example is the Grand Palace, within which is Wat Phra Kaeo, home of the

Buddha images, ready for transit

country's most venerated image, the Emerald Buddha. South of here is Wat Pho, one of the city's oldest temples, while to the north lies Sanam Luang ("field of kings"), the site of royal ceremonies. Alongside Sanam Luang, the National Museum contains Southeast Asia's most impressive artifacts. Two Buddhist universities in temples nearby: Wat Mahathat and Wat Bowonniwet. The latter is famed for its murals combining Western and traditional Thai styles.

SIGHTS AT A GLANCE

Wats

Grand Palace and Wat Phra Kaeo pp80–85 ❶
Wat Bowonniwet ❺
Wat Mahathat ❷
Wat Pho pp92–3 ⓮
Wat Rachabophit ⓬
Wat Rachanadda ❼

Wat Rachapradit ⓭
Wat Saket and the Golden Mount ❽
Wat Suthat and the Giant Swing ⓫

Museums and Galleries

Museum of Siam ⓯
National Gallery ❹
National Museum pp88–9 ❸

Notable Roads and Districts

Bamrung Muang Road ❿
Monk's Bowl Village ❾

Monuments

Democracy Monument ❻

0 meters	500
0 yards	500

GETTING THERE

If you are staying near the river, the easiest way to get to the Old City is by ferry. The Chao Phraya Express piers of Chang and Maharaj are best for the Grand Palace while Tien and Rachinee are close to Wat Pho. Many buses go to the Old City.

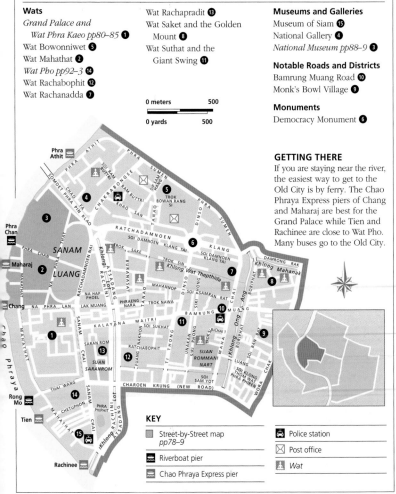

KEY

	Street-by-Street map pp78–9
Riverboat pier
Chao Phraya Express pier

	Police station
Post office
Wat

◁ **The elaborately decorated roof of the Aphonphimok Pavilion, Grand Palace**

Street-by-Street: Around Sanam Luang

สนามหลวง

Sanam Luang ("field of kings" or "royal ground") is one of the few sizeable open spaces in Bangkok. It is the traditional site for royal cremations, the annual kite flying festival, and the Royal Plowing Ceremony *(see p48)*. Spiritually speaking, this area is one of the luckiest in the city, with the Grand Palace, the Lak Muang (City Pillar) shrine, and the Amulet Market bordering Sanam Luang. Neighboring streets overflow with salesmen hawking lotions, potions, and amulets for luck, love, or protection from evil spirits. Astrologers gather to chart your stars or read your palm. Notable sights include Wat Mahathat, Thailand's most revered center of Buddhist studies, and the National Museum, which charts Thailand's fascinating history.

A monument in Sanam Luang

LOCATOR MAP
See Street Finder map 1

Phra Chan Pier

Wat Mahathat
Meditation classes are held at the Buddhist university within this temple's compound. Dating from the 18th century, the wat *is more notable for its bustling atmosphere than its buildings* ❷

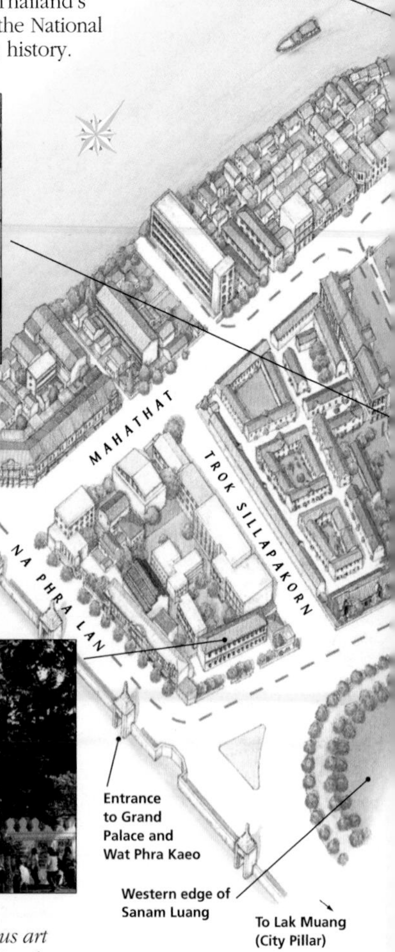

| 0 meters | 500 |
| 0 yards | 500 |

Tha Chang Chao-
Phraya Express Pier

MAHATHAT

TROK SILLAPAKORN

NA PHRA LAN

Silpakorn University of Fine Arts
The entrance to Thailand's most famous art school can be found on Na Phra Lan Road. The university regularly puts on excellent art shows in its exhibition hall. See the signs outside the entrance for details and opening times.

Entrance
to Grand
Palace and
Wat Phra Kaeo

Western edge of
Sanam Luang

To Lak Muang
(City Pillar)

KEY

－ － － Suggested route

AMULETS

The Thais are a highly superstitious people – those who do not wear some form of protective or lucky amulet are firmly in a minority. Amulets come in myriad forms and are sold in specialty markets, often near spiritually auspicious sites. Although many are religious in nature – such as tiny Buddha images and copies of sacred statues – others are designed for more practical purposes, such as model phalluses to ensure sexual potency. Amulets are such a big business that there are even magazines dedicated to them.

A selection of charms sold at stalls around Sanam Luang

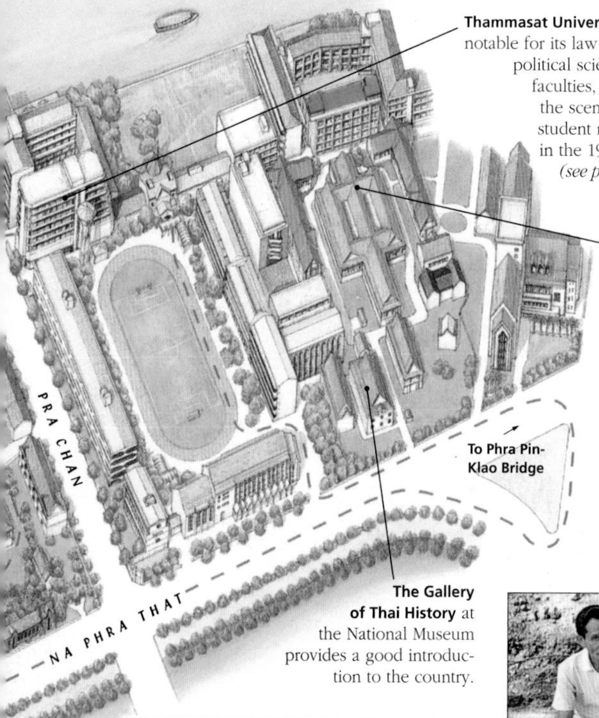

Thammasat University, notable for its law and political science faculties, was the scene of student riots in the 1970s (see p69).

★ National Museum
A magnificent range of arts and crafts from every period of Thai history are displayed in this huge museum ❸

To Phra Pin-Klao Bridge

PRA CHAN

NA PHRA THAT

The Gallery of Thai History at the National Museum provides a good introduction to the country.

Fortune Teller at Sanam Luang
Many Thais set great store by the predictions of fortune tellers and often visit those who gather on Sanam Luang near Wat Phra Kaeo.

★ Kite Flying at Sanam Luang
King Chulalongkorn (1868–1910) was an avid kite flyer and permitted Sanam Luang to be used for the sport. Fiercely contested kite fights can often be witnessed here between February and April.

STAR SIGHTS

★ National Museum

★ Kite Flying at Sanam Luang

Grand Palace and Wat Phra Kaeo ❶

พระบรมมหาราชวังและวัดพระแก้ว

Detail on Phra Mondop Library

Construction of this remarkable site began in 1782, to mark the founding of the new capital and provide a resting place for the sacred Emerald Buddha (Phra Kaeo) and a residence for the king. Surrounded by walls stretching for 1,900 m (2,080 yards), the complex was once a self-sufficient city within a city. The Royal Family now lives in Dusit, but Wat Phra Kaeo is still Thailand's holiest temple – visitors must cover their knees and heels before entering.

Wat Phra Kaeo's skyline, as seen from Sanam Luang

★ **Bot of the Emerald Buddha**
Devotees make offerings to the Emerald Buddha at the entrance to the bot, *the most important building in the* wat.

Emerald Buddha

Chapel of the Gandharara Buddha

Eight *prangs* border the east side of the wat.

★ **Ramakien Gallery**
Extending clockwise all the way around the cloisters are 178 panels depicting the complete story of the Ramakien.

TIMELINE

1750	1800	1850	1900	1950
	1783 Work begins on Wat Phra Kaeo, Dusit Throne Hall, and Phra Maha Monthien	**1855** New buildings epitomize fusion of Eastern and Western styles		**1925** Rama VII chooses to live in the less formal Chitrlada Palace at Dusit. Grand Palace reserved for special occasions
1782 Official founding of new capital	**1809** Rama II introduces Chinese details	**1840s** Women's quarter laid out as a city within a city	**1880** Chulalongkorn, the last king to make major additions, involves 26 half-brothers in renovation of Wat Phra Kaeo	**1932** Chakri Dynasty's 150th year celebrated at palace **1982** Renovation of the complex

Decorative Gilt Figures
Encircling the exterior of the bot are 112 garudas (mythical beasts that are half-man, half-bird). They are shown holding nagas (serpents) and are typical of the wat's dazzling decorative details.

VISITORS' CHECKLIST

Na Phra Lan Rd. **Map** 1 C5. 🚌 1, 3, 25, 33, 39, 53. 🚢 Chang, Tien. ⬜ 8:30am–3:30pm daily. ⬤ ceremonies. 🎫 includes Vimanmek Mansion (see p104) and Ananta Samakhom Throne Room (see p107). 📷 in bot. 🖥 www.palaces.thai.net

Apsonsi
A mythical creature (half-woman, half-lion), Apsonsi is one of the beautiful gilded figures on the upper terrace of Wat Phra Kaeo.

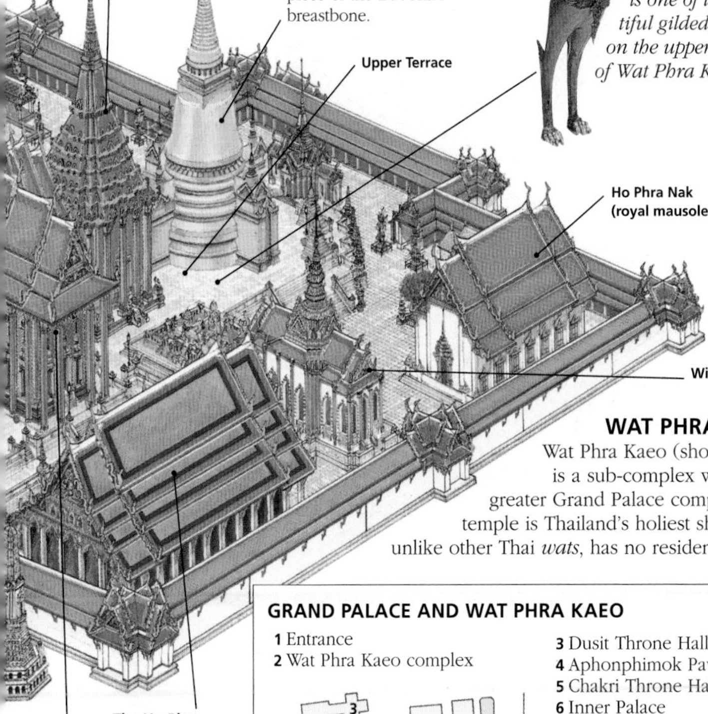

Phra Mondop (library)

The Phra Si Rattana Chedi contains a piece of the Buddha's breastbone.

Upper Terrace

Ho Phra Nak (royal mausoleum)

Wihan Yot

WAT PHRA KAEO

Wat Phra Kaeo (shown here) is a sub-complex within the greater Grand Palace complex. The temple is Thailand's holiest shrine, but unlike other Thai *wats*, has no resident monks.

The Ho Phra Monthien Tham is the auxiliary library.

The Royal Pantheon

GRAND PALACE AND WAT PHRA KAEO

1 Entrance
2 Wat Phra Kaeo complex
3 Dusit Throne Hall
4 Aphonphimok Pavilion
5 Chakri Throne Hall
6 Inner Palace
7 Phra Maha Monthien Buildings
8 Siwalai Gardens
9 Rama IV Chapel
10 Boromphiman Mansion
11 Audience Chamber

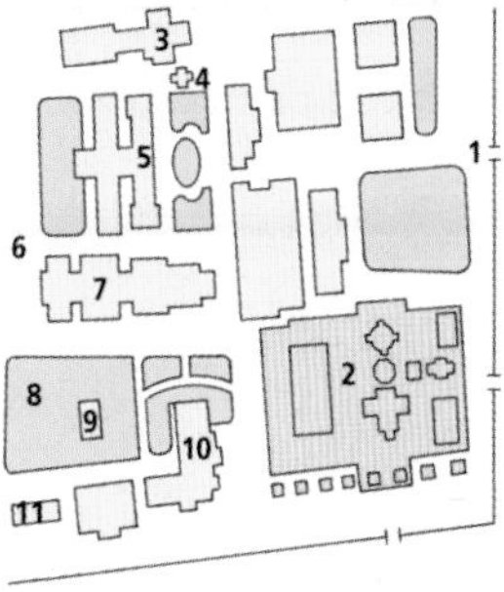

KEY

⬜ Wat Phra Kaeo complex
⬜ Buildings
⬜ Lawns

STAR FEATURES

★ Bot of the Emerald Buddha

★ Ramakien Gallery

Exploring Wat Phra Kaeo

When Rama I established the new capital of Bangkok in 1782 his ambition was to construct a royal temple along the lines of the grand chapels of previous capital cities. Symbolizing the simultaneous founding of the Chakri dynasty, this temple was to surpass its larger Sukhothai and Ayutthaya predecessors in the splendor of its design and decoration. The result of his vision was Wat Phra Kaeo, or Temple of the Emerald Buddha (officially known as Wat Phra Si Rattana Sasadaram), so called because the *bot* houses the Emerald Buddha image, brought here from Wat Arun *(see pp124–5)* in 1785.

Guard outside *chedi*

The Emerald Buddha crowning the ornate gilded altar inside the *bot*

THE BOT AND PERIPHERAL BUILDINGS

The most sacred building within the palace complex, the *bot* of Wat Phra Kaeo was erected to house what is still the most revered image of the Buddha in Thailand: the Emerald Buddha.

The exterior doors and windows of the *bot* are inlaid with delicate mother-of-pearl designs. Along the marble base supporting the structure runs a series of gilt bronze *garudas* (half bird, half human). The staircase of the main entrance is guarded by Cambodian-style stone lions, or *singhas*.

Inside, the surprisingly small image of the Emerald Buddha sits in a glass case high above a golden altar. Carved from a single piece of jade (not emerald), it is 66 cm (26 in) tall and has a lap span of 48 cm (19 in). The Buddha has been attributed to the late Lanna School of the 15th century. It is dressed in one of three costumes: a crown and jewelry for the summer season; a golden shawl in winter; and a gilded monastic robe and headdress in the rainy season. The reigning monarch or a prince appointed by him presides over each changing of the Buddha's attire in a deeply symbolic ceremony.

Inside the *bot* are murals from the reign of Rama III (1824–51). They depict the classic subjects of Thai mural painting, namely the Traiphum (Buddhist cosmology), the Buddha's victory over Mara (the god of death), and scenes from the previous lives of the Buddha – the *jatakas*. Around the temple are 12 open-sided *salas* (small pavilions) built as contemplative shelters.

Southeast of the *bot* is the 19th-century **Chapel of the Gandharara Buddha**. The bronze image of the Buddha calling the rains housed here is used in the Royal Plowing Ceremony in May *(see p46)*. The bell in the nearby belfry is rung only on special occasions such as New Year's Day.

THE UPPER TERRACE

Of the four structures on this elevated terrace, the **Phra Si Rattana Chedi**, at the western end, is the most striking. It was built by King Mongkut (Rama IV) to enshrine a piece of the Buddha's breastbone. The golden tiles decorating the exterior were later added by King Chulalongkorn (Rama V).

The adjacent **Phra Mondop**, used as a library, was built by Rama I as a hall to house Buddhist scriptures. Although the Library is closed to the public, the exterior is splendid in itself. The Javanese Buddha images on the four outer corners are copies of early 9th-century originals, which are now in the museum near the entrance

Gold Angel Guardians decorating the wall of the Phra Mondop

Mural depicting a scene from the Ramakien in the Ramakien Gallery

to the palace complex. Outside the building are memorials to all the kings of the present Chakri dynasty, and bronze elephant statues representing the royal white elephants (*see p106*) from the first five reigns of the dynasty (*see pp64–5*).

To the north of the *mondop* is a model of Angkor Wat in north-west Cambodia (*see pp264–5*). The model was commissioned by Rama IV to show his people the scale and gracious splendor of 12th-century Khmer architecture – Cambodia during his reign being under Thai rule.

The **Royal Pantheon** houses life-size statues of the Chakri kings. Rama IV had intended the hall to hold the Emerald Buddha, but decided that it was too small. The pantheon is open to the public only on Chakri Day (*see p48*).

Ramakien figure outside *chedi*

THE NORTHERN TERRACE

Ho Phra Nak was originally constructed by Rama I in the late 18th century to enshrine the Nak (literally, alloy of gold, silver, and copper) Buddha image that had been rescued from Ayutthaya. Rama III, however, demolished the original hall, preferring to build the present brick and mortar structure to house the ashes of

minor members of the royal family. The Nak Buddha was moved into the neighboring **Wihan Yot**, which is shaped like a Greek cross and decorated with Chinese porcelain.

Also on the Northern Terrace is the **Ho Phra Monthien Tham**, or Auxiliary Library, built by the brother of Rama I. The door panels, inlaid with mother-of-pearl, were salvaged from Ayutthaya's Wat Borom Buddharam. Inside, Buddhist scriptures are stored in fine cabinets.

THE PRANGS, YAKSHAS, AND RAMAKIEN GALLERY

Surrounding the temple complex is the cloisterlike Ramakien Gallery, decorated with lavishly painted and meticulously restored murals. This is Thailand's most extensive depiction of the ancient legend of the Ramakien (*see pp40–41*). The 178 panels were originally painted in the late 18th century, but damage from humidity means that frequent renovation is necessary. The murals are divided by marble pillars inscribed with verses relating the story, which begins opposite Wihan Yot and proceeds in a clockwise direction.

Guarding each gateway to the gallery is a pair of *yakshas* (demons). Placed here during the reign of Rama II, they are said to protect the Emerald Buddha from evil spirits. Each one represents a different character from the Ramakien myth: the green one, for example, symbolizes Tosakan, or the demon king.

The eight different-colored *prangs* on the edge of the temple complex are intricately decorated with Chinese porcelain. They represent the eight elements of the Buddhist religion, including the Buddha, the Dharma (law), the *sangha* (monkhood), and the *bhiksunis* (female Buddhists).

THE LEGEND OF THE EMERALD BUDDHA

In 1434 lightning struck the *chedi* of Wat Phra Kaeo in Chiang Rai in Northern Thailand (*see pp250–51*), revealing a simple stucco image. The abbot of the temple kept it in his residence until the flaking plaster exposed a jadeite image beneath. Upon learning of the discovery, the king of Chiang Mai sent an army of elephants to bring the image to him. The elephant bearing the Emerald Buddha, however, refused to take the road to Chiang Mai, and, treating this as an auspicious sign, the entourage re-routed to Lampang. The image was moved several more times over the next century, then was taken to Wat Pha Kaew in Laos (*see pp294–5*) in 1552. It was not until General Chakri (later Rama I) captured Vientiane in 1778 that the Emerald Buddha was returned to Thailand. It was kept in Wat Arun (*see pp124–5*) for 15 years, before a grand river procession brought it to its current resting place on March 5, 1785.

The small Emerald Buddha inside the *bot*

Exploring the Grand Palace

Built at the same time as Wat Phra Kaeo, the Grand Palace was the king's official residence from 1782 to 1946, although King Chulalongkorn (Rama V) was the last monarch to live here. Today, the royal family resides at Chitrlada Palace (see p106). Throughout the palace's history, many structures have been altered. Within the complex there are a few functioning government buildings, such as the Ministry of Finance, but most others are unused. Important ceremonies are still held in the Dusit Throne Hall and the Amarin Winichai Hall.

Decorative demon guardian

DUSIT THRONE HALL

This cross-shaped throne hall was originally built in 1784 as a reproduction of one of Ayutthaya's grandest buildings, Sanphet Maha Prasat (see pp178–9). Five years later the hall was struck by lightning and rebuilt on a smaller scale. Crowned with a sumptuously decorated tiered spire, it is one of the finest examples of early Rattanakosin architecture (see p35). Inside is a masterpiece of Thai art: the original Rama I teak throne, inlaid with mother-of-pearl. In the south wing is a window in the form of a throne. The hall is used for the annual Coronation Day celebrations (see p48).

APHONPHIMOK PAVILION

King Mongkut (Rama IV) built this small wooden structure as a royal changing room for when he was

giving audiences at the Dusit Throne Hall. The king would be carried on a palanquin to the pavilion's shoulder-high first step. Inside the building he would change into the appropriate apparel for the occasion. The pavilion's simple structure, complemented by its elaborate decoration, makes it a building of perfect proportions: indeed, it is considered a glory of Thai architecture. It inspired Rama V so much so that he had a replica built at Bang Pa-in (see p181).

Elephant statue by Chakri Throne Hall

CHAKRI THRONE HALL

Also known as the Grand Palace Throne Hall, Chakri Maha Prasat was built in Neo-Classical style by the British architect John Chinitz. Rama V commissioned the building in 1882 to mark the centenary of the Chakri dynasty, a fact reflected in the theme

of the sumptuous decoration. The structure was originally intended to have a domed roof, but the royal court decided that a Thai-style roof would be more appropriate, in keeping with the area.

Housed on the top floor of the Central Hall are the ashes of royal monarchs, and the first floor – the only floor open to the public – acts as the main audience hall where the King receives ambassadors and entertains foreign monarchs; artifacts from the King's armory are on display here.

Behind the Niello Throne in the Chakri Throne Room is the emblem of the Chakri dynasty: a discus and trident. The paintings in the room depict diplomatic missions, including Queen Victoria welcoming Rama IV's ambassador in London. The East Wing is used as a reception room for royal guests. The long hall connecting the Central Hall with this wing is lined with portraits of the Chakri dynasty. In the West Wing is the queen's personal reception room. Portraits of the principal queens of Rama IV, Rama V, and Rama VII decorate the hall between the Central Hall and this wing.

PHRA MAHA MONTHIEN BUILDINGS

This cluster of connected buildings, located to the east of the Chakri Throne Hall, is the "Grand Residence" of the palace complex.

The focal point of the 18th-century **Amarin Winichai Hall**, the northernmost building of the group, is Rama I's boat-shaped Busabok Mala Throne. When an audience was present, two curtains hid the throne as the king ascended, and, with an elaborate fanfare, the curtains were drawn back to reveal the king wearing a loose, golden gown and seeming to float on the prowlike part of the throne. In the 19th century two British ambassadors were received in such manner here;

Exterior of the Dusit Throne Hall, with its elegant multitiered spire

Lavish decor of the connecting hall of the Chakri Throne Hall's West Wing

John Crawfurd by Rama II and Sir John Bowring by Rama IV. The hall is now used for some state ceremonies.

Connected to the hall by a gateway through which only the king, queen, and royal children may walk is the **Phaisan Thaksin Hall**. This was used by Rama I as a private hall when dining with family, friends, and members of the royal court. In 1809 a Borom Rachaphisek Ceremony was performed in this hall to mark the coronation of the new king, Rama II. On the high altar is the Phra Siam Thewathirat, a highly venerated guardian figure, placed here by Rama IV.

The third building is the **Chakraphat Phiman Hall**. It served as a residence for the first three Chakri kings. It is still the custom for a newly crowned king to spend a night here as part of his coronation.

INNER PALACE

Behind a gateway to the left of the Chakri Throne Hall is the entrance to the Inner Palace, which is closed to the public. Until the time of Rama VII, the palace was inhabited solely by women of the royal family: principal wives, minor wives, and daughters. Apart from sons, who had to leave the palace on reaching puberty, the king was the only male allowed to live within its walls.

The palace functioned as a small city, with its own government and laws, complete with prison cells. Under the strict guidance of a formidable "Directress of the Inside," a small army of uniformed officers policed the area.

Rama III renovated the overcrowded and precarious wooden structures, and, in the late 19th century, Rama V built small, fantastical Victorian style palaces here for his favorite consorts. Because his successor, Rama VI, had only one wife, the complex was left virtually empty, and it eventually fell into disrepair.

One of the palace buildings that continues to function is the finishing school for the daughters of high-society Thai families. The girls are taught flower weaving, royal cuisine, and social etiquette.

SIWALAI GARDENS

These beautiful gardens, which are sadly now closed to the public, lie east of the Inner Palace and contain the **Phra Buddha Ratana Sathan**, a personal chapel built by Rama IV. The pavilion is covered in gray marble and decorated with white and blue glass mosaics. The marble *bai sema* (boundary stones) are inlaid with the insignia of Rama V, who placed the stones here, Rama II, who had the gardens laid out, and Rama IV.

The Neo-Classical **Borom-phiman Mansion** in the gardens was built by Rama V as a residence for the Crown Prince (later king Rama VI). The building served as a temporary residence for several kings: Rama VII, Rama VIII, and Rama IX (King Bhumibol). Today it is used as a guest house for visiting dignitaries.

AUDIENCE CHAMBER

Visible from outside the palace walls, this chamber – Phra Thinang Sutthaisawan Prasat – is located between Thewaphithak and Sakchaisit gates. It was built by Rama I as a place to grant an audience during royal ceremonies and to watch the training of his elephants. Rama III strengthened the wooden structure with brick, and decorative features were added later. These include the crowning spire and ornamental cast-iron motifs.

Mosaic-decorated Phra Buddha Ratana Sathan in the Siwalai Gardens

Entrance to the Buddhist University at Wat Mahathat

Wat Mahathat ❷

วัดมหาธาตุ

3 Maharaj Rd. **Map** 1 C5.
Tel 0-2972-9473. 🚌 AC: 203, 506.
🚤 Chang Maharaj. 🕐 daily.

This is a large, busy temple complex, interesting more for its atmosphere than for its architecture. Dating from the 1700s, the *wihan* and *bot* were both rebuilt between 1844 and 1851. The *mondop*, which gives the temple its name – "temple of the great relic" – has a cruciform roof, a feature rarely found in Bangkok.

The *wat* is the national center for the Mahanikai monastic sect, and it holds one of Bangkok's two Buddhist universities (meditation classes are offered here at 7am, 1pm, and 6pm in Section Five, near the monks' quarters). There is also a traditional herbal medicine market, and, on weekends, numerous stalls selling a wide range of goods.

National Museum ❸

พิพิธภัณฑสถานแห่งชาติ

See pp88–9.

National Gallery ❹

หอศิลป์แห่งชาติ

4 Chao Fa Rd. **Map** 2 D4. **Tel** 0-2282-2639. 🚌 AC: 506. 🚤 Phra Athit. 🕐 9am–4pm Wed–Sun. ⬤ public hols. 📷 🚫 www.national-gallery.go.th

Thailand's main art gallery, housed in the old mint building, was established in 1977. It concentrates on modern Thai and international art. Initially the gallery suffered from lack of funds, but in 1989 further wings were added. The high-ceilinged, spacious halls now attract exhibitions from all over Asia. Temporary shows of prominent Asian artists are often better than many of the permanent exhibits. Modern art can also be found at the Visual Dhamma Gallery *(see p136)*. Check the *Bangkok Post* for details.

Modern sculpture at the National Gallery

Wat Bowonniwet ❺

วัดบวรนิเวศน์

248 Phra Sumen Rd. **Map** 2 E4.
Tel 0-2281-5052. 🚌 12, 15, 56; AC: 511 (Express). 🕐 8am–5pm daily.

Hidden in quiet, tree-filled grounds, this mid-19th-century temple was constructed by Rama III. The style bears his trademark Chinese influence. A central gilded *chedi* is flanked by two symmetrical chapels, the most interesting of which is next to Phra Sumen Road. The interior murals are attributed to monk-painter Khrua In Khong, who is famous for the introduction of Western perspective into Thai temple murals. As court painter to King Mongkut (Rama IV) he was exposed to Western ideas and adapted these to a Thai setting. The result was a series of murals that on first glance look wholly Western, but that portray the same Buddhist allegories found in traditional Thai murals. For instance, a physician healing a blind man can be interpreted as the illuminating power of Buddhism. The images are all the more remarkable for the fact that Khrua In Khong never traveled to the West. The main Buddha image, Phra Buddha Chinasara, is one of the best examples from the Sukhothai period.

King Mongkut served as abbot here during his 27 years in the monkhood and founded the strict Tammayut sect of Buddhism, for which the temple is now the head-quarters. Since Mongkut, many Thai kings have served their monkhoods at the *wat*, including the current monarch, King Bhumibol (Rama IX). The temple also houses Thailand's second Buddhist university. Across the road from the temple is a Buddhist bookstore that sells English-language publications.

Mid-19th-century, Western-style mural at Wat Bowonniwet

For hotels and restaurants in this region see pp398–402 and pp428–32

Democracy Monument ❻

อนุเสาวรีย์ประชาธิปไตย

Ratchadamnoen Klang. **Map** 2 E4.
🚌 *AC: 503, 509, 511.* ⬜ *daily.*

A focal point during pro-democracy demonstrations, this monument (built 1939) commemorates the revolution of 1932 *(see p68)*. Each feature symbolizes the date of the establishment of Thailand's constitutional monarchy, on June 24, 1932.

The four wing towers are each 24 m (79 ft) high. The 75 cannons indicate the year 2475 of the Buddhist Era (1932), and the pedestal, containing a copy of the constitution, is 3 m (10 ft) high, referring to the third month of the Thai calendar (June).

The structure was designed by Silpa Bhirasi, an Italian sculptor who took a Thai name and citizenship.

Central edifice of Democracy Monument (1939)

Wat Rachanadda ❼

วัดราชนัดดา

Maha Chai Rd. **Map** 2 E4.
🚌 *2, 44, 59; AC: 79, 503, 511.*
⬜ *9am–4pm daily.*

The most interesting feature at Wat Rachanadda (also often spelt Ratchanaddaram) is the metal monastery. Originally conceived as a *chedi* to complement the temple, it evolved into an elaborate meditation chamber modeled

One of hundreds of meditation cells at Wat Rachanat

on a 3rd-century BC Sri Lankan temple (the original is now ruined). Passages dissect each level, running north to south and east to west. The meditation cells are at each intersection.

In the temple's courtyard is Bangkok's best amulet market. Tourists may face disapproval if they attempt to take talismans home as souvenirs. Across the road, behind the old city walls, is the Doves' Village, where singing doves are sold for competitions.

Wat Saket and the Golden Mount ❽

วัดสระเกศและภูเขาทอง

Chakkaphatdi Phong Rd. **Map** 2 F5.
🚌 *8, 15, 37, 47, 49; AC: 38, 543.*
⬜ *7:30am–5:30pm daily.* 📷
🎪 *Golden Mount Fair (Nov).*

Built by Rama I in the late 18th century, Wat Saket is one of the oldest temples in Bangkok. Visitors come to climb the artificial hill topped with a golden tower within the grounds. Rama III built the first Golden Mount, but the soft soil led to its collapse. King Chulalongkorn (Rama V) provided the necessary technology to create the 76-m (250-ft) high representation of the mythical Mount Meru seen today. It is believed to house relics of the Buddha presented to Rama V by the Viceroy of India. A circular staircase lined with strange

monuments and tombs leads to the top, where there is a small sanctuary. The wonderful panoramic view from the gallery takes in the Grand Palace, Wat Pho, and Wat Arun. The octagonal building opposite, Mahakan Fort, is one of 14 original watchtowers of the city walls.

Until the 1960s the Golden Mount was one of the highest points in Bangkok. Today, it still forms a prominent landmark, although it is dwarfed by skyscrapers *(see p121)*.

During the 19th century the grounds of Wat Saket served a macabre function as a crematorium. The bodies of the poor were sometimes left for vultures and dogs. By contrast, a fair with dancing and a candle procession is now held on the grounds in November.

The Golden Mount, a distinctive Bangkok landmark

National Museum ❸

พิพิธภัณฑสถานแห่งชาติ

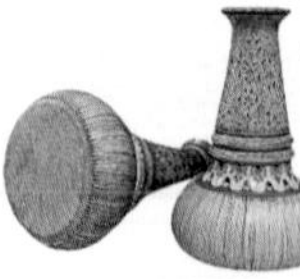

The National Museum has one of the largest and most comprehensive collections in Southeast Asia and provides an excellent introduction to the arts, crafts, and history of Thailand. Two of the museum buildings, the 18th-century Wang Na Palace and Buddhaisawan Chapel, are works of art in themselves. The chapel contains the venerated Phra Buddha Sihing image and the palace an eclectic selection of artifacts from ancient weaponry to shadow puppets. The two wings of the museum are devoted mainly to art and sculpture. Other attractions include galleries of history and prehistory and the Royal Funeral Chariots Gallery. The labeling of the collection is not always helpful, so taking one of the frequent, free guided tours is highly recommended.

Colorful Bencharong drums

Doors of Throne Hall
These beautifully decorated black and gold lacquered doors to the Wang Na Palace date from the 19th century and show a strong Chinese influence.

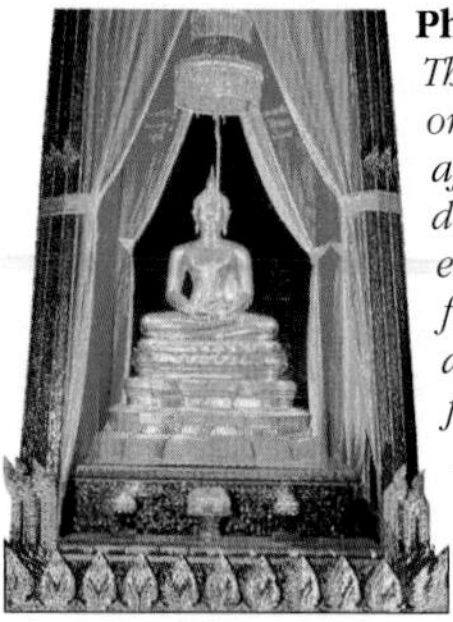

Phra Buddha Sihing
The history of this image, one of Thailand's holiest after the Emerald Buddha, is shrouded in legend. It probably dates from the 13th century and was brought here from Chiang Mai by Rama I in 1787.

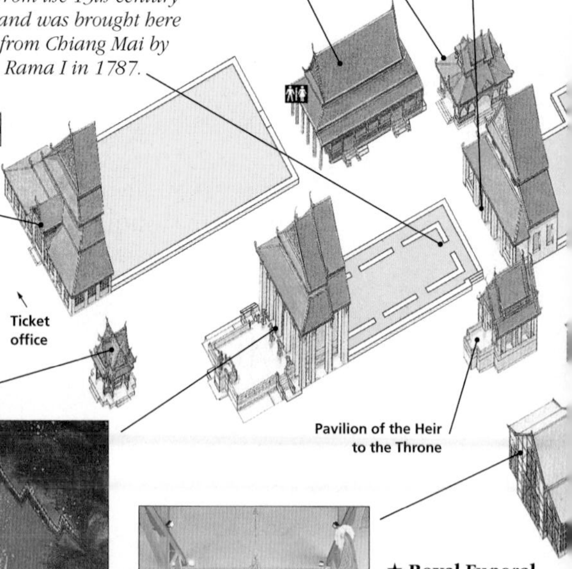

King Rama IV Pavilion

Red Pavilion

The Gallery of Thai History houses the 13th-century Ramkamhaeng Stone. This is thought to be inscribed with the earliest extant example of the Thai script.

Ticket office

King Vajiravudh Pavilion

Pavilion of the Heir to the Throne

★ Buddhaisawan Chapel
Built in 1787, this beautiful building is decorated with some of the best Rattanakosin period murals in Thailand.

★ Royal Funeral Chariots Gallery
Several lavishly decorated, gilded teak chariots used in royal funeral processions can be seen in this gallery, including Racharot Noi, built in 1795.

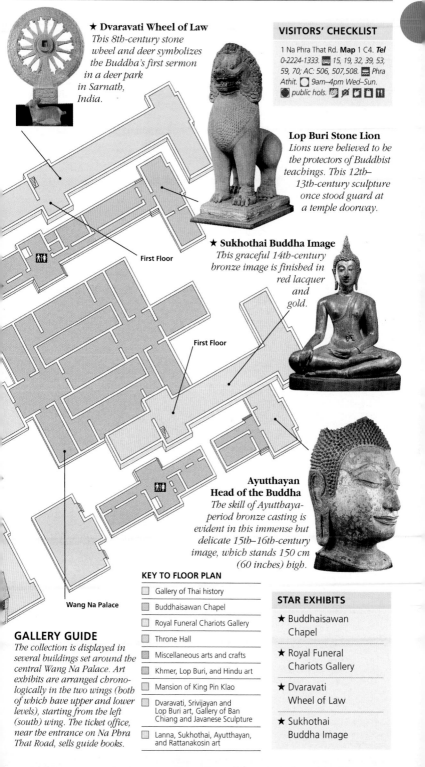

★ **Dvaravati Wheel of Law**
This 8th-century stone wheel and deer symbolizes the Buddha's first sermon in a deer park in Sarnath, India.

VISITORS' CHECKLIST

1 Na Phra That Rd. **Map** 1 C4. **Tel** 0-2224-1333. 15, 19, 32, 39, 53, 59, 70; AC: 506, 507,508. Phra Athit. 9am–4pm Wed–Sun. public hols.

Lop Buri Stone Lion
Lions were believed to be the protectors of Buddhist teachings. This 12th–13th-century sculpture once stood guard at a temple doorway.

First Floor

★ **Sukhothai Buddha Image**
This graceful 14th-century bronze image is finished in red lacquer and gold.

First Floor

Ayutthayan Head of the Buddha
The skill of Ayutthaya-period bronze casting is evident in this immense but delicate 15th–16th-century image, which stands 150 cm (60 inches) high.

Wang Na Palace

KEY TO FLOOR PLAN

- Gallery of Thai history
- Buddhaisawan Chapel
- Royal Funeral Chariots Gallery
- Throne Hall
- Miscellaneous arts and crafts
- Khmer, Lop Buri, and Hindu art
- Mansion of King Pin Klao
- Dvaravati, Srivijayan and Lop Buri art, Gallery of Ban Chiang and Javanese Sculpture
- Lanna, Sukhothai, Ayutthayan, and Rattanakosin art

GALLERY GUIDE
The collection is displayed in several buildings set around the central Wang Na Palace. Art exhibits are arranged chronologically in the two wings (both of which have upper and lower levels), starting from the left (south) wing. The ticket office, near the entrance on Na Phra That Road, sells guide books.

STAR EXHIBITS

★ Buddhaisawan Chapel

★ Royal Funeral Chariots Gallery

★ Dvaravati Wheel of Law

★ Sukhothai Buddha Image

Monk's bowl being heated to blacken and finish the surface

Monk's Bowl Village (Ban Bat) ❾

บ้านบาตร

Bamrung Muang Rd, Soi Ban Bat.
Map 2 F5. ⬛ AC: 508.

Monks' bowls were first used 2,500 years ago and are still widely used today in Buddhist countries for early morning alms-gathering (see p129). Such bowls have been made at Monk's Bowl Village in Bangkok since the late 18th century. The village once stretched as far as Wat Saket (see p87), but modern developments have reduced the village to just four homes and a cluster of small workshops. This area may be hard to find amid the maze of sois, but the bowls are sold at Wat Suthat.

The process of bowl making is time consuming and requires eight pieces of metal, representing the eight spokes of the wheel of Dharma. The first strip is beaten into a circular form to make the rim. Three pieces are then beaten to create a cross-shaped skeleton. Four triangular pieces complete the sides. After being welded in a kiln, the bowl is shaped, filed smooth, and fired again to give an enamel-like surface. About 20 bowls are produced daily in the village.

At the center of the maze of alleyways next to the small village hall is an unusual and intriguing shrine, constructed from old Chinese cylinder bellows, that is dedicated to the "Holy Teacher and Ancestor."

Bamrung Muang Road ❿

ถนนบำรุงเมือง

Map 2 F5. ⬛ AC: 508.

Bamrung Muang, like Charoen Krung (see p114), was an elephant trail until the 20th century, when it became one of Thailand's first paved roads. The stretch between Maha Chai Road and the Giant Swing provides an enlightening peek into the thriving business behind the Buddhist practice of merit-making. Along here the road is lined with shops selling religious paraphernalia: monks' robes, votive candles, and Buddha images of all shapes and sizes, many rather incongruously packaged in cellophane. Monks shop here for temple essentials; other people buy offerings and shrines for the home. Although the religious objects look enticing to tourists, they are not intended as souvenirs: images of the Buddha cannot be taken out of the country without an export license (see p475).

Wat Suthat and the Giant Swing ⓫

วัดสุทัศน์และเสาชิงช้า

Bamrung Muang Rd. **Map** 2 E5. ⬛ 10, 12, 19, 35, 42, 56, 96. ◯ 8:30am–4pm daily (wihan Sat & Sun only).

There are several superlatives for Wat Suthat, a temple that was begun by Rama I in 1807 and completed by Rama III. Its wihan is the largest in Bangkok. The art and architecture beautifully exemplify Rattanakosin style (see p35). Its central Buddha, at 8 m (26 ft) high, is one of the largest surviving Sukhothai bronzes. This image was moved from Wat Mahathat in Sukhothai (see pp58–9) to Bangkok by Rama I. The murals in the immense wihan are some of the most celebrated in

Thailand. Amazingly intricate, they depict the Traiphum (Buddhist cosmology) and were restored in the 1980s. The teak doors to the wihan are carved in five delicate layers and stand 5.5 m (18 ft) high. (One made by Rama II is now in the National Museum.) The cloister around the outside of the wihan is lined with 156 golden Buddha images.

The square in front of Wat Suthat used to feature the Giant Swing, the remains of a swing used for a Brahmin ceremony. After standing for 224 years, this was moved in 2007 to Devasathan Brahmin temple and replaced by a new swing made from six 100-year-old teak trees.

Wat Rachabophit ⓬

วัดราชบพิธ

Fuang Nakhon Rd. **Map** 2 D5. **Tel** 0-2222-3930. ⬛ 2, 60; AC: 501, 502, 512. ⬛ Thien. ◯ 5am–8pm daily.

The circular form of Wat Rachabophit is a successful architectural blend of East and West. Construction of the temple began under King Chulalongkorn (Rama V) in 1869 and continued for over 20 years. The whole complex is splendidly decorated with porcelain tiles, which were made to order in China. The focal point is the central, Sri Lankan-style, gilded chedi,

View through the immense portal of the wihan at Wat Suthat

whose full height from the terrace is 140 ft (43 m).

Inside the *wat* are four Buddha images, each facing one of the cardinal points. Leading off from the circular gallery are the *bot* to the north, the *wihan* to the south, and two lesser *wihans* to the east and west: an unusual layout for a Thai *wat*.

East-West flourishes permeate the complex. The 10 door panels and 28 window panels of the *bot* are decorated with typically Thai mother-of-pearl inlay that illustrates the insignia of five royal orders. The moldings over the door depict King Chulalongkorn's seal. The carved, painted guards on the doors are distinctively *farang* (European), and the interior is decorated in an incongruous Italian Renaissance style.

Accessible through the temple grounds (parallel to Khlong Lot) is a fascinating royal cemetery rarely explored by visitors. The monuments to members of King Chulalongkorn's family are an eccentric mix of Khmer, Thai, and European styles.

Wat Rachapradit ⑬
วัดราชประดิษฐ์

Saran Rom Rd. **Map** 2 D5.
Tel 0-2223-8215. 🚌 AC: 501, 502, 512. 🚤 Thien.
⏰ 5am–10pm daily.

Located in the northeast corner of the former Saranrom Palace gardens (now the Ministry of Foreign Affairs), this charming, peaceful temple is rarely visited

Rows of tiny carved figures on eaves of the *bot* at Wat Rachapradit

"Farang," Wat Rachabophit

by tourists. It was built in the mid-19th century by King Mongkut (Rama IV) and his East-meets-West taste in architecture is apparent in the choice of building materials. The main *wihan*, for instance, is covered in forbidding gray marble. The interior murals were painted in the late 19th century and depict the festivals of the Thai lunar calendar. Among other scenes are some extravagant preparations for the Giant Swing ceremony, people celebrating the annual Loy Krathong water festival, and an image of King Mongkut observing an eclipse of the moon *(see p65)*. Striking carvings adorn the doors, eaves, and gables of the temple. Other notable edifices in the grounds of the *wat* include graceful pavilions, Khmer-style *prangs*, and a gray marble *chedi*. Near to Wat Rachapradit, next to Khlong Lot, is a small gilded boar, a

shrine to Queen Saowapha Phongsi (King Chulalongkorn's consort), who was born in the year of the pig.

Wat Pho ⑭
วัดโพธิ์

See pp92–3.

Museum of Siam ⑮
พิพิธภัณฑ์สยาม

Sanam Chai Rd. **Map** 5 C1.
Tel 0-2225-2777. 🚌 12, 47; AC: 3, 82. 🚤 Thien.
⏰ 10am–6pm Tue–Sun & public holidays. ⦿ Songkram Holiday, New Year's Eve, New Year's Day. ▢
www.museumsiam.com

The Museum of Siam is housed in the former Ministry of Commerce – a handsome Italianate building that was designed by Mario Tamagno. The project was finished in 1922 and was converted into its present incarnation in 2007. A Milanese architect, Tamagno was also the designer of many other important Bangkok landmarks, including the Ananta Samakhom Throne Hall *(see p107)*.

The Museum of Siam is spread over three floors and features excellent permanent interactive exhibits that explore what it means to be Thai through ancient and contemporary history. Buddhism, village life, and politics and communication are some of the themes that are examined.

THE SWING IN ACTION

Sao Ching Cha, the "Giant Swing" at Wat Suthat, was built in 1784 by Rama I. During ceremonies – Brahmin in origin – teams of four would swing in 180-degree arcs up to 25 m (82 ft) high. One participant would try to bite off a sack of gold hung from tall poles. The event, linked to the god Shiva swinging in the heavens, caused many deaths and was abolished in 1935.

Young Brahmins performing on Sao Ching Cha

Wat Pho ⑭

วัดโพธิ์

Officially known as Wat Phra Chetuphon, Wat Pho is not only Bangkok's oldest and largest temple but also Thailand's foremost center for public education. Unlike the Grand Palace (*see pp80–85*), it has a lively and lived-in dilapidated grandeur. In the 1780s Rama I rebuilt the original 16th-century temple on this site and enlarged the complex. In 1832 Rama III built the Chapel of the Reclining Buddha, housing the stunning image, and turned the temple into a place of learning. Today Wat Pho is a traditional medicine center, of which the famous Institute of Massage is a part. Nearby on Chetuphon Road is the temple monastery, home to some 300 monks.

Farang guard

Wihan
The western wihan *is one of four around the* main bot.

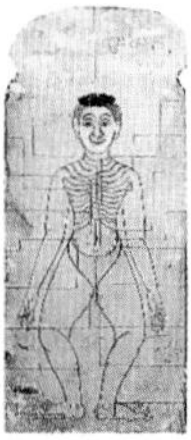

★ Medicine Pavilion
Embedded in the inner walls of this pavilion are stone plaques showing massage points. The pavilion is now a souvenir shop.

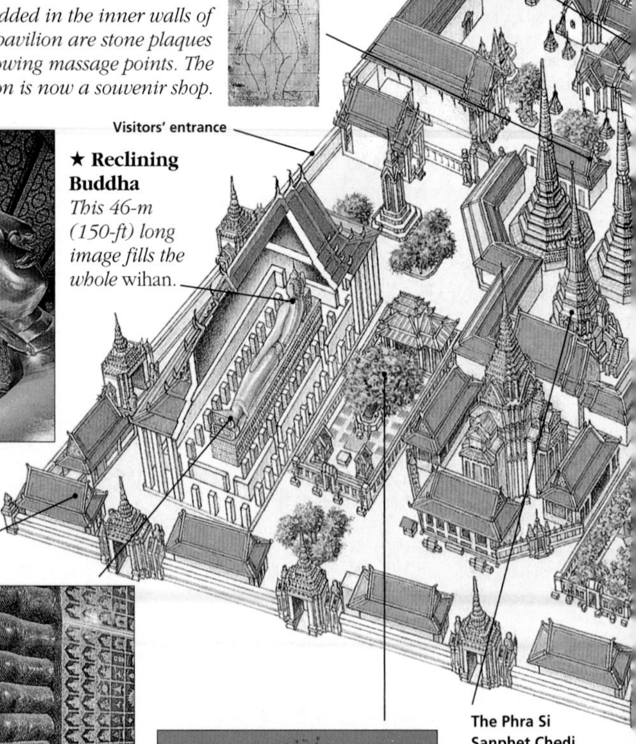

Visitors' entrance

★ Reclining Buddha
This 46-m (150-ft) long image fills the whole wihan.

Small buildings at this end of the *wat* are reserved for children.

The **Phra Si Sanphet Chedi** encases the remains o a sacred Buddha imag

Feet of the Reclining Buddha
The striking, intricate mother-of-pearl images on the soles of the feet of the gilded plaster and brick Reclining Buddha represent the 108 lakshanas, which are the auspicious signs of the true Buddha.

Bodhi Tree
It is said that this gre from a cutting of the under which the Bud meditated in India.

Ceramic Decoration
This porcelain design is on the Phra Si Sanphet Chedi.

VISITORS' CHECKLIST

Sanam Chai Rd. **Map** 5 C1. *Tel* 0-2226-0335. 🚌 *AC: 25, 32, 44, 60, 508.* 🚤 Thien, Chang, Rachinee. 🕐 9am–5pm daily. 🎫 🎥 **Institute of Massage** *Tel* 0-2622-3550-1. 🕐 8:30am–6pm daily. 🎫

Institute of Massage

Main Bot
Wat Pho's bot houses a bronze meditating Buddha image salvaged from Ayutthaya by Rama I's brother. Scenes from the Ramakien (see pp40–41) are carved into the outer base and inner doors.

Visitors' entrance

Miniature Mountains
This tiny stone mountain by the southern wihan is one of several within the complex. The statues of naked hermits are posed in the different positions of healing massage.

Farang guards stand at the compound's inner gates. These huge stone statues with big noses, beards, and top hats are caricatures of Westerners.

TRADITIONAL MASSAGE

Since the 1960s Wat Pho has run the most respected massage school in the city. Traditional Thai massage *(nuat paen boran)* supposedly dates from the time of the Buddha and is related to Chinese acupuncture and Indian yoga. The highly trained masseurs at the *wat* specialize in pulling and stretching the limbs and torso to relieve various ailments ranging from general tension to viruses. Visitors can experience a massage or learn the art through a 10- or 15-day course in Thai or English.

Braving a traditional Thai massage at Wat Pho

STAR FEATURES

★ Reclining Buddha

★ Medicine Pavilion

CHINATOWN

Bangkok's Chinese residents originally lived in the area where the Old City is today. When Rama I decided to move his capital across the river in 1782, the entire community was relocated. Since then the district around Yaowarat and Sampeng roads has been the focus of Chinese life in the city, although now it is also home to a small Indian community. Once the financial center of Bangkok, Chinatown remains a thriving, bustling, noisy area. Between the two great traffic-choked thoroughfares of Yaowarat Road and Charoen Krung Road lies a maze of narrow alleyways

Modern painting of a Chinatown street vendor

packed with market stalls. The most accessible are the wholesale fabric market of Sampeng Lane and the diverse offerings of the vendors along Soi Isara Nuphap. Other major markets in Chinatown include Pak Khlong, Nakorn Kasem, and Phahurat. Near to Hua Lamphong Station is Wat Traimit with its splendid interior and huge gold Buddha image. The area is peppered with Chinese shrines, many of which combine elements of Confucianism, Taoism, Mahayana Buddhism, and animism. Old Chinese noodle shops patronized by mahjong-playing, undershirt-clad men make interesting snack spots.

SIGHTS AT A GLANCE

Wats
Wat Traimit ❹

Markets
Nakorn Kasem ❸
Pak Khlong Market ❶
Phahurat Market ❷

Historic Buildings
Hua Lamphong Station ❺

0 meters 500
0 yards 500

GETTING THERE
Chinatown is easily accessible from the Chao Phraya Express Ratchawong pier, by bus along Charoen Krung Road, or train to Hua Lamphong station.

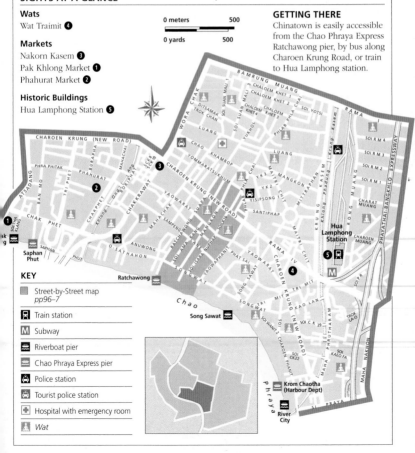

KEY

▨	Street-by-Street map pp96–7
🚉	Train station
Ⓜ	Subway
⛴	Riverboat pier
⛴	Chao Phraya Express pier
🏢	Police station
🏢	Tourist police station
➕	Hospital with emergency room
🛕	Wat

◁ **Bags of dried shrimp in one of Chinatown's numerous, pungent markets**

Street-by-Street: Central Chinatown

เยาวราช

Khanom dao – a soy sweet

This area is Chinatown at its most atmospheric, with its vibrant colors, pungent smells, overwhelming cacophony, and frenetic bustle. A cross-section of the district can be experienced by walking up Soi Isara Nuphap from Ratchawong pier. After Songwat Road, with its old wooden buildings, the street is lined with wholesale spice shops. Past the fabric market of Sampeng Lane, the sidewalk is crowded with fresh and preserved foods. Once over Yaowarat Road, with its countless gold shops and Chinese herbal medicine stores, snack stalls predominate before giving way, after crossing traffic-choked Charoen Krung Road, to sellers of Chinese religious paraphernalia.

Kao Market
Fresh produce, such as mushrooms, is sold at Kao ("old") Market, which has been here since the late 18th century.

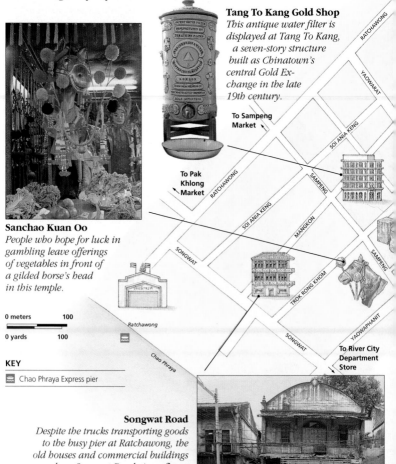

Tang To Kang Gold Shop
This antique water filter is displayed at Tang To Kang, a seven-story structure built as Chinatown's central Gold Exchange in the late 19th century.

To Sampeng Market

To Pak Khlong Market

Sanchao Kuan Oo
People who hope for luck in gambling leave offerings of vegetables in front of a gilded horse's head in this temple.

0 meters   100

0 yards   100

KEY

▣ Chao Phraya Express pier

To River City Department Store

Songwat Road
Despite the trucks transporting goods to the busy pier at Ratchawong, the old houses and commercial buildings along Songwat Road give a flavor of Chinatown as it was in the 19th century. This old wooden warehouse stands opposite Soi Thanam San Chao.

★ Leng Noi Yee
This Buddhist shrine combines elements of Confucianism and Taoism, attracting a wide range of devotees. The main chamber contains several gilded Buddha images.

LOCATOR MAP
See Street Finder map 6

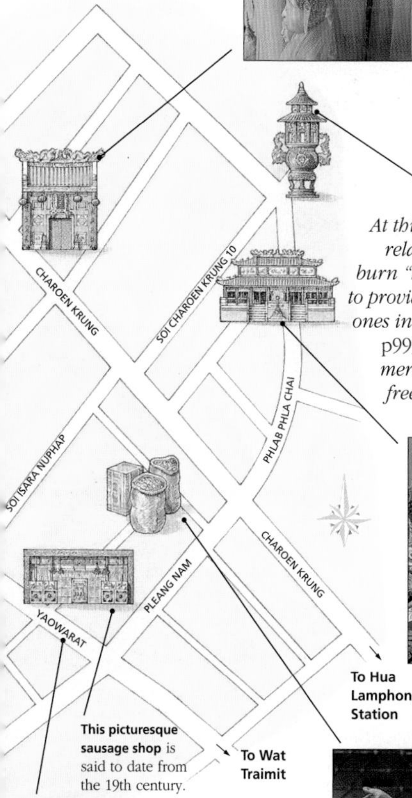

CHAROEN KRUNG

SOI CHAROEN KRUNG 10

PHLAB PHLA CHAI

SOI ISARA NUPHAP

CHAROEN KRUNG

PLEANG NAM

YAOWARAT

Sanchao Dtai Hong Kong
At this popular temple relatives of the dead burn "hell's banknotes" to provide for their loved ones in the afterlife (see p99). Devotees make merit by buying and freeing caged birds.

Li Thi Miew
This atmospheric temple within a courtyard is topped by fierce dragons. Inside, incense smoke swirls around statues of Taoist deities.

This picturesque sausage shop is said to date from the 19th century.

To Wat Traimit

To Hua Lamphong Station

Mai Market
Mai ("new") Market can't boast the pedigree of Kao Market, but it is still a good source of everyday and unusual items like snake parts for Chinese medicine.

★ Yaowarat Road
One of Chinatown's main traffic arteries, this bustling road is packed with gold shops, herbal sellers, cafés, and restaurants.

STAR SIGHTS

★ Leng Noi Yee

★ Yaowarat Road

Vendor selling a wide range of chilies, Pak Khlong Market

Pak Khlong Market ❶

ตลาดปากคลอง

Maharaj Rd. **Map** 5 C2. 🚌 *AC: 501, 512* 🚤 *Rachinee, Pak Khlong.* ⬚ *daily.*

Open 24 hours a day, Pak Khlong Market provides the city with fresh flowers and vegetables. Known for offering the best array of flowers in Thailand, it is a one-stop florist's dream. Deliveries arrive from 1am and by dawn the display has roses, orchids, lotus, jasmine, and Dutch tulips. The widest variety of blooms can be seen at 9am. Visitors can buy bouquets or floral basket arrangements.

Phahurat Market ❷

ตลาดพาหุรัด

Phahurat Rd. **Map** 6 D1. 🚌 *6, 37, 82, 88; AC: 3, 82.*

This predominantly Indian market offers all the tastes, sights, and smells of Bombay. The main bazaar, which spills out around Phahurat and Chak Phet roads, specializes in fabrics. Downstairs, cloth merchants sell anything from tablecloths to wedding saris. The dimly lit upstairs section is devoted to traditional Indian accessories such as sandals and ornate jewelry.

In the surrounding streets are many delicious "hole-in-the-wall" Indian restaurants and samosa stalls. Off Chak Phet Road is Siri Guru Singh Sabha, a traditional Sikh temple.

Nakorn Kasem ❸

นครเกษม

Charoen Krung Rd. **Map** 6 E1. 🚌 *AC: 501, 507.*

Popularly known as Thieves' Market because stolen goods were allegedly once sold here, Nakorn Kasem has discarded its illicit past and now has a miscellaneous collection of shops selling metal wares, musical instruments, and a wide range of ornaments.

Nearby is Saphan Han Market, a covered market along both sides of Khlong Ong Ang. Its specialty is electrical goods. The area is filled with smells wafting from nearby noodle stalls.

Wat Traimit ❹

วัดไตรมิตร

Tri Mit Rd. **Map** 6 F2. 🚌 *1, 4, 11, 25, 53, 73; AC: 501, 507.* ⬚ *9am–5pm daily.*

Also called the Temple of the Golden Buddha, Wat Traimit is houses the world's largest solid gold Buddha. The gleaming 4-m (13-ft) high 13th-century Sukhothai image is made of 18-carat gold and weighs five tons.

The Buddha was discovered by accident in 1955. While extending the port of Bangkok, workers for the East Asiatic Company unearthed what appeared to be a plain stucco Buddha. The image was kept at Wat Traimit under a makeshift shelter for 20 years until a crane dropped it while moving it to a more permanent shelter. The plaster cracked, revealing the gold Buddha beneath. The statue had likely been encased in stucco to hide it from Burmese ransackers – a common practice during the Ayutthaya period (*see pp60–61*).

Local Chinese residents come here to worship the Golden Buddha and to make merit by rubbing gold leaf on the temple's smaller Buddha images.

Wat Traimit, which houses the revered Golden Buddha image

Hua Lampong Station ❺

สถานีหัวลำโพง

Rama IV Rd. **Map** 7 A2. **Tel** *1690.* 🚌 *4, 21, 25, 29, 34, 40, 48, 109; AC: 501, 507, 529.* **www**.*railway.co.th*

King Chulalongkorn (Rama V), a great champion of modernization, was the instigator of rail travel in Thailand. The first railroad line, begun in 1891, was a private line from Paknam to Hua Lampong. Today, the historic station is Bangkok's main rail junction. From here, trains leave for the North, Northeast, the Central Plains, and the South. The city's other station, Bangkok Noi, serves only the South.

The Chinese in Thailand

Warrior on the roof of a temple in Chinatown

The first Chinese immigrants arrived in Thailand as merchants in the 12th century. During the late 18th and early 19th centuries, following years of war in Thailand *(see p64)*, Chinese immigration was encouraged in order to help rebuild the economy. The subsequent integration of the Chinese into Thai society was so successful that by the mid-19th century half of Bangkok's population was of pure or mixed Chinese blood. There have been periods of anti-Chinese feeling and immigration restrictions, but the Chinese still dominate Thailand's commercial sector. Chinese traditions and beliefs remain strong in their communities.

Leng Noi Yee Temple *in Bangkok is an important Mahayana Buddhist shrine that also incorporates elements of Taoism and Confucianism. The temple, with its glazed ceramic gables topped by Chinese dragons, is the focal point of the annual Vegetarian Festival* (see p47).

"Hell's banknotes" *are a form of kong tek – paper replicas of real objects, burned to provide for the dead during their next life.*

Intricate Chinese designs feature on many utensils, such as these pan covers.

Fresh vegetables are essential to many Chinese dishes.

CHINESE SHOP-HOUSES

Shop-houses are a common feature of Chinatown. The family lives on the first floor while the ground floor is devoted to the family business, whether it is a small workshop or a store selling, for example, food or household goods.

Chinese opera, *performed by traveling troupes, features a dramatic mixture of martial arts, acrobatics, singing, and dance.*

Dim sum, *literally "touch the heart," can be sampled in many of the area's Chinese restaurants. The bite-size snacks include shrimp toast and pork dumplings.*

Sign painting *is not just a decorative art form. These good luck messages, written in gold, are said to ward off evil and sickness. They are displayed in great numbers during the Chinese New Year.*

DUSIT

Dusit is the center of Thai officialdom and an oasis of relative calm in a chaotic city. Tree-lined avenues, *khlongs*, old buildings, and the low skyline have all been preserved here. King Chulalongkorn laid out the district along European lines, with grand vistas, broad boulevards, and a geometric road grid surrounding his palaces. A century later is still the royal quarter. Ratchadamnoen Avenue ("royal way") leads up to Vimanmek Mansion and the royal museums in

Detail from gates in Dusit Park

Dusit Park. Nearby is the royal "marble" temple of Wat Benchamabophit and Chitrlada Palace, the King and Queen's residence. Political power is also concentrated in Dusit. The National Assembly, Government House, several ministries, and the Prime Minister's house are located here. By contrast, horse racing at the Royal Turf Club, *muay thai* boxing at Ratchadamnoen Stadium, and animal encounters at the landscaped Dusit Zoo provide popular public entertainment.

SIGHTS AT A GLANCE

Wats and Churches
Dusit's Christian Churches ❷
Wat Benchamabophit ❿
Wat Indrawihan ❹

Museums
SUPPORT Museum ❻
Vimanmek Mansion ❺

Notable Roads
Phitsanulok Road ❾
Ratchadamnoen Avenue ⓫

Landmark Buildings
Chitrlada Palace ❽

Markets
Thewet Flower Market ❸

Parks and Zoos
Dusit Park pp102–3 ❶
Dusit Zoo ❼

GETTING THERE
The Chao Phraya Express calls at Wat Sam Phraya, Wisut Kasat, and Thewet piers. The latter is the most convenient stop for the majority of Dusit's sights. The area is well served by buses, particularly along Ratchadamnoen Avenue and Dusit's other main arteries.

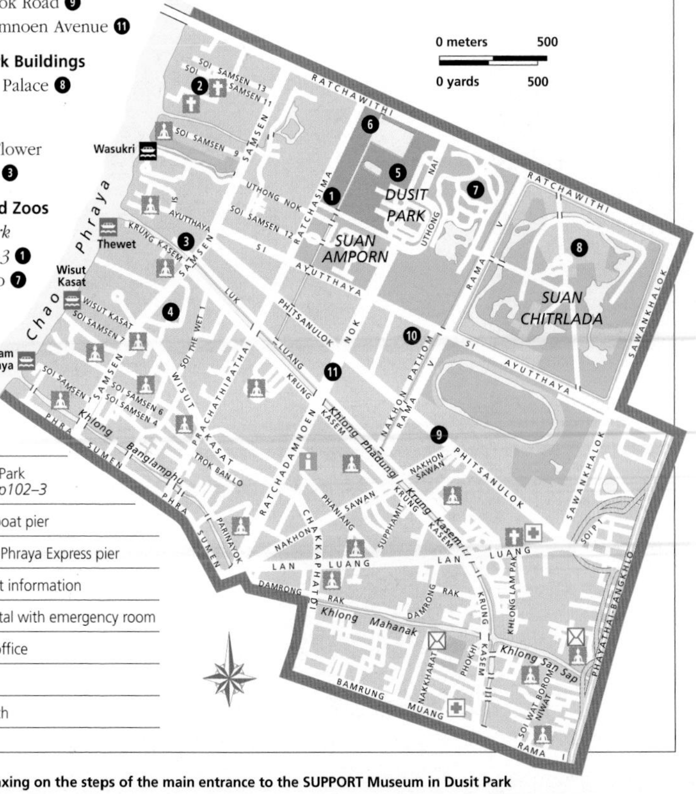

0 meters 500
0 yards 500

KEY
- Dusit Park *See pp102–3*
- Riverboat pier
- Chao Phraya Express pier
- Tourist information
- Hospital with emergency room
- Post office
- Wat
- Church

◁ Nuns relaxing on the steps of the main entrance to the SUPPORT Museum in Dusit Park

Dusit Park ●

แผนผังสวนดุสิต

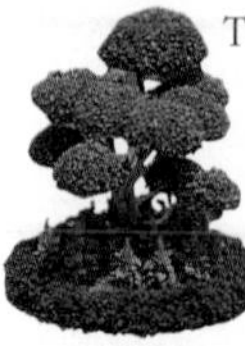

Topiary at Vimanmek

This magnificent park is the major attraction of the Dusit area. King Chulalongkorn (1868–1910), the first Thai sovereign to visit Europe, was determined to Westernize Bangkok, and the manicured gardens, genteel architecture, and teak mansions in Dusit Park all bear testimony to his efforts. Highlights include Vimanmek Mansion – the world's largest golden teak building – and the graceful Abhisek Dusit Throne Hall, which houses the SUPPORT Museum of traditional arts and crafts. A visit to the park and the neighboring zoo (*see p105*) can easily occupy a whole day.

LOCATOR MAP
See Street Finder maps 2, 3

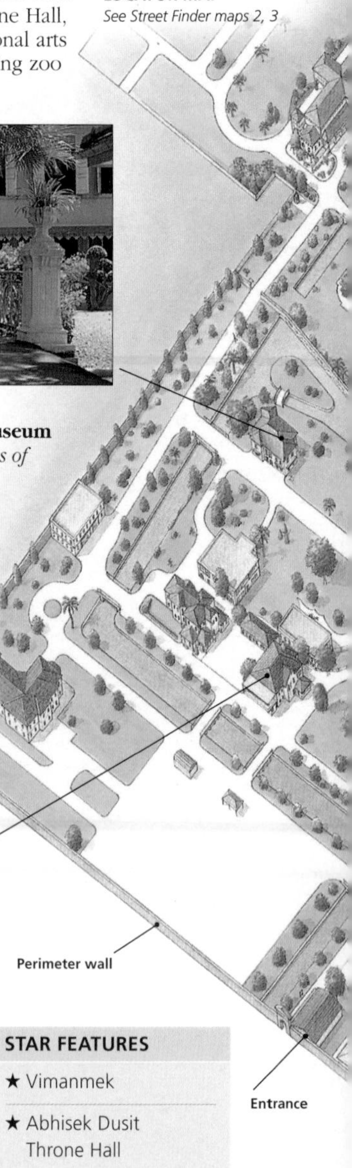

King Bhumibol's Photographic Museums
Most of the photographs in these museums were taken by King Bhumibol, an avid photographer. The royal family features in many.

Royal Paraphernalia Museum
Photographs and paintings of regal figures from the Chakri dynasty, such as this portrait of Maha Uparaja Bovornvijaya Jarn, the deputy king to King Rama V, can be seen in this museum.

Antique Textile Exhibition Hall
This small collection includes a range of fabrics favored by the court of King Rama V, such as satin. There are also displays of the different types of Thai silk from all over Thailand.

Perimeter wall

STAR FEATURES
★ Vimanmek

★ Abhisek Dusit Throne Hall

Entrance

★ Abhisek Dusit Throne Hall

This hall (see p105) is a fancifully ornamented white edifice. The major attraction inside is the SUPPORT Museum, with its collection of traditional, crafted artifacts, such as works using the exquisitely colored wings of jewel beetles.

VISITORS' CHECKLIST

Map 2 F1. 0-2628-6300-9, ext 0#. 56, 70; AC: 70, 510, 515. **Vimanmek Mansion** 9:30am–3:15pm daily (tickets sold till 3pm). compulsory. **SUPPORT Museum** 9:30am–3:15pm daily. **All other buildings** 9am–4pm daily. for royal ceremonies. Royal Mansion ticket (valid 30 days) inc adm to Dusit Park and all buildings. in buildings. **www**.palaces.thai.net

Canal

Bridge

Lakeside Pavilion

An elegant pavilion behind Vimanmek Palace affords a pleasant view across the lake to some particularly fine traditional Thai teak houses. The farther bank is, however, closed to visitors.

★ Vimanmek Mansion

More like a Victorian mansion than a Thai palace, this three-storied, golden teak structure (see pp104–5) was built using wooden pegs instead of nails. The palace is full of intriguing artifacts.

Old Clock Museum

This museum houses the collection of clocks acquired by Kings Rama V and Rama IX on their trips to Europe. It includes timepieces of European, American, and Japanese origin.

0 meters 50

0 yards 50

Dusit's Christian Churches ❷

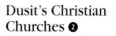
โบสถ์ดุสิตคริสเตียน

Map 2 E1. 🚌 3, 9, 30, 53; AC: 506; MB: 8, 10.

By the bank of the Chao Phraya River, just south of Ratchawithi Road, is a small group of Christian churches.

The first of these, **St. Francis Xavier Church**, is near Krung Thon Bridge. Built in the early 1850s, it is notable for the statue of the saint atop its triple-arched portico frontage. Among its congregation are members of the local Vietnamese Catholic community, who settled here in 1934.

Just south is the smaller **Church of the Immaculate Conception**. It was built in 1837 by French missionaries on a site previously occupied by a Portuguese church.

Behind it is an even earlier church constructed in 1674, during King Narai's reign (see pp60–61), by Father Louis Laneau for the early Portuguese community. Their descendants, and those of some Cambodian refugees who settled here in the late 17th century, still live in the parish. They take part in religious festivals here, hence the church's nickname, the Cambodian Church. It now houses the **Wat Mae Phrae Museum** (no set opening times), which contains a statue of the Virgin Mary, venerated in an annual ceremony held in October.

Porticoed entrance of St. Francis Xavier Church

Modern mural of a reclining Buddha, Wat Indrawihan

Thewet Flower Market ❸

ตลาดดอกไม้เทเวศน์

Krung Kasem Rd. **Map** 2 E2. 🚌 AC: 506. **National Library** Samsen Rd. **Tel** 0-2281-5212. ◯ 9:30am–7:30pm daily.

One of Bangkok's premier plant and garden markets flanks both sides of Khlong Phadung Krung Kasem, west of Samsen Road. It stocks a huge range of goods, including ornamental garden pots, orchids, trees, and pond bases. Although Thewet Market is not as vast as Chatuchak Market (see p135), its prices are generally lower. It is a pleasant place to browse, even if you buy nothing.

Ornamental garden pots at Thewet Flower Market

Around the corner is the **National Library**, which contains a large collection of books in Thai and English. A number of Thai paintings hang in the lobby. The exterior incorporates several traditional Thai architectural touches (see pp34–5), as do many government offices in the area.

Wat Indrawihan ❹

วัดอินทรวิหาร

Wisut Kasat Rd. **Map** 2 E3. 🚌 3, 53; AC: 506. ◯ daily.

You cannot miss the reason for Wat Indrawihan's fame: an impressive 32-m (105-ft) standing Buddha. The statue was commissioned in the mid-19th century by King Mongkut (Rama IV) to enshrine a relic of the Buddha from Sri Lanka. (Relics such as fragments of bone and hair are housed in countless Buddhist monuments worldwide.)

While admittedly not the most beautiful of Buddha images because of its rather flattened features, it stands out attractively against the sky. Its enormous toes make a bizarre altar for the many offerings presented, including garlands of flowers.

Inside the bot of Wat In (a popular abbreviation for the temple) are hundreds of Buddhas of Bencharong (five-color) funerary urns. Traditional-style, modern murals can also be seen inside the bot. In another, smaller building, "lucky" water is sold in plastic bags.

Vimanmek Mansion ❺

พระที่นั่งวิมานเมฆ

Ratchawithi Rd. **Map** 2 F1. **Tel** 0-2628-6300-9 (ext 0#). 🚌 56, 70; AC: 70, 510, 515. ◯ 9:30am–3:15pm daily. ◯ 1–6 Jan. 🎫 (free for Grand Palace ticket holders). 📷 inside. 📷 compulsory. **www**.palaces.thai.net

Constructed entirely without nails, the world's largest golden teak building was reassembled on this site in 1901, after being moved from its original location on Ko Sichang (see pp316–17). It soon became a favored retreat of King Chulalongkorn (Rama V) and his family and concubines while they were waiting for nearby Chitrlada Palace *(see p106)* to be completed. Apart from the king, the mansion was for women only. After closing in 1935 and falling into disrepair, this "celestial residence" was magnificently restored in 1982 at the request of Queen Sirikit for Bangkok's bicentennial celebrations *(see pp68–9)*.

The guided tour takes in 30 of the 81 rooms via circuitous corridors. Highlights include the audience chambers, the music room, sweeping staircases, and the king's apartments, which are contained within an octagonal tower. The palace was the first building in Thailand to have electricity and an indoor bathroom; an early light bulb and a showerhead are two of the items on display.

Treasures from the Rattanakosin era include porcelain, furniture, betel-nut sets, the first Thai alphabet typewriter, hunting trophies, and royal photographs. King Chulalongkorn was known for his taste in Western-style design, and the palace, with its verandas and high ceilings, is reminiscent of a Victorian mansion.

Although the tour allows little time inside, visitors can walk around outside or sit in a lakeside porch, where Thai dancing *(see pp42–3)* and disquieting monkey acrobatics are staged twice daily.

Vimanmek Mansion, the summer residence of Rama V

Domed ceiling of the Ananta Samakhom Throne Hall

SUPPORT Museum ❻

พิพิธภัณฑ์ศิลปาชีพ

Ratchawithi Rd. **Map** 2 F1.
Tel *0-2628-6300.* 🚌 *AC: 510, 515.*
⏰ *9:30am–3:15pm daily.* 📷

Housed in the Abhisek Dusit Throne Hall beside Vimanmek Palace (and included on the same ticket), the SUPPORT Museum is a showcase for traditional crafts that have been saved from decline by Queen Sirikit, founder of the Promotion of Supplementary Occupations and Related Techniques (SUPPORT). One such craft is *yan lipao* weaving, which originated in Nakhon Si Thammarat *(see pp378–9)*. The fine reed used in *yan lipao* lends itself to intricate patterns, its sheen giving the end product a luster.

Crafts on display include nielloware, rattan, bamboo, celadon, lacquerware, and an art form that uses the iridescent green-blue wings of jewel beetles. Some of the designs were created by members of the royal family. One of the training centers for SUPPORT is at the Bang Sai Folk Arts and Crafts Center near Bang Pa-in *(see p181)*. South Abhisek Dusit is another throne hall, **Ananta Samakorn**. Dating from 1912,

Black bear in Dusit Zoo

this ornate, Italianate building once housed the parliament. Today it is used for royal receptions and private functions. Its spectacular interior is open to the public only on Children's Day, the second Saturday in January.

Dusit Zoo ❼

สวนสัตว์ดุสิต (เขาดิน)

Rama V & Ratchawithi rds.
Map 3 A2. ***Tel*** *0-2281-2000.*
🚌 *AC: 510, 515.* ⏰ *8am–6pm daily.* 📷 🌐 **www**.zoothailand.org

Forming a green wedge between Dusit Park and Chitrlada Palace are the lush gardens of Dusit Zoo. One of Asia's better zoos, it has reasonable space for birds and large mammals such as tigers, bears, elephants, and hippos, although some of the other enclosures are much more confining. There are also elephant rides and several animal-feeding shows. The grounds were originally the private botanical gardens of Rama V, and some varieties of tropical flora are still cultivated here. The lawns, lakes, and wooded glades are ideal for relaxing strolls and watching Thai families enjoying a day out.

Chitrlada Palace ❽

พระตำหนักจิตรลดา

Ratchawithi & Rama V rds. **Map** 3 B2.
🚌 18, 28; AC: 510. ⬤ to public.

The permanent residence
of the king and queen is an
early 20th-century palace set in
extensive grounds (closed to
the public), east of Dusit Zoo.
Although the palace is hidden
from view, the buildings used
by King Bhumibol (Rama
IX) for agricultural and
industrial experiments
are visible. In 1993
he became the first
monarch in the
world to earn a
patent – for a
waste water aerator.

The royal white
elephants (there
are currently 11) are
trained and housed on
the palace grounds.

A portrait of King Bhumibol

The perimeter is illuminated
from the King's Birthday
(Dec 5) to New Year.

Phitsanulok Road ❾

ถนนพิษณุโลก

Map 2 E2. 🚌 16, 23, 201, 505.

A number of important state
institutions are located along
this major avenue, which
cuts through the heart of
Dusit. Traveling northwest

past the Mission Hospital at
the Sawankhalok Road end,
the first of interest is **Ban
Phitsanulok**. This mansion
has been the official residence
of the prime minister since it
was restored in 1982. It was
originally built in 1925 by
Rama VI for Major General
Phraya Anirutheva. Designed
by the same Italian architects
who built the Ananta Samakorn Throne Hall *(see p105)*,
it is a riot of Venetian Gothic,
with floral-shaped mullioned
windows, spindly cren-
ellations, and a sweep-
ing curved wing. It
is not open to the
public, and guests
rarely stay over-
night because the
mansion is believed
to be haunted.

On the opposite
side of the road
is the grassy oval of
the **Royal Turf Club**,
one of Thailand's two major
horse-racing tracks *(see p117)*.
Races alternate between the
two tracks, and are held here
from 12:30 to 6:30pm every
other Sunday. The stands fill
with bettors from all levels
of Thai society. Experiencing
the banter and furious betting
can often be as much fun as
watching the race itself. The
most prominent annual event
that takes place here is the
King's Cup, also known as
the Derby Cup, on the first or
second weekend of January.

**Filling in the results at the end
of a race at the Royal Turf Club**

Government House, to the
west, just past the Nakhon
Pathom Road turning, is a
fanciful, cream-colored Neo-
Venetian style building. It
is now used to house the
prime minister's office, and
it is closed to the public.

Wat Benchama-bophit ❿

วัดเบญจมบพิตร

69 Rama V Rd. **Map** 3 A3.
Tel 0-2282-7413. 🚌 3, 16, 23,
505. ⬤ 8:30am–5:30pm daily. 📷

European influence on Thai
architecture *(see p35)* is
exemplified by Wat Benchamabophit, the last major temple
to be built in central Bangkok.
In 1899 King Chulalongkorn
(Rama V) commissioned his
brother Prince Naris and the
Italian architect Hercules
Manfredi to design a new *bot*

ROYAL WHITE ELEPHANTS

The importance of
the white elephant
(chang samkhan) in
Thailand derives from
a 2,500-year-old tale.
Queen Maya, once
barren, became
pregnant with the
future Buddha after
dreaming of a white
elephant entering her
womb. Ever since the
13th century, when
King Ramkamhaeng
gave the animal great
prestige, the reigning
monarch's importance has been judged in
part according to the number of white elephants he owns. Indeed, the white elephant's
status as a national icon was symbolized by

Old manuscript depicting a white elephant

its presence on the
Siamese flag until
1917. The origin of
the phrase "white ele-
phant," meaning a
large, useless invest-
ment, lies in the Thai
tradition according to
which all white ele-
phants must belong
to the king. They
cannot be used for
work and, therefore,
have to be cared for
at huge expense.

Though referred to as
white, the elephants are not fully albino. But
tradition states that seven parts of their body
– the eyes, palate, nails, tail hair, skin, hairs,
and testicles – must be close to white.

Singhas guarding the entrance to Wat Benchamabophit

Ratchadamnoen Avenue ⑪

ถนนราชดำเนิน

Map 1 D4. 🚌 *15, 33, 39, 70, 159, 201; AC: 511, 503, 157, 170, 183.*

Planned by King Mongkut (Rama IV) in the style of a European boulevard, this thoroughfare has three parts.

The first section, Ratchadamnoen Nai ("inner"), starts at Lak Muang and skirts **Sanam Luang** *(see pp78–9)*, before veering east at the Royal Hotel as Ratchadamnoen Klang ("middle"). From here it passes the **Democracy Monument** *(see p87)* and 1930s mansions – a vista featured in the movie *Good Morning, Vietnam.*

Just across Khlong Banglamphu, Ratchadamnoen Nok ("outer") turns north into the Dusit area. This stretch, shaded by trees, is flanked by ministries, the main TAT headquarters and **Ratchadamnoen Boxing Stadium** *(see p45)*. Just before the ornate double bridge over Khlong Phadung Krung Kasem is the Thai-influenced modern building of the United Nations Economic and Social Commission for Asia and the Pacific (ESCAP).

The avenue ends at the domed **Ananta Samakhom Throne Hall** *(see p105)*, which looms up beyond the Chulalongkorn Equestrian Statue in the parade ground, the site of December's Trooping of the Colors ceremony *(see p51)*.

Ratchadamnoen Avenue is decorated and illuminated in December as part of King Bhumibol's birthday festivities.

and cloister for the original Ayutthaya-period temple which stood on the site. The nickname for the new *wat* ("Marble Temple") is derived from the gray Carrara marble used to clad the walls.

Laid out in cruciform with cascading roof levels, the *bot* is elegantly proportioned. It contains another successful fusion of traditions: intricate Victorian-style stained-glass windows depicting scenes from Thai mythology. In the room of the ashes of Rama V is the most revered copy of Phitsanulok's Phra Buddha Chinarat *(see pp160–61)*, with a pointed halo. In the cloister are 53 different Buddha images, originals and copies of images from around Thailand and other Buddhist countries, assembled by Rama V.

Within the *wat* is one of the three sets of doors inlaid with mother-of-pearl that were salvaged from Wat Borom Buddharam in Ayutthaya. The building in which Rama V lived as a monk features

murals depicting events that occurred during his reign.

Wat Benchamabophit is a popular location for witnessing monastic rituals, from Buddhist holiday processions to the daily alms round *(see p129)*, in which merit-makers donate food to the monks lined up outside the *wat* along Nakhon Pathom Road. This is a reversal of the usual practice where the monks go out in search of alms.

Annual Trooping of the Colors ceremony, Ratchadamnoen Avenue

Buddhist monks in the forecourt of the European-inspired Wat Benchamabophit ▷

DOWNTOWN

The center of Bangkok's vast and continually expanding downtown is the area spanning Silom and Ploen Chit roads. The business district originated in the 19th century in the Old Farang Quarter of Charoen Krung Road, where charming colonial buildings have been conserved around the Oriental Hotel. The concrete canyon of Silom is the preserve of business people by day, but after dark its northern end is the heart of city nightlife. Farther north, showcase stores line Ploen Chit and Rama I roads while the stalls of Silom Road and Siam Square provide cheaper shopping. Amid the tower blocks, Lumphini Park provides green relief, and a few traditional Thai buildings remain, such as Jim Thompson's House and Suan Pakkad Palace.

SIGHTS AT A GLANCE

Wats, Shrines, and Churches
Assumption Cathedral ②
Erawan Shrine ⑫
Maha Uma Devi Temple ⑤
Wat Pathum Wanaram ⑬

Museums and Libraries
Bangkok Art and Culture Center ⑮
Jim Thompson's House pp120–21 ⑯
Neilson-Hays Library ⑥
Suan Pakkad Palace ⑱

Notable Roads and Districts
Charoen Krung (New) Road ③
Patpong ⑦
Pratunam ⑰

Siam Square ⑭
Silom Road ④

Parks and Sports Grounds
Lumphini Park ⑨
Royal Bangkok Sports Club ⑪

Historic Buildings
Chulalongkorn University ⑩
Mandarin Oriental Hotel ①

Zoos
Snake Farm ⑧

GETTING THERE
Many buses run along the main roads. The Chao Phraya Express stops at Si Phraya, Wat Muang Khae, and Oriental piers. Avoid any heavy traffic jams by taking the Skytrain.

KEY

Street-by-Street map *pp112–13*

Ⓜ Subway

🚉 Skytrain station

🚤 Riverboat pier

🚤 Chao Phraya Express pier

🚓 Police station

Tourist police station

Hospital with emergency room

⊠ Post office

Wat

Church

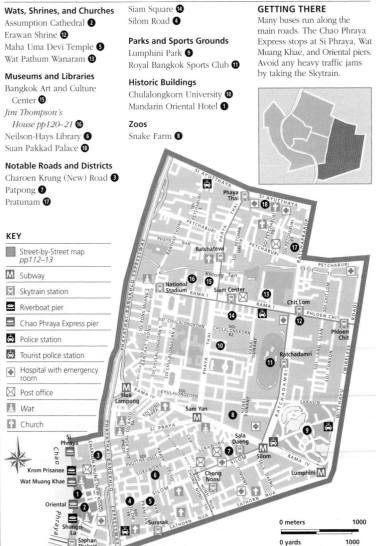

◁ Office buildings and shopping centers, as seen from Lumphini Park

Street-by-Street: Old Farang Quarter

ย่านที่อยู่ของฝรั่งสมัยก่อน(ย่านเจริญกรุง)

This area was Bangkok's original port and foreign commercial district in the 19th century. In 1820 Portugal was granted land in Bangkok, which resulted in the construction of the Portuguese Embassy. Embassies of other countries, such as France, soon followed. These outside influences created an amalgam of Western and Eastern architectural styles. Charoen Krung (New) Road, the first road in Thailand to be paved, cuts through the Old Farang Quarter and is home to gem traders, tailors, and antique dealers. The elegant Assumption Cathedral faces Bangkok's only European-style square. The Quarter's back streets are surprisingly quiet and contain some attractive wooden houses.

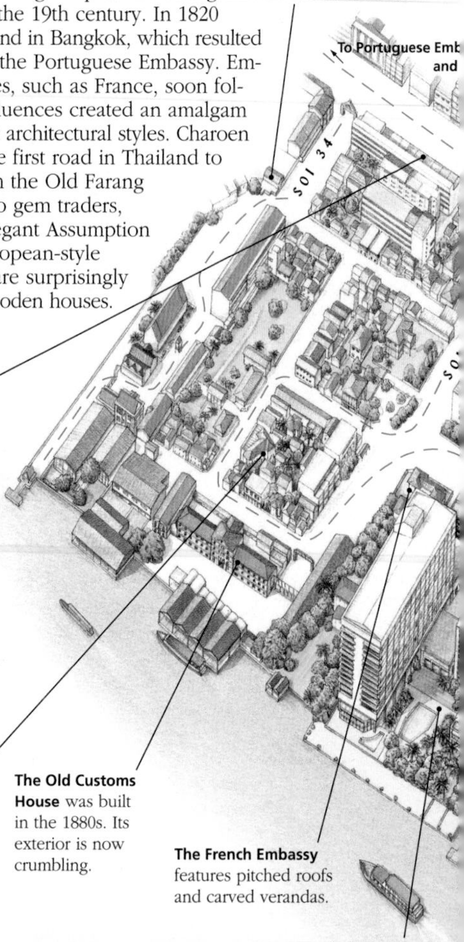

Emblem on gate of French Embassy

Harmonique restaurant is one of a row of Chinese shop-houses built around 1900.

To Portuguese Emb and

House of Gems
is a tiny shop/museum selling rocks and fossils. Geological oddities – such as dinosaur droppings and tektites (glassy meteorites) – can be seen here.

The Haroon Mosque
is a quaint stucco building with a Muslim graveyard. The mosque, which faces Mecca, is off a street lined with wooden houses.

The Old Customs House was built in the 1880s. Its exterior is now crumbling.

The French Embassy features pitched roofs and carved verandas.

STAR SIGHTS

★ Mandarin Oriental Hotel

★ Assumption Cathedral

★ Mandarin Oriental Hotel
The world-renowned Mandarin Oriental Hotel was established in 1876 by two Danish sea captains. In 1958 a new structure (the Tower Wing) was added, and in 1976 the ten-story River Wing opened ❶

For hotels and restaurants in this region see pp398–402 and pp428–32

The China House, *one of Bangkok's most expensive restaurants, is in a building dating from the reign of King Vajiravudh (see p67). The structure next door, the Commercial Co. of Siam, was erected in the same era.*

LOCATOR MAP
See Street Finder map 6

★ Assumption Cathedral
This elegantly decorated cathedral was built in 1910. The cathedral's Rococo interior features a high, vaulted ceiling and a striking marble altar from France ❷

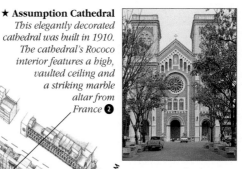

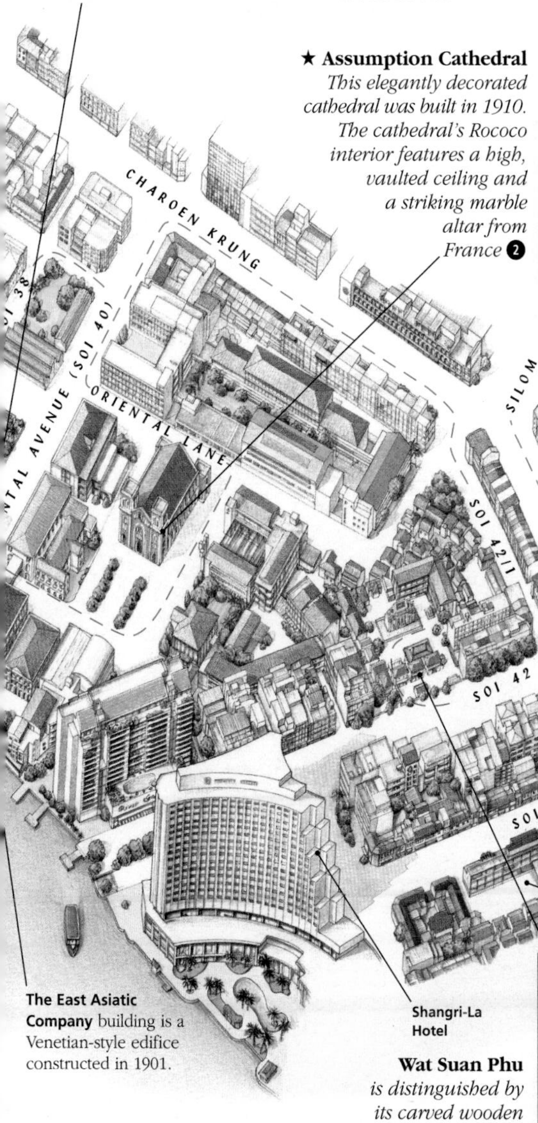

To
Taksin
Bridge

Bangrak
Market

Shangri-La
Hotel

The East Asiatic Company building is a Venetian-style edifice constructed in 1901.

Wat Suan Phu *is distinguished by its carved wooden buildings and the Phra Bodhisattva Kuan-Im, a Chinese shrine over a carp pond.*

KEY

 Suggested route

hotel's eight highly acclaimed restaurants (*see p430*). *Khon* performances (*see pp42–3*) are staged here as guests dine. The hotel runs a respected school of Thai cookery.

Assumption Cathedral ❷

วัดอัสสัมชัญ

Oriental Lane, off Charoen Krung Rd. **Map** 6 F4. 🚌 *35, 75.* ⬜ *daily.*

This Romanesque-style brick edifice was built in 1910 on the site of an earlier cathedral. Its rose window is flanked by twin squat towers. The richly ornamented, Rococo interior is dominated by a lofty, barrel-arched blue ceiling patterned with gold starbursts.

The cathedral faces a tree-shaded piazza, the site of several other Western-style buildings. These include the modern Assumption College, the Neo-Classical Catholic Mission, and the Renaissance-style Catholic Center.

Charoen Krung (New) Road ❸

ถนนเจริญกรุง

Map 6 F2. 🚌 *1; AC: 504.*

Skirting the Chao Phraya River – from Wat Pho through Chinatown and on to Yannawa – Charoen Krung, or New Road (as it is often also called) is one of Bangkok's oldest thoroughfares.

Linking the Customs House and many trading companies, the road was once the center of Bangkok's European community. At their insistence it became Thailand's first paved highway. Still home to the gem and antique trades, today the road is choked with traffic pollution and noise, but side streets, lined with trees and old wooden buildings, can be blissfully serene. Along the road is the imposing **General Post Office**, whose light-brown stone façade is adorned with reliefs of *garudas* (mythical beasts, half bird, half human).

Neo-Classical façade of the Authors' Wing of the Mandarin Oriental Hotel

Mandarin Oriental Hotel ❶

โรงแรมโอเรียนเต็ล

Oriental Ave, off Charoen Krung Rd. **Map** 6 F4. **Tel** 0-2659-9000. 🚌 *35, 75.* 🚢 *Oriental.* **www**.mandarin oriental.com/bangkok

Repeatedly voted the world's best hotel for its service and attention to detail, the Mandarin Oriental was Thailand's first large hotel. It was established in 1876 and completely rebuilt in 1887. More wings have since been added. The hotel owes much of its charm to the Armenian Sarkies brothers, creators of the luxurious Raffles Hotel in Singapore, and boasts lavish decor and a spectacular setting on the banks of the Chao Phraya River.

The original, white-shuttered wing contains the renowned Authors' Suites. Somerset Maugham was one such author who stayed here in the 1920s. Recovering from a bout of malaria, he wrote of the "dust and heat and noise and whiteness and more dust" of Bangkok, though his perception of the city was to change once he was able to explore the *wats* and *khlongs*.

Classic, English-style high tea is served in the Authors' Lounge of the hotel, a riot of potted plants and wicker chairs. A teak barge shuttles back and forth to the Sala Rim Naam on the opposite bank, one of the

The airy and luxurious lobby of the Mandarin Oriental Hotel

In front is a statue of King Chulalongkorn. The coin and stamp stalls (open Sundays) outside the post office and the **Bangrak Market** (open daily), selling clothing and fruit, give the area vibrancy.

Silom Road ❹
ถนนสีลม

Map 7 A4. 🚌 *AC: 177, 504, 514, 532, 544.* Ⓜ *Silom.* 🚊 *Saladaeng (skytrain).*

The commercial heart of Bangkok, Silom Road is becoming a polluted canyon of skyscrapers, shopping malls, and elevated railway lines, though the area used to consist of orchards flanking a canal. One feature that remains unchanged is the many thousands of barn swallows that nest here from October to March.

Towards the river end of the road, and also on parallel Surawong Road, are several gem and silk shops. Near Patpong *(see p116)* is the Dusit Thani Hotel that overlooks Lumphini Park and the bustle of the local nightlife. Close by is Convent Road, taking its name from the **Carmelite Convent**, and also home to the Gothic-style **Anglican Christ Church**, built in 1904.

Street vendor pushing his cart

Maha Uma Devi Temple ❺
วัดศรีมหาอุมาเทวี

Corner of Silom and Pan rds. **Map** 7 B4. 🚌 *AC: 76, 502, 504.* 🕑 *7am–6pm daily.* 🎎 *Deepavali (Nov).*

Tamils founded this colorful Hindu temple during the 1860s. They were part of an influx of Indians who decided to move to Bangkok when India was handed over to the British Crown in 1858.

The main temple building is topped by a gold-plated copper dome above a 6-m (20-ft) high façade depicting various Hindu gods. Always buzzing with activity, and often with

Multicolored deities on the roof of Maha Uma Devi Temple

live Indian music, the temple is also the focus for Deepavali (Festival of Lights) celebrations in November. An oil-lamp ritual is held most days at noon, and on Fridays at 11:30am there is a *prasada* (vegetarian ceremony), in which blessed food is distributed to devotees.

Although some Thais might call the temple Wat Khaek ("Indians' temple"), a common cultural heritage means that many local Thais and Chinese also regularly worship here. The Hindu deities Shiva and Ganesh feature in Thai Buddhism, and Hindus regard the Buddha as one of the incarnations of Vishnu.

Neilson-Hays Library ❻
ห้องสมุดเนลสันเฮยส์

195 Surawong Rd. **Map** 7 B4. **Tel** 0-2233-1731. 🚌 *16, 93.* 🕑 *9:30am–5pm Tue–Sun.* www.neilsonhayslibrary.com

Housed within an elegant building beside the British Club is the Neilson-Hays Library. Its 20,000 volumes form one of Southeast Asia's finest English-language collections.

The library was built in 1921 in honor of Jennie Neilson-Hays, who was the mainstay of the Bangkok Library Association between 1895 and 1920. The internal domed rotunda is used as a modern art gallery.

WESTERN WRITERS IN BANGKOK

Western impressions of Thailand were for a long time heavily influenced by just one author – Anna Leonowens. An English teacher at the court of King Mongkut (Rama IV), Leonowens wrote the book that inspired the musical *The King and I*. However, the portrayal of the king as a comic figure stirred up anger in the country, and the book is now regarded as an unreliable historical source. Less controversially, Joseph Conrad wrote about his journey up the Chao Phraya in *The Shadow Line*, and Somerset Maugham described his impressions of Thailand in *The Gentleman in the Parlour*. These are just two of the Western authors commemorated by suites at the Oriental Hotel. Others include Noël Coward, Gore Vidal, Graham Greene, and Barbara Cartland. The Oriental has also ventured into other literary projects: it is the site for the annual prize-giving ceremony of the SEAWrite Award, established in 1969 to promote contact between writers in Southeast Asian countries.

Joseph Conrad in 1904

Looking for bargains at a night market in Patpong

Patpong ❼

พัฒน์พงษ์

Silom Rd, Patpong 1 and 2. **Map** 7
C3. 🚌 *AC: 76, 177, 504, 514.*
Ⓜ *Silom.* 🚊 *Saladaeng (skytrain).*

The private streets of Patpong
1 and 2, named after the one-
time owner, Chinese millionaire
Khun Patpongpanit, comprise
what is probably the world's
most notorious red light
district. In the 1960s the area
was the home of Bangkok's
entertainment scene – the
go-go bars sprang up to satisfy
airline crews and US GIs on
leave during the Vietnam War.
Since the 1970s, the sex

shows have been sustained
mainly through tourist patronage. A less visible homosexual
scene exists in adjacent Silom
Soi 6, while Soi Taniya's hostess bars are frequented
mainly by Japanese clients.

The tourist police department monitors Patpong, and
the area is surprisingly safe. A
night market, with stalls selling souvenirs and original and
fake fashions, gives the area a
thin veneer of respectability.
A bookstore in the center of
Patpong is one of Southeast
Asia's major outlets for books
on feminism and exploitation.
Many visitors come to Patpong
out of curiosity rather than to
indulge in the flesh trade.

Snake Farm ❽

สวนงู

Rama IV Rd. **Map** 7 C3. **Tel** *0-2252-*
0161. 🚌 *AC: 50, 507.* Ⓜ *Silom.*
🚊 *Saladaeng (skytrain).*
⭘ *8:30am–4:30pm Mon–Fri,*
8:30am–noon Sat, Sun & public hols
(shows at 10:30am, 2pm). 🏷️ 📷

The Queen Saowapha Snake
Farm is run by the Thai Red
Cross. It makes snakebite
serums and informs the public about local snakes. Unlike
the tourist-oriented farms, the
emphasis is on education.
Demonstrations of venom
milking take place twice daily
(once daily on weekends), pre-
ceded by an explanatory slide
show. Handlers open a snake's
mouth and pierce the cellophane lid of a glass jar with its
fangs. The milky venom then
squirts harmlessly into the jar.

Cobra before milking, Snake Farm

SEX WORKERS AND THEIR CLIENTS IN THAILAND

Historically, prostitution in Thailand was
reinforced by the institution of polygamy. Both
are now illegal, but the use of prostitutes by
Thai men is still widespread. Every town has
at least one massage parlor. The glitzy brothels
of Patpong and such towns as Pattaya and
Hat Yai may form the foreign perception of
the Thai sex industry, but they are a relatively
recent development, dating from the presence
of US servicemen in Thailand during the
Vietnam War. Some estimates put the number
of sex workers as high as two million, but a

more realistic figure is 250,000, one fifth of
whom are male. The majority of prostitutes
work for Thai clients, but a few service the
many tourists who come for so-called "sex
holidays." Increasingly, concern about exploitation, pedophilia, AIDS, and sex tourism are
being voiced around the world, and countries
such as Sweden now prosecute their nationals
caught paying for sex with children abroad.

Many prostitutes come from the poorest
regions of Thailand or neighboring countries
such as Burma. The income, and a somewhat
fatalistic attitude, can outweigh any social
disapproval they may face. But some do not
become involved in the industry willingly,
and cases of beatings and imprisonment are
not uncommon. Health problems, stigma,
lack of skills, and death from AIDS *(see p483)*
spell grim prospects for all sex workers.
Despite a government campaign and the work
of programs by charities such as Empower,
AIDS statistics for the mid-1990s estimate the
number of prostitutes infected at 14 percent
for the whole country, and up to 70 percent
for provinces such as Chiang Rai.

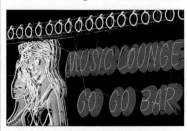

Gaudy nightclub sign in central Bangkok

Perfecting the art of tai chi chuan early one morning in Lumphini Park

Lumphini Park ❾

สวนลุมพินี

Map 8 D3. 🚌 *14; AC: 50, 507.* Ⓜ *Silom, Lumphini.* 🚊 *Saladaeng (skytrain).* ◯ *5:30am–9pm daily.*

Named after the Buddha's birthplace in Nepal, Bangkok's main greenbelt sprawls around two boating lakes. Dominating the Silom Road corner of the park is a statue of Rama VI.

The best time to visit is early morning, when it is used by Thais for jogging and Chinese for practicing tai chi chuan. The superstitious can be seen consuming fresh snake blood and bile to keep ill health at bay, purchased from stalls along the park's northern edge. The park is a relaxing place to stroll and observe elderly Chinese playing chess, and impromptu games of *takraw* (a type of volleyball in which the hands may not be used).

Chulalongkorn University ❿

มหาวิทยาลัยจุฬาลงกรณ์

Phya Thai Rd. **Map** 7 C3. 🚌 *16, 40, 47, 50; AC: 501; MB: 1.* **Tel** *0-2215-3555.* **Imaging Tech Museum** *Tel 0-2218-5580.* ◯ *10:30am–3:30pm Mon–Fri.* 🚫 **Art Gallery** *Tel 0-2218-2961.* ◯ *daily.* ◯ *public hols.* **Museum of Ecology** *Tel 0-2218-5442.* ◯ *8:30am–4:30pm Mon–Fri.*

Dedicated to the modern-minded king who founded it, this is Thailand's oldest, richest, and most prestigious university. Chulalongkorn's central gardens, between the busy Phya Thai and Henri Dunant roads, are the site of several attractive buildings and a pond that is often used during the festival of Loy Krathong (see p50).

The **Imaging Technology Museum**, south of the lake, features hands-on photographic displays, including a room where you can develop and print your own film, and exhibitions of high-quality photography from Thailand and other countries. Nearby are an auditorium, used mainly for classical concerts, a contemporary **Art Gallery**, which stages various temporary exhibitions, and a **Museum of Ecology**.

Royal Bangkok Sports Club ⓫

ราชกรีฑาสโมสร

Henry Dunant Rd. **Map** 8 D2. 🚌 *16, 21; AC: 141.* **Tel** *0-2652-5000.* ◯ *9am–6pm alternate Sundays for races only.* 🚫 **www.rbsc.org**

Considered to be Thailand's most exclusive social institution, the RBSC has a waiting list to prove it. It offers a wide range of sports to its members – including rugby, soccer, and field hockey – who form some of the top Thai teams in these sports. Nonmembers may enter to watch horse races at the club, one of Thailand's two principal race courses; the other is the Royal Turf Club on Phitsanulok Road (see p106).

Gambling is virtually a national institution in Thailand, and the RBSC gives Bangkokians the perfect opportunity to indulge in one of their favorite pastimes. On race days, thousands of bettors from all social classes flock to the track. As the start of the race draws near, betting becomes furious, and huge electronic screens track the odds on each horse and the total money wagered. Visitors are welcome to join in, and should watch the screens for clues as to which horse to bet on; you may have to ask for help to fill out one of the Thai-language betting slips.

Horses on the home stretch, Royal Bangkok Sports Club

The vast interior of the Siam Center, one of Thailand's first shopping malls

Erawan Shrine ⓬

พระพรหมเอราวัณ

Ratchadamri Rd. **Map** 8 D1. 🚌 AC: 501, 504, 505. 🚇 Rachadamri or Siam (skytrain).

Drivers take their hands off the steering wheel to *wai* (a gesture of respect) as they pass the Erawan Shrine, such is the widespread faith in the luck that this landmark brings. The construction of the original Erawan Hotel in the 1950s, on the site now occupied by the Grand Hyatt Erawan Hotel, was plagued by a series of mishaps. In order to counteract the bad spirits believed to be causing the problems, this shrine dedicated to Indra and his elephant mount, Erawan, was erected in front of the hotel. Ever since, the somewhat gaudy monument has been

Dancers in traditional Thai costume performing at the Erawan Shrine

decked with garlands, carved wooden elephants, and other offerings in the hope of, or thanks for, good fortune. By the shrine are women in traditional costume. Anyone wishing to express gratitude for good fortune can pay the dancers a fee, and they will do a thank you dance around it.

Near the shrine, and along Phloen Chit and Sukhumvit roads, are several of Bangkok's most upscale shopping complexes *(see pp138–9)*, including Sogo, Siam Center, World Trade Center, Gay Sorn Plaza, Amarin Plaza, Le Meridien, and the swankiest of them all, the Siam Paragon.

Wat Pathum Wanaram ⓭

วัดปทุมวนาราม

Rama I Rd. **Map** 8 D1. 🚌 AC: 25, 501, 508. 🚇 Siam (skytrain).
⏰ 7am–6pm daily.

The main reason for visiting the Pathum Wanaram temple is to see Phra Meru Mas, a reconstruction of the crematorium of the late Princess Mother. Following her cremation at Sanam Luang *(see pp78–9)* in March 1996, her remains were transferred to these grounds in an elaborate procession. The crematorium is a rare example of ancient craftmanship, featuring ornate stencils and lacquered sculptures. It represents Mount Meru, the heavenly abode of the gods.

Siam Square ⓮

สยามสแควร์

Rama I Rd. **Map** 7 C1. 🚌 AC: 25, 501, 508. 🚇 Siam (skytrain).

Street shopping is fast disappearing in Bangkok as shopping malls proliferate. The principal exception to this phenomenon is the network of *sois* (alleys) collectively known as Siam Square, between Chulalongkorn University *(see p117)* and the Siam Center.

The square is packed with independent shops and stalls selling, in particular, music, books, accessories, and clothing – much of it by enterprising young Thai designers.

Rama I Road, on one side of the square, is the showcase for Thailand's movie industry. Three grand theaters – the Scala, the Lido, and the Siam – are located here. On the western edge of the square, on Phaya Thai Road, is the **Mahboonkrong Center** (MBK), which houses a department store and various shops and stalls. Beyond it is the **National Stadium**, Thailand's main arena for major soccer and other sports events. However, the future of the entire district looks uncertain: it is feared that the land may be redeveloped when its lease expires.

Bangkok Art and Culture Center ⓯

หอศิลปวัฒนธรรมแห่งกรุงเทพฯ
จาวมตรี

939 Rama I Rd. **Map** 7 C1. **Tel** 0-22 14-6630. 🚌 AC: 15, 16, 501, 508, 529. 🚇 National Stadium (skytrain).
⏰ 10am–6pm Tue–Sun. 🎫 for special exhibitions and performances.
🅿 🍴 🛍 www.bacc.or.th

The Bangkok Art and Culture Center offers visitors an enjoyable insight into Thai culture and society. This striking eleven-story building is home to galleries, performance spaces, and a library. The center displays over 300 contemporary works of art by Thai and international artists and hosts regular exhibitions alongside an exciting events program.

Bargain-price clothing for sale at Pratunam Market

Jim Thompson's House 🄰

บ้านจิมทอมป์สัน

See pp120–21.

Pratunam 🄱

ประตูน้ำ

Map 4 E5. 🚌 *12; AC: 504.*

Pratunam district is worth a brief visit. The lively and colorful **Pratunam Market** is a vast maze of stalls, stores, and workshops, trading mostly in clothing and fashion accessories. Just west of the market is the Modernist **Baiyoke Tower**, which reigned briefly as the tallest building in Bangkok from 1987 until 1995. Despite evidence of

settling in the surrounding ground, permission was granted for construction of the adjacent **Baiyoke Tower II**, which was completed in 1997.

Suan Pakkad Palace 🄲

วังสวนผักกาด

352 Si Ayutthaya Rd. **Map** 4 D4. **Tel** 0-2245-4934. 🚌 AC: 201, 513. 🚉 *Phayathai (skytrain).* 🕐 *9am–4pm daily.* 🎫 🌐 www.suanpakkad.com

This palace, a group of five traditional teak houses, was originally the home of Prince and Princess Chumbhot. The houses were assembled in the 1950s within a lush garden landscaped out of a cabbage patch – *suan pakkad* in Thai – that gives the palace its name. Each building has been converted into a museum, and together they house an impressive private collection of art and artifacts that once belonged to the royal couple.

The eclectic assortment ranges from Khmer sculpture, betel-nut sets, and pieces of antique lacquered furniture, to Thai musical instruments and exquisite shells and crystals. More important, perhaps, is the first-class collection of whorl-patterned red and white Bronze Age pottery, excavated

from tombs at Ban Chiang *(see p272)* in Northeast Thailand. The highlight for most visitors, though, is the Lacquer Pavilion, which was built from two exquisite temple buildings retrieved by Prince Chumbhot from Ayutthaya province.

Immaculately crafted, charmingly detailed black and gold lacquered murals inside each edifice depict scenes from the Buddha's life and the Ramakien *(see pp40–41)*. They also portray ordinary Thai life from just before the fall of Ayutthaya in 1767 *(see pp60–61)*. These murals are some of the only ones to survive from the Ayutthaya period. Scenes include foreign traders exchanging goods, graphic battle scenes, and gruesome depictions of hell.

Elegant façade of the Lacquer Pavilion at Suan Pakkad Palace

BANGKOK'S MODERN ARCHITECTURE

An apparently endless mass of dull concrete towers, monotonous rows of shop-houses, and gaudy mock-classical edifices give Bangkok the overall impression of a sprawling urban jungle rather than the Oriental splendor visitors might expect.

Nonetheless, there are some modern buildings within the city that were designed by visionary architects. Postmodern architecture of an international standard is particularly noticeable along Sathorn Tai and Silom roads. Other interesting buildings include the Thai Airways headquarters and the triple-towered "Elephant Building."

One of Bangkok's most progressive design companies is Plan Architecture, responsible for striking buildings such as the Baiyoke Towers I and II, the bullet-shaped Vanit Building II on

One of the Baiyoke Towers, in downtown Bangkok

Soi Chidlom, and the narrow Thai Wah II Tower on Sathorn Tai Road. Thailand's most famous, and perhaps most witty, modern landmark is probably the Bank of Asia's head office on Sathorn Tai Road, nicknamed the "Robot Building" *(see p69)*.

Two sophisticated examples of Thai Modernism, both of which are hotels, were designed by Westerners. The roof of the Siam Inter-Continental was designed to resemble a traditional "Mongkut" crown, and the gardens of the Sukhothai evoke the serene waterscape of the old capital of the same name *(see pp194–7)*.

In the 21st century, Bangkok's skyline continues to change, with additions such as the Siam Paragon, Central World, and many flashy apartment buildings and chic hotels.

Jim Thompson's House ⑯

บ้านจิมทอมป์สัน

One of the best-preserved traditional Thai houses in Bangkok and finest museums in the country is the former home of Jim Thompson. The entrepreneurial American revived the art of Thai silk weaving (see pp266–7) following its demise during World War II. His house stands in a flower-filled garden across from the ancient silk weavers' quarter of Ban Khrua. In 1959 Thompson

Khmer
singha **in
the garden**

dismantled six teak houses in Ban Khrua and Ayutthaya province and reassembled them here in an unconventional layout. Thompson

was an avid collector of antiquities and artworks from all over Southeast Asia. His distinguished array, which spans 14 centuries, is attractively displayed, and left much as it was when he mysteriously disappeared in 1967. Unlike many other domestic museums, this feels like a lived-in home.

Master Bedroom
Fine 19th-century paintings of the jataka *tales line the walls of this room.*

First floor

Ground floor

Guest bedrooms

★ Jataka Paintings
This panel, in the entrance hall, is one of eight early 19th-century paintings in the house showing scenes from the Vessantara jataka (see p30). *These depict Prince Vessantara as an incarnation of the Buddha.*

★ Burmese Carvings
This wooden figure of an animist Nat spirit is among Thompson's extensive collection of Burmese images. When Buddhism developed in Burma it incorporated the preexisting worship of Nat spirits.

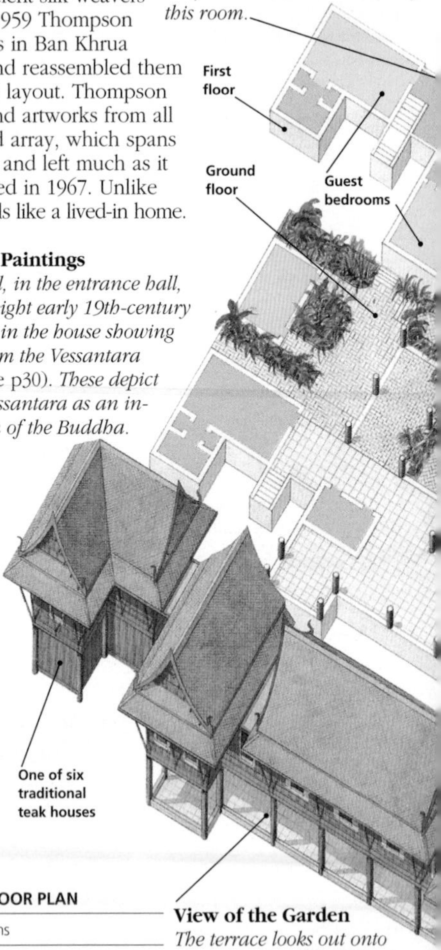

One of six traditional teak houses

KEY TO FLOOR PLAN

	Bedrooms
	Study
	Entrance hall
	Drawing room
	Dining room
	Secure room
	Bencharong room
	Silk Pavilion
	Other exhibition space

View of the Garden
The terrace looks out onto the garden, Khlong San Sap, and across to Ban Khrua.

STAR EXHIBITS

- ★ Jataka Paintings
- ★ Burmese Carvings
- ★ Dvaravati Torso of the Buddha

Drawing Room
Situated on the right is a 14th-century U Thong sandstone head of the Buddha, while the 18th-century carved wooden figures in the alcoves are of Burmese spirits.

VISITORS' CHECKLIST

6 Soi Kasemsan 2, Rama I Rd. **Map** 3 C5. **Tel** 0-2216-7368. 15, 48, 204; AC: 508. National Stadium (skytrain). 9am–5pm daily. compulsory.

The *khlong* (canal) was once used by silk weavers, who dried threads of silk on poles along the banks.

Porcelain Chamberpot
This cat, made of Chinese porcelain, is in the guest bedroom.

Dining Room
Beautiful blue and white Ming porcelain adorns the walls of this room.

★ **Dvaravati Torso of the Buddha**
This torso, made of limestone, is in the garden. Dating from the early Dvaravati period (7th century), it is said to be one of the oldest surviving Buddha images in Southeast Asia.

Spirit house with offerings

WHO WAS JIM THOMPSON?
An architect by profession, Thailand's most famous American came here in 1945 as the Bangkok head of the Office of Strategic Services (OSS), a forerunner of the CIA. In 1948 he founded the Thai Silk Company Ltd, turning the ailing industry into a thriving business once again. Thompson became a social celebrity in Bangkok and finally achieved mythical status following his disappearance on Easter Sunday 1967 while walking in the Cameron Highlands in Malaysia. Explanations for his vanishing include falling from a path or having a heart attack to more sinister suggestions of CIA involvement.

Jim Thompson inspecting Thai silk in 1964

trance

The teak houses, the oldest dating from 1800, were erected with some walls reversed so that exterior carvings now face the interior.

THON BURI

K nown originally as Ban Kok ("village of the wild plum"), Thon Buri was the capital of Thailand for 15 years between 1767 and 1782. When Rama I moved his capital across the river its original name followed, and, though Thais refer to the capital as Krung Thep, it remains known as Bangkok to foreigners. Thon Buri wasn't linked by bridge to Bangkok until 1932 and was officially incorporated into the city only in 1971. Today this area preserves a dis-

Chinese statue at Wat Arun

tinct identity, offering a sleepier version of Bangkok proper. The best way to explore Thon Buri is by boat. Meandering down the intricate network of canals, the visitor sees scenes of river life – stilt houses, small temples, mansions, and floating shops. On Khlong Bangkok Noi is the Royal Barge Museum with its lavishly decorated boats. Farther south there are some interesting riverside *wats* along the Chao Phraya River, the most prominent and famous of which is Wat Arun.

SIGHTS AT A GLANCE

Wats and Churches
Church of Santa Cruz ❼
Wat Arun pp126–7 ❺
Wat Kalayanimit ❻
Wat Prayun ❽
Wat Rakhang ❹
Wat Suwannaram ❶

Museums
Museums at the Siriraj Hospital ❸
Royal Barge Museum ❷

Monuments
Taksin Monument ❾

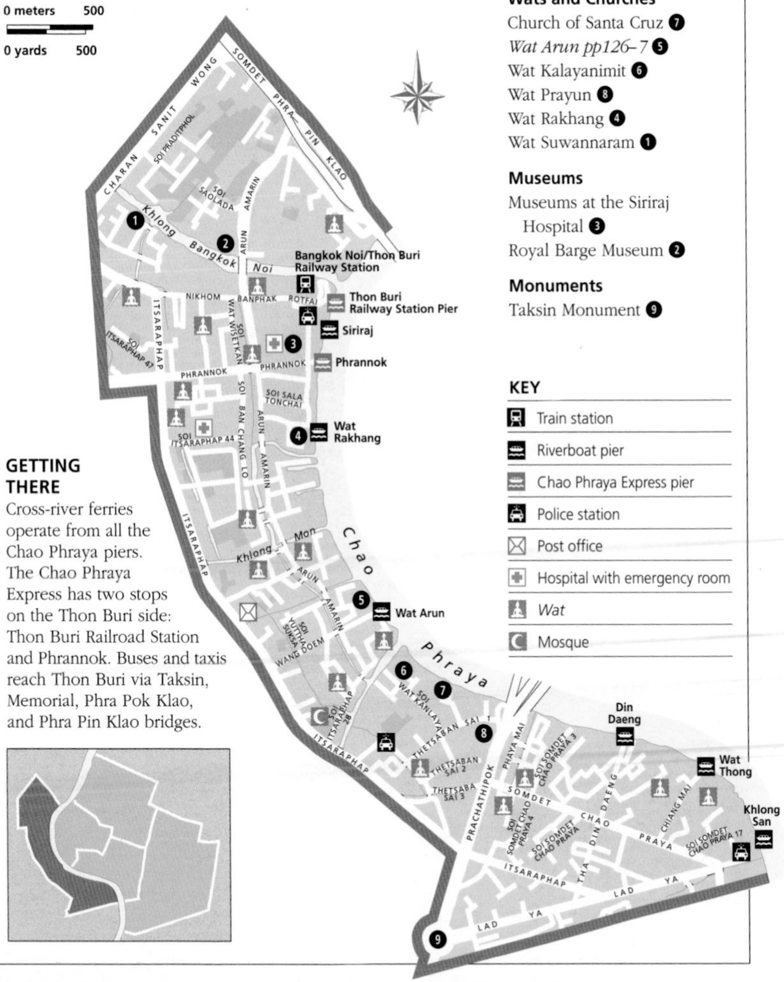

KEY

🚆	Train station
⛴	Riverboat pier
🛳	Chao Phraya Express pier
🚓	Police station
✉	Post office
✚	Hospital with emergency room
🛕	*Wat*
☪	Mosque

GETTING THERE
Cross-river ferries operate from all the Chao Phraya piers. The Chao Phraya Express has two stops on the Thon Buri side: Thon Buri Railroad Station and Phrannok. Buses and taxis reach Thon Buri via Taksin, Memorial, Phra Pok Klao, and Phra Pin Klao bridges.

0 meters   500
0 yards   500

Bangkok Noi/Thon Buri Railway Station
Thon Buri Railway Station Pier
Siriraj
Phrannok
Wat Rakhang
Wat Arun
Din Daeng
Wat Thong
Khlong San

◁ Detail of the elaborate ceramic decoration, made up of thousands of pieces of broken porcelain, on Wat Arun

Buddha in classic *bhumisparsa* mudra posture, Wat Suwannaram

Wat Suwannaram ❶

วัดสุวรรณาราม

Charan Sanit Wong Rd, Khlong Bangkok Noi. **Map** 1 A3. 🚌 *hire a long-tail from any pier.* ◯ *daily.*

Wat Suwannaram was constructed by Rama I on the foundations of a temple dating from the Ayutthaya era. It was renovated by Rama III and finally completed in 1831. The temple complex provides a graceful example of early Rattanakosin architecture *(see p35)*, in which a few traces of the Ayutthaya style still linger. The well-restored murals of the main *wihan*, some of the best of the early 19th century, are attributed to two renowned painters of the third reign, Luang Vichit Chetsada and Krua Khonpae.

Western perspective had not permeated Thai mural painting at the time: scenes are depicted as aerial views with figures shown at the same size whether they are in the foreground or background. On the side panels are depictions of the last ten tales of the *jataka* (the Buddha's previous lives). On the south wall are the Buddhist cosmological kingdoms, and the entrance wall is dominated by a lively scene of the Buddha's victory over Mara. Notice the hairstyles of the third reign (1824–51): the heads of both sexes are shaven to leave a small patch of hair at the top. Also, look for a Christian cross on a hermit's hut, evidence that missionaries were active in Thailand at the time.

Hongsa, on prow of the king's barge

Royal Barge Museum ❷

พิพิธภัณฑ์เรือพระที่นั่ง

Khlong Bangkok Noi. **Map** 1 B3. **Tel** 0-2424-0004. 🚌 7, 9,19. 🚤 *hire a long-tail from Chang pier.* ◯ *9am–5pm daily.* 🚫 📷

Housed within a huge warehouse-like structure is a collection of Thailand's most ostentatious boats, the royal barges. Paintings of fabulous Ayutthayan barges *(see pp60–61)* engaged in battles and stately processions, together with archive photographs of royal barge ceremonies in Bangkok over the last 150 years, have provided some of the most splendid visions of Thailand presented to the world via postcards and tourist brochures. Nowadays, though, the vessels are rarely seen cruising the Chao Phraya River, since they have been housed in the museum since 1967. The barges are reproductions of some built 200 years ago by Rama I, who had copied Ayutthayan originals.

In 1981 most of the royal barges underwent an expensive face-lift. They came out in all their gilded glory during the 1982 Bangkok Bicentennial celebrations *(see p68)*, for the King's 60th birthday in 1987, and for the Golden Jubilee of his reign on November 7, 1996. For such auspicious occasions more than 50 barges sail in a lengthy procession down the Chao Phraya. Most of the 2,000 oarsmen – dressed in traditional uniforms – are sea cadets, a fitting crew for boats that were once the naval fleet.

The vessel in the center of the museum, Supphanahongsa ("golden swan"), is the most important royal barge. Made from a single piece of teak, it is over 50 m (165 ft) long and weighs 15 tons. In action it requires a highly trained crew of 64. The mythical, swanlike bird Hongsa rears up from its prow. Anantanagaraj, a barge bearing a multiheaded *naga* and a Buddha image, is reserved for conveying monks'

Superbly detailed 19th-century mural at Wat Suwannaram

Ferocious figurehead on a gun barge built in the reign of Rama I

robes. Narai Song Suban Rama IX is the first barge to be built during the present king's reign. It is 44 m (145 ft) long and can carry 50 people.

Museums at the Siriraj Hospital ❸

พิพิธภัณฑ์โรงพยาบาลศิริราช

Arun Amarin Rd. **Map** 1 B4. **Tel** 0-2419-7000 (Forensic), 0-2419-8523 (Congdon). 🚌 81, 91. 🚢 Phrannok and Wanglang. ⬜ 8:30am–4pm Mon–Fri. ● public hols. ∅ **www**.si.mahidol.ac.th/museums

Ten medical museums are located at this hospital, of which the **Museum of Forensic Medicine** is the best known. It houses gruesome objects, such as the preserved

figure of Si-oui, a man who suffocated and ate seven children. Thai parents often threaten naughty children with his ghost. In the **Congdon Museum of Anatomy** are still-born Siamese twins. Such twins are so-named because the famous Chan and In, who toured the world in the mid-19th century, were from Siam, as Thailand was then known.

Wat Rakhang ❹

วัดระฆัง

Soi Wat Rakhang. **Map** 1 B5. 🚌 57, 83. 🚢 Chang to Wat Rakhang. ⬜ daily.

Wat Rakhang was the last major temple to be constructed by Rama I in the early 19th century. The fine murals in the main *wihan*, which were painted between 1922 and 1923 by a monk Phra Wanawatwichit, include recognizable scenes of Bangkok. Though the capital has changed much since then, the Grand Palace, which stands just across the river from Wat Rakhang, is easy to identify. In the murals, the palace is shown in the middle of an imaginary attack. There is also an elaborate depiction of a royal barge procession.

The raised wooden library (*ho trai*) of Wat Rakhang, in the west of the compound, was used as a residence by Rama I before he became king. The building's eave supports, delicately carved bookcases, and gold and black doors are period masterpieces. Inside the library are murals depicting scenes from the Ramakien and a portrait of Rama I.

Wooden façade of the raised library at Wat Rakhang

LIVING ON WATER: THE ERA OF THE THAI KHLONGS

Ayutthaya and Bangkok, both on the flood plain of the Chao Phraya River, were cities that grew along countless little canals and streams known as *khlongs*. Bangkok was once a floating city. In the 1840s all but about ten percent of its population of 400,000 lived on the *khlongs*. Houses built on rafts could be moored wherever there was space (*see p37*).

Stilt houses lining the banks of the *khlongs* provided a somewhat more stable habitat. Although roads now cover most of Bangkok's eastern waterways, many still exist in Thon Buri, where life still largely revolves around the *khlongs*. Children splashing in the water are a common sight, and early each morning water-borne vendors cruise up and down, selling everything from Chinese pastries and coffee to fruit, vegetables, and cooking utensils. The favored *khlong* vessel today is the long-tailed powerboat – one was memorably commandeered by Roger Moore as James Bond in the movie *The Man with the Golden Gun*. Visitors can easily charter their own from Chang pier to explore the Thon Buri *khlongs*.

Bangkok in the 1890s, before the age of roads and land-based dwellings

Wat Arun ❺

วัดอรุณ

Ceramic flower on main prang

Wat Arun, named after Aruna, the Indian god of dawn, is a striking Bangkok landmark. It owes its name to the legend that, in October 1767, King Taksin arrived here at sunrise from the sacked capital, Ayutthaya. He soon enlarged the tiny temple that stood on the site into a Royal Chapel to house the Emerald Buddha *(see pp82–3)*. Rama II and Rama III were responsible for the size of the current temple: the main *prang* is 79 m (260 ft) high and the circumference of its base is 234 m (768 ft). In the 19th century King Mongkut (Rama IV) added the ornamentation created with broken pieces of porcelain. The monument's style, deriving mainly from Khmer architecture *(see pp264–5)*, is unique in Thailand.

Multicolored Tiers
Rows of demons, decorated with pieces of porcelain, line the exterior of a minor prang.

CENTRAL MONUMENT OF WAT ARUN
The monument's design symbolizes Hindu-Buddhist cosmology. The central *prang* (tower) is the mythical Mount Meru, and its ornamental tiers are worlds within worlds. The layout of four minor *prangs* around a central one is a symbolic mandala shape.

★ River View of Temple
This popular image of Wat Arun, as seen from the Chao Phraya, appears on the ten-baht coin and in the Tourism Authority of Thailand (TAT) logo.

Top terrace

One of the eight entrances

Minor *prangs* at each corner of the *wat*

Chinese Guards
These figures, at the entrances to the terrace, complement the Chinese-style porcelain decorating the prangs.

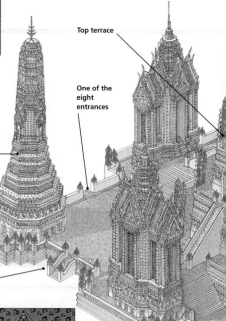

STAR FEATURES

★ Ceramic Details

★ River View of Temple

Gallery of the Bot
Elsewhere in the temple complex are the usual buildings found in a wat. This image of the Buddha in the main bot sits above the ashes of devotees.

Indra's weapon, the *vajra* or thunderbolt, at the crest

SYMBOLIC LEVELS

The Devaphum (top) is the peak of Mount Meru, rising above four subsidiary peaks. It denotes six heavens within seven realms of happiness.

The Tavatimsa Heaven (central section), where all desires are fulfilled, is guarded at the four cardinal points by the Hindu god Indra.

The Traiphum (base) represents 31 realms of existence across the three worlds (Desire, Form, and Formless) of the Buddhist universe.

Stairs on the Central Prang
The steep steps represent the difficulties of reaching higher levels of existence. Visitors can climb halfway up when restoration work allows.

Small Cove
On the second level of the central prang are many small coves, inside which are kinnari, mythological creatures, half bird, half human.

Decoration of the Four Minor Prangs
Inside the niches of each minor prang are statues of Nayu, the god of wind, on horseback.

Mondops at the cardinal points

★ Ceramic Details
Much of the colorful porcelain decorating the prangs was donated by local people. The flowers above and below the "demon bears" are said to evoke the vegetation of Mount Meru, home of the gods.

Wat Kalayanimit ❻
วัดกัลยาณิมิตร

Soi Wat Kanlaya. **Map** 5 B2. 🚌 2, 8;
AC: 2 to Pak Klong Talad, then cross
the river by ferry at the pier.
🕐 8:30am–4:30pm daily.

This dilapidated temple
com plex is one of the five
temples built in Bangkok by
Rama III (1824–51). Rama
liked Chinese design, as can
be seen from the statuary
dotted around the courtyard
(brought to Thailand as ballast
on empty rice barges returning
from China) and the Chinese-
style polygonal *chedi*.

The complex's immense
wiban contains a large sitting
Buddha image. In the temple
grounds is the biggest bronze
bell in Thailand.

Near the *wat*, on the other
side of Khlong Bangkok Yai,
is **Wichai Prasit Fortress**, built
to guard the river approach
to Thon Buri when Ayutthaya
was the dominant city in
Thailand (*see pp60–61*).

Thailand's biggest bronze bell, in
the bell tower of Wat Kalayanimit

Church of Santa Cruz ❼
วัดซางตาครู้ส

Soi Kudi Chin. **Map** 5 C2. 🚌 2, 8 to
Pak Klong Talad then cross the river
by ferry at the pier, or express boat to
Saphan Phut pier. 🕐 6am and 7pm
Sun (for Mass). 📷 inside the church.

This pastel yellow church is
one of the most prominent reminders of the community of

Newly released turtles feeding on fruit in the pond at Wat Prayun

Portuguese merchants and missionaries who lived here in the
mid-19th century. The church
was built in the late 18th
century, when Thon Buri was
the capital of Thailand (*see
pp64–5*). It was rebuilt by
Bishop Pallegoix in 1834, and
again in 1913. The church is
known in Thai as Wat Kuti
Chin ("Chinese monastic residence"), from the Chinese
influences in its architecture.

Although only a few houses
of Portuguese origin remain
in the muddle of alleyways
surrounding the temple, the
Portuguese legacy can still be
seen in the private Catholic
shrines that are tucked away
among Thai shop-houses.

Wat Prayun ❽
วัดประยุร

Pratchatipok Rd. **Map** 5 C2. 🚌 6,
43, or express boat to Saphan Phut
pier. 🕐 7am–4:30pm daily.

The unusual artificial hill at
the entrance to this temple
was created on a whim of
Rama III. While reading by
candlelight, the king observed
the interesting wax
formation of the
melting candle. He
then asked one of
his courtiers, Prayun
Bunnag, to create a
hill in the same
shape. The hill is
dotted with bizarre
shrines, miniature
chedis, *prangs*, grot-
toes, and tiny temples, but is
perhaps most memorable for
its ornamental pond, filled

Detail of King Taksin
monument

with hundreds of turtles.
Devotees buy the turtles nearby and then release them into
the pond. This act of setting
free confined creatures (more
commonly releasing caged
birds) is a way of gaining
merit for future lives.

The temple *bot*, although in
a state of disrepair, has doors
and window shutters decorated
with mother-of-pearl. The large
chedi has a circular cloister
surmounted by smaller *chedis*.

Taksin Monument ❾
อนุสาวรีย์พระเจ้าตากสิน

Pratchathipok Rd. **Map** 5 C4.
🚌 21, 40, 43, 82.

Located on the busy Wong-
wian Yai traffic circle, this
20th-century equestrian statue
commemorates King Taksin
(ruled 1767–82), who moved
the capital to Thon Buri after
the destruction of Ayutthaya
by the Burmese in 1767.

In 1950 the commission to
design the monument was giv-
en to Professor Silpa Bhirasri,
the Italian "father" of Thai
modern art who
took a Thai name
and citizenship.
The striking statue
took three years
to complete and
was finally un-
veiled in 1954.
Each year, on
December 28 –
the anniversary
of King Taksin's Coronation –
many Thais come to pay
homage at the statue.

Popular Buddhist Rituals

The act of merit-making is an essential part of religious life in Thailand *(see pp30–31)*. Practiced both by monks and lay people, it reflects an awareness that good deeds lead to good outcomes, such as happiness, either in this life or the next (as a more fortunate rebirth). To accumulate merit is a way of taking responsibility for one's own *karma* (destiny). Becoming a monk, even for a short period, or sponsoring the ordina-

Child offering a lotus bud

tion of a monk, is the highest form of making merit, and a devout Buddhist monk adheres to strict rules in his daily life. In some rituals – such as the alms round – the lives of monks and lay people interact. Other everyday habits of ordinary people focus on the local temple: the shared act of decorating a Buddhist shrine strengthens community ties. Devout lay people, meanwhile, may meditate and worship at a private shrine in their own home.

The daily alms round (bintabat) *takes place shortly after dawn, when monks leave their temples to search for their daily meal. Giving food to monks is a popular way for lay people to earn merit and practice generosity (the act of dana). Monks are permitted to eat only food that has been offered to them, and they must consume it before noon.*

Meditation *purifies the mind and clears it of distractions. It is practiced regularly by all monks and some lay people.*

Shaving the head *is a ritual for monks on the day of the full moon. This mural shows a novice being shaved for ordination.*

Gold leaf *put on the Buddha image honors his teachings.*

Pavilion at Wat Phra Kaeo

Offerings for the Buddha are usually symbolic. Lotus buds represent the purity of the Buddha's thoughts.

Incense sticks, in groups of three, symbolize the Buddha, the *dharma* (teachings), and the *sangha* (monkhood). Candles stand for the light of understanding.

VISITS TO THE WAT

Many lay people in Thailand go to their local *wat* at least once a week. Typically they make offerings to an image of the Buddha, listen to the monks chanting and to a *dharma* talk, and receive blessings. Food is prepared to offer to the monks and as a communal meal. The local community often funds building or restoration projects.

FARTHER AFIELD

Many interesting sights lie outside central Bangkok. Extending eastward is Sukhumvit Road, with a plethora of shops, restaurants, small galleries, and museums. Shopaholics will also not want to miss the superb Chatuchak Market or the spectacle of Damnoen Saduak Floating Market, west of the city. To the south and east are a clutch of theme and amusement parks, including the Erawan Museum and the Ancient City, a tranquil park with replicas of Thai monuments. At the Crocodile Farm reptile wrestling is the major attraction, and Safari World offers further wildlife encounters. Culture lovers will enjoy the art and antiques in the Prasart Museum. Pleasant day trips include the green suburb of Nonthaburi and, to the west, the relaxed provincial towns of Ratchaburi and Nakhon Pathom. The latter is the site of the world's tallest Buddhist monument, Phra Pathom Chedi. Another popular excursion is west to the Thai culture shows and elephant rides at the Rose Garden.

Thai classical dancer

SIGHTS AT A GLANCE

Towns
Nakhon Pathom ❹
Nonthaburi ❺
Ratchaburi ❶

Museums and Cultural Theme Parks
Ancient City ⓫
Erawan Museum ⓭
Prasart Museum ❿
Rose Garden ❸

Notable Roads
Sukhumvit Road ❼

Swimming Pools
Siam Park ❾

Markets
Chatuchak Market ❻
Damnoen Saduak Floating Market ❷

Zoos
Crocodile Farm ⓬
Safari World ❽

GETTING THERE
Many tour companies offer day trips to popular sights such as the Rose Garden, Safari World and Ancient City. Local bus routes also serve most sights.

KEY

▢	Main sightseeing area
▢	Built-up area
✈	Airport
═	Highway
═	Major road
═	Minor road

20 km = 12 miles

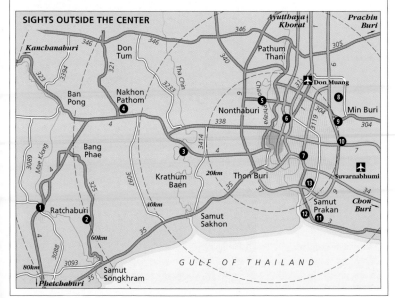

SIGHTS OUTSIDE THE CENTER

Ayutthaya, Khorat
Prachin Buri
Kanchanaburi
346
Don Tum
Pathum Thani
346
305
323 3394
321
340
Ban Pong
Nakhon Pathom ❹
Tha Chin
3233
Don Muang ✈
❺ Nonthaburi
❽
Min Buri
6
304
304 (3119)
338
❻
❾
Bang Phae
3414
❸
4
❿
Mae Klong 3089
325
❼
7
Krathum Baen
20km
Thon Buri
35
Suvarnabhumi ✈
3097
❶ Ratchaburi
40km
Samut Sakhon
37
⓭
9
34
❷
35
⓬
Samut Prakan
⓫ 3
Chon Buri
60km
3008
G U L F   O F   T H A I L A N D
80km   3093
35
Samut Songkhram
Phetchaburi

Palm-shaded Wat Mahathat, the main sight at Ratchaburi

Ratchaburi ❶

ราชบุรี

Ratchaburi province. 🚶 195,977.
🚌 🚆 ℹ️ *TAT, Ratchaburi (0-3451-1200).*

Originally an estuarial port at the mouth of the Klong River, Ratchaburi is now 30 km (19 miles) from the ocean. During the Ayutthaya period *(see pp60–61)* the town was sacked twice, in 1765 and 1767, by invading Burmese armies en route to besiege the capital city of Ayutthaya.

Nowadays, Ratchaburi makes a pleasant place to stop on the way to Kanchanaburi and the Western Seaboard. Some visitors stay overnight if visiting Damnoen Saduak Floating Market the next morning.

The town has few sights, but Wat Mahathat is worth a visit. Its *prang*, allegedly modeled on the main *prang* at Angkor Wat *(see pp264–5)*, dates from the 15th century, although the temple complex may have been founded as early as the 8th or 9th century. Inside the *prang* are traces of murals from the 15th century, and partially restored stucco work.

Artifacts in the **Ratchaburi National Museum** include archaeological finds such as fine Khmer sculptures and stucco decorations excavated from Muang Khu Bua, a Dvaravati site south of Ratchaburi.

🏛 **Ratchaburi National Museum**
Woradej Rd. *Tel* 0-3232-1513. 🕐
9am–4pm Wed–Sun. 🔴 *public hols.*
🌐 www.thailandmuseum.com

Environs
The caves of Khao Ngu, 6 km (4 miles) northwest of Ratchaburi on Highway 3087, contain some early Dvaravati art. The splendid reliefs of Buddha images found in Tham Rusi and Tham Fa Tho are probably of greatest interest. Aggressive macaques gather in the area around the caves.

Damnoen Saduak Floating Market ❷

ตลาดน้ำดำเนินสะดวก

2 km (1 mile) W of Damnoen Saduak, Ratchaburi province.
🚌 🚆 🚐 *or join tour from Bangkok.* 🕐 *4am–11am daily.*
ℹ️ *TAT, Phetchaburi (0-3247-1005).*

Like the numerous floating markets in Bangkok, the Damnoen Saduak market is also organized almost exclusively for tourists.

Located near Damnoen Saduak – 100 km (62 miles) southwest of Bangkok – the market is a labyrinth of narrow *khlongs* (canals). The small wooden boats are paddled mainly by female traders, some of whom are dressed in traditional blue farmers' shirts – *mo hom* – and conical straw hats. The fresh produce, including fruit, vegetables, and spices, comes straight from the farm. For the benefit of the tourists, some boats sell souvenir straw hats and refreshments.

The floating market actually consists of three markets. The largest, **Ton Khem**, is on Khlong Damnoen Saduak. On the parallel *khlong* is **Hia Kui**, where structures anchored to the banks function as warehouses selling souvenirs to large tour groups. To the south, on a smaller *khlong*, is **Khun Phitak**, which is the least crowded market.

The best way of getting around the three markets is by boat: trips can be taken along the *khlongs* or to see nearby coconut plantations. The best time to arrive is between 7am and 9am, when the Floating Market is in full swing.

Trading Thai-style at the bustling Damnoen Saduak Floating Market

For hotels and restaurants in this region see pp398–402 and pp428–32

Thai Fruits and Vegetables

Thailand's climate and soil conditions are conducive to the cultivation of a huge variety of fruits and vegetables throughout the year. Well known tropical fruits, including papaya, watermelon, mango, and pineapple, are unmistakable, but the orchards and farms of Thailand also offer a wealth of produce that may be less familiar to many visitors. Among the not-to-be-missed treats are the mangosteen, the grapefruitlike pomelo, the much-prized durian, and the sweet-fleshed, hairy rambutan. Thai fruits are sold sliced as snacks by street vendors everywhere, and the full range of fresh produce can be seen at most markets.

Bright red, fresh rambutans

Longans *have a transparent, succulent flesh around a smooth pit.*

Mangoes *can be eaten unripe and sour (green) or ripe and sweet (yellow).*

Mangosteens *are a favorite with Thais. Their tasty flesh has a melt-in-the-mouth texture.*

Durians *are the king of Thai fruit. The pungent smell and flavor are an acquired taste.*

Guavas, *crisp and sour fruits, are best enjoyed with a sweet chili dip or as a refreshing juice.*

Jackfruits, *similar in appearance to durians, only larger, have a sticky flesh with a tangy flavor.*

Gourds
Pea eggplant
Baby tomatoes
Eggplant

Thai vegetables *include several types of* makhua *(the tomato and eggplant family). Gourds and eggplant are frequently used in curries.*

Scallions
Cilantro
Chilies

Thai cuisine *makes liberal use of chilies, galingle, tamarind, and lemon grass to flavor dishes, balancing spiciness with coconut milk and sugar. Cilantro and scallions are popular garnishes.*

The peaceful, immaculately maintained Rose Garden

Rose Garden ❸
สวนสามพราน

Off Hwy 4, 32 km (20 miles) W of Bangkok. *Tel 0-3432-2544.* 🚌 M: 15; AC: to Nakom Pathom or Suphan Buri, or join tour from Bangkok. 🕐 8am–6pm daily (show at 2:45pm). 🌐 www.rosegardenriverside.com

This well-manicured garden, west of Bangkok, is part of the Rose Garden Country Resort. Although you can play tennis or golf and swim here, the chief attraction for visitors is the daily show of culture. Packed into the one-hour show are traditional Thai dancing (*see pp42–3*), ancient sword fighting, a Thai wedding, the ordination of a monk (*see p30*), and Thai boxing (*see pp44–5*). The model Thai village within the grounds is a showcase for fruit-carving, basket weaving, and other crafts.

Environs

Just north of the Rose Garden, the **Samphran Elephant Ground and Zoo** features crocodile wrestling and elephant rides. Farther west, on the way to Nakhon Pathom, the **Thai Human Imagery Museum** has fiberglass statues of historical Thai figures, including the Chakri kings (*see pp64–5*) and some renowned monks.

🐘 **Samphran Elephant Ground and Zoo**
Tel 0-2295-2938. 🕐 daily. 🖼
www.elephantshow.com

🏛 **Thai Human Imagery Museum**
Pinklao-Nakhonchaisri Hwy, km 31. *Tel 0-3433-2607.* 🕐 daily. 🖼

Nakhon Pathom ❹
นครปฐม

Nakhon Pathom province. 🏠 167,500. 🚉 🚌 ℹ️ TAT, Bangkok (0-2694-1222), TAT, Kanchanaburi (0-3451-1200). 🕐 daily. 🎉 Food and Fruit Fair (Sep 1-7); Phra Pathom Chedi Fair (Nov).

Some 67 km (42 miles) to the west of Bangkok, Nakhon Pathom was a major center of the Dvaravati Kingdom, which thrived from the 6th to the 11th centuries AD (*see pp56–7*).

The highlight of the town is the **Phra Pathom Chedi**, on Phetkasem Highway. This huge monument, housing a large standing Buddha image, is one of the most important places of pilgrimage in Thailand. The original *stupa* (a non-Thai *chedi*) on this site is thought to have been built sometime between the 2nd century BC and the 5th century AD. It commemorated the first Buddhist missionaries in Thailand, allegedly sent here from India in the 3rd century BC. The building fell into decay in the 11th century and was not restored until the early 19th century when King Mongkut had the old shrine encased in a *chedi*. The spire was completed by King Chulalongkorn. The *chedi*, dominates the town and at 120 m (395 ft) in height is the tallest Buddhist monument in the world.

Southeast of the *chedi* is the **Phra Pathom Chedi National Museum**, which has a fascinating collection of locally excavated pieces from the Dvaravati period, including stone Wheels of the Law 23 els from Chedi Chula Prathon, a 7th–8th century monument east of town.

West of the *chedi* is the early 20th-century **Sanam Chan Palace**. Parts of the palace are open to the public, and the peaceful grounds are a good place from which to view the palace's unusual mix of architectural styles.

🏛 **Phra Pathom Chedi National Museum**
Khwa Phra Rd. *Tel 0-3424-2500.* 🕐 Wed–Sun. ⬤ public hols. 🖼

🏛 **Sanam Chan Palace**
Off Phetkasem Hwy. *Tel 0-3424-4237.* 🕐 daily. 🖼

Nakhon Pathom's *chedi*, the world's tallest Buddhist monument

Nonthaburi pier, as seen from the Chao Phraya River

Nonthaburi ❺

นนทบุรี

Nonthaburi province. 🏠 46,500.
🚉 🚌 🚢 🛈 TAT, Bangkok
(1672); TAT, Ayutthaya (0-3524-
6076). 🚢 daily. 🎉 Fruit Fair
(Apr–Jun).

Approximately 10 km
(6 miles) north of
Bangkok, Nonthaburi
offers a relaxing slice
of provincial life. The
town is best reached
by riverboat from one
of Bangkok's express
piers. The journey
takes 50 minutes and
offers several inter-
esting sights, the first
of which is the Royal
Boat House near Wat
Sam Phraya pier,
where some of the
royal barges are kept. Others
are housed at the Royal Barge
Museum in Thon Buri (see
pp124–5). Past the Krung
Thon Bridge is a small community of rice barges on the
east bank, and shortly before
Nonthaburi pier is **Wat Khian**,
a temple that is half-sub-
merged in the river.

Nonthaburi has a pleasant,
provincial atmosphere that
contrasts with the chaos and
pollution of the capital just
down the river. The town is
particularly well known for the
quality of its durian fruit (see
p133) – reflected in the unusual decoration of the lamp-
posts on the promenade. You
may find the famously smelly
fruit for sale in Nonthaburi's
colorful, lively market by the
side of the river. A round-trip
boat ride from Nonthaburi

Door of *bot*, Wat
Chalerm Phrakiet

along Khlong Om will take
you on a slow-paced journey
through durian plantations
and past riverside houses. The
tiny river island of **Ko Kret**,
accessible only by boat, is
home to a community of
craftsmen, who are famous
for their distinctive
style of pottery.
Another worthwhile
excursion from
Nonthaburi is the
river journey to **Wat
Chalerm Phrakiet**, on
the west bank of the
Chao Phraya. The
wat occupies the site
of a 17th-century for-
tress, built by Rama
III in the 19th cen-
tury for his mother.
A particularly striking
feature is the intricate
detailing, including
porcelain tilework, on the
doors, gables, and window
frames of the *bot*. Behind is
a *chedi*, added by Rama IV.
The grounds have Chinese-
style wooden statues, including one of Santa Claus.

Chatuchak Market ❻

ตลาดจตุจักร

Chatuchak district. 🚌 AC: 38, 502,
503, 509, 510, 512, 517, 518, 521,
523. Ⓜ Kampangphet. 🚇 Mo Chit
(skytrain). 🛈 TAT, Bangkok (1672).
🕐 7am–6pm Sat & Sun.
www.chatuchak.org

Thailand's biggest market is
staged each weekend in a
northern suburb of Bangkok,
between the Northern Bus
Terminal and Bangsu Railroad
Station. It moved here in 1982
because it had outgrown its
original site on Sanam Luang
(see pp78–9). This chaotic
mass of more than 6,000 stalls
occupies the space of over
five football fields. It is always
full of throngs of eager shoppers, many of whom spend a
whole day browsing among
the merchandise displays.

The huge variety of goods
for sale ranges from seafood
to antiques, and from Siamese
fighting fish to second-hand
jeans. The plant section offers
a good introduction to Thai
flora, while the food stalls
display every conceivable
ingredient of Thai food, fresh
from the farm or the sea. The
antique and hill-tribe sections
sell a good selection of artifacts
and textiles, both fake and
genuine, from all over Thailand
and neighboring countries.

The market has been re-
ferred to as the "wildlife supermarket of the world," due to
the sale of some endangered
species here, such as leaf
monkeys. Despite efforts to
stop this, it is still continuing.

Traditional Thai wooden figures for sale at Chatuchak Market

Sukhumvit Road ❼
ถนนสุขุมวิท

Phra Khanong district. 🚇 🚌 *AC:*
38, 501, 508, 511, 513.

This road begins at the
eastern end of Bangkok's
downtown and continues all
the way to the Cambodian
border in Trat province *(see
p323)*. In Bangkok it is the
main thoroughfare of an
expanding business quarter
popular with foreigners.

Though it is a long way from
Bangkok's best-known sights,
the area has numerous good
quality, moderately priced
hotels and restaurants, and
a few attractions of its own.

Foremost of these is the
Siam Society, which was
founded in the early 1900s (by
a group of Thais and foreign
residents under the
patronage of Rama
VI) to research, re-
discover, and pre-
serve Thai culture.
Within the grounds
are two traditional
teakwood Northern
Thai houses that
comprise the coun-
try's only genuine
ethnological
museum. The
Kamthieng House,
a farm dwelling,
was transported
piece by piece in the 1960s to
Bangkok from the bank of
the Ping River, near Chiang
Mai. The Sangaroon House is
a later addition donated by
the architect Sangaroon Ratagasikorn who – inspired by
the utilitarian beauty of rural

*Sculpture at the
Queen's Park*

*A mock-up of a traditional sleeping
area in the Kamthieng House*

utensils – amassed a sizeable
collection. It is a good example of Central Plains style *(see
p36)*. Also on the grounds is
a reference library on Thai
culture, open to
visitors. The *Jour-
nal of the Siam
Society* is one of
Asia's most respect-
ed publications on
art history, culture,
and society.

Located next to
the Eastern Bus
Terminal, the
**Bangkok Planetar-
ium**, with its hands-
on exhibitions, may
be of some interest
to those people
who have time to spare while
waiting for a bus.

The **Queen's Park** (or Benjasiri Park) is between sois 22
and 24, while the larger **King's
Royal Park** is farther out toward
Samut Prakan. With its botanical gardens and area for
water sports, this park is one
of Bangkok's most pleasant
oases. The park also has an
exhibition on the king's life.

🏠 **Siam Society**
131 Soi Asoke, Sukhumvit Rd, Soi 21.
Tel 0-2661-6470. ⬜ Tue–Sat.
www.siam-society.org

🏠 **Bangkok Planetarium**
928 Sukhumvit Rd. **Tel** 0-2391-0544.
⬜ Tue–Sun. ⬛ public hols. 🈲
www.bangkokplanetarium.com

🌿 **Queen's Park**
By Soi 22, Sukhumvit Rd. ⬜ daily.

🌿 **King's Royal Park**
Soi Udomsuk, Sukhumvit Rd,
Soi 103. **Tel** 0-2328-1385.
⬜ daily. 🈲 🍴

Bangkok's Mass Transit System along busy Sukhumvit Road

Safari World ❽
ซาฟารีเวิลด์

99 Ramindra Road, Minburi district.
Tel 0-2914-4100. 🚌 60, 71 & *AC:
501 to Fashion Island Center, then*
songthaew. ⬜ 9am–5pm daily. 🈲
www.safariworld.com

This car-safari park offers eight
different natural habitats over
a 5-km (3-mile) drive. Animals
on view include tigers, elephants, giraffes, lions, zebras,
and rare species such as
white pandas. A marine park
features dolphin shows. There
are also elephant and orang-
utan shows, and a bird park.

Siam Park ❾
สวนสยาม

101 Mu 4 Sukha Phiban 2 Rd, Minburi
district. **Tel** 0-2919-7200-1. 🚌 *AC:
519.* ⬜ 10am–6pm Mon–Fri,
9am–7pm Sat, Sun & public hols. 🈲
www.siamparkcity.com

Siam Park is a great place to
cool off from the heat of the
Thai sun. Its attractions
include huge waterslides, a
gentle whirlpool, and an artificial lake. Water permeates
Thai culture in many ways, not
least at Songkran (New Year),
when everyone gets soaked
on the streets *(see p48, p236)*.

The facilities are well maintained, and there are restaurants and lifeguards. There is
also an amusement park with
rickety fairground rides and a
small zoo. As Bangkok families
descend upon the park in
numbers at the weekend, it's
best to visit during the week.

Prasart Museum ⑩

พิพิธภัณฑ์ปราสาท

9 Soi Krungthepkretha 4a,
Bang Kapi district. Tel 0-2379-3607.
⬛ M: 10. ◯ Tue–Sun. 📷 🚫 🎥
compulsory (book in advance).

The privately owned Prasart
Museum is known to
relatively few tourists and
Bangkokians, but the journey
out to this elegant museum,
set in landscaped tropical
gardens, will be worthwhile
for anyone who loves Thai
art. The collector, Prasart
Vongsakul, started to acquire
Thai antiques in 1965 when
he was only 12 years old.

Ornate interior of Lanna Pavilion at
the Prasart Museum

Ancient City ⑪

เมืองโบราณ

Sukhumvit Rd, Bangpu, Samut Prakan
province. Tel 0-2709-1644. ⬛ AC:
511 to the end of the line, then take
the 36 mini bus. ◯ 8am–5pm daily.
📷 🚻 www.ancientcity.com

Muang Boran, or "Ancient
City," is an outdoor cultural
theme park financed and
created in the early 1970s by
the art-loving philanthropic
owner of Thailand's largest
Mercedes-Benz dealership.
    The park makes a surpris-
ingly worthwhile visit. The
peaceful grounds, shaped
roughly like Thailand itself,
display numerous replicas
of important monuments in
Thailand as well as actual
buildings and sculptures that
have been restored to their
former grandeur. Replicas
are one third real size.

All the Thai art periods are
represented, including a few
mythical and literary ones
such as at the Garden of Phra
Aphaimani, inspired by a 19th-
century verse play (see p318).
Some of the buildings, for
example the Sanphet Prasat
Palace, which once stood
near Wat Phra Si Sanphet in
Ayutthaya (see pp178–9), are
reconstructions of monuments
destroyed centuries ago in
battle and so provide the only
testaments to past glories.

Crocodile Farm ⑫

ฟาร์มจระเข้

Old Sukhumvit Highway, Samut
Prakan province. Tel 0-2703-4891.
⬛ AC: 511 to Samut Prakan, then
songthaew, or join tour from
Bangkok. ◯ 8am–5pm daily. 📷
www.worldcrocodile.com

The largest of Thailand's (and,
supposedly, the world's) crocodile farms, this breeding park/
zoo is home to some 30,000
reptiles. Fresh- and saltwater
species, from South American
caimans to crocodiles from
the Nile, can be seen here.
    In the breeding section you
can see crocodiles hatching
and in various stages of
growth. You can also see them
transformed into handbags
and key rings in the souvenir
shop. Wrestling shows are
held regularly, and feeding
time happens at 4:30–5:30pm.
A visit to the crocodile farm
is popularly combined with
a day trip to the Ancient City.

Wrestling, the most spectacular
show at the Crocodile Farm

Erawan Museum ⑬

พิพิธภัณฑ์ช้างเอราวัณ

Sukhumvit Road, Samut Prakan
province. Tel 0-2380-0305.
⬛ 25, 142, 365; AC: 102, 507,
511, 536. ◯ 8am–6pm daily.
📷 www.erawan-museum.com

A monumental three-headed
bronze elephant stands
astride the Erawan Museum,
making it visible for miles
around. Inside is a large
collection of ancient religious
objects, including a number
of priceless Buddha statues.
    The exterior of the building's
lower story is decorated
with tiny pink enamel tiles
in the style of Thai Benjaron
ceramics. An elaborate double
staircase, which takes you
up inside the body of the elephant, dominates the upper
levels. There is also an elevator
that travels up one of the hind
legs. Outside, the tranquil
gardens contain ponds and
fountains in a variety of styles.

Reconstruction of the Prince of Lampang's Palace, Ancient City

SHOPPING IN BANGKOK

Shopping center sign

Bangkok is a veritable shoppers' paradise with its profusion of retail outlets, high quality of goods, and surprisingly low prices. Staff in department stores are super-attentive – some might say overly so – and whether it's designer clothes, traditional crafts, or electronic equipment you're after, there are some great deals to be had. Don't miss the fun of bargaining in the open-air markets, where vendors will often drop their prices by 30 percent or more. Beware of the energy-sapping heat and humidity of mid-afternoon, and limit your buying spree to one or two locations per day.

Crowds thronging Mahboonkrong shopping mall

PRACTICAL INFORMATION

Opening hours are usually early morning to mid-afternoon in fresh markets, 10am–10pm in shopping malls, and 24 hours in convenience stores. Credit cards are accepted in shopping malls and modern boutiques, but market vendors expect cash payment. VAT refunds are available, but the shop where the item is bought must fill out a form for customs, which can be time-consuming, so it is only worth it for significant savings. Bargaining is expected at street stalls and markets, but prices are fixed in department stores and boutiques. For more information, see page 450.

SHOPPING DISTRICTS

Boutiques and markets are scattered all over the city, but an especially high concentration of shopping outlets can be found around Siam Square and Silom, Ploenchit, and Sukhumvit Roads.

SHOPPING MALLS

CentralWorld leads the way in the race to be Bangkok's best and biggest mall; indeed,

this is Southeast Asia's largest shopping complex. Another favourite shopping destination is **Siam Paragon**, where you can buy anything from a sports car to a bowl of noodles. **Mahboonkrong** (or MBK) feels more like a street market spread over eight floors. Other centrally located malls are **Siam Center** and **Siam Discovery**, **Emporium**, **Silom Complex**, **Amarin Plaza**, **Gaysorn Plaza**, and **Erewan**.

A stall at Chatuchak Market, the country's biggest open-air market

MARKETS

No self-respecting shopaholic can claim to know Bangkok without having experienced the city's vast **Chatuchak**

Market (see p135), said to be the world's largest open-air market. Pick up a map and be selective, since you'll never get round it all in a day.

Bangkok's night markets in the Khao San, Patpong, and Sukhumvit Sois 3–15 regions, which consist of simple stalls set up each evening on the sidewalk, make it possible to combine souvenir shopping with dining and clubbing in case you're pushed for time.

Jim Thompson, one of the most reputable outlets for silk products

SILK AND COTTON

Thai silk is renowned for its high quality, unique designs, and reasonable price. Be aware that in the night markets, some items that claim to be silk are, in fact, made of synthetic fabric. To be sure you're getting the real thing, it pays to visit a reputable shop, such as **Jim Thompson**, which has outlets in many top hotels. If you know what you're looking for, head for **Phahurat Market**, where prices are cheaper.

Thai cotton is also a good deal. The eye-catching designs on items like bedspreads and cushion covers make it a distinctive souvenir.

CLOTHES

With prices only a fraction of what they are in the West, it makes sense to stock up on clothes, either off the peg in shopping malls or tailor-made to order. Tailors abound in all tourist areas, but workmanship varies, so visit a reputable tailor such as **Raja's Fashions** or **Marzotto**, and allow several days for preparation and fittings.

ANTIQUES

Examples of ancient crafts are available in many shops, but few of these are genuine antiques, for which a permit from the Fine Arts Department is required for export. A couple of reliable outlets are the **River City Complex**, which has four floors of antique furniture, carvings, and old maps, and **Oriental Plaza**, with rare collectibles like sculptures and prints.

THAI CRAFTS

From silverware to celadon, from lacquerware to woodcarvings, from basketware to hand-woven textiles, the variety of Thai crafts is rich indeed. Good places to see a wide range of crafts include **Chatuchak Market** (see p135), **Narayana Phand**, **Silom Village**, and **Nandakwang**.

Hand-painted umbrellas can be found in many craft centers

GEMS AND JEWELRY

As with antiques, extreme caution should be exercised when buying gems or jewelry, since potential customers are often exposed to sophisticated scams. Serious shoppers should browse the glittering displays of jewelry at **Peninsula Plaza** or the gem boutiques at reliable hotels.

ELECTRONIC GOODS

Computer equipment, video games, cameras, and mobile phones are on sale in shopping malls throughout the city, but one place that specializes in such goods is **Pantip Plaza**. Customers should be aware that some items on sale, such as software, are pirated and offer no money-back guarantee.

BOOKS

Book addicts should explore the massive selection at **Asia Books** and **Kinokuniya Books**. Other bookstore chains with outlets in central Bangkok are **B2S** and **Bookazine**.

DIRECTORY

SHOPPING MALLS

Amarin Plaza
Ploenchit Rd.
Map 8 D1.
Tel 0-2256-9111.
www.amarinplaza.com

CentralWorld
Ratchadamri Rd.
Map 8 D1.
Tel 0-2635-1111.
www.centralworld.co.th

Emporium
Sukhumvit Soi 24–26.
Tel 0-2269-1000. www.emporiumthailand.com

Erewan
Ploenchit Rd. **Map 8 D1.**
Tel 0-2250-7777.
www.erewanbkk.com

Gaysorn Plaza
Ploenchit Rd.
Map 8 D1.
Tel 0-2656-1149.
www.gaysornplaza.com

Mahboonkrong (MBK)
Phayathai Rd.
Map 7 C1.
Tel 0-2217-9111.
www.mbk-center.co.th

Siam Center/ Siam Discovery
Rama I Rd. **Map 7 C1.**
Tel 0-2658-1000.
www.siamcenter.co.th

Siam Paragon
Rama I Rd.
Map 7 C1.
Tel 0-2690-1000.
www.siamparagon.co.th

Silom Complex
Silom Rd.
Map 8 D4.
Tel 0-2632-1199.
www.silomcomplex.net

SILK AND COTTON

Jim Thompson
9 Surawong Rd.
Map 7 C3.
Tel 0-2632-8100.

Phahurat Market
Phahurat.
Map 6 D1.

CLOTHES

Marzotto
3 Soi Shangri-La Hotel,
Charoen Krung Rd.
Map 6 F5.
Tel 0-2233-2880.

Raja's Fashions
1/6 Sukhumvit Soi 4.
Map 8 F2.
Tel 0-2253-8379.
www.rajasfashions.com

ANTIQUES

Oriental Plaza
Charoen Krung Rd.
Map 6 F4.

River City Complex
23 Trok Rongnamkaeng
Yotha Rd.
Map 6 F3.
Tel 0-2237-0077.
www.rivercity.co.th

THAI CRAFTS

Nandakwang
Sukhumvit Soi 23.
Tel 0-2259-9607.
www.nandakwang.com

Narayana Phand
Ratchadamri Rd.
Map 8 D1.
Tel 0-2252-4670.

Silom Village
Silom Rd.
Map 7 A4.
Tel 0-2235-8760.
www.silomvillage.co.th

GEMS AND JEWELRY

Peninsula Plaza
Ratchadamri Rd.
Map 8 D1.
Tel 0-2253-9762.

ELECTRONIC GOODS

Pantip Plaza
Petchburi Rd.
Map 4 D5.
Tel 0-2250-1555.
www.pantipplaza.com

BOOKS

Asia Books
Sukhumvit Soi 15–19.

B2S
CentralWorld,
Ratchadamri Rd.
Map 8 D1.

Bookazine
Silom Complex, Silom Rd.
Map 8 D4.

Kinokuniya Books
Siam Paragon
(also in Emporium
and CentralWorld).
Map 7 C1.

Bangkok's Markets

Markets are a fundamental part of Bangkok life. Both specialty and general markets provide great browsing, whether you are interested in flowers or fabrics, sarongs or stamps. Do not try to take in too many markets in one outing – focus on one area and explore that in depth. Nancy Chandler's *Market Map and Much More*, readily available in Bangkok, can be a great help in planning a market sortie.

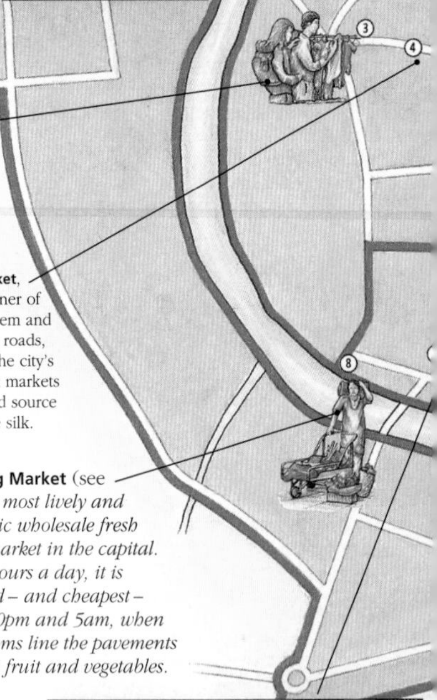

Market vendor selling Thai flowers

Thewet Flower Market *(see p104), located in a sedate backwater of the city, offers a riotously colorful spectacle of flowers and plants from all over Thailand.*

Banglamphu Market *is a typical neighborhood market with general stalls displaying food, shoes, clothes, and assorted bric-a-brac.*

Khao San Road Market *may take up only one tiny road, but it has become a legend among backpackers as a source of almost anything imaginable. In addition to rucksacks, hiking boots, and other travelers' equipment, it is good for second-hand books, jewelry, clothes, bags, and pirated cassette tapes.*

Bo Be Market, on the corner of Krung Kasem and Lan Luang roads, is one of the city's main cloth markets and a good source of Chinese silk.

Pak Khlong Market (see p98) *is the most lively and atmospheric wholesale fresh produce market in the capital. Open 24 hours a day, it is best viewed – and cheapest – between 10pm and 5am, when exotic blooms line the pavements along with fruit and vegetables.*

KEY TO MARKET LOCATIONS IN BANGKOK

Banglamphu Market ②
Bangrak Market ⑬
Bo Be Market ④
Kao Market ⑩
Khao San Road Market ③
Nakorn Kasem (Thieves' Market) ⑤
Pak Khlong Market ⑧
Patpong/Silom Market ⑫
Phahurat Market ⑦
Pratunam Market ⑪
Sampeng Lane Market ⑨
Stamp Market ⑥
Thewet Flower Market ①

Phahurat Market (see p98) *is the commercial hub of Bangkok's Indian community. Fabric sellers and tailors predominate, and the air is filled with the aroma of Indian food and spices.*

Nakorn Kasem (see p98), *otherwise known as the Thieves' Market, in Chinatown was once a focus for stolen goods. Today, it is a good place to pick up pots and pans, antiques, ceramics, and furniture. Hard bargaining and a sharp eye for spotting fakes is recommended.*

| 0 meters | 500 |
| 0 yards | 500 |

Pratunam Market (*see pp118–19*) occupies a maze of covered stalls. It is particularly good for cheap Indian fabrics and sewing accessories, and it also has general domestic items.

Kao Market *(see pp96–7)* between Yaowarat Road and Sampeng Lane, has been supplying the Chinese community with traditional ceremonial and decorative items – from lanterns to paper models for cremations – for more than 200 years.

⑪

Sampeng Lane Market *(Soi Wanit) in a former red light district has bargain-priced quality fabrics, toys, household goods, Chinese decorative items, and stationery.*

⑩

The Stamp Market is held every Sunday outside the General Post Office on Charoen Krung Road. Thailand has long been issuing fine stamp designs, collected by philatelists around the world.

⑥   ⑫

Patpong/Silom Market *(see pp115–16)* is a neon-lit jumble of stalls displaying cheap souvenirs and fake goods. Stalls on Silom Road have fashionable clothes.

⑬

Bangrak Market (see p115) *is a small but thriving local bazaar. Many of the top hotels buy their fruit, vegetables, meat, and seafood from here. The market also has fabric and clothes stands.*

ENTERTAINMENT IN BANGKOK

Bangkok provides a bewildering range of entertainment, from classical puppet theater to nightclubs. One of the most popular choices for short-stay visitors is a cultural show accompanied by a Thai meal, but there are plenty of alternatives, such as transvestite cabaret shows or an unusual cocktail at one of the city's bars with a view. Many restaurants and bars feature live music, ranging from traditional Thai ballads to rock classics, while the city's discos provide a melting pot in which locals and foreigners discover mutual tastes. If you are going to any event that starts at a particular time, be sure to plan your journey well in advance to beat Bangkok's notorious traffic.

A traditional Thai puppet show at the Joe Louis Theater

GENERAL INFORMATION

For information about upcoming events, consult the English-language newspapers **Bangkok Post** and **The Nation**, or pick up one of the free magazines, like **BK**, that are distributed at tourist locations. Tickets for events are usually easy to come by: ask at your hotel desk or at any travel agent, or book online at www.thaiticketmaster.com. For more information, see p458.

CULTURAL SHOWS AND THEATER

If you're in the mood for a cultural extravaganza, then book for the nightly show at **Siam Niramit**, which features spectacular sets and more than 500 elaborately dressed performers. More intimate performances take place at the riverside **Patravadi Theatre**, where traditional and modern dance techniques are blended to clever effect. Classical dance shows with buffet or à la carte dinners can be enjoyed at **Sala Rim Nam** and **Silom Village**, while the city's top cabaret location

is **Calypso Cabaret**. For performances of *khon*, or classical masked drama, head for the **Sala Chalermkrung Theatre** or the **National Theatre**.

Puppet shows may seem like entertainment for kids, but the puppeteers at the **Joe Louis Theater** are so accomplished that most adults will be as enthralled as their children.

MUAY THAI

Those who prefer visceral rather than intellectual entertainment should head to the local Thai boxing ring. Thai boxing, or *muay thai*, is the national sport, and bouts always draw a large crowd.

Spectators like to bet on the outcome of the matches, and cheer excitedly for their chosen fighter.

At **Ratchadamnoen Stadium** and **Lumphini Stadium**, you can watch the boxers prepare for their bouts with slow, mindful movements to the accompaniment of wailing instruments.

CINEMAS

It may seem strange to travel all the way to Thailand and end up going to the cinema, but with their air-conditioned interiors, comfortable seats, and cheap prices, they can make the perfect antidote to a tiring shopping spree. Most cinemas these days are located in shopping malls, such as the **Paragon Cineplex** in Siam Paragon and the **Major Cineplex** in Central World Plaza, though a few independent cinemas still exist, such as the **Scala** and **Lido** in Siam Square, which occasionally show arthouse or independent films. The Thai national anthem is played before every showing, and everybody is expected to stand, including foreign visitors. The website www.movieseer.com has details of what films are showing.

The colorful foyer of the Major Cineplex in CentralWorld

The crowded dancefloor at the popular Bed Supperclub

BARS AND NIGHTCLUBS

Bangkok has an astonishing range of bars, from the hole-in-the-wall **Ad Here the 13th**, with an in-house band playing funky music, to the super-chic **Sky Bar**, where the city's high-flyers sip cocktails and gaze down on their domain from the 63rd floor. Competition for custom is fierce, and many bars feature live bands in an effort to draw in the crowds – for example, **Saxophone** offers a heady mix of jazz, blues, and reggae, while **Hard Rock Café** has bands playing covers of rock classics. Visitors itching to shake their stuff at a disco are also catered for at venues like **Bed Supperclub**, **Q Bar**, **Café Democ**, and at the gay nightclub **DJ Station**. Sophisticated travelers looking for an elegant environment should make their way to **Diplomat Bar**, **Moon Bar**, or **Syn Bar**.

Bangkok has long been known for its tolerance of a wide variety of sexual tastes, and Silom Sois 2 and 4 are lined with gay bars, such as **Telephone Pub**. The three main areas of hostess and go-go bars are the infamous **Patpong 1 and 2** (off Silom Road), **Nana Plaza** (Sukhumvit Soi 4), and **Soi Cowboy** (Sukhumvit Soi 21–23). Many are curious to drop into one of these bars, but it's best to avoid the upstairs bars on Patpong, where scams often leave foreign visitors with an empty wallet.

The neon lights of Soi Cowboy, one of Bangkok's red-light districts

DIRECTORY

CULTURAL SHOWS AND THEATER

Calypso Cabaret
Asia Hotel, Phayathai Rd.
Map 3 C5. **Tel** 0-2216-8973. www.calypso cabaret.com

Joe Louis Theater
Suan Lum Night Bazaar,
Rama IV Rd.
Map 8 E4.
Tel 0-2252-9683/4.

National Theatre
Rachinee Rd.
Map 1 C4.
Tel 0-2224-1342.

Patravadi Theatre
69/1 Soi Wat Rakhang.
Map 1 B5.
Tel 0-2412-7287/8.

Sala Chalermkrung Theatre
Charoen Krung Rd.
Map 6 D1.
Tel 0-2222-0434.

Sala Rim Nam
Oriental Hotel,
48 Oriental Avenue.
Map 6 F4.
Tel 0-2659-9000.

Siam Niramit
Ratchada Theatre,
19 Tiam Ruammit Rd.
Tel 0-2649-9222.
www.siamniramit.com

Silom Village
Silom Rd. **Map** 7 A4.
Tel 0-2235-8760.
www.silomvillage.co.th

MUAY THAI

Lumphini Stadium
Rama IV Rd. **Map** 8 E4.
Tel 0-2251-4303. www.
muaythailumpini.com

Ratchadamnoen Stadium
Ratchadamnoen Nok Rd.
Map 2 F4.
Tel 0-2281-4205.
www.rajadamnern.com

CINEMAS

Lido
Siam Square.
Map 7 C1.
Tel 0-2252-6498.

Major Cineplex
Central World Plaza,
Ratchadamri Rd.
Map 8 D1.
Tel 0-2635-1111.

Paragon Cineplex
Siam Paragon,
Rama I Rd.
Map 7 C1.
Tel 0-2515-5555.

Scala
Siam Square.
Map 7 C1.
Tel 0-2251-2861.

BARS AND NIGHTCLUBS

Ad Here the 13th
13 Samsen Rd.
Map 2 D3.

Bed Supperclub
Sukhumvit Soi 11.
Tel 0-2651-3537.
www.bedsupperclub.com

Café Democ
Ratchadamnoen Klang Rd.
Map 2 E4.
Tel 0-2622-2571.

Diplomat Bar
Conrad Hotel,
Wireless Rd.
Map 8 E2.
Tel 0-2690-9999.

DJ Station
Silom Soi 2. **Map** 7 C4.
Tel 0-2266-4029.
www.djstation.com

Hard Rock Café
Siam Square.
Map 7 C1.
Tel 0-2251-0797.
www.hardrockcafe.co.th

Moon Bar
Banyan Tree Hotel,
South Sathorn Rd.
Map 8 D4.
Tel 0-2679-1200.

Q Bar
Sukhumvit Soi 11.
Tel 0-2252-3274.

Saxophone
3/8 Victory Monument.
Map 4 E3.
Tel 0-2246-5472.

Sky Bar
63rd Floor, State Tower,
Silom Rd.
Map 7 A5.
Tel 0-2624-9555.
www.lebua.com

Syn Bar
Swissotel Nai Lert Park,
Wireless Rd.
Map 8 E1.
Tel 0-2253-0123.

Telephone Pub
Silom Soi 4. **Map** 7 C4.
Tel 0-2234-3279.
www.telephonepub.com

BANGKOK STREET FINDER

The quickest way to get around Bangkok for humans and canines

inding your way around Bangkok can be a challenge. The lack of standard transliterations for Thai words means that the street names listed here will not always match those seen on street signs. Additionally, some streets are known by more than one name – for example, Charoen Krung Road is New Road and Wireless Road is Witthayu Road. Most major roads *(thanons)* have numerous numbered (and sometimes named) *sois* and *troks* (minor roads and lanes) leading from them. Odd numbered *sois* usually lead off one side of a road, even numbers off the other. Be warned that there can be considerable distances between *sois* – for instance, *sois* 6 and 36 off Phetchaburi Road are more than 3 km (2 miles) apart. Major sights, markets, and ferry piers are also listed in this gazetteer.

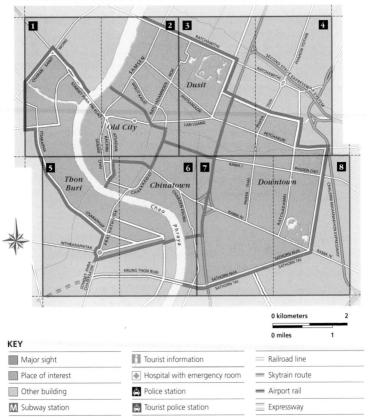

KEY

Major sight	Tourist information	Railroad line
Place of interest	Hospital with emergency room	Skytrain route
Other building	Police station	Airport rail
Subway station	Tourist police station	Expressway
Railroad station	Wat	Road under construction
Skytrain station	Hindu temple	Street market
Airport rail link	Church	
Riverboat pier	Mosque	
Chao Phraya Express pier	Post office	

0 kilometers 2
0 miles 1

0 meters 400
0 yards 400

Scale for Street Finder pages

A

Aksin, Sois 1–2 **8 F5**
Ama Kang, Soi **6 E2**
Amulet Market **1 C5**
Anantanak **3 A5**
Anglo Plaza, Soi **7 B4**
Annoparumit, Soi **4 F3**
Anuman Rajdhon,
  Soi **7 B4**
Anuwong **6 D2**
Aram Si, Soi **4 D4**
Ari, Sois 1–5 **4 E1**
Ari Samphan, Soi **4 D1**
Ari Samphan, Sois 1–2 **4 E1**
Ari Samphan, Sois 3–10 **4 D1**
Arun Amarin **1 B3**
  continues **5 B1**
Asoke Din Daeng **4 F3**
Asoke-Rachadapisek
  Expressway **4 D2**
Assumption Cathedral **6 F4**
Atsadang **2 D5**
  continues **5 C1**
Atsawin, Sois 1–2 **1 A2**
Attaphannorapha, Soi **4 E4**
Atthakan Prasit, Soi **8 E4**
Atthawimon, Soi **4 F3**

B

Baiyoke Towers **4 E5**
Bamrung Muang **2 E5**
  continues **3 A5**
Bamrung Rat **6 E1**
Ban Bat, Soi **2 E5**
Ban Chang Lo, Soi **1 B5**
Ban Dok Mai, Trok **2 F5**
Ban Dok Mai, Trok 1 **2 F5**
Ban Dok Mai, Trok 2 **2 E5**
Ban Lo, Trok **2 E4**
Ban Mo **5 C1**
Banbab, Trok **7 A5**
Bandit, Soi **7 A5**
Bangkok Bank, Soi **6 F1**
Bangkok Christian
  Hospital **7 C4**
Bangkok Noi/Thon Buri
  Railroad Station **1 B4**
Bangkok Shopping
  Complex **6 F5**
Bangrak Market **6 F5**
Banthat Thong **7 A2**
  continues **3 C5**
  Soi 36 **7 A2**
  Sois 24, 26, 28, 30, 32,
    34, 38, 40 **7 B2**
Boonphongsa, Soi **1 B2**
Boonphongsa, Soi 1 **1 B2**
Bophit Pimuk, Soi **6 D1**
Boriphat **6 D1**
  continues **2 E5**
Bowan Rang Si, Trok **2 D4**
Bowon Niwet **2 D4**
Bun Chu, Soi **4 F3**
Bun Chu 1, Soi **4 F3**
Bun Chuai, Soi **4 D2**
Bun Prarop, Soi **4 E4**
Bung Makkasan **4 F4**
Bunsiri **2 D5**
Buranasat **6 D1**
Burapha **6 D1**
Burirom, Sois 1, 2, 5 **6 E1**

C

C.S.T., Soi **4 E4**
Central Hospital **6 E1**
Central Post Office **6 F4**
Central Supermarket **6 D1**
Chai Samoraphum, Soi **4 E3**
Chaiyot, Soi **6 D1**
Chak Phet **6 D1**
Chakkaphatdi Phong **2 F4**
Chakkrawat **6 D1**
Chakrabongse **2 D4**

Chalerm Mahanakhon
  Expressway **4 F5**
  continues **8 F2**
Chalermlap Market **4 E5**
Chaloem Khet 1–3 **3 A5**
Chaloem Khet 4 **2 F5**
Cham Niam Suk, Sois 1–3 **5 A4**
Champravit Market **2 E2**
Chamsai, Soi **4 D4**
Chan, Trok **2 F5**
Chang Pier **1 C5**
Chang Tong, Trok **2 D5**
Chanong Krung, Trok **7 A2**
Chanpravit Market **2 E2**
Chao Fa **1 C4**
Chao Khamrop **6 E1**
Chao Phraya **2 D3**
  continues **5 B1**
Charan Sanit Wong **1 A2**
  Sois 32, 34, 41 **1 A3**
  Sois 36, 43, 45 **1 A2**
  Sois 38, 40 **1 B2**
  Sois 42, 49, 55,
    57–57/1 **1 B1**
  Sois 44, 46, 48, 50–
    50/1, 52 **1 C1**
Charat Muang **7 A1**
Charat Wiang **7 A5**
Charoen Chai, Trok 2 **6 F1**
Charoen Krung (New Rd) **6 D1**
  Soi 39 **7 A3**
  Sois 1, 2 **6 D1**
  Sois 8–15, 19, 21, 23 **6 E1**
  Sois 16, 18 **6 E2**
  Sois 20, 22, 24, 26, 28,
    29, 31, 33, 35, 37 **6 F3**
  Sois 30, 32, 34, 36, 38 **6 F4**
  Sois 42–42/1, 46, 48,
    50–53 **6 F5**
  Sois 43, 45 **7 A4**
Charoen Muang **7 A1**
Charoen Nakhon **6 E4**
  Sois 1–12 **6 D4**
  Sois 13–15, 17–20 **6 E5**
Charoen Phanit **6 F3**
Charoen Rat **5 C4**
  Sois 4, 8 **5 C4**
  Sois 3, 5, 7, 9, 11–16,
    18, 20, 22 **6 D4**
  Sois 17, 24, 26, 28, 30 **6 E4**
Charoen Suk, Soi **1 A1**
Charoen Wiang **7 A5**
Charoenkit, Soi **7 A3**
Charoenphol Market **3 B5**
Charun Wiang **7 A5**
Chawakul, Soi **3 C4**
Chawakun, Soi **4 E3**
Cherdchungam, Soi **1 A5**
Chetuphon **5 C1**
Chiang Mai **6 E3**
Chinda Thawin, Soi **7 B3**
Chit Lom, Soi **8 E1**
Chitrlada Palace **3 B2**
Chitta Kasem, Trok **6 F2**
Chom Sombun, Soi **7 B3**
Chong Nonsi Nua **7 C4**
Chong Nonsi Tai (Narathi
  watrachanakarin **7 C4**
Chongraknorasi, Soi **8 D4**
Chuaphloeng **8 F5**
Chulalongkorn Hospital **8 D3**
Chulalongkorn
  Monument **2 F2**
Chulalongkorn University **7 C3**
Chulalongkorn, Soi 1,
  3–6, 8, 10, 12, 14, 16 **7 B3**
Chulalongkorn, Soi 7, 9,
  18, 20, 22 **7 B2**
Chulalongkorn, Sois 11, 15,
  42, 44, 48, 50, 52, 54 **7 B3**
Chulalongkorn, Sois
  19, 60 **7 C3**
Chulalongkorn, Sois
  62, 64 **7 C1**

Chulin, Soi **2 E5**
Chung Charoen Phanit **6 E1**
Church of Santa Cruz **5 C2**
Convent Road **7 C4**

D

Daeng Bunga, Soi **4 D4**
Damnoen Klang Tai, Soi **2 D4**
Damrong Rak **2 F4**
  continues **3 A4**
Decho **7 B4**
Democracy Monument **2 E4**
Din Daeng 1 **4 F3**
Din Daeng Pier **6 D2**
Din Daeng, Soi **4 F3**
Dinso **2 E5**
Ditsamak **2 F5**
Dumake Pier **6 F5**
Dusit Park **2 F2**
  continues **3 A2**
Dusit Zoo **3 A2**

E

Ek-Ong, Soi **1 B1**
Erawan Shrine **8 D1**
Expressway **3 C5**

F

Fuang Nakhon **2 D5**

G

Gay Sorn Plaza **8 D1**
Goethe Institute **8 E4**
Golden Mount **2 F5**
Government House **2 F3**
Grand Palace and Wat
  Phra Kaeo **1 C5**

H

Hasadin, Soi **4 E5**
Henri Dunant **7 C3**
Hiranruci, Soi **5 B4**
Hua Lamphong Station **7 A2**
Hutayana, Soi **8 D5**

I

Inthraraphitak **5 B4**
  Sois 1–3 **5 B4**
Isara Nuphap, Soi **6 E2**
Isetan Shopping
  Complex **4 E5**
Itsaraphap **1 A4**
  continues **5 A1**
  Soi 1 **6 D4**
  Sois 2, 4–4/1, 6, 8 **6 D3**
  Sois 3, 5, 9–14, 16,
    18, 20, 22, 24 **5 C3**
  Sois 15, 17–17/1, 19 **5 B3**
  Sois 21, 28, 30, 32, 34 **5 B2**
  Sois 23, 27, 29, 36, 38 **5 A2**
  Sois 31, 33, 40, 42 **5 A1**
  Sois 37, 39, 41, 43,
    44, 45 **1 A5**
  Sois 46, 47 **1 A4**

J

Jack Chia, Soi **8 F5**
Jim Thompson's House **3 C5**

K

Ka-Om **2 F4**
Kaeo Fa, Soi **7 A3**
Kai Chae, Trok **2 D3**
Kalatan **6 F2**
Kalayana Maitri **2 D5**
Kao Lan **6 F2**
Kao Market **6 E2**
Kasaemsi, Soi **2 E3**
Kasem San, Soi 1 **7 C1**
Kasem San, Soi 2–3 **7 B1**
Khai, Trok **2 E5**
Khang Ban Manang-
  khasila, Soi **3 B4**

Khang Pam Nam Man
  Shell, Soi **5 A4**
Khang Rong Rap
  Chamnam, Soi **5 C3**
Khang Wat Welurachin,
  Soi **5 B4**
Khao **2 E1**
Khao San **2 D4**
Khao San Market **2 D4**
Khlai Chinda, Soi **5 C4**
Khlong Bang Jag **2 D1**
Khlong Bang Nam Chon **5 A5**
Khlong Bang Ramru **1 A1**
Khlong Bang Sakai **5 B3**
Khlong Bang Yikhan **1 A1**
Khlong Bangkok Noi **1 A3**
Khlong Bangkok Yai **5 B2**
Khlong Banglamphu **2 E4**
Khlong Chong Nonsi **7 B3**
Khlong Lam Pak **3 A4**
  Soi Khlong Lam Pak **3 A4**
Khlong Lot **2 D5**
  continues **5 C1**
Khlong Mahanak **2 F4**
  continues **3 A5**
Khlong Mon **5 A1**
Khlong Ong Ang **2 E5**
  continues **6 D1**
Khlong Phadung Krung
  Kasem **2 E2**
  continues **3 A4 & 6 F1**
Khlong Samre **5 A5**
Khlong Samsen **3 B1**
Khlong San **6 E3**
Khlong San Pier **6 E3**
Khlong San Sap **3 B5**
Khlong Sathorn **8 E4**
Khlong Thom, Soi **5 C3**
Khlong Thom Market **6 E1**
Khlong Wat Chaeng **5 A1**
Khlong Wat
  Ratchasittharam **5 A3**
Khlong Wat Thepthida **2 E5**
Khlong Wat Thong **1 A3**
Khlong Wat Thong
  Phleng **6 D4**
Khlongthom Wat
  Sommanat **2 F4**
Khrut, Trok **2 D5**
Kit Phanit **7 A3**
Klong Thom Pathum
  Nongkha, Soi **6 F2**
Klong Thom Wat Phra
  Phiren, Soi **6 E1**
Klong Thom, Soi **6 F2**
Kolit, Soi **4 D4**
Kradang Nga, Trok **2 F4**
Krai Si **2 D4**
Krai, Trok **6 D2**
Krai, Trok **6 E2**
Kraisih, Soi **8 F5**
Kraithamas, Soi **6 D2**
Krom Chaotha (Harbour
  Department) Pier **6 F3**
Krom Prisanee Pier **6 F4**
Krung Kasem **2 E2**
  continues **3 A4 & 6 F1**
Krung Man **3 A5**
Krung Thon Buri **5 C5**
  Soi 1 **5 C4**
  Soi 4 **5 C5**
  Sois 3, 8 **6 D5**
  Sois 5, 10 **6 E5**
Kudi Chain, Soi **5 C2**
Kumarin Ratchapaksi, Soi **1 B3**

L

La-O, Trok **7 A2**
Lad Ya **5 C4**
  Sois 1–3, 5 **5 C4**
  Sois 6, 8, 10–13, 15 **6 D4**
  Sois 14, 16 **6 E4**
  Soi 17 **6 D3**
  Soi 21 **6 E3**

Lak Muang 2 D5
Lamphun Chai 6 F2
Lan Luang 2 F4
  continues 2 E5
Lang Krasuang Market 5 C1
Lang Samoson Thapok,
  Soi 2 F2
Lang Suan, Soi 8 E2
Lang Suan, Sois 1–7 8 E2
Lang Wat Hua Lamphong,
  Trok 7 B3
Loet Panya, Soi 4 E4
Luang 6 E1
  continues 2 E5
Luk Luang 2 E2
  continues 3 A4
Lukmahadthai 2 D1
Lumphini Boxing
  Stadium 8 E4
Lumphini Park 8 D3

M

Maekhong, Soi 1 B1
Maen Si, Soi 2 F5
Maen Si, Sois 1–2 2 F5
Maha Chai 2 E5
  continues 6 D1
Maha Nakhon 7 A3
  Sois 4, 6, 8 7 A3
Maha Phrutharam 6 F3
Maha Uma Devi
  Temple 7 B4
Mahachak 6 E1
Mahanak Market 3 A5
Mahannop 2 D5
Mahannop, Trok 2 D5
Maharaj Market 1 C4
Maharaj Pier 1 C4
Mahathat 1 C5
  continues 5 C1
Mahatlek Luang,
  Sois 1–3 8 D2
Mahesak 7 A4
Mai Market 6 E2
Maitri, Trok 6 F1
Maitri Chit 6 F1
Makham, Trok 1–2 6 F2
Makkasan Railroad
  Station 4 F5
Man Sin, Sois 1–4 3 C4
Manawitthaya, Trok 5 C5
Mangkon 6 E2
  Soi Mangkon 6 F1
  Sois 1–2 6 F1
Matum, Soi 1 B5
Mayom, Trok 2 D4
Meksawat, Soi 8 F5
Memorial Bridge 5 C2
Ming Bamrung Muang,
  Soi 1 A5
Mit Anan, Soi 3 C1
Mittraphan 6 F2
Mo Daeng, Soi 1 A4
Momchuan, Trok 3 A5
Monk's Bowl Village 2 F5
Montri, Soi 5 B3
Moobangbangyikhan
  Thaohouse, Soi 1 B2
Moobankhunpan, Soi 6 E5
Moobanmahawong
  Patthana, Soi 1 B2
Morchub, Soi 5 B5
Morleng, Soi 4 F4
Morsun, Trok 7 A3
Museums at the Siriraj
  Hospital 1 B4

N

Na Hap Phoel 2 D5
Na Phra Lan 1 C5
Na Phra That 1 C4
Nai Loet, Soi 8 F1
Nai Thongbai, Trok 5 C4
Nak Bamrung, Soi 3 A5

Nakhon Chaisi 3 B1
Nakhon Kasem, Sois 3–4 6 D1
Nakhon Pathom 3 A3
Nakhon Sawan 2 F4
  continues 3 A4
Nakkharat 3 A5
Nakorn Kasem 6 E1
Nam Banyat, Soi 2 E3
Nana, Soi 6 F2
Nana Market 2 D3
Nangleng Market 2 F4
Nang Lueng, Trok 2–3 2 F4
Nantha, Soi 8 D5
Narayana Phand
  Shopping Complex 8 D1
Naret 7 B3
National Arts Gallery 2 D4
National Library 2 E2
National Museum 1 C4
Nawa, Trok 2 D5
Nawang, Soi 6 D1
Nawat Hua Lamphong,
  Soi 7 C3
Neilson-Hays Library 7 B4
New Bobe Shopping
  Complex 3 B5
New Road (Charoen
  Krung) 6 D1
New World Department
  Store 2 D3
Ngam Duphli, Soi 8 E5
Ni Chong Sawatdi 6 F3
Nikhom Banphak Rotfai 1 B4
  Sois 1–6 1 A4
Nikhom Makkasan 4 F5
Nitcharot, Soi 1 C1
Noen Khai Luang, Soi 1 A4
Nom Chit, Soi 4 D4
Nopphamat, Soi 1 A4

O

O-Sathahon 6 D2
Oriental Pier 6 F4
Oriental Hotel 6 F4
Oriental Plaza 6 F4

P

Pak Khlong Pier 5 C2
Pak Khlong Market 5 C1
Palana, Soi 7 A4
Pan 7 B5
Parinayok 2 E4
Pata Department Store 4 E5
Patpong 1–2 7 C3
Patravadi Theatre 1 B5
Peninsula Plaza 8 D1
Petchaburi 3 C4
  Sois 1, 2, 4, 6 3 B4
  Sois 3, 5, 7 3 C4
  Sois 9, 11, 13, 15, 18,
  20 4 D5
  Sois 10, 12, 14 3 C5
  Sois 17, 19, 21–26, 28,
  30, 32 4 E5
  Sois 27, 29, 31, 33,
  35, 37 4 F5
Petchaburi Market 3 C5
Phadung Dao 6 F2
Phadung Krung Kasem
  Market 3 A5
Phahon Yothin 4 E2
  Sois 1, 3 4 E2
  Sois 2, 4 4 F1
  Soi 5 4 E1
Phahurat 6 D1
Phahurat Market 6 D1
Phalittaphon, Soi 6 E2
Phan Trachit, Trok 2 6 F2
Phaniang 2 F4
Phanu Rang Si, Soi 6 F2
Phat Sai 6 F2
Phattana Chang, Soi 1 A4
Phatu Nokyung, Soi 5 B1

Phaya Mai 5 C3
  Soi Phaya Mai 5 C3
Phaya Nak 3 B5
  Soi Phaya Nak 3 C5
Phaya Thai 7 C2
  continues 4 D5
Phayathai-Bangkhlo
  Expressway 3 B5
  continues 7 A1
Phet Kasem 5 A4
  Sois 1–3 5 A4
  Soi 4 5 A3
Phet Phloi, Trok 7 A3
Phi Rom, Soi 6 D2
Phiphat, Soi 7 C4
Phiphat, Sois 1–2 7 C4
Phiphit, Soi 2 E4
Phisamai, Soi 3 A1
Phithaksin, Soi 5 C4
Phitsanulok 2 E2
  continues 3 A4
Phlab Phla Chai 6 F1
  continues 3 A5
Phloen Chit 8 E1
Pho Phanit 6 E1
Pho Sua, Trok 2 D5
Pho, Soi 5 C2
Phok Siri, Soi 3 C1
Phokhi 3 A5
Phra Athit 1 C3
Phra Athit Pier 1 C3
Phra Chan 1 C4
Phra Chan Pier 1 C4
Phra Chen, Soi 8 E3
Phra Nakharet, Soi 7 A3
Phra Nang, Soi 4 E3
Phra Phinij, Soi 8 D5
Phra Phiphit 5 C1
Phra Phitak 5 C1
Phra Pin Klao (Wat Dao
  Dung) Pier 1 C3
Phra Pin Klao Tatmai 1 A1
Phra Pok Klao Bridge 6 D2
Phra Sumen 2 D3
Phraeng Nara 2 D5
Phraeng Phuton 2 D5
Phraeng Sanphasat 2 D5
Phrannok 1 A4
Phrannok Market 1 A4
Phrannok Pier 1 B4
Phrasan Saraban, Soi 4 F4
Phrasi, Soi 3 B5
Phraya Damrong, Soi 7 A3
Phraya Maha Ammat,
  Soi 3 A5
Phraya Si, Soi 5 C1
Phun Suk, Soi 8 E5
Phuttha-Osot, Soi 7 A4
Phyanakhonratchaseni,
  Soi 7 A2
Phyaphiren, Soi 8 F5
Phyasingseni, Trok 7 A2
Phyautit, Soi 3 A1
Pichai 3 A1
Pichai Soi 1 7 B5
Pichai Soi 2 7 C5
Pikul, Soi 7 B5
Pinthipphimanwes, Soi 1 B2
Plaeng Nam 6 E2
Plukchit, Soi 8 F4
Plukchit, Sois 1–2 8 F4
Polalit, Soi 4 E4
Polit Sapha, Soi 6 F2
Polo, Soi 1 8 E3
Polo, Sois 2, 4–5 8 E3
Pongchitt, Soi 5 A4
Prachathipathai 2 E3
Prachathipok 5 C3
Prachum, Soi 7 A4
Pradit, Soi 7 A4
Praditphol, Soi 1 A3
Pradu, Soi 6 F2
Prakobphol, Sois 1–2 1 C3
Pramongkut Hospital 4 D2

Pramot, Soi 7 A4
Pramot, Sois 1–3 7 A4
Pramuan 7 A5
Prasaan, Soi 7 A4
Prasart Court, Soi 8 D5
Prasat Suk, Soi 8 F5
Pratunam Market 4 E5
Pridi, Soi 8 E5
Prinya 1 B1
Prok Wat Arun,
  Sois 1–3 5 B1
Prong Chai, Soi 8 E5

R

Rachawadi, Trok 5 C4
Rachawat Market 3 B1
Rachinee Pier 5 C2
Rachini 2 D5
  continues 5 C1
Ram Buttri 2 D4
Ram Buttri, Soi 2 D3
Rama I 7 A1
Rama IV 7 A2
  continues 6 F2
Rama V 3 A3
Rama VIII Bridge 1 C2
Ramathibodi Hospital 3 C3
Rang Nam 4 E4
Ratchabophit 2 D5
Ratchadamnoen Boxing
  Stadium 2 F3
Ratchadamnoen Klang 2 D4
Ratchadamnoen Nok 2 F4
Ratchadamri 8 D2
  Soi Ratchadamri 8 D1
Ratchaprarop 4 E4
  Soi Ratchaprarop 4 E4
Ratchasi, Trok 2 F5
Ratchasima 2 F2
Ratchataphan, Soi 4 E4
Ratchawithi 3 A1
  continues 2 E1
Ratchawong 6 E2
Ratchawong Pier 6 E2
Ratruam Charoen, Soi 5 C4
Rattanasisang, Soi 1 A5
Ratutit, Soi 7 A2
Ratying Charoen, Soi 5 C4
River City Department
  Store 6 F3
River City Pier 6 F3
Rong Che, Soi 5 A5
Rong Lao Pier 2 D3
Rong Liang Dek, Trok 3 A5
Rong Liang Dek Market 3 A5
Rong Mai, Trok 1 C4
Rong Mo Pier 5 B1
Rong Muang 7 A1
  Sois 1–5 7 A1
Rong Rian Chanthana
  Suksa, Soi 5 B4
Rongrian King Phet,
  Soi 3 C5
Rongrian Ratprasong,
  Soi 4 F3
Rongrian Sudarak, Soi 3 C5
Ronnachai, Sois 1–2 3 C1
Royal Bangkok Sports
  Club 8 D2
Royal Barge Museum 1 B3
Royal Chalermkrung
  Theater 6 D1
Royal Turf Club 3 A3
Ruam Pradit, Soi 3 B1
Ruam Rudi, Soi 8 F2
Ruam Rudi, Sois 1–4 8 F2
Ruam Rudi, Soi 5 8 F3
Ruamit, Soi 4 F3
Ruen Rudi, Soi 8 F1

S

Sa Nam Rhao 4 E2
Saeng Uthai Thip, Soi 4 F3
Saengmuang, Soi 5 C4

Saha Mit, Soi 7 A3
Sailom, Soi 4 F1
St. Francis Xavier Church 2 E1
Saint Louis, Sois 1–3 7 B5
Saithi 2 8 D5
Sake, Trok 2 D4
Saksin, Soi 5 C5
Sala Daeng 8 D4
Sois 1–2 8 D4
Sala Tonchai, Soi 1 B5
Salakhin, Trok 7 A2
Sam Sen Railroad
Station 3 C1
Sam Yot, Soi 6 D1
Sama Han, Soi 8 F2
Sampaya, Soi 5 C5
Sampeng Lane 6 E2
Samran Rat, Soi 2 E5
Samran, Soi 4 E5
Samsen 2 D3
Sois 1–3, 5, 7 2 D3
Sois 4, 6, 10 2 E3
Sois 9, 11, 13 2 E1
Soi 12 2 F2
San Chao Maepla
Taphian, Soi 7 A4
Sanam Chai 5 C1
Sanam Khli, Soi 8 E3
Sanam Luang 1 C4
Sanan Sin, Soi 1 A4
Sanchao Arneaw, Soi 5 C5
Sanchao, Soi 1 B1
Sangkhalok 2 F1
Sanguan Suk, Soi 3 B1
Santi Phra, Soi 7 B3
Santi Phap, Soi 1 7 B3
Santi, Soi 1 B1
Santiphap 6 F1
Santisuk, Soi 1 A4
Santisuk, Soi 4 E3
Saolada, Soi 1 A3
Sap 7 B3
Saphan Luang, Trok 5 C4
Saphan Phut 5 C2
Saphan Phut Pier 5 C2
Saphan Tia, Soi 7 B3
Saphankhu, Soi 8 F4
Saphran Khao Fruit
Market 3 A4
Saran Rom 2 D5
Saraphi, Soi 2 5 C4
Saraphi, Soi 3 5 C5
Saraphi, Soi 3 Tatmai 6 D5
Sarasin 8 E3
Sathithorn, Soi 1 B1
Sathorn Pier 6 F5
Sathorn Nua
(North) 7 A5
Sathorn Tai
(South) 7 A5
Satsana, Soi 4 D1
Satsana, Soi 1–5 4 D1
Sawang 7 A2
Sois 1, 3, 5, 7 7 A3
Sawankhalok 3 B4
Sawansawat, Soi 8 F5
Senarak, Soi 4 D3
Set Siri, Soi 2 3 C1
Setthakan, Soi 5 C1
Shangri-La Pier 6 F5
Si Ayutthaya 3 B3
continues 2 F2
Soi 1 4 E4
Si Bamphen, Soi 8 E5
Si Phom, Soi 5 B4
Si Phraya Pier 6 F4
Si Praya 7 A3
continues 6 F3
Si Thamathirat 6 E1
Si Wiang 7 A5
Siam Center 7 C1
Siam City 4 D4
Siam Square 7 C1
Sois 1–6, 9–11 7 C1

Sillapakorn, Trok 1 C5
Silom 7 A4
Soi 19 7 A5
Sois 1, 3–8 7 C4
Sois 9–14, 16, 18, 20 7 B4
Sois 17, 22, 24, 26, 28,
30, 32 7 A4
Silom Plaza 7 B4
Silom Village
Complex 7 A4
Silpakorn University 1 C5
Sin, Trok 2 E4
Sip Sam Hang 2 D4
Siri Phong 2 E5
Sirichai, Trok 1–2 2 E5
Siriraj Pier 1 B4
Sirung, Soi 8 F5
Sithongdi, Soi 1 B1
Sitthiprasat, Soi 8 F5
Snake Farm 7 C3
Soda, Soi 3 A1
Soem Sinkha 6 E1
Sombun Panya, Soi 7 B3
Somdet Chao Praya 6 D3
Sois 1–2, 4 5 C3
Sois 3, 5–8, 10–12,
14, 16, 18 6 D3
Sois 13, 15, 17 6 D3
Somdet Phra Chao
Taksin 5 B5
Sois 3, 5 5 C4
Sois 4–4/1, 6, 8, 10,
12, 14, 18 5 B5
Sois 7, 9, 11 5 C5
Song Phra, Soi 7 B3
Song Sawat 6 F2
Song Sawat Pier 6 E2
Songwat 6 E2
Sot Phinsan, Soi 4 E3
Sra Song, Soi 2 E5
St. Francis Xavier
Church 2 E1
Stadium Charusathian 7 B2
Suan Amporn 2 F2
Suan Chitrlada 3 B3
Suan Mali, Sois 1–3 2 E5
Suan Ngen, Soi 3 C2
Suan Oi, Sois 1–5 2 F1
Suan Pakkad Palace 4 D1
Suan Rommani Nart 2 E5
Suan Saranrom 5 C1
Suandusit, Soi 3 B2
Suanphlu, Soi 8 D5
Suanphlu, Sois 1–2 8 D5
Suapa 6 E1
Sukhat, Soi 2 D5
Sukhom Tharam 3 B1
Sukhumvit 8 F1
Sois 1, 3 8 F1
Sois 2, 4 8 F2
Sukon, Sois 1–2 6 F2
Sukon, Trok 6 F2
Sukothai 3 A1
Sois 1–2 3 B1
Sois 3–4 3 B2
Soi 5 3 C2
Suksa Witthaya, Soi 7 B5
Sung, Trok 6 F5
Sunthonphimol, Soi 7 A2
Suphan 3 A1
Supphakorn, Soi 3 A4
Supphamit 3 A4
SUPPORT Museum 2 F1
Surasak 7 A5
Surawong 7 A4
Surawong Center 7 C3
Sutcharit, Soi 3 B1
Sutcharit, Soi 2 3 B2
Sutcharit Nua, Soi 3 B1
Suthisuksa, Soi 3 A3
Suwannaram Market 1 A3
Suwannin, Soi 1 C2
Suwichandamri, Soi 1 C3
Swatdi, Soi 7 A2

T

Taksin Bridge 6 F5
Taksin Monument 5 C4
Talad Charoen Phon,
Soi 3 B5
Taladsiwanich, Soi 4 F3
Talat Sesaweech, Soi 5 B4
Tambon Mahathat, Soi 1 C5
Tambon Nakhon, Soi 1 C4
Tambon Taweephol,
Soi 1 C5
Tambonwanglang,
Soi 1 1 B5
Tanao 2 D5
Tanarak, Soi 7 B5
Tani 2 D4
Taniya 7 C4
Taphanyao, Trok 6 D2
Tha Din Daeng 6 D3
Sois 1, 3–11, 13,
15–18/1 6 D3
Soi 2 6 D4
Soi 20 6 D2
Tha Klang, Soi 5 C2
Tha Tian, Soi 5 B1
Thai Wang 5 C1
Thammasat University 1 C4
Than Thawan, Soi 7 C4
Thanam San Chao, Soi 6 E2
Thanasilp, Soi 8 D5
Thaneethaphisek, Soi 5 A1
The Wet, Soi 1–3 2 E3
Thep Hatsadin, Soi 4 E4
Thepharak, Soi 1 B3
Thepnakarin, Soi 1 B2
Therd Damri 3 C1
Thetsaban Sai 1 5 C2
Thetsaban Sai 2–3 5 C3
Thewet Pier 2 D2
Thewet Flower Market 2 E2
Thewi Worayat, Soi 2 F5
Thian Siang, Soi 7 C5
Thoet Thai 5 A5
Thon Buri Railroad
Station Pier 1 C4
Ti Thong 2 D5
Tien Pier 5 B1
Tokyo Department
Store 7 C1
Tonson, Soi 8 E2
Tri Mit 6 F2
Tri Phet 6 D1
Trong Kham Talat Si
Thon, Soi 5 A4
Tuk Din, Trok 2 E4

U

Udomsap, Soi 1 A1
Ulit, Soi 8 F2
Unakan 2 E5
Uruphong, Soi 3 B4
Uruphong, Soi 3 3 B5
Uthai, Soi 6 D2
Uthai Thip, Soi 4 F3
Uthong Nai 3 A2
Uthong Nok 2 F2

V

Vichaigut Hospital 4 D1
Vimanmek Palace 2 F1

W

Wanawan, Trok 6 D4
Wang Doem 5 A2
Wang Lang, Trok 1 B4
Wangchao Sai 6 F1
Wanit, Soi 2 6 F3
Wasukri Pier 2 E1
Wat Amarin Market 1 B4
Wat Amonkiri, Soi 1 C2
Wat Amphawan, Soi 3 B1
Wat Arun 5 B1
Wat Arun Pier 5 B1

Wat Benchamabophit 3 A3
Wat Borom Niwat, Soi 3 B5
Wat Bowonniwet 2 E4
Wat Daowadungsaram,
Soi 1 C3
Wat Duangkhae, Soi 7 A2
Wat Hong, Soi 5 B2
Wat Indrawihan 2 E2
Wat Kalayanimit 5 B2
Wat Kanlaya, Soi 5 C2
Wat Khahabodi, Soi 1 C2
Wat Klang, Soi 5 A5
Wat Klang Market 5 A4
Wat Mahathat 1 C5
Wat Makog, Soi 4 D3
Wat Muang Khae Pier 6 F4
Wat Nak Klang, Soi 5 A1
Wat Pathum Wanaram 8 D1
Wat Phichininat, Soi 2 D1
Wat Pho 5 C1
Wat Phothi Nimit, Soi 5 A5
Wat Phraya Tham, Soi 5 A1
Wat Prayun 5 C2
Wat Rachabophit 2 D5
Wat Rachanat 2 E4
Wat Rachapradit 2 D5
Wat Rakhang 1 B5
Wat Rakhang Pier 1 B5
Wat Rakhang Khositaram,
Soi 1 B5
Wat Ratchakhru, Soi 5 A5
Wat Ratchinatda, Trok 2 E4
Wat Saket 2 F5
Wat Sam Phraya Pier 2 D3
Wat Sommanat, Soi 2 F4
Wat Suthat and the
Giant Swing 2 D5
Wat Suwannaram 1 A3
Wat Taphan, Soi 4 E3
Wat Thong Pier 6 E3
Wat Traimit 6 F2
Wat Tri Thotsthep, Trok 2 E3
Wat Wisetkan, Soi 1 B4
Wat Yai Si Suphan, Soi 5 B4
Wattana Yothin, Soi 4 E3
Wattana, Soi 1 A4
Watthanasin, Soi 4 E5
Watthanawong, Soi 4 E5
Wiraya, Soi 3 C4
Wireless Road
(Witthayu) 8 E2
Wiset San, Soi 5 C4
Wisut Kasat 2 E3
Wisut Kasat Pier 2 D2
Witthayu (Wireless) Road 8 E2
Wiwat Wiang, Soi 6 E1
Wongwian Lek Market 6 D2
Wongwian Yai Railroad
Station 5 B4
Wora Chak 2 F5
Woraphong, Soi 2 E3
Worarak, Soi 3 B1
Worarit, Soi 3 C5
World Trade Center 8 D1
Wutthi Chai, Trok 3 A4
Wutthi Suksa, Soi 5 C4
Wutthipan, Soi 4 E4

Y

Yaowaphanit 6 E2
Yaowarat 6 E1
Yen Akat 8 E5
Yen Akat, Soi 1 8 E5
Yenchit, Trok 6 D4
Yisipsong Karakadakhom
1–3, 5 6 F1
Yommarat Market 3 B4
Yommarat, Soi 8 D4
Yommaratsukhum 6 E1
Yotha 6 F3
Yotha 1 6 F3
Yothi 3 C3
Yotsi, Soi 3 A5
Yuttha Suksa, Soi 5 A1

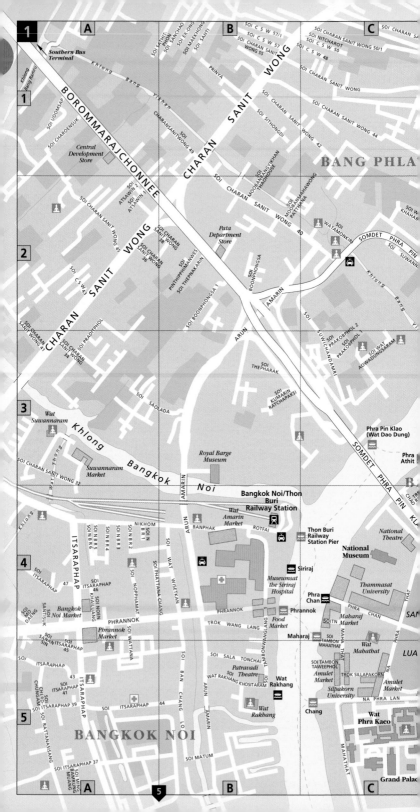

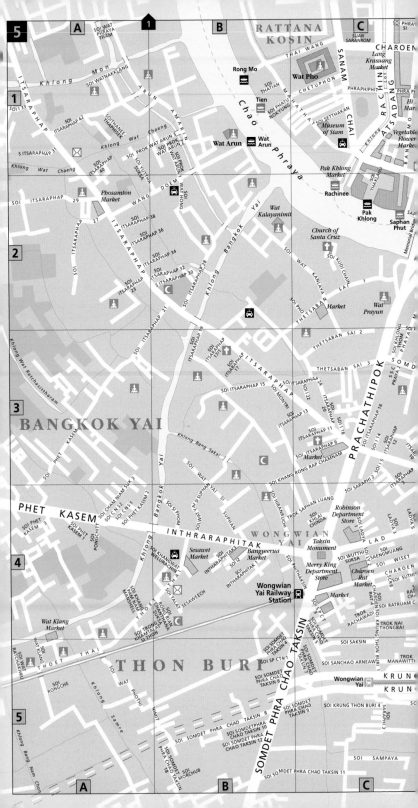

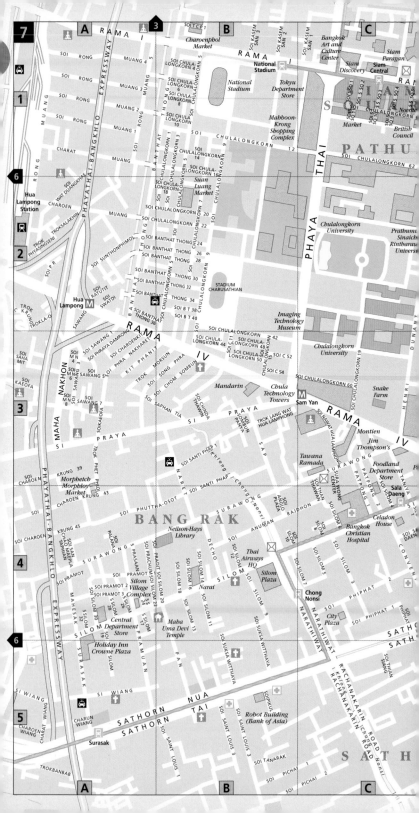

THE CENTRAL PLAINS

INTRODUCING THE CENTRAL PLAINS 158–163
SOUTH CENTRAL PLAINS 164–185
NORTH CENTRAL PLAINS 186–201

Introducing the Central Plains

The fertile plains stretching northward from Bangkok are the nation's rice basket and the historic heartland of the Tai people. Here lie the impressive ruined cities of the old Sukhothai *(see pp58–9)* and Ayutthaya kingdoms *(see pp62–3)*. Today this is the country's most wealthy and densely populated region, with fast-expanding towns surrounded by fields of sugar cane and rice. In the forested hills that border the Central Plains are national parks with spectacular waterfalls and a wide range of wildlife, providing a pleasant scenic contrast.

Si Satchan
Chalien
Historical

Kamphaeng Phet

SOUTH
CENTRAL
PLAINS
(see pp164–185)

Kanchanaburi

Si Satchanalai-Chalieng Historical Park (see pp198–200) *encompasses the ruins of one of the most important Sukhothai cities, as well as the remains of an earlier Khmer settlement.*

Kamphaeng Phet (see pp192–3) *contains a wealth of Sukhothai-era monuments and ruins and, within the old city walls, a fine museum displaying ceramics such as this 15th-century pot.*

Kanchanaburi (see pp170–71) *is near the site of the infamous bridge built over the Khwae Yai River during World War II. A museum and cemetery in the town provide a moving testament to the Asian laborers and Allied troops who died.*

◁ The remains of a *bot*, featuring a huge, seated Buddha image, Wat Mahathat, Sukhothai

Sukhothai Historical Park (see pp194–7) *is one of Thailand's most memorable sights. Within the vast, abandoned city are the remains of 40 wats.*

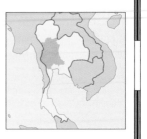

Sukhothai Historical Park

NORTH CENTRAL PLAINS *(see pp186–201)*

Lop Buri (see pp174–5) *is an ancient city within easy reach of Bangkok. Although it is not as geared to tourism as Ayutthaya or Sukhothai, it has a variety of Sukhothai and Khmer ruins, such as Prang Sam Yot.*

Khao Yai National Park (see pp184–5), *the first, and still one of the most popular national parks in the country, ranks among the best places to see Thai wildlife.*

Lop Buri

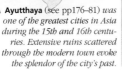

Khao Yai National Park

Ayutthaya

Ayutthaya (see pp176–81) *was one of the greatest cities in Asia during the 15th and 16th centuries. Extensive ruins scattered through the modern town evoke the splendor of the city's past.*

0 kilometers 50

0 miles 25

Sukhothai Art

The prolific artisans of the Sukhothai School (late 13th–15th centuries) adapted stylistic elements from Sri Lanka, Burma, and other neighboring countries to produce some of Thailand's finest works of art. Numerous Buddha images of immense beauty and fluidity were cast in bronze. The "Walking" Buddha – a posture that is otherwise rare in Buddhist art – is perhaps the best-known artistic achievement of the period. The Sangkhalok *(see p200)* ceramics industry also flourished, and its fine wares, including pale blue-green celadons, were exported all over Asia until the middle of the 16th century.

The Walking Buddha *posture possibly represents the Buddha's descent from Tavatimsa Heaven after he had visited his mother.*

Bronze *replaced stone as the preferred material for Buddha images during the Sukhothai period. It allowed a far more delicate detailing of the Buddha's hair and facial features.*

PHITSANULOK BUDDHA

Located in Wat Phra Si Rattana Mahathat in Phitsanulok, this 14th-century Buddha image, known properly as Phra Phuttha Chinarat, is one of the most revered in all of Thailand, second only to the Emerald Buddha in Bangkok. Cast in bronze and later gilded, the serene figure is a supreme example of late Sukhothai art.

This bronze Vishnu, *a Hindu god, is in the classic Sukhothai style. Brahmin priests, who presided over some court ceremonies, probably ordered figures like this to be made.*

Wedge-shaped joints

The flame like "halo" around Phra Phuttha Chinarat, ending in *naga* heads, is unique.

Fingers all of the same length

Sukhothai *bai* **semas** *(boundary stones, see p33) were fashioned from slate into leaf shapes. This one, at Wat Sorasak in Sukhothai, is inscribed with details of a land grant.*

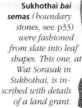

Monochrome ceramic gable decorations, *such as this one from Wat Phra Phai Luang, Sukhothai, are a typical architectural flourish from the period.*

Ceramic finials, *found on many roofs, were sometimes fashioned as dragons. Such decorations show a fusion of Khmer and Chinese styles.*

Sangkhalok ware, *such as this delightful, brown monochrome elephant, are often well preserved. Fine pieces like this were produced from the mid-14th century onward, when exports boomed.*

King Vajiravudh *(1910–25) was highly active in the early archaeological work at Sukhothai: he was a totally untrained but enthusiastic excavator.*

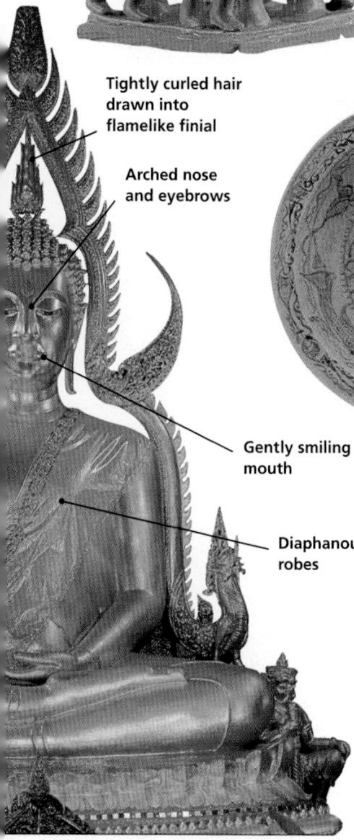

Tightly curled hair drawn into flamelike finial

Arched nose and eyebrows

Fish-and-flower motifs, *painted beneath the glaze, were popular for bowls and plates. Such items were exported as far afield as Japan.*

Gently smiling mouth

Diaphanous robes

Figurines *sometimes feature a bulge by the mouth, which may depict the chewing of fermented tea. Female figures are common, often carrying babies.*

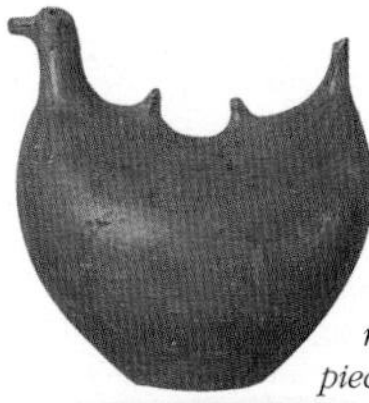

Pouring vessels, *known as* kendis, *were sometimes zoomorphic, like this earthenware piece in the shape of a duck.*

THE BAN KO NOI KILNS

The remains of 200 brick kilns were excavated at Ban Ko Noi *(see p199)* near Si Satchanalai in 1980–87. Some contain the pots that were being fired when the kilns were abandoned. There are also a number of kiln sites at Sukhothai.

Entrance

Chimney

Foreigners in Ayutthaya

European illustration of a Siamese official

Throughout the 16th and 17th centuries Ayutthaya was one of the most important trading centers in Asia, attracting not only merchants but also missionaries, adventurers, and mercenaries from around the world. Portuguese visitors arriving in the 16th century found a riverine city of canals and magnificent flotillas of barges. They brought firearms to trade and military advisers to help Ayutthaya against the Burmese. The Dutch and English followed in the 17th century and established trading warehouses. The Japanese came to buy animal hides, while French Jesuits and Persians competed for religious converts. Some foreigners, including Constantine Phaulkon, sought political influence.

St. Joseph's Church (see p180) *stands south of Ayutthaya's main island. Originally built during the reign of King Narai (1656–88) by French missionaries, it has been restored many times since.*

Lacquerware *was a specialty of Ayutthaya. Like other aspects of life in the city, the decorative arts reflected the influence of foreigners or* farangs. *These doors depict* farang *traders.*

MAP OF AYUTTHAYA

The involvement of Europeans in Siamese affairs led to the publication of several maps of Ayutthaya. This French map, probably an 18th-century copy of one drawn in the 17th century, shows the location of the French, Portuguese, and Siamese quarters. The European spelling of Ayutthaya at that time was Iudia.

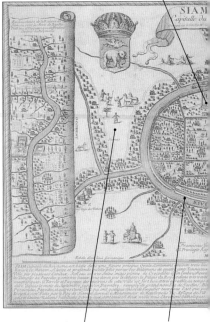

Royal Palace

Siamese quarter

Chao Phraya River

The first French *to arrive in Ayutthaya, in 1662, were Jesuit missionaries. In 1681 the French asked permission for a full diplomatic mission to visit the city. It arrived in 1685, headed by the envoy from Louis XIV, Chevalier de Chaumont. A Siamese envoy later returned with him to France. This painting shows him being received at court by the Sun King, Louis XIV.*

French Jesuit missionaries *came to Ayutthaya to convert King Narai to Catholicism. They failed in this but encouraged him to cultivate an interest in astronomy. This illustration shows him watching a lunar eclipse in 1685. Following the Jesuits' tutelage he watched a partial solar eclipse in 1688. Narai favored the Jesuits and gave them land to build churches and schools.*

Chilies *were first imported from South America by the Portuguese, who established a trading treaty with the Siamese in 1516. They quickly grew in popularity, and today chilies are an essential ingredient in numerous Thai dishes.*

Siamese quarter

Chinese quarter

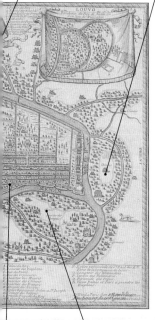

French quarter

Portuguese quarter

Royal barges *and other boats crowded the waterways of Ayutthaya. Often the first sight that greeted visitors to the city was a convoy of royal barges. As a result, Ayutthaya became known as the "Venice of the East."*

The VOC *(Dutch East India Company) first visited Ayutthaya in 1604. A trading warehouse was set up in 1634, but by the 1670s trade had declined. The warehouse in Ayutthaya was later destroyed by the Burmese.*

CONSTANTINE PHAULKON

The influence of foreigners in Ayutthaya was greatest under King Narai (1656–88). Most notorious of those who came to Ayutthaya was the Greek adventurer Constantine Phaulkon, who arrived in 1678 in the employ of the English East India Company. Attracting the attention of Narai, he quickly moved on to become the king's personal confidant and chief minister. He later advised Narai against Dutch and English interests in Ayutthaya. The French, meanwhile, were allowed to station 600 soldiers in the kingdom. Amid much political wrangling in court, Narai was viewed as cultivating strong ties with Louis XIV, whose ambition was to convert him and Siam to Catholicism, and some people feared a French takeover. When Narai died in 1688 all ties with Westerners were cut, and Phaulkon was executed.

Constantine Phaulkon, prostrate before the Siamese king, Narai

SOUTH CENTRAL PLAINS

For centuries, the broad flood plain of the Chao Phraya, which bisects the South Central Plains north to south, has been Thailand's rice basket as well as its most densely populated region. The river remains a vital link between the country's cultural heartland and its present-day capital, Bangkok. The old capital of Ayutthaya, upstream from Bangkok, is the region's most popular sight._

Ayutthaya was one of the greatest mercantile centers in Asia during the 14th–18th centuries. Its fabulous temples and palaces, built around the confluence of the Chao Phraya, Lop Buri, and Pasak Rivers, were regarded with wonder by foreigners. In 1767 it was sacked by the Burmese, and the capital was forced to move downstream to Bangkok. The remains of monuments from the earlier period stand among more modern buidings and each day attract hundreds of visitors on round-trips from Bangkok.

Kanchanaburi, to the west of Bangkok, is another popular day trip from the capital. During World War II the Japanese built a railroad from here to the Three Pagodas Pass near Burma, along an old Burmese invasion route. Little of the railroad was ever used, but at Kanchanaburi visitors can see poignant reminders of this grueling episode, when thousands of Asian laborers and Allied POWs died.

Despite these and other noteworthy sights, the region still has relatively few tourist facilities. Towns such as Lop Buri – an old Khmer outpost with several Khmer *prangs* – and the pilgrimage site of Phra Phutthabat are unknown to the majority of tourists. There is some accommodation in the Khwae Noi River Valley, along the route to the Three Pagodas Pass. This region is surrounded by a vast expanse of forest and grassland, including two wildlife sanctuaries and the Erawan, Sai Yok, and Chaloem Rattanakosin national parks. At the eastern edge of the South Central Plains, Khao Yai, the oldest national park, is the best place in Thailand to see wild elephants and many other animals.

The bridge over the Khwae Yai River at Kanchanaburi, a poignant reminder of World War II

◁ Wat Mahathat, built in 1384, one of the largest temples at the ancient site of Ayutthaya

Exploring the South Central Plains

The Chao Phraya River basin is fertile terrain, perfect for rice production. It is no coincidence that the kingdoms of Lop Buri and, later, Ayutthaya, the capital of which is the main sight of the region, were founded here. East of the wide plain, Khao Yai is the country's oldest and most accessible national park. Kanchanaburi, in the west, is the site of the notorious Death Railroad of World War II. From there, a road winds up to the Three Pagodas Pass on the Burmese border, passing near numerous national parks and wildlife sanctuaries.

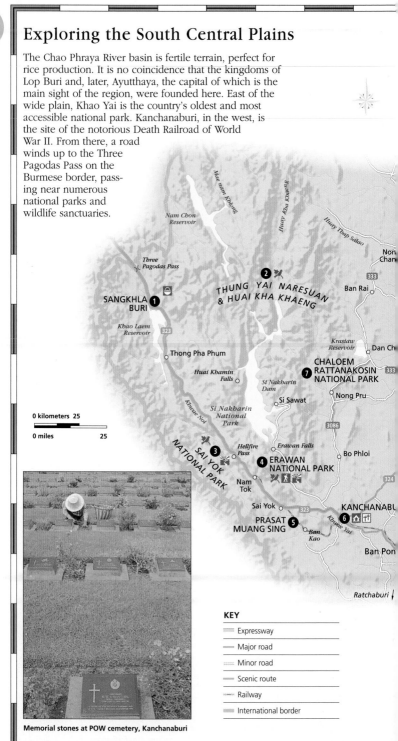

Mae nam Khlong

Nam Chon Reservoir

Huay Kha Khaeng

Huay Thap Salao

Non Chan

Three Pagodas Pass

THUNG YAI NARESUAN & HUAI KHA KHAENG ➋

Ban Rai

333

SANGKHLA BURI ➊

Khao Laem Reservoir 323

Krasiaw Reservoir

Dan Ch

Thong Pha Phum

CHALOEM RATTANAKOSIN NATIONAL PARK ➐

333

Huai Khamin Falls

St Nakharin Dam

Si Sawat

Nong Pru

Si Nakharin National Park

Khwae Noi

3086

SAI YOK NATIONAL PARK ➌

Hellfire Pass

Erawan Falls

Bo Phloi

ERAWAN NATIONAL PARK ➍

324

Nam Tok

Sai Yok 323

KANCHANABl

Khwae Yai

➏

PRASAT MUANG SING ➎

Ban Kao

Ban Pon

Ratchaburi ↓

Memorial stones at POW cemetery, Kanchanaburi

KEY

▬▬	Expressway
▬▬	Major road
▪▪▪	Minor road
▬▬	Scenic route
▪▪▪	Railway
▬▬	International border

GETTING AROUND
Many hotels in Bangkok arrange day tours of
Ayutthaya and Kanchanaburi. Boat tours up the
Chao Phraya River, from Bangkok to Ayutthaya
via Bang Pa-in, are also popular. Roads from
Bangkok fan out across the region, providing fast
and easy access by bus or car, though leaving
Bangkok itself is time consuming. Kanchanaburi,
Ayutthaya, and Lop
Buri can be
all reached
by rail.

Buddhas at Wat Yai Chai Mongkhon, Ayutthaya

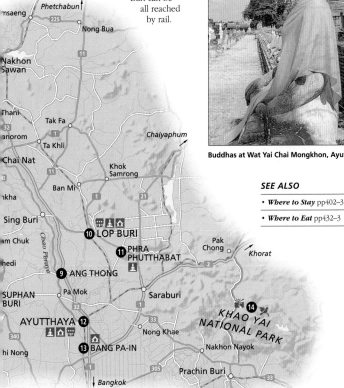

SEE ALSO

- *Where to Stay* pp402–3
- *Where to Eat* pp432–3

Chanthara Phisan Hall, on grounds of King Narai's Palace, Lop Buri

SIGHTS AT A GLANCE

Ang Thong ❾
Ayutthaya pp176–81 ⓬
Bang Pa-in ⓭
Chaloem Rattanakosin
  National Park ❼
Erawan National Park ❹
Kanchanaburi ❻
*Khao Yai National Park
  pp184–5* ⓮
Lop Buri pp174–5 ❿
Phra Phutthabat ⓫
Prasat Muang Sing ❺
Sai Yok National Park ❸
Sangkhla Buri ❶
Suphan Buri ❽
Thung Yai Naresuan ❷

On the way to market, Three Pagodas Pass

Sangkhla Buri ❶

สังขละบุรี

Kanchanaburi province. 🏔 36,000. 🚌 from Kanchanaburi. 🛈 TAT, Kanchanaburi (0-3451-1200). 🛍 daily.

In the center of Sangkhla Buri is a market where, among other things, you can buy Burmese curries and samosas, as well as books written in the Mon language.

However, the main attraction of this isolated trading town, which is populated by Mon and Karen tribespeople (see p206) as well as Thais, is its serene lakeside location. The lake is actually a large reservoir, formed by the damming of the Khwae Noi River farther downstream. Sometimes, late in the dry season,

the drowned remains of old villages and forests can be seen sticking up out of the calm surface of the lake's waters.

The north shore of the lake is overlooked by the unusual *chedi* of **Wat Wangwiwekaram**. In the covered gallery beside it a daily market sells goods, including *lungis* (sarongs) and simple woodcarvings from Myanmar (Burma), Indonesia, and elsewhere. Visitors can reach the *wat* on foot by crossing a wooden bridge that spans the wide, shallow inlet of the lake. A large settlement, consisting predominantly of Mon tribespeople, has grown up in close proximity to the *wat*. An interesting daily market is held here in the early morning.

Environs

At the **Three Pagodas Pass**, 23 km (14 miles) northwest of Sangkhla Buri, right on the Myanmar border, are situated three small, physically unimpressive, whitewashed *chedis*. For centuries this pass, which is less than 300 m (985 ft) above sea level, was used as an invasion route. During World War II, the Burma-Siam Railroad (see pp170–71) passed through here, and the route the track took can still be seen beside the Myanmar border. Nowadays, the pass is a quiet trading (and smuggling) route between the Indian Ocean to

the west and mainland Southeast Asia. Visitors to this region are usually permitted to cross the border on a one-day visa (see p475) to the Myanmar town of Pyathonzu. However, visitors should note that the relations between Thailand and Myanmar are often uneasy, at times verging on the hostile, and mean that this situation is prone to change at any time.

Thung Yai Naresuan and Huai Kha Khaeng ❷

เขตรักษาพันธุ์สัตว์ป่าห้วยขาแข้ง

Kanchanaburi, Tak and Uthai Thani provinces. 🛈 TAT, Tak (0-5551-4341); Kanchanaburi (0-3451-1200); Forestry Dept (0-2562-0760). 🚌 from Kanchanaburi. 🌐 www.huaikhakhaeng.net

These two huge, adjacent wildlife sanctuaries, covering 6,220 sq km (2,400 sq miles) and surrounded by a further 6,000 sq km (2,320 sq miles) of protected forest, form one of the most important conservation areas in Southeast Asia. They are listed jointly as a UNESCO World Heritage Site and are home to some of Thailand's largest remaining wild elephant herds, as well as several endangered carnivores, such as tigers, clouded leopards, and Malaysian sun bears. The enormous gaur, a species of wild cattle, and the country's last wild buffalo herds also

Herd of wild buffalo, native to Thung Yai Naresuan and Huai Kha Khaeng wildlife sanctuaries

Tourist accommodations in the tranquil Sai Yok National Park

live within the sanctuary. Rare species of gibbon can also be seen. At Huai Kha Khaeng there is a nature trail, but neither wildlife sanctuary is geared up for large numbers of visitors – permission for large parties to enter the parks can be obtained from Bangkok Forestry Department.

Sai Yok National Park ❸

อุทยานแห่งชาติไทรโยค

Kanchanaburi province. Park HQ off Hwy 323, 100 km (62 miles) NW of Kanchanaburi. *Tel* 0-3451-6163-4. 🛈 TAT, Kanachanaburi (0-3451-1200); Forestry Dept (0-2562-0760 or **www**.dnp.go.th for bungalow bookings). 🚆 🚌 from Kanchanaburi. 🌐

Sai Yok was the site of a large Japanese army barracks and POW labor camp during World War II. The 500-sq km (190-sq mile) national park was established in 1980 and today is renowned for its tranquil river scenery and the impressive Sai Yok Yai waterfall, which tumbles into the Khwae Noi River near to the park headquarters.

Accommodation is available in park bungalows or on pleasant houseboats, and boats can be chartered – at some expense – to some nearby caves. The caves are home to the 3-cm (1-inch) long Kitti's hog-nosed bat, considered by some to be the world's smallest mammal, and which was discovered in 1973 by Thai naturalist Kitti Thonglongya.

Environs
The Burma-Thailand Railroad Memorial Trail, south of Sai Yok, pays tribute to prisoners who died during the excavation of the Konyu railroad cut. Near to the cut, which was given the name "Hellfire Pass" by the many prisoners of war who labored through the night by torchlight, was the "Pack of Cards Bridge." This rickety 300-m (985-ft) long, 25-m (82-ft) high structure was built at perilous

Plaque in memory of POWs, Hellfire Pass

speed with green timber and, as a result, heavy loss of life – the structure collapsed three times during its construction.

The trail, set up with funding from the Australian government, winds up to Konyu cutting through a bamboo grove. The railroad track has long since been removed.

Erawan National Park ❹

อุทยานแห่งชาติเอราวัณ

Kanchanaburi province. Park HQ off Hwy 3199, 65 km (40 miles) NW of Kanchanaburi. *Tel* 0-3457-4222. 🛈 TAT, Kanchanaburi (0-3451-1200); Forestry Dept (0-2562-0760 or **www**.dnp.go.th for bungalow bookings). 🚆 🚌 from Kanchanaburi. 🌐

In the lush forest of the 550- sq km (210-sq mile) Erawan National Park, the nearest park to Kanchanaburi,

are the beautiful **Erawan falls**, which drop through a series of cascades and shady rock pools. While park rangers still find occasional tiger prints, visitors are more likely to see pig-tailed and rhesus macaques, and some 80 bird species. The Visitors' Center offers a slide show about the park, and there is a pleasant, 2-km (1-mile) hiking trail which climbs up beside the falls. This is one of Thailand's most popular national parks, and at weekends and holidays it gets very crowded. The large limestone cavern of Tham Wang Badan, situated on the west side of the park, contains many colorful stalactites and stalagmites.

Environs
The Huai Khamin falls, which are in nearby **Si Nakharin National Park**, do not receive as many visitors as the Erawan falls but, are nonetheless quite impressive. Visitors can make boat trips onto the Si Nakharin reservoir, either from the Kradan pier or from Si Sawat, a small market town situated on the eastern shore of the reservoir.

🏕 **Si Nakharin National Park**
108 km (67 miles) N of Kanchanaburi.
Tel 0-3451-6667-8. ⬜ daily. 🌐

The Erawan falls, named after the Hindu god Indra's elephant mount

Central sanctuary of Prasat Muang Sing near Kanchanaburi

Prasat Muang Sing ❺

ปราสาทเมืองสิงห์

Off Hwy 323, 43 km (27 miles) W of Kanchanaburi, Kanchanaburi province. ℹ️ *TAT, Kanchanaburi (0-3451-1200).* 🚌 *from Kanchanaburi to Tha Kilen, then songthaew.* ⏰ *daily.* 📷

The ruins of Muang Sing beside the Khwae Noi River date from around the 13th century and mark the westernmost point of expansion of the Khmer Empire *(see pp264–5)*. Earthen ramparts surround an inner wall of laterite that forms a rough rectangle about 1 sq km (245 acres). Near the center of this are the ruins of the Buddhist sanctuary, Prasat Muang Sing. Like most Khmer temples it faces east, in alignment with the city of Angkor.

Although the Muang Sing temple complex looks Khmer, some art historians believe it was actually built by local artisans in imitation of the occupying Khmers – the sanctuary, for example, lacks the stylistic details that are normally associated with Khmer sites. It was probably built after the reign of Jayavarman VII (1181–1220) as the Khmer Empire began to decline and its power in this region was fading. A museum at the site displays artifacts excavated here.

Environs

Southeast of Muang Sing is Ban Kao, a prehistoric settlement discovered in the 1940s by Dutch archaeologist van Heekeren, a prisoner on the Burma-Siam Railroad. The **Ban Kao Museum** houses stone tools and ornaments.

🏛️ **Ban Kao Museum**
35 km (22 miles) W of Kanchanaburi.
⏰ *8am–4:30pm Wed–Sat.* 📷

Kanchanaburi ❻

กาญจนบุรี

Kanchanaburi province. 👥 *108,000.* 🚌 🚉 ℹ️ *TAT, Saeng Chuto Rd, Kanchanaburi (0-3451-1200).* ⏰ *daily.* 🎉 *Khwae River Bridge Week (Nov/Dec).*

Though surrounded by beautiful limestone hills and vast expanses of sugar cane, Kanchanaburi is best known for its associations with the infamous Burma-Siam Railroad. Constructed in 1942–3 it crosses over the Khwae Yai River just to the north of Kanchanaburi town center. At the small station beside the bridge are a number of steam locomotives dating from the period. There is also a memorial to those who died during the war, which was erected by the Japanese administration in 1944. Today, 77 km (47 miles) of the railroad remain, and the trip along it from Kanchanaburi to Nam Tok is one of the most interesting in Thailand. The **Thailand-Burma Railroad Center** is a small museum charting the history of this railroad. The building

Sign, Kanchanaburi station

of the railroad cost the lives of more than 100,000 Asian laborers and 12,000 Allied prisoners of war. The **Kanchanaburi War Cemetery**, contains the graves of almost 7,000 mostly British and Australian prisoners and is one of two war cemeteries in the town. It is immaculately maintained by the Commonwealth War Graves Commission.

The smaller of the two cemeteries, **Chong Kai Cemetery**, contains 1,740 graves and lies on the north bank of the Khwae Noi River, a short ferry ride from the center of town. Nearby is **Wat Tham Khao Pun**, overlooking the river and the Burma-Siam Railroad, which at this point heads south toward Ban Kao and Prasat Muang Sing. In the grounds of the *wat* complex a network of narrow passages leads through a cave system filled with Buddha images.

In the **JEATH War Museum**, housed in Wat Chai Chumphon, visitors can see three replicas of the bamboo huts used to house prisoners of war in the camps that sprang up along the Burma-Siam Railroad during the war. The huts display paintings, sketches, and photographs of life in the camps and along the railroad line. JEATH is an acronym for Japan, England, Australia and America, Thailand, and Holland, some of the countries whose nationals worked on the railroad. Many survivors

Steel bridge over the Khwae Yai River, Kanchanaburi

and victims' relatives visit Kanchanaburi each year.

Accommodations here include riverside raft houses.

⚑ Kanchanaburi War Cemetery
Saeng Chuto Rd. ☐ *daily.*

⚑ Chong Kai Cemetery
Ban Kao Rd. ☐ *daily.*

🏛 JEATH War Museum
Wisuttharangsi Rd. ☐ *daily.* 🗺

🏛 Thailand-Burma Railroad Center
73 Jaokunneu Rd. ☐ *daily.* 🗺

Farmers cultivating crops in the hills around Kanchanaburi

Chaloem Rattanakosin National Park ❼

อุทยานแห่งชาติเฉลิมรัตนโกสินทร์

Kanchanaburi province. Park HQ off Hwy 3086, 97 km (60 miles) NE of Kanchanaburi. 🛈 *TAT (0-3451-1200); Forestry Dept (0-2562-0760 or* **www. dnp.go.th** *for bungalow bookings).* 🚌 *from Kanchanaburi to Nong Preu, then songthaew.* ☐ *daily.* 🗺

This beautiful and isolated national park is one of Thailand's smallest, at just 59 sq km (23 sq miles). The main trail runs beside a stream which passes through a cavern, Tham Than Lot Noi, to emerge in a thickly forested, steep-sided ravine. The path continues for 2,500 m (8,200 ft), climbing steeply beside the Trai Trung falls to Tham Than Lot Yai, a limestone sinkhole, and a small Buddhist shrine. On weekday mornings you may find that you are the only visitor in this delightful spot.

THE BRIDGE OVER THE KHWAE YAI RIVER AND THE BURMA-SIAM RAILROAD

The first railroad bridge over the Khwae Yai River, near Kanchanaburi, was built of wood, using Allied and Asian slave labor. In 1943 it was abandoned for an iron bridge, which was repeatedly bombed and damaged by the US Army Air Force from late 1944 on. In 1945, after only a short period in service, the bridge was put out of commission. After the war this infamous river crossing was immortalized in David Lean's movie, *The Bridge on the River Kwai* (1957). The bridge was part of an immense project, the 414-km (255-mile) Burma-Siam Railroad, conceived by the Japanese after the Allies blockaded sea routes in 1942. It ran from Nong Pladuk, 50 km (30 miles) southeast of Kanchanaburi, to Thanbyuzayat near the coast in Burma. Built under appalling conditions, it operated for only two years. Around 60,000 Allied prisoners of war and 300,000 Asian laborers were forced to work 18-hour shifts on its construction, with many losing their lives to cholera, malaria, malnutrition, and most tragically to maltreatment. It is said that one man died for each tie laid. One reason for the brutal regime was that the Japanese followed a samurai code. They despised the disgrace of surrender and treated the

Painting by prisoner of war in the JEATH War Museum, Kanchanaburi

Allied prisoners of war as if they had forfeited all human rights. The present-day bridge at Kanchanaburi was rebuilt, as part of Japanese war reparations, with two girders from the Japan Bridge Company of Osaka. It has now become a place of pilgrimage for veterans. Kanchanaburi has two cemeteries and a museum, the latter, in particular, presenting a moving evocation of this harrowing episode of World War II history.

Prisoners of war on the wooden bridge over the Khwae Yai River (c.1942–3)

The beautifully tended Chong Kai Cemetery, Kanchanaburi

The Chinese shrine of San Chao Pho, Suphan Buri

Suphan Buri ❽

สุพรรณบุรี

Suphan Buri province. 🏯 *111,000.*
🚉 🚌 ℹ *TAT, Suphan Buri (0-3553-6030); TAT, Ayutthaya (0-3524-6077).* 🎎 *Don Chedi Fair (Jan 25).*

Suphan Buri came to prominence with the rise of Ayutthaya in the 14th century. The attractive art and architecture of the town are known to few tourists.

Near the center of town is the beautiful *prang* of Wat Phra Si Rattana Mahathat, restored in the Ayutthaya period and again in the 20th century. At Wat Pa Lelai, on the edge of Suphan Buri, is a Buddha image from the Dvaravati period *(see pp56–7).* To the east is San Chao Pho Lak Muang, a Chinese shrine. Wat Phra Rup, on the other side of the Suphan Buri River, houses a reclining Buddha image and a carved wooden Footprint of the Buddha. The *bot* of nearby Wat Pratu San contains striking 19th-century murals of the Buddha's life.

Environs

The large white monument of **Don Chedi**, 31 km (20 miles) from Suphan Buri, marks the site of the battle of Nong Sarai, between the Burmese and Thai forces led by King Naresuan *(see p62).* The **U Thong National Museum** houses 6th- to 11th-century Dvaravati artifacts and Khmer art.

🏛 **U Thong National Museum**
7 km (4 miles) SW of Suphan Buri.
◷ *Wed–Sun.* 🎫

Ang Thong ❾

อ่างทอง

Ang Thong province. 🏯 *41,600.*
🚉 ℹ *TAT, Ayutthaya (0-3524-6077).* 🏨 *daily.*

This small town is a useful base from which travelers who are interested in Thai images of the Buddha can visit three little known but rewarding sites nearby. To the south of Ang Thong, **Wat Pa Mok** houses a reclining Buddha image from the 15th century. **Wat Khun In Pramun** is to the northwest. In its grounds is a huge reclining Buddha image, about 50 m (165 ft) long, dating from the Ayutthaya period.

At **Wat Chaiyo Wora Wihan**, to the north of Ang Thong, a *wihan* houses a third enormous, seated image of the Buddha from the Rattanakosin period, called the Phra Maha Phuttha Phim.

Wat Pha Mok, which houses a 15th-century Buddha, near Ang Thong

Lop Buri ❿

ลพบุรี

See pp174–5.

Phra Phutthabat ⓫

พระพุทธบาท

Saraburi province. ℹ *TAT, Ayutthaya (0-3524-6077); TAT, Saraburi (0-3642-2768-9).* 🚌 *from Saraburi, then samlor.* ◷ *7am–6pm daily.* 🎎 *Phra Phutthabat Fair (Mar).*

In the early 17th century, King Song Tham of Ayutthaya sent a group of monks to Sri Lanka to pay homage to a Footprint of the Buddha. (According to legend, these Footprints show where the Lord Buddha walked upon the Earth.) The monks were surprised to be told by the Sri Lankans that, according to scriptures, there was a footprint in Thailand. Song Tham, on hearing this, ordered a search for the footprint. It was found by a hunter pursuing a wounded deer – the animal vanished into the undergrowth only to re-emerge healed. On closer inspection, the hunter found a water-filled pool shaped like a footprint. He drank from it and was miraculously cured of a skin disease. The king, on learning of this, had a temple built on the site, which subsequently became one of the most sacred places of worship in Thailand.

Today, the 1.5-m (5-ft) long Footprint, Phra Phutthabat, lies in an ornate *mondop*, restored in the late 18th century after the earlier buildings were destroyed by the Burmese in 1765. A museum here displays offerings by pilgrims, who flock to the sight each year. Phra Phutthabat is also the name of the small town here.

Bell, Phra Phutthabat

Environs

At **Phra Phutthachai** ("Buddha's shadow"), about 40 km (25 miles) southeast of Phra Phutthabat, a faint Buddha image, probably painted by a hermit, adorns a cliff face. Pilgrims often visit this site on their way to Phra Phutthabat.

Gestures of the Buddha

Buddha images throughout Thailand for the most part follow strict rules laid down in the 3rd century AD. There are four basic postures: standing, sitting, walking, and reclining; the first three are associated with daily activities of the Buddha, the last with the Buddha's final moments on earth as he achieved *nirvana*. These postures can be com- bined with hand and feet positions to create a variety of attitudes *(mudras)*, that represent key Buddhist themes. King Rama III (1824–51) drew up a list of 40 attitudes to be used by sculptors, but many of these are rare. Most images in Thailand represent a dozen or so atti- tudes, the seated image in *bhumispar- sa mudra* occurring most frequently.

Exposition (vitarkha mudra) *symbolizes the first public discourse given by the Buddha, to five ascetics in a deer park in India. On this Sukhothai-era image, the thumb and forefinger form a circle – the "turning of the wheel of law" (see p31).*

TOUCHING THE EARTH

Bhumisparsa is the most common *mudra*. It symbolizes an important episode in the Buddha's life when he sat in meditation under a Bodhi tree in Bodh Gaya, India, refusing to move until he attained Enlightenment. While his enemy, Mara, of- fered temptations such as nubile maidens and feasts, the Buddha touched the ground to attract the atten- tion of the Earth goddess, so that she could see his resistance. Just after this he achieved Enlightenment.

Right hand pointing to the Earth

Left hand resting in lap

Legs in lotus position

Meditation (dhyana mudra) *is signified with a sitting pos- ture, shown by this modern Buddha image from South- ern Thailand. Both hands are positioned palms up, the right over the left, as still practiced by meditating Buddhists.*

Reassurance (abhaya mudra) *symbolizes the Buddha's offer of protection to his followers. The raised right hand is also representative of an episode in which the Buddha settled a heated dispute over water.*

Restraining the waters *is a variation of* abhaya mudra. *The two hands of this Ayutthayan Buddha image are held palms forward, fingers pointing upward. It refers to an episode when the Buddha calmed the floodwaters of the Nairanjana, a tributary of the Ganges in northern India.*

Reclining *Buddhas, such as this one at Ayutthaya, usually represent the point of* parinirvana *or ultimate* nirvana.

Street-by-Street: Lop Buri ⑩

ลพบุรี

One of Thailand's oldest cities, Lop Buri was known as Lavo in the Dvaravati period *(see pp56–7)* and subsequently became an important outpost of the Khmer Empire *(see pp264–5)*. The Khmer *prang* on the grounds of Wat Phra Si Rattana Mahathat, and those of Prang Sam Yot, date from this time. With the decline of the Khmer Empire and the rise of the Sukhothai Kingdom *(see pp58–9)*, Lop Buri struggled to retain its independence, until, in the 14th century, it was linked by marriage to the emerging state of Ayutthaya *(see pp62–3)*. It reached its political peak in the 17th century when the Ayutthayan King Narai (1656–88) preferred to stay at Lop Buri rather than his official palace at Ayutthaya. Today, the thriving modern town of Lop Buri lies to the east of the old city.

Wat Sao Thong Thong
The wihan at this wat was modified by King Narai so the buildng could be used as a Christian chapel – he replaced Thai windows with Western-style Gothic designs.

The market sells vegetables and other foodstuffs.

★ **King Narai's Palace**
Abandoned after Narai's death, parts of the palace, including the Chanthara Phisan Hall, were later restored by King Mongkut (see p65).

★ **Samdej Phra Narai National Museum**
This museum is housed in the partially restored, colonial-style Phiman Mongkut Hall of King Narai's Palace. It has a superb collection of Lop Buri Buddha images, and collections of Dvaravati, Khmer, and Ayutthayan art.

STAR SIGHTS

★ King Narai's Palace

★ Samdej Phra Narai National Museum

★ Wat Phra Si Rattana Mahathat

★ Prang Sam Yot

KEY

– – – Suggested route

Phaulkon Residence

This house was built by King Narai for his favored minister, the Greek Constantine Phaulkon. Phaulkon encouraged Narai to forge close ties with the French, often excluding other foreigners, though his motive was perhaps to aid Louis XIV's attempt to convert Narai to Christianity. When this came to light it alarmed the Ayutthayan court and Phaulkon was executed (see p163).

VISITORS' CHECKLIST

Lop Buri province. 🚗 *165,000.*
🚉 *Na Phra Kan Rd.* 🚌 *Phra Narai Maharat Rd.* 🛈 *TAT, Phra Yam Chamkat Rd. (0-3642-2768).* 🏛
daily. 🎉 *King Narai Festival (Feb).*
Somdej Phra Narai National Museum *Tel* 0-3641-1458. ◻
9am–4pm Wed–Sun. ● *public hols.* 🏛 **King Narai's Palace**
◻ *daily.* 🏛 **Wat Phra Si Rattana Mahathat** ◻ *daily.* 🏛 🛈
Phaulkon Residence ◻ *daily.* 🏛
🌐 www.thailandmuseum.com

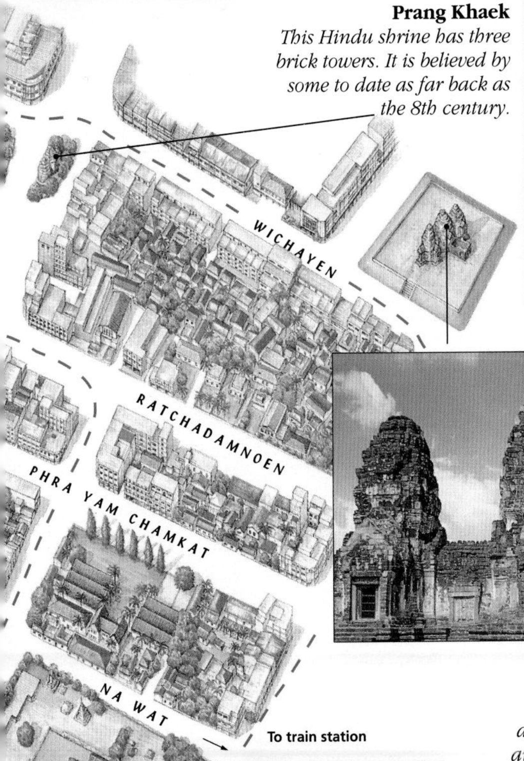

Prang Khaek

This Hindu shrine has three brick towers. It is believed by some to date as far back as the 8th century.

WICHAYEN

RATCHADAMNOEN

PHRA YAM CHAMKAT

NA WAT

To train station

★ Prang Sam Yot

The Lop Buri style was a variation by local artisans, of already established Khmer art and architecture; this shrine is archetypal. The three prangs were originally consecrated as a Hindu shrine; Buddha images were added later to two of them.

★ Wat Phra Si Rattana Mahathat

This wat complex encloses ruins from two distinct eras. At its center is a 12th-century, Khmer prang, decorated with finely detailed stucco work. The site also includes Ayutthayan chedis and a wihan added by King Narai.

0 meters 75

0 yards 75

Ayutthaya ⑫

พระนครศรีอยุธยา

Ayutthayan bracelet

The city of Ayutthaya was founded around 1350 by Ramathibodi I (1351–69), who came here to escape an outbreak of smallpox at Lop Buri. By the early 15th century Ayutthaya had become a major power. Sukhothai (*see pp58–9*) fell to Ayutthaya in 1438. Western traders arrived in the early 16th century (*see pp162–3*), and evidence of Ayutthaya's splendor comes from their accounts. In the early 18th century, after years of war, decline set in, and in 1767 the Burmese sacked the city. Today, the ruins stand among the modern buildings of the provincial town.

Stucco and brick *singhas* around the main *chedi* of Wat Thammikarat

🏛 Wat Phra Mahathat

วัดพระมหาธาตุ

Corner of Chi Kun Rd and Naresuan Rd. ◯ *daily.* 🎫

Wat Phra Mahathat is one of the largest and most important *wat* complexes in Ayutthaya. It was almost certainly founded in the late 14th century by King Borommaracha I (1370–88). Other buildings were subsequently added by his successor, Ramesuan (1388–95).

European-style Pisai Sayalak Tower, behind the Chan Kasem Palace

🏛 Wat Ratchaburana

วัดราชบูรณะ

Cheekun Rd. ◯ *daily.* 🎫

Across the road from Wat Mahathat is Wat Ratchaburana, its *prang* now restored. It was built in the early 15th century by King Borommaracha II (1424–48) on the cremation site of his two brothers, who died in a power struggle. Both of them had wanted to succeed their father, Intharacha I (1409–24), to the throne.

Robbers looted the crypt in 1957 and escaped with a huge cache of gold artifacts, only a few of which were recovered. A steep, narrow staircase descends to the crypt where visitors can see the faded remains of Ayutthayan frescoes (*see p60*).

🏛 Chan Kasem Palace

วังจันทรเกษม

Uthong Rd, opposite the night market. ◯ *Wed–Sun.* 🎫

In the northeast corner of the main island stands the Chan Kasem Palace or Wang Na. It was built in 1577 by the illustrious Naresuan, the son of King Maha Thammaracha (1569–90), before he became king. When Naresuan came to the throne in 1590, the palace became his permanent residence. The buildings seen today, however, date from the reign of King Mongkut (1851–68), as the palace was razed by the Burmese in 1767. It houses a large collection of Buddha images and historical artifacts. Behind the Chan Kasem Palace is the **Pisai Sayalak Tower**, once used as an astronomical observatory by King Mongkut.

🏛 Wat Thammikarat

วัดธรรมิกราช

Uthong Rd. ◯ *daily.* 🎫

At this picturesque site are the dilapidated remains of a large, early Ayutthayan, octagonal *chedi* surrounded by stucco and brick lions, or *singhas*. Beside the *chedi* is the ruin of a *wihan*, slowly succumbing to weeds and trees. A beautiful U Thong Buddha head recovered from here is now in the Chao Sam Phraya National Museum (*see p178*).

🏛 Wang Luang

วังหลวง

Uthong Rd. ◯ *daily.* 🎫

To the west of Wat Thammikarat is Wang Luang, the northern extension of the royal palace built by King Borommatrailokanat (1448–88) in the mid-15th century. Successive monarchs added a number of pavilions and halls. Wang Luang was razed by the Burmese in 1767. The best preserved of the buildings of the former royal palace is the **Trimuk Pavilion**. It was built during the reign of King Chulalongkorn (1868–1910) on the site of earlier foundations.

19th-century Trimuk Pavilion, on the grounds of Wang Luang

For hotels and restaurants in this region see pp402–3 and pp432–3

Wat Phra Si Sanphet

See pp178–9.

Wihan Phra Mongkhon Bophit

วิหารพระมงคลบพิตร

Si Sanphet Rd. ☐ daily. 📷
This *wat* contains one of Thailand's largest bronze Buddha images. Now gilded, it probably dates from the late 15th century, though it has undergone numerous restorations. In 1767 Burmese invaders destoyed much of the *wihan* and damaged the image's head and right hand. The image was left open to the sky until the 1950s, when the *wihan* was rebuilt.

Wat Phra Ram

วัดพระราม

Si Sanphet Rd. ☐ daily. 📷
A chronicle relates that Wat Phra Ram was built in 1369 on the cremation site of King Ramathibodi (1351–69) by his son, Ramesuan. The elegant *prang* visible today, however, is the result of later renovation by King Borommatrailokanat (1448–88). The *prang* is decorated with *garudas*, *nagas*, and walking Buddha images. Surrounding it are *wihans* and a *bot*. The *wat* casts beautiful reflections in nearby lily ponds.

15th-century, corncob-shaped *prang* at Wat Phra Ram

VISITORS' CHECKLIST

Phra Nakhon Si Ayutthaya province. 🏠 60,900. 🚆 Off Bang Ain Rd. 🚌 Naresuan Rd. 🚌 ℹ️ TAT, Si Sanphet Rd, Ayutthaya (0-3532-2730-1). ☐ daily.

Wat Lokaya Sutharam

วัดโลกยสุธาราม

W of main island. ☐ daily. 📷
This *wat* is the site of a 42-m (140-ft) long, whitewashed reclining Buddha image. Large Buddha images such as this do not always depict the Buddha's death, but sometimes, as in this instance, an occasion when the Buddha grew 100 times in size to confront the demon Rahu. The image now lies in the open air, the original *wihan*, having been destroyed by the Burmese; 24 octagonal pillars are all that remain of this *wihan*. The *wat* also houses the ruins of a *bot* and *chedis*.

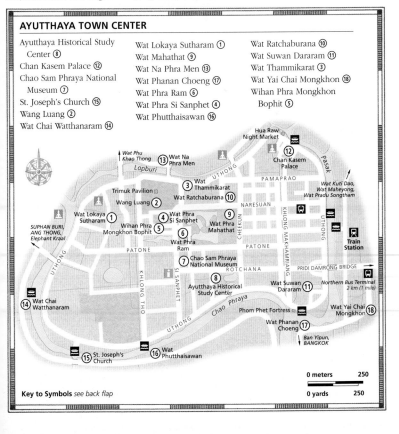

AYUTTHAYA TOWN CENTER

Ayutthaya Historical Study Center ⑧
Chan Kasem Palace ⑫
Chao Sam Phraya National Museum ⑦
St. Joseph's Church ⑮
Wang Luang ②
Wat Chai Watthanaram ⑭

Wat Lokaya Sutharam ①
Wat Mahathat ⑨
Wat Na Phra Men ⑬
Wat Phanan Choeng ⑰
Wat Phra Ram ⑥
Wat Phra Si Sanphet ④
Wat Phutthaisawan ⑯

Wat Ratchaburana ⑩
Wat Suwan Dararam ⑪
Wat Thammikarat ③
Wat Yai Chai Mongkhon ⑱
Wihan Phra Mongkhon Bophit ⑤

Key to Symbols *see back flap*

Chao Sam Phraya National Museum

พิพิธภัณฑ์เจ้าสามพระยา

Intersection of Rotchana Rd and Si Sanphet Rd. ◯ *Wed–Sun.*
www.thailandmuseum.com

Among the exhibits here is a small collection of gold artifacts, including a jewel-encrusted sword, gold slippers, and jewelry. Discovered in the crypt of Wat Ratchaburana's central *prang* when it was looted in 1957, they

Deity on wooden door-panel

are among the few items from the *wat* to have survived the sack of Ayutthaya by the Burmese *(see pp62–3)*. Other artifacts include bronze Buddha images and wooden door panels from *wats* around Ayutthaya.

Ayutthaya Historical Study Center

ศูนย์ศึกษาประวัติศาสตร์อยุธยา

Rotchana. ◯ *daily.*
This study center houses interesting audiovisual displays depicting Ayutthaya's history and trading relations. There is also a reconstructed model of Wat Phra Si Sanphet. Another part of the study center stands in what was the Japanese quarter at the time when Ayutthaya was at the height of its power.

Wat Suwan Dararam

วัดสุวรรณดาราราม

Near Pomphet. ◯ *daily.*
This temple was completely destroyed by the Burmese but later rebuilt by Rama I (1782–1809). The *ubosot* is usually locked, but it is worth requesting the key to see the murals commissioned by Rama VII (1925–35), depicting scenes from the time of King Naresuan. Among them is a mural of the Battle of Nong Sarai, which was fought against the Burmese in 1593 *(see p62)*.

Nearby is a section of the old city defenses, Phom Phet, which were a strategically important lookout post over the Chao Phraya River.

Wat Phra Si Sanphet

วัดพระศรีสรรเพชญ์

Founded by King Borommatrailokanat during the 15th century as a state temple, Wat Phra Si Sanphet was later added to by his son, Ramathibodi II, who built two *chedis* to house the relics of his father and brother. The third *chedi* was built by Borommaracha IV to house the remains of Ramathibodi II. The site was extended by subsequent rulers until the Burmese sack of 1767 *(see pp62–3)*. Partially renovated in the 20th century, many of its treasures are now kept in museums.

The Prasat Phra Narai was cruciform in shape. All that remains of it today are the foundations.

The ashes of Ramathibodi II (1491–1529) are enshrined in this *chedi*, built in the mid-16th century by Borommaracha IV.

RECONSTRUCTION

Overgrown with weeds and trees until the beginning of the 20th century, Wat Phra Si Sanphet is still a ruin, albeit partially restored. This artist's impression gives an idea of its glory before it was sacked.

Drawing of Chedis
Lying empty after it was sacked by the Burmese, Ayutthaya became the focus of scholarly interest. Henri Mouhot, who drew this image, was one of many late 19th-century visitors. Wat Phra Si Sanphet has been under the protection of the Thai Fine Arts Department since 1927.

Wooden Door
This door was probably once situated in the entrance to Wihan Phra Si Sanphet and dates from the reign of Ramathibodi II. A collection of such doors is displayed in the Chao Sam Phraya Museum.

Three Chedis
Apart from the ashes of kings, caskets of precious Buddha images and royal regalia were buried in the chedis' *central chambers.*

The ashes of Borommaracha III (1463–88), the brother of Ramathibodi II, are buried in this *chedi*.

Entrance to Chedi
The entrance chamber to the chedi *is a scaled-down version of a Khmer* mandapa *(entrance chamber to a Khmer sanctuary). Ayutthayan builders modified many older architectural features, such as Khmer* prangs *and Sri Lankan bell-shaped* chedis.

The ashes of Borommatrailokanat (1448–88) are buried in this *chedi*, the only one to survive the Burmese sack. The other two had to be restored.

Stairway leading to entrance of hollow *chedi*

A Footprint of the Lord Buddha was housed in this elegant, spired *mondop*.

Wihan Phra Si Sanphet
The main wihan *– the entrance to the* wat *– once housed the principal Buddha image of Phra Si Sanphet.*

Exploring Ayutthaya: the Outer Sites

Buddha, Wat Na Phra Men

The central island of Ayutthaya stands at the confluence of the Chao Phraya, Lop Buri, and Pasak Rivers. The town's most imposing sites are to be found on the central island. However, a short *samlor* ride by bridge over any of the rivers, which more or less encircle it, will bring you to many more sites of interest. Wat Na Phra Men is one of Ayutthaya's most beautiful *wats*, and St. Joseph's Church offers a glimpse of Ayutthaya's connections with Western trading powers (*see pp162–3*) during the city's heyday. The main part of modern Ayutthaya sprawls to the east of the island, over the Pasak River and beyond.

A roundup of wild elephants at the elephant kraal (1890)

🔲 Wat Na Phra Men

วัดหน้าพระเมรุ

Opp Royal Palace, nr Muang Canal. **Tel** 0-3525-2163. ⬜ *daily.* 📷
Across a bridge to the north of the main island is Wat Na Phra Men, one of the most beautiful of Ayutthaya's monasteries, and one of the few to survive the Burmese sacking of the city in 1767 (*see p60*). Thought to date from the reign of Intharacha II (1488–91), it was restored during the reign of King Borommakot (1733–58), and again in the mid-19th century. In the *wiban* is a Dvaravati seated Buddha image, Phra Kanthararat, that was moved here from Nakhon Pathom in the mid-16th century. The murals covering the *wiban* walls have now almost completely disappeared. Its doors are from the early 19th century. In the adjacent *bot* is a gilded Buddha image, probably from the reign of King Prasat Thong (1629–56).

🔲 Elephant Kraal

พระที่นั่งเพนียด

NW on Hwy 309. ⬜ *daily.* 📷
Farther to the north is the elephant kraal. It is thought that the original structure, built by King Yot Fa (1547–8), stood within the confines of the old city wall. The present kraal, built later, was in use well into the 19th century – wild elephants would be driven here for training as pack animals or war mounts for senior officers. In the middle of the stockade is a shrine where the elephant guardian is thought to live.

🔲 Wat Phu Khao Thong

วัดภูเขาทอง

2 km (1 mile) NW on Hwy 309. ⬜ *daily.* 📷
To the west, the original *chedi* of Phu Khao Thong was constructed by King Bayinnaung of Burma to celebrate his capture of Ayutthaya in 1569. Additions were made in 1744–5 by the Thai King Borommakot.

🔲 Wat Chai Watthanaram

วัดไชยวัฒนาราม

W bank of Chao Phraya River, SW of main island. ⬜ *daily.* 📷
This *wat* was built by King Prasat Thong in 1630. The central *prang* is surrounded by eight smaller ones, decorated with stucco reliefs depicting images such as the Buddha preaching to his mother in the Tavatimsa Heaven. All the *prangs* have been restored.

🔲 St. Joseph's Church

โบสถ์เซนต์ยอเซฟ

SW of main island on the Chao Phraya River. ⬜ *daily.*
St. Joseph's, overlooking the Chao Phraya River, has been the site of Catholic worship for over 300 years. The original 17th-century structure was destroyed by the Burmese in 1767. The present church was built during the 19th century.

🔲 Wat Phutthaisawan

วัดพุทไธศวรรย์

S of main island. ⬜ *daily.* 📷
East from St. Joseph's is Wat Phutthaisawan, also located on the river bank. It has a restored 14th-century *prang* surrounded by a cloister filled with Buddha images.

🔲 Wat Kuti Dao

วัดกุฎีดาว

E of railway station. ⬜ *daily.* 📷
This *wat* originally dated from the early Ayutthaya period, but the ruins here today are of an 18th-century renovation by King Phumintharacha. The *chedi* is flanked by a *wiban* and a *bot* with distinctive arched windows and doors.

Bell-shaped *chedi*, part of the ruined Wat Kuti Dao

For hotels and restaurants in this region see pp402–3 and pp432–3

Reclining Buddha in a ruined *wihan* at Wat Yai Chai Mongkhon

Wat Pradu Songtham
วัดประดู่ทรงธรรม
N of railroad station, E of main island. ☐ *daily.*
Inside the *wihan* of Wat Pradu Songtham are the remains of murals dating from the early Rattanakosin period (*see p35*). These recount the life of the Buddha and also show images of daily life, including one of a performance of the Ramakien at a fair. Outside is a bell tower topped by a small *chedi* from the late Ayutthaya period.

Wat Maheyong
วัดมเหยงค์
E of main island. ☐ *daily.*
The partially reconstructed ruins of Wat Maheyong date from the reign of King Borommaracha II (1424–48). The principal, bell-shaped *chedi* shows a clear stylistic link with earlier Sukhothai *chedis*, while all around the rectangular base are the remnants of stucco elephants. Other *chedis* at this site also show Sukhothai influence.

Wat Yai Chai Mongkhon
วัดใหญ่ไชยมงคล
E of main island. ☐ *daily.* 📷
The *chedi* here, one of the largest in Ayutthaya, was built by King Naresuan (1590–1605) to celebrate his victory over the Burmese at Nong Sarai in 1593 (*see pp62–3*). Flanking steps up to the *chedi* are two *mondops* housing seated Buddha images. On the northeast side of the *wat* is a ruined *wihan* containing a reclining Buddha.

Wat Phanan Choeng
วัดพนัญเชิง
S of main island. ☐ *daily.*
This *wat* has been renovated over the years and houses the large, 14th-century, seated image of Phra Chao Phanan Choeng. The *wihan* was built in the mid-19th century.

Ban Yipun
บ้านญี่ปุ่น
S of main island.
☐ *daily.* 📷
Once the site of a 17th-century Japanese settlement, today a museum here displays exhibits that explain Ayutthaya's foreign relations at the time.

Bang Pa-in ⑱
บางปะอิน

Phra Nakhon Si Ayutthaya province. 🚇 59,000. 🚉 🚌 🚤 ℹ TAT, Ayutthaya (0-3532-2730-1). ☐ *daily.*
www.palaces.thai.net

Visitors to Bang Pa-in stop off, for the most part, just to visit **Bang Pa-in Palace**, whose exuberant 19th-century buildings stand in stark contrast to nearby Ayutthaya. It is thought that a royal palace was first built at Bang Pa-in by King Prasat Thong (1629–56), to mark the birth of his son and successor, King Narai. With the defeat of Ayutthaya by the Burmese in 1767 the site fell into ruin; the present buildings date from the reigns of Mongkut (1851–68) and Chulalongkorn (1868–1910).

The beautiful pavilion, Phra Thinang Aisawan Thipha-at ("divine seat of personal freedom"), at the center of an ornamental lake, was built for Chulalongkorn in 1876, together with the Phra Thinang

Warophat Phiman ("excellent and shining abode"), to the left. Behind are the terra-cotta- and white-striped lookout tower, Ho Withun Thasana, built by Chulalongkorn in 1881, and the Chinese-style mansion, Phra Thinang Wehat Chamrun, built as a gift for him by an as-

sociation of Chinese merchants in 1889. Visitors can cross a canal by cable car to Wat Niwet Tham Prawat, which was built by Chulalongkorn in 1877–8.

Bang Pa-in Palace
พระราชวังบางปะอิน
Bang Pa-in district. ☐ *daily.* 📷 🍴

The Phra Thinang Aisawan Thipha-at pavilion, Bang Pa-in Palace

Monks looking out over the ornamental lake of the Phra Thinang Aisawan Thipha-at pavilion, Bang Pa-in ▷

Khao Yai National Park ⓮

อุทยานแห่งชาติเขาใหญ่

Established in 1962, Khao Yai was then Thailand's sole national park. Today there are well over 100, but this one remains popular. Set over 2,000 sq km (770 sq miles), the park has a wide variety of habitats, including submontane evergreen forests and grasslands. There are also several mountains of around 1,000 m (3,300 ft), including Khao Khieo. The abundant wildlife includes many

Begonia flower

endangered mammals such as elephants, gibbons, tigers and Malaysian sun bears, as well as more than 300 bird species. Visitors are advised to hire a guide for trips to more remote parts. The surrounding area offers luxurious resorts, golf courses, and even vineyards.

White-Handed Gibbon
These tailless apes use their long arms to move swiftly and agilely through the trees.

SARABURI

Elephant salt lick •

Watchtower •

Watchtower •

Radar station •

Khao
Khieo
1,287 m
(4,223 ft)

BANGKOK

NAKHON NAYOK

Endangered Species
Khao Yai is home to about 20 of the 500 or so tigers left in Thailand. These noble animals can be found surprisingly close to the park's headquarters; visitors should treat them with respect.

Siamese Fireback Pheasant
Thailand's national bird, this pheasant spends its days on the ground where it feeds on small insects, seeds, and fruit. It roosts in the trees at night.

Deciduous forest
grows in the park's low-lying areas.

Haeo Suwat Waterfall
Located along the upper reaches of the Lam Takhong River, this waterfall is one of many dotted around Khao Yai. From March to May each year many varieties of orchids can be seen flowering around the waterfall. Elephants have been known to drown while crossing near waterfalls when the rains are very heavy.

Submontane Evergreen Forest

This type of forest often contains deciduous trees such as chestnuts. It grows at Khao Yai's highest altitudes, 1,000 m (3,300 ft) to 1,351 m (4,450 ft) above sea level.

VISITORS' CHECKLIST

Khorat, Nakhon Nayok, Saraburi & Prachin Buri provinces. Park HQ off Hwy 1, NE of Bangkok. ⓘ TAT, Khorat (0-4421-3666); Park HQ (08-6092-6529); Forestry Dept (0-2562-0760 or **www**.dnp. go.th for bungalows). Pak Chong, then bus or songthaew. in bad weather.

KHORAT

AK CHONG

Sambar Stag

Sambar are the largest species of deer in Thailand and are primarily forest dwellers. Though hunted by tigers and leopards, humans are its main predator. It is now common only in well-protected conservation areas.

Semievergreen rainforest can be seen above 600 m (1,950 ft).

Khao Kamphaeng 974 m (3,196 ft)

Khao Wong 146 m (479 ft)

Earthball Fungus

This parasitic fungus is found in humid evergreen forests all over Southeast Asia. Unlike many parasites, its presence actually encourages the growth of its host.

PRACHIN BURI

0 kilometers 10

0 yards 10

KEY

Expressway

Major road

Minor road

Park border

ⓘ Park headquarters

Ⓐ Camping and bungalows

Water sports

Vista

Lam Takhong River

Rainfall in Khao Yai National Park is usually in excess of 3,000 mm (120 inches) per year. Streams swollen by the rains flow off forested slopes forming rivers, among them the Lam Takhong River. Wildlife living around this river includes kingfishers, cormorants, elephants, and macaques.

NORTH CENTRAL PLAINS

The farther north the visitor travels through the Central Plains the more sparsely populated the countryside becomes – the landscape here is typified by gentle, rolling hills and rice farms. There are few interesting modern cities in this region. Its major attractions are ancient city ruins, relics of an illustrious past when competing princedoms and city-states fought each other for land and power.

Visitors to Thailand traveling north from Bangkok tend not to stop off in the North Central Plains, but instead press on to the major destination of Thailand's second city, Chiang Mai. However, some of the most fascinating ruins in Southeast Asia are found here.

In the 13th century, during the reign of King Ramkamhaeng *(see p58)*, one city, Sukhothai, came to dominate the region to such an extent that its influence was felt far beyond Thailand's present borders. But its power was shortlived, and by the mid-14th century the region was once more a collection of fiefdoms. The ruins the kingdom left behind at Sukhothai, and at its satellite cities of Kamphaeng Phet and Si Satchanalai, still inspire wonder. They have been extensively restored and turned into well-managed historical parks.

Other places of interest in the region include the prosperous trading center Phitsanulok, which is at the heart of a transportation network connecting the region to Bangkok and the north. This, and other towns, support a local rice-farming economy.

The hillier areas, in the west and northeast of the region, are the setting for a number of national parks and wildlife sanctuaries. These provide a much needed refuge for endangered plant and animal species *(see pp28–9)* whose habitats are threatened by the impact of illegal logging and the widespread loss of land to agriculture.

Around Mae Sot the influence of Myanmar (Burma) is felt; the town is characterized by Myanmar architecture, and a common sight is Karen and Shan tribespeople and Myanmar who cross the border at this point to trade.

Farmer raking unhusked rice, a typical rural scene in the North Central Plains

◁ Reclining and sitting Buddha images at Wat Phra Kaeo, Kamphaeng Phet

Exploring the North Central Plains

This part of the country acts as a bridge between the crowded
heartland of modern Thailand to the immediate south and the
rolling hills of the North. The region has no big cities,
and most tourists do no more than overnight in small,
provincial towns near the magnificent ruins of ancient
Sukhothai, the first Thai capital. Predominantly, this
is rice-farming country, flanked to the east, north,
and west by hills. National parks in some of the
hilly areas help protect endangered flora and fauna.
Magnificent forest scenery and spectacular waterfalls can be found along the western border with
Myanmar (Burma), around Mae Sot and remote
Umphang. Here, a hint of Myanmar spills
across the border in the shape of Karen
and Shan tribespeople and
Myanmar architecture,
goods, and food.

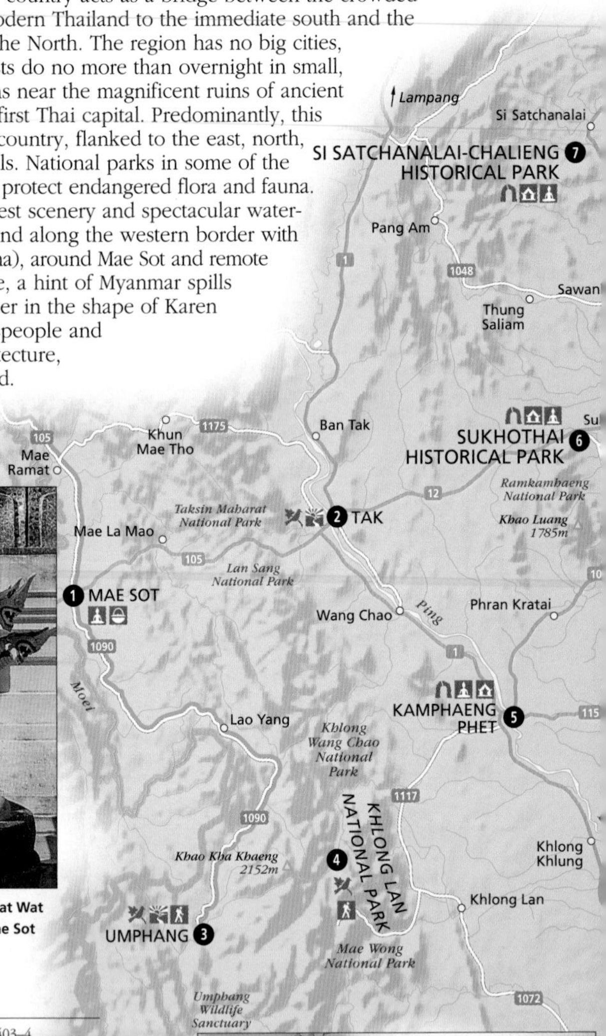

Lampang

Si Satchanalai

SI SATCHANALAI-CHALIENG 7
HISTORICAL PARK

Pang Am

1

1048

Sawan

Thung
Saliam

Khun
Mae Tho   1175   Ban Tak

Su

SUKHOTHAI 6
HISTORICAL PARK

Mae
Ramat

105

*Taksin Maharat
National Park*

2 TAK

12

*Ramkambaeng
National Park*
*Khao Luang
1785m*

Mae La Mao

105

*Lan Sang
National Park*

10

1 MAE SOT

Wang Chao

Ping

Phran Kratai

1090

Moei

Lao Yang

*Khlong
Wang Chao
National
Park*

KAMPHAENG 5
PHET

1

115

**Buddha under *naga* at Wat
Chumphon Khiri, Mae Sot**

1090

*Khao Kha Khaeng
2152m*

4

KHLONG LAN NATIONAL PARK

1117

Khlong
Khlung

Khlong Lan

UMPHANG 3

*Mae Wong
National Park*

1072

SEE ALSO

• **Where to Stay** pp403–4

• **Where to Eat** pp433–4

KEY

━━ Major road

┈┈ Minor road

━━ Scenic route

╍╍ Railway

▰▰ International border

△ Summit

*Umphang
Wildlife
Sanctuary*

**Wat Traphang Thong, a monastery surrounded by a lotus-
filled pond at Sukhothai Historical Park**

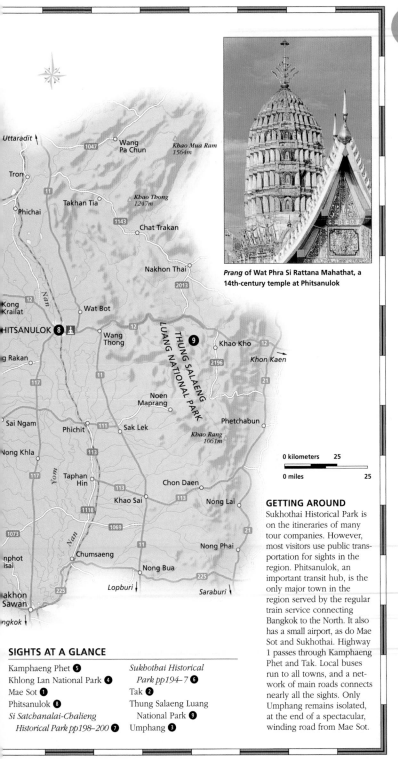

Prang of Wat Phra Si Rattana Mahathat, a 14th-century temple at Phitsanulok

0 kilometers   25

0 miles   25

GETTING AROUND

Sukhothai Historical Park is on the itineraries of many tour companies. However, most visitors use public transportation for sights in the region. Phitsanulok, an important transit hub, is the only major town in the region served by the regular train service connecting Bangkok to the North. It also has a small airport, as do Mae Sot and Sukhothai. Highway 1 passes through Kamphaeng Phet and Tak. Local buses run to all towns, and a network of main roads connects nearly all the sights. Only Umphang remains isolated, at the end of a spectacular, winding road from Mae Sot.

SIGHTS AT A GLANCE

Kamphaeng Phet ⑤
Khlong Lan National Park ④
Mae Sot ①
Phitsanulok ⑧
Si Satchanalai-Chalieng Historical Park pp198–200 ⑦

Sukhothai Historical Park pp194–7 ⑥
Tak ②
Thung Salaeng Luang National Park ⑨
Umphang ③

Wat Chumphon Khiri, Mae Sot, Tak province

Mae Sot ❶
แม่สอด

Tak province. 🏛 70,000. ✈
🚌 ℹ️ TAT, Tak (0-5551-4341).
🛍 daily.

In the mid-19th century Myanmar and Shan merchants, crossing the Moei River from Myanmar (Burma) in the west, helped to establish Mae Sot as a prosperous market town. Trade in Myanmar hardwoods and gemstones, both legal and smuggled, has brought considerable wealth to this small town. Today Mae Sot retains the feel of a frontier town and makes a relaxing stopover for travelers. Gem traders, usually ethnic Chinese, can often be seen huddled on Mae Sot's pavements, negotiating with buyers from Bangkok and other parts of Thailand. Because of its location and trading history, Mae Sot has a distinct Myanmar flavor, evident in architecture and market goods.

Trilingual shop signs can be seen on the streets, Myanmar-language publications are sold in shops, and Myanmar people wearing traditional sarongs (lungis) can be seen walking along the streets. During the morning food market – one of Thailand's most picturesque and colorful – Karen and Myanmar traders haggle with Thais and Indians.

North of the market is **Wat Chumphon Khiri**, which has a magnificent Myanmar *chedi* decorated with golden mosaic tiles. On the southeast side of town is the Muslim quarter; at its center is the small **Nurul Islam Mosque**.

Dotted around the town are a number of other temples that have both Karen and Shan characteristics.

Environs
Some 3 km (2 miles) west of Mae Sot is **Wat Thai Watthanaram**. In the rear courtyard is a huge, Myanmar-style, reclining Buddha image built in 1993 and a gallery of 28 seated Buddha images. A further 1 km (1,100 yards) beyond Wat Thai Watthanaram, a bridge over the Moei River links Mae Sot to the Myanmar border town of Myawadi. Clustered around the foot of the bridge is a market selling an odd mix of Thai, Myanmar, Indonesian, and Chinese goods.

Southeast of Mae Sot are the **Pha Charoen falls**, a very popular spot for picnicking and swimming.

Monks in the grounds of Wat Bot Mani Sibunruang, Tak

Tak ❷
ตาก

Tak province. 🏛 78,000. ✈ 🚌
ℹ️ TAT, Taksin Rd, Tak (0-5551-4341). 🛍 daily.

During much of the 13th century, Tak was a western outpost of the Sukhothai Kingdom. After the death of King Ramkamhaeng and the

Reclining, Myanmar-style Buddha in the courtyard of Wat Thai Watthanaram, near Mae Sot

For hotels and restaurants in this region see pp403–4 and pp433–4

One of many waterfalls in the Umphang Wildlife Sanctuary

Umphang ❸
อุ้มผาง

Tak province. 🚶 *23,000.* 🚌 *Mae Sot, then songthaew.* 🛈 *TAT, Tak (0-5551-4341).* 🏠 *daily.*

Part of Umphang's charm lies in the journey, as the road from Mae Sot is one of Thailand's most scenic. The village – its population consisting largely of Karen tribespeople – is surrounded by the lush forests of **Umphang Wildlife Sanctuary**, rich in bird life and small mammals. Umphang has become popular for rafting, hiking, and elephant treks, but its isolation has kept most of the tourist hordes away. Here too are many cascades and rapids (including one of the country's highest waterfalls, **Thi Lo Su**), caves, and Karen settlements. Several agencies in Umphang or Mae Sot can arrange treks. Visitors should avoid school vacations, when this region is crowded and accommodations scarce.

🏞 Umphang Wildlife Sanctuary
150 km (93 miles) S of Mae Sot on Hwy 1090. 🛈 *Forestry Dept (0-2562-0760).* 📷

---

subsequent collapse of the Sukhothai Empire *(see pp58– 9)*, the town came under the influence of the Lanna Kingdom *(see pp62–3)* to the north. Today Tak sprawls along the left bank of the Ping River, and much of the Lanna influence can still be seen in the teak houses hidden away in quiet lanes at the southern end of town. The houses here date from the late 19th and early 20th centuries.

Wat Bot Mani Sibunruang also shows Northern influences with its finely decorated, Lanna-style *bot* and a small *sala* containing a much re-vered Buddha image called Luang Pho Phutthamon.

Nearby is a statue of King Taksin, a former governor of Tak, who, after the sacking of Ayutthaya by Myanmar in 1767, established a new capital at Thon Buri, now part of Bangkok *(see pp64–5)*.

Environs
The 105-sq km (40-sq mile) **Lan Sang National Park** has tracks leading to several beautiful waterfalls. These are best visited during or soon after the rainy season *(see pp26– 7)*; at other times of year there is little water. To the north of Lan Sang National Park is the **Taksin Maharat National Park**, the highlight of which is a steeply descending trail to the huge *ton krabak yai*, or big krabak tree, which is some 50 m (165 ft) tall, and

has a girth of 16 m (50 ft). The park offers bird-watching opportunities, boasting a variety of species including the tiger shrike and forest wagtail. Also in the park are the nine-tiered Mae Ya Pa falls.

🏞 Lan Sang National Park
20 km (12 miles) W of Tak, off Hwy 105. 📷

🏞 Taksin Maharat National Park
15 km (9 miles) W of Tak, off Hwy 105. 🛈 *Forestry Dept (0-2562-0760).* 📷

THAILAND-MYANMAR (BURMA) BORDER REFUGEES

There are nine official refugee camps on Thailand's western border, including three main camps around Mae Sot–Mae La, Noe Po, and Umpium. Together, these camps are home to about 100,000 Myanmar refugees. The Karen tribespeople, who have long occupied an area straddling Myanmar and Thailand, are Myanmar's largest ethnic minority. The British were supposed to grant the Karen an autonomous homeland within Myanmar after World War II, but this did not happen. Following pro-democracy demonstrations in Myanmar in 1988, and the subsequent crack down, opposition MPs and ethnic minorities fled east to refugee villages. It is in such villages that the Karen organize their struggle for an independent state. The Thai government does not openly condemn Myanmar, and the Thai army does not usually intervene on behalf of the Karen.

Boy soldiers in the rebel army of the Karen tribespeople

Waterfall in Khlong Lan National Park, Kamphaeng Phet province

Khlong Lan
National Park ❹

อุทยานแห่งชาติคลองลาน

Kamphaeng Phet province. Park HQ 6 km (4 miles) off Hwy 1117, S of Kamphaeng Phet. 🛈 TAT, Tak (0-5551-4341); Forestry Dept (0-2562-0760 inc bungalow bookings). 🚌 from Kamphaeng Phet to Klonglan, then songthaew. 💻 www.dnp.go.th

This 300-sq km (116-sq mile) national park was formed in 1982. Formerly, the area was controlled by Communist insurgents, and inhabited by a number of hill tribes. Initially, the tribes lived within the park but were later relocated because they were regarded as a threat to the wildlife, which includes gaur, tiger, and the Asiatic black bear.

The highlight of the park is the Khlong Lan waterfall, which is easily accessible from the park headquarters. It falls 95 m (310 ft) into a pool ideal for a refreshing swim. At the foot of the road leading up to the waterfall is a small market selling Hmong handicrafts – a government rehabilitation scheme for the hill tribes relocated from the park.

The adjacent **Mae Wong National Park** is good for hiking and bird-watching, and there are some facilities for visitors. Until the late 1980s it was populated by Hmong, who have also been relocated. Park staff confirm that the number of birds and mammals is steadily increasing. An old road running through the center of the park is now overgrown, but it does make a good hiking trail. Simple accommodations in bungalows are available near the park headquarters.

> 🦌 **Mae Wong National Park**
> Park HQ SW of Kamphaeng Phet, off Hwy 1117. 🛈 Forestry Dept (0-2562-0760, inc bungalow bookings). 💻 www.dnp.go.th

Kamphaeng
Phet ❺

กำแพงเพชร

Kamphaeng Phet province. 👥 164,000. ✈ 🚌 🛈 TAT, Tak (0-5551-4341). 🍴 daily. 🎉 Nop Phra-Len Plang (Feb), Kluay Khai Muang Kamphaeng (Sep).

There has been a settlement at this site on the banks of the Ping River since the 11th century, when a northern prince, fleeing an attack by Myanmar in the area of present-day Fang (see p242), brought his followers here. The community initially survived as an outpost of the Khmer Empire (see p56) and, during the 13th century, as part of the Sukhothai Kingdom.

On the east bank lie the impressive remains of the **Old City**, dating from the early 15th century, and which once formed part of a satellite city to the mighty Sukhothai (see pp194–7). Located within its walls is the **Kamphaeng Phet National Museum**. In this collection are several fine 16th-century bronzes of Hindu deities, including a standing image of Shiva and torsos of Vishnu and Lakshmi. There are also stucco and terra-cotta fragments from Kamphaeng Phet's many ruins.

The Old City walls also enclose two important ruins from the late Sukhothai period. Close to the National Museum, **Wat Phra Kaeo** is the Old City's largest site, containing the ruins of several wihans, a

Renovated stone elephant at Wat Phra Kaeo, Kamphaeng Phet

Kamphaeng Phet National Museum and surrounding gardens

bot at the eastern end, a *chedi* from the late Sukhothai period, and the laterite cores of a number of Buddha images. At the western end of the site are three more partly restored Buddha images. Neighboring **Wat Phra That** has a fine late Sukhothai, octagonal-based *chedi*. One admission charge covers all ruins in the Old City.

The modern town of Kamphaeng Phet, for the most part, sprawls to the south of the Old City. It mostly comprises commercial buildings, though it also has a riverside park and a few traditional wooden houses, as well as some tourist-oriented facilities.

A *samlor* ride northwest of the Old City are the **Aranyik Ruins**, the area of many forest *wats* once used by a meditational order called the Forest Dwelling Sect. Built during the 14th–16th centuries, the sheer number of ruins at Aranyik attest to the popularity of the sect, which achieved prominence in Thailand during the Sukhothai era. With the assistance of UNESCO, parts of the site have now been restored and landscaped.

The *wihan* at Wat Phra Non, near the entrance, once contained a large reclining Buddha, but this is so badly damaged as to be almost indiscernible. Nevertheless, a number of laterite columns from the *wihan* are still standing. On each side of the *mondop* at Wat Phra Si Iriyabot are images of the Buddha in different postures, though all are damaged. The standing

Buddha on the west side has been partially restored. In the ruined *bot* of Wat Sing (found in the northern part of the Aranyik site) is the laterite core of a Buddha image.

Most impressive of the Aranyik *wats* is **Wat Chang Rop**, consisting mostly of the remains of a very large, square-based *chedi*, flanked by the forequarters of some elephants in laterite. On a few of these, the original stucco decoration has been restored. However, little of the Sri Lankan-style bell-shaped *chedi* is still standing. Among two dozen or so other sites dotted around Aranyik, many of

them scarcely visible in thick undergrowth, Wat Awat Yai is one of the few now cleared of vegetation.

In the modern part of town, other monuments, such as the Sukhothai brick *chedi* of **Wat Kalothai**, can be seen tucked away in quiet lanes. Many such sites have now fallen into disrepair, but their sheer quantity is an indication of the importance of Kamphaeng Phet during the Sukhothai and Ayutthaya periods.

West of the city, the large, white, Myanmar-style *chedi* of **Wat Phra Boromathat** was built in the late 19th century on the site of three 13th–14th-century *chedis*, the earliest of which was constructed by King Si Intharathit of Sukhothai (c.1240–70) to house some relics of the Lord Buddha. Also to the west are the laterite walls of **Thung Setthi Fort**, which once protected this side of the city.

🏛 **Kamphaeng Phet National Museum**
Old City, behind Wat Phra Kaeo.
Tel 0-5571-1570. ⬤ 8:30am–4pm
Wed–Sun. ⬤ *public hols.*
🖳 www.finearts.go.th

🏛 **Aranyik Ruins**
NW of Old City. ⬤ *daily.* 🖳

🏛 **Thung Setthi Fort**
Off Hwy 1, W of town. ⬤ *daily.*

KAMPHAENG PHET'S HISTORICAL SITES

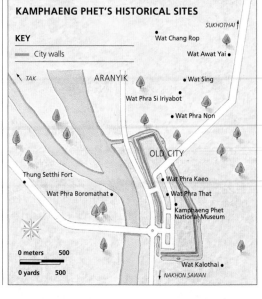

KEY

▭▭▭ City walls

SUKHOTHAI ↑

Wat Chang Rop

Wat Awat Yai ●

↖ TAK   ARANYIK

● Wat Sing

Wat Phra Si Iriyabot

● Wat Phra Non

OLD CITY

Thung Setthi Fort

Wat Phra Boromathat ●

● Wat Phra Kaeo

● Wat Phra That

Kamphaeng Phet National Museum

Wat Kalothai ●

↓ NAKHON SAWAN

0 meters   500
0 yards   500

Sukhothai Historical Park ⑥

อุทยานประวัติศาสตร์สุโขทัย

The UNESCO World Heritage site of Old Sukhothai lies to the west of the modern town. It is a potent reminder of the ancient Sukhothai Kingdom, which arose in the early 13th century from what had been a distant outpost of the Khmer Empire. Under the leadership of the Tai warrior King Ramkamhaeng, the city came to dominate the Central Plains *(see pp58–9)*. The abandoned city that can be seen today is the best preserved and most popular sight in Central Thailand. Ongoing restoration has revealed the amazing symmetry of its layout and offers the visitor a remarkable insight into a time when Thai art and culture reached its apex.

Buddha, Wat Traphang Ngoen

Exploring Sukhothai Historical Park

The site of Old Sukhothai has around 40 temple complexes spread over an area of about 70 sq km (28 sq miles). At its center is the walled Royal City, protected by moats and ramparts. Many of the most important ruins are within this inner compound. The layout of Old Sukhothai, as with many major Thai cities (*muangs*), follows fixed principles: a large, central *wat* complex surrounded concentrically by walls, river, rice fields, and, beyond, forested mountains. Another example of this, on a smaller scale, is Si Satchanalai *(see pp58–9)*.

One way to see the ruins of the Royal City is by bicycle: shops beside the old east gate rent them by the day for a small fee. A quick test ride is advised as some are in poor condition, and an early start is recommended to avoid the midday heat.

The Royal City

Entering from the east, the first *wat* within the city walls is Wat Traphang Thong, which is situated on an islet in a small lotus-filled lake. The Sri Lankan-style *chedi* dates from the mid-14th century, and a small *mondop* beside it enshrines a stone Footprint of the Buddha, still worshiped by resident monks.

The **Ramkamhaeng National Museum** houses photographs, taken around

Khmer-style, laterite *prangs*, part of Wat Si Sawai

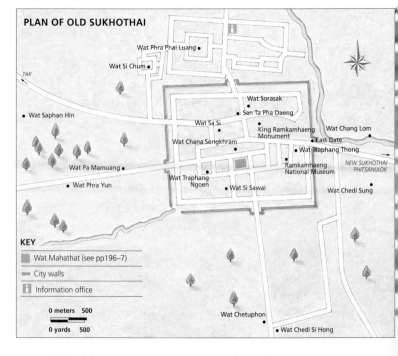

PLAN OF OLD SUKHOTHAI

- Wat Phra Phai Luang
- Wat Si Chum
- TAK
- Wat Saphan Hin
- Wat Sorasak
- San Ta Pha Daeng
- Wat Sa Si
- King Ramkamhaeng Monument
- Wat Chang Lom
- Wat Chana Songkhram
- East Gate
- Wat Traphang Thong
- Wat Pa Mamuang
- Ramkamhaeng National Museum
- NEW SUKHOTHAI PHITSANULOK
- Wat Phra Yun
- Wat Traphang Ngoen
- Wat Si Sawai
- Wat Chedi Sung

KEY
- Wat Mahathat (see pp196–7)
- City walls
- Information office

0 meters 500
0 yards 500

- Wat Chetuphon
- Wat Chedi Si Hong

Façade of the Ramkamhaeng National Museum

1900–1920, of Sukhothai's ruins prior to renovation and a large collection of artifacts. At the heart of the moated city is **Wat Mahathat** *(see pp196–7)*, the most important *wat* complex in Sukhothai.

Nearby, Wat Takuan has a restored, Sri Lankan bell-shaped *chedi*. Several Buddha images found in the vault of the *chedi* are thought to date from the early Sukhothai period, though they remain something of a mystery.

To the southwest, at Wat Si Sawai, are three 12th–14th-century Khmer-style *prangs*, thought to predate the Tai takeover of the city.

The *bot* of Wat Traphang Ngoen, mentioned in Ramkamhaeng's famous Inscription No. 1 *(see p58)*, lies in an artificial rectangular lake.

Copper Buddha images and Chinese pottery were recovered from Wat Sa Si, also at the center of an artificial lake. These are now in the Ramkamhaeng National Museum.

Nearby, Wat Chana Song-khram has a restored, squat Sri Lankan-style *chedi*. A smaller *chedi* here dates from the Ayutthaya period.

To the north of Wat Mahathat is the modern **King Ramkamhaeng Monument**. Beyond lies San Ta Pha Daeng, a 12th-century Khmer shrine that once housed sandstone Hindu icons, now in the Ramkamhaeng National Museum.

Wat Sorasak, a small, brick, bell-shaped *chedi*, dates from the early 15th century. The square base is supported by 24 stucco elephants.

East of the Royal City

Wat Chang Lom, a bell-shaped *chedi* similar to one at Si Satch-analai *(see p200)*, has 36 brick and stucco elephants around its base. It represents mythical Mount Meru, supported by elephants. Beyond is Wat Chedi Sung, a beautiful *chedi* with a high, square base typical of the late Sukhothai era.

North of the Royal City

Wat Phra Phai Luang, a Khmer-style complex, is thought to be part of the original mid-13th century settlement, built when this region was part of the Khmer Empire. Only one of the three laterite *prangs*, decorated with stucco fragments, is extant. Nearby, the *mondop* of Wat Si Chum has an immense seated Buddha peering through an opening.

Reconstructed stucco elephant heads at Wat Sorasak

LOY KRATHONG AT SUKHOTHAI

Loy Krathong *(see p50)* occurs at the November full moon to mark the end of the rainy season and the main rice harvest. The festival has its origins in the Hindu tradition of thanking the water god for the rains. *Krathongs*, bowls fashioned out of banana leaves holding lighted candles, are floated on water after dark. Though celebrated all over Thailand, the most exuberant festivities take place at Old Sukhothai. Nowadays, the festival includes folk dancing and sound-and-light shows.

Loy Krathong festivities at the Sukhothai Historical Park

Wat Mahathat

วัดมหาธาตุ

Wat Mahathat was the spiritual center of the Sukhothai Kingdom. The central *chedi* was founded by Si Intharathit (c.1240–70), first king of Sukhothai, and rebuilt in the 1340s by Lue Thai (1298–1346) to house relics of the Buddha. Buildings were added to the complex by successive kings: by the time it was abandoned in the 16th century it had some 200 *chedis* as well as numerous *wihans* and *mondops*.

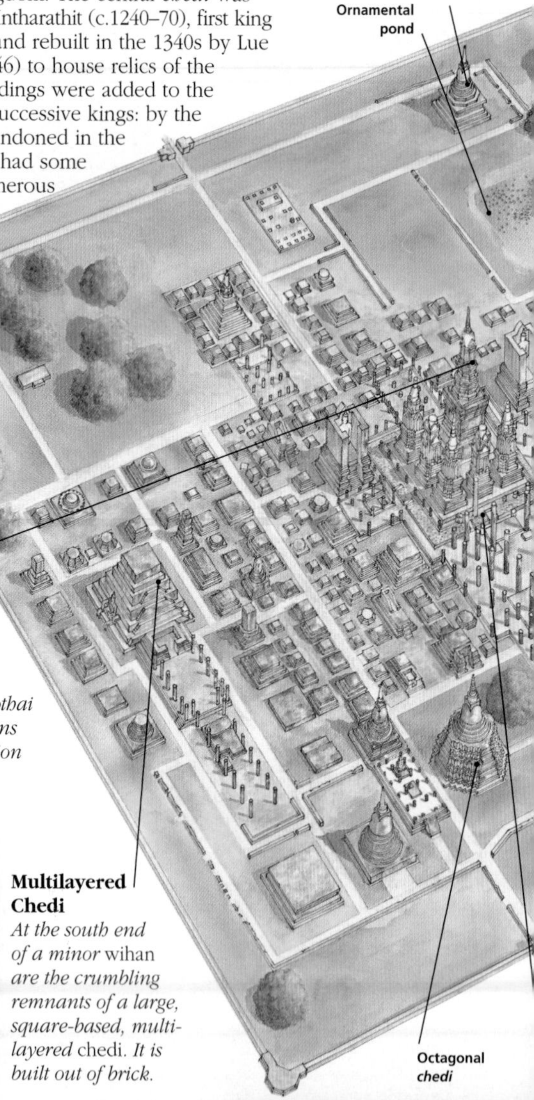

Arch on east-facing *chedi*

Bell-shaped *chedi*

Ornamental pond

★ Lotus-Bud Chedi
At the epicenter of the wat complex is this classic Sukhothai lotus-bud chedi. The remains of beautiful stucco decoration can be seen in patches.

Multilayered Chedi
At the south end of a minor wihan are the crumbling remnants of a large, square-based, multi-layered chedi. It is built out of brick.

Octagonal *chedi*

STAR FEATURES

★ Frieze of Walking Monks

★ Lotus-Bud Chedi

★ Phra Attharot Buddha Images

★ Frieze of Walking Monks
A stucco frieze runs around the square base of the central group of chedis. It depicts monks processing around the shrine – a ritual called pradaksina.

Remains of Bot
To the north of the central chedi are the remains of a bot, with a large, seated Buddha. Like all major Buddha images in Thailand, it faces east.

Perimeter wall

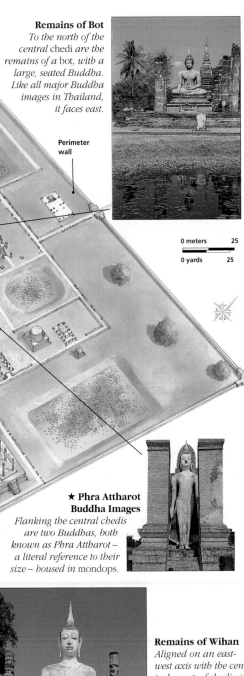

0 meters   25
0 yards   25

★ Phra Attharot Buddha Images
Flanking the central chedis are two Buddhas, both known as Phra Attharot – a literal reference to their size – housed in mondops.

Remains of Wihan
Aligned on an east-west axis with the central group of chedis is the main wihan. The only remains today are columns that once supported a roof and a seated Buddha image.

Exploring the Outer Sights

Along a low ridge of hills, around 3.5 km (2 miles) west of the ramparted royal city is another string of ruins that form part of the Sukhothai Historical Park. Most important of these is **Wat Saphan Hin**, where a 12.5-m (41-ft) high Buddha image, Phra Attharot, similar to the Buddha images of the same name at Wat Mahathat, stands on a low summit. There is another large image, similar to Phra Attharot, at Wat Phra Yun, though the head and hands are missing.

Closer to the west city wall is Wat Pa Mamuang, of arch-eological importance for the inscriptions discovered here relating to King Lo Thai.

To the south are the ruins of Wat Chetuphon, where a *mondop* contains the remains of four Buddha images *(see p173)*; two are in good condition, but of the other two, one is missing below the waist and the other has virtually disappeared. At Wat Chedi Si Hong, the base of the laterite brick *chedi* is lined with elephants and divinities.

Beyond the southern edge of the Historical Park loom the hills of **Ramkamhaeng National Park**. Covering 342 sq km (133 sq mile), this is home to serow, gaur, and wild pig.

🦌 **Ramkamhaeng National Park**
S of Sukhothai off Hwy 101.
Tel 0-5591-0000. 🛈 *Forestry Dept (0-2562-0760 inc bungalow bookings).* 📷 **www**.dnp.go.th

Farmer cultivating rice in the fields surrounding Sukhothai

Si Satchanalai-Chalieng Historical Park ❼

อุทยานประวัติศาสตร์ศรีสัชนาลัย-ชะเลียง

During the 13th century, the Sukhothai Kingdom consolidated its power in the Central Plains by building a number of satellite cities. The most important of these was Si Satchanalai. Today, its ruins lie on the right bank of the Yom River, 7 km (4 miles) south of modern Si Satchanalai. One of the best examples of a Thai *muang (see pp58–9)*, it was laid out along fixed cosmological lines – temple complexes lay at its heart, surrounded by city walls, rivers, and forest. It is considered by many historians to be the apogee of Thai city planning. The nearby ruins of Chalieng are thought to be an earlier Khmer settlement, an outpost of that empire dating from the time of Jayavarman VII (1181–1220). At the height of the Sukhothai Kingdom, Si Satchanalai was twinned with the city of Sukhothai. A royal road, the Phra Ruang, linked the two.

Laterite columns and central chedi at Wat Nang Phaya

The central, lotus-bud *chedi* of Wat Chedi Chet Thaeo

Exploring the Park

The ruins of Si Satchanalai are not as grandiose as those of Sukhothai but are in some ways more interesting. They have not been as extensively restored, and fewer tourists visit the site. The ruins evoke a once powerful city that, although not a seat of government of the Sukhothai Kingdom, was the city of the deputy king and an important commercial center in the 14th and 15th centuries. Its most important trade was in ceramics *(see pp160–61)*, for which it was renowned all over Southeast Asia and China.

Today, the ruins at Si Satchanalai cover an area of roughly 45 sq km (18 sq miles) and are surrounded by a moat 12 m (40 ft) wide. A good way to tour the site is by bicycle; there is a bicycle rental store located halfway between Si Satchanalai and Chalieng. Visitors can also ride around the ruined city

on the back of an elephant. An information center located in front of the Ram Narong Gate houses a small exhibition of artifacts found at the site and photographs of Si Satchanalai's many monuments.

The Main Wats

At the heart of the moated city a huge Sri Lankan-style, bell-shaped *chedi* forms the centerpiece of **Wat Chang Lom** *(see p200)*. To the south is **Wat Chedi Chet Thaeo**, around whose central lotus-bud *chedi* are many smaller ones in different styles, some containing stucco Buddha images. One of these *chedis* is a smaller version of the famous lotus-bud *chedi* at Wat Mahathat at Sukhothai *(see pp196–7)*.

At **Wat Nang Phaya**, the *wihan* is decorated with fine stucco reliefs from the Ayutthaya period, especially on the exterior. There is also a Sri Lankan-style, 15th–16th-century *chedi*. The *wihan's* grille-like windows here are

SRI LANKAN INFLUENCE

During the Sukhothai period, Theravada Buddhism, which had developed independently in Sri Lanka, arrived in Thailand. With it came Sri Lankan, bell-shaped *chedis*, reliquary towers symbolizing the ringing out of the teachings of the Buddha. The three-tiered base symbolizes hell, earth, and heaven; rings on the spire represent the 33 levels of heaven. A second layer of symbolism designates the base as the Buddha's folded robes, the *stupa* as his alms bowl and the spire as his staff. The entire *chedi* also symbolizes Mount Meru.

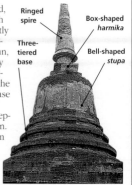

Ringed spire

Box-shaped *harmika*

Three-tiered base

Bell-shaped *stupa*

Sri Lankan-style *chedi* of Wat Suwan Khiri, overlooking Si Satchanalai

For hotels and restaurants in this region see pp403–4 and pp433–4

also characteristic of Ayutthaya, and less complete examples of this style can be seen elsewhere around the park. Nearby stands Wat Lak Muang, a small, Khmer-style shrine built as the city foundation shrine.

Minor Wats

On a low, wooded hill north of Wat Chang Lom stands Wat Khao Phnom Phloeng, once the site of ritual cremations. Also among the ruins are a seated Buddha, a *chedi*, and a number of columns that once supported a *wihan* roof.

On a hill top, farther west, all that remains of Wat Suwan Khiri is a single *chedi*, though there are great views from here of the rest of the city.

Beyond the City Walls

Farther west, on a mountain outside the city walls, is a row of ruined monasteries reached by a shady path. At the top of the path is the large, ruined *chedi* of Wat Khao Yai Bon.

There are many other minor ruins scattered inside and outside the moated site, and while some have been restored, others comprise little more than the base of a *wihan* or *chedi*. The *mondop* of Wat Hua Khon, for example, once contained seven stuccoed standing Buddha images; today only three are still plainly identifiable. North of the old Tao Mo Gate is Wat Kuti Rai.

There are two rectangular *mondops* here, both built entirely from laterite. Their pediments retain holes for beams, suggesting that they were once linked to other buildings. Inside one *mondop* is a seated Buddha image.

To the north are the kiln sites of Ban Pa Yuang and Ban Noi, where some of the finest Sangkhalok ceramics were produced. A sign of the times is that villagers nearby sell modern replicas to supplement their farming incomes.

Chalieng

Situated 1 km (1,090 yds) to the southeast is the settlement of Chalieng, predating the city of Si Satchanalai and in all likelihood built by the Khmers (*see pp264–5*) as a staging post for travelers. Some of the ruins that can be seen today date from later.

The laterite shrine of **Wat Chao Chan** was built in the Bayon style as a Mahayana Buddhist structure. The *wihan* and *mondop*, now ruins, were added later and reflect a move toward Theravada Buddhism.

Surrounded on three sides by a tight bend of the Yom River, the most important of the Chalieng sites is **Wat Phra Si Rattana Mahathat**, the buildings of which reflect a range of architectural styles from Sukhothai to Ayutthayan. The original Sukhothai lotus-

Ancient kiln site, north of the walled city at Ban Pa Yuang

bud *chedi* was built over with a huge Khmer-influenced, Ayutthayan *prang*, one of the finest structures of its type in Thailand. Nearby, a seated Buddha, sheltered under the head of a *naga*, sits inside a half *chedi*. Also close by are remains of stucco reliefs of walking Buddhas, said to be some of the very finest examples of Sukhothai sculpture.

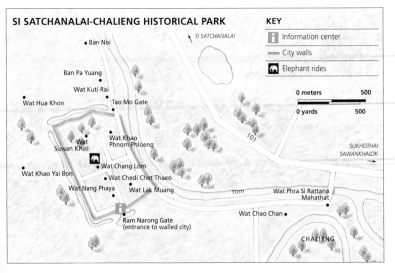

SI SATCHANALAI-CHALIENG HISTORICAL PARK

KEY

ℹ️	Information center
—	City walls
🐘	Elephant rides

0 meters 500
0 yards 500

- Ban Noi
- SI SATCHANALAI
- Ban Pa Yuang
- Wat Kuti Rai
- Wat Hua Khon
- Tao Mo Gate
- 101
- Wat Suwan Khiri
- Wat Khao Phnom Phloeng
- SUKHOTHAI SAWANKHALOK
- Wat Khao Yai Bon
- Wat Chang Lom
- Wat Chedi Chet Thaeo
- Wat Nang Phaya
- Wat Lak Muang
- Yom
- Wat Phra Si Rattana Mahathat
- Wat Chao Chan
- Ram Narong Gate (entrance to walled city)
- CHALIENG

Wat Chang Lom

วัดช้างล้อม

Built in the reign of Ramkamhaeng, this monument is thought to be the first Sri Lankan-style *chedi* of the Sukhothai Kingdom. The style was later copied throughout Si Satchanalai and Sukhothai.

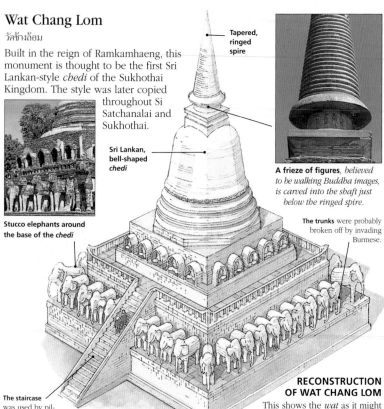

Tapered, ringed spire

Sri Lankan, bell-shaped *chedi*

Stucco elephants around the base of the *chedi*

A frieze of figures, *believed to be walking Buddha images, is carved into the shaft just below the ringed spire.*

The trunks were probably broken off by invading Burmese.

The staircase was used by pilgrims wishing to make the symbolic journey between earth and heaven.

RECONSTRUCTION OF WAT CHANG LOM

This shows the *wat* as it might have looked in the Sukhothai era. It stood in the center of Si Satchanalai.

Exploring Sawankhalok

With the introduction of new firing techniques by Chinese potters, the kilns around Si Satchanalai and Sukhothai became some of the most important producers of ceramics in Southeast Asia. At their most prolific, during the 14th–16th centuries, as the Sukhothai Kingdom came under the control of the Kingdom of Ayutthaya, it is thought that over 200 potteries lined the banks of the Yom River. They produced a variety of pottery termed Sangkhalok – a derivation of Sawankhalok, the name that was given to Si Satchanalai during the period of Ayutthaya's rule in the region. Today the name applies only to the small town

Sangkhalok pottery

of Sawankhalok, where the **Sawankha Woranayok National Museum** is located. This houses an expansive selection of Sangkhalok ceramics *(see pp160–61)*, which includes plates, storage jars, bowls, temple roof tiles, figures used in religious ceremonies, and everyday statues that may have been toys. A large number of the ceramics on display were salvaged from ships wrecked in the Gulf of Thailand on their way to trade with India, China, the Philippines, and Indonesia. The museum also contains a collection of religious sculptures taken from Sawankhalok's nearby Wat Sawankharam – many were donated to the *wat* by the villagers who unearthed them.

Exploring Si Satchanalai National Park

Founded in 1981, this park covers an area of 213 sq km (82 sq miles). Dotted around the park are the Tad Dao, Tad Duen, Huai Sai, and Huai Pa Cho waterfalls. The Tara Wasan and Kang Khao caves are also worth visiting. The park is good for bird-watching with more than 70 species recorded. Few large mammals inhabit the park, but there may be a small number of wild elephants living here.

🏛 **Sawankha Woranayok National Museum**
Sawankhalok, 17 km (11 miles) S of Si Satchanalai. ◯ Wed–Sun. 🏛

🌿 **Si Satchanalai National Park**
N of Si Satchanalai-Chalieng Historical Park, off Hwy 101, (0-2562-0760 or www.dnp.go.th for bungalow bookings). ◯ daily. 🏛

Green and ocher roof tiles at Wat Phra Si Rattana Mahathat, Phitsanulok

Phitsanulok ❽

พิษณุโลก

Phitsanulok province. 🏯 *183,000.*
✕ 🚌 🚍 ℹ️ *TAT, 209/7–8
Borommatrailokanat Rd, Phitsanulok
(0-5525-2743).* 🛶 *Wed, Sat.*
🎎 *Phra Buddha Chinarat (Jan/Feb),
Phitsanulok Boat Races (Oct).*

Many visitors pass
through this town
since it is an important
transport hub, con-
necting Bangkok and
the Central Plains to
Northern Thailand.

There has been a
settlement here from
as early as the mid-
14th century, when
**Wat Phra Si Rattana
Mahathat** was built on
the bank of the Nan River.
Initially, this *wat* complex,
also called Wat Yai, probably
housed a Sukhothai lotus-bud
chedi, which was later replaced by the tall Ayutthayan
prang that can be seen today.
It was built by the Ayutthayan
king Borommatrailokanat
(1448–88), who ruled from
Phitsanulok after 1463 in
order to wage a military campaign against the Kingdom
of Lanna *(see pp62–3).* The
golden tiles on the antefixes
of the *wat* were added during
a later renovation by King
Chulalongkorn (1868–1910).

Inside the west *wihan* is
the revered Buddha image
Phra Buddha Chinarat *(see
pp160–61)*, made of gilded
bronze and dating from the
14th century. It attracts pilgrims
from all over Thailand, and,
consequently, a small industry
of religious paraphernalia has

The Phra Buddha
Chinarat image

grown up around it. In the
gallery outside the *prang* are
dozens of Buddha images.
Across the road, in the *bot* of
Wat Ratchaburana, are some
faded 19th-century murals,
depicting scenes from the
Ramakien *(see pp40–41)*.

**Sergeant Major Thawee's
Folk Museum** houses a
collection of rural folk
crafts – wood and bam-
boo animal traps, farm
tools, and basketry.
Across the street is
the affiliated **Buddha
Foundry**, where
visitors can watch
bronze Buddha im-
ages being forged.

Environs
Five kilometers (3 miles)
south of Phitsanulok is the
Ayutthayan, laterite *prang* of
Wat Chulamani. It was built
by King Borommatrailokanat
in 1464, a year after he moved
his capital from Ayutthaya to
Phitsanulok. He was ordained
as a monk here in 1465 after

abdicating in favor of his son.
Eight months later he returned
to the throne; until his death
in 1488, he ruled Ayutthaya
from Phitsanulok.

🏠 **Sergeant Major Thawee's
Folk Museum**
26/43 Wisuth Kasat Rd. **Tel** 0-
5521-2749. 🕐 *Tue–Sun.* 📷
Buddha Foundry 🕐 *Mon–Sat.*

Thung Salaeng Luang National Park ❾

อุทยานแห่งชาติทุ่งแสลงหลวง

Phitsanulok province, Park HQ off
Hwy 12, 80 km (50 miles) E of
Phitsanulok. ℹ️ *TAT, Phitsanulok (0-
5525-2743); Forestry Dept (0-2562-
0760 or www.dnp.go.th for bungalow bookings).* 🚌 *from Phitsanulok
to Nakhon Thai, then songthaew.* 📷

With its open fields intersper-
sed with forest, this 1,262-sq
km (487-sq mile) park offers
good hiking and bird-watching.
Barking deer can also be
seen, and elephants are sometimes found at the salt licks.
The cascades of Kaeng Sopha
lie 9 km (6 miles) from the
park headquarters. Farther
west are the Poi falls and
smaller Kaeng Song rapids.

Environs
At **Khao Kho**, to the east,
is a rehabilitation project
for the Hmong, displaced
through involvement in anti-
Communist fighting in the
1970s–80s. The King takes
great interest in the program
and has a palace nearby.

The thinly forested Thung Salaeng Luang National Park

NORTHERN
THAILAND

INTRODUCING
NORTHERN THAILAND 204–211

NORTHWEST HEARTLAND 212–237

FAR NORTH 238–259

Introducing Northern Thailand

Northern Thailand, home of the ancient Lanna king-dom *(see pp62–3)*, offers a great diversity of activities. The old Lanna capitals of Chiang Mai and Chiang Rai are filled with ancient monuments and museums, and markets selling the distinctive local textiles and handicrafts. Smaller towns, such as Nan and Lamphun, offer a more low-key charm. Away from the main settle-ments, the scenery of Northern Thailand is stupendous: mountains, forests (some of them teak), rice fields set in verdant valleys and several spectacular national parks. The more adventurous visitor can join a trek to remote villages inhabited by hill tribes where elements of lifestyle have changed little in hundreds of years.

Mae Hong Son (see pp216–17), *a rapidly developing tourist center, is particularly popular with budget travelers. The town's main attraction is its beautiful mountain setting.*

Chiang Mai (see pp224–7) *is justly famed for its 300 temples, fine shopping, distinctive Northern cuisine, and (despite its size) relaxed pace of life.*

Mae Hong Son

Chiang Mai

NORTHWEST HEARTLAND
(see pp212–237)

Doi Inthanon National Park

Lampang

Doi Inthanon National Park (see pp230–31) *incorporates the highest mountain in Thai-land. Visitors come for the stun-ning scenery, including several waterfalls, and rich wildlife.*

Lampang (see pp234–7) *is a thriving town which hosts colorful festivals. It contains a number of important wats and a museum of Lanna artifacts.*

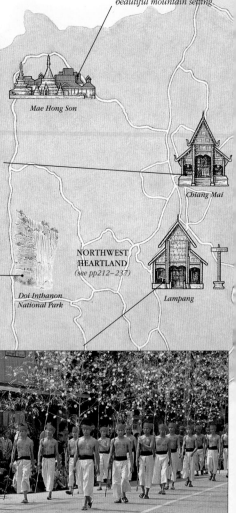

◁ The Elephant Training Center, southeast of the town of Chiang Dao

Doi Tung (see p243), *a mountain set in beautiful forested country, is crowned by an important pilgrimage site.*

Doi Tung

Chiang Rai

FAR NORTH
(see pp238–259)

Chiang Rai (see pp250–51) *has long dwelled in the shadow of nearby Chiang Mai, but is now rapidly developing into a significant tourist center in its own right. Its monuments may not be as numerous as those of Chiang Mai, but the city is an excellent source of hill-tribe handicrafts and a major starting point for trekkers.*

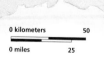

Nan

0 kilometers   50

0 miles   25

Nan (see pp254–5) *is a wealthy, sleepy town with several quirky wats, a good museum, and a spectacular mountain setting. Every October the Nan River is filled with colorful canoes taking part in the Lanna boat races.*

The Hill Tribes of Thailand

Ceremonial mask

There are six main groups of hill dwellers living in Northern Thailand: the Akha, Hmong, Lisu, Karen, Lahu, and Mien. These seminomadic peoples, some 500,000 in total, began to arrive here at the end of the 19th century, pushed out of their native Tibet, Myanmar, and China by civil war and political pressures. Though widely referred to as hill tribes, this label is rather general as each group has its own heritage, language, religion, and culture. The future of the hill tribes is uncertain. Traditionally, most use the slash-and-burn method (swiddening) to grow crops, abandoning land once it is exhausted. But competing pressures on land are drawing them into the Thai market economy. Many hill-tribe teenagers have moved to Chiang Mai to work in or set up craft workshops.

This 1890s portrait *is of Lahu women. Most hill tribes still wear traditional dress, though Western clothing is widely available.*

Bamboo sections are pounded rhythmically to honor leaders during the Swing Ceremony.

Young Lisu women *and girls wear black turbans adorned with multicolored threads, mainly for important celebrations such as New Year. Silver jewelry, sewn onto their clothes, is a display of the family's wealth.*

This Hmong house *has been accidentally destroyed by fire. To improve living conditions and economic opportunities, and to stop swiddening, the government aims to integrate hill tribes into the Thai way of life.*

FESTIVALS AND GATHERINGS
Colorful ceremonies mark rites of passage such as birth, death, and marriage. Here, the Akha gather for a festival.

New Year is the most important date *in the Lisu calendar. A tree is planted in front of each house in the village. A shaman and a priest then perform a ritual to cleanse the village of the past year's bad elements, while young people dance around the trees.*

In the past, *some hill tribes earned extra income from opium production. They are now encouraged to grow "new" crops such as cabbage.*

Akha houses *are characterized by a large porch connected to a square living area with a stove. They are usually constructed on high ground near the tribe's rice fields.*

Akha people *strive to maintain a traditional way of life, the "Akha Way." This is proving more difficult as fertile land disappears and animal numbers are depleted. Here, a villager carries out the vital chore of collecting wood.*

An ornate headdress, decorated with silver or, increasingly, aluminum, is worn by Akha women.

A sash, weighed down with coins and beads, distinguishes women from girls.

While many Lahu women *no longer wear traditional dress on a daily basis, they still weave distinctive shoulder bags* (yam) *from brightly colored fabrics.*

Mien clothing *is particularly distinctive. Women embroider colorful patterns onto black or indigo cloth and stitch red pompons onto caps worn by children.*

Karen *typically build houses in lowland valleys, cultivating by crop rotation rather than slash-and-burn. They are the largest and least nomadic tribe.*

SPIRITUAL BELIEFS

Many hill-tribe beliefs and practices are based on animism. Villages often have two religious leaders: a priest, who performs rituals and communes with the local guardian spirit, and a shaman, who has the power to consult directly with the spirit world. Rituals influence most decisions in a village, including where it is sited. But as tribes are drawn into modern life, traditional practices and medicine are coming under threat.

Mien tools used during shamanistic ceremonies

Northern Arts and Crafts

Pale green celadon bowl

Northern Thailand is famous for its handicrafts. The high quality of crafts produced today, such as wooden carvings, silverware, fabrics, ceramics, silk, and lacquerware, reflects centuries of Northern Thai, or Lanna, expertise. The region's ethnic minorities and hill tribes *(see pp206–7)* also produce distinctive embroidery, paintings, and silverware. Chiang Mai *(see pp224–7)* is the main crafts center, while villages such as Bo Sang and San Kamphaeng *(see pp228–9)* specialize in particular crafts. In factory-shops, visitors can watch crafts being made. Antiques and excellent copies are sold in outlets in Chiang Mai. Though teak logging has been strictly controlled in Thailand since 1989, wooden crafts produced from imported teak are still widely sold.

Ornate Akha *headdresses feature silver coins and hollow baubles that are expertly crafted by the men of the hill tribe.*

Animal figures, *intricately carved from wood (in many cases teak), often feature in Northern wats. Such wooden crafts are still produced throughout the North, despite the ban on unregulated teak logging.*

Northern lacquerwork *typically consists of a red lacquer-coated wood or bamboo base decorated with a yellow pattern. This is a 19th- or 20th-century box.*

Curved legs were designed to fit over the back of the elephant, near its head.

ROYAL HOWDAH

Before the advent of the car, elephants were used for transportation in Thailand. People sat in howdahs, or elephant chairs, on the elephants' backs. Howdahs stood some 1.5 m (5 ft) high, and their decoration revealed their passengers' status. The most basic form consisted of a seat with raised sides. Howdahs used for transporting royalty and aristocrats, such as this one from Northern Thailand, featured ornate wood carving and usually had a roof.

Umbrellas are the main craft items *produced in Bo Sang. They are made of lacquered paper, stretched over a bamboo frame, then painted with traditional motifs such as elephants.*

Betel sets *consist of several containers used to hold the ingredients for betel-chewing (a popular activity in Southeast Asia) – betel leaf, limestone ash, and the narcotic areca palm fruit. A gold set was a sign of status.*

A roof made from lacquered woven bamboo offered shelter from the heat.

Wooden roof brackets, *seen on religious buildings, are for decoration rather than support. They often depict* nagas *(serpents) and other animals.*

Silver ceremonial *jewelry is worn for village festivals and other important occasions. While hill tribes still use old silver, melted down from Indian and Burmese coins, many Thai silversmiths in Chiang Mai nowadays rely on imported silver of a lower quality.*

Handles were used for support during bumpy rides. Royal elephant seats were more comfortable than ordinary ones.

Delicately fashioned wood carving featured only on elephant chairs used by affluent members of society.

In Thailand *even everyday items are decorated, such as this wooden clapper, which is painted with a flower motif. A clapper is traditionally worn by water buffalo so they can be located if they stray.*

TEXTILES OF NORTHERN THAILAND

Embroidering a striped Lahu bag

Textile production in Northern Thailand dates from the early Lanna period, and the region is known for its silk and cotton. Chiang Mai and San Kamphaeng are centers for silk clothing – also made in the Northeast *(see pp266–7)* – including the traditional *pha sin* (woman's sarong). Outlets also sell furnishings and cottonware produced in Pasang *(see p229)* such as the *pha koma* (man's sarong). Chiang Khong factory-shops produce Thai Lue cotton fabrics in stunning colors *(see p249)*, while hill tribes make and sell brightly patterned fabrics. Most textiles can be bought as lengths or as ready-made items.

A traditional cotton design

A 19th-century *pha sin*

Birds of Northern Thailand

Northern Thailand lies on the Eastern Asia Flyway, a major flight path for migrating birds. Thailand boasts some ten percent of the world's bird species, 380 of which have been recorded in the hills around Chiang Mai. Most of these are migratory birds that have flown south in winter to the warmer climes of Thailand's forested hills. Steps have been introduced to protect bird habitats under threat from deforestation. But many sites in the north, especially Doi Suthep *(see pp222–3)* and Doi Inthanon *(see pp230–31)* national parks, still provide a habitat for numerous bird species.

SELECTED MIGRATION ROUTES

— Arctic warblers

— Siberian rubythroats

— Herons

Changeable hawk-eagle

The red-breasted parakeet, of deciduous woodlands, is threatened by the illegal trade in birds.

Black-crowned night-herons *are nocturnal birds. They have a black crest, nape, and back, whitish underparts, and gray wings. Resident in various countries, they migrate to low altitudes in Northern Thailand.*

Red-wattled lapwings, *named for the red patch of skin in front of the eye, reside near streams and in open forest. When alarmed they emit a loud, shrill call.*

Teak tree

Silver pheasants *live at various altitudes, typically over 700 m (2,300 ft). Their red feet and long tail distinguish them from other types of pheasants. They are also bred in captivity to be sold for food – because of their depleted numbers, pheasants are protected.*

Pheasant-tailed jacanas *have long legs, toes, and claws that enable them to walk on leaves in lowland rivers, foraging for food.*

Purple herons are wetland birds that can be seen near forest streams. They have a slender, rufous (red-brown) neck.

0–500 M (0–1,640 FT) ABOVE SEA LEVEL

Coral-billed ground-cuckoos are difficult to observe because they are rare, shy birds.

Long-tailed broadbills, *so called for their short heavy bill and long tail (unique in broadbills), live at high altitudes in Northern Thailand. They feed on insects, probing for them in trees or catching them while in flight.*

Asian paradise flycatchers *can be resident or migratory, nesting on upper slopes. The females and immature males have a brown body and a black head. Fully developed males are more stunning in color, with a white tail and a blue beak.*

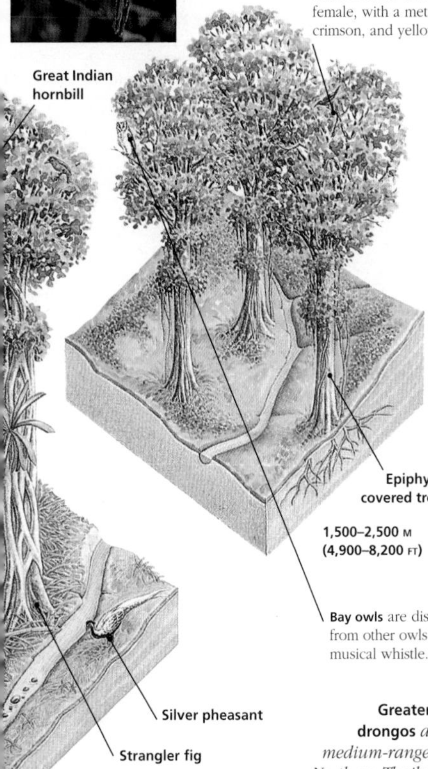

Gould's sunbirds live at high altitudes. The male is far more colorful than the female, with a metallic blue, crimson, and yellow body.

Great Indian hornbill

Siberian rubythroats *migrate to the upper slopes of Northern Thailand's evergreen forests. The characteristic red patch on the throat is present only in the male.*

Epiphyte-covered trees

1,500–2,500 M
(4,900–8,200 FT)

Bay owls are distinguished from other owls by a loud, musical whistle.

Silver pheasant

Strangler fig

500–1,500 M
(1,640–4,900 FT)

Greater racket-tailed drongos *are resident at medium-range elevations in Northern Thailand. They feed almost entirely on insects, flying out repeatedly from the same branch, often in small groups. Their long tails are tipped with a vane or "racket" that ripples as the bird flies.*

BIRD HABITATS AT DIFFERENT ALTITUDES

Deciduous dipterocarp trees clothe the foothills of Northern Thailand. Here, teak forests provide a habitat for kalij pheasants, wagtails, and parakeets, and migratory wetland birds such as herons. Higher up the slopes, bazas, hornbills, hill mynas, and shikes are drawn to mixed evergreen and deciduous forests. Oaks and epiphytic plants, such as ferns, thrive on the hilltops, where arctic warblers, owls, and other small birds live.

TIPS FOR BIRD-WATCHING

• The best time to see birds is during the "winter" months, from January to April, when resident birds are mating and most migratory species arrive. Avoid the wet season (June–October), when heavy rain and leeches can be a problem.
• National park headquarters provide leaflets detailing bird-watching trails. Guided trips can often be arranged.
• Take binoculars, plenty of water, insect repellent, and a compass. Try to wear dark green or inconspicuous clothing.
• Many birds are shy, so be patient. Walk quietly to avoid rustling leaves, and do not walk straight toward the bird.

NORTHWEST HEARTLAND

Northwest Thailand is the heartland of Lanna Thai. The ancient city of Chiang Mai, famed for its many fine temples and handicrafts, is the focal point for visitors. This and smaller towns are set in verdant valleys among thickly forested mountains. The Northwest is also home to a number of ethnic minorities, and the rich mix of diverse cultures and scenery is most enticing.

Chiang Mai, superbly sited in the Ping River Valley, was once the capital of the Lanna Kingdom. In the 12th–18th centuries this kingdom, strongly influenced by Burma (now Myanmar), ruled over what is now northern Thailand, and local Thais remain proud of their Lanna heritage. Indeed, the silverwork, woodcarving, pottery, and other crafts of the North are regarded by many as the most exquisite in Thailand. Nowhere in the country are crafts more readily available than in Chiang Mai and its environs.

Chiang Mai is also a useful base from which to explore the mountains and villages. Trekking to hill-tribe villages is a popular, though controversial, activity. Although most trekkers are genuinely interested in hill-tribe culture, there is a danger that villages will become dependent on tourism and that traditional ways of life will be lost forever.

In the west, close to the Myanmar border, the remote towns of Mae Hong Son and Mae Sariang are in some ways more Myanmar than Thai. The *wats*, for instance, have multiroofed *chedis* reminiscent of Myanmar temples. North of Chiang Mai, the streets of Chiang Dao are lined with two-story teak buildings, a reminder that the surrounding countryside was once rich in teak forests. To the south of Chiang Mai, Lanna influence can again be seen in temples and museum artifacts within the cities of Lampang and Lamphun. The latter also has surviving traces of the older Kingdom of Haripunchai.

Thailand's highest mountain, Doi Inthanon, lies west of Chiang Mai, within a national park with good facilities. Here can be seen dramatic waterfalls and a wide range of wildlife, including hundreds of migratory birds.

Boy lighting a candle at Wat Phra That Lampang Luang, one of several major *wats* in the Northwest

◁ Woman cleaning umbrellas in the handicraft village of Bo Sang, near Chiang Mai

Exploring the Northwest Heartland

The Northwest Heartland is a geographically spectacular region. Towering mountains, many with densely forested slopes, stretch to the Myanmar (Burma) border and contrast with the gentler scenery of the Ping and Taeng River valleys. Trekking in this beautiful landscape, with its wealth of wildlife and fascinating hill-tribe villages, is a major activity in the Northwest Heartland. Cultural attractions are also plentiful, including the ancient temples of Chiang Mai, Lamphun, and Lampang, and the unmissable Wat Phra That Lampang Luang.

SIGHTS AT A GLANCE

Bo Sang **13**
Chiang Mai pp224–7 **11**
Doi Chiang Dao **7**
Doi Inthanon National Park pp230–31 **16**
Doi Saket **12**
Doi Suthep pp222–3 **10**
Lampang **20**
Lamphun **15**
Mae Aw **4**
Mae Hong Son pp216–17 **1**
Mae Sariang **18**
Mae Surin National Park **2**
Mae Taeng Valley **9**
Pai **6**
Phrao **8**
Ping River Valley **17**
San Kamphaeng **14**
Soppong **5**
Thai Elephant Conservation Center **21**
Tham Pla **3**
Uttaradit **22**
Wat Phra That Lampang Luang pp234–5 **19**

Vachirathan Waterfall, Doi Inthanon National Park

SEE ALSO

• *Where to Stay* pp404–7

• *Where to Eat* pp434–7

For additional map symbols *see back flap*

Fang
109
Pang Makham
Pom
107
Na Wai
1150
Wiang Pa
Pao
7 DOI CHIANG
DAO
8 PHRAO
Chiang Dao
1001
9 MAE TAENG VALLEY
Mae Taeng
Luang
Chiang
Rai
118
DOI
HEP
10
12 DOI SAKET
San Kamphaeng
Hot Springs
11
13 BO SANG
NG MAI
14 SAN KAMPHAENG
1147
15 LAMPHUN
Pasang
Chiang
Rai
11
21 THAI ELEPHANT
CONSERVATION CENTER
n Hong
Hang Chat
20 LAMPANG
WAT PHRA THAT
LAMPANG LUANG **19**
Kor Kha
Som Ngam
11
Phrae
Mae Tun
Thung Hua
Chang
Den Chai
Dong Ya Thao
Li
Sop Prap
101
106
Thoen
11
UTTARADIT **22**
Sukhothai
ing
nal
k
Wang
Bhumibol
Reservoir
1
Sam Ngao
Ping
75
Tak

Elaborately decorated pillars inside the *bot* of
Chiang Mai's Wat Chiang Man

GETTING AROUND
The highways around Chiang Mai are well
maintained, and most other roads in this
area are reasonable. Lampang and Mae
Hong Son have domestic airports, and
there is an international airport at Chiang
Mai, the main transportation hub. Many
trains and buses run each day between
Chiang Mai and Bangkok (11–13 hours
by train, via Uttaradit and Lampang;
about ten hours by bus). Frequent
local bus services link most
towns and villages in the
region. Isolated sights are
best reached by *song-
thaew*, and guided
treks and organized
tours are a good
way of seeing
larger areas.

KEY
— Major road
---- Minor road
— Scenic route
---- Railway
▬▬ International border
△ Summit

Elephants at the Thai Elephant Conservation Center

Street-by-Street: Mae Hong Son ❶
แม่ฮ่องสอน

Beautifully located in a valley ringed by forested mountains, Mae Hong Son sprang up in 1831 from a small camp where elephants were tethered. The town was largely isolated until it was linked by a paved highway to Chiang Mai in 1965. The province has traditionally been dominated by nearby Myanmar (Burma), as shown by its architecture. Shan and Karen people, who make up most of the population, continue to move across the border to live in Mae Hong Son and its environs. Today, the tranquil town is growing as a resort and trekking center. In the cool season, you may need to wear a sweater or jacket here.

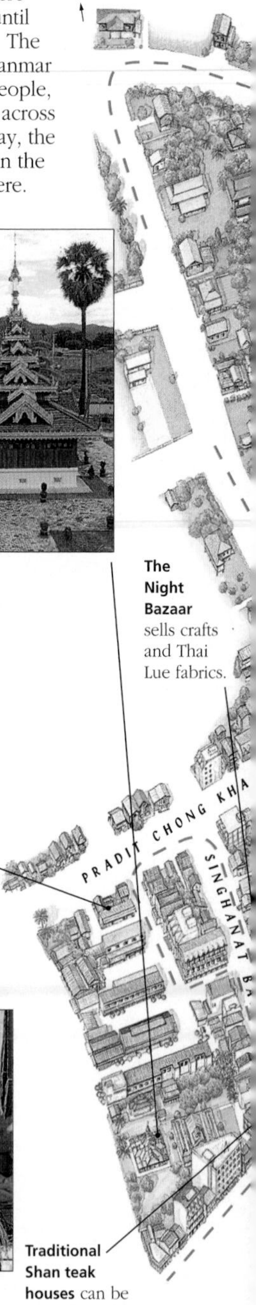

To Airport

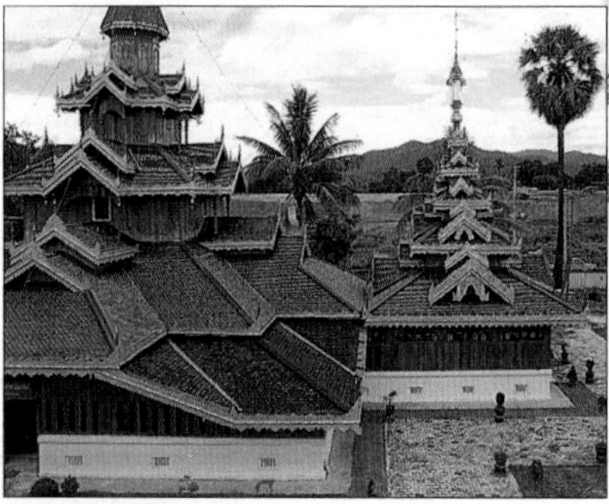

★ **Wat Hua Wiang**
This teak temple has a Myanmar-style, multi-roofed design. The bot – *in an advanced state of decay – houses an important brass image of Buddha, Phrachao Para La 'Khaeng, that was transported here from Myanmar.*

The Night Bazaar sells crafts and Thai Lue fabrics.

PRADIT CHONG KHA

SINGHANAT BA

Daily Market
This lively, pungent market, which almost spills onto the airport runway, sells a range of fresh produce, Myanmar textiles, and trekking supplies. Local hill tribes are often seen here.

THE PADAUNG WOMEN

Many tours from Mae Hong Son visit the "long-neck women" of the area. These women, of the Padaung, or Kayan, tribe, are distinguished by their long necks, lengthened from childhood by brass rings. Among the explanations for this old practice are that it protects the women from tiger attacks and that it enhances their looks. The practice began to die out until the Padaung realized tourists would pay to see the women. Some organizations condemn such visits.

"Long-neck women" of the Padaung tribe

Traditional Shan teak houses can be seen along this street.

Chong Kham Lake
This lake, which was originally a bathing pool for elephants, can be especially stunning in the early-morning mists that enshroud the town.

VISITORS' CHECKLIST

Mae Hong Son province. 48,000. ✈ 1 km (1,100 yds) NW of Chong Kham Lake. 🚌 Khumlum Phraphat Rd. 🅸 TAT, Mae Hong Son (0-5361-2982-3); SinghanatBamrungRd(0-5361-1952). 🚌 early–9am daily. 🎎 Poi Sang Long Festival (late Mar/early Apr); Chong Para Festival (Oct). **www**.travelmaehongson.org

★ Wat Chong Kham
Wat Chong Kham (c.1827), which was built by the Shan, features a multi-roofed chedi. The wat houses a revered 5-m (16-ft) seated Buddha image.

CHAMNANSATIT

Post office

Fitness park

Wat Doi Kong Mu, on a hill top to the west of town, has superb views of the town and area.

To Wat Doi Kong Mu

M PHRAPHAT

★ Wat Chong Klang
Built in the late 19th century, this temple has distinctive white and gold chedis. Painted glass panels depicting the jataka tales (see p30) can be seen on request.

0 meters	25
0 yards	25

KEY

– – – Suggested route

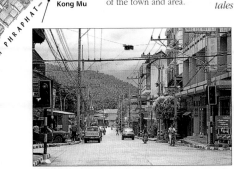

Khumlum Phraphat Road
Craft shops, restaurants, and tour companies line Mae Hong Son's main street. Hill-tribe textiles and antiques are among the items for sale.

STAR SIGHTS

★ Wat Hua Wiang

★ Wat Chong Kham

★ Wat Chong Klang

The spectacular Mae Surin waterfall in Mae Surin National Park

Mae Surin National Park ②

อุทยานแห่งชาติน้ำตกแม่สุรินทร์

Mae Hong Son province. Park HQ 2.5 km (2 miles) off Hwy 108, 8 km (5 miles) N of Mae Hong Son. 🛈 TAT, Mae Hong Son (0-5361-2982-3); Forestry Dept (0-2562-0760 or **www**.dnp.go.th for bungalow bookings). 🚌 from Khun Yuam then songthaew. ⬜ daily. 📷

This small park is the highlight of the area south of Mae Hong Son. Much of its lowland forest provides a habitat for the Malaysian sun bear, Asiatic black bear, and barking deer. Bird species include drongos and hornbills.

Mae Surin waterfall, which at 100 m (330 ft) is one of the highest in Thailand, is reached from the Khun Yuam district. on a dirt road. Also accessible from this road is Thung Bua Thong ("wild sunflower meadow"), which blooms in November and December.

Raft trips along the Pai River, which flows through the park, can be arranged at guesthouses in Mae Hong Son and Pai.

Tham Pla ③

ถ้ำปลา

Mae Hong Son province. Off Hwy 1095, 17 km (11 miles) N of Mae Hong Son. 🛈 TAT, Chiang Mai (0-5324-8604). 🚌 Mae Hong Son, then songthaew, or join tour. 📷

Located north of Mae Hong Son, this scenic spot can be visited on a day trip from the town. Tham Pla ("fish cave") is actually a pool and stream at the base of a limestone outcrop, so named because of the huge carp that live in it.

Visitors make merit by buying papaya to feed to the fish. The peaceful surrounding gardens are perhaps the site's most attractive feature.

Mae Aw ④

แม่ออ

Mae Hong Son province. 🚶 7,000. 🚐 Mae Hong Son, then songthaew, or join tour. 🛈 TAT, Mae Hong Son (0-5361-2982-3). 🚌 daily.

Situated in the mountains near the Myanmar border, Mae Aw is a remote settlement built by members of the Kuomintang, or KMT (see p242). Apart from superb views, the village offers an intriguing insight into life in an isolated border village. But fighting still sometimes breaks out between rival factions over control of the local opium trade, following the overthrow of Khun Sa (see p233) in 1996.

The best way to get to Mae Aw is with a tour from Mae Hong Son or by jeep. Before you come, check with the local tourist information office that there is no fighting in the area.

Soppong ⑤

สบปอง

Mae Hong Son province. 🚶 15,000. 🚐 from Mae Hong Son. 🛈 TAT, Mae Hong Son (0-5361-2982-3). 🚌 daily.

The village of Soppong (sometimes called Pang Mapha on local maps) is perched 700 m (2,200 ft) up in the mountains. With its fine views, surrounding teak forests, and air of

Highway 1095 as it passes through Soppong

Muslim children in Pai, part of the town's mixed community

Pai ⑥
ปาย

Mae Hong Son province. 🏠 27,000. 🚌 from Mae Hong Son. ℹ TAT, Mae Hong Son (0-5361-2982-3). 🏛 daily.

Set in a beautiful valley, the town of Pai has become one of the region's most popular destinations. Although still very much a haven for backpackers, Pai is increasingly attracting larger resorts. Halfway between Chiang Mai and Mae Hong Son, the old Shan settlement is home to several hill tribes and is renowned for trekking and rafting.

The yellow and white tiles and multilayered roofs of **Wat Klang**, between the bus station and the Pai River, are typical of Shan temples. The hilltop **Wat Phra That Mae Yen**, just east of Pai, was also built by the Shan. The carved wooden doors of the main *wihan* depict scenes from nature and human life. The temple has sweeping views of the valley.

Guided treks of the area *(see p221)* can be arranged at many guesthouses in town.

tranquility, Soppong is becoming an increasingly popular resort. Many trekkers pass through here on the way to visit local hill-tribe villages populated by Lisu and Shan (a minority originally from Myanmar). The village itself has a thriving market where local tribespeople congregate daily.

Environs
Tham Lot, north of Soppong, is one of the largest cave systems in Southeast Asia. The three adjoining caverns form a vast subterranean canyon, which is cut through by a large stream. The distinctive stalactites and stalagmites are especially impressive. The discovery of artifacts and huge carved teak coffins indicates that the caves were inhabited thousands of years ago. Visitors may cross the stream by raft or by elephant. Guided visits can be arranged at local guesthouses.

🏞 Tham Lot
8 km (5 miles) N of Soppong, Mae Hong Son province. ◯ daily. 🔦 (for guide and lantern).

THAILAND'S ENDANGERED WILDLIFE

With its diversity of landscapes, Thailand is an ideal habitat for a vast range of flora and fauna. In the 20th century, however, poaching and deforestation led to the extinction of many species, including the kouprey (a type of wild cattle) and Schomburgk's deer. Some animals are caught for food; some, including gibbons, are sold as pets, while others, like snakes, are killed through fear. Of Thailand's 282 mammal species, about 40 are endangered, and while laws exist to protect these animals, they are not always enforced. Almost all of Thailand's large mammals are in danger of extinction, and many others, including the white-handed gibbon, are, at best, rare. This alarming state of affairs is not confined to mammals: ten percent of the country's 405 reptiles and amphibians are also endangered.

Rock python – its favored forest habitat is rapidly disappearing

A rare white-handed gibbon

TIGERS IN THAILAND
The increasing demand for dried tiger parts in traditional Chinese medicines has led to the worldwide demise of this great creature. Of the few thousand tigers that remain in Asia, about 500 are estimated to be living in Thailand, particularly in the Khao Yai National Park *(see pp184–5)*. In 1995 the Royal Forest Department established a conservation project to try to prevent the tiger from dying out altogether in Thailand.

Pavilions and carp-filled pool in front of Tham Chiang Dao

Doi Chiang Dao **⑦**

ดอยเชียงดาว

12 km (7.5 miles) W of Chiang Dao, Chiang Mai province. **⚑** TAT, Chiang Mai (0-5324-8604). **🚌** from Chiang Mai to Chiang Dao, then songthaew. **www**.chiangmai-thai.com/TAT.htm

At 2,195 m (7,200 ft), this is the third-largest mountain in Thailand. Home to several Lisu and Karen villages, Doi Chiang Dao features both tropical and pine forests. Today, this peak and the surrounding area, characterized by rugged limestone scenery and dense teak forest, are more of an attraction than the nearby town, Chiang Dao.

Running for some 14 km (8.5 miles) under the mountain is a network of caves, **Tham Chiang Dao**, best reached from Chiang Dao town. Most of the caves house statues of the Buddha that, over the years, have been left

by Shan pilgrims from Myanmar. The highlight of the bat-inhabited caves, however, is their huge stalactites and stalagmites. Lanterns and guides can be hired in order to make the most of these impressive features. The tours take visitors along an illuminated walkway through the caves.

Near the caves is a temple, **Wat Tham Chiang Dao**, with a Buddhist meditation center and a small room displaying gongs and other instruments. Beyond a huge tamarind tree, by a pond, is an old Myanmar-style *chedi*. Nearby, a small market offers a wide selection of locally gathered forest roots, herbs, and spices.

East of Doi Chiang Dao, and dominated by the peak, is **Chiang Dao town**, with its traditional teak buildings along the main street. It was founded in the 18th century as a place

Façade of Wat Tham Chiang Dao, near Doi Chiang Dao

of exile for *phi pop*, ("spirit people"), who were suspected of being possessed by evil spirits. In fact, the symptoms of their true illnesses, such as malaria, had been mistaken as signs of madness.

The **Elephant Training Center Chiang Dao**, southeast of Chiang Dao, is located in a wooded area beside a stream. The daily displays feature elephants bathing, and lifting and dragging logs. Elephant rides may also be taken.

Tham Tup Tao, 48 km (30 miles) north of Chiang Dao, are two large caverns. Tham Pha Kao ("light cave") houses two large Buddha images and a stalagmite carved in the shape of a group of elephants. Inside Tham Pha Chak ("dark cave"), which can be explored only by lantern, is a bat colony.

🜨 Tham Chiang Dao
Off Hwy 107, 5 km (3 miles) NW of Chiang Dao. ⬜ daily. 🎫 🎥

🏛 Elephant Training Center Chiang Dao
E of Hwy 107, 15 km (9.5 miles) SE of Chiang Dao, Chiang Mai province. **Tel** 0-5329-8553. ⬜ daily (displays 9–10am and 10–11am). 🎫 **www**.chiangdaoelephantcamp.com

🜨 Tham Tup Tao
W of Hwy 107, Chiang Mai province. ⬜ daily. 🎫 🎥

Phrao **⑧**

พร้าว

Chiang Mai province. 👥 46,000. 🚌 from Chiang Mai. **⚑** TAT, Chiang Mai (0-5324-8604). 🏠 daily.

This small market town is a meeting place for Thai traders and hill-tribe people. Phrao was previously relatively isolated, but today Highway 1150 connects it with Wiang Pa Pao *(see p252)*, making it more accessible. Phrao is still off the main tourist track. The town's principal sight is its covered market, which sells traditional textiles and locally grown fruit and vegetables.

Environs
Heading east toward Wiang Pa Pao, Highway 1150 runs through spectacular forest scenery. Several Lisu and Hmong hill-tribe villages can be seen.

ORCHIDS IN THAILAND

Seen on logos throughout Thailand, the orchid is the country's most famous flower. There are over 1,300 varieties of wild orchid in Thailand, most of which are dependent on forests. But while their natural habitat is threatened by deforestation, millions are being cultivated for export to overseas markets.

A pink orchid, one of the most popular colors for the overseas markets

Export began in the 1950s, and burgeoned in the 1980s when the first orchid farms were established. In 1991 the value of exports peaked at about $80 million. Since then, as consumer trends have changed in important markets such as Japan, this figure has started to decline.

A leisurely rafting trip along the Taeng River

Mae Taeng Valley ⑨

แม่แตง

Chiang Mai province. 🚌 🚐 *Chiang Mai, then songthaew.* 🛈 *TAT, Chiang Mai (0-5324-8604).*

The area around Mae Taeng, especially the vicinity of the Taeng River to the northwest of the town, is very popular with trekkers. The land has been terraced and irrigated to improve agricultural production, and the variety of crops grown has created an attractive contrast of landscapes. However, most trekkers come here not only for the peaceful surroundings but also to witness everyday scenes in the region's many Lisu, Karen, and Hmong villages. Other activities, including river rafting and elephant rides, can be combined with treks in the area. Established in 1995, the **Elephant Nature Park**, in the beautiful Mae Taeng Valley, is home to dozens of rescued elephants. Founder Lek Chailert's efforts to save the endangered Asian elephant have received praise and awards from around the world. The center welcomes volunteer workers.

🐘 **Elephant Nature Park**
10 km (6 miles) W of Hwy 107. **Tel** *0-5327-2855.* ◯ *daily.* 🖳 www. elephantnaturefoundation.org

Hmong women, wearing their distinctive woven textiles

Tourists enjoying an elephant ride, Chiang Dao

TREKKING AROUND CHIANG DAO

Northern Thailand is renowned for its trekking *(see p464)*. Treks in the area around Chiang Dao and Mae Taeng often combine visits to hill-tribe villages with an elephant ride or raft trip through the stunning scenery. Most three-day treks from Chiang Mai, which can be arranged by guesthouses or trekking companies in the city, incorporate this area. Among the region's interesting towns are Mae Taeng, Phrao, and Chiang Dao, all of which have long been at the interface between the Thai-dominated lowlands and the uplands, where the hill tribes live. It is vital to trek with a guide who is familiar with the area and hill-tribe etiquette. Typical routes, lasting two to three days, are marked below.

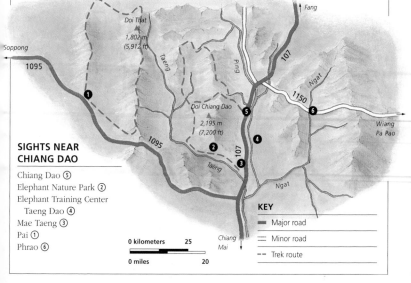

SIGHTS NEAR CHIANG DAO

Chiang Dao ⑤
Elephant Nature Park ②
Elephant Training Center
    Taeng Dao ④
Mae Taeng ③
Pai ①
Phrao ⑥

↑ Fang

Doi Thai
1,802 m
(5,912 ft)

Soppong ←

1095

Taeng

Ping

107

Ngat

1150

Doi Chiang Dao
2,195 m
(7,200 ft)

⑤

⑥

Wiang
Pa Pao

1095

②

④

107

③

Taeng

Ngat

0 kilometers   25

0 miles   20

Chiang
Mai ↓

KEY

━━ Major road

═ Minor road

-- Trek route

Doi Suthep ❿

ดอยสุเทพ

Doi Suthep is a much-visited, thickly forested mountain in the twin-peaked Doi Suthep-Doi Pui National Park. Near its 1,601-m (5,250-ft) summit is Wat Phra That Doi Suthep, one of the most revered Buddhist shrines in Northern Thailand. The mountain is also popular with birdwatchers and trekkers. From Chiang Mai, a paved road snakes up the hillside to a village with restaurants and souvenir shops. From here, there is a choice of a steep climb or the funicular to the *wat*. Minor attractions on Doi Suthep include waterfalls, a Hmong village, and, farther along the road, the English-style gardens of Phuping Palace.

Buddha image by *chedi*

Murals in Cloister
The murals depict scenes from the Buddha's life

★ Central Chedi
This striking gold-plated Lanna structure is a 16th-century extension of the original. The four multi-tiered gold umbrellas around it, onto which pilgrims apply gold leaf (see p30), are adorned with intricate filigree.

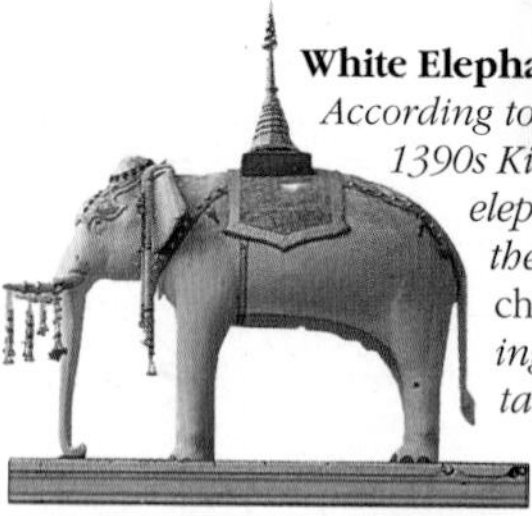

White Elephant Monument
According to legend, in the 1390s King Ku Na's elephant selected the site of the chedi by marching up the mountain, trumpeting and turning three times.

WAT DOI SUTHEP
Enshrining sacred relics, the *wat* at the top of Doi Suthep, founded in the 14th century, is regarded by many as the symbol of Lanna Thailand (*see pp62–3*).

Naga Staircase
Flanked by nagas, this sweeping staircase has 304 steps. The less energetic can take the funicular up to the temple.

STAR FEATURES

★ Central Chedi

★ Panoramic Views

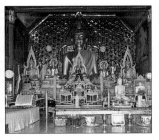

Buddha Images in the Main Wihan
The gold Buddha images in the 16th-century wihan *are the most important within the temple complex. The huge image in the back is surrounded by several smaller ones.*

VISITORS' CHECKLIST

16 km (10 miles) NW of Chiang Mai, Chiang Mai province. *TAT, Chiang Mai (0-5324-8604); Forestry Dept (0-2562-0760 or* **www.**dnp.go.th *for bungalows).* *Chiang Mai then* songthaew. **Wat Doi Suthep** *5:30am–7:30pm daily.* **www.**doisuthep.com **Palace Gardens** *8:30–11:30am & 1–3:30pm Mon–Fri.* **Phuping Palace** *to public.*

Library
Funicular

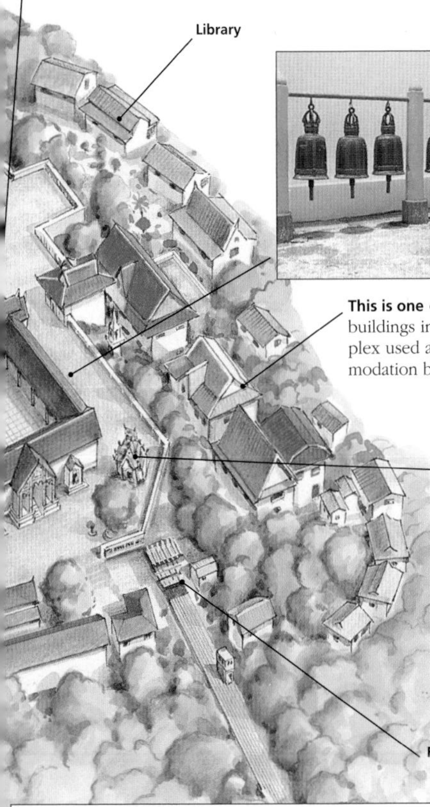

Temple Bells
The original use of these small bells was to call the monks and the people to worship. Today, there is a constant tinkling from visitors ringing them for good luck.

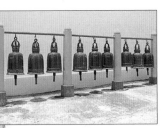

This is one of several buildings in the complex used as accommodation by monks.

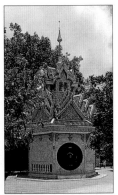

Bell Tower
This decorative bell tower, near the steps up to the main wihan, *is distinctive for its multicolored, layered roof.*

WILDLIFE AROUND WAT DOI SUTHEP

Black-collared starling, a resident of the park

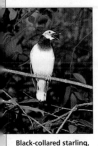

With its rich and varied wildlife, Doi Suthep-Doi Pui National Park is a great attraction for nature lovers. Despite the deforestation of the western side of the park due to agriculture and the building of tourist accommodations, the park is rich in plants, butterflies, and birds such as the green cochoa. Though people have killed or driven out many indigenous mammals, 60 species still live here, including the Burmese ferret badger.

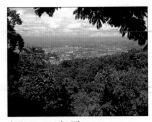

★ Panoramic Views
From the edge of the temple complex there are breathtaking views of the forests of Doi Suthep-Doi Pui National Park and of Chiang Mai city, situated to the southeast.

Street-by-Street: Chiang Mai ⓫

เชียงใหม่

Typical Chiang Mai lantern

Thailand's second most important city, Chiang Mai (literally, "new city"), was chosen in 1292 by King Mengrai to replace Chiang Rai *(see pp250–51)* as the capital of his Lanna Kingdom *(see pp62–3)*. Under Mengrai, Chiang Mai became a major base for Theravada Buddhism. It was during this period and the subsequent reign of King Tilok that many fine *wats* were built within the walled city, which is still the most atmospheric area. To-day, visitors are increasingly drawn to Chiang Mai not only for its beautiful temples, but also for its excellent shopping and trekking facilities and upscale hotels and restaurants.

To Suan Dok Gate

Mengrai Kilns *(see p453)* sells a wide range of ceramics.

To Mengrai Kilns

SAMLAN

SOI 7

Old Chiang Mai
The first bridge across the Ping River was built in 1950. Others were later added to cope with the city's growth.

Wat Muen Ngon Kong
This wat has exquisite lattice-work and a Lanna chedi topped by a Burmese finial.

Wat Phra Chao Mengrai has a decorated ceremonial gate.

KEY

— — — Suggested route

STAR SIGHTS

★ Wat Phra Sing

★ Wat Chedi Luang

Wat Phan Waen
A typical Northern Thai temple, Wat Pan Waen is set within peaceful com-pounds, which provide relief from the city heat. The doors of the wihan are decorated with religious images.

★ Wat Phra Sing
This wat *was built in 1345 to house King Kham Fu's ashes. The Wihan Lai Kham is a superb Lanna structure with carved and gilded pediments. Murals inside depict everyday life in 19th-century Chiang Mai.*

VISITORS' CHECKLIST

Chiang Mai province. 84,000. 3 km (2 miles) SW of Chiang Mai. Charoen Muang Rd. Chiang Mai Arcade. TAT, 105/1 Chiang Mai–Lamphun Rd (0-5324-8604). main office: same address as TAT (0-5324-8974). daily. Bo Sang Festival (Jan), Flower Festival (Feb), Songkran (mid-Apr), Intakin Festival (May), Yi Peng Festival (Nov).

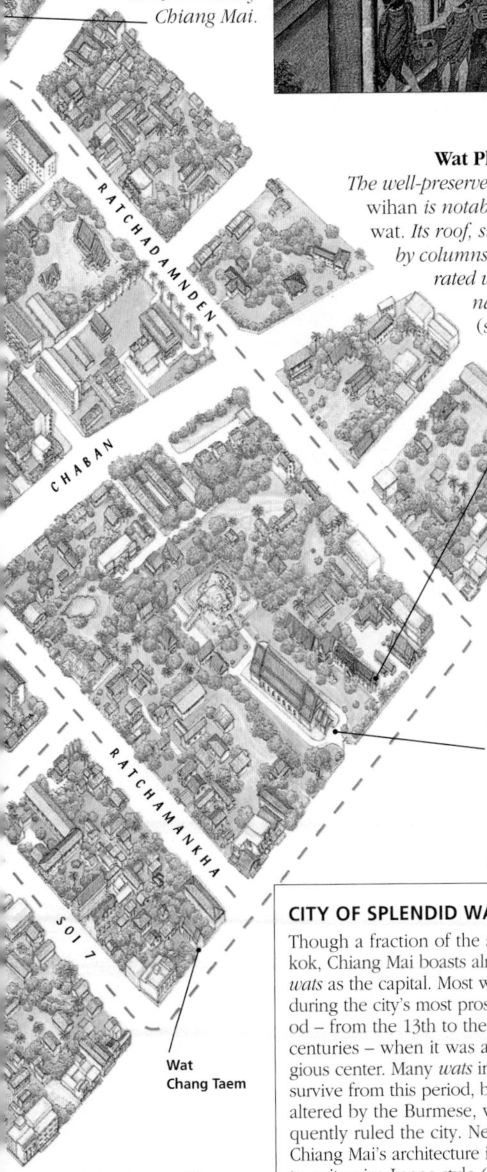

Wat Phan Tao
The well-preserved Lanna wihan is notable at this wat. Its roof, supported by columns, is decorated with Lanna cho fas (see p35).

★ Wat Chedi Luang
The spacious, triple-roofed wihan houses panels depicting scenes from the jataka tales (see p30).

Wat
Chang Taem

0 meters 100

0 yards 100

RATCHADAMNDEN

CHABAN

RATCHAMANKHA

SOI 7

CITY OF SPLENDID WATS

Though a fraction of the size of Bangkok, Chiang Mai boasts almost as many *wats* as the capital. Most were built during the city's most prosperous period – from the 13th to the mid-16th centuries – when it was a major religious center. Many *wats* in Chiang Mai survive from this period, but most were altered by the Burmese, who subsequently ruled the city. Nevertheless, Chiang Mai's architecture is still thought to epitomize Lanna style *(see pp62–3)*, with features such as elaborate woodcarvings on temple pillars and doors.

The 19th-century Wihan
Lai Kham, Wat Phra Sing

Exploring Chiang Mai

Myanmar carving

Often called the "rose of the North," Chiang Mai is shedding its sleepy backpacker-haven reputation and carving out a new identity for itself. The town has expanded rapidly and boutique hotels and trendy restaurants are springing up everywhere, bringing new style and sophistication. Chiang Mai boasts an exquisite location, circled by mountains. Its stunning *wats*, notably Wat Chedi Luang and Wat Phra Sing; historic sites; bustling markets; and lively nightlife make it an exciting destination. The town thrives on its crafts trade (*see pp208–9*), as seen in the wide range sold at Warorot Market and the Night Bazaar, and along Tha Phae Road.

One of the murals inside Wat Phra Sing's Wihan Lai Kham

Wat Phra Sing
วัดพระสิงห์

Samlan Rd, near Suan Dok Gate. ◯ *daily.*
Construction of this temple, the largest in Chiang Mai, began in 1345, though the *bot* dates from 1600. The Wihan Lai Kham ("gilded hall"), decorated with murals of everyday life, houses the revered golden Phra Buddha Sing. Like its namesakes in Bangkok (*see p88*) and Nakhon Si Thammarat (*see p379*), the image is said to have originated in Sri Lanka.

Wat Chedi Luang
วัดเจดีย์หลวง

Phra Pok Klao Rd. ◯ *daily.*
Within the compound of this temple is the spot where King Mengrai was killed by lightning in 1317. The revered Emerald Buddha image was briefly housed in the *wat* in the 15th century – a previous attempt to bring it to Chiang Mai failed (*see p83*). The *chedi*, once 90 m (295 ft) high, was damaged by an earthquake in 1465.

Wat Chiang Man
วัดเชียงมั่น

Off Ratcha Phakhinai Rd. ◯ *daily.*
King Mengrai dedicated this residence as a wat, the city's oldest, while his new capital was being built. It features Lanna teak pillars and a *chedi* surrounded by stone elephant heads. The *wihan* houses the Phra Kaeo Kao, thought to have been carved in Northern India in the 6th century BC.

Tha Phae Gate
ประตูท่าแพ

Tha Phae Gate marks the beginning of Tha Phae Road, the commercial hub of Chiang Mai. Located here are bookstores, department stores, and handicraft shops. Farther east, the road becomes Highway 1006, along which are shops and factories selling silk, celadon, lacquerware, and other crafts.

Suan Dok Gate
ประตูสวนดอก

This is the city's western gate, marking the start of Suthep Road, along which three important temples are situated.

Night Bazaar
ไนท์บาซาร์

Chang Khlan Rd. ◯ *6–11pm daily.*
With its wide range of goods at competitive prices, this easily rivals Bangkok's Chatuchak Market (*see p135*). Inside are endless stalls selling hill-tribe crafts, leather goods, and clothing. The top floor specializes in antiques. Beware of fakes (*see p451*), especially at the stalls outside the market. This is also a good place to try Chiang Mai's Myanmar-influenced cuisine. Shops on Wualai Road, south of Chiang Mai Gate, sell the best silverware and textiles.

Warorot Market
ตลาดวโรรส

N of Tha Phae Rd. ◯ *daily.*
During the day, this covered market sells local food, clothing and hill-tribe crafts, often at lower prices than the Night Bazaar. Fruits, spices, and tasty dishes are all available. By night, it is the site of a colorful flower market.

Shoppers browsing around Chiang Mai's lively Warorot Market

For hotels and restaurants in this region see pp404–7 and pp434–7

Environs

There are many sights outside the city center that are worth a visit. Most can be reached by local transport. For longer excursions, most hotels and guesthouses offer treks to hill-tribe villages (see pp206–7). There are also many tour operators on Tha Phae Road.

To the north of the city is the **Chiang Mai National Museum**. Its varied collection ranges from Haripunchai terra-cottas to Lanna heads of the Buddha.

Sited on the grounds of Chiang Mai University is the **Tribal Research Institute**. Its small museum and library detail the history of the area's ethnic minorities. Treks to hill-tribe villages can also be arranged here.

On Kaew Narawat Road, to the northeast of the city, is **McCormick Hospital**. This working hospital is typical of Chiang Mai's 19th- and 20th-century architecture, much of which was built by missionaries and officials of the British teak logging companies who came here from Myanmar (Burma).

Just west of Suan Dok Gate, on Suthep Road, is **Wat Suan Dok**. The temple was built in 1383 to house relics of the Buddha, while the open-sided *wihan* was restored in the 1930s. The small *chedis* contain ashes of members of Chiang Mai's former royal family. Farther along Suthep Road, in a picturesque forest, is the 14th-century **Wat U Mong**. Some of the original underground tunnels leading to the monks' cells can still be explored. Also of note is a disturbing image of a fasting Buddha. This temple and nearby **Wat Ram Poeng** offer meditation courses. The latter's library keeps versions of the Theravada Buddhist canon in English, Chinese, and other languages.

Wat Chet Yot, distinctive for its seven-spired *chedi*, is set in spacious grounds. Its stuccoed

Facade of the 14th-century Wat Suan Dok

design is based on the Maha-bodhi Temple of Buddh Gaya in India, where the Buddha achieved Enlightenment.

🏛 Chiang Mai National Museum
Off Superhighway. *Tel* 0-5322 1308. ☐ 9am–4pm Wed–Sun. ● public hols.

🏛 Tribal Research Institute
Chiang Mai University, off Huai Kaew Rd. *Tel* 0-5321-0872. ☐ 8:30am–noon & 1–4:30pm Mon–Fri. ● public hols.

Buddha image, National Museum

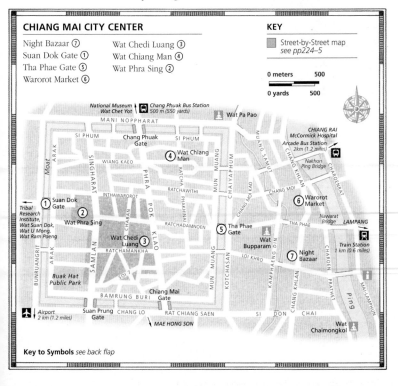

CHIANG MAI CITY CENTER

Night Bazaar ⑦
Suan Dok Gate ①
Tha Phae Gate ⑤
Warorot Market ⑥
Wat Chedi Luang ③
Wat Chiang Man ④
Wat Phra Sing ②

KEY

☐ Street-by-Street map see pp224–5

0 meters   500
0 yards   500

Key to Symbols see back flap

Doi Saket

ดอยสะเก็ด

Off Hwy 1019, 16 km (10 miles) NE
of Chiang Mai, Chiang Mai province.
🛈 *TAT, Chiang Mai (0-5324-8604).*
🚌 🚉 *Chiang Mai, then songthaew.*
◯ *daily.* 🎫

Forming a triangle with Bo
Sang and San Kamphaeng,
the mountain of Doi Saket
is an ideal sight to combine
with these two towns on a
day trip from Chiang Mai.

    The main reason for visiting
Doi Saket is its hilltop temple,
Wat Doi Saket, which offers
stunning views of the Chiang
Mai valley. The *wat* is reached
by a steep staircase of 300
steps, flanked on either side by
a *naga*. The temple complex
includes a modern *wihan*,
painted in red and gold, and a
white *chedi*. There is a huge,
seated Buddha on the hill top
and seven smaller Buddhas,
one for each day of the week.

**Red and gold modern *wihan* of the
hill top Wat Doi Saket**

Women constructing ornamental umbrellas in the village of Bo Sang

Bo Sang ⑬

บ่อสร้าง

9 km (6 miles) E of Chiang Mai,
Chiang Mai province. 🏠 *2,600.*
🚌 *from Chiang Mai.* 🛈 *TAT,
Chiang Mai (0-5324-8604).* ◯ *daily.*
🎪 *Umbrella Fair (Jan).*

Bo Sang is known throughout
Thailand as the "umbrella village" on account of the decorative umbrellas produced here.
The village is made up almost
entirely of shops and factories
involved in this craft.

    Each umbrella has a wooden
handle, bamboo ribs, and a
covering of oiled rice paper,
silk, or cotton. Craftsmen will
usually add names or a personalized design in bold colors if
requested. The annual fair
includes competitions, exhibitions, and a beauty contest.

    Other handicrafts, including
silverware, celadon (a
grayish-green porce-
lain), and lacquerware,
are also sold here.
Aside from its umbrella

making, Bo Sang is also the
heart of a farming community.
In the wet season (June to
October), the rice fields are a
deep green color. From
November to January, the
fields dry out and turn gold-
en. Farmers then thresh the
rice by hand.

    Many houses in and around
Bo Sang are traditional, wood-
en Northern Thai structures
(see p36) with spacious rooms.
They are typically built on
stilts and set in small gardens.

San Kamphaeng ⑭

สันกำแพง

13 km (9 miles) E of Chiang Mai,
Chiang Mai province. 🏠 *44,000.*
🚌 *from Chiang Mai.* 🛈 *TAT,
Chiang Mai (0-5324-8604).* ◯ *daily.*

This village, with its old, wood-
en buildings and narrow streets,
is renowned for its silk and
handicraft products. There are
many factories here selling
good-quality silk, teak

NAGAS: MYTHICAL SERPENTS

Naga figures, seen throughout Thailand, are protective
serpents. Acting as guardians against bad spirits, they often
flank the walls of temples or the staircases up to them, and
may also be carved on roofs, doors, gables, and windows.
The significance of *nagas* is deep-rooted throughout Buddhist Asia, though their meaning may vary slightly according
to the country, with overlaps between Buddhism and Hinduism.
In Buddhism, their origins can be traced back to an episode in
the *jataka* tales *(see p31)* in which a *garuda*, or mythical bird,
attacks and subdues a *naga* that is trying to harm the Buddha.
The *naga* subsequently becomes the Buddha's guardian. Its
protective powers are shown when Mucilinda, a king of the
nagas, grows several heads to shelter the Buddha from a
thunderstorm. *Nagas* are also believed to control rainfall and
are worshiped as givers of water during Songkran *(see p236).*

**Two-headed *naga* of
Wat Chedi Luang,
Chiang Saen
*(see p248)***

Geyser bursting through the ground at the San Kamphaeng Hot Springs

furniture, silverware, lacquer-ware, jade, or celadon. Prices can be high, though bargaining (see p479) often reduces the cost significantly. An interesting feature of most of the silk factories are their exhibits of the silk-making process. The whole procedure is shown (see pp266–7), from silk moths, through the un-raveling of the cocoons, to the weaving of dyed silk thread on traditional wooden looms.

Environs
To the east of San Kam-phaeng, just past the village of Mu Song, are the caves of **Tam Muang On**, with impressive stalactites and stalagmites. Farther east are the **San Kamphaeng Hot Springs**, offering therapeutic baths in hot mineral water. Here, gey-sers spurt to incredible heights.

🏖 **Tam Muang On**
14 km (8.5 miles) E of San Kamphaeng. ☐ daily.

🏖 **San Kamphaeng Hot Springs**
20 km (12.5 miles) E of San Kamphaeng. ☐ daily. 🈁

Lamphun ⑮
ลำพูน

Lamphun province. 🏛 97,000. 🚉
🚌 ℹ TAT, Lamphun (0-5356-0906). ☐ daily. 🎪 Lamyai Festival (Aug).

This ancient town was the capital of the Haripunchai Kingdom from AD 750–1281. Today, Lamphun is made up of large wooden houses beside the Kuang River and is char-acterized by its peaceful atmosphere, ancient temples, and surrounding countryside of rice fields.

Lamphun's most important temple is **Wat Phra That Haripunchai**. The present compound was probably founded in AD 1044 by King Athitayarai of Hari-punchai, though the 46-m (150-ft) high cen-tral chedi, topped by a nine-tier umbrella of pure gold, is thought to date from 897. In the 1930s, the temple was reno-vated by Khrubaa Siwichai, one of the most revered monks

Buddha head, Lamphun Na-tional Museum

in Northern Thailand. One unusual structure is the rare, pyramid-shaped chedi in the northwest of the compound. The large bot houses a reclin-ing Buddha image, while a 15th-century Lanna Buddha is kept in the main wihan. Adjoining it is a 19th-century library, with a staircase flanked by nagas. To the right of the library is an open pavilion dis-playing a huge gong cast in 1860, alleged to be the largest in the world. Outside the main compound is a smaller bot, inside of which is a so-called "happy Buddha," a fat, smiling Chinese-style image.

The nearby **Lamphun National Museum** is small but excellent. It has carvings and artifacts from many periods, especially the Dvaravati, Haripunchai, and Lanna king-doms. Modern artifacts include an ornate black and gold how-dah (see pp208–9) and naga decorations. The collection of Buddha images covers many schools of sculpture.

Wat Chama Thewi (or Wat Kukut), just west of Lamphun on Highway 1015, is noted for its two chedis, thought to be among the oldest in Thailand. Both built in 1218, they are the last surviving examples of Dvaravati architecture. The larger, tiered structure is adorned with Buddha images, and the smaller one is deco-rated with Hindu gods.

🏛 **Lamphun National Museum**
Inthayongyot Rd. **Tel** 0-5351-1186. ☐ Wed–Sun. 🈁

Environs
Pasang, a small town 30 km (19 miles) south of Lamphun, produces excellent cotton-wear of unique designs, especially sarongs and shirts. They are sold through many outlets in the town. Lamphun province, in particular the town of Nong Chang Kheun, to the north, is renowned for its lamyai, or longan (see p133) fruit. It is cele-brated in a festival that features competitions and a Miss Lamyai beauty contest.

Doi Inthanon National Park ⑯

อุทยานแห่งชาติดอยอินทนนท์

The rare *hyper-icum garrettii*

Doi Inthanon, at 2,565 m (8,400 ft), is the highest mountain in Thailand. It is located in the 272-sq km (105-sq mile) Doi Inthanon National Park, and, only 58 km (36 miles) from Chiang Mai, is a popular destination for one-day excursions. The park has many types of habitat and a wide range of mammals, such as leopard cats, pangolins, and flying squirrels. The area is also popular for bird-watching, being home to nearly 400 bird species, many from North Asia (including mountain hawk eagles and Eurasian woodcocks). Karen and Hmong peoples *(see pp206–7)* also live here. In contrast to the rest of Thailand, the climate on Doi Inthanon can be chilly, so visitors to the park are advised to take warm clothing.

Twin Chedis

This shrine is inside one of twin chedis of Phra That N amataneedon, built for Kir Bhumibol's 60th birthday.

Doi Inthanon
2,565 m (8,400 ft) ▲

Siri
wa

Mae Pan
waterfall

MAE CHAEM

Spectacular View
Walkers on Doi Inthanon are treated to impressive views. On a clear day it is possible to see for many miles over the forested landscape.

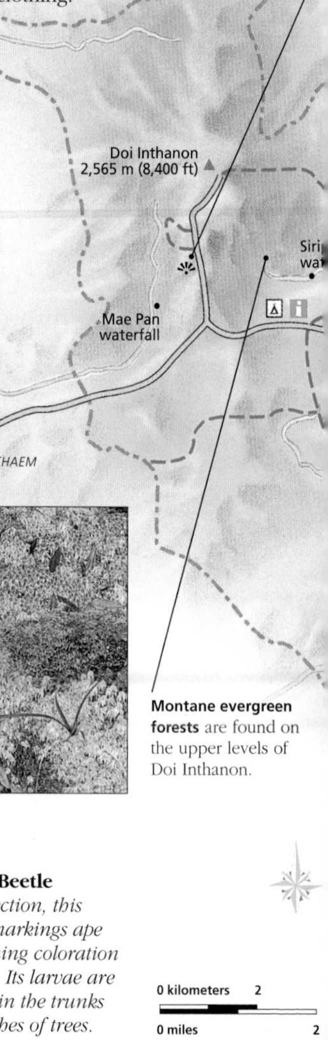

Sphagnum Moss
Doi Inthanon's cool climate allows plants such as mosses, ferns, and lichens to thrive. At the mountain's summit, sphagnum mosses form a kind of bog, the only habitat of this kind in Thailand.

Montane evergreen forests are found on the upper levels of Doi Inthanon.

Timber Beetle
For protection, this beetle's markings ape the warning coloration of wasps. Its larvae are hatched in the trunks or branches of trees.

0 kilometers   2

0 miles   2

Orchids

Wild orchids are in abundance on Doi Inthanon. On the higher slopes of the mountain, 2,500 m (8,200 ft) above sea level, pink and white orchids (see p220) can be seen draped over the branches of evergreen trees.

VISITORS' CHECKLIST

Chiang Mai province. Park HQ off Hwy 1009 (which is off Hwy 108), S of Chiang Mai. **Tel** TAT, Chiang Mai (0-5324-8604); Forestry Dept, Bangkok (0-2562-0760 or www.dnp.go.th for bungalow bookings). 🚌 from Chom Thong to Mae Klang falls, then songthaew to Doi Inthanon summit. ⭕ 6am–6pm daily. 📷 🍴 🚻

White-Crested Laughing Thrush

This bird takes its name from its distinctive white crest. Its common habitat is the forest crowning the upper slopes of Doi Inthanon.

Deciduous and sub-montane forests are found in low-lying areas of the national park.

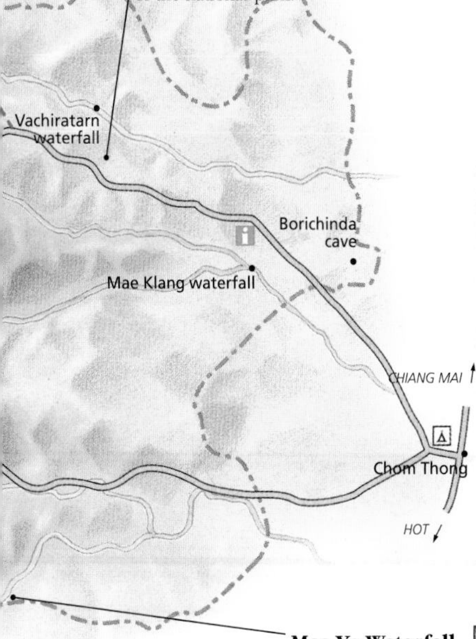

Vachiratarn waterfall

Borichinda cave

ℹ️

Mae Klang waterfall

CHIANG MAI ↑

🏕️

Chom Thong

HOT ↙

Hmong Tribespeople

The Hmong (see p206) have been here since the 1890s. Their slash-and-burn agriculture has led to deforestation, but government programs to reduce this are now underway.

Mae Ya Waterfall

This is estimated to be the highest waterfall in the whole of Thailand. Falling over 250 m (820 ft), Mae Ya waterfall is also one of the most beautiful sights at Doi Inthanon.

KEY

▬▬▬ Road

– – Trail

— ∙ — Park border

ℹ️ Park headquarters

🏕️ Camping and bungalows

〽️ Vista

Rural landscape around Hot, a town in the Ping River Valley

Ping River Valley ❶

หุบเขาแม่น้ำปิง

Chiang Mai province. ℹ TAT, Chiang Mai (0-5324-8604). 🚌 Chiang Mai, then songthaew.

Nearly 600 km (370 miles) long, the Ping River is one of the major waterways in Northern Thailand. It rises on the Myanmar border and flows on to the Bhumibol Reservoir before merging with the Wang, Yom, and Nan rivers. This becomes the Chao Phraya River at Nakhon Sawan, in the Central Plains. The valley is a rural area where traditional life can still be observed.

Wooden carving on the *bot* of Wat Phra That Si Chom Thong

Chom Thong, just south of Chiang Mai, at the junction of Highway 108 and the road to Doi Inthanon National Park (*see pp230–31*), is a small but busy town. It boasts one major sight, **Wat Phra That Si Chom Thong**. The *wat* was built to enshrine a relic of the Buddha and is still an important pilgrimage site for Buddhists. Many will try to make the journey at least once a year. This *wat* is also widely considered to be one of the most beautiful in Northern Thailand. The gilded *chedi*, built in 1451, is of Myanmar design, as is the mid-16th-century *bot*, which features intricate woodcarvings

depicting flowers, birds, and *nagas* (*see p228*). A meditation center and a room displaying thrones, religious antiques, and weapons are also located within the temple complex.

The deep Chaem River Valley, west of Chom Thong, is known locally for its many varieties of butterfly and moth. Several villages, spread along the twisting road within the valley, are known collectively as the town of **Mae Chaem**. The town, once famous for weaving, is now modernizing rapidly. Its main temple, **Wat Pa Daet**, is worth visiting for its well-preserved Lanna buildings and extensive murals.

At the southern end of the valley is the small town of **Hot**. Originally located 15 km (10 miles) farther downstream, the town was relocated to its present site in 1964, when the land was flooded to form the Bhumibol Reservoir. Today, this reservoir is a major source of Thailand's electricity. Ruins of the original town can still be seen beside the reservoir, though they are limited to only a few *chedis*. Excavation of the site has turned up amulets, stucco carvings and gold jewelry. These artifacts are now on display in Chiang Mai's National Museum (*see p227*). Modern-day Hot, meanwhile, is an important market town and a useful staging post for journeys westward to the town of Mae Sariang.

Mae Sariang ❶

แม่สะเรียง

Mae Hong Son province. 🏠 48,000. 🚌 ℹ TAT, Chiang Mai (0-5324-8604). 🛒 daily.

Mae Sariang is a pleasant town on the Yuam River. The area has historical links with nearby Myanmar, a fact that is reflected in Mae Sariang's architecture and by its large community of Myanmar Muslims. People of the Karen hill tribe – the area's main ethnic group – can be seen in the central market.

Two temples near the bus station have Myanmar features: multilayered roofs and vivid orange and yellow exterior ornamentation. **Wat Chong Sung** (also called Wat Uthayarom) was built in 1896, while **Wat Si Bunruang** dates from 1939.

Environs

The area around Mae Sariang is mountainous and forested, with many winding roads. Organized trips by boat or *songthaew* (which can be arranged in town) make the 45-km (30-mile) journey from Mae Sariang to **Mae Sam Laep**, a Karen settlement on the Myanmar border next to the Salawin River. This river was once infamous for drug running and gem smuggling. Today, Mae Sam Laep is a staging post for the (mostly illegal) teak log trade. Political troubles in Myanmar have made this area a zone for refugees, though some Myanmar minorities, such as the Lawa, have lived here longer than Thais.

Chedi of the 19th-century Wat Chong Sung in Mae Sariang

The History of Opium in Thailand

Opium was first grown in Northern Thailand in the late 19th century, when hill tribes *(see pp206–7)* arrived from Southern China, where the drug was a major commodity. Grown on poor soil at high altitudes and easily transported, it was in fact their most profitable cash crop. Opium production was outlawed in Thailand in 1959, but flourished nonetheless during the Vietnam War. It was during this lucrative period that power struggles erupted

Opium poppies

for control of the Golden Triangle's *(see pp246–7)* poppy fields. The KMT *(see p242)*, allowed by the Thai government to control the illicit drugs trade, and the Shan United Army, based in Burma (now Myanmar), were the largest of the many contenders, including the Thai, Burmese, and Lao armies. Opium production has been cut by more than 80 percent since the 1960s, and most hill tribes now grow other crops, but Thailand is still used as a channel for opium produced in nearby countries.

Smoking opium *in custom-built dens became popular in parts of Asia – especially China – in the 19th century.*

Britain and China *fought the Opium Wars of 1839–42 and 1856–60 over British rights to import opium from India. After the wars the drug was legalized in China and freely traded.*

Short sickles, used to score poppy heads, are just some of a number of poppy-cultivating implements exhibited in the House of Opium.

The thin hillside soil easily supports poppies, which favor the low-nutrient, high-alkaline conditions at altitudes of over 1,000 m (3,300 ft).

OPIUM PRODUCTION
This mural in the House of Opium Museum, Sop Ruak *(see p248)*, is one of a series showing traditional poppy harvesting for opium production, a process normally carried out in December and January. The museum also houses artifacts depicting the war between the KMT and the Shan United Army.

Since the 1980s, *cash crops, including cabbage, tea, and coffee, have begun to replace poppies grown for opium production. Today, fields of these new crops are a common sight in Northern Thailand.*

King Bhumibol, *concerned about opiate addiction and the illegal drug trade in his country, has been particularly active in encouraging replacement crops.*

Wat Phra That Lampang Luang ⑲
วัดพระธาตุลำปางหลวง

Buddha in Wihan Phra Phut
A huge Buddha image sits inside the 13th-century wihan*, the oldest building on the site.*

China cow by the main *chedi*, where devotees make merit

One of the most famous temples in Northern Thailand, Wat Phra That Lampang Luang is also one of the most attractive. The main buildings were constructed in the late 15th century on the site of an 8th-century fortress. This had been built on a mound to protect it from attack and was further fortified by three parallel earthen ramparts separated by moats. The ramparts are still visible in the village around the present *wat*. In 1736 a local hero, Tip Chang, successfully defended the temple from the Burmese. The buildings are distinctive for their graceful architecture and richly colored interiors, while the revered Phra Kaeo Don Tao image, allegedly carved from the same jadeite block as the Emerald Buddha *(see p83)*, is kept in the museum behind the main complex.

Wihan Phra Phut
With its beautifully carved façade and two-tiered roof, this wihan, *from 1802, is a masterpiece of Lanna architecture.*

Bodhi tree

Main entrance

Five Buddhas in Wihan Luang
The huge, open-sided main wihan, *which dates from 1496, has an elegant, three-tiered roof. Inside are five seated Buddha images.*

STAR FEATURES

★ Main Chedi

★ Murals in Wihan Nam Tam

Main Staircase
Flanked by nagas, *this stairway leads up to a 15th-century ceremonial gatehouse.*

Ho Phra Phuttabat
This small, elevated mondop houses a sculpture of the Buddha's Footprint, which is worshipped by pilgrims during important festivals. Women may not enter the building.

VISITORS' CHECKLIST

Off Hwy 1, 18 km (11 miles) SW of Lampang, Lampang province. ℹ️ TAT, Lampang (0-5421-8823 or 0-5422-6812). 🚌 Lampang, then songthaew or taxi, or join tour from Lampang, Chiang Mai, or Lamphun. ⏰ 7:30am–5pm daily. 🎉 Luang Wiang Lakhon (Nov).

Bot

Wihan Phra Chao Sila

★ **Main Chedi**
The subtle green and blue hues of the 15th-century chedi are due to centuries of rainfall, which have oxidized the copper. Inside is a hair, said to be from the Buddha.

★ **Murals in Wihan Nam Tam**
These faded murals, which depict 16th-century life and scenes from the jataka *tales (see p30), adorn the walls of what may be Thailand's oldest surviving wooden structure.*

Wihan Ton Kaew

Ku in Wihan Luang
The Buddha image, Phra Chao Lang Thong, which dates from 1563, sits in this gilded brick ku (Lao-style prang).

Pillar Detail
This black lacquered pillar, inlaid with gold, is typical of the intricate decoration of the whole temple complex.

Horse-drawn carriages, a popular tourist attraction in Lampang

Lampang ⑳
ลำปาง

Lampang province. 👥 94,000. ✈️ 🚉 🚌 ℹ️ *TAT, Lampang (0-5421-8823 or 0-5422-6812).* 🚌 *daily.* 🎏 *Luang Wiang Lakon (Feb).*

The second-largest town in Northern Thailand, Lampang is still growing rapidly as a trading center. It offers much of the historic interest of Chiang Mai, but without the overt commercialization. Lampang is also a good base for excursions and travel within Northern Thailand.

The town was originally inhabited in the 7th century. The following century, when it was still called Kelang Nakorn, it became part of the Haripunchai Empire, which centered on Lamphun (*see p229*). In the 19th century, British traders came here from Myanmar and turned the town into a teak production center, bringing Myanmar workers with them. The result was the many teak houses and Myanmar-style temples seen throughout the town today. Teak furniture is just one of the traditional crafts still produced in Lampang; others are cottonware and ceramics.

Modern Lampang is distinctive for its brightly colored horse-drawn carriages, another surviving tradition. This mode of transportation was introduced to Lampang in the 19th century, and it is the only town in Thailand that uses it.

One of the most important temples in Northern Thailand is **Wat Phra That Lampang Luang** (*see pp234–5*), to the southwest of the town, which is famous for its impressive 19th-century murals.

Lampang town focuses on the south side of the Wang River, although the main sights are found to the north of it. Of its temples, the most interesting is **Wat Phra Kaeo Don Tao**. The *wat* is thought to have been built about the same time the town was founded, but only the 50-m (165-ft) *chedi* survives from the original buildings. The distinctive *mondop* is notable for its nine-tier teak roof with intricate carvings and a bronze Buddha in the Mandalay style.

Between 1436 and 1468 the temple housed the revered Emerald Buddha, or Phra Kaeo (*see p81*), which was later moved to Bangkok's Wat Phra

Kaeo. During the same period, a similar jasper Buddha image, now in Wat Phra That Lampang Luang, was kept here. Within the compound is the **Lanna Museum**, displaying religious Lanna artifacts.

Ban Sao Nak ("many pillars house"), southeast of Wat Phra Kaeo Don Tao, is a Lanna structure built in 1896. It takes its name from the 116 square teak pillars supporting the building. Now a museum, it is furnished with Myanmar and Thai antiques. The sumptuous decoration includes lacquerware, ceramics, and silverware. **Wat Pongsanuk Tai**, to the west of Ban Sao Nak, is a distinctive late 18th-century

Interior of Ban Sao Nak, Lampang, decorated with antique crafts

SONGKRAN FESTIVITIES IN THE NORTH

Celebrated nationwide, but most exuberantly in and around Chiang Mai, Songkran (*see p46*) is one of Thailand's major festivals. Held over three days from April 12th–14th (though celebrations carry on until the 15th in towns such as Chiang Mai), Songkran marks the start of the Buddhist New Year. This public holiday has, over the centuries, evolved from a purely religious event, in which Buddha images are bathed with water to purify them, into a much greater celebration of water in the hot season. Nowadays, buckets of water are thrown over everyone in the streets (unsuspecting tourists make the best targets). Some of Songkran's original customs, such as younger Thais paying respect to their elders and monks by sprinkling their hands with perfumed water, are also maintained.

River procession in Lampang, part of the Songkran festivities

Performance at the Thai Elephant Conservation Center near Lampang

Lanna temple with a copper *chedi*. An enclosure in the *mondop* contains a Bodhi tree that is surrounded by four Buddha images.

The 19th-century Myanmar-style **Wat Si Chum**, located in the south of the city, is constructed mostly from beautifully carved teak. The exquisite lacquerwork inside the main chamber shows life in Lampang during the 19th century.

🏛 Lanna Museum
Phra Kaeo Rd. *Tel* 0-5321-1364.
⬜ *daily*. 📷

🏛 Ban Sao Nak
Ratwana Rd. ⬜ *daily*. 📷

Thai Elephant Conservation Center ㉑
ศูนย์ฝึกลูกช้าง

Off Hwy 11, 38 km (24 miles) NW of Lampang, Lampang province.
ℹ *TAT, Lampang (0-5421-8823).*
Tel 0-5424-7875. 🚉 🚌 *Lampang, then songthaew.* ⬜ *daily; shows 9:30–11am (2pm Sat & Sun).* 📷

This is one of the best elephant training camps in Northern Thailand. About 12 animals, three to five years old, arrive here each year to be trained, and there are about 100 in total. Although their ability peaks between the ages of 40 and 50, the elephants may remain at the camp until the official retirement age of 60.

During the five-year training period the elephants learn a variety of tasks, including stacking, carrying, and pushing logs. Nowadays, such chores are part of the performances put on for tourists. Visitors can feed the elephants fruit and take one- to three-day *mahout* (elephant driver) training courses. There is also a small museum focusing on the culture and the history of elephants in Thailand *(see p253).*

Environs
On the opposite side of the highway, the **Thung Kwian Forest Market** sells a wide range of plants and medicinal and culinary herbs, as well as lizards, beetles, and snakes. Government campaigns have attempted to end the sale of endangered species *(see p219)*, but some, such as pangolins (scaly anteaters), are still sold here.

Poster for Thai Elephant Conservation Center

🏛 Thung Kwian Forest Market
Off Hwy 11, 35 km (22 miles) NW of Lampang. ⬜ *daily*.

Uttaradit ㉒
อุตรดิตถ์

Uttaradit province. 🚶 *102,000.* 🚉
🚌 ℹ *TAT, Uttaradit (0-5525-2743).*
🛒 *daily.* 🎉 *Langsat Fair (Oct).*

This provincial capital, relatively free of modern development and tourist paraphernalia, features on few visitors' itineraries. Nevertheless, the town's location makes it a convenient staging post between the North Central Plains and Northern Thailand.

Uttaradit rose to prominence during the Sukhothai era, and just prior to the collapse of the kingdom at the end of the 13th century the town marked its northern border. Uttaradit's most famous citizen was King Taksin, who was born here in the mid-18th century. He reunited Thailand after Myanmar sacked Ayutthaya in 1767. The town is made up of old teak buildings and narrow streets. The main temple of interest is **Wat Tha Thanon**, behind the train station. Inside is the Luang Pho Phet, a revered bronze Lanna Buddha.

To the west of Uttaradit is **Wat Phra Boromathat**, which is also known as Wat That Thung Yang. Its *wihan* is an example of the Lao Luang Prabang architectural style.

Uttaradit province is famous for the quality of its agricultural produce, particularly the *langsat* fruit.

Busy main street of Uttaradit, the birthplace of King Taksin

FAR NORTH

The Far North of Thailand is known as the Golden Triangle – the meeting point of Thailand, Myanmar, and Laos and an area historically associated with opium production. Nowadays, this picturesque region with numerous hill-tribe villages attracts large numbers of trekkers. Less well known delights in the Far North include, southeast of the Golden Triangle, quiet towns such as Phrae and Nan.

The fertile flood plains of the Mekong, which touch the tip of the Far North before running east into Laos, contrast with the breathtaking beauty of the mountains in the west and east of the area. Here can be found remote villages inhabited by hill tribes such as the Mien and Akha, who still preserve their traditional way of life. There are also settlements populated by ex-Chinese Nationalist soldiers and their descendants, who migrated here after Mao Tse-tung's Communist army won the Chinese civil war in 1949.

Chiang Rai is the main town in the Far North. Though not picturesque, it has a few sights and is used as a trekking base. Of greater interest are the towns strung out by the Mekong along the Myanmar and Lao borders, including the ancient city of Chiang Saen and Chiang Khong, a Thai Lue settlement.

Most visitors to northern Thailand travel from Chiang Mai to Chiang Rai, and then north to the Golden Triangle; thus some sights to the east are relatively unknown. The old, walled settlement of Phrae, for instance, with some of Thailand's largest teak buildings, is visited by few tourists, despite being easily accessible from the Central Plains and Chiang Mai. The town of Nan is more remote, set in a valley far from the main highway to the Golden Triangle. The diversion is worthwhile, if only to see the murals at Wat Phumin. Northeast of here, Doi Phu Kha National Park offers superb birdwatching. To the south of Nan, and far from the beaten track, is extraordinarily diverse scenery ranging from the earth pillars of Sao Din and Phrae Muang Phi to the vast Sirikit Reservoir.

Thai Lue farmer plowing the fields in the time-honored way

◁ Young Lisu women sporting their elaborate and colorful traditional costumes

Exploring the Far North

Thailand's northernmost region is, for many people, synonymous with the Golden Triangle. This area around the meeting point of three national borders still conjures up images of untamed wilderness, remote hill-tribe villages, and opium barons. There remains more than a grain of truth in this reputation, but the Far North is also developing rapidly as a tourist destination, centered around the one-time capital of the Lanna Kingdom, Chiang Rai. The major attraction for visitors is the spectacular geography of the region, best explored on foot or motorbike. Touring through the mighty forested mountains along the Myanmar (Burma) and Lao borders, and beside the winding Mekong, as it skirts the tip of the region, is a richly rewarding experience.

SIGHTS AT A GLANCE

Chiang Khong **9**
Chiang Rai pp250–51 **10**
Chiang Saen **8**
Doi Phu Kha National Park **16**
Doi Tung **4**
Fang **1**
The Golden Triangle Apex
  (Sop Ruak) **7**
Mae Sai **5**
Mae Salong **3**
Mae Saruai **11**
Nan pp254–7 **17**
Ngao **14**
Nong Bua **15**
Phayao **13**
Phrae pp258–9 **18**
Sirikit Reservoir **19**
Tha Ton **2**
Wiang Pa Pao **12**

Tours
Golden Triangle **6**

KEY

━━	Major road
⋯⋯	Minor road
━━	Scenic route
⊶⊶	Railway
▬▬	International border
△	Summit

Tachil
MAE SAI **5**
DOI TUNG **4**
MAE SALONG **3**
Doi Hua Mae Raeng 2249 m
GOLDEN TRIANGLE
1089   Mae Chan
2 THA TON
Kok
1 FANG
CHIANG RAI **10**
△ *Doi Ang Khang 1300 m*
San Ton Phao
107
Chiang Mai
Pa Sak
118
11 MAE SARUAI
Tha Ko
109
WIANG PA PAO **12**
Lao
Mae Chai
118
Mae Khachan
PHAYAO
Pong Nam Rong
120
Wang
Huay Khi
Chiang Mai
Chae Hom   NGA
Kiu Lom Dam
Cham Pui
1
Thasi
Lampang
10

0 kilometers	25
0 miles	15

A gathering of Lisu tribeswomen in traditional costume

Buddha image and 19th-century murals in Wat Nong Bua, Nong Bua

GETTING AROUND

Chiang Rai, Nan, and Phrae are all served by domestic airports. Highway 1 (which becomes Highway 110 at Chiang Rai, heading north) is Thailand's major north–south road. Other highways in the Far North are the 101 and the 103. A scenic boat trip operates along the Kok River between Tha Ton and Chiang Rai. An alternative way of getting to smaller, out-of-the-way places, is to join an organized trip. There are no train services in the region.

SEE ALSO

• *Where to Stay* pp407–9

• *Where to Eat* pp437–9

Ornate pavilion at Wat Phra Bat in the center of Phrae

Karen tribespeople trading their wares at Fang's daily market

Fang ❶
ฝาง

Chiang Mai province. 🏠 *111,000.*
🚌 *from Chiang Mai.* ℹ️ *TAT, Chiang Mai (0-5324-8604).* 🏪 *daily.*

This town was founded as a trading center in 1268 by King Mengrai, who took advantage of the site's location at the head of a valley. At the beginning of the 19th century the town was destroyed by Burmese raiders, and it lay deserted until 1880. Today Fang is effectively a border town between the areas inhabited by Thais and hill tribes *(see pp206–7)*. The local Mien, Karen, and Lahu tribes sell their goods at Fang's market, and this has made it an important trading center.

Fang is characterized by teak houses. The influence of nearby Myanmar is seen in many structures, such as **Wat Jong Paen**, located in the north of town. The most impressive temple in Fang, it features a Myanmar-style, multiroofed *wihan.*

Environs
Drug trading in the Fang area has been significant in the past, and fighting between rival drug factions in Myanmar still occasionally spills across the border. It is wise to check the situation with the local tourist office before venturing on a guided trek. Sights in the region include, some 10 km

(6 miles) west of Fang, sulfur springs, whose natural energy is used to power a nearby geothermal plant. To the southwest of Fang, Highway 1249 leads to the peak of **Doi Ang Khang**, via several Lisu, Lahu, and Hmong hill-tribe villages.

Tha Ton ❷
ท่าตอน

Chiang Mai province. 🏠 *21,000.*
🚌 *from Chiang Mai to Fang, then songthaew.* ℹ️ *TAT, Chiang Mai (0-5324-8604).*

Located on a bend in the Kok River, picturesque Tha Ton is essentially a staging post for riverboats that make regular trips from here to Chiang Rai. Excursions can be arranged at guesthouses in town, and may often be combined with visits to nearby tribal villages or hot springs. Tha Ton's chief tourist attraction is **Wat Tha Ton**, which is notable for a huge white Buddha with a striking golden topknot. The temple dominates the town from its hillside location to the west, offering splendid panoramic views.

Imposing white Buddha overlooking Tha Ton

Environs
The road leading from Tha Ton to Doi Mae Salong, 43 km (26 miles) to the northeast, takes in impressive mountain scenery and villages along the Myanmar border.

Mae Salong (Santikhiree) ❸
ดอยแม่สะลอง (ดอยสันติคีรี)

Chiang Rai province. 🏠 *15,000.*
🚌 *Chiang Rai, then songthaew.* ℹ️ *TAT, Chiang Rai (0-5375-4991 or 0-5371-7433).* 🏪 *daily.*

One of the main settlements in Northern Thailand, the hillside town of Mae Salong is also one of the most scenic. Mae Salong was founded in 1962 by the Kuomintang (KMT), or Chinese Nationalist Army, following their defeat in China by Mao Zedong in 1949. It became a center for exiled Chinese soldiers, who used it as a base for incursions into China. The Thai military agreed to let the KMT stay if they helped to suppress Communism, which they believed would become rife among the hill tribes at the time of the Vietnam War. In return for their help, the KMT were allowed to control and tax the local opium trade. As a result, the area around Mae Salong was relatively lawless and dangerous until the 1980s.

When Khun Sa, the opium warlord *(see p233)*, retreated to Myanmar in the early 1980s, the Thai government began to have some success in pacifying the area. This was helped when, soon after the end of this turbulent period, Mae Salong was officially renamed Santikhiree ("hill of peace"), in an attempt to rid the town of its former image. The new term is used for both the town and the 1,200-m (3,950-ft) peak

Chinese medicinal herbs and spices for sale at Mae Salong market

Modern temple on the hill top of Doi Mae Salong

that rises above it, Doi Mae Salong. A temple has been built at the summit, giving spectacular views of the surrounding rolling hills, which are dotted with hill-tribe villages. Akha and Mien villagers can be seen at the market in Mae Salong, but the town's main population is made up of old KMT soldiers and their descendants. The sight of low, Chinese-style houses made of bamboo and the sound of Yunnanese (a Chinese dialect) give the overall impression that Mae Salong is more of a Chinese than Thai town.

A road built to Mae Salong in the early 1980s made the settlement less isolated. Opium production is now suppressed, having been replaced by cash crops such as cabbage, tea, and Chinese herbs and medicines. This produce is sold in the town's market.

Doi Tung ❹

ดอยตุง

Chiang Rai province. ℹ TAT, Chiang Rai (0-5371-7433). 🚌 from Mae Chan or Mae Sai to turn-off for Doi Tung, then songthaew to summit.

The mountain of Doi Tung is an impressive limestone outcrop dominating the Mekong flood plain near Mae Sai. The narrow road snakes through monsoon forest, winding its way up to the 1,800-m (5,900-ft) peak. On a clear day the views of Myanmar and lowland Thailand from the summit are stunning.

The name of the mountain means "flag peak," so called because in AD 911 King Achutarat of Chiang Saen ordered a giant flag to be flown from the summit to mark the site where two *chedis* were to be built, allegedly to house a piece of the Buddha's collarbone. Still a major pilgrimage site, the *chedis* are at the heart of **Wat Phra That Doi Tung**, which was renovated in the early 1900s. Also here is a large, rotund Chinese-style Buddha image. Pilgrims throw coins into its navel to make merit.

The area around Doi Tung has historically been the site of opium production, the poppy fields guarded by hill tribespeople and the KMT. The area has become the focus for a rural development project aimed at increasing central government control over the area. In 1988 **Doi Tung Royal Villa** was built on the mountain as part of a plan to increase tourism in the area and to discourage nearby hill tribes from producing opium. Originally a summer residence for the late mother of King Bhumibol, the villa has an attractive flower garden and a restaurant. While the plan has largely succeeded, local villagers have become dependent on hand-outs from the development project and from tourists.

Doi Tung is now connected to the other main settlements of the area by good roads. These make fascinating driving into regions that were once the preserve of drug barons. Mae Salong and Mae Sai may be reached by these routes, via Lahu and Akha hill-tribe villages. Although a strong Thai army presence has reduced drug trading in the area substantially, visitors are advised not to leave main roads.

🏠 **Doi Tung Royal Villa**
Hwy 1149. ⏰ 7am–5:30pm daily.
🌿 **Gardens** ⏰ 6am–6pm. 🌿

The hillside of Doi Tung, cultivated with new crops aimed at replacing opium as the main source of income

Terraced plantation adjoining a formal garden, on a hillside in the beautiful Golden Triangle region ▷

Mae Sai ❺

แม่สาย

Chiang Rai province. 👥 58,000.
🚌 ℹ️ TAT, Chiang Rai (0-5371-7433).
🏪 daily.

The northernmost town in Thailand, Mae Sai is separated from Myanmar (Burma) only by a bridge. The town bustles with traders from the neighboring country who come here to sell their wares. Among the handicrafts are lacquerware, gems, and jade items, mostly made in Myanmar. Though the town itself is nondescript, there are good views over the Sai River to Myanmar. **Wat Phra That Doi Wao** also has a good vista.

Environs

For about $10 in US currency, visitors may usually cross the bridge to the Myanmar town of **Tachilek**. Check the current political situation with the Myanmar Embassy (see p475), as this determines whether visitors can travel farther into Myanmar. Tachilek is like Mae Sai and thrives on its market selling a variety of goods.

South of Mae Sai is **Tham Luang**, a large cave complex with crystals that change color in the light. Farther south are more caves, **Tham Pum** and **Tham Pla**, with lakes inside.

🏞️ **Tham Luang**
Off Hwy 110, 6 km (3.5 miles)
S of Mae Sai. ☐ daily. 📷 🎫

🏞️ **Tham Pum and Tham Pla**
Off Hwy 110, 13 km (8 miles)
S of Mae Sai. ☐ daily. 📷 🎫

Tobacco-curing houses near the Myanmar border, outside Mae Sai

Golden Triangle Driving Tour ❻

The Golden Triangle is a 195,000 sq-km (75,000 sq-mile) area spanning parts of Thailand, Laos, and Myanmar (Burma), th three countries of the "triangle." The area is historically connected to the opium and heroin trades (thus "golden"), but it has much more to interest visitors. This tour takes in its best features: superb views of the "apex" of the Golden Triangle, where the three countries meet; hill-tribe villages nestling amid stunning mountain scenery; and the historical towns of Chiang Saen and Chiang Khong.
Illicit opium trading is thought to continue the region, however, and visitors should take extra ca near the Myanmar border, which can be dangerous.

Lanna carving, Chiang Saen

Saam Yekh Akha ③
As in every Akha village, small sculpture of people, representing human life, decorate the village gate These are meant to warn spirits that only humans may enter.

Doi Mae Salong ②
This mountain, the site of the mainly Chinese settlement of Mae Salong (see pp242–3), is set amid beautiful rolling scenery.

Pha Dua
This Mien villa sells textiles and han crafts. Visitors may also s elaborate rituals and ce monies based on the local tribe's religion, a mixture animism and Chinese Taois

Tha Ton ①
Located near the Myanmar border, Tha Thon (see p242) is a staging post between the lowlands and the mountains. A huge white Buddha image, visible from miles around, faces eastward over the town and surrounding countryside.

0 kilometers   15
0 miles   10

TIPS FOR DRIVERS

Tour length: 200 km (125 miles).
Stopping-off points: Mae Sai, Chiang Saen, and Chiang Khong all have restaurants, guesthouses, and gas stations. Smaller roads may be difficult for travel, especially in the wet season, so it is best to use the numbered roads above.

Mae Sai ⑥
Wat Phra That Doi Wao, on a hilltop out-
side Mae Sai, is the town's best temple.
The *bot* features carvings of the Buddha.

Doi Tung ⑤
This impressive mountain is the
site of the Doi Tung Royal Villa
(see p243), which has a colorful,
English-style flower garden.

Sop Ruak ⑦
This village *(see p248)*, with its daily market,
thrives on its location at the meeting point
of Thailand, Myanmar, and Laos.

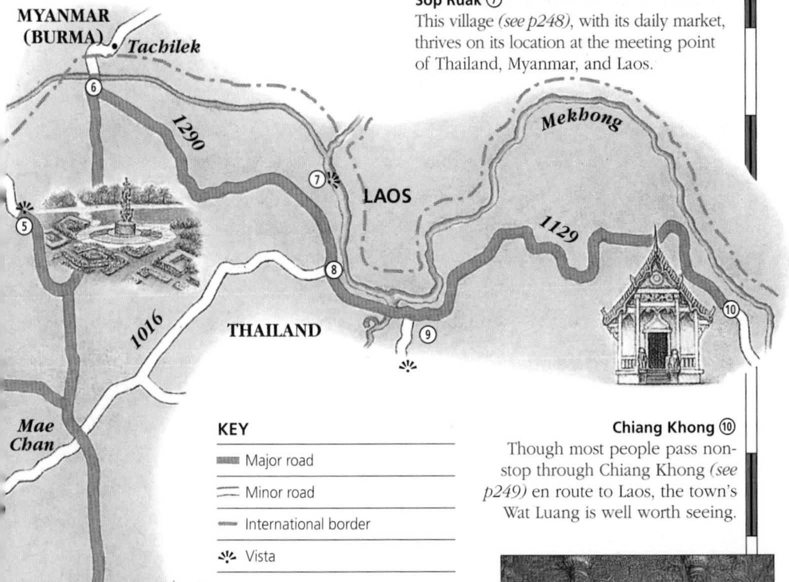

MYANMAR (BURMA) • *Tachilek*

Mekhong

LAOS

1290

1016

1129

THAILAND

Mae Chan

110

Kok

ang Rai

KEY

▬▬▬	Major road
══	Minor road
⚬⚬⚬	International border
☀	Vista

Chiang Khong ⑩
Though most people pass non-
stop through Chiang Khong *(see
p249)* en route to Laos, the town's
Wat Luang is well worth seeing.

Wat Phra That Pha Ngao ⑨
This 10th-century temple *(see p249)*
is superbly sited on a hilltop south
of Chiang Saen, and offers exhilarating views of the surrounding
countryside. It is distinctive for its
bas relief work on the *wihan* and
its *chedi* of shiny white marble.

Chiang Saen ⑧
Visitors should not miss this town
(see pp248–9) of ruined temples
and teak trees, once the capital of a
small kingdom. Today it boasts an
excellent branch of the National Museum and a daily market specializing
in Thai Lue fabrics and souvenirs.

Farmers using traditional methods to cultivate rice in paddies near Chiang Saen

The Golden Triangle Apex (Sop Ruak) ❼

สามเหลี่ยมทองคำ (สปรวก)

68 km (42 miles) NE of Chiang Rai, Chiang Rai province. 🚌 *from Chiang Saen.* 🚤 *from Chiang Saen.* ℹ *TAT, Chiang Rai (0-5371-7433).*

The apex of the Golden Triangle is the point at which the borders of Thailand, Myanmar (Burma), and Laos meet. The junction, at a bend in the Mekong River, is near the village of **Sop Ruak**. Historically, the "Golden Triangle" referred to a much wider region – the area of Northern Thailand, Myanmar, and Laos in which opium was produced *(see p233)*. Nowadays, though, the term refers to a much smaller area and is associated with Sop Ruak village.

Sop Ruak, eager to take advantage of its location, is growing rapidly as a tourist spot, as evidenced by its many shops, restaurants, and hotels. A museum, the **House of Opium**, displays artifacts relating to opium production. It details a battle between the KMT army *(see p242)* and the now-deposed opium lord, Khun Sa *(see p233)*, over control of the local opium trade. The battle, which established the notoriety of the Golden Triangle, took place in 1967.

But the area's main attraction is the Mekong. Boat trips give views of Laos and of the Golden Triangle Paradise Resort in Myanmar. The resort, with a casino, was built in Myanmar as gambling is illegal in Thailand.

Lanna carving, National Museum

🏠 House of Opium
212 House of Opium, SE of Sop Ruak village center. ◻ *7am–7pm daily.* 📷

Mural in the House of Opium showing tools used to harvest poppies

Chiang Saen ❽

เชียงแสน

Chiang Rai province. 🏠 *47,000.* 🚌 🚤 ℹ *TAT, Chiang Rai (0-5371-7433).* 🛒 *daily.*

One of the oldest towns in Thailand, Chiang Saen is set beautifully on the bank of the Mekong River. The town was founded in 1328 by Saenphu, the grandson of King Mengrai, as a powerful fortification with many temples. There is evidence, however, from some of Chiang Saen's monuments, that suggests the town may be much older. In 1558 Chiang Saen was captured by the Burmese. It was liberated by King Rama I in 1804, who burned it to the ground to prevent its recapture. The present town was established in the early 1880s. Today, Chiang Saen is a quiet and peaceful settlement boasting an impressive number of monuments that survived the razing. The Fine Arts Department in Bangkok lists 66 ruins inside the walled town and 75 beyond.

The largest temple in Chiang Saen is **Wat Phra That Chedi Luang**. Its 58-m (190-ft) octagonal *chedi*, built between the 12th and the 14th centuries, is a classic Chiang Saen (more commonly known as Lanna) structure. Beside the temple is a small market selling textiles and souvenirs made by the Thai

Lue, an ethnic minority from China who came to the area in the 18th century. Also nearby is the **Chiang Saen National Museum**, with a collection of stone carvings from the Lanna period, Buddha images, and artifacts relating to hill-tribe culture *(see pp206–7)*.

The town's most attractive temple is **Wat Pa Sak**, ("teak forest temple"), located outside the old walls to the west. The monument consists of seven separate ruined structures set among teak trees, which give the *wat* its name. The *chedi*, built in 1295, is the oldest in town. It is carved with flowers and mythological beasts.

On a hill to the northwest of Chiang Saen is **Wat Phra That Chom Kitti**, which may date from 10th century. The temple has little of architectural interest, it gives fine views of the town and the Mekong.

Just south of Chiang Saen is the hilltop **Wat Phra That Pha Ngao**. This temple, with a white pagoda, offers stunning views of the river and the Golden Triangle region.

🏛 **Chiang Saen National Museum**
Phahon Yothin Rd. ○ *Wed–Sun.* ● *public hols.* 💰

🛕 **Wat Pa Sak**
Near Chiang Saen Gate. ○ *daily.* 💰

Typical Thai Lue fabrics for sale in Chiang Khong

Chiang Khong ❾

เชียงของ

Chiang Rai province. 👥 *52,000.* 🚌 ⛴ ℹ *TAT, Chiang Rai (0-5371-7433).* 🧺 *daily.*

On the banks of the Mekong River, Chiang Khong town is all that remains of the much larger territory of Chiang Khong, most of which was lost to the French in 1893 when they claimed it as part of French Indochina (the rest of this land now forms part of Laos). A growing border town, Chiang Khong is largely dominated by events in Laos. The town was one of the key points of arrival for refugees after the Communist victory in Laos in 1975 *(see p295)*. There is a large Thai Lue community here too, and shops sell their distinctive, multicolored textiles. Chiang Khong's main temple is the 13th-century **Wat Luang**, in the town center. On a hillside just northwest of town is a cemetery where some 200 Chinese KMT soldiers, killed in battles against Communists in the area since the 1960s, are buried.

Environs

Visitors can take a ferry to **Huay Xai**, just inside the Lao border. Visas can be obtained on arrival at Huay Xai immigration at a cost of $35. You will need a passport-size photo. An important trading center, Huay Xai boasts the 19th-century **Wat Chan Khao Manirat**.

THAILAND'S TEAK INDUSTRY

The use of teak *(Tectona grandis)* in Thailand dates back many centuries. Its favorable properties, including strength and resistance to pests and disease, made it a natural choice for use in buildings and furniture, while its fine grain traditionally lent itself to intricate carving. However, reckless overlogging has led to disastrous deforestation, and, as a result, most commercial teak logging and export was banned in 1989. Pockets of teak may still be seen in its natural habitat – low-lying deciduous forests of up to 600 m (1,950 ft) in elevation, with rich, moist soil (such forest is characteristic of Northern Thailand) – or in large new plantations. The trees are easily recognizable by their huge size – they can grow up to 100 m (330 ft) when mature – and by their large, floppy leaves, which fall off during the dry period of November to May. Thailand's historic use of teak is evident in rural parts of the country, as in the old wooden houses of provincial towns, including Phrae *(see pp258–9)* and Ngao *(see p252)*, both located in the North.

Transporting teak logs on the Chao Phraya River

Lowland teak forest in Northern Thailand

Chiang Rai ❿

เชียงราย

Detail of carved peacock, Wat Phra Sing

This ancient town was founded in 1262 by King Mengrai. He decided that the site, in a basin between mountains, would be ideal for the new capital of the Lanna Kingdom *(see pp60–61)*. However, the capital was transferred to Chiang Mai only 34 years later, and Chiang Rai declined in importance. Today it is known as the "gateway to the Golden Triangle." While the modern town may lack the charm and architectural interest of Chiang Mai, it has a number of sights worthy of attention.

Exploring Chiang Rai

Evidence of the town's historic importance can be seen in monuments such as Wat Phra Kaeo. However, modern development is becoming increasingly prominent. The construction of hotels for tourists, who use Chiang Rai as a trekking base, and of second homes for the wealthy people of Bangkok, has made the town one of the fastest growing in Thailand. Economic activity in the area is expected to grow even further as trade increases with China, just 200 km (120 miles) to the north. Development focuses mainly on the area between the old market off Suk Sathit Road and Phahon Yothin Road, with the newest hotels on the outskirts of town and by the airport. Resorts have been built on many of the islands in the Kok River. A popular night bazaar is held in the center of town. Visitors can buy a range of crafts, enjoy a meal, and watch cultural performances. The nearby fresh fruit market is also open at night.

🔳 Wat Phra Kaeo

วัดพระแก้ว

Trirat Rd. 🔘 *daily.*

This is the city's most revered temple. According to legend, lightning struck and cracked the *chedi* in 1354, revealing a plaster cast statue encasing the Emerald Buddha (actually made of jadeite). Today Thailand's most holy Buddha image is housed in Bangkok *(see p83)*. A replica, presented in 1991, is now kept here. The *wat* dates from the 13th century and is also notable for its fine *bot*, decorated with elaborate woodcarving, and the Phra Chao Lang Thong, one of the largest surviving bronze statues from the early Lanna period *(see pp62–3)*.

🔳 Wat Chet Yot

วัดเจ็ดยอด

Chet Yot Rd. 🔘 *daily.*

This small temple, named for its unusual, seven-spired *chedi*, is similar in appearance to its namesake in Chiang Mai *(see pp226–7)*. The front veranda of the main *wihan* has a mural depicting astrological scenes.

🔳 Wat Phra Sing

วัดพระสิงห์

Singhakhlai Rd. 🔘 *daily.*

Built in the late 14th century, Wat Phra Sing is a typical Northern wooden structure, with low, curved roofs. The main *wihan* houses a replica of the Phra Sing Buddha in Chiang Mai's Wat Phra Sing *(see p226)*. Also of interest are the carved medallions below the windows of the *bot*, which depict birds and animals. Around the Bodhi tree are images of the Buddha.

Staircase leading up to a seated Buddha image at Wat Mungmuang

🔳 Wat Mungmuang

วัดมุ่งเมือง

Uttarakit Rd. 🔘 *daily.*

A rotund Buddha image with one hand raised in the *vitarkha mudra* position *(see p173)* dominates this *wat*. The murals in the main *wihan*, depicting local mountain scenery and scenes of flooding and pollution, reflect the concern of Thais at the rapid growth of their cities, an issue of particular relevance in Chiang Rai.

🔳 Wat Phra That Doi Thong

วัดพระธาตุดอยทอง

At-am Nuai Rd, Doi Chom Thong Hill. 🔘 *daily.*

This temple, built in the 1940s, is located on a hill top outside the town. It is on this spot that King Mengrai is said to have decided upon the location of his new capital. In the *wihan* is Chiang Rai's original *lak muang*, or "city pillar," traditionally erected in Thailand to mark the founding of a new city.

Wihan of Wat Phra Sing, housing a replica of Chiang Mai's Phra Sing Buddha

Overbrook Hospital, an example of Chiang Rai's colonial architecture

Overbrook Hospital
โรงพยาบาลโอเวอร์บรุ๊ค
Singhakhlai Rd. **Tel** 0-5371-1366.
This working hospital is typical of the colonial architecture created by Westerners in the 19th and 20th centuries, when the city was a base for missionaries and traders. Such buildings are slowly being swamped in Chiang Rai as modern development proceeds apace. This trend is likely to continue as ever more trekkers and package tourists, demanding ever more comprehensive facilities, are attracted to the wild beauty of the mountainous Golden Triangle region *(see pp246–8).*

Hill Tribe Museum
พิพิธภัณฑ์ชาวเขา
620–625 Thanalai Rd.
Tel 0-5374-0088. ☐ daily. ☒
This small museum and crafts center was established in 1990 by the non-profit Population and Community Development Association (PDA), also known for raising awareness of Thailand's AIDS problem *(see p116).* In addition to informing tourists of the plight of hill tribes *(see pp206–7),* volunteers at the center work with the tribespeople themselves, educating them on how to cope with threats to their traditional lifestyle from a rapidly modernizing society. The center displays and sells hill-tribe crafts *(see pp208–9).* These can also be bought at the market and in shops around the center of town.

Environs
Chiang Rai is growing as a base for visiting the rest of the Far North. Vehicle rental, guided treks, and organized excursions can

Tourists riding an elephant at Ruamit

be arranged through tour companies and many of the guesthouses in town. Also available are boat trips on the Kok River, including excursions to the village of **Tha Ton** *(see p242).* **Ruamit**, some 20 km (12 miles) west of Chiang Rai, can be reached by an hour-long boat ride. This village was originally inhabited solely by the Karen tribe, although many different hill tribes now live here. Elephants can then be taken to travel overland to other Akha and Mien villages.

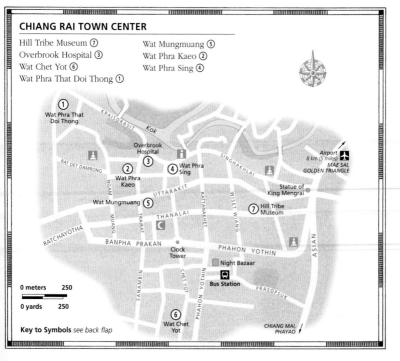

CHIANG RAI TOWN CENTER

Hill Tribe Museum ⑦
Overbrook Hospital ③
Wat Chet Yot ⑥
Wat Phra That Doi Thong ①
Wat Mungmuang ⑤
Wat Phra Kaeo ②
Wat Phra Sing ④

① Wat Phra That Doi Thong
KRAISORASIT
Kok
Overbrook Hospital
SINGHAKHLAI
Airport 8 km (5 miles)
MAE SAI, GOLDEN TRIANGLE
RAT DET DAMRONG
② Wat Phra Kaeo
④ Wat Phra Sing
UTTARAKIT
NGAM
Wat Mungmuang ⑤
MUANG
TRAIRAT
RATTANAKHET
THANALAI
WISET WIANG
Statue of King Mengrai
⑦ Hill Tribe Museum
RATCHAYOTHA
BANPHA PRAKAN
SANAMBIN
CHET YOT
PHAHON YOTHIN
Clock Tower
Night Bazaar
Bus Station
PRASOPSUK
ASIAN
PHAHON YOTHIN
⑥ Wat Chet Yot
CHIANG MAI, PHAYAO

0 meters   250
0 yards   250

Key to Symbols see back flap

Mae Saruai ⑪
แม่สรวย

Chiang Rai province. 👥 84,000. 🚌
Chiang Rai, then songthaew. 🛈 TAT,
Chiang Rai (0-5371-7433). 🏪 daily.

Situated on a plain between
mountains and jagged limestone outcrops, this small market town is a popular meeting
place for hill tribes, particularly
Akha (see pp206–7). Mae
Saruai is modernizing rapidly,
and new agriculture, including
flower production, is replacing
traditional crops such as rice.

Environs
Cars can be rented in Chiang
Rai to visit the Akha hill-tribe
villages. The remote ones are
accessible on motorcycles or
by trekking. Ban Saen
Chareon, 10 km (6 miles) west
of Mae Saruai, was the subject
of a major study of the Akha.

Wiang Pa Pao ⑫
เวียงป่าเป้า

Chiang Rai province. 👥 61,000.
🚃 🚌 Chiang Mai, then songthaew; or
🚌 Chiang Rai, then songthaew. 🛈
TAT, Chiang Rai (0-5371-7433). 🏪 daily.

This important market town is
picturesquely located in a long,
thin valley surrounded by
mountains. The town is composed mainly of two-story teak
buildings, typical of Northern
Thailand, and has quiet back
streets shaded by teak trees.
Many hill-tribe villagers who
live in the area, especially Lisu
and Akha, come to trade at its

The main street in Mae Saruai, with its two-story buildings

market. Wiang Pa Pao's main
tourist attraction is **Wat Si
Suthawat**, to the east of the
main road through town. This
spacious old temple, with distinctive, curled *nagas* flanking
the sweeping staircase that
leads up to the main *wihan*,
is surrounded by teak trees.

Phayao ⑬
พะเยา

Phayao province. 👥 21,000. 🚌 🛈
TAT, Chiang Rai (0-5371-7433). 🏪 daily.

This quiet provincial capital,
spectacularly sited beside a
large lake, was possibly first
settled in the Bronze Age. Later
abandoned, it was resettled
in the 12th century, when it
became an independent city
state. Today, Phayao is divided into two parts. The
older district is confined
to the promontory jutting
into the lake. With its
narrow streets and teak
houses, it is more pleas-
ant than the newer part.
Wat Si Komkam, situ-
ated just north of town by
the lake, dates from the
12th century. Its mod-
ern *wihan* houses a
16th-century, 16-m
(52-ft) Buddha image, which
is thought to be the largest in
the whole of Northern Thailand. The *wihan* is surrounded
by 38 heads of the Buddha in
the Phayao style – distinguished by their rounded heads
and pointed noses – dating
from the 14th century.

Ngao ⑭
งาว

Lampang province. 👥 53,000. 🚌
from Lampang or Chiang Rai. 🛈 TAT,
Lampang (0-5422-1813). 🏪 daily.

Like many towns in Northern
Thailand, Ngao's historical
association with the teak trade
is evident in its buildings. The
suspension bridge over the
Yom River offers wonderful
views of the town, with its
teak houses on stilts backing
onto the fertile river valley.
Ngao's principal temple is
Wat Dok Ban, on the east side
of town. It is distinctive for
its wall surrounded by about
100 kneeling angel figures
of different colors.

Environs
Mae Yom National Park,
northeast of Ngao, is centered on the Yom River,
one of Northern Thai-
land's main waterways.
More than 50 species
of birds have been ob-
served in the park, as
well as many mammals,
including the serow (a
type of antelope), pan-
golin (scaly anteater),
wild pigs, and barking
deer. Within the park is the
Dong Sak Ngan Forest, notable
for its tall teak trees. The forest
can be reached only on foot.

**Angel at Wat
Dok Ban, Ngao**

🏕 **Mae Yom National Park**
18 km (11 miles) NE of Ngao.
🛈 Forestry Dept (0-2579-0529).
⚪ daily. 🅿

Chedi and wihan of Wat Si Suthawat, Wiang Pa Pao's main temple

Elephants in Thailand

As well as playing a very important practical role in Thai history, elephants have traditionally been of great spiritual significance. They were first mentioned centuries ago in Hindu and Buddhist texts and since then have enjoyed a higher status in Thailand than any other animal. However, although wild elephants have been protected by law since 1921, deforestation and, to a lesser extent, poaching have reduced their numbers to just a few thousand. The introduction of machines for logging, followed by a ban on most commercial logging in 1989, has led to a sharp fall in the number of captive elephants, too. While tourists may still come across these being ridden by *mahouts*, a surer way to see them is at shows at elephant camps.

White elephant on a former Siamese flag

Elephants were used in war, as depicted in this old manuscript

WORKING ELEPHANTS

Although most logging is officially banned in Thailand, elephants are still used for transporting logs in some areas. They are often looked after by one handler for all their life, and cause less damage than modern machinery.

Able to run *up to 20 km (12 miles) an hour, elephants were frequently used by hunters.*

This 19th-century training manual *shows how to tame wild elephants.*

SACRED ELEPHANTS

The spiritual significance of elephants derives from Ganesh, the Hindu god of knowledge and the remover and creator of obstacles, who is a young boy with an elephant's head. The significance of white elephants *(see p106)*, the most revered of all, has its roots in Buddhism. Only the king may own them.

Mural of elephants *in one of the Buddhist heavens, Wat Suthat, Bangkok (see pp90–91).*

Royal white elephants, *said to represent the monarch's power, are the most sacred elephants.*

Nong Bua

หนองบัว

Nan province. 🏠 *5,100.* 🚌 *Nan, then songthaew.* ℹ️ *TAT, Chiang Rai (0-5371-7433).* 🛕 *daily.*

This picturesque town, situated on a flat, fertile plain beside the Nan River, is characterized by traditional teak houses on stilts and neat vegetable gardens. It is one of a number of towns in Nan province inhabited by the Thai Lue, an ethnic minority related to the Tai people of Southern China, who began to settle in the region in 1836.

Wat Nong Bua, which was built in 1862, has features typical of a Thai Lue temple, including a two-tiered roof and a carved wooden portico. Its murals are thought to be the work of the same artists who painted those at Wat Phumin *(see pp256–7)*. Though the murals at Wat Nong Bua are more faded than Wat Phumin's, their depictions of 19th-century life are just as fascinating. As at Wat Phumin, scenes from the *jataka* tales *(see pp30–31)* are also featured here.

To the west of town is a textile factory, where traditional Thai Lue fabrics are made using hand-operated looms. The distinctive, multicolored fabrics are for sale in the adjacent store.

Nong Bua is the site of a two-day festival held every three years in December (2014, 2017 and so on), during which the villagers pay homage to their ancestors.

A 19th-century mural depicting a hunting party, Wat Nong Bua

Doi Phu Kha National Park ⑯

อุทยานแห่งชาติดอยภูคา

Visitors' Center off Hwy 1080, 85 km (42 miles) NE of Nan. ℹ️ *TAT, Chiang Rai (0-5371-7433); Forestry Dept (0-2562-0760 or* **www**.dnp. go.th). 🚌 *Nan, then songthaew.*

Ranged around the 2,000-m (6,550-ft) peak of Doi Phu Kha, this is one of the youngest national parks in Thailand. For years, the area was widely considered to be a hotbed of Communist infiltration. Some of the hill-tribe villagers here were suspected of sympathizing with the Communists and were kept isolated from visitors. Tourism in the park is therefore still in its infancy. Doi Phu Kha has two main attractions, the most obvious

Short-tailed magpie, Doi Phu Kha National Park

being its beautiful scenery, such as caves and waterfalls. The visitors' center provides information on forest walks and opportunities for bird-watching.

The other points of interest in the park are the tribal villages, particularly Mien and Hmong *(see pp206–7)*, and lowland ethnic minorities such as the Htin and Thai Lue.

There are few good roads or tourist facilities in the park. The more adventurous will be rewarded by an area relatively free of development.

Nan ⑰

น่าน

Nan province. 🏠 *60,000.* ✈️ 🚌 ℹ️ *TAT, Chiang Rai (0-5371-7433).* 🛕 *daily.* 🎉 *Nan Provincial Fair (Oct/Nov), Nan Boat Racing (late Oct or early Dec). Golden Orange Festival (Dec/Jan).*

Nan developed as an isolated kingdom in the 13th and 14th centuries. It fell under the influence of the Sukothai and Lanna kingdoms *(see pp58–61)*, then surrendered to Burmese control in 1558. In 1788 the town became a vassal state of Bangkok, though it kept its autonomy and independent rulers until it officially became part of Thailand in 1931. Today, Nan is a prosperous town on the Nan River.

Wat Phumin *(see pp256–7)*, in the south of town, is without doubt the most important sight in Nan. Just north of it (on highway 101) is the **Nan National Museum**, which is housed in an impressive

Thai Lue farmers working in the rice fields around Nong Bua

former royal palace dating from 1903. The ground floor is dedicated to the ethnic groups of Nan province, including the Hmong and Mien hill tribes. The second floor has a comprehensive selection of artifacts relating to the history of the region, including weapons. Notable items include a "black" elephant tusk weighing 18 kg (40 lb), supported by a sculpted *khut* (mythological eagle). Thought to date from the 17th century, the tusk is actually dark brown.

The collection of Buddhas includes some rare Lanna and Lao images. Also exhibited are sky rockets made by local farmers for the Bun Bang Fai (Rocket Festival) *(see pp46–7)* held each May in Northeast and parts of Northern Thailand. Unusually for Thai

Facade of the *bot* of the 14th-century Wat Suan Tan in Nan

museums, many of the exhibits are labeled in English. Nearby is **Wat Chang Kham Wora Wihan**, with a magnificent 14th-century *chedi* resting on sculpted elephant heads. The *bot* and the *wihan* are guarded by *singhas* (mythological lions).

Among Nan's other temples is **Wat Suan Tan**, in the northwest of town, with a 40-m (130-ft) *chedi*, crowned by a white *prang* – a rounded, Khmer-style tower that is very rarely seen in Northern Thailand. Housed in the *wihan* is a bronze Buddha image, Phra Chao Thong Thip. The image was made to the order of the king of Chiang Mai in 1449 after he conquered Nan. According to legend, the monarch gave the city's craftsmen just one week to make it.

Just southeast of Nan is the revered **Wat Phra That Chae Haeng**. Dating from 1355, the temple is set in a square compound on a hill top overlooking the Nan valley. Its gilded Lanna *chedi* is just over 55 m (180 ft) high. This, and the huge *nagas* (serpents) flanking the staircase, can be seen from several miles around. The multilayered roof of the *wihan* is Lao in style.

🏛 **Nan National Museum**
Hwy 101. ⬜ *Wed–Sun.* 🎟

"Black" elephant tusk in Nan National Museum

Environs

Despite its many attractions, the mountainous province of Nan was once one of the most remote and inaccessible areas in Thailand. Better roads have now greatly improved connections to the province, making it one of the country's fastest-growing tourist destinations.

To the north of Nan is **Tham Pha Tup Forest Reserve**, a limestone cave complex set in a forested area. There are some 17 caves here, which are impressive for their stalactites and stalagmites. About half of them can be reached by marked trails.

Another natural feature of the region is **Sao Din**, literally "earth pillars," which are located off Highway 1026, about 30 km (19 miles) to the south of Nan. These sculpted clay columns, created by erosion, stick out of depressions in the ground. The pillars have the same eerie appearance as those at Phrae Muang Phi in Phrae province *(see p259)* and have been used as a backdrop for many Thai films.

🦅 **Tham Pha Tup Forest Reserve**
Off Hwy 1080, 12 km (7 miles) N of Nan. 🛈 *Forestry Dept (0-2562-0760 or www.dnp.go.th).* ⬜ *daily.* 🎟

TRADITIONAL BOAT RACES IN NAN

Each year, at the end of October, boat races take place on the river at Nan. The races are the highlight of the two-week Nan Provincial Fair, which attracts visitors from all over Thailand. The tradition of the boat races is thought to have begun toward the end of the 19th century and marks the start of the Krathin season *(see p50)*, when the city's menfolk present new robes to the local monks. The boats, some 30 m (98 ft) in length, can hold up to 50 rowers. Each one is carved from a single log and decorated to look like a dragon-serpent or *naga* *(see p228)*. The sides are brightly painted with traditional motifs.

Boats competing during annual races on the Nan River

Wat Phumin
วัดภูมินทร์

One of the most beautiful temples in northern Thailand, Wat Phumin was founded in 1596 by the ruler of Nan. The *wat* was renovated in the mid-19th century and again in 1991 and is notable for its cross-shaped design, elaborate coffered ceiling, and carved doors and pillars. The highlight, however, is undoubtedly its murals. These were originally thought to have been painted by Thai Lue *(see p254)* artists during the 19th-century renovation. But the apparent depiction of French troops, unknown in the area before the French annexation of part of Nan province in 1893, suggests a date in the mid-1890s. Three main themes can be picked out from the murals: the life of the Buddha, the *jataka (see p30)* tale of his incarnation as Khatta Kumara, and scenes depicting everyday life in Nan.

Rich Official
This lavishly dressed man, smoking a pipe, may depict the ruler of Nan who commissioned the murals.

★ Central Buddha Images
Four identical gilded Sukhothai images (see pp160–61) sit back-to-back facing the cardinal points.

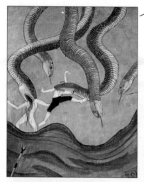

Descending Serpents
This mural shows poisonous snakes sent by angry gods to punish an unruly king in the story of Khatta Kumara.

Decorative Pillars
These red, black, and gold pillars are all carved with the same floral pattern. The bases of some pillars feature elephant motifs while others depict devas *(Hindu gods).*

STAR FEATURES

★ Central Buddha Images

★ Story of the Buddha Mural

Courting Couple

This mural gives an insight into clothing worn in 19th-century Nan. The tattooed man with a Thai Lue hair-style may be one of the artists.

★ Story of the Buddha Mural

The mural on the northern wall above the main door is particularly outstanding. Located at the very top of the image is the Buddha, and on a lower plane are his disciples. In the bottom half, Khatta Kumara and his friends are depicted on their way to a city with a palace, which Khatta later rebuilds after its destruction by snakes and birds.

Nagas (serpents) flank the steps at the front and back of the building.

Main entrance

The Arrival of Europeans in Nan

This scene shows characters wearing European clothes. The figures in berets may be French, and the mural could be a direct reference to the takeover of part of Nan province by the French in 1893.

Boy, Mother, and Elephant's Footprint

In this scene, Khatta Kumara is with his mother. She bore him after drinking the god Indra's urine from an elephant's footprint. Indra had descended to earth in the form of an elephant.

Street-by-Street: Phrae ⓲

แพร่

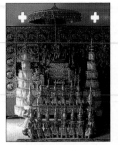

With its distinctive charm and identity, Phrae is appealing yet surprisingly seldom visited. The town was built beside the Yom River in the 12th century and remained an independent city state until it came under Ayutthayan control. In the 18th century, the town was taken by Myanmar (Burma) and later became a base for Myanmar and Lao teak loggers. Myanmar influence is obvious in Phrae's temples, which also have Lanna features. The town prospers on agricultural produce from the surrounding fertile valley, as shown by the growing commercial district outside the walled town. Remains of the old city walls and moat can be seen in the northeast of town.

Buddhist shrine inside the museum at Wat Luang

★ Wat Luang
Phrae's oldest temple (12th century) is entered through a section of old city wall. The octagonal Lanna *chedi is notable for its elephant caryatids. Swords, jewelry, and photographs are displayed in the museum.*

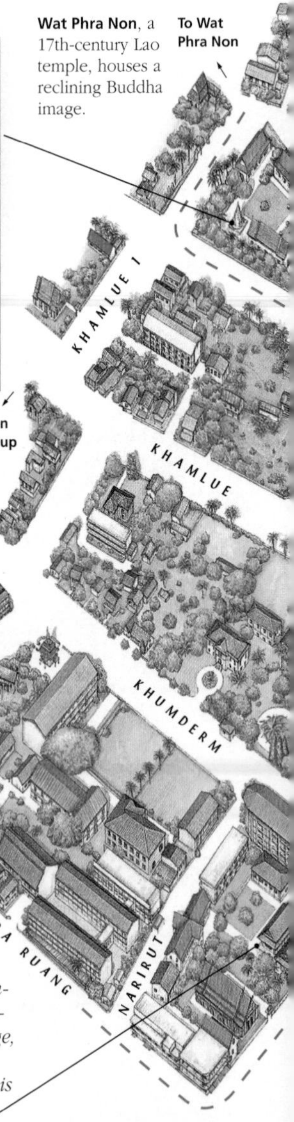

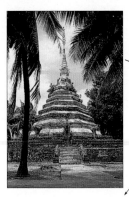

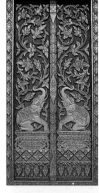

Wat Phra Ruang
Several architectural styles are blended at this temple. The cruciform bot *is more characteristic of temples in nearby Nan. The Lao* wihan *has delicately carved doors, shown here. The* chedi *is Lanna.*

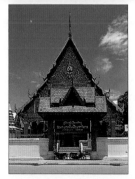

Wat Phra Bat
The Lao bot *of Wat Phra Bat dates from the 18th century, while the* wihan, *housing a revered Buddha image, is modern. Part of a Buddhist university, the temple is often bustling with monks.*

To Wat Phra Non
To Ban Prathup Chai
KHAMLUE I
KHAMLUE
KHUMDERM
PHRA RUANG
NARIRUT

Wat Phra Non, a 17th-century Lao temple, houses a reclining Buddha image.

For hotels and restaurants in this region see pp407–9 and pp437–9

VISITORS' CHECKLIST

Phrae province. 85,000. 2 km (1 mile) SE of Phrae. off Yantarakitkosok Rd. TAT, Chiang Rai (0-5371-7433). daily. Phra That Chaw Hae (Mar); Songkran (Apr).

Wat Si Chum
The plain interiors of the bot and wihan contrast with the ornate Buddha images inside. Unfortunately, the chedi is in a state of ruin.

★ **Teak Houses**
These teak houses are typical of Phrae. Their roofs are decorated with kalae, a feature of Northern Thai houses (see p36).

Public Park
This park is ideal for relaxing after visiting Phrae's sights. Unusually for Thai towns, it is located in the center.

To Wat Chom Sawan and old city walls

0 meters 100
0 yards 100

KEY
– – – Suggested route

STAR SIGHTS
★ Wat Luang
★ Teak Houses

Environs
Wat Chom Sawan, in the northeast of Phrae, is an early 20th-century Shan temple with a distinctive, copper-crowned Myanmar *chedi*.

To the west of Phrae is **Ban Prathup Chai**, one of Thailand's largest teak houses, with its ornate pillars. The structure was assembled in the mid-1980s; even though teak logging was not banned then *(see p249)*, spare logs from nine other houses were used to build it.

To the southeast is **Wat Phra That Chaw Hae**, thought to date from the 12th–13th centuries. Staircases flanked by *nagas* and stone lions lead through a teak forest up to the hilltop *wat*. The temple is named after the satinlike cloth *(chaw hae)* that worshipers wrap around the 33-m (110-ft) gilded *chedi*. Inside is the revered Phra Chao Than Chai, believed to grant wishes.

Phea Muang Phi is a popular excursion from Phrae. This surreal landscape *(muang phi means "ghost city")* consists of pillars of soil and rock that rise from the ground like mushrooms. Like Sao Din in Nan province *(see p255)*, they are the result of the erosion of clay beneath a hard crust.

Ban Prathup Chai
1 km (1,100 yards) W of Phrae. daily.

Wat Phra That Chaw Hae
8 km (5 miles) SE of Phrae, Phrae province. Phrae, then songthaew. daily.

Phea Muang Phi
Off Hwy 101, 18 km (11 miles) NE of Phrae, Phrae province. Phrae, then songthaew.

Sirikit Reservoir ⑲
เขื่อนสิริกิติ์

45 km (28 miles) SE of Phrae, Uttaradit province. Nan or Uttaradit, then songthaew.

Named after Queen Sirikit and set amid splendid scenery, this reservoir and dam were created in the mid-1970s on the Nan River, a tributary of the Chao Phraya. Built to control flooding, the dam also provides electricity and water to farmers in the area.

NORTHEAST
THAILAND

INTRODUCING
NORTHEAST THAILAND 262–267

KHORAT PLATEAU 268–281

MEKONG RIVER VALLEY 282–303

Introducing Northeast Thailand

The Khorat Plateau, which takes up most of the Northeast, is mostly barren scrubland; its main focus is the city of Khorat. To the north and east of this region and separating it from neighboring Laos is the Mekong River Valley. Along the Thai side of the river lie small towns and villages, some with small docks and beaches. Known locally as Isan, the Northeast has an extremely rich history. One of the first areas in the world where rice was cultivated, silk woven, and bronze produced, it fell under Khmer rule in the 9th–13th centuries. Isan's proximity to Laos and Cambodia and its largely infertile land mean that it is seen by many Thais as a poor relation. Most of its people are ethnically Lao and are known for their friendly openness.

Nong Khai

Phu Kradung National Park

KHORAT PLATEAU
(see pp268–281)

Phu Kradung National Park (see pp286–7), *with a steep-sided plateau at its center, is home to fabulous animal and plant life.*

Prasat Hin Phimai (see pp276–7), *dating from the 11th–12th centuries, is one of the most extensively restored Khmer temple complexes in Thailand.*

Prasat Phir

Prasat Hin Khao Phnom Run

Prasat Hin Khao Phnom Rung
(see pp280–81), covering a huge area, is one of Thailand's finest examples of Khmer architecture.

◁ **The ruins of Prasat Hin Muang Tam reflected in one of its four surrounding lotus-filled ponds**

Nong Khai (see pp292–3) *is a developed commercial town that has retained a peaceful riverside atmosphere.*

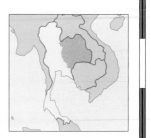

MEKONG RIVER VALLEY
(see pp282–303)

Wat Phra That Phanom

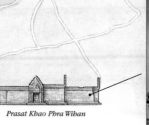

Wat Phra That Phanom (see p297) *was, according to legend, built shortly after the death of the Buddha. It is the Northeast's most sacred shrine.*

Prasat Khao Phra Wihan

Prasat Khao Phra Wihan (see p302) *enjoys a stunning location on a mountain spur on the border between Thailand and Cambodia.*

0 kilometers   50

0 miles   25

The Lost Khmer Temples

**Lintel at
Phnom Rung**

When Europeans first saw mysterious ruins in the forests far east of Ayutthaya, they thought they had found an ancient Chinese, or even Greek, civilization. It was not until the 19th century that the history of the Khmers, who ruled an area covering much of modern Cambodia and Northeast Thailand from the 9th–14th centuries, began to be uncovered. The Khmers are now acknowledged to have been among the world's greatest architects. Many sites can be visited in Thailand today; in Cambodia, restoration of Angkor, the old capital, is ongoing.

THE KHMER EMPIRE

• *Major Khmer sites*

Bas-reliefs of battles *adorning the walls of many Khmer sites not only display the creative and technical abilities of the Khmer craftsmen, but have also helped scholars to write Khmer history. The Khmers' main adversaries were the Thais: in 1444 Ayutthaya finally took Angkor, and the Khmer Empire was vanquished.*

**At the center of Angkor
Thom** stands the Bayon, with its distinctive, colossal heads.

Restoration *of the most important of Thailand's 300-odd Khmer monuments was begun in 1925. The Thai Fine Arts Department has overseen work at temple complexes such as Phimai (see pp276–7) in the late 20th century.*

ROMANCE OF THE GREAT TEMPLES

Khmer temple complexes were built to symbolize kingship and the universe and are awesome in their scale and beauty. The Thais borrowed elements of Khmer temple design *(see p34),* and a scale model, made in 1922, of Angkor Wat, the largest complex, stands at Bangkok's Wat Phra Kaeo *(see pp80–83).* European views of romantic ruins abound, as exemplified by engravings such as this made in 1866–8. A reconstruction of Angkor Wat was also the centerpiece of the 1931 Colonial Exposition in Paris.

A shivalinga was the main object of worship at the center of many Khmer temples. It is a phallus representing the creative force of the Hindu god Shiva.

THE REDISCOVERY OF ANGKOR

In about 1550 a Cambodian king is said to have come upon the ruins of Angkor while hunting for elephants. He cleared part of the site where his ancestors had once held court. Before long, news filtered to Europe from Portuguese and Spanish missionaries of a vast hidden city. But few ventured into the jungle, and the artistic feats of the Khmers were to remain largely unknown for another 300 years. Interest in the ruins increased when France colonized Indochina. Henri Mouhot (1826–61) earned the dubious posthumous status of "discoverer" of Angkor on publication of his engravings and drawings of the site that he made in 1860. From his work France decided to finance proper exploration. Louis Delaporte, George Coedès, Jean Boisselier, and Henri Parmentier were among others who spent much of their lives piecing together Khmer history.

The French scholar Parmentier in 1923

Scenes from the Ramayana, *an ancient Indian epic, are found at many Khmer temples, and probably directly inspired the Thai version, the Ramakien (see pp40–41).*

The 19th-century artists were particularly inspired by imagery of the jungle encroaching upon the ruins.

The scale of the humans shown in the engraving is fairly accurate. The larger statues in the foreground are imaginary.

Marc Riboud, *a photographer for the renowned Magnum agency, visited Angkor in the 1960s and 1980s. He took some of the most evocative and widely published pictures of Angkor before and after the war in Cambodia.*

The gently smiling faces *of the Buddha at the Bayon of Angkor Thom have found their way onto posters, book covers, and, here, the score of a 1921 foxtrot.*

Silk Production

Leaves from the
mulberry bush

Finds at the prehistoric site of Ban Chiang *(see pp54–5)* indicate that silk production in Northeast Thailand may predate even that of China, where sericulture probably originated in about 2700 BC. In Thailand, silk production was beginning to die out until an American, Jim Thompson *(see pp120–21)*, revived it in the 1940s. Today, all manner of silk products are available, with silk shirts and sarongs popular with visitors. The silk industry is centered mostly in the Northeast, due to the suitability of soil in these areas for growing mulberry bushes, the main diet of the silkworm. Silk production in these areas is still based on traditional methods and comprises the stages outlined here.

2 *In three to four weeks the eggs grow into silkworms. These are placed on large, woven bamboo trays and, protected from mice, ants, flies, and bright light, feed on mulberry leaves. In the larval stage, while they are still growing, each silkworm sheds its skin four times and increases its weight 10,000-fold.*

Silkworm moth
(Bombyx mori)

1 *Female silkworm moths spend their short life of about four days mating and laying eggs.*

SILKWORMS

REELING	DYEING

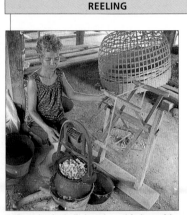

5 *The individual silk threads are lifted out of the pot using a special forked bamboo pole. They are twisted together to form a single, larger thread, which is then reeled onto a spool.*

6 *Silk skeins are inspected and graded. The outer layer of cocoon gives the coarsest yarn and is used for furnishings. The best silk, from the middle and inner layers, is used for weaving.*

7 *The raw silk is soaked in soapy water to remove the sericin, a gumlike coating, leaving it softer and lighter.*

8 *The yarn is then dyed. The strength of the dye depends on the number of times the yarn is dipped in the solution. Tie-dyed yarn (ikat) is achieved by wrapping segments of yarn with dye-resistant strings, according to the design required. The thread is then dried and the strings removed, revealing the pattern.*

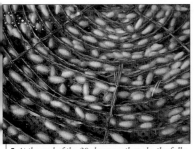

3 *At the end of the 30-day growth cycle, the fully developed silkworms are ready to spin a cocoon. They are moved to a large, circular, bamboo tray with a frame that leaves them just enough space to attach their cocoons. Silkworms build their cocoons from a single white or yellow fiber secreted from the mouth at a rate of 12 cm (4.5 in) per minute.*

Cocoons, which are spun in about 36 hours

4 *Cocoons have to be reeled within ten days or the moths will begin to hatch and damage the silk. The cocoons are placed in a pot of water just below boiling point. This kills them and releases the silk threads.*

COCOONS

PLYING	WEAVING

9 *Up to six threads can be plyed together to form a single thread, the weft.*

10 *The silk is woven on upright looms with foot treadles. The coarse weft is woven into fine, even warps, which even in traditional workshops are often prefabricated and imported from Japan, Korea, and Europe – the production of the warp is a time consuming business by any method. The combination of fine and coarse threads gives the fabric its unique luster.*

TOOLS FOR SILK WEAVING

During the silk-weaving process, the fibers must be kept clean and free from obstructions that could tangle and damage them. Each implement has a unique and vital function: delicate brushes with ornamental wooden handles help to keep the silk free from particles of dust. Carved wooden pulleys, which are attached to traditional looms, insure that the fibers run smoothly while they are being woven.

Decorative silk brushes

Traditional pulley

11 *The distinctive, brightly colored silk is then made into umbrellas, scarves, ties, shirts, and sarongs, and sold around Thailand (see p457).*

KHORAT PLATEAU

Though one of the most infertile areas of Thailand, and home to the nation's poorest people, the Khorat Plateau is rich in culture and historic sites from the days when the Khmer Empire held sway over the region. The people are welcoming, the cuisine fiery hot, often served with glutinous rice and raw vegetables, and the silk and cotton handicrafts are exquisite.

The vast, sandstone Khorat Plateau dominates the Northeast, a region that the Thais call Isan. The plateau, which is about 200 m (660 ft) above sea level, takes up almost a third of Thailand's land mass and is home to about a third of the population. The uneven rainfall of the region causes both floods and droughts and permits the cultivation of only one rice crop per year. As a result there is much rural poverty.

Although few tourists visit the region, there is much of historical interest to be discovered. To the north, at Ban Chiang, lies a site that has revolutionized archaeologists' views of prehistoric Southeast Asia. The Northeast is now thought to be one of the first areas in the world where rice growing, bronze making, and silk weaving were pioneered. Silk production has flourished again since the mid-20th century, and visitors are drawn to modern-day weaving villages where a wide range of silk and cotton goods are sold.

In the 9th century AD, the Khorat Plateau came under Cambodian control, which was to endure until the end of the 13th century. It was during this period that the region's splendid Khmer temples were built. The magnificent stone temples at Phnom Rung and Phimai, which once stood on a road linking the plateau with the Khmer capital of Angkor, have now been evocatively restored.

Bung Phlan Chai, a scenic lake in the center of Roi Et town

◁ Balustraded stone windows at Prasat Hin Muang Tam

Exploring the Khorat Plateau

The Khorat Plateau occupies most of Northeast Thailand. It is a broad stretch of barren, arid hills some 300 m (985 ft) above sea level, separated from the Central Plains to the west by the Phetchabun mountain range. Much of the region is characterized by red earth and scrub forest. Khorat city, regarded as the gateway to the Northeast, is the center of the region's transportation network. Other towns and sights of interest in the region can be reached by road from here, though distances are considerable. North of Khorat lie the towns of Khon Kaen and Roi Et; farther north still, the prehistoric site of Ban Chiang. East of Khorat the main attractions are the Khmer temples of Phimai and Phnom Rung. Nearby are Ta Klang and Surin, which are linked to the elephant trade.

SIGHTS AT A GLANCE

Ban Chiang ❷
Ban Ta Klang ⓭
Dan Kwian ❽
Khon Kaen ❸
Khorat ❼
Prasat Hin Khao Phnom Rung (see pp280–81) ⓫
Prasat Hin Muang Tam ❿
Prasat Hin Phimai (see pp276–7) ❻
Prasat Ta Muen and Prasat Ta Muen Tot ❾
Roi Et ❹
Surin ⓬
Udon Thani ❶
Yasothon ❺

The exquisitely restored Prasat Hin Phimai

| 0 kilometers | 50 |
| 0 miles | 25 |

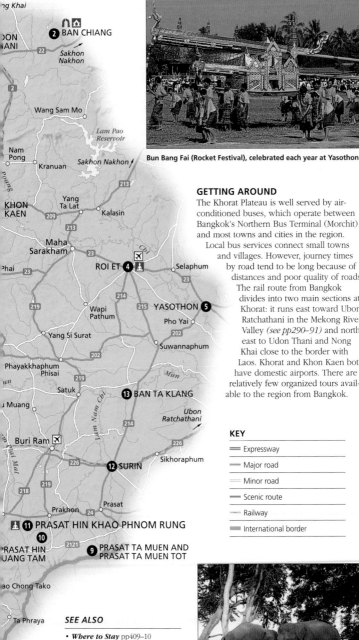

Bun Bang Fai (Rocket Festival), celebrated each year at Yasothon

GETTING AROUND

The Khorat Plateau is well served by air-conditioned buses, which operate between Bangkok's Northern Bus Terminal (Morchit) and most towns and cities in the region. Local bus services connect small towns and villages. However, journey times by road tend to be long because of distances and poor quality of roads. The rail route from Bangkok divides into two main sections at Khorat: it runs east toward Ubon Ratchathani in the Mekong River Valley *(see pp290–91)* and northeast to Udon Thani and Nong Khai close to the border with Laos. Khorat and Khon Kaen both have domestic airports. There are relatively few organized tours available to the region from Bangkok.

KEY

▬▬	Expressway
▬▬	Major road
┈┈	Minor road
▬▬	Scenic route
∾∾∾	Railway
▬▬	International border

SEE ALSO

- *Where to Stay* pp409–10
- *Where to Eat* pp439–40

Elephants at Surin, part of the mass roundup *(see p278)* that takes place annually

Nong Prachak Park, one of the more peaceful parts of Udon Thani

Udon Thani ❶

อุดรธานี

Udon Thani province. 170,000. ✈ 🚌 🚃 🅿 TAT, Mukmontri Rd, Udon Thani (0-4232-5406). 🏛 daily.

During the Vietnam War Udon Thani changed from a sleepy provincial capital into a booming support center for a nearby American airbase. Since the withdrawal of the GIs in 1976, Udon has retained a little of that past vibrancy, together with some rather nondescript streets, lined with Western-style coffee shops, nightclubs, and massage parlors. It has continued to grow as an industrial and commercial center within the region. The most attractive part of town is **Nong Prachak Park**, where there are some open-air restaurants. The town makes a good base for travelers wanting to visit nearby Ban Chiang.

Ban Chiang pot, c.2000 BC

Ban Chiang ❷

บ้านเชียง

Udon Thani province. 4,680. 🚌 from Udon Thani. 🅿 TAT, Udon Thani (0-4232-5406). 🏛 daily.

The principal attraction for visitors to Ban Chiang is its archaeological site *(see pp54–5)*. It was discovered by accident in 1966 by an American sociologist who tripped over some remains. The finds provided archaeological evidence that northeast Thailand may have been one of the world's earliest centers of bronze production. Spearheads from the site are thought to date from around 3600 BC, while ceramics, dating from between 3000 BC and AD 500, testify to a high degree of technical and artistic skill.

Today, a collection of these artifacts is on display, together with ornaments such as bangles and rings, at the **Ban Chiang National Museum**.

A short walk from the museum, 2 km (1 mile) through dusty streets lined with quaint wooden shophouses, two covered excavation sites lie in the grounds of **Wat Pho Si Nai**. Here the main exhibits are graves containing skeletal remains and ceramics used for symbolic purposes in burial. Bodies were wrapped in perishable material and laid on their backs. Pots were then arranged along the edge of the grave and over the bodies themselves. Other grave goods found at the burial site include pig skulls and mandibles, jewelry, tools, weapons, and river pebbles.

Research associated with the discoveries at Wat Pho Si Nai indicates that the inhabitants of Ban Chiang were a strong, long-legged people with wide foreheads and prominent cheekbones with an average life expectancy of 31 years. The main causes of death were diseases such as malaria. As with other early peoples of Southeast Asia, the exact ethnic origins of the population of Ban Chiang remain a mystery.

🏛 **Ban Chiang National Museum**
On edge of Ban Chiang. *Tel* 0-4220-8340. 🕘 9am–4pm Wed–Sun. 🎫

Khon Kaen ❸

ขอนแก่น

Khon Kaen province. 240,000. ✈ 🚌 🚃 🅿 TAT, 15/5 Prachasamoson Rd, Khon Kaen (0-4324-4498). 🏛 daily. 🎉 Silk Festival (10 days Nov/Dec). www.khonkaen.com

Once the quiet capital of one of the poorest provinces in the northeast of Thailand, this place has changed into a bustling town. Located at the heart of the region, it has consequently been a focus of regional development projects – the town now boasts

Khon Kaen National Museum, home to Ban Chiang and Dvaravati relics

the largest university in the northeast, in addition to its own television studios. There are a number of modern hotels and shopping complexes, all of which nestle rather incongruously among the town's more traditional streets and market places.

Places of interest to tourists include **Khaen Nakhon Lake**, an artifical lake beside which are some restaurants. **Khon Kaen National Museum** has a collection of Ban Chiang artifacts and a number of Dvaravati *(see pp56–7)* stelae carved with excerpts from the life of the Buddha, as well as examples of local folk art.

🏛 **Khon Kaen National Museum**
At intersection of Kasikhon Thungsang Rd and Lungsun Rachakhan Rd.
○ Wed–Sun. ● public hols. 📷

Roi Et ➍
ร้อยเอ็ด

Roi Et province. 🚶 119,000.
🚉 ℹ TAT, Khon Kaen
(0-4324-4498). 🚌 daily.

Founded in 1782, Roi Et literally means "one hundred and one," a name that is thought to be an exaggeration of 11, the number of vassal states over which the town once ruled. Today it is a steadily growing provincial capital. The modern skyline is dominated by an immense brown and ocher image of the Lord Buddha, the Phraphutthа-rattana-mongkol-maha-mani, which is situated within the grounds of **Wat Buraphaphi-ram**. Measuring 68 m (225 ft) from its base to the tip of its flame finial, this giant standing Buddha is reputed to be one

The Phraphuttha-rattana-mongkol-maha-mani image at Roi Et

of the tallest in the world. The climb up the statue offers an impressive view of the town and surrounding area. Silk and cotton are both good buys in Roi Et and can be found along Phadung Phanit Road.

THE KHAEN

Originating in Laos, and played widely in Northeast Thailand, the *khaen* is a large, free-reed panpipe and is constructed primarily of bamboo. Although the length and pitch of the *khaen* are not standardized, the number of pipes and the tuning are. Each *khaen* is pitched according either to the personal preference of the player, or to the range of the singer it accompanies, and has a range of two octaves – this gives a total of 15 pitches. Whereas most arts in Thailand are formally taught, *khaen* players tend to learn their skills by listening to relatives and neighbors in the village. There is no written music for the *khaen*, its repertoire having been passed down through oral transmission. It was traditionally played by young men on their way to woo their sweethearts or by blind beggars in the hope of receiving a few coins for their performances. Women never play the *khaen*.

Craftsmen *assemble the* khaen *from bamboo reeds dried in the sun. Wax from the* khisut, *an insect, is used to glue the reeds together and attach them to the carved windchest.*

Phin (a type of guitar)   *Ponglang* (a type of xylophone)

Khaen

The *khaen* consists varying lengths of bamboo, each producing a different pitch.

Holes in the reeds are fingered to create different levels of pitch.

Notes are made by blowing into this carved windchest.

Orchestra with *khaen*, *phin*, and *ponglang* players

Bun Bang Fai or "Rocket" Festival held each year at Yasothon

Yasothon ⑤

ยโสธร

Yasothon province. ⋔ *108,000.*
🚌 **i** *TAT, Ubon Ratchathani
(0-4524-3770).* 🏛 *daily.* 🎆 *Bun
Bang Fai (Rocket) Festival (May).*

Like many provincial towns
across Thailand, Yasothon
has only a few tourist sights.
There are one or two temples
that are worth visiting, in particular **Wat Thung Sawang**
and **Wat Mahathat Yasothon**.
Situated in the center of the
town, the latter is home to the
Phra That Phra Anon *chedi*,
thought to have been built

in the 7th century to house
the relics of Phra Anon, the
closest disciple of the Buddha.
    Yasothon is best known,
however, as the principal
venue for the Bun Bang Fai or
"Rocket" Festival *(see pp47–8)*.
As a result of harsh weather
in Northeast Thailand, this
festival, the principal function
of which is to appease a Hindu
rain god, is one of great symbolic importance. Local people invest enormous sums of
money in the construction of
huge bamboo rockets. The
gunpowder that goes into the
rockets is pounded by young
girls in the temple grounds,

and, perhaps surprisingly, it is
Buddhist monks who possess
the expertise of building and
firing the rockets. The rockets
are paraded on floats through
the streets, surrounded by
revelers, then shot into the
clouds to "fertilize" them. The
festival's sexual overtones
come out in bawdy humor
and flirtation, not encouraged
at other times. The owners of
those rockets that fail to go
off are ritually coated in mud.

Prasat Hin Phimai ⑥

ปราสาทหินพิมาย

See pp276–7.

Khorat ⑦

โคราช

Khorat province. ⋔ *207,000.* ✈
🚌 **i** *TAT, 2102–4 Mittraphap Rd,
Khorat (0-4421-3666).* 🏛 *daily.* 🎆
*Thao Suranari Festival (late Mar/early
Apr), Phimai Boat Racing (Oct/Nov).*

In former times, Khorat, or
Nakhon Ratchasima, was two
separate towns, Khorakh-
apura and Sema; they were
joined during the reign of

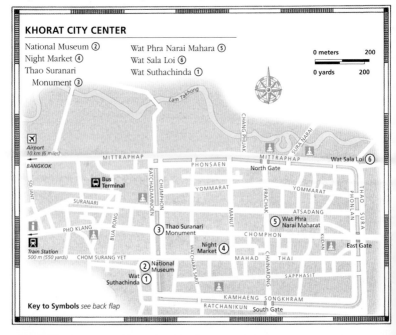

KHORAT CITY CENTER

National Museum ②
Night Market ④
Thao Suranari
    Monument ③

Wat Phra Narai Mahara ⑤
Wat Sala Loi ⑥
Wat Suthachinda ①

0 meters   200

0 yards   200

Lam Takhong

CHANG PHUAK
SURA NARAI

✈ Airport
10 km (6 miles)

BANGKOK

MITTRAPHAP   MITTRAPHAP   Wat Sala Loi ⑥
                                              North Gate

RATCHADAMNOEN

SOI JIANT

SURANARI

🚌 Bus
Terminal

CHUMPHON

PHONSAEN

YOMMARAT   YOMMARAT

PRACHAK

MANUT

ATSADANG

⑤ Wat Phra
Narai Maharat

THAO SURA

PHONLAN

PHO KLANG

BUA RONG

③ Thao Suranari
Monument

WAT CHARA YARIT

CHOMPHON

KUDAN

East Gate

i

🚉 Train Station
500 m (550 yards)

CHOM SURANG YET

② National
① Museum

Wat
Suthachinda

Night ④
Market

MAHAD   THAI

CHAINARONG

SAPPHASIT

KAMHAENG SONGKHRAM
RATCHANIKUN South Gate

Key to Symbols *see back flap*

Ornate pediment and façade of the bot at Wat Phra Narai Maharat

King Narai (1656–88). Today Khorat is a rapidly expanding business center. Its development stems from playing host to a nearby US airbase during the Vietnam War. At first sight Khorat appears to the visitor as a sprawl of confusing roads and heavy traffic. The city center has little of interest save for the **Night Market** that sells good-value street foods and local handicrafts.

At the city's western gate, Pratu Chumphon, is the **Thao Suranari Monument**, built in memory of Khunying Mo, a woman who successfully defended Khorat against an attack by an invading Lao army in 1826. While her husband, the deputy governor of Khorat, was away on business in Bangkok, Prince Anuwong of Vientiane (*see pp294–5*) seized the city. Khunying Mo and her fellow captives allegedly served the Lao army with liquor and were then able to kill them in their drunken stupor with whatever weapons were at hand. The Lao invasion was therefore held at bay until help arrived. Khunying Mo was given the title of Thao Suranari or "brave lady" from which the monument, built in 1934, derives its name. It shows Khunying Mo standing, hand on hip, on a tall pedestal. The

Thao Suranari Monument

base of the statue is adorned with garlands and ornamental offerings made by local people in their respect for her; a week-long festival, including folk performances of dancing, theater, and song is also held in her honor each year.

Located in the grounds of **Wat Suthachinda** is Khorat's **Maha Weerawong National Museum**. The artifacts on display here range from skeletal remains of human corpses, Dvaravati and Ayutthaya Buddha images, ceramics, and wood carvings, and were donated to Prince Maha Weerawong, from whom the museum derives its name.

Though quite a modern city, Khorat has a number of other Buddhist temples. In the *wihan* of **Wat Phra Narai Maharat** is a sandstone image of the Hindu god Vishnu, originally found at Khmer ruins near to the city.

One of the most strikingly innovative, modern Buddhist temples in northeast Thailand is **Wat Sala Loi**, or the "temple of the floating pavilion," on the banks of the Lam Takhong River. Designed in the form of a Chinese junk, the main *wihan* of this *wat* has won architectural awards. It was constructed entirely from local materials, including distinctive earthenware tiles made only at the nearby village of Dan Kwian. The original site on which

Wat Sala Loi now stands dates back to the time of Khunying Mo, and her ashes are still buried here, a fitting resting place for the heroine without whom present-day Khorat would possibly not exist.

Just outside Khorat, **Wat Khao Chan Ngam**, is the site of prehistoric finds, while at **Wat Thep Phitak Punnaram**, a large white Buddha overlooks the road.

🏛 **Maha Weerawong National Museum**
Ratchadamnoen Rd. ⭘ 9am–4pm Wed–Sun. ⬤ public hols. 📷

Dan Kwian ❽
ด่านเกวียน

Khorat province. 👥 2,300.
ℹ TAT, Khorat (0-4421-3666).

Southeast of Khorat is Dan Kwian, first inhabited in the mid-18th century by the Mon people traveling east from the Burmese border. Since then it has become famous for its rust-colored pottery, derived from the high iron content of the local clay.

Today Dan Kwian is essentially a collection of ceramics factories, many of which can export large items for tourists. Shops selling the local pottery line the highway at the entrance point to the village. Items for sale include jewelry, elaborately decorated vases, often in the form of upstanding fish, chicken-shaped plant pots, leaf-shaped wind chimes, and traditional water jars.

LUCKY KHORAT CATS

Silver-colored Khorat cats are named after the Khorat Plateau. They are one of the most prized breeds in Thailand. A pair of Khorat cats is sometimes given as a wedding present in the Northeast, as they are believed to bring good fortune to their owners. They are mentioned in a book of cat poems written during the Ayutthaya period. Khorat cats were first introduced to the West in 1896, but did not gain the same popularity as their cream-colored relatives, who are still known as the original Siamese cats.

Thai stamp bearing a picture of a Khorat cat

Prasat Hin Phimai ⑥

ปราสาทหินพิมาย

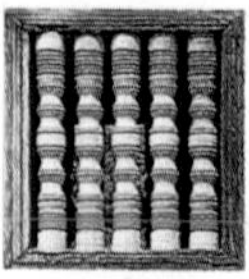

Balustraded window

In the small town of Phimai, on the banks of the Mun River, lies one of Thailand's most extensively restored Khmer temple complexes. There is no definitive date for the construction of this temple, but the central sanctuary is likely to have been completed during the reign of Suryavarman I (1001–49). Prasat Hin Phimai lies on what was once a direct route to the Khmer capital at Angkor, and, unusually, is oriented in a southeasterly direction to face that city. Originally a Brahmanic shrine dedicated to Shiva, Prasat Hin Phimai was rededicated as a Mahayana Buddhist temple at the end of the 12th century. Its famous lintels and pediments depict scenes from the Ramayana (see p40), and, unique among Khmer temples, Buddhist themes. Restoration of the site was carried out by the Fine Arts Department in 1964–9.

Front View of Central Sanctuary
The white sandstone edifice is topped with a rounded prang, the style of which may have influenced the builders of Angkor Wat (see pp264–5).

Naga Bridge
This symbolic bridge leads to the main entrance of the temple complex. The line of nagas that flank either side of the bridge are mythical guardian spirits.

CENTRAL SANCTUARY
The word *prasat*, which is used to refer to the central sanctuary, also describes the temple complex as a whole.

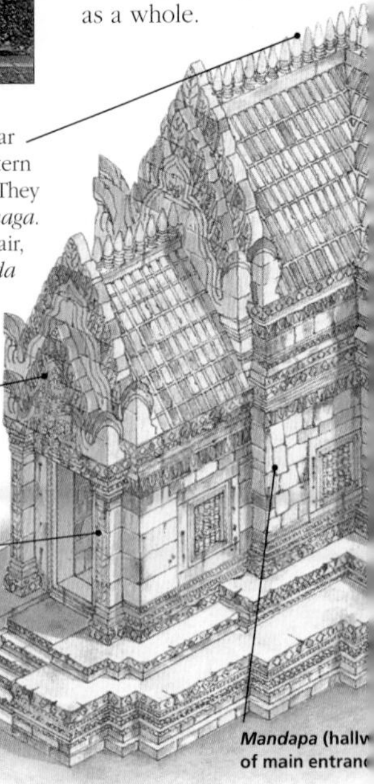

Rama and Lakshman appear on the lintel over the western entrance to the *mandapa*. They have been tied up with a *naga*. The monkeys below despair, while above them a *garuda* (a mythical creature, half bird, half human) and more monkeys come to the rescue.

Southern Pediment
The southern pediment of the mandapa *shows a dancing Shiva, a classic Khmer theme. His mount, Nandin the bull, is to the right.*

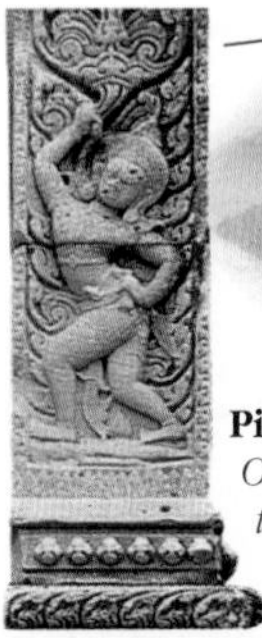

STAR FEATURES

★ Buddha under Naga

★ Northern Pediment

★ Northern Porch

Mandapa (hall of main entrance

Pilaster with Vajarasattva
On the southern face of the mandapa, *this pilaster shows a Vajarasattva (guardian spirit), holding a thunderbolt and a bell, protecting the door.*

Rama and his monkeys, building the causeway to Lanka – a scene from the Ramayana *(see p40)* – can be seen on the western pediment of the prang.

Prang (tower)

★ **Northern Porch**
The centerpiece of the northern porch is this lintel depicting a three-headed, six-armed Vajarasattva. Below him crouch a group of dancing girls.

VISITORS' CHECKLIST

Centre of Phimai town, Khorat province. **Tel** 0-4447-1568.
TAT, Khorat (0-4421-3666).
Khorat, then songthaew.
7am–6pm daily.
Phimai Temple Festival (Nov).

★ **Northern Pediment**
This scene from the Ramayana includes Vishnu holding a conch, a lotus, a discus, and a staff.

★ **Buddha under Naga**
Seated atop a coiled naga and protected by an umbrella formed by the beast's head, this reproduction of a 13th-century Buddha is in the Bayon (see p264) style.

The God of Justice, on the pediment of the eastern porch, judges a feud between Rama and Tosakan *(see p41)*, good and evil.

Trilokayavijaya, the most important Mahayana Bodhisattva (Enlightened being), can be seen on the interior lintel of the eastern porch.

Novice Monks
Though Prasat Hin Phimai does not function as a working wat, it is sometimes the setting for Buddhist gatherings and celebrations.

PLAN OF COMPLEX

1 Central sanctuary
2 Inner compound
3 Outer compound
4 Royal pavilions
5 Gopuras (entrance pavilions)
6 Naga (serpent) bridge

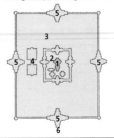

Prasat Ta Muen and Prasat Ta Muen Tot **9**

ปราสาททาเมือนและตาเมือนโต๊ด

Off Hwy 214, Surin province.
🛈 TAT, Khorat (0-4421-3666).
🚍 🚌 Surin, then preferably by organized tour. ◯ daily. 🎫

In the district of Ta Muen, in Surin province, the remains of two Khmer *prasats* stand 100 m (330 ft) apart. One, Prasat Ta Muen, is a laterite chapel marking what would once have been a resting place on the long, arduous road between Angkor (*see pp264–5*) and Prasat Hin Phimai (*see pp276–7*). The other, Prasat Ta Muen Tot, is more decayed and was originally a hospital to care for travelers along this route. Both were built by King Jayavarman VII (1181–1220).

Although both *prasats* are today largely in ruins, with their brickwork gripped and overrun by the roots of towering fig trees, they are potent reminders of the powerful Khmer Empire that once held

Border police who act as armed escorts for visitors, Prasat Ta Muen

sway over the Khorat Plateau. Because of their location along the rather dangerous Cambodian border, Ta Muen and Ta Muen Tot are best seen as part of a tour organized by one of the guesthouses in Surin, and may require a military escort. They are not easily accessible to lone tourists and cannot be visited at times of disputes and skirmishes between the various rival factions in the area.

THE SURIN ELEPHANT ROUNDUP

In the third weekend of November, Surin is transformed by the annual Elephant Roundup. The first roundup was held here in 1960, though nowadays the elephants are used less as working animals than as performers. Some 150 to 200 elephants from local farms are led into Surin by their riders. Shows include demonstrations of how elephants are captured and raised. There are war parades celebrating King Naresuan of Ayutthaya (1590–1605), who fought the Burmese on elephant back. Soldiers, dressed in Ayutthayan costume, march toward an imagined enemy with spears and shields poised. There are also demonstrations of the elephants' strength and intelligence, as well as a chance for spectators to take rides.

Elephants and riders in traditional costume, Surin

Prasat Hin Muang Tam **10**

ปราสาทหินเมืองต่ำ

Off Hwy 214, Buri Ram province.
🛈 TAT, Khorat (0-4421-3666).
🚌 from Surin to Prakhon Chai, then songthaew. ◯ daily. 🎫

Muang Tam, or "the lower city," stands at the foot of Khao Phnom Rung, an extinct volcano on top of which lies the Khmer site of Prasat Hin Khao Phnom Rung (*see pp280–81*). Muang Tam postdates the earliest stages of construction of the more elaborate and well-preserved temple above and was built in brick, sandstone, and laterite between the 10th and 12th centuries as a residence for the local governor. Today little remains, and at first sight Muang Tam appears to be nothing more than an exotic heap of decaying brickwork.

The remains of four brick sanctuaries surround what would once have been a central temple containing religious icons. The reliefs on the Muang Tam lintels indicate that these icons were most likely to have been Hindu. The lintel over the northern sanctuary shows Shiva and his consort Parvati riding on Nandin the bull, another lintel depicts the four-headed Hindu god of creation, Brahma.

All the sanctuaries in the complex face east and are encircled by galleries (now collapsed). On each side there are also four *gopuras* or entrance pavilions. Beyond these lie four L-shaped ponds, decorated at each corner with majestic, multiheaded *nagas*. The ponds themselves are filled with colorful lotus blossoms.

An immense reservoir or *baray*, 1,200 m (3,950 ft) wide and 500 m (1,650 ft) long, is situated to the north of Muang Tam, pointing to the fact that this site probably once supported a sizeable population.

Prasat Hin Khao Phnom Rung ⓫

ปราสาทหินเขาพนมรุ้ง

See pp280–81.

Boiling silkworm cocoons to release the silk threads, Surin

Surin ⓬

สุรินทร์

Surin province. ⚏ *214,000.* ▯ ▱ ℹ *TAT, Khorat (0-4421-3666).* ▱ *daily.* ⚐ *Elephant Roundup (Nov).*

Surin is famous for its silk, its elephants, and its first ruler, Phraya Surin Phakdi Si Narong Wang, from whom it derives its name. A modern statue in the town depicts the leader dressed to go into battle. A member of the Suay tribe, Phraya Surin became ruler of Surin in 1760 when, according to legend, he was instrumental in recapturing an escaped royal white elephant (*see p106*).

The process of silk production (*see pp266–7*) can be seen in the surrounding villages.

There are over 700 patterns used by silk weavers in Surin province. Rhomboid designs are especially popular.

During the 1970s, when the Khmer Rouge seized control of, and terrorized, neighboring Cambodia, thousands of Cambodian refugees crossed the Banthat mountains into Surin province and took up residence there, alongside already established Lao refugees, Thais, and Suay tribespeople. Although most immigrants have been repatriated, some remain.

Surin's main attraction is the annual Elephant Roundup, at the **Surin Sports Park**. At other times of the year, artifacts associated with elephant capture and training can be seen at the **Surin Museum**, including buffalo-hide ropes used by Suay tribesmen to catch wild elephants. There are also exhibits of the protective clothing and amulets, inscribed with magical incantations, worn during elephant hunts. The capture and training of elephants in Surin is traditionally a male preserve. In fact, women are strictly forbidden to touch the paraphernalia of the hunt, in case they destroy the magic needed to catch the elephants.

Statue of Phraya Surin

🏛 **Surin Museum**
Chitramboong Rd. **Tel** 0-4451-3358. ◯ 9am–4pm Wed–Sun.

Road sign advertising Ban Ta Klang, the Elephant Village

Ban Ta Klang ⓭

บ้านตากลาง

Surin province. ⚏ *15,000.* ℹ *TAT, Khorat (0-4421-3666).* ▱ *daily.* ⚐ *Elephant Roundup (Nov).*

The Suay tribes people make up the population of Ban Ta Klang, which is also known as the Elephant Village, a name that reflects the Suay people's skill in capturing and training wild elephants. The Suay are thought to have migrated to Thailand from Central Asia in the early 9th century and to have been the first people to make use of elephants for building, in particular for the construction of Khmer temples. Nowadays, Ban Ta Klang is the primary training ground for the Surin Elephant Roundup. Every October, approximately one month before the roundup in Surin itself, Suay tribesmen begin to practise their skills. In the days leading up to the roundup, the training becomes intense. To participate in the roundup, the riders must walk their elephants the 50 km (32 miles) or so south to the outskirts of Surin.

An elephant feeding while the trainer takes a break, Surin

Prasat Hin Khao Phnom Rung ⓫

ปราสาทหินเขาพนมรุ้ง

Carved stone elephants

Crowning the extinct volcano of Khao Phnom Rung is the splendid Khmer temple complex Prasat Hin Khao Phnom Rung. A Hindu temple, it was built here to symbolize Shiva's abode on Mount Krailasa; hence the processional way leading to the central sanctuary, its stairways, and *naga* bridges extending in total for 200 m (655 ft). The temple's construction

began early in the 10th century, and, like other Khmer sites, it lies on a route to Angkor Wat in Cambodia *(see pp264–5)*. Its buildings are aligned so that at Songkran *(see p48)*, the rising sun can be seen through all 15 doors of the western *gopura*.

Western Porch Pediment
This carving shows monkeys rescuing Sita in a chariot that is itself a model of the temple.

★ **Central Sanctuary**
The corncob-shaped prang of the central sanctuary is the cosmological summit of the processional way.

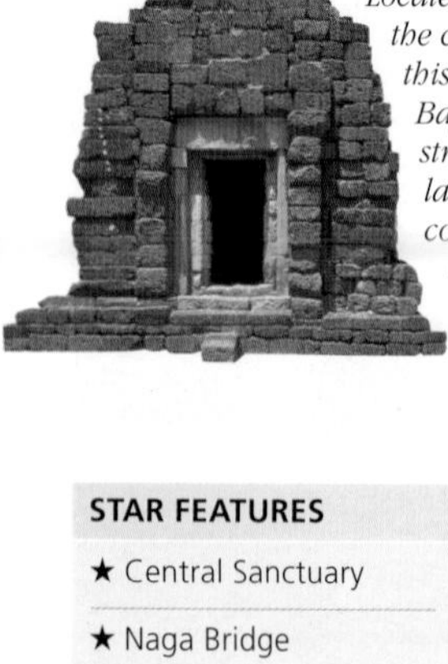

Brick Sanctuary
Located just southeast of the central sanctuary, this 13th-century Bayon-style, laterite structure was a late addition to the compound. It was built as a library.

STAR FEATURES

★ Central Sanctuary

★ Naga Bridge

★ Ornamental Ponds

★ Processional Way

★ **Naga Bridge**
This naga bridge, which is located inside the main temple compound, links the east-facing entrance gopura to the central sanctuary. The body of the naga forms the bridge's balustrade.

Pediment over Porch of Mandapa
The carving on this pediment represents Shiva Nataraja, the dancing Shiva, his ten arms splayed out in a dance of death and destruction.

VISITORS' CHECKLIST

50 km (31 miles) S of Buriram, off Hwy 24, Buriram province.
TAT, Khorat (0-4421-3666).
from Khorat or Surin to Ban Ta Ko, then songthaew.
6am–6pm daily.
Phnom Rung Festival (Apr).

Nandin the Bull
This image of Nandin the bull, the mythical mount of the Hindu deity Shiva, is located in the first, eastern chamber of the central sanctuary.

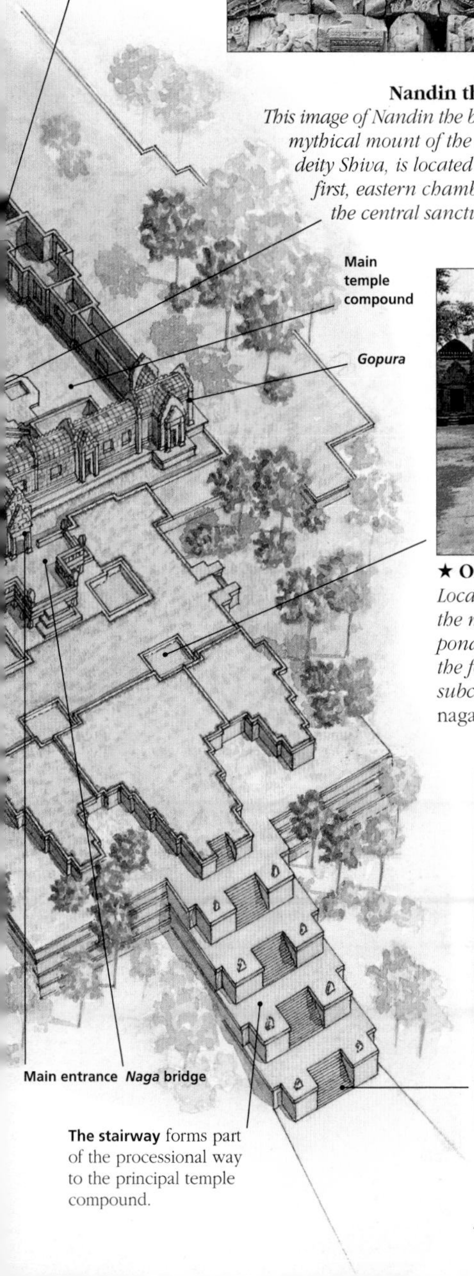

Main temple compound

Gopura

★ Ornamental Ponds
Located at the front of the entrance to the main temple compound are four ponds. They supposedly represent the four sacred rivers of the Indian subcontinent. In the background, a naga bridge leads into the complex.

Main entrance Naga bridge

The stairway forms part of the processional way to the principal temple compound.

★ Processional Way
This processional walkway was built to symbolize the spiritual journey from earth to Hindu heaven.

MEKONG RIVER VALLEY

S ome 2,000 km (1,250 miles) from its source in the Tibetan Himalayas, having passed through China, Myanmar (Burma), northern Thailand, then Laos, the Mekong River reaches Chiang Khan in Northeast Thailand. From here the river forms the border with Laos until it flows into Cambodia. Although relatively few tourists visit this border country, it has many natural and cultural attractions.

The agricultural basin of the Mekong River Valley stands in contrast to the dusty, parched Khorat Plateau to the south and west and the rugged mountains on the Lao side of the river. The Mekong River Valley's relatively fertile land means fruit and vegetables can be produced on a marketable scale. Furthermore, due to its distance from Bangkok, the area has escaped widespread development and remains one of the most beautiful, unspoilt regions in the country.

Lively Nong Khai is the most important border town in the region and the access point to the Lao capital, Vientiane. The stretch of river to the west of here is dotted with numerous picturesque towns and villages with traditional teak houses. At Phu Phrabat Historical Park (near Ban Phu), a variety of mesmerizing sandstone rock formations can be seen. Nearby are the extraordinary huge Buddhist and Hindu statues of Wat Khaek.

As the river winds its way east and then south, past Nakhon Phanom, it passes one of the most important Buddhist pilgrimage sites in Thailand, Wat Phra That Phanom. The temple supposedly dates from the death of the Lord Buddha in 543 BC.

Farther downriver is Pha Taem, a cliff face painted with huge prehistoric figures and unusual geometrical patterns. Not far away, at Khong Chiam, the Mun River flows into the Mekong, creating the phenomenon of the "two-colored river." From here the Mekong flows into Laos and then Cambodia. The Cambodian border with Thailand has been the scene of skirmishes between rival factions and, as a result, it is not always possible to reach one of the most magnificent of all Khmer monuments, Prasat Khao Phra Wihan.

View from Nakhon Phanom, looking over the Mekong River and into Laos

◁ Distinctive rock formations – a feature of the Northeast – near Phu Kradung

Exploring the Mekong River Valley

The mighty Mekong River forms a 750-km (465-mile) border between Northeast Thailand and Laos. The valley along which it flows is a relatively fertile area in an otherwise arid region of Thailand. It is possible to follow the length of the Mekong from Chiang Khan to Pha Taem by road. Some of the most attractive areas are west of Nong Khai, where visitors pass through sleepy towns and villages of pretty wooden houses. South of the northern stretch of the Mekong lie the Phu Rua, Phu Kradung, and Phu Hin Rong Kla national parks. Farther south is Ubon Rachathani, by far the largest city in the region.

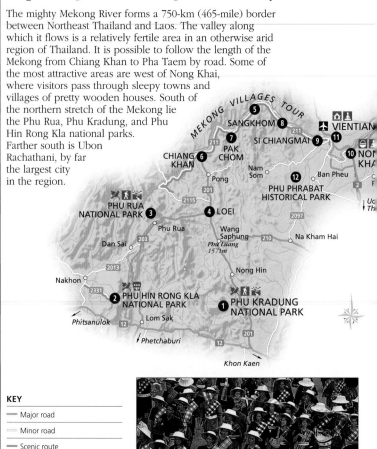

MEKONG VILLAGES TOUR

SANGKHOM **8**
SI CHIANGMAI **9**
VIENTIAN
PAK CHOM **7**
CHIANG KHAN **6**
Nam Som
Ban Pheu
Pong
PHU PHRABAT HISTORICAL PARK **12**
NONG KHAI
PHU RUA NATIONAL PARK **3**
LOEI **4**
Phu Rua
Wang Saphung
Na Kham Hai
Dan Sai
Phu Luang 1571m
Nong Hin
Nakhon
PHU HIN RONG KLA NATIONAL PARK **2**
PHU KRADUNG NATIONAL PARK **1**
Phitsanulok
Lom Sak
Phetchaburi
Khon Kaen

KEY

━━━ Major road

┈┈┈ Minor road

━━━ Scenic route

━━━ Main railway

▬▬▬ International border

△ Summit

The colorful Phi Ta Khon Festival, held in Loei

SIGHTS AT A GLANCE

Chiang Khan **6**
Chong Mek **20**
Khong Chiam **19**
Loei **4**
Mukdahan **17**
Nakhon Phanom **14**
Nong Khai pp292–3 **10**
Pak Chom **7**
Pha Taem **18**
Prasat Khao Phra Wihan **22**

Prasat Prang Ku **23**
Phu Hin Rong Kla National Park **2**
Phu Kradung National Park pp286–7 **1**
Phu Phrabat Historical Park **12**
Phu Rua National Park **3**
Renu Nakhon **15**
Sakhon Nakhon **13**

Sangkhom **8**
Si Chiangmai **9**
Sirindhorn Dam **21**
Ubon Ratchathani **24**
Vientiane pp294–5 **11**
Wat Phra That Phanom **16**

Tour
Mekong Villages Tour **5**

GETTING AROUND

Nong Khai, Loei, Nakhon Phanom, and Ubon Ratchathani are the best bases from which to tour the area. Two train lines run through the region: a direct line, which divides at Khorat, connects Bangkok to Ubon Ratchathani and to Udon Thani. Travelers can pick up a connection from Udon Thani to Nong Khai. The best way to get around is by bus, rented car, or *songthaew*. Long-tail boats run on some sections of the Mekong River.

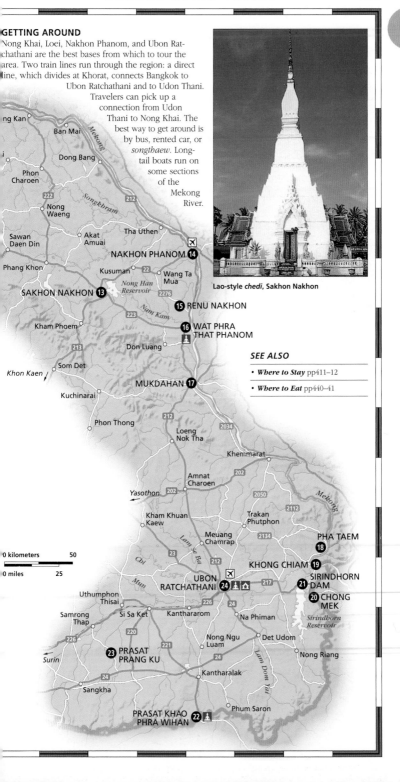

Lao-style *chedi*, Sakhon Nakhon

ng Kan

Ban Mai

Dong Bang

Mekong

Phon Charoen

222

Songkhram

212

Nong Waeng

Sawan Daen Din

Akat Amuai

Tha Uthen

Phang Khon

Kusuman 22

Wang Ta Mua

✈ NAKHON PHANOM 14

Nong Han Reservoir 2276

SAKHON NAKHON 13

Nam Kam

223

15 RENU NAKHON

Kham Phoem

213

16 WAT PHRA THAT PHANOM

Don Luang

Som Det

Khon Kaen

Kuchinarai

MUKDAHAN 17

Phon Thong

212

Loeng Nok Tha

2034

Khemmarat

Yasothon

Amnat Charoen

202

202

2050

Mekong

Kham Khuan Kaew

Lam Se Bai

Meuang Chamrap

2134

212

202

2112

Trakan Phutphon

PHA TAEM 18

| 0 kilometers | 50 |
| 0 miles | 25 |

Chi

23

Mun

KHONG CHIAM 19

UBON RATCHATHANI ✈ 24

217

SIRINDHORN DAM 21

Uthumphon Thisai

Si Sa Ket

Kanthararom

226

24

Na Phiman

20 CHONG MEK

Sirindhorn Reservoir

Samrong Thap

220

221

Nong Ngu Luam

Det Udom

Lam Dom Yai

Nong Riang

Surin

226

23 PRASAT PRANG KU

24

Kantharalak

Sangkha

24

PRASAT KHAO PHRA WIHAN 22

Phum Saron

SEE ALSO

- *Where to Stay* pp411–12
- *Where to Eat* pp440–41

Phu Kradung National Park ❶

อุทยานแห่งชาติภูกระดึง

Thai flower

There are two legends connected to Phu Kradung, or "bell mountain": the first is that the sound of a bell, said to be that of the god Indra, once rang out from its peak; the second is that the mountain rings like a bell when struck with a staff. This steep-sided, flat-topped mountain is now a national park covering 348 sq km (135 sq miles), its 60-km (37-mile) plateau 1,350 m (4,450 ft) above sea level. This plateau has a climate cool enough for plants that cannot survive in other parts of Thailand; many animals also live in its thin pine forests and grasslands.

Asiatic Black Bear
This bear lives in forests all over Southeast Asia; it feeds on ants, insect larvae, nuts, and fruit.

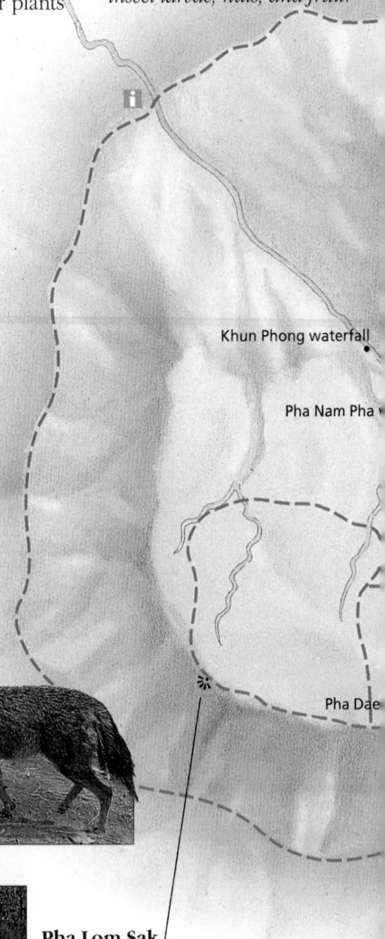

Khun Phong waterfall

Pha Nam Pha

Waterfalls
Waterfalls are dotted all over Phu Kradung. They are most impressive in October (the end of the rainy season).

Asian Jackal
Thailand has two wild dogs. The handsome Asian jackal, which lives on Phu Kradung, has a bushy tail. The other common species is the red dog.

Pha Dae

Pha Lom Sak
This unusually shaped sandstone ledge is situated on the southern edge of the plateau. It provides beautiful vistas over the rolling hills and valleys. In summer, lines of people gather to photograph this popular and scenic attraction.

Pha Nok An
"Swallow cliff," situated at the eastern edge of the plateau, offers breathtaking sunrise views. Its name refers to the many families of swallows who build their nests under the cliff's overhang.

VISITORS' CHECKLIST

Loei province. Park HQ about 8 km (5 miles) off Hwy 2019, on Hwy 2019. ⓘ TAT, Udon Thani (0-4232-5406); Forestry Dept (0-4287-1333 inc bungalow bookings). 🚌 Bus to Pha Nok Kao then songthaew. Access to plateau on foot only. ⏲ mid-Jul–early Sep (rainy season). 📷 🛉 🍴

Pitcher Plants
Common in Phu Kradung, carnivorous pitcher plants gather nutrients lacking in the local acidic soil by "eating" insects.

Phen Pop Mai waterfall

Tharn Yai waterfall

Tharn Sawan waterfall

Anodat pond

Phone Phop waterfall is named after the first World Champion Thai boxer, Phone Kingphet, who stumbled upon it when he was training. Phone chose the plateau as a training ground because its cool climate prepared him for fights abroad.

LOEI

Park entrance

THE BALLAD OF PHU KRADUNG

Phu Kradung was the inspiration for a long poem in 1969 by the award-winning Thai poet and artist Angkhan Kalyanaphong, who eulogized its unspoiled, natural beauties. *Lam Nam Phu Kradung* ("the ballad of Phu Kradung") reflects Angkhan's interest in nature and Buddhism. This excerpt translates poorly into English:

"Each time the sun went down I would sit at the Makduk cliff
And watch the beams of colored light
Pierce the clouds and set alight the sky."

Sa Anodat pond, one of many inspiring sights

0 kilometers 10

0 miles 10

KEY

═══ Road

– · Trail

ⓘ National park office

🄰 Camping and bungalows

🔆 Vista

Rapids in Phu Hin Rong Kla National Park

Phu Hin Rong Kla National Park ❷

อุทยานแห่งชาติภูหินร่องกล้า

Phitsanulok province. Park HQ off Hwy 2331, 31 km (19 miles) SE of Nakhon Thai. 🛈 TAT, Phitsanulok (0-5525-2743); Forestry Dept (0-2562-0760 or www.dnp.go.th for bungalow bookings). 🚍 from Loei or Phitsanulok to Nakhon Thai, then songthaew. 🏍️

Covering an area of 307 sq km (120 sq miles), Phu Hin Rong Kla National Park has a wide variety of flora and fauna and an unusual open-air museum with exhibits of the Communist camp based here in the 1960s and '70s. The spread of Communism in Southeast Asia from the 1950s alarmed the Thai goverment, and hostilities between the Communist Party of Thailand (CPT) and the military commenced in 1964. Soon after, the open forests of the Phu Hin Rong Kla mountain range became a CPT stronghold. An average elevation of 1,000 m (3,300 ft), proximity to Laos – run by the Communist Pathet Lao from 1975 (see p295) – and the access this facilitated to headquarters, at Kunming in China, all made it an ideal site. The CPT was active after 1976, when thousands of students fled here after a coup in Bangkok. By 1979, disillusioned with Communism, many began to take advantage of an amnesty from the Thai government. Dwindling support and government attacks on Phu Hin Rong Kla in the early 1980s led the site to fall to the authorities in 1982.

Two years later it opened as a national park. Its highest peak, Phu Man Khao, rises to a height of 1,620 m (5,300 ft).

Unusual rock formation at Phu Rua National Park

Phu Rua National Park ❸

อุทยานแห่งชาติภูเรือ

Loei province. Park HQ off Hwy 203, 60 km (30 miles) W of Loei. 🛈 TAT, Udon Thani (0-4232-5406); Forestry Dept (0-2562-0760 or www.dnp.go.th for bungalow bookings). 🚍 from Loei to Phu Rua village, then songthaew. 🏍️

Phu Rua or "boat mountain" gets its name from its peak, which is shaped like a junk. It stands some 1,365 m (4,500 ft) above sea level and offers spectacular views of the town of Loei to the south and toward Laos. A modern Buddha image sits looking out over the plains in contemplation of their beauty.

It is possible to drive to the summit of Phu Rua, passing several bizarre rock formations on the way. The most remarkable is Hin Ta or "tortoise rock," with two huge sandstone boulders stacked one on top of the other, surmounted by a third, giving the structure the appearance of a giant mushroom.

For the traveler with time to explore the 121 sq km (47 sq miles) of this national park, a number of marked trails lead through a beautiful landscape of meadows, rock gardens, and pine and evergreen forests. Views across the surrounding lowlands can be seen from Phu Kut and the cliffs of Pha Lon Noi, Pha Dong Tham San, Pha Yat, and Pha Sap Thong. There are also several waterfalls located around the park, namely Huai Phai, Huai Ta Wat, and Lan Hin Taek.

Animals at Phu Rua National Park include barking deer, wild pigs, a wide variety of birds, including pheasant, and the rare tao puru, or Siamese big-headed turtle. Phu Rua is also famed for being one of the coolest areas of Thailand, with a record low temperature of -4° C (25° F) having been recorded here in 1981.

Relics of the war between the military and the CPT, Phu Hin Rong Kla

Rolling hills near Loei, typical of this part of the Northeast

Loei ❹

เลย

Loei province. 🏔 86,000. ✈ 🚍 🚉
TAT, Udon Thani (0-4232-5406). 🗓 daily.
🎭 Cotton Blossom Festival (Feb), Phi Ta
Khon Festival, Rocket Festival (May/Jun).

In Thai, the word *loei* means "beyond" or "to the farthest extreme," a fitting name for a town and province that lie in the northernmost part of Northeast Thailand, straddling the edge of the Khorat Plateau. Though the province is administrated as part of Isan (the Northeast), its climate and landscape are more similar to those of Northern Thailand. In winter it is cold and foggy, in summer searingly hot. In the past, bureaucrats who had fallen out of favor with the Siamese government, based in Bangkok, were posted to the remote town of Loei as punishment for their inefficiency. One fortunate aspect of Loei's isolation is that it firmly retains its traditional flavor.

Lying along the west bank of the Loei River, Loei has a few sights of interest to visitors. There is a lively market by the bridge across the river, and next to the bridge is the **Lak Muang** or "city pillar." The town also has an old Chinese shrine, **Chao Pho Kut Pong**, a popular place of worship for the local people. The surrounding valley is rich in minerals and also produces some of the finest cotton in Thailand. Examples of this can be bought in Loei, in shops along Charoenraj Road and Ruamchai Road.

Loei also has a reasonable amount of cheap accommodations, making it a good base from which to visit Phu Rua and Phu Kradung *(see pp286–7)* national parks.

PHI TA KHON FESTIVAL

Phi Ta Khon costume

Although a less lively version of this festival is held in the provincial capital of Loei in July, its real home is in the town of Dan Sai, 80 km (50 miles) to the west. Here Phi Ta Khon takes place in June at the beginning of the rainy season *(see pp47–9)*. Its purpose is to make Buddhist merit and call for rain. The festival's origins are in the Buddhist tale of Prince Vessandorn, the Lord Buddha's final incarnation before he attained *nirvana*. Apparently, when Vessandorn returned to his city, the welcoming procession was so enchanting that the spirits emerged to celebrate. Today, the young men of Dan Sai dress up as spirits *(phi ta khon)*, draped in robes of patchwork rags and sporting painted masks made out of coconut tree trunks with huge, gaping mouths, beaklike noses, and wicker-basket crowns. During the three-day festival, they make playful jibes at onlookers as they parade a sacred Buddha image around the town. Monks also recite the story of Vessandorn to the crowd. On the third day, the "spirits" bring the festival to a close by circumambulating the main building of the local *wat* three times, before finally casting their colorful masks into a nearby river.

Young men, dressed as spirits, preparing to parade a sacred Buddha around Loei town

Phi Ta Khon "spirits" making fun of onlookers

Ornate, Lao-style facade of Wat Tha Kok, Chiang Khan

Chiang Khan ❻

เชียงคาน

Loei province. 🏛 52,000. 🚌 from Loei or Nong Khai. 🛈 TAT, Udon Thani (0-4232-5406).

Chiang Khan consists of two 2-km (1-mile) long parallel streets running along the south bank of the Mekong River and lined with run-down teakwood shop-houses, restaurants, and temples. Those temples most worth a visit are Wat Santi, Wat Pa Klang, built over 100 years ago by Lao immigrants, Wat Si Khun Muang, Wat Tha Kok, and Wat Mahathat. The latter is the oldest temple in Chiang Khan, its *bot* having been built in 1654. Like Wat Tha Kok, it shows French colonial influence in its colonnades and shutters.

Wat Tha Khok has a beautiful, painted ceiling. Its exterior walls are stained red, like the river, from dust. This possibly stems from deforestation in nearby Laos, which exposes the local red topsoil.

Environs
Located 2 km (1 mile) farther east from Wat Tha Kok along the Mekong River is Wat Tha Khaek. Neglected for years, this temple is now undergoing major reconstruction in a mixture of traditional and modern styles. A further 2 km (1 mile) down river are the scenic Kaeng Kut Khu rapids.

Pak Chom ❼

ปากชม

Loei province. 🏛 29,000. 🚌 from Loei or Nong Khai. 🛈 TAT, Udon Thani (0-4232-5406). 🛒 daily.

Pak Chom is little more than a picturesque settlement of ramshackle wooden buildings clustered by the bank of the Mekong River, 40 km (25 miles) northeast of Chiang Khan. It's a good place to stop for refreshments and to enjoy the scenery. In the 1970s and 1980s the town had a somewhat higher profile thanks to Ban Winai, a Lao-Hmong (*see p206*) refugee camp of some 15,000 inhabitants. It was established when these tribes people fled Laos in the wake of the Pathet Lao (*see p295*), who overthrew the Lao monarchy and took control of the country in 1975. In 1992 the camp was disbanded and the Hmong moved to Chiang Kham in the Chiang Rai province of Northern Thailand.

Mekong Villages Tour ❺

As well as villages, this tour takes in temples, lush forest, and great river views. No river in the world is quite like the 4,025-km (2,500-mile) Mekong, with its distinctive red waters. Its source is in the Himalayas, and it separates Laos and Thailand for 750 km (470 miles) before flowing through Cambodia and Vietnam out into the South China Sea. Rich in agriculture, its floodplain has been a source of wealth in an otherwise infertile region.

TIPS FOR TRAVELERS

Length: 120 km (75 miles).
Stopping-off points: Chiang Khan has a couple of restaurants, and four or five good guesthouses serving food. Pak Chom, Sangkhom, and Si Chiangmai all have good guesthouses offering food. Some guesthouses rent out bicycles. Food vendors can be found in most villages and towns.
Public transport: Local buses run between the main towns along the route. It is also possible to travel from Chiang Khan to Pak Chom by long-tail boat.

Ban Muang ④
Fishermen casting their nets are a common sight at this point in the Mekong River.

Pha Baen ②
This small village is one of many with picturesque wooden buildings and river views.

Pak Chom ③
The journey along the stretch of river between Chiang Khan and Pak Chom can be made by road or by long-tail boat.

Chiang Khan ①
Many of the temples and shop-houses in Chiang Khan show Lao influences.

KEY

▰▰ Tour route

▭ Other roads

▱ Rivers

Sangkhom 🛈
สังคม

Nong Khai province. 🏘 *19,000.*
🚌 *from Loei or Nong Khai.* 🛈 *TAT,
Udon Thani (0-4232-5406).*

The main attractions of this
town are its peace and quiet
and its location in a particularly lush part of the Mekong
River Valley. Ranged along
the bank of the river are some
quaint wooden buildings.
Sangkhom also makes a good
base for excursions into the
surrounding countryside.

Environs
The **Than Thip falls** are a
major highlight of this area.
Just outside Sangkhom, 3 km
(2 miles) off the main highway, they are hidden in the
middle of jungle and banana
groves. The two main, and
most accessible, levels of this
waterfall have pools at their
bases, making them ideal for a
refreshing swim. More intrepid
travelers can explore a further
three levels higher up the falls.

Topiary in the gardens of the Fisheries Department, near Si Chiangmai

Si Chiangmai 🛈
ศรีเชียงใหม่

Nong Khai province. 🏘 *23,000.*
🚌 *from Loei or Nong Khai.* 🛈 *TAT,
Udon Thani (0-4232-5406).* 🏠 *daily.*

This town overlooks the
Lao capital of Vientiane *(see
pp294–5)* on the other side
of the Mekong River and has
a large population of Lao and
Vietnamese refugees. Its main
claim to fame is as the world's
largest producer of spring roll
wrappers. When the weather
is good, they can be seen along
the roadsides, spread out on
bamboo racks to dry in the sun.

Environs
Located 5 km (3 miles)
outside Si Chiangmai are
the gardens of the **Fisheries
Department**, featuring unusual elephant-shaped topiary.

Than Thip Falls ⑤
Situated close to Sangkhom,
the Than Thip Falls, with
their numerous pools, make a
delightful refreshment stop.

LAOS

Sangkhom ⑥
In beautiful surroundings, this
town is favored by back-
packers, who stay in bam-
boo huts by the river.

THAILAND

Wat Hin Mak Peng ⑦
This *wat* complex is the site of
a famous meditation center. It is
popular with Thai pilgrims, and
much of its wealth comes from
donations by affluent visitors.

0 kilometers	10
0 miles	5

Si Chiangmai ⑧
In this town there is a
Roman Catholic cathedral serving
a large population of Christian
Lao and Vietnamese refugees.

Nong Khai

หนองคาย

Now one of the busiest commercial centers in the Northeast, this once sleepy border town continues to grow, benefitting from lively border trade with Laos. The construction, in 1994, of the Friendship Bridge, the first bridge to span the Mekong River between Thailand and Laos, was a factor in an increase in trade between the two countries. Nevertheless, the town center retains much of its original charm, and Nong Khai's main attraction for travelers is still its peaceful riverside character.

Village Weaver shop sign

Relative peace and quiet on Nong Khai's Meechai Street

Exploring Nong Khai

Nong Khai's streets and *sois* are lined with traditional wooden shop-houses. Its most vibrant neighborhood is around the Sadet riverboat pier, with its market and adjacent restaurants overlooking the Mekong River. An influx of prosperity in the town is made obvious by the burgeoning number of restaurants as well as modern shopping centers and banking facilities.

Intricate carving on the rear of the Lao-style Wat Si Muang

Indochina Market

ตลาดอินโดจีน

Off Rimkhong Rd, Tha Sadet. ⬜ *daily*.
This market remains the focus of lively, local trade carried out between Thailand and Laos. Reciprocal visa arrangements allow merchants from either country to visit Vientiane *(see pp294–5)* or Nong Khai for up to three days. Merchandise that can be bought at the market includes clothing, pots and pans, foodstuffs, pestles and mortars, fishing nets, and tables woven from bamboo.

Prap Ho Monument

อนุสาวรีย์ปราบฮ่อ

Janjopthit Rd.
The Prap Ho Monument, a symbol of municipal pride, was built to honor those who held off Ho Chinese invasions in 1855 and 1877. Built in 1886, and bearing Thai, Lao, Chinese, and English inscriptions, it is the site of annual celebrations on March 5.

Prajak Road

ถนนประจักษ์

Along Prajak Road, visitors can pay a call at the Village Weaver shop, where traditional silk weaving is carried out. The factory/shop specializes in *mut mee*, the name given to a method of tie-dying used in the Northeast. It was established as part of a program to encourage local girls to stay and work in Nong Khai, rather than moving to larger urban centers such as Bangkok. There is also a market on Prajak Road, to the rear of the bus station.

Wat Si Muang

วัดศรีเมือง

Off Meechai Rd. ⬜ *daily*.
The temple buildings and *chedi* of Wat Si Muang are Lao in style. The *wat* has an ornate shrine at the main entrance, cluttered with Buddhist merit offerings. Wat Si Muang is one of many such temples that line the main Meechai Road leading west toward Wat Pho Chai.

Wat Pho Chai

วัดโพธิ์ชัย

Pho Chai Rd. ⬜ *daily*.
The somewhat gaudy Wat Pho Chai lies in the southwest of the city, adjacent to a street market of the same name. Its main chapel sports imposing *naga* balustrades and a pair of roaring lions at the top of the entrance stairs, protecting the highly revered Luang Pho Phra Sai Buddha image housed inside.

Guardian lion, Wat Pho Chai

This solid gold Buddha with a ruby-studded, flame finial was originally molded in the ancient Lao kingdom of Lan Xang. It later resided in Vientiane *(see pp294–5)*. In 1778 it was taken by Prince Chakri, later Rama I (1782–1809), following the first Thai invasion of Laos. As he attempted to ferry it across the Mekong, it fell into the river and, according to legend, miraculously resurfaced. After it had been rescued it was placed in Wat Pho Chai. Murals in the temple give a pictorial account of this story.

Luang Pho Phra Sai Buddha image, housed in Wat Pho Chai

cooperation, it links Ban Chommani on the western outskirts of Nong Khai to Tha Na Laeng on the opposite bank, some 20 km (12 miles) from Vientiane. By the foot of the bridge, on the Thai side, is a stretch of sand known as Chommani beach, a popular spot for picnicking Thais during the dry season, when the waters of the Mekong River are low.

Closer to the town center is the Lao *chedi* of **Phra That Nong Khai**, which collapsed into the Mekong River in 1847. Over the years it has slowly drifted farther and farther into the middle of the river to the point where it can now be seen only when the water is low.

By far the most unusual site of interest at Nong Khai lies some 5 km (3 miles) to the east of the town. **Wat Khaek**, also known as Sala Kaew Ku, was founded in 1978 by the charismatic Luang Pu Bunleua Surirat. This Thai-Brahmin shaman allegedly trained under a Hindu guru in Vietnam, moved on to Laos, and was then forced to Thailand by the hostile attentions of the Pathet Lao *(see p295)*. Wat

🏛 Other Wats

Apart from its major sights, Nong Khai has a number of minor *wats* worth a visit. All of them have Lao-influenced architecture and include **Wat Haisoke**, **Wat Lamduan** and **Wat Si Sumang**, which all offer views of the Mekong River, and **Wat Si Khun Muang**.

Environs

Though always a major crossing point for tourists and traders bound for the Lao capital of Vientiane, Nong Khai gained significance as a commercial border post with the opening of the **Friendship Bridge** in 1994. Built with Thai, Lao, and Australian

VISITORS' CHECKLIST

Nong Khai province. 🏠 83,000. 🚌 3 km (2 miles) W on Kaeo Worawut Rd. 🚉 Praserm Rd. 🛈 TAT, Udon Thani (0-4232-5406). 🏛 daily. 🎉 Nong Khai Festival (Mar), Bun Bang Fai (Rocket) Festival (May); Naga Fireballs (Oct).

Khaek is essentially an open-air theme park of enormous, concrete Hindu and Buddhist sculptures.

Among the giant gods, saints, and demons that are depicted here are Rahu, the god of eclipses and, tallest of all, a 25-m (82-ft) high seven-headed *naga* with a tiny Buddha seated on its coils. The atmosphere of a walk through this eccentric collection of images is intensified by incense and piped music. The shrine building is an exhibition hall on two floors that contains, among other things, numerous photographs of the Luang Pu or "Venerable Grandfather." He is said to have such charisma that anyone drinking holy water offered by him will immediately donate all their belongings to the temple.

Seven-headed *naga*, Wat Khaek

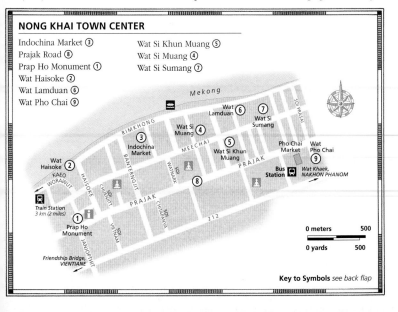

NONG KHAI TOWN CENTER

Indochina Market ③
Prajak Road ⑧
Prap Ho Monument ①
Wat Haisoke ②
Wat Lamduan ⑥
Wat Pho Chai ⑨

Wat Si Khun Muang ⑤
Wat Si Muang ④
Wat Si Sumang ⑦

Mekong

Wat Lamduan ⑥ ⑦ Wat Si Sumang

RIMKHONG

Wat Si ④ Muang

③ Indochina Market

MEECHAI

⑤ Wat Si Khun Muang

Pho Chai Market

Wat Pho Chai ⑨

Wat Haisoke ②

KAEO WORAWUT

HAISOKE

CHUBUT

BANTERNGJIT

WATNAK

SOI WATNAK

PRAJAK

⑧

Bus Station 🚏

Wat Khaek, NAKHON PHANOM

Train Station 3 km (2 miles) 🚉 🛈

① Prap Ho Monument

JANYOTPHIT

PRAJAK

SOI VIETNAM

SOI CHUBUT

SOI CHIARAWA

212

Friendship Bridge, VIENTIANE

0 meters 500
0 yards 500

Key to Symbols *see back flap*

Vientiane ⑪

เวียงจันทน์

Temple door

In its 1,000-year history, Vientiane has come under Khmer, Vietnamese, Thai, and French colonial influence. It was capital of the Lan Xang Kingdom in the 16th century and later a vassal of Ayutthaya. The Thais sacked Vientiane in 1828. In 1893 the French annexed Laos and made Vientiane its capital. Laos gained independence in 1953; in 1975 it became a Socialist Republic. A day trip from Nong Khai (see pp292–3), today Vientiane shows a side of Southeast Asia that is fast disappearing.

Exploring Vientiane

Vientiane has been isolated from change for generations. However, it has now seen some radical changes thanks to cross-border trade with Thailand, encouraged by the Friendship Bridge (see p293), and investment from China and Japan. Vientiane is shaking off its sleepy image, but so far it has also remained blissfully free from mass commercialism and uncontrolled development.

Vientiane was one of three important French Indochinese cities; the others were Ho Chi Minh City (or Saigon) and Phnom Penh. French colonial influence can still be felt in the city, with its broad, tree-lined boulevards and shuttered villas.

Shop-house in Vientiane

🏛 Haw Pha Kaew

Setthathirat Rd. ⬜ daily. ⬤ public hols. 🈵
This temple was once home to the Phra Kaeo or Emerald Buddha (see p83), which was taken by the Thais in 1778 and placed in Wat Phra Kaeo in Bangkok. (Phra Kaeo is the preferred transliteration in Thai; Pha Kaew in Lao.) A replica, a symbol of renewed friendship, was given to Laos by Thailand in 1994. The sack of 1828 left the temple in ruins. Restored in the 20th century, it is now a museum. The beautifully carved main door is all that remains of the original wat.

🏛 Wat Sisaket

Lane Xang Rd. ⬜ daily. ⬤ public hols. 🈵
This wat, built in 1818, was one of the few buildings to survive the sack of 1828. It is now the oldest wat in Vientiane and one of the most interesting to visit. Its most memorable feature is the 2,052 tiny Buddha images made of terra-cotta, bronze, and wood that fill niches in the walls of the cloister. Over 300 Buddha images also rest on a long shelf below the niches.

🏛 Lao Revolutionary Museum

Samsenthai Rd. ⬜ 8am–noon, 1–4pm daily. ⬤ public hols. 🈵
Artifacts and photographs here detail the period of French colonialism, independence in the 1940s and '50s, and the rise of the Pathet Lao.

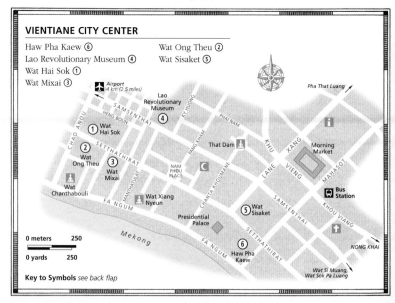

VIENTIANE CITY CENTER

Haw Pha Kaew ⑥
Lao Revolutionary Museum ④
Wat Hai Sok ①
Wat Mixai ③
Wat Ong Theu ②
Wat Sisaket ⑤

Airport
4 km (2.5 miles)

Lao Revolutionary Museum ④

① Wat Hai Sok
② Wat Ong Theu
③ Wat Mixai
Wat Chanthabouli
Wat Xiang Nyeun

That Dam
NAM PHOU PLACE

Presidential Palace

⑤ Wat Sisaket
⑥ Haw Pha Kaew

Pha That Luang

Morning Market

Bus Station

NONG KHAI

Wat Si Muang, Wat Sok Pa Luang

Mekong

SAMSENTHAI
HENG BOUN
CHAO ANOU
SETTHATHIRAT
MANTHATURAT
FA NGUM
KY HUONG
PANG KHAM
PHAI NAM
CHANTA KHOUMANE
KHU XANG
LANE VIENG
SAMSENTHAI
MAHASOT
KHOU VIANG

0 meters   250
0 yards   250

Key to Symbols see back flap

Wat Mixai

Setthathirat Rd. ◯ daily.
Its gates flanked by two *nyaks* or guardian giants, parts of this *wat* complex were built in 19th-century Rattanakosin style.

Wat Ong Theu

Setthathirat Rd. ◯ daily.
One of the most important *wat* complexes in all Laos, Wat Ong Theu was originally founded in the early 16th century. Destroyed in 1828, it was rebuilt in the 19th and 20th centuries. The *wat* houses a large, 16th-century bronze Buddha image, with two standing Buddhas either side of it. The *wat* also houses a school for monks.

Wat Hai Sok

Setthathirat Rd. ◯ daily.
Like other *wats* in Vientiane, Wat Hai Sok has undergone restoration. Its most distinctive feature is an impressive five-tiered roof.

Environs

The **Pha That Luang**, which perches, somewhat out of the way, half-way up a hill on the north-eastern outskirts of the city, is the most important national and Buddhist monument in Laos. According to legend a *chedi* was built here in the 3rd century BC to house a breastbone of the Lord Buddha. More tangible

VISITORS' CHECKLIST

Vientiane province, Laos. 🚶 6 million. ✈ 4 km (2.5 miles) W of center. 🚌 off Khu Vieng Rd. 🚤 from Nong Khai. 🛈 corner of Setthathirat Rd and Pang Kham Rd. 🛍 daily. 🎉 Bun That Luang Festival (mid-Nov). **Currency:** kip, Thai baht, US dollar. **Visas and permits:** A visa is issued on arrival at Wattay Airport in Vientiane for a fee of US$35. A passport photo is required. Visitors to Vientiane can also enter via the Friendship Bridge, just outside Nong Khai in Thailand, crossing by bus. A visa is issued on arrival here too. Visas are valid for one month and allow you to travel freely throughout Laos.

evidence suggests this was the site of a Khmer *prasat*. The present structure was built in 1566, when Vientiane became the capital of the Lan Xang Kingdom. It was damaged in the 18th and 19th centuries and restored, albeit badly, by the French in 1900. A better restoration of the site was undertaken in the 1930s.

Wat Si Muang, to the southeast of the city center, is the most popular place of worship in Vientiane. According to legend, the site was chosen by Lao sages in 1563.

Wat Sok Pa Luang is known for its instruction in *vipassana*, a type of Buddhist meditation.

Ho Nang Ussa, a rock formation in Phu Phrabat Historical Park

Phu Phrabat Historical Park ⑫
อุทยานประวัติศาสตร์ภูพระบาท

Off Hwy 2021, 10 km (6 miles) W of Ban Pheu, Udon Thani province. 🛈 TAT, Udon Thani (0-4232-5406). 🚌 from Nong Khai or Udon Thani to Ban Phu, then songthaew. ◯ daily. 🎫

The distinctive sandstone formations that are the central attraction of this historical park cannot fail to leave their imprint on the imagination. The local population has shrouded the site in many fantastic myths and legends. According to one of these, Princess Ussa was sent to Phu Phrabat by her father to study. However, she fell in love with Prince Barot. Outraged, her father challenged the prince to a temple-building duel, but lost. A huge sandstone slab in the park, known as Kok Ma Thao Barot, is supposedly Prince Barot's stable. The mushroom-shaped Ho Nang Ussa apparently represents Princess Ussa's residence, where she pined away many long years in exile.

The 6,000-year-old human history of this site is testified to by cave paintings found on the underside of two natural rock shelters, known locally as Tham Wua and Tham Khon or "ox cave" and "people cave."

At the entrance to the historical park stands a crude replica of Wat Phra That Phanom (*see p297*); the **Wat Phraphutthabat Bua Bok** houses the Bua Bok Buddha Footprint and is an important pilgrimage site for local Thais.

THE PATHET LAO

The Lao Patriotic Front was formed after World War II and, with ties to Ho Chi Minh's Communist Party in Vietnam, opposed French rule. In 1953 Laos was declared a constitutional monarchy, backed by France and the US. The LPF's armed wing, the Pathet Lao, mounted an armed struggle against the government in the 1960s. During the Vietnam War the US repeatedly bombed Laos in order to stamp out Pathet Lao support for the North Vietnamese. With the withdrawal of American forces from the region in 1975, the Pathet Lao staged a bloodless coup and declared Laos the Lao People's Democratic Republic.

Poster supporting the Lao People's Democratic Party

Wat Phra That Choeng Chum, the main *wat* in the old, once Khmer, town of Sakhon Nakhon

Sakhon Nakhon ⑬

สกลนคร

Sakhon Nakhon province.
🏙 120,000. ✈ 🚌 🛈 *TAT, Nakhon Phanom (0-4251-3490).* 🛍 *daily.*
🎎 *Wax Castle Ceremony (Oct).*

There are two sights of interest in the friendly town of Sakhon Nakhon. **Wat Phra That Choeng Chum** is a beautiful temple complex with a large *bot* and *wihan*, a 10th-century Khmer *prang*, and a whitewashed, 24-m (80-ft) Lao-style *chedi* built during the Ayutthaya period.

The old *prang* is reached through a door in the *wihan*. Etched into the *prang's* base is an ancient Khmer inscription, and around it are Lao and Khmer images of the Buddha. Also in the compound is an interesting display of *luk nimit*, which are Brahmin foundation markers that somewhat resemble giant cannon balls.

The five-layered, 11th-century Khmer *prang* of **Wat Phra That Narai Cheng Weng** was built as a Hindu monument. The name Cheng Weng is taken from the princess responsible for its construction; Narai is a Thai and Khmer name for Vishnu. The most important lintel – over the only entrance, to the east – shows Shiva dancing to the destruction of the universe,

as he tramples the head of a lion. On the northern portico is a splendid depiction of Vishnu, with a lotus and baton in two of his four hands.

Nakhon Phanom ⑭

นครพนม

Nakhon Phanom province.
🏙 114,000. ✈ 🚌 🛈 *TAT, 1841 Soontornvijit Rd, Nakhon Phanom (0-4251-3490).* 🛍 *daily.* 🎎 *Illuminated Boats Procession (Oct).*

Nakhon Phanom – "city of hills" – is a good town in which to spend a few relaxing days by the Mekong. In the dry season a beach by the river, **Hat Sai Tai Muang**, becomes exposed, and it is possible to walk out almost as far as Laos. However, this town cannot be used as a place to procure a few visa for, or as an entry point into, Laos.

To celebrate the end of the rains, during the night of the full moon in the 11th lunar month, there is a resplendent procession of illuminated boats on the river here. Measuring some 10 m (33 ft) in length, the boats are traditionally crafted from bamboo or banana trees. They are filled with lighted candles, incense, kerosene lamps, and offerings of fragrant flowers and candies.

Renu Nakhon ⑮

เรณูนคร

Nakhon Phanom province.
🏙 39,000. 🚌 *from Nakhon Phanom.* 🛈 *TAT, Nakhon Phanom (0-4251-3490).* 🛍 *Wed.*

Renu Nakhon is a village known primarily for its weaving and fine embroidery. At the popular Wednesday market, colorful cottons and silks are sold by the *phun*, a measure 75 cm (2 ft) long. Ready-made garments and furnishings from all over the Northeast and Laos are also sold. There is a more permanent gathering of textile stalls around **Phra That Renu**. This was built in 1918 and modeled loosely on the nearby *chedi* at That Phanom.

Shop selling a range of locally made textiles, Renu Nakhon

Wat Phra That Phanom ⑯

วัดพระธาตุพนม

This *wat*, in the remote town of That Phanom, is the most revered shrine in Northeast Thailand, famous for its central, Lao-style brick and plaster *chedi*. The *chedi* was constructed some 1,500 years ago, but according to legend it was built eight years after the death of the Buddha in 535 BC, when local dignitaries erected it as a burial place for his breastbone. The monument has been restored many times, most recently after devastating rains in 1975. Each year at the full moon of the third lunar month, during a farming holiday, a week-long temple festival attracts thousands of pilgrims from Thailand and Laos.

VISITORS' CHECKLIST

Center of That Phanom, Nakhon Phanom province. 🛈 *TAT, Nakhon Phanom (0-4251-3490).* 🚌 *from Nakhon Phanom, Sakhon Nakhon, or Mukdahan.* 🕕 *6am–7pm daily.* 📅 🎆 *Phra That Phanom Festival (Feb/Mar).*

Stone Lion
One of two on either side of the outer compound's central path, this fierce mythical beast is a temple guardian who wards off evil forces.

Pilgrims at Wat Phra That Phanom
Thousands come to pay homage at festival time and throughout the year. Many devotees are from Laos – the monument is the second most sacred site to them, the first being That Luang in Vientiane.

Gold decoration in the shape of a multi-leaved lotus flower represents the path to Enlightenment.

The *chedi* **is** studded with gemstones and gold rings.

CENTRAL CHEDI

The famous 57-m (185-ft) high *chedi* at the center of the temple is in the shape of a stylized, elongated lotus bud. The present structure, rebuilt in 1977, is modeled on That Luang in Vientiane, Laos.

Golden Buddha Image
In abhaya mudra *posture (see p173) and shaded by an umbrella, this image sits near the entrance to the inner compound.*

A *chat*, **or ceremonial umbrella**

Numerous Buddha images line the inner compound wall of the *chedi*. Pilgrims paste squares of gold leaf onto them as a way of making merit.

Stone panels carved in the 10th century tell the legends of the five men who supposedly built the *chedi* in the 6th century BC.

The market along the river at Mukdahan, where Lao and Vietnamese merchandise is sold

Mukdahan ⑰

มุกดาหาร

Mukdahan province. 👥 *83,000.* 🚌 ℹ️ *TAT, Nakhon Phanom (0-4251-3490).* 🍽 *daily.* 🎋 *Ruam Pao Thai Ma Kham Wan Chai Khong Fair (Jan).*

Mukdahan is the capital of one of Thailand's newest provinces, created in 1980 from areas that were formerly part of Nakhon Phanom and Ubon Ratchathani provinces.

The most interesting street is Samran Chai Khong Road, along the Mekong River front. It faces the second-largest city in Laos, Suwannakhet, on the opposite bank. In 2007, a

Seated Buddha at Wat Yot Kaew Siwichai, Mukdahan

second Friendship Bridge opened across the river, linking Mukdahan with Suwannakhet. Visitors can obtain a visa on arrival to enter Laos. Mukdahan is a busy trading center, and both Lao and Thai boats can be seen at the pier, loading and unloading their goods.

A market also runs most of the length of the riverside, between **Wat Si Mongkol Tai** and **Wat Yot Kaew Siwichai**. Goods for sale may be disappointing because there are few examples of traditional Lao and Vietnamese merchandise. Expect an excess of plastic ephemera, though the market is worth a visit for the local sweetmeats and its colorful atmosphere.

Wat Si Mongkhol Thai was built in 1956 by Vietnamese immigrants in the town and is distinguished by statues of mythical creatures at the entrance to its main chapel.

The gaudier Wat Yot Kaew Siwichai houses an enormous, seated, golden Buddha image. The figure sits in an open-fronted *wihan* with paneled glass on two of its sides. Near Wat Yot Kaew Siwichai, on Song Nang Sathit Road, is the Chinese **Chao Fa Mung Muang shrine**, home to Mukdahan's guardian center. Also here is the **Lak Muang**, or City Pillar, which is usually draped in colorful plastic garlands.

Environs

Excellent views of the entire provincial capital can be captured from the 500-m (1,650-ft) peak of **Phu Manorom**. A pavilion at the top of the hill shelters a replica of the Buddha's Footprint.

🏞 **Phu Manorom**
Off Hwy 2034, 5 km (3 miles) S of Mukdahan. ⚪ *daily.* 📷

Pha Taem ⑱

ผาแต้ม

18 km (11 miles) N of Khong Chiam, Ubon Ratchathani province. ℹ️ *TAT, Ubon Ratchathani (0-4524-3770).* 🚌 *from Ubon Ratchathani to Khong Chiam, then tuk-tuk.* ⚪ *daily.* 📷

The route, 18 km (11 miles) from Khong Chiam up to Pha Taem or "painted cliff," is a circuitous one, really accessible only by rental car or *tuk-tuk.* Along the way, a few kilometers before you arrive at the cliff top, an unusual, sandstone rock formation can be seen at the side of the road. Known as Sao Chaliang, it is reminiscent of the Ho Nang Ussa at Phu Phrabat Historical Park (*see p295*).

At the end of the journey, an unmarked trail leads from the parking lot to the cliff face. This is decorated with huge figures and geometrical designs. Painted in an indelible red pigment derived from soil, tree gum, and fat, the paintings are thought to date back some 4,000 years. Covering 170 m (560 ft) along the cliff face, they include depictions of fish traps, wild animals, giant cockroachlike fish, angular human beings, and a 30-m (98-ft) stretch of handprints. The artists who created these decorations are thought to be related to the early inhabitants of Ban Chiang (see p272) and were rice cultivators rather than cave dwellers.

Prehistoric cliff-painting, Pha Taem

Pha Taem is particularly beautiful at sunset, when it has tremendous views across the Mekong and of the wild Lao jungle beyond.

Khong Chiam ⓳
โขงเจียม

Ubon Ratchathani province. 🏠 30,000. 🚌 🛈 TAT, Ubon Ratchathani (0-4524-3770). 🏪 daily.

Khong Chiam is near the confluence of the muddy red Mekong and the indigo-blue Mun rivers, which creates the phenomenon of the *maenam song si* or "two-colored river."

Making wicker fish traps, Khong Chiam

The differing colors of the rivers derive from the amounts of sand and clay suspended in their waters. Scenic views are offered from the bank at **Wat Khong Chiam**, and boat trips out to the confluence point itself allow a full appreciation of the blend of colored waters, clearest in April. It is also possible to cross from Khong Chiam to the Lao town on the opposite side of the river, but this cannot be used by travelers as an official crossing point into Laos.

Visitors to Khong Chiam can also watch traditional conical fish traps being made out of wicker.

Chong Mek ⓴
ช่องเม็ก

Ubon Ratchathani province. 🏠 4,900. 🚌 from Ubon Ratchathani. 🛈 TAT, Ubon Ratchathani (0-4524-3770). 🏪 daily.

Situated on the border between Thailand and Laos, Chong Mek is one of the few places at which tourists can cross into Laos. Other Lao entry points include Nong Khai (see pp292–3), Chiang Khong (see p249), and Mukdahan (see p298).

Visitors can obtain a visa on arrival, valid for one month, for a fee of US$35 and a recent passport photograph.

Since the border crossing opened at Chong Mek, a vibrant market and shopping area has sprung up, attracting busloads of Thai tourists who also cross into Laos to visit the nearby town of Pakse.

For those who do not have a visa, it is possible, even without a passport, to walk some 200 m (660 ft) over the border to browse around the open-air market and duty-free shops that are set up there.

In the market, there may be groups of old women selling rare plants and flowers. However, many of the plants are, sadly, taken from the Lao jungle. Visitors to the market are advised not to buy these.

Boat on the Sirindhorn Dam

Sirindhorn Dam ㉑
เขื่อนสิรินธร

Ubon Ratchathani province. 🛈 TAT, Ubon Ratchathani (0-4524-3770). For information about tourist accommodation call 0-4536-6085. 🚌 from Ubon Ratchathani to Chong Mek, then songthaew.

Named after the second daughter of King Bhumibol, the Sirindhorn Dam was built in 1971. The reservoir it created is 43 km (27 miles) from north to south; the turbines produce 24,000 kilowatts of electricity.

There is a park at the dam HQ, and a restaurant and bungalows. It is possible to walk out over the dam and to take a boat on the reservoir.

Dams in Thailand have been funded by the World Bank since the 1950s to meet Thailand's ever-increasing need for electricity. They are given support mainly by politicians and the business community. Residents and environmental groups have begun to campaign against the construction of new dams.

Prasat Khao Phra Wihan ②

ปราสาทเขาพระวิหาร

Off Hwy 221, S of Ubon and Sisaket, just inside Cambodia. ⓘ *TAT, Ubon Ratchathani (0-4524-3770).* 🚌 *from Ubon or Sisaket to Kantharalak, then songthaew.* ⬜ *daily.* 📷

The extraordinary site of this early Khmer temple, laid out along a spur of the Dongrek Mountains, makes it one of the most distinctive Khmer structures outside of Angkor *(see pp264–5).* Possibly older than Angkor, sadly, it was long the victim of disputes between Thailand and Cambodia. After much disagreement between the two countries, in 1962 a decision was taken by the World Court: while the easiest access to the temple is through Thailand, the temple stands firmly in Cambodia.

During the mid-1970s, the years of the Khmer Rouge regime in Cambodia, the temple became a strictly no-go area. After the Vietnamese invaded Cambodia in 1978, conflicts between rival factions continued in the area until the late 1980s. The site was finally cleared of land mines and opened to the public in the early 1990s, but as civil unrest

Three ruined *prangs*, all on a single base, at Prasat Prang Ku

continues in Cambodia, this magnificent temple is forced to close down periodically.

When Khao Phra Wihan is open, tourists can walk through army checkpoints to ascend a series of grand staircases, pass through stone *gopuras,* and then walk along an 850-m (2,800-ft) *naga-lined* causeway to arrive at the central sanctuary, or *prasat.* Dedicated to the Hindu god Shiva, it is now largely in ruins. The *prang* in particular is in need of restoration. Views from the sheer cliffs here, over the Cambodian plateau, are exhilarating. If the temple is closed, elegant Khmer reliefs carved in the cliff can be viewed from the Thai side of the border.

Stone relief on the Cambodian sight of Prasat Khao Phra Wihan

Prasat Prang Ku ②

ปราสาทปรางค์กู่

Off Hwy 2234, 70 km (43 miles) SW of Si Sa Ket, Si Sa Ket province. ⓘ *TAT, Ubon Ratchathani (0-4524-3770).* 🚌 *from Ubon or Sisaket to Kantha-ralak, then songthaew.* ⬜ *daily.* 📷

Located in the district of Prang Ku in Si Sa Ket province, this 11th-century Khmer monument comprises three brick *prangs* on a single platform. The most remarkable feature is a well-preserved lintel, divided horizontally into two sections by the tails of two long *nagas.* In the

center stands Vishnu on his mount, a *garuda.* On either side of the *garuda* are two lions with garlands of flowers in their open mouths. The top half of the lintel is decorated with dancing deities. In front of Prasat Prang Ku is a 1-km (1,100-yd) long Khmer *baray* (reservoir), a welcome feeding ground for birds.

Ubon Ratchathani ②

อุบลราชธานี

Ubon Ratchathani province. 👥 *118,000.* ✈ 🚂 🚌 ⓘ *TAT, 264/1 Khuan Thani Rd, Ubon Ratchathani (0-4524-3770).* 🍴 *daily.* 🎉 *Ubon Candle Festival (late Jul).* **www**.*tatubon.org*

From the 10th century, Ubon Ratchathani province, often simply known as Ubon, was part of the Khmer Empire. It later fell under the control of the Ayutthaya Kingdom *(see pp60–61).* The provincial capital, the city of Ubon Ratchathani was founded by Lao immigrants on the northern bank of the Mun River at the end of the 18th century, and Lao influence can still be seen in the architectural features of some of the city's religious buildings. Following the rapid growth of Ubon during the Vietnam War, when it played host to a nearby American air base, the city is, today, one of the largest in Thailand.

At first sight, Ubon appears to be a great concrete sprawl, but the **Ubon National Museum** is one of the best in the Northeast, and some fascinating

A beautifully preserved stone *gopura,* Prasat Khao Phra Wihan

temples are dotted around the city. The museum is housed in the former country residence of King Vajiravudh (1910–25) and contains displays of Khmer, Hindu, and Lao Buddhist iconography, as well as traditional tools, utensils, and handicrafts. One of the rarest and most impressive exhibits is a giant bronze drum, dating back as far as the 4th century AD, that was used originally for ceremonial purposes.

The most interesting of Ubon's temples is **Wat Thung Si Muang** on account of its teakwood library. Founded by King Rama III (1824–51) the *wat* houses 150-year-old murals showing some of the *jatakas* (see p30). The complex also includes a *mondop* with a Buddha Footprint.

In 1853 King Mongkut (1851–68) gave his support to the construction of **Wat Supattanaram Worawihan** as the first temple in the

Figure atop Wat Supattanaram

Northeast dedicated to the Thammayut sect – a strict branch of Theravada Buddhism – of which the king was also a member. It consists of a highly eclectic blend of architectural styles, having been built by Vietnamese craftsmen who were under instruction to incorporate an unusual mixture of Khmer, Thai, and European architectural influences.

The more modern **Wat Phra That Nong Bua** was built in 1957 to commemorate the 2,500th anniversary of the death of the Lord Buddha. Its two four-sided, white-washed towers are decorated with standing Buddha images in niches and reliefs of tales of the Buddha in his previous lives. Ubon also has several other interesting temples: **Wat Cheng**, with its elegant Lao-style wooden carvings; **Wat Si Ubon Rattanaram**, built in 1855 and housing a topaz Buddha image, originating from Chiang Saen; and the main

Carved Buddha images in niches at **Wat Phra That Nong Bua**

temple, **Wat Maha Wanaram**, in which local people worship.

Ubon becomes a place of pilgrimage at the beginning of Buddhist Lent, when, during the Ubon Candle Festival (see p49), large, sculpted candles are carried through the streets.

🏛 **Ubon National Museum**
Khuan Thani Rd. *Tel* 0-4525-5071.
⏰ 9am–4pm Wed–Sun. ● public hols. 🖥 www.thailandmuseum.com

UBON RATCHATHANI CITY CENTER

Ubon National Museum ②
Wat Cheng ④
Wat Maha Wanaram ⑤
Wat Si Ubon Rattanaram ③
Wat Supattanaram Worawihan ①
Wat Thung Si Muang ⑥

0 meters   50
0 yards   50

Wat Phra That Nong Bua
SURIYAT
Airport 500 m (550 yards)
CHAYANGKUN
PHADAENG
SOI SUMPASIT 2
SAPPHASIT
④ Wat Cheng
⑤ Wat Maha Wanaram
YASOTHON
PHICHIT RANGSAN
SURAPHA NAI
PHONPHAEN
THEP YOTHI
LUANG
Bus Station
PHALO CHAI
SURASAK
NAKHON BAN
③ Wat Si Ubon Rattanaram
⑥ Wat Thung Si Muang
PHALO RUNGRIT
SI NARONG
SI NARONG
Ubon National Museum ②
RATCHABUT
YUTTHAPHAN
LUANG
KHUAN THANI
PHROMRAT
① Wat Supattanaram Worawihan
UPPARAT
PHROM THEP
PHROMRAT
Night Market
Train Station 2km (1.2 miles)
Mun

Key to Symbols see back flap

THE GULF OF
THAILAND

INTRODUCING THE GULF OF THAILAND
306–311

EASTERN SEABOARD 312–323

WESTERN SEABOARD 324–341

Introducing the Gulf of Thailand

Thais and foreigners flock to the Gulf's resorts to relax on the many superb beaches and eat delicious seafood. Bangkok weekenders have long favored Cha-am and Hua Hin, while Pattaya draws lovers of sports and hectic nightlife. The towns of Chaiya and Phetchaburi contain architectural and artistic treasures and have the lively ethnic and cultural mix typical of the Western Seaboard and farther south. Inland, breathtaking flora and fauna abound in beautiful, crowd-free national parks. Thailand's once-idyllic islands have been experiencing a huge surge in popularity. Ko Samui has suffered badly from uncontrolled development and mass tourism, and Ko Samet and Ko Chang have also witnessed dramatic changes.

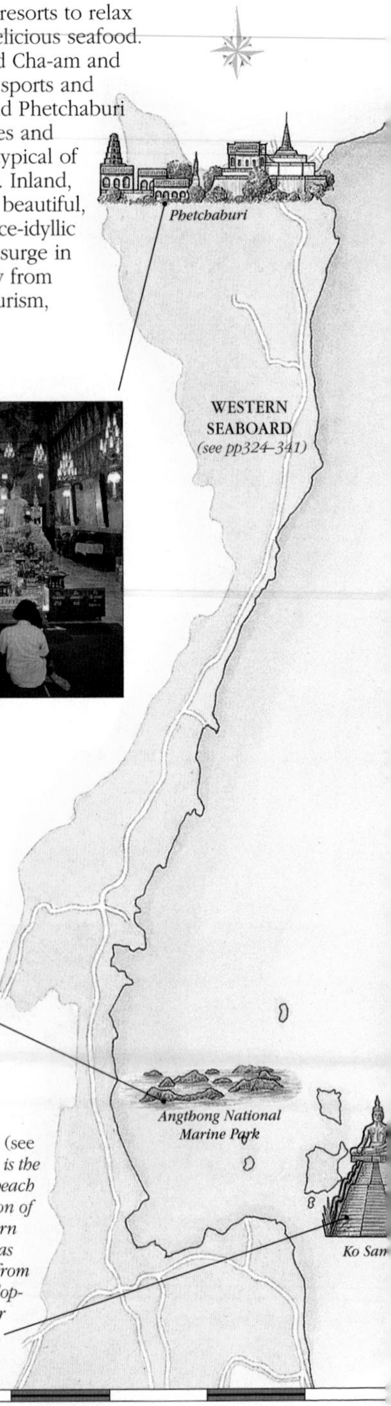

Phetchaburi

WESTERN SEABOARD
(see pp324–341)

Phetchaburi (see pp328–30) *is an important cultural center with more than 30 wats, including the splendid Wat Mahathat, founded in the 14th century. Despite a history dating back to the 11th century and an attractive old quarter, the town receives few visitors.*

Angthong National Marine Park (see pp340–41), *easily accessible from Ko Samui, is a stunning group of tiny islands teeming with wildlife.*

Angthong National Marine Park

Ko Samui (see pp336–8) *is the premier beach destination of the Western Gulf. It has suffered from overdevelopment over the years.*

Ko Sam

◁ View of Ban Lamai beach, Ko Samui

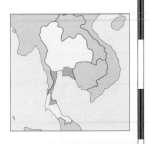

EASTERN
SEABOARD
(see pp312–323)

Pattaya

Ko Samet

Ko Chang

Ko Samet (see pp318–19) *is a popular island destination, particularly with Thais, since it is within comfortable driving distance from Bangkok.*

Pattaya (see p317) *attracts an unlikely mix of families eager to take advantage of the beaches and excellent sports facilities, and hedonists equally eager to enjoy the renowned nightlife of the discos, go-go, and beer bars.*

Ko Chang (see pp322–3) *is the largest of an archipelago of 52 islands. It has experienced considerable development and is now a popular mainstream destination.*

0 kilometers   50

0 miles   25

Beach Life and Leisure in the Gulf

Thai beach culture dates from the 1920s with the opening of both the railroad from Bangkok to Hua Hin and the first golf club, the Royal Hua Hin, designed by Scottish railroad engineer A.O. Robins. Hua Hin and its modern neighbor, Cha-am, continue to attract Thai weekenders from Bangkok, whose leisure pursuits center more around seafood dining than swimming and sunbathing. Foreigners, meanwhile, are attracted to the Gulf's clear waters and fine sands, and exceptionally good water sports. The development of resort hotels and golf courses in the Gulf continues to boom, to the alarm of many environmentalists. However, it is still possible to find seclusion and simplicity, such as on Ko Chang.

Windsurfing, one of many sports available at Jomtien

Bangpra Golf Course, *Pattaya, is one of many courses within the forested hills of Chon Buri province (see p464).*

Cha-am (see p330) *has become increasingly developed but is still overshadowed by nearby Hua Hin.*

The Sofitel Centara Grand Resort & Villas (see p331), *formerly famed as the Railway Hotel, has been restored to its original 1920s colonial-style elegance.*

BANGKOK

Kiarti
• Golf

Samut Songkhram

Royal Lakesi
Golf Cour

Ch
Bu

Sawang Resort Golf Course

• Phetchaburi

Bangpra
Golf Cours

Pattaya

② Cha-am

Springfield Golf Course

Royal Hua Hin Golf Course

① Hua Hin

BEST BEACHES OF THE NORTHERN GULF

Hua Hin Beach ①
Thailand's first beach resort. Good for the charm of the town and its seafood restaurants.

Cha-am Beach ②
Popular with Thai weekenders but quiet during the week. Outstanding seafood restaurants.

Jomtien Beach, Pattaya ③
A 14-km (9-mile) long beach. Suitable for families and has excellent water sports facilities.

Glass Sand Beach (Hat Sai Kaeo), Ko Samet ④
Longest and liveliest beach on the island with

sand so clean it squeaks when walked on. Beautifully clear water, and good for water sports.

White Sand Beach (Hat Sai Khao), Ko Chang ⑤
The best and busiest beach on an unspoiled island. Fishing, snorkeling, and boat trips.

PATTAYA

Thailand's biggest, brashest resort attracts single males and family package tourists in equal numbers. The former are drawn by the neon-lit go-go bars and a reputation acquired when Pattaya was used for R&R by US servicemen during the Vietnam War. Families, meanwhile, are attracted by the restaurants, golf courses, and beaches, particularly Jomtien beach (south of Pattaya beach), which has the best water sports facilities in the country.

Si Racha
Ko Sichang
• Laem Chabang
Golf Course
• Pattaya
• Phoenix
Golf Course
Eastern Star
• Golf Course
Rayong
Sattahip

0 kilometers   20
0 miles   10

Water sports – a major attraction of Pattaya

Ko Chang (see pp322–3) is Thailand's second-largest island after Phuket. This former backpacker haven has become increasingly developed and now receives more than 700,000 visitors a year.

Diving is possible all year round in the Gulf of Thailand along the east coast, unlike Ko Samui and the Andaman coast, which are more affected by monsoons (see pp26–7).

ayong
344
Ko Samet   Chanthaburi
4
317
3
Trat
Ko Chang
5
318

0 kilometers 25
0 miles   25

Thai Gemstones

Since the 15th century, Chanthaburi ("city of the moon") has been known to Western travelers for its abundance of gemstones. As a trading city its history dates back to the Khmer Empire in the 9th century *(see pp56–7)*. Along with

Star ruby ring

Bangkok, Chanthaburi is world-renowned as a gem center, and for its skilled gem cutters. The gemstones – mainly rubies and sapphires, with associated deposits of zircon, spinel, and garnet – are found in alluvial deposits either on the surface or up to 6 m (20 ft) underground. Although rubies and sapphires are now overmined around Chanthaburi, farmers have previously found gemstones while plowing. Over 70 percent of the world's rubies have come from Thailand.

GEM-MINING AREAS

■ *Ruby and sapphire mines*

Examining gemstones *in the host rock helps formulate the correct cutting plan. This ensures that the best yield and shapes are obtained.*

This machine is pumping gravel and water that may contain gemstones such as rubies.

Simple grinding wheels *are often used in small businesses, which are commonly run from the owner's home. More sophisticated operations use modern equipment such as diamond saws.*

MINING FOR GEMSTONES

In Chanthaburi, gem stores can arrange visits to mines. Due to over-mining locally, many of the stones cut in Chanthaburi come from mines in Cambodia or Vietnam

FACETING GEMSTONES

Thai workers have a worldwide reputation for their skill and dexterity in faceting (precisely cutting) gemstones, often using simple equipment and judging angles by eye. A modern faceting machine may use a diamond blade or laser to improve speed and accuracy. After cutting, the stones are sorted and graded by size and quality, with quality being determined by sparkle, color, brilliance, and the presence or absence of imperfections.

Modern faceting equipment used to cut gemstones

Most gem buyers *prefer to buy gems "in the rough," using their expertise to judge the potential of the uncut material. Later the buyers arrange the cutting of the stones, often in their own workshops. Untrained buyers should beware of potential scams (see p480).*

Bargaining *in gem-mining towns such as Bo Rai (see p321) is common practice. Since opinions differ as to the potential of rough material and the quality of cut stones, bargaining is hard but good natured.*

Designing and making jewelry *from gems demands a delicate touch and a keen eye, qualities renowned in Thai craftsmen and women. Most jewelry is made to highlight the beauty of the gems.*

Whole families can often be seen searching for gemstones. Children may begin helping at a very young age.

Pans are often used to scoop up gravel that may contain gemstones. The gemstones sink to the bottom of the pan.

Of all the Thai gemstones, *deep blue sapphires and blood-red rubies are highly prized, as are unusually colored (such as yellow) sapphires. Sometimes the color is enhanced permanently by heating the stones to almost 2,000° C (3,650° F).*

Star sapphire

Star ruby

Green sapphire

Zircon

Ruby

Peridot

Yellow sapphire

EASTERN SEABOARD

The Eastern Seaboard of the Gulf of Thailand, stretching from Bangkok to the Cambodian border, is a region of contrasts. Remarkably picturesque and unspoiled islands lie within easy reach of brash, over developed resorts; oil refineries and industrial complexes are scattered along much of the coast, but not far inland are little-visited and spectacular national parks.

The Eastern Seaboard was a frontier between the Khmer and Sukhothai empires in the early 15th century. As Khmer power waned, large numbers of ethnic Tais settled here and discovered gem-rich deposits in the lush countryside. Chanthaburi became a centre for gem trading and in the 18th and 19th centuries had to expel first Burmese then French occupying forces. Numerous Vietnamese refugees have since settled in the town.

Though still a forested region with orchards, gem-mining, and fishing communities, the Eastern Seaboard has seen dramatic changes in the late 20th century as the oil and tourist industries have grown dramatically. However, some seaside towns have retained their charm, and in Si Racha excellent seafood can be sampled in open-air restaurants overlooking the bay. In contrast to this are the neon lights of Pattaya, an infamous destination for US marines on R&R during the Vietnam War. Despite a seedy image, it is an excellent center for water sports. South and east of Rayong there are beautiful mountainous islands and dense rainforest sheltering a wealth of fauna and flora. Trails, waterfalls, and eerie limestone caves characterize Khao Chamao, Khao Kitchakut, and Khao Sabap national parks.

The relaxed island of Ko Samet is a popular vacation destination, with its squeaky-sand beaches. Farther south, Ko Chang has many beautiful beaches and has become increasingly popular, attracting hundreds of thousands of visitors each year.

Temple boys in a shrine cave within the Khao Chamao-Khao Wong National Park

◁ Enjoying the good life on the blissfully quiet Ko Chang

Exploring the Eastern Seaboard

Blessed with miles of idyllic beaches and soaring temperatures, the Eastern Seaboard is a sun-lover's paradise. Whether you want to unwind and sample the local seafood or try out water sports, there is much to choose from. Beach resorts range from the chaotic Pattaya, with its lively nightlife, to lesser-known islands such as Ko Chang, which is part of a stunning national marine park. The three other national parks in this region, characterized by tropical forests, mountains, and waterfalls, are home to a wealth of wildlife. The main town in the area is Chanthaburi, center of the thriving gem mining industry.

Prachinburi

Nakhon Ratchasima

Si Maha Phot

Ka

Chachoengsao   Sanam Chai Khet

Bangkok

Thung Ya Ch

Bang P

Phanat Nikhom

Chon Buri

KHAO KHIEO OPEN ZOO ❶

KO SICHANG ❸   ❷ SI RACHA

Bang Phra Reservoir

Khao Ya 777

Khlong Prasit

Naklua   Bang Lamung

PATTAYA ❹

KHAO CHAMAO-KHAO WONG NATIONAL PARK

Wang Chang

❶❶

Ban Chang

Klae

RAYONG ❺

Sattahip   Ko Saket   Ban Phe   Ko Me Kla

KO SAMET ❻   Ko

KEY

▬▬	Motorway
▬▬	Major road
⋯⋯	Minor road
▬▬	Scenic route
⌁⌁	Main railway
▬▬	International border
△	Summit

Relaxing on Ko Samet's beautiful white beaches

SIGHTS AT A GLANCE

Bo Rai ❶❷
Chanthaburi ❶❶
Khao Chamao-Khao Wong
    National Park ❼
Khao Khieo Open Zoo ❶
Khao Kitchakut National Park ❾
Khlong Yai ❶❺
Ko Chang ❶❸
Ko Samet ❻
Ko Sichang ❸
Namtok Philo National Park ❶❶
Pattaya ❹
Rayong ❺
Si Racha ❷
Trat ❶❹
Wat Khao Sukim ❽

GETTING AROUND

The Eastern Seaboard's transport system is comprehensive on the mainland and connects to the main islands. A twice daily train service runs from Hua Lamphong Station in Bangkok to Si Racha and Pattaya. Chon Buri and Sattahip are served by domestic airports. Buses are the easiest way to get around the Eastern Seaboard: there is a regular service from Bangkok's Eastern Bus Terminal to the main towns. To visit places not on bus routes, charter a *songthaew* from a local bus station. Transportation in the mainland towns is provided by *songthaews*, rickshas, and *tuk-tuks*. Several ferries leave Ban Phe each day for Ko Samet. On the island, *songthaews* service the main beaches, and fishing boats can be hired to surrounding islands. Ko Chang and Ko Mak are reached by ferry from Laem Ngop. Infrastructure on these islands is poor, though motorcycles and *songthaews* can be hired to get around the rough roads.

Aranyaprathet

Wang Nam Yen

Khao Soi Dao Wildlife Sanctuary
Pong Nam Ron

9 KHAO KITCHAKUT NATIONAL PARK

WAT KHAO SUKIM

10 CHANTHABURI

12 BO RAI

11 NAMTOK PHLIO NATIONAL PARK

Khlung

14

13

15

The opulent interior of the main hall of Wat Khao Sukim

SEE ALSO

• **Where to Stay** pp412–15

• **Where to Eat** pp441–3

0 kilometers 25

0 miles 15

Bungalows on palm-fringed Ko Chang

Khao Khieo Open Zoo **❶**

สวนสัตว์เขาเขียว

Off Route 3144, 10 km (6 miles) SE of Chon Buri, Chon Buri province. *Tel* 0-3829-8195. 🚉 🚌 *Chon Buri, then* samlor. ⬤ *8am–6pm daily; Night Safari 6–9pm daily.* 📷

This open zoo has over 50 species of birds and animals, including deer, zebras, and tigers. The animals inhabit spacious, semifree enclosures, and the birds are kept in a large aviary. The zoo is in a peaceful, hilly setting amid woodland scenery and is best reached by car.

For bird enthusiasts, 20 km (12 miles) south of Khao Khieo is the beautiful wild marshland of **Bang Phra Reservoir**, where the brown-spotted wimbrel can be seen in winter.

Si Racha **❷**

ศรีราชา

Chon Buri province. 🏠 *27,000.* 🚉 🚌 🚢 ℹ *TAT, Pattaya (0-3842- 7667).* 🚢 *daily.*

Famed for its seafood and its spicy Si Racha sauce *(nam phrik si racha)* – Thailand's answer to Tabasco – this small seaside town is the launching point for trips to Ko Sichang. Running off busy Jermjompol Road, Si Racha's main waterfront street, are several tentacle-like piers. At the end of the piers are breezy, open-air restaurants ideal for sampling the local delicacies: oysters *(hoi nang rom)* or mussels *(hoi thot)* dipped in Si Racha sauce.

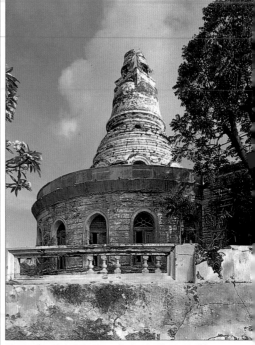

Wat Atsadangnimit, Rama V's meditation chamber on Ko Sichang

On a rocky promontory, which is also an occasional ferry pier, is **Ko Loi**, a Thai-Chinese Buddhist temple. Of interest are a Buddha Footprint, an image of Kuan Yin (the Chinese goddess of mercy), and a pond full of turtles. Buddhists feed the turtles as an act of merit-making *(see p129)*.

The streets of Si Racha (and Ko Sichang) resonate to the sound of spluttering motorcycle rickshas. They are unique to the area – their sidecars are positioned at the rear.

Ko Sichang **❸**

เกาะสีชัง

Chon Buri province. 🏠 *4,600.* 🚢 *from Si Racha.* ℹ *TAT, Pattaya (0-3842-7667 or 0-3842-8750).*

A former haunt of King Chulalongkorn (Rama V), this small island, with a rugged coastline, once functioned as the customs checkpoint for Bangkok-bound ships. Now it is a relatively quiet place with some architectural ruins and a handful of guesthouses catering to visitors who want to avoid the bustle and commercialism of the resorts.

There is only one ramshackle fishing village, **Tha Bon**, on the eastern side of the island. Just north of it is the **Chinese Temple**, with colorfully decorated shrine caves.

On the west coast of the island are the quiet beaches of **Hat Sai Khao** and **Hat Tham**. On the southern side, sprawling over a hillside, are the overgrown ruins of **Rama V's Summer Palace**. The palace was built in the 1890s but abandoned after a fleeting

Motorcycle rickshas provide the transport on Si Racha and Ko Sichang

occupation by the French in 1893. In 1901 it was moved and reconstructed as Viman-mek Palace at Dusit Park in Bangkok *(see pp102–5)*. The only structure of the palace complex to remain intact is the circular **Wat Atsadang-nimit**, at the top of the hill and crowned by a crumbling *chedi*. This was once a meditation chamber used by King Chulalongkorn.

The island also has a well-known temple, **Wat Thamyaiprig**. Its gardens provide crops for the locals, and it has large underground rainwater tanks to meet the islanders' needs, since there is no other water source.

The deserted rocky hilltop offers pleasant walks and fine views. It is home to nesting seabirds and the yellow squirrel, which is endemic here.

Boats to Ko Sichang take 40 minutes from Si Racha's pier.

Pattaya ❹

พัทยา

Chon Buri province. 👥 94,000. 🚌 🚐 ⛴ 🛈 *TAT, 609 Mu 10 Phra Tamnak Rd, Pattaya (0-3842-7667).* 🗓 *daily.* 🎉 *Pattaya Festival (Apr).*

Pattaya's faded beauty is now difficult to discern. The once-idyllic beaches attracted visitors as early as the 1950s and later became a destination for US troops on R&R during the Vietnam War. Now dubbed "Patpong by the Sea" *(see p116)*, the town has become

A jet ski sitting ready for use on one of Pattaya's beaches

one of Thailand's infamous red-light districts, with a menagerie of go-go bars and glitzy transvestite shows.

Despite its seedy image, Pattaya still attracts many families, who come for the good, cheap accommodations, extensive beaches (though the sea is often polluted), excellent restaurants, and the best sports facilities in Thailand.

Pattaya consists of three bays. At its center is the 3-km (2-mile) long **Pattaya beach**. Pattaya Beach Road is packed with fast-food restaurants and souvenir shops. Walking Street, or "the strip," is where the sex industry plies its trade. North Pattaya Road, on the other hand, is more sedate, with open-air drinking spots called bar beers.

Parrot fish, a common sight for divers in Pattaya's waters

Many tourists prefer the more family-oriented 14-km-long **Jomtien beach**, around the southern headland of Pattaya. This is also the best place for water sports, as the sea here is cleaner. Scores of companies offer water- and jet-skiing, windsurfing, sailing, parasailing, game-fishing, and scuba diving. Other activities include golf, target shooting, horseback riding, and tennis.

Quieter **Naklua bay**, to the north of Pattaya beach, has a fishing village that, despite tourism, has kept its charm.

The 2006 opening of Suvarnabhumi Airport, between Bangkok and Pattaya, sparked a building boom that led to the construction of several of Thailand's tallest skyscrapers.

Picnicking Thais relaxing at Suan Son, a beach park near Rayong

Rayong ❺

ระยอง

Rayong province. 👥 95,000. 🚌 ⛴ 🛈 *TAT, 153/4 Sukhumvit Rd, Rayong (0-3865-5420).* 🗓 *daily.* 🎉 *Fruit Fair (May).*

Rayong is a busy and prosperous fishing town best known locally for its statue of Thailand's most famous poet, Sunthorn Phu *(see p319)*.

The main attractions lie outside the town. For good beaches, head 25 km (16 miles) southeast to **Ban Phe**. A 20-km (12-mile) coast road winds along from here to Laem Mae Phim.

From Ban Phe there are boats to Ko Samet *(see pp318–19)*. Ferries also run to nearby **Ko Saket, Ko Man Nok** and **Ko Man Klang** – the latter two islands are part of the Laem Ya-Mu Ko Samet National Park. The park authorities have managed to limit excessive development here, although jet-skiing is gradually eroding the coral reef.

Five km (3 miles) past Ban Phe is the beach park of **Suan Son** ("pine park"). This has crystal-white sand beaches and is a popular picnic area for Thais. It offers seafood snacks and homegrown water sports such as wave riding on inner tubes.

Rayong province is known for its succulent fruit, particularly the pineapple and durian *(see p319)*, and its *nam pla* (fish sauce) and *nam phrik kapi* (shrimp paste).

Ko Samet **6**

เกาะเสม็ด

Rayong province. 🏠 *1,464.* 🚢 *from Ban Phe (Rayong) to Ao Wong Duan and Ao Phrao.* 🚌 *TAT, Rayong (0-3866-4585).* 🗓 *daily.*

Ko Samet, blessed as it is with clear blue waters and crystalline sand, is popular with foreigners and Thai weekenders. Because it is only 6 km (4 miles) long and 3 km (2 miles) wide, most of the island is accessible on foot. The interior's dense jungle, home to the usual geckos and hornbills, is riddled with trails.

Despite attaining national park status in 1981, in common with all Thai resorts and islands, Ko Samet has suffered from development and has experienced a huge increase in high-quality accommodation.

The small fishing town of **Na Dan**, which links Ko Samet to Ban Phe on the mainland, was an ancient checkpoint for Chinese junks. Legend has it that its calm, sheltered waters were once the hunting ground of pirates. Several beaches on Ko Samet offer one-way boat trips back to Ban Phe.

The kite-shaped island's finest beaches are on the east coast. With its clear shallow waters, **Hat Sai Kaeo** ("glass sand beach") is the longest and liveliest beach. Water sports on the beach include windsurfing. Boat

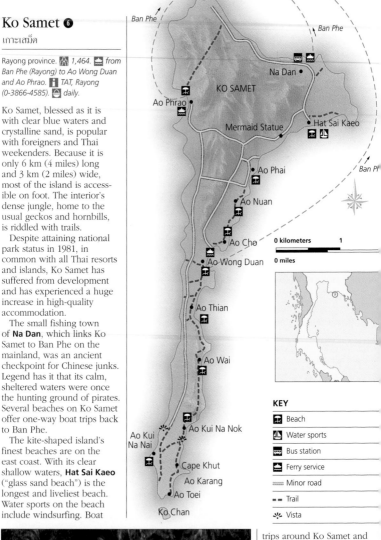

KEY

🏖	Beach
🏄	Water sports
🚌	Bus station
⛴	Ferry service
▬	Minor road
--	Trail
🌿	Vista

trips around Ko Samet and snorkeling day trips to nearby islands leave from here.

Heading southward along the east coast are the equally popular **Ao Phai** and **Ao Nuan**. Near the first is a wind-battered statue of the prince and the mermaid in *Phra Aphaimani*, a poem by Sunthorn Phu, Thailand's most famous poet.

Farther south, the bays are less crowded, with the exception of the wide beach at **Ao Wong Duan** ("moon bay"), which can get quite busy. At the narrow isthmus of **Ao Kui**, solitude and beauty are guaranteed. It is merely a short

Sunset walk along the coast of picturesque Ko Samet

stroll between sunrise and sunset vistas of Ao Kui Na Nok and Ao Kui Na Nai. The island's best coral is found just off the southern tip.

The only area to have undergone development on the largely inaccessible west coast is **Ao Phrao** ("paradise bay"). Due to its isolation, the beach here doesn't receive as many overnight visitors as those on the east coast.

There have been reports of malaria on Ko Samet in the past, so precautions are necessary. A health clinic, located near Na Dan, can deal with any urgent prob-

Upscale bungalows on peaceful Ao Phrao, Ko Samet

Khao Chamao-Khao Wong National Park **7**

อุทยานแห่งชาติเขาชะเมา–เขาวง

Rayong province. Park HQ 17 km (11 miles) N of Hwy 3 at Klaeng. TAT, Rayong (0-3866-4585). Forestry Dept, Bangkok (0-2562-0760 or 0-3889-4378 inc bungalow bookings). Rayong or Chanthaburi, then songthaew. www.tat-rayong.com

The two mountains in this national park, Khao Wong and Khao Chamao, loom above the farming lowlands of the Eastern Seaboard.

Tigers, elephants, and Asiatic black bears find refuge in the park's tropical, broadleaved, evergreen forests, away from farmers and hunters. Also resident is the *tor soro* carp. Folklore claims that the name of Chamao mountain, which

means "to get drunk," derives from the curious giddy feeling induced by eating the carp.

Park highlights include the pools of the **Khao Chamao waterfall** and the 80 or so **Khao Wong caves**. Tham Pet ("diamond cave") and Tham Lakhon ("theater cave"), situated 4 km (2 miles) southeast of the park headquarters, are the most spectacular of these limestone caverns. When the waters are low it is possible to proceed to **Hok Sai waterfall** and camp on the summit.

There are few developed trails in the park. The best route climbs alongside the cascading Khao Chamao waterfall and ends near the top of the falls at Chong Kaep. From the park's northwest station former elephant trails lead through the fertile and wildlife-rich forest of the stunning Khlong Phlu valley.

Wat Khao Sukim's cable car, which transports visitors up to the temple

Wat Khao Sukim **8**

วัดเขาสุกิม

Khao Bay Si, Tha-Mai district, 20 km (13 miles) N of Chanthaburi, off route 3322. TAT, Rayong (0-3866-4585). Chanthaburi, then songthaew.

This huge, pale orange *wat* is perched on the side of Sukim mountain. The temple, the home of Luang Pho Somchai, one of Thailand's most popular meditation masters, is reached via a cable car or the *naga*-lined staircase. Inside are a number of tables inlaid with mother-of-pearl, while exhibits housed in a museum include an ostentatious display of jewelry and a collection of Bencharong, Khmer, and Ban Chiang pottery. They show the surprising wealth that a revered monk can accumulate from donations by merit-makers.

THE POETRY OF SUNTHORN PHU

Sunthorn Phu (1786–1855) is Thailand's most respected poet. His long, lyrical travel verses, often with a moral lesson, made him the favorite poet of kings Rama II and Rama III. The epic *Phra Aphaimani*, Sunthorn Phu's first poem, was inspired by the surroundings of Ko Samet (then called Ko Kaew Pisadan), where he settled. The poem tells the story of a prince, Phra Aphaimani, exiled to an underwater kingdom ruled by a giantess, who is in love with him. Helped by a mermaid, the prince escapes by fleeing to Ko Samet. The giantess follows, but is defeated when the prince plays his magic flute, sending her to sleep. The prince is subsequently betrothed to a beautiful princess.

Statue on Ko Samet depicting characters in *Phra Aphaimani*

Khao Kitchakut National Park **9**

อุทยานแห่งชาติเขาคิชฌกูฏ

Chanthaburi province. Park HQ off Hwy 3249, 24 km (15 miles) NE of Chanthaburi. ![] *Park HQ (0-3945-2074).* ![] *Chanthaburi, then songthaew.* ![]

Covering an area of just 59 sq km (23 sq miles), this is one of Thailand's smallest national parks. It encompasses Khao Kitchakut, a granite mountain just over 1,000 m (3,300 ft) high. The park's best known site, the 13-tier **Krathin waterfall**, is located near park headquarters. From here a relatively easy trail can be taken to the top.

More ambitious hikers and large numbers of pilgrims make the arduous four-hour climb to the summit of the impressive Phrabat mountain. They come to see two sights: an image of the Buddha's Footprint, which is etched here in granite, and a strange collection of natural rock formations shaped like an elephant, a large turtle, a pagoda, and a monk's bowl.

Khao Kitchakut is near the much larger, but less visited, **Khao Soi Dao Wildlife Sanctuary** (745 sq km, 290 sq miles). Both protected areas enclose some of the last surviving tracts of a once-great lowland forest. They are vital to the economy of the region as their slopes collect water for orchards. They also provide protection for many endangered species, including sun bears, spot-bellied eagle owls, silver pheasants, spiny-breasted giant frogs, binturongs (bear cats), and elephants. The upland forests of Khao Soi Dao provide a habitat for the tree-dwelling pileated gibbon.

Logo of the Thai national parks

🦌 Khao Soi Dao Wildlife Sanctuary

Off Hwy 317, 25 km (16 miles) NW of Chanthaburi. ![] *TAT, Rayong (0-3865-5420).* ![] *Chanthaburi, then songthaew.* ![]

A refreshing shower at the base of Krathin waterfall, Khao Kitchakut

Shrine inside the Church of the Immaculate Conception, Chanthaburi

Chanthaburi **10**

จันทบุรี

Chanthaburi province. ![] 48,000. ![] ![] *TAT, Rayong (0-3865-5420).* ![] *daily.* ![] *Fruit Festival (May/Jun).*

Surrounded by verdant chili and rubber plantations, this prosperous and friendly town is arguably Thailand's most charming settlement. Known as a center for gem trading (*see pp310–11*) since the 15th century, Chanthaburi has attracted a wide ethnic mix. Vietnamese refugees form the largest group. They came in three waves: in the 19th century, fleeing the anti-Catholic persecutions of Cochin China; in the early 20th century, escaping French colonial rule; and after the 1975 victory in South Vietnam by North Vietnamese Communists. The Vietnamese quarter, running parallel to the river on Rim Nam Road, is lined with latticework wooden shop-houses.

The monarch most revered in the town today is King Taksin. In the 18th century he expelled the Burmese from the town, their last Thai stronghold, thus reuniting Thailand. Two monuments celebrate Taksin and his famous victory: **San Somdej Prachao Taksin** on Tha Luang Road is a huge statue in the shape of Taksin's hat. **Taksin Park** sports a dynamic bronze statue of the king in battle as seen on the 20-*baht* note.

On the bank of the Chanthaburi River is the **Church of the Immaculate Conception**, a French-style Catholic cathedral built on the site

MAYTIME FRUIT FESTIVALS

Held in three neighboring provinces – Rayong, Chanthaburi and Trat – this annual fruit festival, lasting for a few days in either May or June (whenever the harvest is ripe), is a colorful, celebratory affair. These provinces are known for their flavorsome rambutan, durian, and mangosteen, which all come into season during May. Stalls selling the produce of local orchards are set up on the main streets of each town. Parades of floral-and-fruit floats are held along with gaudy beauty pageants, which are a ubiquitous element of every provincial Thai festival. Contests for the ripest durian or most beautifully shaped fruit, among other titles, are a highlight of the year for local farmers and a great spectacle for tourists. Visitors can also see cultural shows and excellent displays of local handicrafts. In Chanthaburi there are many stalls selling one of the specialties of the province: intricately woven straw mats.

Fruit festival float, Chanthaburi

of an 18th-century missionary chapel. It is the largest cathedral in the country and a legacy of French occupation. The French held Chanthaburi hostage from 1893 to 1904 as a guarantee that Thailand would relinquish her hold on Lao and Cambodian land. To keep the country intact, King Chulalongkorn reluctantly agreed to surrender the territories.

The **Gem Quarter** *(talat phloi)*, at the intersection of Si Chan and Thetsaban 4 roads, attracts gem traders from all over the world. On weekends a rainbow array of gemstones from Burma, Cambodia, and the rich mines of Chanthaburi province are traded at street stalls. However, most of the best quality stones are dispatched directly to Bangkok.

Statue of King Taksin, Chanthaburi

Namtok Phlio National Park ⑪
อุทยานแห่งชาติน้ำตกพลิ้ว

Chanthaburi province. Park HQ off Hwy 3, 14 km (9 miles) SE of Chanthaburi. 🛈 *TAT, Rayong (0-3865-5420); Forestry Dept (0-2562-0760 or* **www**.*dnp.go.th for bungalow bookings).* 🚌 *Chanthaburi, then* songthaew. 🚲

Immensely popular with Thais, this 135-sq km (52-sq mile) park contains some of Thailand's richest rainforest. It is also a haven for wildlife, with over 156 species of birds and 32 of mammals, including the Asiatic black bear, tiger, leopard, barking deer, and macaque. The park's other attractions are its spectacular waterfalls – the most impressive being **Phliu waterfall**. Facing this are two *chedis*: the Alongkon *chedi* and a 3-m (10-ft) high pyramid-shaped *chedi*, built by King Chulalongkorn in honor of one of his queens, Sunantha, who drowned at Bang Pa-in *(see p181)* in 1876. The region was much loved by Chulalongkorn.

A harder hike is required to reach the 20-m (66-ft) roaring Trok Nong falls and the forest-encircled Klang waterfall. The entrance road to the park is lined with souvenir shops.

Bo Rai ⑫
บ่อไร่

Trat province. 🏠 *25,000.* 🚌 🛈 *TAT, Trat (0-3959-7259-60).* 🛒 *daily.*

This small town used to be the thriving center of the Eastern Seaboard's gem trade. The surrounding mines, once renowned for the quality of their rubies *(tab tim)*, have almost dried up, so today the Bo Rai gem trade is small. Only one morning market of any significance, the **Khlong Yaw market**, remains. The market has a reverse system of buying and selling – buyers sit at makeshift tables and vendors stroll around displaying their wares.

Sadly, gem mining has destroyed large areas of Trat province, exposing the topsoil and leaving acres of despoiled land in rusty-orange mud.

Customer carefully inspecting a vendor's gems in Bo Rai market

Bungalows amid coconut trees along Khlong Phrao, Ko Chang

Ko Chang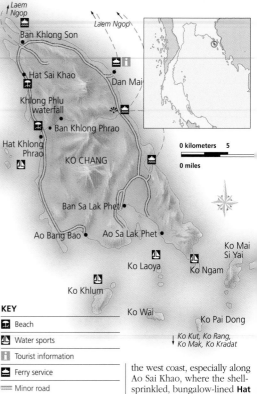

เกาะช้าง

Trat province. 🏠 5,800. 🚤 from Laem Ngop. 🚌 TAT, Trat (0-3959-7259-60).

Mountainous Ko Chang is the largest of the 50 or so islands that form the Ko Chang National Marine Park, which covers an area of 650 sq km (250 sq miles), two-thirds of which is ocean. Mangroves, cliffs, and clear waters make this one of Thailand's most scenic islands and the ideal place for a varied holiday. Increased development means that Ko Chang now has no shortage of quality hotels, resorts, and spas.

Since Thai-Chinese agricultural families first settled on Ko Chang in the mid-19th century, most of the island's wildlife has been destroyed, although some small mammals, including the barking deer, stumptailed macaque, and small Indian civet, remain. Also resident are some 75 bird species, and reptiles and amphibians such as monitor lizards, pythons, king cobras, and the endemic Ko Chang frog.

Inland exploration is difficult because of the rugged terrain. The coast road, which was begun in the early 1990s, is the first construction to improve accessibility on the island. Ko Chang's best beaches are on the west coast, especially along Ao Sai Khao, where the shell-sprinkled, bungalow-lined **Hat Sai Khao** ("white sand beach"), the island's longest and busiest beach, is located. An information center on the beach arranges boat trips, fishing, and snorkeling. Most guesthouses also offer fishing, snorkeling, and motorcycle rental. **Hat Khlong Phrao**, south of here, is more attractive and quieter. Nearby is a fishing village, Ban Khlong Phrao. Because tourism is growing only gradually on the island, fishing is still the main industry.

The beaches in the south are still relatively isolated. Of these, the beach at the sheltered bay of **Ao Bang Bao**, in the southwest corner, is particularly beautiful. East of here is a long beach encircling a bay, Ao Sa Lak Phet, where there are a few fishing villages and bungalows. The wrecks of two Thai Navy ships can be visited off the coast here.

Of the island's many waterfalls, two are worth the hike. On the east coast, near the park headquarters, is the three-tiered **Than Mayom waterfall**, which has good views of the

KEY

🏖 Beach

🏄 Water sports

ℹ️ Tourist information

⛴ Ferry service

▭▭ Minor road

🌄 Vista

View of Hat Khlong Phrao, one of the best beaches on Ko Chang

For hotels and restaurants in this region see pp412–15 and pp441–3

island. The other is **Khlong Phlu waterfall**, along Khlong Phrao on the west coast. The uppermost level, accessible by a gentle 3-km (2-mile) hike, has a freshwater pool.

For snorkelers, divers, and day-trippers there are stunning smaller islands off the coast of Ko Chang, with a good variety of hard and soft corals and a proliferation of giant clams.

Ko Kut, the second largest island within the group, falls outside the park boundaries. It has excellent beaches and breathtaking waterfalls.

The rocky, coral-lined coast of **Ko Wai**, south of Ko Chang, is popular for fishing. Around **Ko Rang**, farther south, is a cluster of rocky coral islets.

Ko Mak, a predominantly flat island, is covered mainly in coconut plantations. It has a secluded beach on the northwest bay, a fishing village, and good coral reefs.

Barrel sponge, seen off Ko Chang

Northeast of Ko Mak is the coconut-fringed **Ko Kradat**, a tiny island with some of the prettiest beaches in the island cluster. Although the entire island is a privately owned resort with expensive hotels, bungalows can also be hired.

Sandflies and mosquitoes are a problem on the islands, so precautions are necessary.

Trat ⑭
ตราด

Trat province. 👥 72,000. 🚏 ⛴ ℹ️ *TAT, Trat (0-3959-7259-60).* 🛍️ *daily.* 🎪 *Rakham Fruit Fair (May–Jun).*

This provincial capital is a small but busy commercial town. Most tourists pass through Trat only en route to Ko Chang. However, the town's popularity is likely to increase in line with that of the archipelago. Trat has several attractions, including its markets, most of which are centered around Tait Mai and Sukhumvit roads. The covered market on Sukhumvit Road has a good selection of food and drink stalls. Also of interest are the gem-mining villages around Trat, such as Bo Rai, where rubies are mined *(see pp310–11).* Local guesthouses can arrange trips. Located about 2 km (1 mile) southwest of Trat is **Wat Bupharam** ("flower temple"), set in pleasant grounds with large, shady trees. Some of the original buildings within the temple complex, including the *wihan*, the bell tower, and the monks' residences, or *kutis*, date from the late Ayutthaya period *(see pp60–61).*

Durian vendor at one of Trat's bustling markets

Khlong Yai ⑮
คลองใหญ่

Trat province. 👥 15,000. ℹ️ *TAT, Trat (0-3959-7259-60).* 🛍️ *daily.*

This picturesque seaside town near the Cambodian border sports a handful of bustling markets and stalls selling delicious noodles with seafood.

The road from Khlong Yai to the border checkpoint of **Hat Lek** passes through spectacular scenery, with mountains on one side and the sea on the other. Tourists can now enter Cambodia at Hat Lek. A visa on arrival is available with a valid passport, recent photo, and US$30. However, border guards often demand higher fees, so it is wise to apply for a visa in advance at Bangkok's Cambodian Embassy.

Fishing trawlers, harbored on Ko Chang, which provide the main source of income on the island

WESTERN SEABOARD

The rolling landscape of the Western Seaboard extends some 600 km (370 miles) from Bangkok to Surat Thani. Its major attraction is the islands that make up the beautiful Ko Samui archipelago, such as Ko Pha Ngan, Ko Tao, and the Ang Thong National Marine Park. Yet visitors should not ignore the many charms of the mainland – lively towns, fine beaches, and national parks.

Miles of remote sandy beaches dominate long stretches of the Western Seaboard, which unites the Buddhist heartland of the nation with the maritime, Muslim-influenced South. Temples reflecting pre-Thai influences, simple fishing villages, verdant fruit orchards, and sand-rimmed resorts characterize this region.

The Tenasserim Mountains, rising to 1,329 m (4,350 ft), form a spine down the peninsula. They absorb much of the rain that falls during the southwest monsoon, keeping the coastal strip relatively dry. However, this coastal region is still a fertile growing area, famed for its pineapples, corn, sugar cane, "lady-finger" bananas, asparagus, and mangosteens.

Beaches easily reached from the capital cater primarily to weekenders from Bangkok. Particularly popular are the casuarina-lined waterfronts of Cha-am and Hua Hin. The latter was Thailand's first beach resort. The many golf courses within easy reach of these two tourist centers make this area arguably the country's premier golf destination. Farther south, the stunning islands of the Ko Samui archipelago offer excellent diving and sunbathing, and a well-developed tourist infrastructure.

Trekkers and bird-watchers will be drawn to Khao Sam Roi Yot and Kaeng Krachan national parks, where migratory birds rest and feed in the salt marshes from August to April.

Among the most interesting of the towns along the Western Seaboard is Phetchaburi, with its crumbling architectural remnants of the Khmer, Mon, Ayutthaya, and Rattanakosin epochs. Farther to the south, Chaiya still contains archeological remains that reveal its important role in the Srivijaya Empire *(see pp346–7)*.

Fishing boats in the bay of the peaceful town of Prachuap Khiri Khan

◁ Devotees making offerings inside Phetchaburi's Wat Mahathat

Exploring the Western Seaboard

This long, narrow coastal strip, backed by mountains along the Burmese border, stretches from the cultural center of Phetchaburi to the commercial town of Surat Thani. In the north is one of Thailand's oldest beach resorts, Hua Hin, while farther north still is the modern resort of Cha-am. The area also offers natural beauty inland in the huge, hilly Kaeng Krachan National Park and the limestone outcrops of the coastal Khao Sam Roi Yot National Park. The islands of the stunning Ko Samui archipelago are the major attractions farther south. Ko Samui itself is the main resort island, while Ko Tao and Ko Pha Ngan are popular with backpackers. For spectacular, unspoiled island scenery, it is hard to beat the beautiful Angthong National Marine Park.

SIGHTS AT A GLANCE

Angthong National
 Marine Park **13**
Cha-am **3**
Chaiya **9**
Chumphon **5**
Hua Hin **5**
Kaeng Krachan National Park **2**
Khao Sam Roi Yot
 National Park **6**
Ko Pha Ngan **12**
Ko Samui pp336–8 **11**
Ko Tao **14**
Mareukathayawan Palace **4**
Phetchaburi pp328–30 **1**
Prachuap Khiri Khan **7**
Surat Thani **10**

Towering stacks of TV aerials on the houses along the Phet River in the center of Phetchaburi

Lapping up the sun on Ko Samui's Chaweng beach

GETTING THERE

Most of the attractions in the region are easily accessible from the main highways 4 and 41. The major towns are linked to each other and Bangkok by bus services and trains (Bangkok to Hua Hin is 3–4 hours by bus or train; Bangkok to Surat Thani is 11 hours by bus, 11–13 hours by train). Ko Samui, Surat Thani, Prachuap Khiri Khan, and Hua Hin have domestic airports. There are several flights a day between Bangkok and Hua Hin and Ko Samui. *Songthaews* and bicycle rickshas can be hired for trips to local sights. Cha-am, Hua Hin, and Ko Samui have car rental facilities. Surat Thani and Don Sak are the main gateways to the Ko Samui archipelago. Ko Tao is also accessible via Chumphon. The train/bus/ferry journey from Bangkok to Ko Samui takes 16 hours.

SEE ALSO

- *Where to Stay* pp415–18
- *Where to Eat* pp443–6

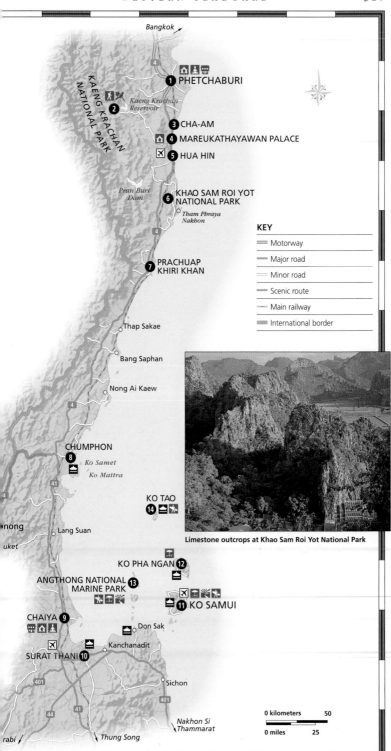

Bangkok

KAENG KRACHAN NATIONAL PARK

Kaeng Krachan Reservoir

1 PHETCHABURI

2

3 CHA-AM

4 MAREUKATHAYAWAN PALACE

5 HUA HIN

Pran Buri Dam

6 KHAO SAM ROI YOT NATIONAL PARK

Tham Phraya Nakhon

7 PRACHUAP KHIRI KHAN

Thap Sakae

Bang Saphan

Nong Ai Kaew

CHUMPHON

8 Ko Samet

Ko Mattra

KO TAO **14**

nong

Lang Suan

uket

KO PHA NGAN **12**

ANGTHONG NATIONAL MARINE PARK **13**

CHAIYA **9**

Don Sak

11 KO SAMUI

SURAT THANI **10**

Kanchanadit

Sichon

rabi

Thung Song

Nakhon Si Thammarat

KEY

═══ Motorway

─── Major road

⋯⋯ Minor road

─── Scenic route

➤─➤ Main railway

▬▬▬ International border

Limestone outcrops at Khao Sam Roi Yot National Park

0 kilometers 50

0 miles 25

Street-by-Street: Phetchaburi ❶

เพชรบุรี

Detail, Phra Nakhon Khiri

Settled since at least the 11th century, Phetchaburi (often spelled Phetburi) is one of Thailand's oldest towns. It has long been an important trading and cultural center, and Mon, Khmer, and Ayutthayan influences can be seen in its 30 temples. During the 19th century it became a favorite royal retreat, and King Mongkut built a summer house here on a hill, Khao Wang, west of the center. This is now part of the Phra Nakhon Khiri Historical Park (*see p330*). Other major sights are the 17th-century Wat Yai Suwannaram, the five Khmer *prangs* of Wat Kamphaeng Laeng, and an old quarter that has retained much of its original charm. Despite such attractions, accommodation is scant. Most visitors come on day trips from Bangkok, 123 km (76 miles) away.

To Phra Nakhon Khiri Historical Park

Phra Song Road
Several wats *are located on this busy road.*

N O K

Wat Mahathat
The five white Khmer-style prangs of this much-restored 14th-century temple dominate the town's central skyline. The figures of angels and gods decorate the roofs of the main wihan *and* bot.

STAR SIGHTS

★ Phra Nakhon Khiri Historical Park

★ Wat Kamphaeng Laeng

★ Wat Yai Suwannaram

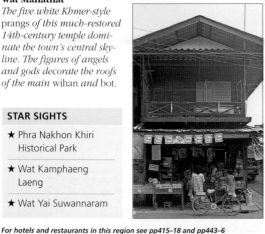

To Wat Tho

Wooden Shop-Houses
Concrete may have replaced wood in many Thai towns, but attractive wooden buildings, many lining the river bank, are still a feature of Phetchaburi.

★ **Phra Nakhon Khiri Historical Park**

As an avid astronomer, King Mongkut had this observatory conveniently built next to his hilltop summer palace; this is now a museum (see p330). The magnificently landscaped and forested surrounding park offers extensive views of Phetchaburi.

VISITORS' CHECKLIST

Phetchaburi province. 🏠 80,000.
🚉 Rot Fai Rd, 1.5 km (1 mile) NW
of town. 🚌 Chisa-in Rd, near
Chomrut Bridge. 🛈 TAT, Cha-am
(0-3247-1005). 🏛 daily. 🎉
Phra Nakhon Khiri Fair (8 days in
early Feb).

To Wat Chisa-in

OEN KASEM

CHISA-IN

PHET

PHANIT JEROEN

PONGSURIYA ROAD

HRA SONG

MATAYAWONG

To Wat
Kamphaeng Laeng

Market

To Wat Yai Suwannaram

★ **Wat Yai Suwannaram**
Built during the Ayutthaya period (see pp60–61), the temple is notable for the lovely original murals of Hindu gods in the bot. A scripture library stands on stilts in the middle of a large pond on the grounds.

| 0 meters | 75 |
| 0 yards | 75 |

KEY

— — — Suggested route

★ **Wat Kamphaeng Laeng**
This is one of the few surviving Khmer shrines in Thailand outside the Northeast. The five laterite prangs of the temple, in varying states of disrepair, are typically Khmer in design and may date from the 12th century. Originally a Hindu temple, it was later adapted for Buddhist use.

Phra Nakhon Khiri, Rama IV's ambitious 19th-century palace complex

Exploring Phetchaburi's Outer Sights

Phetchaburi is divided by the Phet River, which weaves its way past this provincial capital's 30 historic temples. Many, especially the Ayutthayan *wats*, are excellently preserved, their pinnacles dominating the skyline. In the distance, to the west, three large hills loom imperiously over the city.

Phra Nakhon Khiri, locally referred to as Khao Wang, translates as the "celestial city of the mountain." This palace complex, perched on top of 92-m (302-ft) Maha Samana hill, was commissioned by King Mongkut (Rama IV) as a summer house in the 1850s. Extravagant use of European, Chinese, and Japanese architectural styles make this a bold study in Thai and foreign architecture. Set among natural woods, rocks, and caverns, it also offers fine vistas of Phetchaburi town and panoramic views of the province.

The complex extends over three peaks. The Royal Palace and the Ho Chatchawan Wiangchai, an observatory tower (Rama IV was an accomplished amateur astronomer), are both perched on the west rise; the Phra That Chomphet, a white *chedi* erected by Rama V, stands on the central rise; and Wat Maha Samanaram, containing some fine murals, takes up the east rise. In 1988 the complex was made a Historical Park. A cable car takes visitors up the steep ascent to the palace complex.

A short distance north of town is **Tham Khao Luang**, a cave containing stalactites,

chedis, and Buddha images. To the right of the cave's mouth lies **Wat Bun Thawi**, notable for its intricately carved wooden door panels.

🏛 **Phra Nakhon Khiri**
Khao Wang, Phetchaburi.
Tel 0-3242-5600. ◯ daily. ◻

🕳 **Tham Khao Luang**
Hwy 3173, 3 km (2 miles) N of
Phetchaburi. ◯ daily. ◻ donation.

Kaeng Krachan National Park ❷

อุทยานแห่งชาติแก่งกระจาน

Phetchaburi province. Park HQ off
Hwy 3175, 60 km (37 miles) S of
Phetchaburi. 🛈 TAT (0-3247-1005);
Forestry Dept (0-2562-0760 or **www.**
dnp.go.th for bungalow bookings). 🚌
◻ Phetchaburi then songthaew. 🅿

Thailand's largest national park is home to at least 40 species of large mammal, such as tiger, leopard, elephant, gibbon, two types of Asiatic bear, and two types of leaf-monkey (langur). Established in 1981, this 2,920-sq km (1,150-sq mile)

Tiger, one of many species at Kaeng Krachan National Park

preserve covers nearly half of Phetchaburi province and contains some of the most pristine tracts of tropical evergreen forest in the country.

The park is relatively unknown to tourists but offers some excellent hiking.

Its western flank is marked out by the dramatic Tenasserim mountain range and the Thai-Burmese border. Streams and rivers are the water source for the 45-sq km (17-sq mile) **Kaeng Krachan reservoir**, which can be explored by boat. Thousands of migratory birds coming from as far afield as China and Siberia rest, feed, and breed in the salt marshes.

Horse for hire at Cha-am beach

Cha-am ❸

ชะอำ

Phetchaburi province. 👥 20,000.
🚌 🚕 🛈 TAT, 500/51 Phetkasem
Rd, Cha-am (0-3247-1005). 🛥 daily.

Since the mid-1980s Cha-am has experienced a dramatic surge in popularity. It has been developed from a quiet fishing and market village into a lively playground for Bangkok weekenders. Tall condominiums and huge resort hotels have sprung up alongside the long, sandy beach. During the week, however, it can be remarkably quiet.

The resort caters primarily to Thais, who focus their attentions on eating and drinking rather than swimming. At umbrella-shaded tables strung along the beach like a high tide mark, visitors feast on delicious grilled fish, squid, shrimp, and mussels. Spicy dips and cold beer complete the culinary adventure.

Those who prefer more formal eating will find restaurants serving the same range of succulent fare at the northern end of the beach.

Mareukathayawan Palace ❹
พระราชนิเวศน์มฤคทายวัน

Off Hwy 4, 9 km (5 miles) S of Cha-am. ■ *TAT, Cha-am (0-3247-1005).* ▦ *from Cha-am.* ◻ *8:30am–4:30pm daily.* ▨ *donation.* ▨ *in bedroom.*

Mareukathayawan Palace ("the palace of love and hope") was the summer residence of Rama VI. Built midway between Cha-am and Hua Hin, this grand golden teak building was designed by an Italian architect and constructed in just 16 days in 1923. However, it was abandoned when Rama VI died two years later and stood neglected for decades. The palace has undergone restoration since the 1970s and is now close to its original appearance.

The building is cool and airy; its wooden halls, verandas, and royal chambers are decorated simply and painted in pastel shades. Although the palace is easily accessible, it is rarely visited by tourists.

Hua Hin ❺
หัวหิน

Prachuap Khiri Khan province. ▦ *33,000.* ✈ ▦ ▦ ▮ *Municipality Tourist Office, 114 Phetkasem Rd, Hua Hin (0-3247-1005).* ▦ *daily.*

Hua Hin was Thailand's first beach resort. Its rail connection to Bangkok, completed in 1911, was key to its success, making the 190-km (118-mile) journey from Bangkok a manageable seaside excursion. A nine-hole golf course and the splendid colonial-style Railway Hotel were built in 1922 and 1923.

Hua Hin Station, vital to the resort's early success

Following the international trend for recuperative spa resorts at the time, Hua Hin became a popular retreat for minor Thai royalty, Bangkok's high society, and affluent foreigners. Prince Chulachakrabongse built a summer palace in the town which he called **Klai Klangwon** (meaning "far from worries") in 1926. It is still used by the Royal Family and is not open to the public. Hua Hin's fortunes declined after World War II, but its historical connections have

helped it become popular again with a new generation of Bangkokians. Hua Hin is also a hit with Scandinavian retirees, who are catered for by new holiday homes and condominiums. There has also been a marked rise in boutique resorts, spas, and restaurants.

For an insight into the Hua Hin of the 1920s, visit the Railway Hotel, now called the **Sofitel Centara Grand Resort & Villas**. By the 1960s it had fallen into disrepair, but a sensitive restoration of the elegant 1920s decor, museum tea room, and topiaries won it an Outstanding Conservation Award from the Architects' Association of Thailand in 1993. Before its refurbishment the hotel and its environs were used in the making of the film *The Killing Fields*, where it stood in for the Phnom Penh Hotel.

South of Hua Hin's main beach lies Khao Takiap (or "chopstick hill"), which is covered with miniature *chedis* and shrines. Nearby stands **Wat Khao Lad**, fronted by an impressive 20-m (66-ft) standing Buddha, which faces the sea.

The majestic open hall and first-floor gallery in the north wing of Mareukathayawan Palace

Khao Sam Roi Yot National Park ❻

อุทยานแห่งชาติเขาสามร้อยยอด

Prachuap Khiri Khan province. Visitors' Centre off Hwy 4, 37 km (23 miles) S of Pranburi. 🛈 TAT, Cha-am (0-3247-1005); Forestry Dept (0-2562-0760 or **www.dnp.go.th** for bungalow bookings). 🚌 Pranburi, then songthaew. 🛆 🛅

This small coastal park sits in the narrowest part of the Thai peninsula, overlooking the Gulf of Thailand. Covering 98 sq km (38 sq miles), it is a region of contrasts: sea, sand, and marsh backed by mountains and caves. The park is best known for its distinctive limestone pinnacles (Khao Sam Roi Yot means "mountain of 300 peaks") that rise vertically from the marshland to a height of 650 m (2,150 ft).

The park's wetlands provide a sanctuary for water birds. Millions of migratory birds flying from Siberia to Sumatra and Australia rest, feed, and breed here, between August and April. It is home to many other animals such as the rare dusky langur, the nocturnal slow loris, and the crab-eating macaque. **Tham Phraya Nakon** houses a grand pavilion, built for King Rama V in 1896, and **Tham Sai** contains fossilized falls.

Beware monkeys sign, Khao Sam Roi Yot

Wat Chong Kra Chok, overlooking sedate Prachuap Khiri Khan

Prachuap Khiri Khan ❼

ประจวบคีรีขันธ์

Prachuap Khiri Khan province. 🏠 60,000. 🚍 🚌 🛥 🛈 TAT, Cha-am (0-3247-1005). 🛆 daily.

Prachuap Khiri Khan means "town among the mountain chain." And it is certainly true that its coastal sugar-loaf limestone outcrops at either end of a sandy bay give it a "little Rio" appearance. The local economy relies primarily on fishing; freshly caught seafood can be purchased from a number of good restaurants and stalls along the promenade. This peaceful administrative town has pleasant swimming beaches to the north and south of its main bay. The top of the delightful **Wat Chong Kra Chok** – perched on one of the surrounding hills – offers the best view of the area. About 200 macaques live on the hill, and every evening they climb to the top to feed from the lovely frangipani trees.

Chumphon ❽

ชุมพร

Chumphon province. 🏠 84,000. 🚍 🚌 🛥 🛈 TAT, Chumphon (0-7750-1831). 🛆 daily. 🎏 Luang Suan Buddha Image Parade and Boat Race (5 days in Oct).

Chumphon is regarded by some as the point of cultural transition between the heartland of the Buddhist Tai peoples, and the peninsular south of the country, where Muslim culture is strong. The town was the home of Prince Chumphon, the Father of the Royal Thai Navy, who died in 1923. Nearby, the 68-m (225-ft) long **HMS Chumphon** torpedo boat, decommissioned in 1975, has been preserved. It forms a distinctive landmark.

The reefs around the 47 tiny islands off Chumphon's 222-km (140-mile) long coast are becoming increasingly popular with divers. Tour companies in town will arrange diving day trips to such islands as **Samet, Mattra, Ngam Yai**, and **Ngam Noi**. Chumphon is also the most convenient place from which to get a ferry to Ko Tao (*see p341*).

CHAIYA'S ROLE IN THE SRIVIJAYA EMPIRE

Srivijayan votive tablet

The Mahayana Buddhist Empire of Srivijaya (*see pp56–7*) dominated the whole Malaysian peninsula and parts of Indonesia between the 7th and 13th centuries AD. Although the majority of scholars now believe that Palembang in Sumatra was the Srivijayan capital, discoveries of temple remains and some exquisite stone and bronze statues (many now in the National Museum in Bangkok) in Chaiya provide evidence of Chaiya's importance. Its strategic geographical position, as a then coastal port, meant the town played an important role in the east-west trade between India, the peninsula, and China. In fact, Chaiya was mentioned in the writings of the Chinese monk I Chinga, who, while visiting the area in the late 7th century, testified to its religious and cultural sophistication. It is known that some of Chaiya's rulers were connected by marriage to those of central Java. Furthermore, it is possible that the name "Chaiya" originated as a contraction of "Siwichaiya" (a different transliteration of Srivijaya), which follows the local tendency to emphasize the final syllable of a word.

8th-century bronze found at Chaiya

A line of Buddha images at Phra Boromathat Chaiya, one of the few remaining temples from the Srivijaya period

Chaiya ❾

ไชยา

Surat Thani province. 🏠 34,000.
🚉 🚌 🛈 TAT, Surat Thani (0-7728-8818). 🛒 daily. 🎎 Chak Phra Festival (Oct–Nov).

Despite the somewhat dreary look of the small railroad town of Chaiya, the settlement is actually one of the oldest and most historically significant in Southern Thailand. A number of superb examples of sculpture dating from the Srivijaya period (7th–13th centuries) have been found here.

Many of the sculptures show clear Mon and Indian influences, depicting figures such as Bengali-style Buddha images and multiarmed Hindu deities. These, and a variety of votive tablets, can be seen at the **Chaiya National Museum**. It also holds examples of Ayutthayan art. The museum is 2 km (1 mile) west of Chaiya and a ten-minute walk from the train station.

Right beside the museum is **Phra Boromathat Chaiya** *(see pp346–7)*, an important Srivijayan temple. Within the main compound is the central *chedi*, which has been painstakingly restored. Square in plan, it has four porches that ascend in tiers and are topped

with small towers. The 8th-century *chedi* is built of brick and vegetable mortar. Although the site is old, it is the memory of Phra Chaiya Wiwat, a locally venerated monk who died in 1949, that attracts the majority of worshipers today.

🏛 Chaiya National Museum
Phra Boromathat Chaiya.
Tel 0-7743-1066. 🛒 Wed–Sun.
🛑 public hols. 🎫

Environs
The International Dhamma Hermitage *(see p467)* at **Wat Suan Mok**, southwest of Chaiya, is a popular retreat for Buddhists from all over the world. Its attraction is its back-to-basics religious philosophy established by the *wat's* founder, Buddhadhasa Bhikkhu, who died in 1993. Within the temple a regimen

Murals relating the story of the Buddha at Wat Suan Mok

of physical labor underpins a simple monastic life devoid of elaborate religious ceremony. Ten-day residential meditation retreats are held here, starting on the first day of each month.

🏕 Wat Suan Mok
7 km (4 miles) S of Chaiya off Hwy 41. **Tel** 0-7743-1552. 🛒 daily.

Surat Thani ❿

สุราษฎร์ธานี

Surat Thani province. 🏠 31,000.
✈ 🚉 Phun Phin, 14 km (9 miles) W of Surat Thani, then bus. 🚌 ⛴ Ban Don (in town); Thong, 6 km (4 miles) E of town. 🛈 TAT, 5 Talat Mai Rd, Surat Thani (0-7728-8818). @ tatsurat@tat.or.th 🎎 Rambutan Fair (Aug), Chak Phra Festival (Oct–Nov).

Surat Thani, a business center and port dealing in rubber and coconuts, first grew to prominence in the Srivijaya period since it was strategically located at the mouth of the Tapi and Phum Duang Rivers. The riverside is still intriguing today with its numerous small boats ferrying people to the city's busy waterfront markets, which sell fresh products and flowers. But Surat Thani is best known as a transportation gateway to the beaches of Ko Samui and Ko Pha Ngan.

Lofty palm trees and clear blue waters of a near-deserted beach on Ko Samui ▷

Ko Samui ⓫

เกาะสมุย

Coconuts, a key crop on Samui

Ko Samui is situated 400 miles (700 km) south of Bangkok, in the Gulf of Thailand. It is the country's third-largest island, after Phuket and Ko Chang. A backpackers' haven in the 1970s, Samui has now seen tourism become its main income earner. With rapid development, the arrival of major hotel chains, and persistent promotion by the TAT, Samui has become one of the most popular islands in South-east Asia. The island is also attracting foreign investors building luxury homes for wealthy businessmen from Hong Kong, Singapore, and Taiwan. This trend may lead to Samui moving increasingly upmarket.

Nathon

Nathon is Samui's capital and main ferry port. The island was first settled in the 1850s by Chinese merchants who had come in search of trade in cotton and coconuts. Nathon was founded around 1905, when the site was chosen as the island's administrative center.

Few visitors stay here, except in order to take an early morning boat to Surat Thani on the mainland. The town has a supermarket, post office, and money changing facilities.

The main transport route on the island is the 50-km (31-mile) circular road, which passes through Nathon. *Songthaews* departing from Nathon ferry port travel either northward (clockwise) toward Chaweng beach and the airport, or southward (counterclockwise) toward Lamai.

The 12-m (38-ft) "Big Buddha" on Ko Faan, just off the Samui coast

Maenam

This 4-km (2-mile) long beach is the most westerly stretch of sand on the north coast. It has extensive views of Ko Pha Ngan *(see p339)*. Visitors flock here for the excellent windsurfing opportunities, which are aided by the strong directional breezes that blow on-shore

KEY

🏖	Beach
🌊	Water sports
ℹ	Tourist information
🛕	Wat
✈	Airport
🚌	Bus station
⛴	Ferry service
▬	Main road
▬	Minor road
☀	Vista

Maenam, on the north coast, one of the quietest beaches on Ko Samui

For hotels and restaurants in this region see pp415–18 and pp443–6

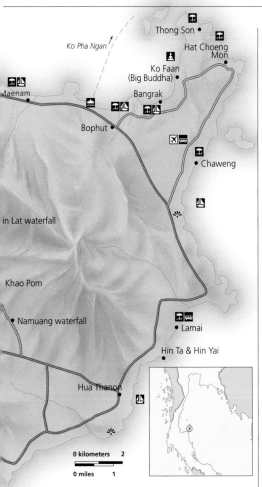

Ko Pha Ngan

Thong Son

Hat Choeng Mon

Ko Faan (Big Buddha)

Bangrak

Maenam

Bophut

Chaweng

in Lat waterfall

Khao Pom

Namuang waterfall

Lamai

Hin Ta & Hin Yai

Hua Thanon

0 kilometers   2

0 miles   1

VISITORS' CHECKLIST

Surat Thani province. 42,000.
23 km (14 miles) from Nathon.
from Surat Thani, Tha Thong
and Don Sak. TAT, Nathon (0-
7742-0504) or TAT, Surat Thani (0-
7728-8818); Songserm (0-2808-
0734), Nathon (0-7742-0157, for
ferry bookings). 3 km (2 miles)
S of Nathon (0-7742-1281).
daily. www.samui.sawadee.com

**Paragliding over Chaweng beach,
one of many activities**

Asian tourists, who come here
to make merit *(see p129)*. A
gaudy bazaar of souvenir stalls
and cafés has sprung up at
the foot of the *naga* staircase
leading to the Buddha image.

Thong Son and Choeng Mon
Farther along the coast, on
Samui's northeastern cape, is
a series of secluded rocky
coves. Hat Thong Son is a
peaceful inlet with marvelous
views across to Ko Pha Ngan.
Most of the accommodation
on the headland is concentrated at Ao Choeng Mon, an
attractive bay with a pleasant
beach and good swimming.

during the northeasterly
monsoon from December to
February. However, the beach
is narrow and not as attractive
as others on the island.

Bophut
Bophut has better facilities
than Maenam. Its village, at
the eastern end of the next
bay to the east, includes bungalows, a bank, bars, restaurants, and a range of water
sports. The tranquil 2-km
(1-mile) long beach is popular
with families and backpackers.
From Bophut there is a daily
boat service to Hat Rin, a
beach on Ko Pha Ngan.

Bangrak
Adjacent to Bophut is Bangrak,
also known as "Big Buddha"
beach. The sea is not as clear
here as it is off Chaweng and

Lamai beaches *(see p338)*, but
it does offer plenty of budget
accommodations. A causeway
links the eastern end of Bangrak beach to the tiny island
of Ko Faan, home to the
large, gold-covered Big Buddha. The imposing statue is
popular with islanders and

Palm trees shading typical beachside huts on Ko Samui

Exploring Ko Samui: the East Coast and Minor Sights

The beautiful beaches and buzzing nightlife of Chaweng and Lamai on Samui's east coast draw tourists from all over the world. Many visitors never stray from these resorts, leaving the quieter beaches on the south and west coasts, the island's *wats,* and Samui's spectacular mountainous and forested interior relatively untouched.

Muslim fishermen landing their boats on Samui's east coast

Chaweng

Chaweng is the longest, busiest, and most beautiful beach on the island, stretching 5 km (3 miles) down the east coast. Its warm waters, white sands, and back-to-nature beach bungalows have attracted budget travelers for many years. Today, though, more and more upscale developments are being built to accommodate package tourists.

At the northern end of Chaweng is a tranquil 1-m (3-ft) deep lagoon, ideal for children and novice windsurfers. The long, inviting sweep of the middle and southern end

of the beach is bordered by coconut palms. Chaweng is at its most scenic along its southern section where large boulders alternate with discreet sandy coves. For the active, the beach has a wide range of sports including windsurfing, canoeing, paragliding, scuba diving, tennis, and volleyball.

Chaweng has the most developed tourist infrastructure on Samui with travel agencies, banks, supermarkets, and car and bike rental among the facilities available. Although it does attract a few families, Chaweng is still predominantly visited by young travelers. Many come to enjoy the ever-increasing numbers of bars, restaurants, and clubs.

Lamai

Samui's second largest beach caters primarily to the European budget tourist. The main focus is at the center of the 4-km (2-mile) long beach. Behind the beach are riotous bars, nightclubs, and restaurants serving Western food.

Lamai village is at the quieter, northern end of the beach, away from the crowds. It still has many old teak houses with thatched roofs. The village's main sight is Wat

Lamai Cultural Hall, built in 1826, which has a small folk museum dedicated to arts and crafts found on Samui.

On the southern promontory of Lamai beach are the Hin Ta and Hin Yai rock formations that are famous for their similarity in shape to male and female sexual organs.

South and West Coasts

There are many quiet beaches with simple huts along the south and west coasts, such as around Thong Krut. Another is Thong Yang which – although only 1.5 km (1 mile) south of the pier where the vehicle ferries from Don Sak dock – which is perfect for those seeking peaceful seclusion.

Swimming in Namuang waterfall, in the center of Samui

The Interior

For visitors tiring of the beach, the interior of Samui offers an adventurous alternative. The mix of dense tropical forest and large coconut plantations seems impenetrable, but there are rough trails – which can be negotiated by four-wheel-drive vehicle or by motorcycle – and two roads leading to Samui's picturesque waterfalls.

Namuang, an impressive 30-m (98-ft) high waterfall, is a popular destination for picnics and swimming. It is situated 10 km (6 miles) from Nathon and 5 km (3 miles) from the circular coast road. Hin Lat, 3 km (2 miles) from Nathon, is smaller than Namuang and less interesting. Both falls are at their most spectacular in December or January at the end of the rainy season, when they swell with rainwater.

Chaweng, the longest and most attractive beach on Ko Samui

For hotels and restaurants in this region see pp415–18 and pp443–6

Ko Pha Ngan ⑫

เกาะพะงัน

Surat Thani province. 🏯 8,400.
🚤 from Nathon on Ko Samui to
Tong Sala. 🛈 TAT, Surat Thani
(0-7728-8818). 🎪 daily.

Ko Pha Ngan is 15 km
(9 miles) north of Ko Samui,
and is two-thirds its size. The
island has the same tropical
combination of powdery
beaches, accessible coral reefs,
and rugged, forested interior.
Budget travelers come to enjoy a bohemian life, staying
in rattan huts beside idyllic
bays. The island is much less
developed for tourism than
Samui, due mainly to its bad
road system. Much of it is accessible only by sea or along
rutted tracks by pickup truck.

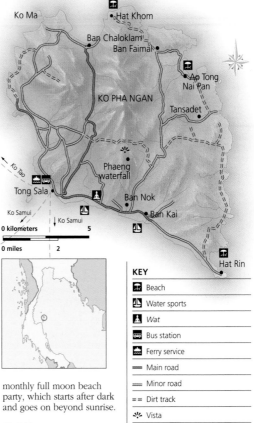

Tong Sala
This town is the entrance port
to Ko Pha Ngan, and, like
Nathon on Ko Samui, acts as a
service town with a bank, post
restante, supermarket, travel
agent, and photoprocessing
store. Next to the pier, an
armada of *songthaews* waits to
take visitors around the island.

Hat Rin
The greatest number of bungalows on the island is at Hat
Rin, located at the southeastern
tip, 10 km (6 miles) from Tong
Sala. It has become a popular
destination with backpackers,
many of whom now consider
Samui's resorts to be too
commercialized. Hat Rin has
two wide beaches flanking
the headland. Its accommodations are often fully booked
for a week either side of the

**The white sands of Hat Rin beach
on Ko Pha Ngan**

monthly full moon beach
party, which starts after dark
and goes on beyond sunrise.

Chaloklam
A strong smell of dried, salted
fish emanates from Chalo-
klam's storefronts. Asian visitors often stop here to
buy fish after visiting
the revered Chao Mae
Koan Im shrine in the
center of the island.
In Chaloklam, fishing-
related activities such
as mending nets and
gutting fish coexist
with shop-houses
selling pizza and
other tourist snacks.
The beaches near the
town tend to be rath-
er dirty but improve farther to
the east, especially as far out
of town as Khom beach.

**Dried fish at
Chaloklam village**

Tong Nai Pan
Although the majority of the
beaches are on the east side
of the island, most are accessible only from a rough track
running along the coast. The
twin bays of Tong Nai Pan Noi
and Tong Nai Pan Yai in the

northeast offer arguably the
most attractive scenery. They
can be reached by pickup
truck from Tong Sala
or, between January
and September, by
long-tail boats, which
sail from Maenam
beach on Ko Samui.

Tansadet, 3 km
(2 miles) to the south,
is the island's biggest
stream and waterfall.
It owes its name,
"royal stream," to
the ten visits King
Chulalongkorn made
between 1888 and 1909. Since
then most Thai monarchs have
left large stone inscriptions on
rocks alongside the stream –
finding the signatures requires
scrambling among the rocks.
The stream has two falls, Sam-
pan and Daeng. Both are suitable for swimming, but heavy
rainfall from September to December makes the stream bed
too dangerous to walk along.

KEY

📷 Beach

🏄 Water sports

🛕 *Wat*

🚌 Bus station

⛴ Ferry service

━━ Main road

═══ Minor road

= = Dirt track

🌿 Vista

Angthong National Marine Park ⓭

อุทยานแห่งชาติทางทะเลอ่างทอง

Surat Thani province. Park HQ on Ko Wua Talab. ⚓ *from Ko Samui.* ℹ *TAT, Surat Thani (0-7728-8818); Park HQ (0-7728-6025); Forestry Dept (0-2562-0760 inc bungalow bookings).* ⬤ *Nov–Dec.*

KEY

🏖	Beach
🏄	Water sports
ℹ	Tourist information
⚓	Ferry service
- -	Trail
⚝	Vista

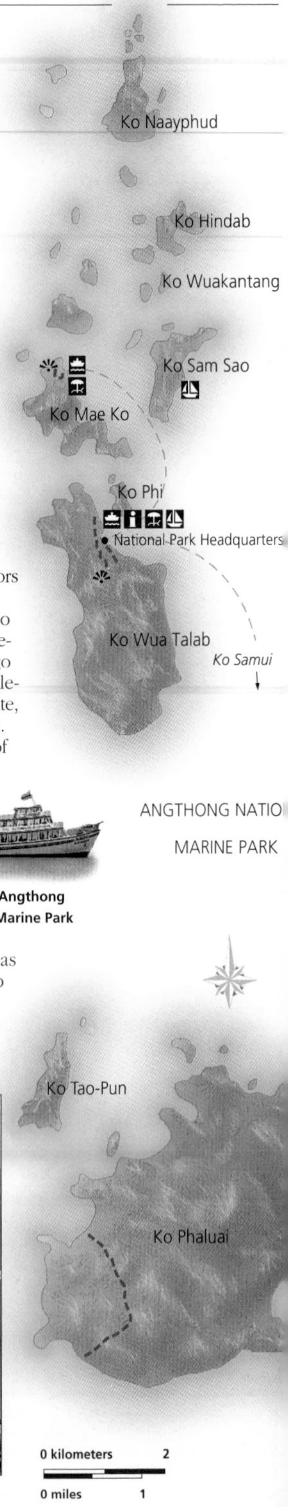

The 40 virtually uninhabited islands of the Angthong National Marine Park display a rugged beauty distinct from palm-fringed Ko Samui 31 km (19 miles) away to the southeast. The Angthong ("golden basin") islands, covering an area of 102 sq km (39 sq miles), are the submerged peaks of a flooded range of limestone mountains that, farther south in Nakhon Si Thammarat province, rise to 1,835 m (6,000 ft).

Angthong's pristine beauty owes much to being the preserve of the Royal Thai Navy, and therefore off-limits until 1980 when it was declared a National Marine Park. Now naval boats have been replaced by tourist ferries. Most visitors come on day-trips from Ko Samui to relax on the mica-white sands, explore the lush forests and limestone caves, sea canoe around the islands' jagged coastlines, and snorkel among the colorful fan corals.

Another attraction is the abundant wildlife, both on land and in the sea. Leopard cats, squirrels, long-tailed macaques, sea otters, and pythons may be glimpsed, and a lack of natural predators has made the endearingly friendly dusky langur easy to spot. Among the 40 bird species found in the archipelago are the black baza, the edible-nest swiftlet, the brahminy kite, and the Eurasian woodcock.

Divers taking advantage of the excellent coral off **Ko Sam Sao** will probably see short-bodied mackerel *(pla thu)*, a staple of the Thai diet. The sea around the islands is favored by the fish as a breeding ground. It is also possible to spot dolphins, although they are wary of humans because fisherman catch them for their meat.

Ferry to Angthong National Marine Park

Ko Naayphud

Ko Hindab

Ko Wuakantang

Ko Sam Sao

Ko Mae Ko

Ko Phi

● National Park Headquarters

Ko Wua Talab

Ko Samui

ANGTHONG NATIO

MARINE PARK

Ko Tao-Pun

Ko Phaluai

0 kilometers	2
0 miles	1

View from a trail on Ko Wua Talab, Angthong National Marine Park

For hotels and restaurants in this region see pp415–18 and pp443–6

Boat for carrying visitors from the ferry to the beach on Ko Mae Ko

The park headquarters, and the islands' only tourist accommodations and facilities, are located on the largest island, **Ko Wua Talab** ("sleeping cow island"). A steep 400-m (1300-ft) climb from here leads to a vista offering wonderful panoramas of the whole archipelago and beyond to Ko Pha Ngan, Ko Samui, and the mainland. The view is at its best at sunrise and sunset. Another fairly tough climb leads to Tham Buabok ("waving lotus cave"), so named because of the shape of some of its stalactites and stalagmites.

On **Ko Mae Ko** there is a swimming beach as well as the stunning Thale Noi, a wide turquoise lake bordered by sheer cliffs. This is the "golden basin" that gives the islands their name.

Cowrie shell, Ko Tao

Ko Tao ⓮

เกาะเต่า

Surat Thani province. 🏠 1,300. 🚢 from Chumphon or Ko Samui. 🛈 TAT, Surat (0-7728-8818).

Located 40 km (25 miles) north of Ko Pha Ngan, "turtle island" is the smallest and prettiest of the islands in the Samui archipelago that offer visitors accommodations.

Ko Tao's major attraction is its superb offshore diving. Excellent visibility, a wide range of diving sites, and a rich variety of coral and marine life make for some of the most rewarding diving in the country. The main dive sites are Green Rock, Chumphon Pinnacle, and Southwest Pinnacle. Many sites are suitable for beginners thanks to the shallow inshore bays and clear waters. In May water visibility can approach 40 m (130 ft), which is often claimed to be the maximum possible. The island has about ten dive companies that operate all year round, although the main season is from December to April.

The island itself is rugged, with dense forest inland, quiet coves along the east coast, and a fine sweep of sandy beach on the west side. Plenty of simple bungalow accommodation is available, although it can be difficult to find a room in tourist season.

Just to the northwest of Ko Tao lie three immensely scenic islands known collectively as **Ko Nang Yuan**. Linked by sandbars and surrounded by coral, these are a delightful place to linger for a few days.

Diving among the rich marine life and fine coral off Ko Tao

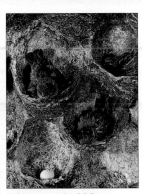

Birds' nests: a regional delicacy

BIRD'S-NEST SOUP

Unlike such misleadingly named delicacies as Bombay duck, the main ingredient of bird's-nest soup is, indeed, birds' nests. Not just any nest will do, however. Only the homes of birds such as the brown-rumped swift, the edible-nest swiftlet, and the sea swallow are acceptable. When these delicate, saliva-thread constructions are cooked they are transformed into smooth, noodlelike strands that are considered to have aphrodisiac properties by peoples throughout Southeast and East Asia. Such is the perceived potency of the soup that the nests change hands for huge sums of money. A government license is required to collect the nests, and many of the most important sites, such as those in caves on Ko Phi Phi Ley (see p373) are protected by armed guards. The dangerous job of nest harvesting is allowed only between February and April and in September, when agile collectors must scale the cave walls on flimsy bamboo scaffolds.

SOUTHERN THAILAND

INTRODUCING
SOUTHERN THAILAND 344–351

UPPER ANDAMAN COAST 352–373

DEEP SOUTH 374–389

Introducing Southern Thailand

The narrow peninsula of Southern Thailand, stretching from Ranong, on the Myanmar border, to Malaysia, is a unique region with a rich, multicultural heritage. Forested mountains run along much of the interior, and the hinterland and islands of Phangnga Bay in the Andaman Sea form Thailand's most spectacular natural landscape. Here the shallow waters are dotted with limestone stacks and craggy islands 300 m (985 feet) high. Some of the country's best sandy beaches and diving sites are also found along the southern coasts and around the Andaman islands. Though the beach resorts of Phuket and Krabi draw the most visitors to the area, the South also offers historic cultural sites, such as the towns of Songkhla and Nakhon Si Thammarat. Sadly, many parts of the region's coast were hit by the tsunami in 2004 and some 5,300 people were killed. The Thais responded rapidly, though, and most of the reconstruction was completed by 2006.

UPPER ANDAMAN COAST (see pp352–373)

Phangnga Bay

Phuket

Phangnga Bay (see pp364–7), *with its weird and wonderful towering limestone stacks, is one of Southern Thailand's most famous natural beauty spots. Due to massive erosion the bay can no longer be accessed by tourist boats, but can be viewed from a distance.*

Phuket (see pp358–63) *is Thailand's largest island and richest province. Prosperous even during the 19th century, when Chinese merchants used the island as a base for sea trade, today it is one of the most popular tourist resorts in Thailand. Phuket is now a largely upscale destination with luxury hotels, restaurants, and shops lining many of the island's stunning beaches. A wide range of water sports is available, including superb diving facilities.*

◁ **A row of golden, seated Buddha images in the interior courtyard of Wat Wang, near Phatthalung town**

Nakhon Si Thammarat (see pp378–9), *once the regional capital of the Srivijaya Empire (see pp346–7), is today the South's cultural center. Despite some fine sights, including Southern Thailand's holiest shrine, Wat Mahathat, and one of the few remaining nang talung shadow puppet theaters, the city is still not visited by many tourists.*

Songkhla National Museum (see pp384–5), *contains an eclectic collection of ceramics, art, and furniture. It occupies the one-time deputy governor's residence, a splendid 19th-century Chinese-style mansion.*

Nakhon Si Thammarat

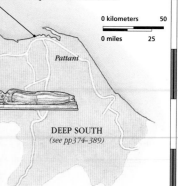

***Korlae* fishing boats** (see p388), *with painted bulls, are a colorful feature of the Muslim South. Some of the best ones can be seen at Pattani, once an independent Muslim state.*

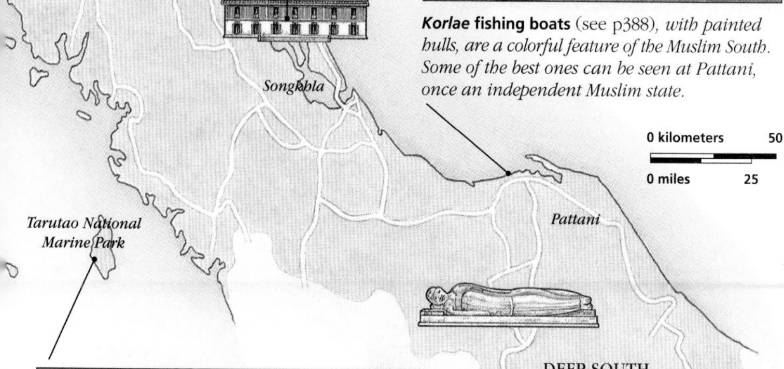

Songkhla

0 kilometers	50
0 miles	25

Tarutao National Marine Park

Pattani

DEEP SOUTH
(see pp374–389)

Tarutao National Marine Park (see p386) *has a wide diversity of wildlife and offers some of the most stunning, unspoiled beaches and island scenery in Thailand.*

The Peninsula as a Cultural Crossroads

For over 2,000 years, the peninsula that is now divided between Malaysia, Thailand, and Myanmar has been a major cultural crossroads. Finds from the Isthmus of Kra (especially the historic trading centers of Nakhon Si Thammarat, Chaiya, Sathing Phra, and Takua Pa) testify to strong links with China, India, the Middle East, and even the Roman Empire before the first millennium AD. In the 7th–13th centuries the Hindu-Buddhist Srivijaya Empire held sway over much of the region. After Srivijaya's decline, Burma and Siam, both Buddhist, pushed south, while Islam, brought by Arab traders, made a lasting impact in the southernmost part of the peninsula. There was even greater cultural diversity from the 16th century, when the British, Dutch, Portuguese, and other colonial powers developed trade routes through the Straits of Malacca.

Islam, the main religion in Malaysia, widely practiced in Southern Thailand today – minarets compete with Buddhist shrines in many towns.

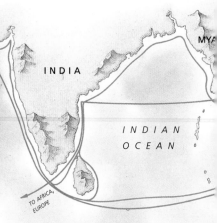

Prehistoric paintings can be found in Phangnga Bay (see pp364–7) and other parts of the peninsula. Humans have lived here at least since the last Ice Age, when the peninsula did not exist as such – the area from Borneo to Sumatra was then dry land.

TRADE ROUTES

The Straits of Malacca have always been a natural channel for sea routes. Chinese, Indian, and Arab vessels were trading, gathering provisions, and "wintering" at posts along the peninsula at least 2,000 years ago. European ships joined them from the 16th century. As seafaring technology developed ships became less dependent on some ports, which subsequently declined.

Ceremonial drums found at the ancient cities of Chaiya and Nakhon Si Thammarat and in Sumatra, were made in Dong Son in North Vietnam c.500 BC, testifying to early trade.

| 0 kilometers | 1,000 |
| 0 miles | 500 |

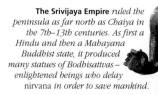

The Srivijaya Empire ruled the peninsula as far north as Chaiya in the 7th–13th centuries. As first a Hindu and then a Mahayana Buddhist state, it produced many statues of Bodhisattvas – enlightened beings who delay nirvana in order to save mankind.

KEY

— Local routes (c. 5th century BC onward)

— Major routes during the Srivijaya period (7th–13th centuries AD)

— Major European routes (16th century onward)

This Dutch East India Company cannon *is in Nakhon Si Thammarat, an ancient town in Southern Thailand (see pp378–9). The company traded all over Southeast Asia and was drawn to the peninsula by access to Chinese and Japanese goods.*

SRIVIJAYAN ARCHITECTURE

The Srivijaya Empire controlled trade at ports such as Chaiya *(see pp332–3)* and Takua Pa, on the Isthmus of Kra. Numerous Srivijayan artifacts have been found in the Gulf and South of Thailand, but most *chedis*, which were built of stucco and brick, have been built over. The main example to survive is an outstanding, complete *chedi* at Wat Phra Boromathat in Chaiya. Cruciform in shape, it has four tiers, decreasing in size

Chedi **of the Javan-influenced Wat Phra Boromathat, Chaiya**

as they ascend. On each corner is a smaller *chedi*. Built in the 9th–10th centuries, it has been restored many times, most recently in 1930.

TO CHINA

VIETNAM

AILAND

CAMBODIA

SOUTH CHINA SEA

MALAYSIA

BORNEO

SUMATRA

JAVA

AFRICA, EUROPE

TO THE SPICE ISLANDS (MOLUCCAS)

This European engraving *shows a march in Pattani (see p388), one of several Muslim states in the peninsula that lost autonomy to Bangkok in the early part of the 20th century.*

The Thais and Burmese *battled over the northern peninsula after Srivijaya waned. A fight for Phuket, or Junkceylon (see pp358–63), took place in 1785.*

European trade *led to extensive mapping of Southeast Asia. This 17th-century French map shows the local trade route up the east coast of the peninsula, from Batavia (Jakarta) in Java to the city of Ayutthaya in Siam.*

Coral Reefs

Red saddleback anemonefish

Thailand's best coral reefs are found in the Andaman Sea. These reefs, which are composed of countless tiny marine animals, grow extremely slowly: 1 m (3 ft) of coral reef can take 1,000 years to form. As a coral reef is an excellent source of food and shelter, it provides the base for a unique and diverse marine ecosystem. The reef consists of reef builders (mainly hard corals, whose limestone skeletons form the basis of the reef) and reef dwellers, such as sea urchins, whose remains may also help build the reef when they die. Although the 2004 tsunami did damage many reefs, especially those of the Surin, Similan, and Phi Phi islands, initial reports of great devastation were inaccurate.

Snorkeling *is a low-cost and easy way to explore a coral reef. Many reefs can be found in relatively shallow, clear water, which is excellent for snorkeling.*

Gobies – *small, spiny-finned fish with large heads – live mainly in tropical waters. They often share sand burrows with shrimp.*

Coconut grove

West-facing wall

The clown triggerfish *has an upright spine in its dorsal fin. The spine is raised to wedge the fish under rocks and ledges; this stops predators from pulling the fish out.*

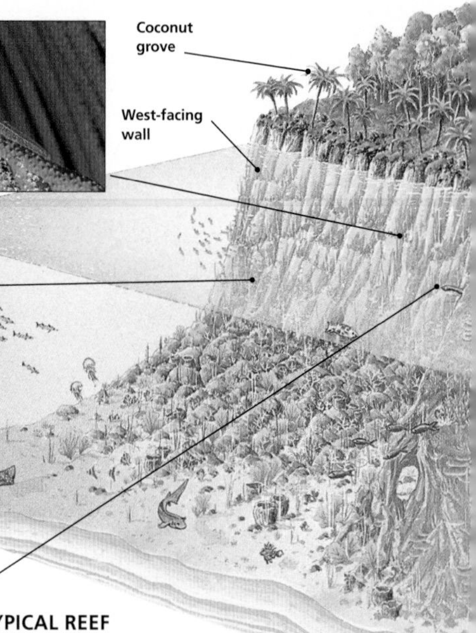

A TYPICAL REEF

On the island's east side, the reef flat slopes away from the beach, rises to a crest, then slopes steeply to the sea bed. Mostly hard corals are found on the east side. The reef's west walls tend to be much steeper and rockier than the east side. Its boulders provide protection for soft corals and nooks in which creatures such as eels live.

Moray eels *are voracious predators, biding in crevices and lunging out at unsuspecting prey swimming by. Food left between a moray's teeth may be picked clean by hungry cleaner shrimp.*

Leopard sharks, *also known as zebra sharks, pose no threat to people. At Shark Point, near Ko Phi Phi, divers often see these timid creatures resting or cruising along the outskirts of the coral reef.*

Scuba diving *is an excellent way to experience diverse reef ecosystems (see p462). In the South, Phuket has the most diving operators offering instruction, equipment rental, and trips to offshore islands such as Ko Phi Phi. When exploring a coral reef, you should not touch the delicate corals, as this causes permanent damage to the reef.*

Many species of sea bird *gather around islands with coral reefs to feed on the abundant fish life. This is a great egret, a large wading bird that feeds by stabbing small fish with its razor-sharp bill.*

Rays *are often seen around coral reefs. Manta rays have impressive wingspans of up to 6 m (20 ft), while blue-spotted rays have a poisonous spine in their tail.*

Sandy beach

Reef flat

Reef crest

Snapper *often follow schools of feeding goatfish, devouring any small fish that escape the latter.*

Reef slope

CORAL: THE REEF'S BUILDING BLOCK

Coral is made of the skeletons of polyps, small animals related to sea anemones and jellyfish. Polyps are unusual in that they build their skeletons outside their bodies. As the polyps divide, the coral colony slowly builds up. There may be as many as 200 different species of coral in a reef, divided into hard corals such as brain coral, and colorful soft corals, which have no stony outer skeleton.

Hard, rocklike coral

Soft, plantlike coral

Giant hermit crabs *are soft-bodied crustaceans. They protect their bodies by living and moving around the sea bed in the empty shells of mollusks such as whelks.*

Mangrove Forests

White-throated kingfisher

Mangrove forests develop only in the tropics, in brackish and saltwater areas of estuaries. In Thailand they are found in pockets of the South, particularly at Phangnga Bay *(see pp364–7)*. Mangrove species are the only trees to have adapted to the inhospitable conditions of these muddy, intertidal zones. The forests typically cover networks of channels and levees created from the buildup of silt that becomes trapped in the cagelike root systems of the trees. Though often dismissed as wasteland, in its natural state a mangrove forest is a vital ecosystem – a fertile spawning, nursing, feeding, and sheltering ground for crustaceans, fish, birds, snakes, and even mammals. "Primary" mangrove grows to over 25 m (80 ft) high. However, most mangrove in Thailand is "secondary," meaning it has been cut by humans and reaches only 5–10 m (16–33 ft).

The characteristic stiltlike roots *of most mangrove trees support the tree against the constant movement of tidal waters. As well as holding the trunk of the tree above the high tide level, the roots trap nutrient-rich sediments.*

The upward-growing roots *(pneumatophores) of some trees have special "breathing" pores used during low tide.*

Sonneratia are sturdy trees, tolerant of high salinity.

Avicennia are sustained by large cable root systems below the mud.

Rhizophora *species* are associated with soft mud under strong tidal influence.

Breathing roots, or pneumatophores, can excrete excess salt.

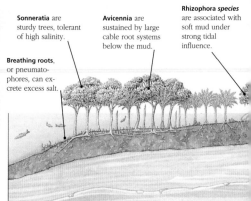

The mud skipper, *so called for its skipping gait across mud flats at low tide, is the ubiquitous mangrove dweller. It can survive for short periods out of water.*

CROSS SECTION OF A MANGROVE LEVEE

This cross section shows a typical gradation of trees in a Thai mangrove forest. The waters are at high tide, a time when small fish and invertebrates feed in the sheltered, nutrient-rich waters around the roots of the trees. At low tide, when the roots of the trees are exposed, crabs and wading birds scour the mud flats for trapped fish and decaying matter.

The estuarine crocodile *was once king of the mangroves. Nowadays it is bred in farms and is very rarely seen in the wild.*

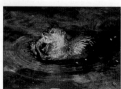

Small-clawed otters *are often spotted in mangrove regions. They eat the smaller inhabitants such as mollusks and crabs.*

Male fiddler crabs *sift the silt with their one enlarged claw, selecting tiny organic particles to eat. As with most other types of crab, their colorful claws are also used in courtship displays.*

Rhizophora **trees**, *such as these at Phangnga Bay, are common in Thai mangrove forests. Their colonizing ability is largely due to the unusual shape of their seed pods. With dagger-shaped stalks, these penetrate the ooze rather than floating away with the tide.*

Yellow-ringed cat snakes, *like other mangrove snakes, are adept swimmers and tree climbers. They rest by day and hunt fish and frogs by night.*

Nipa palms thrive in soft mud away from wave action. Nipa is used by Thais to wrap tobacco and as an ingredient in candies and alcohol.

Bruguiera **trees** grow in compacted mud that is inundated with water only during high spring tides.

Crab-eating macaques *inhabit Thai mangrove forests; they are capable swimmers and forage for crabs at low tide. Seeds also form part of the macaques' diet.*

THE DESTRUCTION OF THAILAND'S MANGROVE FORESTS

Despite the provision of a national mangrove management program (set up in 1946), some 60 percent of Thailand's mangrove has been cleared since the 1960s – just 300,000 acres were thought to remain by 1996. Not only has this loss of habitat decimated marine life, but coastal erosion has also started to become a problem in parts of the South. Without the roots of mangrove trees to trap it, estuarine silt is deposited over a progressively larger area, and seawater seeps over more and more of the land. The rate of loss peaked in the late 1980s with the boom in tiger shrimp farming in former mangrove areas. After clearing mangrove trees to make way for shrimp farms, farmers use the tide-flushed mangrove channels to discharge nutrient-rich excreta from the prawn pools. This reduces oxygen levels in the adjacent natural breeding grounds of shrimp, fish, and crabs. Charcoal production is also to blame: tall mangrove species have been select-cut for decades in order to be incinerated and turned into charcoal. The fuel is sold cheaply in Thailand or shipped to Singapore for distribution within Asia. Road and harbor construction are other factors responsible for the loss of mangrove forests in Thailand.

Shrimp farm in a former area of mangrove forest

UPPER ANDAMAN COAST

The abiding image of Thailand's Andaman Coast is of long sandy beaches backed by swaying palms and a verdant hinterland of rainforest. Centered on Ko Phuket, the upper half of this coast has many attractions. This region suffered the most from the 2004 tsunami, in particular Ranong, the Surin, Similan, and Phi Phi islands, but rebuilding and environmental restoration work has been swift.

The Andaman Coast around Phuket has long been a magnet for Thais and foreigners. Merchants were drawn by its strategic position on the spice routes between East and West *(see pp346–7)*; prospectors came for the rich tin deposits. This is a lush, fertile region. Much of the interior is cloaked in rainforest, and rubber, coffee, cashew, banana, and durian plantations are common.

The outstanding natural beauty of the Andaman Coast is known the world over. The biggest draw in the region is Phuket, now a resort island, which has superb beaches, excellent diving facilities, and the most developed tourist infrastructure in Southern Thailand. Over the last 20 years, many traditional sea gypsy and Muslim fishing villages on Phuket and around Krabi have been transformed into vacation resorts. Long-tail boats take visitors to sights like the extraordinary limestone stacks of Phangnga Bay. In remote mangrove channels – accessible only by canoe – otters, monkeys, and sea eagles still live undisturbed.

There is outstanding scenery and diving around Ko Phi Phi, though it is now firmly on the tourist trail. Visitors wanting sand and sun without the crowds head for relatively undeveloped islands such as Ko Lanta. Unspoiled beach resorts can be found along the stretch of coast from Ranong to Phuket, and the virgin rainforest of Khao Sok National Park is located inland. West of here, the Ko Surin and Ko Similan archipelagos offer some of the world's best dive sites.

The southwest monsoon, which lasts from about June to October, makes some of the outer islands inaccessible.

A typical beach scene in this part of Thailand: sun, sand, and water sports

◁ Not just a vacation island – the productive rice paddies of Phuket

Exploring the Upper Andaman Coast

This part of Thailand's Andaman Sea coast contains some of the most inviting beach scenery in Southeast Asia. Using the international resort of Phuket as a base, visitors have 12 long sandy beaches on their doorstep and a full range of shopping, dining, entertainment, land and water sport services. The towering limestone stacks of Phangnga Bay can readily be explored in a day. An alternative base is quieter Krabi, which combines fine beaches with spectacular cliff landscapes. The idyllic island scenery of Ko Phi Phi is accessible from Krabi and Phuket. The monsoon forests of the Tenasserim mountain range provide a backdrop to the little frequented beaches of Khao Lak. Avid divers and snorkelers can visit the remote Similan and Surin archipelagos acclaimed for their superlative corals and aquatic life.

Ko Chang

Ko Phayam

4 KO SURIN

Khao Lang Ki.

Khura

K
NATIO

Takua Pa

Yachting off the coast of the unspoiled Similan archipelago

| 0 kilometers | 25 |
| 0 miles | 15 |

4 KO SIMILAN

3 Khao Lak

Tap Lamu

Phangng

Thai Muang

Ko Khao
Phing Khan

402

Thalang

Ko

PHUKET 5

Patong   Phuket

A deserted beach on Ko Phi Phi – still possible t find despite its ever-increasing popularity

Chumphon

NONG

*Kaeng
Krung
National
Park*

*Chiaw
Lan Lake*

*Surat
Thani*

SIGHTS AT A GLANCE

Ao Nang **8**
Khao Lak Coast **3**
Khao Phanom Bencha
  National Park **7**
Khao Sok National Park **2**
Khlong Thom **10**
Ko Lanta **12**
Ko Phi Phi **11**
Ko Surin and Ko Similan **4**
Krabi **9**
Phangnga Bay pp364–7 **6**
Phuket pp358–63 **5**
Ranong **1**

SEE ALSO

• **Where to Stay** pp418–20

• **Where to Eat** pp446–9

The thickly forested hillside and limestone
cliffs near Khao Sok National Park

GETTING THERE

Most visitors make use of Phuket's modern airport,
and Phuket or Krabi make the best bases to explore
the Upper Andaman Coast. Reliable air-conditioned
bus services link Phuket, Krabi, Phangnga, and
Ranong, although car rental in Phuket or Krabi is
much more convenient. There is no railroad in
the region. Ko Similan is accessible from Phuket,
Ko Surin from Ranong and also by air from
Phuket. Thailand's water taxi, the long-tail boat,
is the best way to explore smaller bays once in
the Phi Phi, Phangnga Bay, or Ko Lanta areas.

Surat Thani

Phra Saeng

Thung Yai

Thung Song

**KHAO PHANOM
BENCHA NATIONAL PARK 7**

9 KRABI

Lam Thap

Nakhon Si
Thammarat

**10 KHLONG
THOM**

*Ko Phi Phi
Don*

11 KO PHI PHI

*Phi
Ley*

Wang Wiset

Trang

*Ko Lanta
Yai*

12 KO LANTA

Ko Lanta

KEY

▬▬▬	Major road
▭▭▭	Minor road
▬▬	Scenic route
▬ ▬	Main railway
▲	Summit

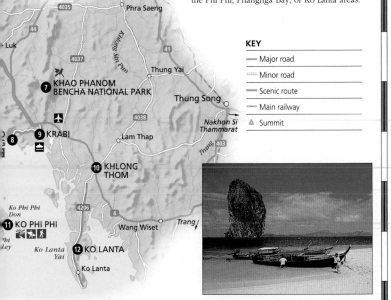

Long-tail boats on a beach on Ko Poda, near Krabi

Collecting water from one of Ranong's geothermal springs

Ranong ❶

ระนอง

Ranong province. 🏔 69,000.
🚌 🚢 ✈ daily. ℹ TAT, Chumphon (0-7750-1831).

Ranong was originally settled in the late 18th century by Hokkien Chinese who were hired to work as laborers in the region's tin mines. The area grew rich, and Ranong is now a major border town. From here Thai nationals may travel to **Victoria Point** in Myanmar (Burma) on a half- or full-day boat trip. Referred to as Kaw Thaung by the Burmese, the town is well known for bargain duty-free goods and handicrafts. Officially, foreigners may not go to Victoria Point without a visa, but this is not always enforced.

In Ranong, the natural hot springs are the main attraction. They rise beside the Khlong Hat Sompen River at **Wat Tapotaram**, 1 km (1,100 yds) east of the town center, and are channeled into three concrete tubs called Mother, Father, and Child. At an average temperature of 65° C (150° F), the water is too hot for bathing. A short walk down the river, the Jansom Thara Spa Resort Hotel has tapped and cooled the water to 42° C (110° F). Those not staying at the hotel can use the spa for a nominal fee.

Khao Sok National Park ❷

อุทยานแห่งชาติเขาสก

Surat Thani province. Park HQ off Hwy 401, 40 km (25 miles) E of Takua Pa. ℹ TAT, Surat Thani (0-7728-8818) or Forestry Dept (0-2562-0760 or **www**.dnp.go.th for bungalow bookings). 🚌 from Surat Thani or Takua Pa. 🅿

Together with nearby preserves, Khao Sok National Park forms the largest and most dramatic tract of virgin forest in South Thailand. The 738-sq km (285-sq mile) park rises to a height of 960 m (3,150 ft) and includes 100 spectacular islands, formed when the Rachabrapha Dam was built in 1982.

Elephants, tigers, bears, boars, and monkeys live in the park, along with at least 188 species of birds, including hornbills and the argus pheasant. Sightings of the larger mammals are usually at night and animal tracks, are regularly seen along the park's many marked trails.

Barking deer at Khao Lak

Sadly, poaching of tigers and elephants persists despite the efforts of national park officers. The area is popular with tourists eager to trek, canoe, watch birds, and spot animals. The park also contains interesting flora, such as the rare giant Rafflesia flower. Many of the hiking trails are suitable for all levels, with more demanding hikes for the experienced. Khao Sok receives the brunt of both summer and winter monsoons, causing a long wet season from May to November. The best time to visit is between January and April.

Khao Lak Coast ❸

เขาหลัก

Phangnga province. ℹ TAT, Phuket (0-7621-1036). 🚌 from Takua Pa or Phuket.

The coastline south of Takua Pa consists of long stretches of rocky and sandy beaches. Commercial development is on the rise and a variety of accommodation can now be found here. Khao Lak, halfway between Takua Pa and Thai Muang, has a fine beach and is a good base from which to explore the area. The nearby **Khao Lak (Lam Ru) National Park** is famous for its scenery: steep ridges of monsoon forest extend to the winding coast. Barking deer and small bears are among the wildlife living in the forest but, sadly, the park is plagued by encroachment and poaching.

The Similan Islands are only 4 hours away by boat, and many visitors come here to book their dive trips. Between November and April, Tap Lamu fishing port and Hat Khao Lak operate as ferry points for Ko Similan.

Badly hit by the 2004 tsunami, this coast has now made a full recovery.

🌿 **Khao Lak (Lam Ru) National Park**
HQ 25 km (16 miles) S of Takua Pa. ℹ Forestry Dept (0-2562-0760). 🅿

Khao Sok, a wilderness of virgin forest, limestone cliffs, and waterfalls

Similan's boulders, under which are massive underwater grottoes

Ko Surin and Ko Similan ❹

เกาะสุรินทร์และสิมิลัน

*Phangnga province. ℹ TAT, Phuket
(0-7621-1036) or Forestry Dept
(0-2562-0760 inc bungalow
bookings for Similan). Surin 🚤
from Khuraburi Pier, 2 km (1 mile) off
Hwy 4. 🚤 Similan 🚤 from Tap
Lamu, off Hwy 4, 39 km (24 miles)
S of Takua Pa; or by diving trips
from Khao Lak Coast or Ko Phuket.
◯ Best time for diving is Dec–early
May. ▣ mid-May–mid-Nov. 🚤*

Ko Surin and Ko Similan,
60 km (37 miles) off the west
coast and 100 km (62 miles)
apart, are the most remote
islands in Thailand. Because
of the southwesterly
monsoon, from May to
October they are virtually
inaccessible. In season, however, the two archipelagos
offer some of the best diving
sites in the world and some
of the most spectacular wildlife and scenery in Thailand.

The five **Surin** islands are
virtually uninhabited, home
only to a few sea gypsies
and national park officials.
There is a park dormitory on
Ko Surin Nua, but most
people camp on the islands.

The two largest islands, Ko
Surin Nua and Ko Surin Tai,
are heavily forested with tall
hardwood trees. Sea eagles,
monitor lizards, and crab-eating
macaques are common sights.
The surrounding sea offers an
outstanding array of soft corals
and frequent sightings of

shovel-nose rays, bow-
mouthed guitar fish, and whale
sharks. However, overfishing
has led to the depletion of the
marine life of Ko Surin, and
many divers maintain that the
best sightings of sealife are
around the Similans instead.

Of the nine **Similan** islands
4, 7, 8, and 9 were damaged
by the 2004 tsunami but are
still open to tourists and divers.
The name Similan is thought
to derive from the Malaysian
word *sembilan*, meaning nine,
and the islands are numbered
Ko 1 through to Ko 9. Ko 4
(Ko Miang) has the park HQ,
a restaurant, bungalows, and
campsite (with a supply of two-
person tents). Also important
is Ko 9, where the ranger sub-

station can be found. The
interiors of these islands
consist of crystal-white sand
and lush rainforest, while the
headlands are made up of
distinctive, giant granite
boulders the size of houses.
Beneath these rocks are underwater grottoes and swim-
through tunnels, which appeal
to divers and snorkelers.

The sea bed is decorated
with staghorn, star, and
branching corals, and a range
of fish, including manta rays,
and giant sea turtles. Other,
more threatening, fish include
giant groupers, and poisonous
stonefish, and lionfish. Sharks
around the islands include
black and white tips, leopard
sharks, hammerheads, bull
sharks, and whale sharks.

Diver exploring the colorful coral
around Ko Similan

THE WORLD'S LARGEST FLOWER

Khao Sok is one of the few places in the world where the
giant *Rafflesia kerri* grows. This foul-smelling tropical plant
has no roots or leaves and is wholly parasitic. For most of
the year it lies dormant in the form of microscopic threads
inside the roots of a host tree. Once a year, however,
a small flower breaks the surface of the host's bark. Over a
period of months the bud swells to the size of a watermelon

and eventually opens to
become the world's largest
flower, with a diameter
up to 80 cm (31 inches).
The flower's fetid smell
attracts insects that assist
in the pollination process.
After a few days the
orange-red flower shrivels
to a vile, unsightly, putres-
cent mass. Occasionally a
Rafflesia in flower may be
found at the end of a
marked path at Khao Sok.

Rafflesia flower in full bloom,
Khao Sok National Park

Phuket ❺

ภูเก็ต

Patong beach on Phuket

Thailand's largest island, Phuket first became prosperous thanks to tin production, but tourism is now the major earner. Southeast Asia's most popular vacation destination attracts visitors from across the globe with its stunning beaches, crystal-clear waters, and vibrant nightlife. Phuket has also seen a huge growth in chic boutique resorts and spas. The northern tip of the island is separated from the mainland by only a narrow channel of sea, over which runs the 700-m (765-yd) long Sarasin Bridge.

Half-Buried Buddha
Wat Phra Tong is built around an unusual, gold-leafed Buddha image, half buried in the ground. Legend says that whoever tries to remove it will die.

Game fishing
Tuna, barracuda, and other fish are hunted from boats.

KEY

🏖	Beach
🏄	Water sports
ℹ	Tourist information
🛕	Wat
✈	Airport
🚌	Bus station
⛴	Ferry service
▬▬	Main road
▬▬	Minor road
☀	Vista

STAR SIGHTS

★ Marine Research Center

★ Thai Village

★ West Coast Beaches

★ West Coast Beaches
The clearest waters, best sand, and most luxurious hotels are on the west coast. Patong is the most densely developed resort; Karon and Kata are quieter.

Cape Promthep is the southernmost point on Ko Phuket. The views from this rugged headland are some of the most stunning on the island, particularly at sunset.

Sarasin Bridge •

Hat Sai Kaeo •

Hat Mai Khao •

Hat Nai Yang •

Hat Nai Thon •

Wat Phra

Thalar

Ao Bang Tao

Hat Pansea •

Hat Surin •

Hat Kamala

Phuket FantaSea

Kathu waterfall •

Hat Patong •

• Hat Karon Noi

Wat Chalo

Hat Karon •

Hat Kata Yai

Hat Kata Noi •

Hat Nai Harn •

Cape Promthep   Ko Bo

VISITORS' CHECKLIST

Phuket province. 102,000.
29 km (18 miles) N of
Phuket town. Phangnga
Rd, Phuket town. from Ko
Phi Phi to Phuket Deep Sea Port.
TAT, 191 Thalang Rd
(0-7621-1036). Phuket
Rd (0-7621-7138).
Vegetarian Festival (late
Sep/early Oct, for nine days),
King's Cup Regatta (Dec).
www.phuket.com

The Gibbon Rehabilitation Center in the Khao Phra Taew Forest Preserve encourages once-domesticated gibbons to fend for themselves in the wild.

Ko Ngam

Cape Khut

Gibbon Rehabilitation Center

Ko Raet

Bang Pae waterfall

Ko Naga Yai

Ao Po

Khao Phra Taew Forest Park

Ko Naga Noi

Sai ...terfall

Naga Pearl Farm

...alang Museum

...oines' ...nument

Ao Sapam

Ko Rang Yai

Ko Maphrao Yai

Butterfly Garden and Insect World

Thai Village

...ET TOWN

Ko Sire Gypsy Village

...halong

Phuket Deep Sea Port

→ Ko Phi Phi

Cape Phanwa Marine Research Center

...one

Heroines' Monument
Two brave sisters rallied the women of Phuket to successfully defend the island against Burmese invaders during the Battle of Thalang in 1785.

Phuket Butterfly Garden and Insect World
Numerous species of butterflies are cultivated in a large, covered garden. There is also a silk museum and Thailand's first insect exhibition.

Phuket town is notable for its 19th-century Sino-Portuguese-style residences. It acts as a transit and service center.

★ **Thai Village**
Orchids are sold at this village, and there is a show on Thai culture with elephants, Thai boxing, and classical dancing.

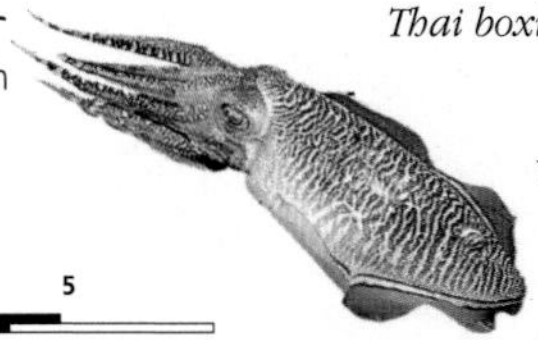

★ **Marine Research Center**
A well-designed aquarium at the center includes salt- and freshwater fish, lobsters, turtles, and mollusks.

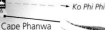

0 kilometers   5

0 miles   5

Phuket Town

Phuket Town grew to prominence around the beginning of the 19th century, when the island's tin resources attracted thousands of Chinese migrants. Many merchants made fortunes from tin, built splendid residences, and sent their children to British Penang to be educated. Hokkien-speaking tin-mining families soon intermarried with the indigenous Thai population. Today, the bustling downtown area retains some of its earlier charm, though, unlike most of the island, it is geared toward residents rather than tourists. The Chinese heritage is preserved in the Sino-Portuguese shop-houses, temples, the local cuisine, and the Vegetarian Festival.

Dragon detail at a temple

One of the grand old Sino-Portuguese mansions in Phuket town

🏠 Chinese Mansions

Thalang, Yaowarat, Dibuk, Krabi, and Phangnga roads.

The heart of Phuket town is the old Sino-Portuguese quarter with its spacious, if now rather run-down, colonial-style residences set in large grounds. Most date from the reigns of Rama IV and Rama V (1851–1910). Among the best examples are those used today as offices by the Standard Chartered Bank and Thai Airways on Ranong Road. Unfortunately, no one has yet seen fit to convert any of the old mansions into a museum, and none can be visited. Many of the commercial Chinese shop-houses are also dilapidated.

🏠 Thavorn Hotel Lobby Exhibition

ห้องแสดงของเก่าโรงแรมถาวร
74 Rasada Rd. **Tel** 0-7621-1334.
◯ daily. 📷

The owner of this hotel in the center of town has assembled a collection of Phuket artifacts and pictures that he now displays in the lobby and adjacent function rooms. Among the exhibits are models of tin mines, pictures of the town center in the 19th century, Chinese treasure chests, and weavers' tables, all of which are imaginatively displayed.

🏠 Fresh Produce Market

ตลาดสด
Ranong Rd. ◯ daily.

The 24-hour wet market is a treat that assaults the senses. The market and adjacent lanes are full of colorful characters hawking condiments, dried herbs and spices, pungent pickled *kapi* fish, squirming eels, and succulent durians.

🌿 Rang Hill

เขารัง
On the top of this hill overlooking the town stands a statue of Khaw Sim Bee Na-Ranong (1857–1913), governor of Phuket for 12 years from 1901. He enjoyed considerable autonomy from Bangkok but is credited with bringing the island firmly under central rule, and also with importing the first rubber tree into Thailand.

🏯 Bang Niew Temple

ศาลเจ้าบางเหนียว
Phuket Rd. ◯ daily.

This temple is where *naga* devotees climb knife ladders during the Vegetarian Festival. The inner compound is devoted to a number of Chinese mythological gods, the most prominent being Siew, Hok, and Lok, who represent longevity, power, and happiness.

PHUKET TOWN'S VEGETARIAN FESTIVAL

At the start of the ninth Chinese lunar month, Phuket town hosts a nine-day Vegetarian Festival accompanied by gruesome rites. The tradition began over 150 years ago when a troupe of Chinese entertainers in Phuket recovered from the plague by adhering to austere rituals practised in China. Today, believers use the festival to purge the body and soul of impure thoughts and deeds. Devotees dress in white, follow a vegetarian diet, and refrain from alcohol and sex. The highlight is the parade of *nagas* (spirit mediums) with their flesh pierced by metal rods. Other *nagas* climb ladders of knives, plunge their hands into hot oil, or walk on burning coals. The worse the suffering, the greater reward for the *naga* and his temple.

Nagas parading through the town

Wat Mongkol Nimit, a typical example of Rattanakosin architecture

VISITORS' CHECKLIST

Phuket province. 102,000.
Southern Bus Terminal, near
Phang Nga Rd. TAT, 191
Thalang Rd (0-7621-1036/2213).
Phuket Rd (0-7621-7138).
daily. Vegetarian Festival
(early Oct, for nine days).

Wat Mongkol Nimit
วัดมงคลนิมิต

Yaowarat Rd. daily.
This large, Rattanakosin-style
temple has finely carved doors.
Its compound acts as a community center where monks
play *takraw* with the laity.

Chui Tui Temple
ศาลเจ้าจุ้ยตุ่ย

Ranong Rd. daily.
A steady flow of people visit
this Chinese temple to shake
numbered sticks from a canis-
ter dedicated to vegetarian god
Kiu Wong In. Each number
corresponds to a preprinted
fate that, according to belief,
the person will inherit.

Environs
Just 3 km (2 miles) to the
north of Phuket town is the
**Phuket Butterfly Garden and
Insect World**. The garden's
warm and humid atmosphere
provides ideal conditions for
hundreds of tropical butterflies. Visitors are also invited
to discover more about insects
and their habitats. Specimens
on show include ants, beetles,
millipedes, and arachnids
such as spiders and scorpions.

The **Thai Village**, located
4 km (2.5 miles) north of
Phuket town, puts on cultural
performances and animal
shows from the different
regions of Thailand.

There are demonstrations
of *muay thai* boxing (see
pp44–5), traditional dancing,
cock fighting, sword fighting,
and a reenactment of a Thai
wedding. The fisherman's, tin
miner's, and rubber-tapping
dances were invented here.
There is also an elephant
show. The village is a good
place to buy *yan lipao (see
p105)* reed grass bags and
ornaments, made by a
weaving method unique to
Southern Thailand. You can
watch the artisans at work.
There is also an **Orchid
Garden**, with orchids for
sale – 40,000 are grown
here each year.

**Phuket Butterfly
Garden and Insect World**
Yaowarat Rd. Tel 0-7621-0861.
9am–5pm daily.

**Thai Village and
Orchid Garden**
Thepkasattri Rd. Tel 0-7621-4860.
Tue–Sun.

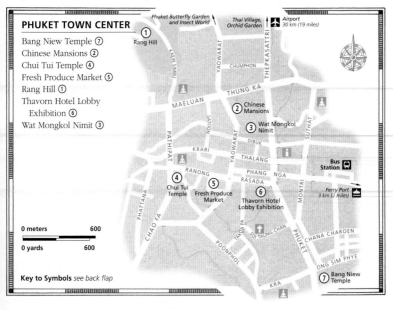

PHUKET TOWN CENTER

Bang Niew Temple ⑦
Chinese Mansions ②
Chui Tui Temple ④
Fresh Produce Market ⑤
Rang Hill ①
Thavorn Hotel Lobby
    Exhibition ⑥
Wat Mongkol Nimit ③

Phuket Butterfly Garden
and Insect World
Thai Village,
Orchid Garden
Airport
30 km (19 miles)

① Rang Hill

KAEW SIMBU
YAOWARAT
CHUMPHON
THEPKASATTRI

MAELUAN
THUNG KA

② Chinese
Mansions

SOONS
YAOWARAT
③ Wat Mongkol
Nimit

PATHIPAT
DIBUK
SUTHAT

KRABI
THALANG

RANONG
PHANG NGA
RASADA

Bus
Station

④ Chui Tui
Temple
⑤ Fresh Produce
Market
⑥ Thavorn Hotel
Lobby Exhibition

MONTRI
Ferry Port
3 km (2 miles)

PHATTANA

CHAO FA

SOI TALING CHAN

PHUKET

CHANA CHAROEN

POONPHOL

ONG SIM PHYE

TAKUA PA

⑦ Bang Niew
Temple

KRA

0 meters   600
0 yards   600

Key to Symbols see back flap

Exploring Phuket

Phuket was called Junkceylon by early European traders, but its modern name may derive from the Malay word *bukit*, meaning hill. On arrival, many visitors head straight for a beach resort and do not leave it for the duration of their vacation – the best of the island's beaches are strung out along the west coast.

Hibiscus flower, typical of Phuket

However, there are several historical and cultural sights to complement the beachside attractions, and the lush, hilly interior is also worth exploring.

High-rise hotel overlooking the popular, tree-lined beach at Patong

Hat Patong

Phuket's most developed beach is the 3-km (2-mile) long Hat Patong. Once a quiet banana plantation, it is now almost a city by the sea. The area has a lively nightlife, with a vibrant mix of hotels, restaurants, discos, and bars. During the day there are many water activities, such as parasailing, waterskiing, diving, and deep-sea fishing.

Although Patong continues to expand, the beaches along the southern headland of Patong bay are far quieter. It is possible to ride to the cape on elephant back.

Hat Karon and Hat Kata

South of Patong, and almost as popular, are the beaches of Karon and Kata. Karon has one long stretch of sand lined with accommodations, and a second beach at tiny Karon Noi. Kata's beaches, along the bays of Kata Yai and Kata Noi, are smaller and prettier, sheltered by rocky promontories. There are a number of good restaurants on the headland between Karon and Kata.

Other Western Beaches

North of Patong, fringed by palm-covered headlands, lie the smaller beaches of Kamala, Surin, and Pansea. Hat Kamala is relatively undeveloped, with some Muslim fishermen's houses and a few restaurants. Just to the south, however, is **Phuket FantaSea**, a huge Las Vegas-style cultural theme complex that hosts a spectacular live night-time stage show with music, dance, special effects and elephants.

Farther north from Hat Kamala, Hat Bang Tao offers a quiet, enchanting retreat, popular with families. Fronted by a few exclusive hotels, the beach is good for water sports.

Round the next few headlands are three beaches: Hat Nai Thon, a gorgeous, undeveloped stretch; Hat Nai Yang, which is visited by Thais on weekends; and Hat Mai Khao, a deserted 12-km (7.5-mile) stretch of sand.

ⓜ Phuket FantaSea
99 Kamala Beach. **Tel** 0-7638-5000.
◯ 5:30–11:30pm Fri–Wed.

Cape Promthep, one of the best vistas on Phuket – a good place for spectacular sunsets

SEA GYPSIES OF THE ANDAMAN SEA

Sea gypsies, known as *chao ley* in Thai, may originate from the Andaman or Nicobar islands, across the Andaman Sea from Thailand. Phuket's sea gypsy population settled the area around 200 years ago, following routes from the Mergui archipelago, west of the Burmese mainland. Today, they can be found in Phuket at Rawai, Ko Sire, near Sapam village, and in northern Phuket's villages of Laem La and Nua. Ethnically, they comprise three groups: Moklen, Moken, and Urak Lawoi. Sea gypsies live throughout the Andaman Sea at Ko Surin, Ko Phra Tong in Phangnga, and farther south at the islands of Phi Phi, Lanta, Talibong, Tarutao, and Langkawi. They speak their own language and have animistic beliefs. Once a year they hold a spiritual cleansing ceremony, placing human mementoes on a small boat before pushing it out to sea to get rid of bad spirits.

Cleaning fish, an everyday part of life for Andaman sea gypsies

Southeastern Capes and Bays

Ao Nai Harn, a bay near the southern tip of Phuket, is the home of the exclusive Phuket Yacht Club. The beach (open to all) is one of the most beautiful on the island. Cape Promthep, 2 km (1 mile) away on the southern tip of Phuket, offers wonderful views, especially at sunset.

Ghost crab at Marine Center

North of Promthep, on the east side of the island, are Hat Rawai, and farther along, Ao Chalong. The sands around this bay are not as white as those on the west coast, but there are many excellent seafood shacks here. Ao Chalong acts as an anchorage for international yachts exploiting its sheltered location, and is also a departure point for boat excursions to the charming islands of Lone, Hai, and Bon, where there is good snorkeling. Farther up the coast at Cape Phanwa is the interesting and much-visited Phuket Aquarium, which forms part of the **Marine Research Center**.

🏛 Marine Research Center
Tip of Cape Phanwa. *Tel* 0-7639-1126. ◯ 9am–4pm daily. 🎟

Northeast Coast

Ko Naga Noi, an island off Phuket's northeast coast, has a tranquil, sandy beach that makes a fine halt for swimming and relaxing. The island is home to the **Naga Pearl Farm**, whose owners give demonstrations of the process of culturing South Sea pearls.

At Phuket's northeasternmost point, on the Cape Khut headland, there are sweeping views of the monoliths of Phangnga Bay *(see pp364–7)*. The placid waters of the narrow channel between Phuket and Phangnga province are exploited by Muslim fishermen who farm sea bass here.

🏛 Naga Pearl Farm
Ko Naga Noi. ◯ daily. 🎟

Thalang

This town in central Phuket was the site of a famous battle in 1785 against the Burmese, which is commemorated by the Heroines' Monument 8 km (5 miles) to the south. A short walk east of the monument is the Thalang Museum, which outlines the rich heritage of Phuket. Among the exhibits are

5th-century religious icons, Chinese porcelain, life-size figures recreated from the Burmese battle, and information on the sea gypsies.

In Thalang itself there is a good market and, nearby, Wat Phra Tong. In the center of the *wat* lies a gold-covered Buddha image, half buried in the ground. Legend has it that disaster will come to anyone who tries to move the image.

🏛 Thalang National Museum
Off Hwy 402, opposite Heroines' Monument. *Tel* 0-7631-1025, 0-7631-1426. ◯ daily. ● public hols. 🎟

Khao Phra Taew Forest Park

Four kilometers (2.5 miles) east of Thalang is the spectacular Khao Phra Taew Forest Park. The preserve is important as it preserves the last of Phuket's primary rainforest.

Within the park are two fine waterfalls. Ton Sai waterfall is the prettiest and is at its best from June to December. On the eastern fringe of the preserve is the Bang Pae waterfall.

Near the latter is the **Gibbon Rehabilitation Center**. This volunteer-run program aims to reintroduce domesticated gibbons into the forest by encouraging them to fend for themselves. Visitors' donations buy food for the gibbons.

🌿 Khao Phra Taew Forest Park
Thalang district. ◯ daily. 🎟

🌿 Gibbon Rehabilitation Center
Near Bang Pae Falls. ◯ daily.

A barrel of limes for sale at Thalang market in central Phuket

Phangnga Bay ⑥

อ่าวพังงา

No one area epitomizes the splendor of the South's landscape as succinctly as 400-sq km (155-sq mile) Phangnga Bay. Its scenic grandeur derives from towering limestone stacks rising sheer from calm, shallow waters up to 350 m (1,150 ft) high. Inside many of the 40-odd stacks are narrow tunnels and sea caves. Inland, too, this coastal area boasts majestic, scrub-clad pinnacles. Phangnga is, in fact, the most spectacular remnant of the once mighty Tenasserim Mountains, which still form a spine through Thailand to China.

Sea eagle, Phangnga Bay

Protected Mangroves
The heavily silted northern end of Phangnga Bay, where several rivers meet the sea, is Thailand's largest and best preserved area of mangrove (see pp350–51).

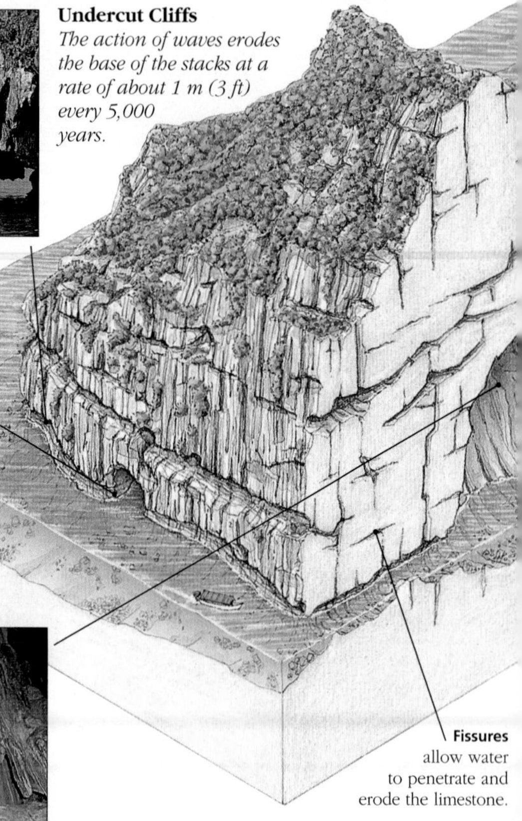

Undercut Cliffs
The action of waves erodes the base of the stacks at a rate of about 1 m (3 ft) every 5,000 years.

Caves form quickly at sea level. Some are exposed only at low tide.

Fissures allow water to penetrate and erode the limestone.

Calcite Deposits in Caves
Within most caves are stalagmites, stalactites, and other structures formed from dripping calcite.

CROSS SECTION OF TYPICAL STACKS IN PHANGNGA BAY

The limestone landscape at Phangnga Bay is known by geologists as drowned karstland. Karst is characterized by its internal drainage system, whereby water finds its way into the interior of the limestone through fissures, then erodes the rock from within. A riddle of tunnels is typical; chasms and vast sea chambers (*bongs*) are also common at Phangnga.

Aerial view of Stacks in Phangnga Bay
The stacks at Phangnga make striking coastal scenery.

Forest scrub clings to cracks in the limestone.

Isolated Stacks
There are a number of sheer, thin stacks in the bay. These columns of rock are splinters of limestone that have been heavily eroded by the sea.

The weakened roof of the cave will eventually collapse.

HOW PHANGNGA BAY WAS FORMED

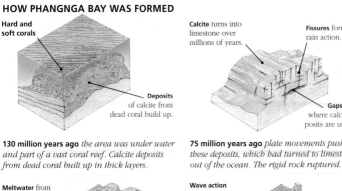

Hard and soft corals

Deposits of calcite from dead coral build up.

130 million years ago *the area was under water and part of a vast coral reef. Calcite deposits from dead coral built up in thick layers.*

Calcite turns into limestone over millions of years.

Fissures form from rain action.

Gaps occur where calcite deposits are uneven.

75 million years ago *plate movements pushed these deposits, which had turned to limestone, out of the ocean. The rigid rock ruptured.*

Meltwater from ice caps begins to flood Phangnga.

The gap erodes into a cave.

20,000 years ago, *at the end of the last Ice Age, the sea level rose, flooding Phangnga. Wave and tide action accelerated the process of erosion.*

Wave action sculpts the stacks.

The cave is much larger.

8,000 years ago *the sea reached its highest level, about 4 m (13 ft) above its present height, sculpting a shelf, visible on most of the stacks.*

Exploring Phangnga Bay

Seashell, Phangnga

Boat tours of the bay once took in the best-known sights, such as the fishing village built over water in the shadow of Ko Panyi, and "James Bond Island," as well as a number of fascinating caves. Some of the eerie caverns contain prehistoric paintings and Buddhist shrines.

Due to massive erosion however, tourist boats are currently banned from large areas of Phangnga Bay though viewing is still possible from a distance. The karst scenery continues inland to the east, where cliffs soar above hidden valleys with cascading rivers.

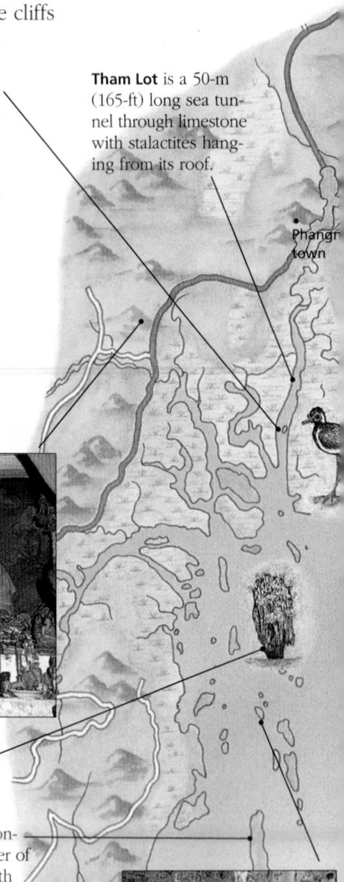

Tham Lot is a 50-m (165-ft) long sea tunnel through limestone with stalactites hanging from its roof.

Phangnga town

★ **Panyi Fishing Village**
About 120 Muslim families live in this village, which is built on stilts above the water. Islanders sell fish sauce, dried shrimp, and shrimp paste.

Suwan Kuha Cave (Wat Tham)
A reclining Buddha, tiny shrines, and chedis are found among stalactites and stalagmites in this cave temple.

Ko Phanak contains a number of sea *hongs* with vegetation-clad walls and marooned snakes and monkeys.

Ko Hong
A vast network of lagoons, chasms, and tunnels runs underneath this island. As a conservation measure access to the area is forbidden at present.

★ **James Bond Island**
This island (Ko Khao Phing Kan) and nearby Ko Tapu ("nail island") both appeared memorably in the 1974 James Bond classic, The Man With the Golden Gun.

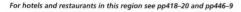
For hotels and restaurants in this region see pp418–20 and pp446–9

Areas of Mangrove
It is possible to explore many mangrove channels in a small boat at high tide, though skillful piloting is required.

Rubber Plantations
Rubber is a major industry around Phangnga. Latex, tapped from rubber trees, is left to harden in shallow trays.

Tham Hua Gralok ("skull cave") contains prehistoric paintings, in black and red pigment, of humans and strange animals.

Ao Luk

Tanboke Koranee National Park
In Ao Luk district, this national park is known for its series of miniature waterfalls amid beautiful limestone scenery.

0 kilometers   10

0 miles   5

STAR SIGHTS

★ Panyi Fishing Village

★ James Bond Island

JAMES BOND AND THE ISLAND HIDEOUT

In the film *The Man With the Golden Gun* (1974), James Bond (Roger Moore) comes to the Orient in search of the villain Scaramanga (Christopher Lee). Bond is eventually taken to Scaramanga's hideout, an island just off China. In fact, the island seen is Ko Khao Phing Kan in Phangnga Bay; the sheer rock nearby, containing the secret weapon, is Ko Tapu.

Scaramanga and Bond

The extraordinary Ko Tapu ("nail island") in Phangnga Bay ▷

Khao Phanom Bencha National Park ➐

อุทยานแห่งชาติเขาพนมเบญจา

Krabi province. Park HQ off Hwy 4, 20 km (12.5 miles) N of Krabi. **ℹ** *TAT, Krabi (0-7562-2163); Forestry Dept (0-2562-0760); Park HQ (0-7566-0716).* **🚌** *Krabi, then local bus.*

This 500-sq km (193-sq mile) national park of mostly tropical monsoon forest is named for the five-shouldered peak of Khao Phanom Bencha, which rises to a height of 1,397 m (4,580 ft).

Despite illegal logging and poaching, the park's rainforest still holds at least 156 species of bird, including the white-crowned hornbill and the striped wren-babbler. Among the 32 mammal species catalogued are the Asiatic black bear, Malaysian sun bear, clouded leopard, wild boar, binturong, and serow.

Clouded leopard in Khao Phanom Bencha

The thundering **Huay To waterfall** and **Huay Sadeh waterfall** are located less than 3 km (2 miles) from the park headquarters. Park attendants can arrange treks to the summit. The climb is difficult but rewarding – from the top there are spectacular views of the surrounding forest.

Ao Nang ➑

อ่าวนาง

18 km (11 miles) W of Krabi town, Krabi province. **ℹ** *TAT, Krabi (0-7562-2163).* **🚌** *Krabi, then songthaew.*

From November to April, Ao Nang sees the arrival of thousands of tourists attracted by the spectacular scenery, pristine beaches, and laid-back atmosphere.

Until the early 1980s, fishing and coconut and rubber plantations were the mainstay for the Muslim villagers at Ao Nang. Today the 2-km (1-mile) sandy beach sports a growing number of hotels, seafood restaurants, scuba diving outlets, and canoe tour companies. Visitors can rent a sea canoe to paddle in the turquoise waters in the shadow of the 100-m (330-ft) rocky eastern end of the bay. Nearby is uncrowded Pai Plong beach. In season, Ao Nang is a pleasant base for day trips by long-tail boat to the striking **Railay-Phra Nang headland**, 3 km (2 miles) to the southeast. Its sheer limestone cliffs, pure white sand, and emerald sea attract many visitors.

Hat Phra Nang, west of the Phra Nang headland, is the most attractive beach in the

Strolling along a beach on Ko Poda, a small island near Ao Nang

area. Rising above it is a high limestone cliff into which **Tham Phra Nang Nok** ("outer princess cave") is carved. Inside is a shrine to the lost spirit of a princess, Phra Nang, whose ship allegedly sank near the beach in the 4th century BC. Today, local fishermen place offerings of incense, fruit, and water at the shrine to bring them a plentiful catch. Inside the cliff is **Sa Phra Nang**, a lagoon reached by a steep path.

Flanking Phra Nang are the white sand beaches of East and West Railay, the latter being much finer. There are boats from West Railay and Phra Nang beaches to **Ko Poda**, southwest of Phra Nang, where striped tiger fish can be fed by hand from the shallow shore, and **Ko Hua Khwan**, or Chicken Island, located farther south. Both islands offer excellent diving and snorkeling.

On **Ko Hong**, 25 km (16 miles) northwest of Ao Nang, the prized nests of the edible-nest swiftlet *(see p341)* are collected from the island's intricate network of caves.

The headquarters of the **Phi Phi-Hat Nopparat Thara National Marine Park**, to the west of Ao Nang, overlook stunning beaches. The park covers an area of 390 sq km (150 sq miles), which includes Ko Phi Phi *(see pp372–3)*, Ko Mai Phai, and Ko Yung (also known as Ko Mosquito).

🚏 Phi Phi-Hat Nopparat Thara National Marine Park
Park HQ 3 km (2 miles) W of Ao Nang. **ℹ** *TAT, Krabi office (0-7562-2163).* **🚌** *Krabi, then songthaew.*

Idyllic bay within the Phi Phi-Hat Nopparat Thara National Marine Park

Krabi ❾

กระบี่

Krabi province. 🏠 68,000. 🚌 ⛴
🚤 ℹ️ TAT, Maharat Rd, Krabi
(0-7562-2163). 🛍️ daily.
www.tourismthailand.org/krabi

This small fishing town, the
capital of beautiful Krabi
province, has an important role
as the ferry embarkation point
for islands such as Ko Lanta to
the south, Ko Phi Phi to the
southwest, and the beaches
around Ao Nang to the west.
Set on the banks of the Krabi
Estuary, the town takes its
name from a sword, or *krabi*,
allegedly discovered nearby.
It is surrounded by towering
limestone outcrops, similar to
those in Phangnga Bay *(see
pp364–7)*, which have become
the symbol of Krabi province.
Among the most notable are
**Kanap Nam twin limestone
peaks**, which stand like sen-
tinels at each side of the river.
To the east, the town is flanked
by mangrove-lined shorelines.
These outcrops and mangroves
can be toured by renting a
long-tail boat from the Chao
Fa pier in the center of town.

Environs
Located 8 km (5 miles) north
of town is **Wat Tham Sua**
("tiger cave temple"), named
after a rock formation that
resembles a tiger paw. It is
one of the most renowned
forest *wats* in Southern
Thailand, with the main
hall, where meditation is
practiced, built inside a cave.

Swimmers enjoying a hot spring spa in the forest near Khlong Thom

A circular path in the nearby
forest hollow offers a pleasant
walk among towering, but-
tressed trees and *kutis*, simple
huts inhabited by monks and
nuns. A 300-m-high staircase
(985-ft) leads to a large
Buddha image and Buddha
Footprint on top of the cliff.
From here there are pano-
ramic views of the province.

Buddha image on the cliff top by
Wat Tham Sua, Krabi province

Khlong Thom ❿

คลองท่อม

Krabi province. 🏠 60,000. 🚌 ℹ️
TAT, Krabi (0-7562-2163). 🛍️ daily.

Some 40 km (25 miles) south
of Krabi town, Khlong Thom
is known locally for the small
museum within **Wat Khlong
Thom**. The temple's abbot has
assembled an array of archaeological icons and weapons
from the area. One of the
most interesting exhibits is
a collection of distinctive
beads called *lukbat*.

A maritime port, Kuan Lukbat, was once located on the
site of Khlong Thom. From the
5th century AD onward, the
port was used by foreign merchants and emissaries crossing the peninsula to Nakhon
Si Thammarat and Surat Thani
(see pp346–7). Few traders
wanted to sail through the
treacherous, pirate-infested
Straits of Malacca, so they
traveled overland instead.

Environs
A bumpy 12-km (7.5-mile)
ride inland from Khlong Thom
leads to a natural hot spring in
the forest – ideal for swimming.

About 8 km (5 miles) farther
on is the rewarding **Tung Tieo
forest trail** in Khao No Chuchi
lowland forest. The well-
marked paths lead through
this protected area, skirting
emerald pools along the way.
The surrounding woodland is
the only known area in the
world where the colorful
ground-dwelling Gurney's
pitta survives. Previously, this
bird was thought to be extinct.

CLIMBING KRABI'S STACKS

Krabi and Ko Phi Phi are the only places in Thailand where
organized rock-climbing takes place. The honeycombed limestone stacks around the Phra Nang headland, near Krabi, and

Ko Phi Phi offer challenging
conditions and attract rock
climbers from around the
world. Only the south of
France is said to offer such
arduous climbs. They vary
in difficulty from an easy "4"
according to the French system, to a very difficult "8b."
Climbers can cool off with
a swim between climbs.

**Climber on Thaiwand Wall,
Tham Phra Nang near Ao Nang**

Ko Phi Phi ⓫

เกาะพีพี

Krabi province. 🏠 7,700. 🛥 from Phuket or Krabi. 🛈 TAT, Phuket (0-7621-2213). 🎭 Chinese New Year (Feb), Songkran (Apr), Loykratong (Nov). **www**.phi-phi.com

Spectacular Ko Phi Phi, pronounced "PP," 40 km (25 miles) south of Krabi town, is in fact two separate islands: Phi Phi Don and Phi Phi Ley. Both islands belong to the **Phi Phi-Hat Nopparat Thara National Park**, which also takes in part of the mainland near Ao Nang *(see p370)*.

The islands are famed for their spectacular landscapes. Rock climbers are attracted by the breathtaking cliffs *(see p371)*, with tall sheer walls of limestone rising to 314 m (1,030 ft) on Phi Phi Don, and 374 m (1,230 ft) on Phi Phi Ley. Nature lovers will find a haven in the islands' coral beds, teeming with sea life.

Phi Phi Don

The two sections of Phi Phi Don, the larger of the two islands, are linked by a 1-km (1,100-yd) isthmus of sand. Here stands the island's original Muslim fishing village, Ban Ton Sai. This area was badly damaged by the 2004 tsunami but the reconstruction work was completed quickly. Since development began on Phi Phi Don following the arrival of the first visitors in the 1970s, the island has given itself up to

KEY

🏖	Beach
🏄	Water sports
⛴	Ferry service
- - -	Trail
🌿	Vista

tourism. However, there is still plenty of natural beauty to enjoy here. A pleasant one-hour coastal walk from Ban Ton Sai leads to Hat Yao ("long

beach"), with tantalizing white sands, vibrant offshore marine life, and unhindered views of the soaring flanks of Phi Phi Ley, 4 km (2.5 miles) away.

It is also worth climbing the steep trails on Phi Phi Don's two massifs, which afford wonderful vistas of the island. The eastern route is well marked and the least strenuous.

Superb coral beds at Hin Pae off Hat Yao, and at Ko Phai ("bamboo island"), to the northeast of Phi Phi Don, provide some of the best diving and snorkeling in Thailand.

To the north is Ban Laem Tong. This village's sea gypsy population still survives on fish caught in the isolated coves of nearby Laem Tong.

A typical view of Ko Phi Phi's stunning scenery, now enjoyed by large numbers of vacationers

For hotels and restaurants in this region see pp418–20 and pp446–9

One of Ko Phi Phi's enticing, dazzling, white-sand beaches

Phi Phi Ley

Unlike Phi Phi Don, Phi Phi Ley remains uninhabited and unspoiled. Boats from Phi Phi Don bring visitors on day trips to see the paintings in Viking Cave. Another feature of the cave are the nests of the edible-nest swiftlet (*see p341*), which are used in bird's-nest soup. Agile collectors climb rickety bamboo scaffolding to reach the nests, which are so valuable that the caves are protected by armed guards and staying overnight on the island is prohibited. There is excellent snorkeling at the coral reefs of Ao Maya.

Environs

Many of the islands in the area shelter endangered bird species such as the white-bellied sea eagle and the *mukimaki* flycatcher.

Ko Lanta 12

เกาะลันตา

Krabi province. 26,000. from Krabi or Bo Muang. TAT, Krabi (0-7562-2163).

Close to the mainland in the southeast corner of Krabi province, Ko Lanta is a group of 52 islands, 15 of which belong to the Ko Lanta National Marine Park. Most of the wildlife can be found on the smaller,

---

CAVE PAINTINGS OF THE ANDAMAN ISLANDS

There are many prehistoric paintings in Phangnga (*see pp364–9*) and Krabi (*see p371*) provinces, especially in caves on the Andaman Islands. Most are stylized red and black outlines depicting human forms, hands, fish, and, in some cases, broken line patterns that are thought to have had symbolic value. Some of the unidentifiable images are of monstrous beings – half-human, half sea-creatures – that still mystify archaeologists. Such paintings may have been drawn as part of magical-religious rituals to bring good fortune for hunting, fishing, food gathering, and tribal battles. Many paintings can be reliably dated to Neolithic times, but the drawings of junklike boats at Phangnga Bay and in the misleadingly named Viking Cave on Phi Phi Ley may be only a few hundred years old.

Paintings of boats in a cave at Phangnga Bay

---

remoter islands. The ramshackle wooden port of Ban Sala Dan is the gateway to **Ko Lanta Yai**, a predominantly Muslim fishing island. Some 25 km (15 miles) long, this is the main island in the archipelago. It is covered with undulating forested hills sweeping down to numerous west-facing sandy bays. The natural beauty has attracted many new resorts, and Ko Lanta Yai is now popular with tourists. However, monkey and lizard footprints are still

A rare white-bellied sea eagle

more common on its beaches than human prints.

The Laem Kaw Kwang headland in the northwest of the island has views across to Ko Phi Phi. At the southern tip, a 3-km (2-mile) coastal trail leads to a solar-powered lighthouse on a steep promontory beside the park headquarters.

Sea gypsies inhabit the nearby village, Ban Sangka-u. They are renowned for their colorful rituals, such as the *loi rua* ceremony. As part of the festivities, a 2-m (6-ft) replica boat is sent out to sea to banish the ill fate built up throughout the past year.

Bungalow accommodations on the unspoiled island of Ko Lanta

DEEP SOUTH

The Deep South of Thailand has more in common with Malaysia than with the distant Thai heartland to the north. Many visitors come here to experience the region's distinct culture, dialect, and food, and to learn about the local history and religion. The scenery, with spectacular mountains in the interior of the peninsula and unspoiled beaches and islands on the west coast, is equally alluring.

In many ways Thailand's Deep South doesn't feel like Thailand at all. The influence of Indian, Chinese, and Malaysian culture can be seen in the region's architecture and ethnic makeup. Skin tones are noticeably darker than the rest of the country. The population speaks an unusually intonated dialect of Thai, and Yawi, a language related to Malay and Indonesian. Also, the food is spicier, characterized by often bitter curries laced with turmeric.

South of Songkhla, especially near the coasts, most people are Muslim, and the minarets of mosques replace the gilded peaks of Buddhist temples. Indeed, Pattani, an important Malay kingdom in the 17th century, is still a center of Islamic scholarship. Even so, Wat Phra Mahathat in Nakhon Si Thammarat, the South's cultural capital, is one of the most revered Buddhist temples in Thailand. Also, numerous Hindu shrines and customs, not least the Hindu-inspired *manohra* dance, are evidence of Nakhon's role as a major religious center on the ocean trade routes between India and China.

Modern Songkhla has become the educational capital of the South. Nearby Hat Yai has grown from an agricultural service and railroad town into an important shopping and entertainment center. However, tourism in the area remains low-key due to spiraling separatist violence perpetrated by Muslim extremists seeking local autonomy. In the troubled southern provinces of Songkhla, Pattani, Yala, and Narathiwat, hostilities are ongoing, and tourists are advised against all but essential travel in these areas.

Two Muslim girls – the Islamic religion is strong in the Deep South

◁ Detail from the staircase to Wat Pha Kho, Sathing Phra

Exploring the Deep South

The eastern lowlands of the Deep South are among the most fertile in the country. Year-round heat and high humidity are ideal conditions for fast-growing coffee beans, pineapples, cashews, rambutans, and oil and rubber palms. The South's commercial capital, Hat Yai, is in this region, but Nakhon Si Thammarat and Songkhla are the cultural centers. In the west, the Trang coast and Tarutao archipelago both have fine sand beaches, spectacular corals, and few visitors by virtue of undeveloped tourist facilities. The east coast offers fewer natural attractions, but charming towns such as Songkhla are well worth visiting. The three provinces south of Hat Yai – Yala, Pattani, and Narathiwat – are strongly influenced by Muslim Malaysia. The differences in language, cuisine, and religion are obvious even to casual visitors. Densely forested mountains near the Malaysian border shelter tigers, elephants, and other wildlife.

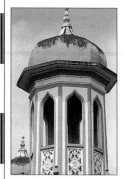

Minaret of Friday Mosque, Nakhon Si Thammarat

SIGHTS AT A GLANCE

Banthat Mountains **5**
Betong **14**
Hat Chao Mai National Park **3**
Hat Yai **9**
Nakhon Si Thammarat pp378–9 **1**
Narathiwat **15**
Pattani **12**
Phatthalung **6**
Songkhla **8**
Tarutao National Marine Park **11**
Thale Ban National Park **10**
Thale Noi Waterfowl Park **7**
Trang **4**
Trang's Andaman Islands **2**
Yala **13**

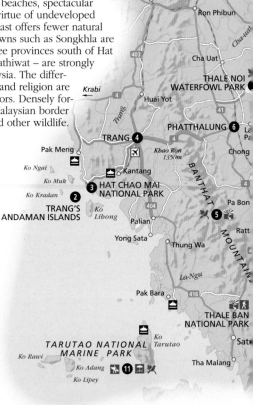

Surat Thani

Tha Sala

Surat Thani

NAKHON SI THAMMARAT **1**

Phal

Thung Song

Ron Phibun

Cha Uat

THALE NOI WATERFOWL PARK

Krabi

Huai Yot

PHATTHALUNG **6**

La

Pa

Chong

TRANG **4**

Pak Meng

Khao Ron 1350m

Kantang

HAT CHAO MAI NATIONAL PARK **3**

Ko Ngai

Ko Muk

Ko Kradan

TRANG'S ANDAMAN ISLANDS **2**

Ko Libong

Palian

Pa Bon

5

Ratt

Yong Sata

Thung Wa

La-Ngu

Pak Bara

THALE BAN NATIONAL PARK

TARUTAO NATIONAL MARINE PARK

Ko Rawi

Ko Tarutao

Sat

Ko Adang **11**

Tha Malang

Ko Lipey

Typically deserted beach in the Tarutao archipelago

GETTING AROUND

Hat Yai is the main transportation
hub of the Deep South. The 930-
km (580-mile) trip to Hat Yai
from Bangkok takes about 14
hours by bus and 17 by train.
Most of the other big towns
have bus and rail connections.
Highways 4 and 41 are the major
north-south roads. Most roads are
paved, and local buses run to
many sights. There are six small
regional airports. Many Singapo-
reans and Malaysians visit the
area on tours; most other visitors
are independent travelers. A
rental car is the easiest way
to get around. The east coast
islands can be reached from Pak
Meng, Pak Bara, and Kantang.

Fishing village in Narathiwat province

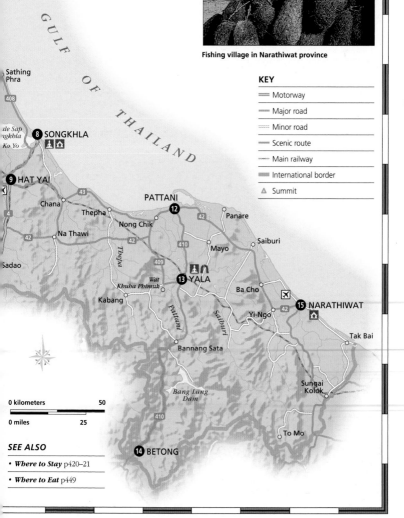

KEY

▬▬	Motorway
▬▬	Major road
▭▭▭	Minor road
▬▬	Scenic route
▬▬	Main railway
▬▬	International border
△	Summit

Sathing
Phra

GULF

408

OF

THAILAND

le Sap
ngkhla
Ko Yo

8 SONGKHLA 🏛 🏠

9 HAT YAI

Chana   43   **PATTANI**

4   Thepha   **12**   Panare

Na Thawi   Nong Chik   42

42   42   410   Mayo   Saiburi

Sadao   409

Wat   🏛 🏠
Khuba Phimuk   **13** YALA

Kabang   Ba Cho   ⊠   **15** NARATHIWAT 🏠

Yi-Ngo   42

Tak Bai

Bannang Sata   Sungai
Kolok

*Bang Lang
Dam*

410   To Mo

0 kilometers   50

0 miles   25

SEE ALSO

• **Where to Stay** p420–21

• **Where to Eat** p449

14 BETONG

Nakhon Si Thammarat ➊

นครศรีธรรมราช

Although Nakhon Si Thammarat is featured on few tourist itineraries, the most historic town in the South is a lively center with several attractions. Under the name of Ligor, it is thought to have been the capital of Tambralinga, a peninsular kingdom prior to the 7th century. From the 7th–13th centuries it was an important city of the Srivijaya Empire *(see pp346–7)*, when it became a religious center with the Sanskrit name Nagara Sri Dhammaraja, meaning "city of the sacred dharma king." Many Indian traders settled in Nakhon – as the town is popularly known – and Hindu shrines are a feature here, together with *nang talung* shadow puppet plays *(see p383)* and intricately etched nielloware *(see p453)*.

Silver figure

The relaxing way to take in Nakhon's sights

🏛 Wat Phra Mahathat
วัดพระมหาธาตุ

Rachadamnoen Rd, 2 km (1 mile) S of train station. ☐ *daily.*

Wat Phra Mahathat is one of Thailand's most sacred temples. Although its age is disputed, the *wat* is thought to be at least 1,500 years old. The present *chedi* dates from the 13th century and was supposedly built to house relics of the Buddha that were brought here from Sri Lanka. It is 77 m (255 ft) high and topped with gold variously estimated to weigh between 600 and 1,000 kg (1,350 to 2,200 lbs).

The Wihan Luang chapel has an intricately painted 18th-century ceiling, although the Wihan Phra Ma hall is perhaps more impressive. It features an elaborate, emerald-inlay door from the Sukhothai period, carved with the figures of Phrom and Vishnu. A small museum displays an evocative but unlabeled selection of archaeological finds, jewelry, and religious sculptures including Dvaravati pieces from the 6th to 13th centuries.

🏛 Nakhon Si Thammarat National Museum
พิพิธภัณฑสถานแห่งชาตินครศรีธรรมราช

Rachadamnoen Rd, 2.5 km (1.5 miles) S of train station. **Tel** 0-7534-1075. ☐ Wed–Sun. ⬤ public hols. 🎟

The centerpiece of this branch of the National Museum is the 9th-century statue of Vishnu in the Pala style of South India. It was found in the base of a tree in Kapong district near Takua Pha in Phangnga, then a major transit point for Indians colonizing the south.

Two rare bronze drums made by the Dong Son people of northern Vietnam are another highlight. The Thai gallery displays religious art from Dvaravati and Srivijayan periods to the Rattanakosin era. Look out for Buddha images in the distinctive local Sing style, characterized by stumpy features and animated faces.

🎭 Shadow Puppet Theater (Suchart House)
บ้านหนังตะลุงสุชาติ

10/18 Si Thammasok Soi 3. **Tel** 0-7534-6394. ☐ *daily.* 🎟

The *nang talung* workshop of Suchart Subsin keeps alive a uniquely Southeast Asian form of entertainment in danger of dying out. Visitors can watch the puppets being cut from leather and buy the finished product. Sometimes impromptu shows are staged.

The gold-topped *chedi* of Nakhon's splendid Wat Phra Mahathat

⚡ Ho Phra I-suan (Shiva)
หอพระอิศวร

Rachadamnoen Rd. ☐ *daily.*
In the hall of this shrine is a
1-m (3-ft) *shivalinga*, a phallic
image of the Hindu god Shiva,
that may date back to the 6th
century AD. The worship of
Shiva was a potent force in
the early peninsular city-states
of the first millennium AD.

⚡ Ho Phra Buddha Sihing
หอพระพุทธสิหิงค์

Rachadamnoen Rd. ☐ *Wed–Sun.*
The Phra Buddha Sing is one
of Thailand's most revered
images. The replica kept in
this shrine is of an original
cast in Sri Lanka in AD 157
and brought to Nakhon at the
end of the 13th century. Local

**Ho Phra Buddha Sing, home of the
sacred Phra Buddha Sing image**

artisans put their characteristic
stamp on the Buddha by giving
it a half smile, a rounder face,
and a full chest. It is similar to
Buddha images in Wat Phra
Sing in Chiang Mai.

⚡ Ho Phra Narai
หอพระนารายณ์

Rachadamnoen Rd. ☐ *daily.*
Five *lingas* (phallic sculptures)
discovered on the site of this
shrine may date from before
AD 1000. They are now in
the Wat Mahathat Museum.

🏠 Tha Chang Road
ถนนท่าช้าง

The tradition of gold
and silver shops along
this road dates from
1804, when migrants
from Saiburi district
moved to Nakhon.
Only skilled gold-
and silversmiths were
allowed to settle here,
to the west of Sanam
Na Muang parade ground.

**Typical
nielloware pot**

⛩ Ancient City Wall & North Gate
กำแพงเมืองเก่า

Just E of Rachadamnoen Rd.
The ancient city wall originally
contained an area 400 m by
2,230 m (440 yds by 2,450 yds).
The red brick North Gate is a
reconstruction of the original.

VISITORS' CHECKLIST

Nakhon Si Thammarat province.
🏠 147,000. ✈ 15 km (9 miles)
N of Nakhon. 🚌 Yommarat Rd.
🚐 off Karom Rd. 🛈 TAT, Sanam
Na Muang, Rachadamnoen Rd,
Nakhon Si Thammarat (0-7534-
6516). 🛍 daily. 🎏 Tenth Lunar
Month Festival (Sep/Oct).

⚡ Wat Sao Thong Tong
วัดเสาธงทอง

Rachadamnoen Rd. ☐ *daily.*
Adjoining the compound of
Wang Tawan Tok tem-
ple, this *wat's* main attraction is the Southern
Thai wooden house,
started in 1888 and
finished in 1901. It is
actually three houses
joined together and
features delicately
carved wooden door
panels, gables, and
window surrounds.
The Architects' Association of
Thailand gave a conservation
award to the building in 1993.

🏠 Bovorn Bazaar
บวรบาซาร์

Rachadamnoen Rd. ☐ *daily.*
The city center bazaar is a
peaceful courtyard and popular meeting place with cafés,
bars, and two good restaurants.

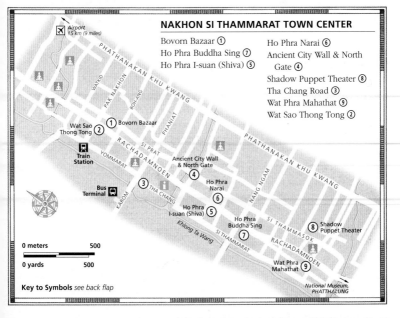

NAKHON SI THAMMARAT TOWN CENTER

Bovorn Bazaar ①
Ho Phra Buddha Sing ⑦
Ho Phra I-suan (Shiva) ⑤

Ho Phra Narai ⑥
Ancient City Wall & North
  Gate ④
Shadow Puppet Theater ⑧
Tha Chang Road ③
Wat Phra Mahathat ⑨
Wat Sao Thong Tong ②

0 meters 500
0 yards 500

Key to Symbols *see back flap*

Lush lowland scenery at Hat Chao Mai National Park

Trang's Andaman Islands **❷**

หมู่เกาะอันดามันจังหวัดตรัง

Trang province. *long-tail from Kantang to Ko Muk, Ko Kradan and Ko Libong, and from Pak Meng to Ko Hai and Ko Muk.* *TAT, Trang (0-7521-5867); Forestry Dept (0-2562-0760).*

Tourist development has barely touched the 50 or so small islands off the coast of Trang province. Their stunning sands, pristine corals, and rich bird and marine life remain the preserve of a handful of solitude seekers.

Forested **Ko Hai**, or **Ko Ngai**, is the island most easily reached from Pak Meng on the mainland and offers the widest choice of accommodation. There are wonderful beaches, particularly on the east coast, and magnificent coral offshore.

Ko Muk, 8 km (5 miles) southeast of Ko Hai, is best known for Tham Morakhot ("emerald cave") on its west coast. A long limestone tunnel leads from the sea to an inland beach surrounded by vegetation-clad cliffs. It can be entered only by boat at low tide.

Arguably the most beautiful and remotest of Trang's Andaman islands, **Ko Kradan** offers white sand beaches and good snorkeling.

Farther south and close to the mainland, **Ko Libong** is the largest of the islands. It is famed for its spectacular birdlife, which is at its best during March and April.

Hat Chao Mai National Park **❸**

อุทยานแห่งชาติหาดเจ้าไหม

Trang province. *TAT, Trang (0-7521-5867); Forestry Dept (0-2562-0760 inc bungalow bookings).* *from Trang to Kantang, then songthaew.*

Around 50 km (31 miles) west of Trang town, the varied coastal landscape of Hat Chao Mai National Park includes mangrove creeks, coastal karsts, and hidden beaches, accessed through caves around Yao and Yongling beaches. The casuarina trees lining Pak Meng beach in the north of the park is popular. This is also the main departure point for boat tours around Trang's islands, nine of which are also under park control. Dugongs can sometimes be spotted between the mainland and the islands.

Trang **❹**

ตรัง

Trang province. *83,000.* *TAT, Trang (0-7521-5867).* *daily.* *Vegetarian Festival (Oct).*

Trang has been a trading center since at least the 1st century AD. It grew to prosperity between the 7th and 13th centuries during the Srivijaya period and remains an important commercial town today. Rubber, palm oil, and fishing are the mainstays of its economy. Tourism has not yet made much impact, although this may change if Trang's Andaman islands start to be more intensively developed.

The town has a strong Chinese character (and good Chinese restaurants) as a result of an influx of immigrant labor in the latter half of the 19th century. Trang's Vegetarian Festival, mirroring its better-known counterpart on the island of Phuket *(see p360),* is renowned for the intensity of its ascetic rites, which include body piercing.

A monument to Khaw Sim Bee Na-Ranong, the first governor of Trang from 1890 to 1901, stands in the Fitness

Tuk-tuk in Trang town

Tranquil landing pier on the estuary of the Trang River

Park at the eastern end of Phatthalung Road. The statue attracts many merit-makers, especially on April 10, the day dedicated to the former governor. The Clarion MP Hotel is notable for being partially built in the shape of an ocean liner.

Environs

Trang province was dependent on tin mining until the first rubber tree seedlings were brought into Thailand around 1901. The first rubber tree can still be seen in Kantang, 22 km (14 miles) southwest of Trang, near a small museum dedicated to Khaw Sim Bee Na-Ranong. Boats run from Kantang to many of the nearby islands.

Dense rainforest on the steep slopes of the Banthat Mountains

Slender rubber trees in one of Trang province's many plantations

Banthat Mountains ❺

เขาบรรทัด

Trang province. ℹ TAT, Trang (0-7521-5867); Forestry Dept (0-2562-0760).

The verdant Banthat Mountains, which run down the peninsula as far as the Malaysian border, mark the eastern boundary of Trang province.

The forested higher elevations of the mountains, which rise to 1,350 m (4,430 ft) at Khao Ron, are one of the few places in South Thailand where the Sakai tribe still maintain their hunter-gatherer existence. These ethnically unique Negrito people speak a language related to Mon-Khmer. Traditionally they live in groups of 10 to 30 in simple lean-to leaf and grass shelters near running water, and hunt with poison blow darts. Forest clearance and exposure to lowland culture has led to some Sakai becoming agricultural laborers.

The mountains are also home to many amphibian and reptile species, including dwarf geckos and wrinkled frogs. Rare birds include hornbills, spiderhunters, hawk cuckoos, and the narcissus flycatcher. A worthwhile excursion is to the **Khao Chong Nature and Wildlife Study Center**, 20 km (12 miles) east of Trang off Highway 4. It contains an impressive open zoo and two waterfalls. Just to the south, a bird sanctuary at **Khlong Lamchan** has a reservoir that attracts many species of duck.

The minor road heading south along the western flanks of the Banthat Mountains gives access to a series of spectacular waterfalls, caves, and shady picnic places. Highlights include the huge **Ton Tay falls**, the spray rainbow that often forms by mid-afternoon over the **Sairung falls**, and the stalactites and stalagmites of **Tham Chang Hai** ("lost elephant cave") near Muansari village in Nayong district.

Much farther south, and easily accessible from Satun, is the spectacular Thale Ban National Park *(see p386)*.

DUGONGS

The once common dugong, or sea cow, was brought to the brink of extinction in Thai waters by hunting and by accidental drowning in commercial fishing nets. Today numbers are slowly increasing. The area around the Trang islands of the Andaman Sea is one of the few places they can be spotted. These herbivores feed on the seagrass beds around Ko Libong and the Trang Estuary. They grow up to 3 m (10 ft) long and can weigh 400 kg (880 lbs). In local folklore, the tears of a dugong act as a love potion.

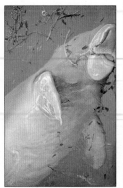

The dugong – a rare, gentle giant now protected by law

Phatthalung ⑥

พัทลุง

Phatthalung province. 🏚 81,000.
🚉 🚌 ⛴ ℹ TAT, Hat Yai (0-7423-
1055). 🛒 daily. 🎭 Phon Lak Phra
Competition (3 days in Oct or Nov).

One of the few rice-growing areas in Southern Thailand, Phatthalung province has earned a steady income from the crop throughout its history. It is better known, though, as the place where *nang talung* (shadow puppetry) was first performed in Thailand – the name *nang talung* may even derive from Phatthalung. This popular form of theater, related to Indonesian shadow puppetry, is performed mainly in Phatthalung and Nakhon Si Thammarat provinces.

Phatthalung town was established in the 19th century during the reign of Rama III *(see pp64–5)*. Today's modern town is set out in a grid and is surrounded by limestone hills to the north and the fertile Thale Luang lake to the east.

Phatthalung lies between two attractive peaks: **Khao Ok Talu** ("punctured chest mountain") to the northeast, and **Khao Hua Taek** ("broken head mountain") to the northwest. According to local legend, these two mountains, "the mistress" and "the wife," fought over Khao Muang (the male mountain), located to the north. It is said that they still nurse their battle scars from this confrontation. In fact, Khao Ok Talu has a naturally occurring tunnel in its peak (the punctured chest), while

Khao Ok Talu ("punctured chest mountain") overlooking Phatthalung

Khao Hua Taek has a dent in its peak (the broken head). In the latter are the Buddhist grottoes of **Wat Tham Kuha Sawan**. Inside the lower cave are statues of monks and the Buddha, while the upper cave has views of Khao Ok Talu and most of Phatthalung and the surrounding area.

Environs

Lush rice fields surround Phatthalung. At **Lam Pam**, a small fishing village 6 km (4 miles) east of Phatthalung, slow-flowing canals empty into the large Thale Luang inland sea. The breezy but peaceful area at Sansuk beach has a few restaurants serving good seafood. Boats can be hired to the nearby islands, Ko Si and Ko Ha.

Two kilometres (1 mile) before Lam Pam is **Wat Wang**, Phatthalung's oldest temple, thought to have been founded at the same time as the town. Next to the *chedi* is a *bot* with faded murals depicting Buddhist and Ramakien themes *(see pp40–41)*.

The restored **Governor's Palace** occupies a peaceful site nearby. Built in 1889, the palace comprises two individual buildings. The outer teak structure, nearer the road, functioned as living quarters for the governor's family. The main building, beside the river, is built around a courtyard with a large tree.

🏠 **Governor's Palace**
Hwy 4047, 4 km (2 miles) E of
Phatthalung. ⏰ 8:30am–4pm daily.

The elevated structures of the Governor's Palace in Lam Pam

For hotels and restaurants in this region see pp420–21 and p449

Thale Noi Waterfowl Park ❼

ทะเลน้อย

32 km (20 miles) NE of Phatthalung, Phatthalung province. ℹ *TAT, Hat Yai (0-7423-1055); Forestry Dept, Bangkok (0-2562-0760 or* **www**.dnp.go.th). 🚍 *from Phatthalung, then hire a long-tail.* ◯ *8:30am–4pm daily.* 📷

The largest wetland bird sanctuary in Thailand, this park serves as a resting and feeding ground for thousands of exotic migratory birds flying to Sumatra and Australia to escape winter in Siberia and China. The best way to explore the watery preserve, covering 30 sq km (12 sq miles), is by long-tail boat, which can be hired from Phatthalung for a two-hour round trip.

Thale Noi has the appearance of a swamp, but it is predominantly a freshwater lake, with a depth of up to 1.5 m (5 ft). Only in periods of high southerly winds does the lake become brackish, when saltier water

Long-tail boat at Thale Noi Waterfowl Park

from Thale Luang and Songkhla Lake to the south is pushed northward.

Dawn is the best time for bird-watching, especially between the months of January and April. Many of the 150 or so species of birds who visit the park arrive during this time, swelling its population to as much as 100,000. In May the population begins to shrink, and from October to December there are only small numbers of native species left. A view-

White-throated kingfisher

ing platform in the lake is the ideal place for bird-watching. Among the birds here are the purple swamp hen, bronze-winged jacana, whistling teal, white-throated kingfisher, the long-legged *nok i-kong*, and the white ibis and gray heron.

One of the major forms of vegetation in the park is *don kok*, a reed which the *nok i-kong* use to build "platforms".

Around 100 families live along the shores of Thale Noi, mostly in raised wooden houses. They make a living from fishing and by weaving bulrush reeds into mats.

SHADOW PUPPETS – NANG TALUNG

Nang talung is the popular Thai version of shadow puppetry, an art form that originated as early as 400 BC in Asia. *Nang talung* performances, which begin late at night and last several hours, are still an essential part of village life in the Deep South. It is the task of a single person, the *nai nag* (puppet master), to create the whole show. Sitting behind an illuminated screen, he maneuvers up to six puppets per scene. The puppets, about 50 cm (20 in) high, are made from leather, or *nang*, which is carved, colored, and rendered movable by joints. The changing tone of the puppeteer's voice differen-

Shadow puppet of a Ramakien character

A puppeteer, sitting behind a screen, using his skills to perform *nang talung*

tiates between the characters, while a band of musicians adds tension to the plot. While the more formal *nang yai* is based on the Ramakien (see pp40–41), *nang talung* takes its inspiration from everyday life, with themes such as family problems. Each story is created by the *nai nag* and includes easily recognizable characters, such as comic figures with exaggerated features. Once a year the apprentices commemorate the puppet master in a *wai kru* ("paying respect to the teacher") ceremony.

The audience's view of *nang talung*

Songkhla 🐚

สงขลา

Songkhla province. 🏘 86,000.
✈ 🚉 at Hat Yai, 36 km (22 miles)
SW of Songkhla. 🚌 🚢 🛈 TAT,
Hat Yai (0-7424-3747). 🎏 daily.
🎎 Chinese Lunar Festival (Sep/Oct).

Once known as Singora ("lion city"), Songkhla grew to prominence during the Srivijaya period (*see pp346–7*). It once had a reputation as a pirate base but gradually attracted Arab, Indian, Khmer, and Chinese traders. The cuisine and language of Songkhla reflect its multicultural heritage, and a subtle Portuguese influence is evident in the architecture of the houses along Nakhon Nok and Nakhon Nai roads.

Wat Chai Mongkhon, Songkhla

Today the city, built on the headland between the Gulf of Thailand and Thale Sap – the country's largest lake – is a fishing port and an administrative and educational center.

Songkhla's main beach, **Hat Samila**, which is presided over by a bronze **mermaid statue**, is pleasant to walk along and it has several good seafood restaurants. Farther south,

at **Khao Seng**, is a Muslim fishing village where colorful *korlae* fishing boats (*see p388*) can be seen. A local myth says that if you can move the Nai Bang's Head boulder on the headland beside the village, you will inherit the gold buried underneath.

The beautiful, evocative building housing the **Songkhla National Museum** is an attraction in itself. It was built in 1878 in the Southern Thai-Chinese style as the residence of deputy Songkhla governor Phraya Suntharanuraksa. A hidden grass courtyard flanks two spiraling staircases leading to the wooden paneled second story where most exhibits are kept. Highlights include Bencharong pottery, earthenware jars recovered from the sea around Songkhla, 7th- to 9th-century Dvaravati plinths and Buddha images, and Ban Chiang pottery said to date from 3000 BC.

The **Patsree Museum** in Wat Matchimawat (sometimes called Wat Klang), south of the National Museum, is no less important. Its 35-cm (14-in) stone image of Ganesh, the elephant god, is thought to date

from the late 6th century, making it the earliest such image found in the peninsula. Chinese painted enamelware from the Qwing Ching dynasty, 15th-century U Thong wares, and 18th-century European plates all indicate the importance of Songkhla's former maritime trade links.

The city's other main temple, **Wat Chai Mongkhon**, has a Buddha relic from Sri Lanka buried beneath it.

Songkhla is an attractive city to walk around, taking in the topiary garden at **Khao Noi** and the view of Thale Sap from the peak of **Khao Tung Kuan**. Restaurants and live music bars can be found around Chaiya Road.

Elaborately decorated door at the Songkhla National Museum

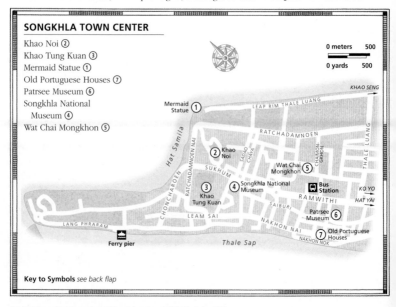

SONGKHLA TOWN CENTER

Khao Noi ②
Khao Tung Kuan ③
Mermaid Statue ①
Old Portuguese Houses ⑦
Patsree Museum ⑥
Songkhla National Museum ④
Wat Chai Mongkhon ⑤

0 meters 500
0 yards 500

KHAO SENG

Mermaid Statue ①
LEAP RIM THALE LUANG
Hat Samila
RATCHADAMNOEN
CHAIMON-GKHON
THALE LUANG
② Khao Noi
SADAO CHAYA
RATCHADAMNOEN NAI
SUKHUM
Wat Chai Mongkhon ⑤
③ Khao Tung Kuan
④ Songkhla National Museum
Bus Station
KO YO
CHONCHAROEN
SAIBURI
RAMWITHI
HAT YAI
LEAM SAI
NAKHON NAI
Patsree Museum ⑥
LANG PHRARAM
Ferry pier
Thale Sap
NAKHON NOK
Old Portuguese Houses ⑦

Key to Symbols *see back flap*

⌂ Songkhla National Museum
Wichianchom Rd. *Tel* 0-7431-1728.
◯ Wed–Sun. ◉ public hols. 📷

⌂ Patrsee Museum
Wat Matchimawat, Saiburi Rd.
◯ Wed–Sun. ◉ public hols. 📷

Environs
The Prem Tinsulanond bridge connects Songkhla with the narrow coastal strip to the north. The longest bridge in Thailand, it traverses Thale Sap via the island of **Ko Yo** on the western side of the lake. The link has boosted the island's active cotton-weaving industry and fish farms.

Ko Yo is home to the excellent **Folklore Museum**, on a hilltop overlooking the lake. The museum, which aims to preserve the rich folk traditions of the South, houses displays on history, ethnology, and religion. Exhibits include fabrics, pottery, and metalware, and traditional arts from the South, such as rattan and brassware from Ranong, Muslim *kris* knives from Pattani, *krajude* grass mats from Chumphon, and dove cages from Songkhla.

Wat Pha Kho, in **Sathing Phra** district, to the north of Songkhla, is believed to be the oldest temple in Songkhla province. Archaeological finds around the *wat* suggest Sathing Phra was once an important port selling ceramics, produced at nearby Pa-o, to Khmer, Cham, and Chinese traders.

⌂ Folklore Museum
Institute of Southern Thai Studies, Ko Yo, 14 km (8 miles) SW of Songkhla. ◯ daily. 📷

Three young devotees venerating a Buddhist shrine in Hat Yai

Hat Yai ❾
หาดใหญ่

Songkhla province. 🏠 70,000. ✈ 12 km (7 miles) W of Hat Yai. 🚉 🚌
🛈 TAT, 1/1 Soi 2, Niphat U-thit Rd, Hat Yai (0-7424-3747). 🚍 next to TAT (0-7424-6733). 🛍 daily. 🎎 Chinese Lunar Festival (Sep/Oct).

The commercial and transport capital of Southern Thailand, Hat Yai wins no prizes for beauty. It has grown affluent due to its strategic railroad junction, its cut-price products, and a constant flow of Malaysian tourists who converge on the city on weekends to enjoy its dining, shopping, and nightlife. Malay, English, Yawi, Hokkien, Mandarin, and the clipped syllables of Southern Thai dialect can be heard around the cosmopolitan downtown area.

Seller displaying produce at Hat Yai market

Be aware that some parlors here advertising "ancient massage" will probably offer more than a quick rubdown.

Hat Yai's cultural attractions are few, so most visitors spend daylight hours shopping in Thailand's third-largest city. Electrical goods at the Kim Yong market, durians and apples from street vendors, and Bangkok-made leather goods and fashions in the department stores are a few of Hat Yai's popular buys. Bullfighting takes place in the city on the first Saturday of every month at different locations. Bulls are pitted against each other, and the winner is the animal that forces its opponent to retreat. The furious betting is often as much of a spectacle as the fight itself.

Wat Hat Yai Nai, 2 km (1 mile) west of the city center, has the third largest reclining Buddha image in the world, measuring 35 m (115 ft) long and 15 m (49 ft) high. You can walk inside the image, entering via a small shrine room. Herbal saunas and massages are offered in the temple grounds.

Environs
Ton Nga Chang ("elephant tusk") waterfall, 24 km (15 miles) west of Hat Yai, takes its name from the two streams of water that tumble over the seven tiers of falls. They are best seen in the cool season, starting in November.

Extensive fish farms beside Ko Yo on Thale Sap lake, near Songkhla

Taking the ferry from Pak Bara to Tarutao National Marine Park

Thale Ban National Park ⑩

อุทยานแห่งชาติทะเลบัน

Satun province. Off Hwy 4184, 37 km (23 miles) from Satun. 📋 TAT, Hat Yai (0-7423-1055); Forestry Dept (0-2562-0760 inc bungalow bookings). 🚌 Satun, then songthaew. 📷

Thale Ban is a lush expanse of dense tropical rainforest scattered with waterfalls that extends over the Banthat Mountains (see p381) close to the Malaysian border. It covers only 102 sq km (40 sq miles) but contains a staggering variety of wildlife including sun bears, tigers, and rare birds such as bat hawks. The park has some marked trails, the Yaroy waterfall, 5 km (3 miles) north of the park headquarters, and several swimming pools.

Satun is the nearest town and gateway to the park. It is within easy reach of Pak Bara, from which ferries depart for Tarutao, and the west coast.

Tarutao National Marine Park ⑪

อุทยานแห่งชาติตะรุเตา

Satun province. 22 km (14 miles) from Pak Bara. 📋 TAT, Hat Yai (0-7423-1055) or Park HQ (0-7478-3485). 🚢 from Pak Bara; regular crossings mid-Nov to mid-Apr only. 📷

The 51 islands of the Tarutao National Marine Park are the most southwesterly in Thailand, located only 8 km (5 miles) from the Malaysian island of Langkawi. Tarutao is famous for its superb diving sites, said to be among the world's best.

Offshore sightings of sperm and minke whales, dugongs, and dolphins are common. There is also a rich concentration of fish life with 92 species of coral fish and around 25 percent of all the world's fish species in the surrounding seas.

For centuries the islands had a more sinister reputation as a lair for pirates. It wasn't until the 1960s that the British Royal Navy finally curtailed the pirate raids. The archipelago, extending over 1,490 sq km (580 sq miles), became Thailand's first national marine park in 1974.

The park includes spectacular, unspoiled scenery, a wide variety of wildlife, and good coral. However, these attractions are accessible to visitors only from mid-November to mid-May as monsoon storms make the ferry trip from Pak Bara too risky at other times.

Hawksbill turtle, a resident of Tarutao

The largest island in the group, 26-km (16-mile) long **Ko Tarutao**, offers the greatest scenic variety. Tropical rainforest covers most of its surface, which reaches a height of 708 m (2,300 ft). Most accommodations and the best facilities for visitors are found near the wonderful, pristine beaches of the west coast.

Ferries from Pak Bara dock at Ao Phante Malaka, which is where the park headquarters, bungalows, two restaurants, and the island's only store are located. Worthwhile excursions from here include the half-hour climb to To-bo cliff with its fine views, particularly at sunset, and the 2-km (1-mile) boat trip to stalagmite-filled Crocodile cave. No crocodiles have been seen for many years, but the island does support a wide variety of fauna, including deer, wild pigs, macaques, otters, and soft-shelled turtles.

Ko Adang and **Ko Lipey** are the only other islands in the park to offer (rudimentary) accommodations and food for visitors.

Rugged Ko Adang, 62 km (39 miles) west of the mainland, rises to 703 m (2,300 ft). It is thickly forested and has many year-round waterfalls, such as the Rattana falls on the southwest coast. Here, you can take a freshwater rock pool swim while overlooking the sea.

The smaller island of Ko Lipey, 2 km (1 mile) south of Ko Adang, has pleasant footpaths through coconut plantations and the immaculate sands of Pattaya beach. It is also home to a community of sea gypsies, displaced from Ko Rawi and Ko Adang when the park was created. Relations between the gypsies and the park authorities are strained.

Ko Kra, off Lipey's east coast, has excellent corals, as does Ko Yang, midway between Rawi and Adang islands.

Tiny Ko Khai ("egg island"), west of Tarutao, has a dramatic rock arch and is surrounded by fine sands. These are a major breeding ground for sea turtles, hence the island's name.

Colorful corals, part of a reef in the Tarutao National Marine Park

For hotels and restaurants in this region see pp420–21 and p449

Seafood of the South

One of the greatest culinary treats Thailand provides is the abundant fresh seafood of the South. Throughout the year, a wide range of fish, crabs, lobsters, mussels, shrimp, squid are available along both the Gulf of Thailand and Andaman Sea coasts. Although flash-frozen and container-freighted seafood is available

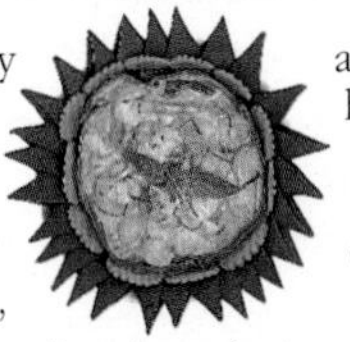

Ho mok, a seafood soufflé with Thai basil

all over the country today, it is hard to beat the flavor of a freshly caught fish, simply cooked and served up whole on a plate by the shore. Nor does it have to be expensive: for every five-star restaurant offering lobster bisque there are half a dozen street cafés serving an enormous range of seafood cooked in an amazing variety of styles.

Hoi nang rom sot, *a simple Thai hors d'oeuvre of fresh oysters, is served out of the shell with slices of zesty lime.*

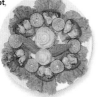

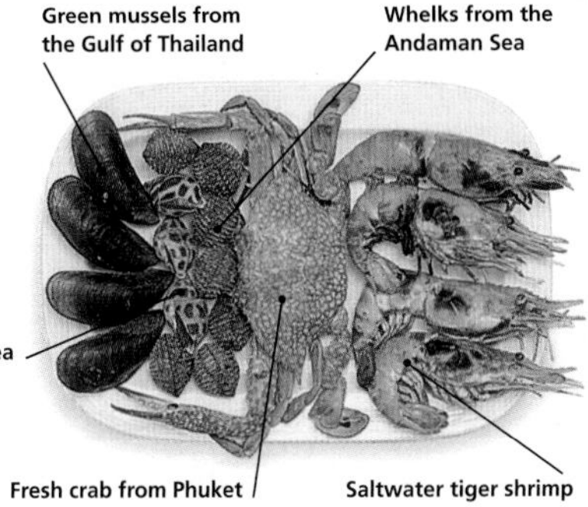

Green mussels from the Gulf of Thailand

Whelks from the Andaman Sea

Andaman Sea cockles

Fresh crab from Phuket

Saltwater tiger shrimp

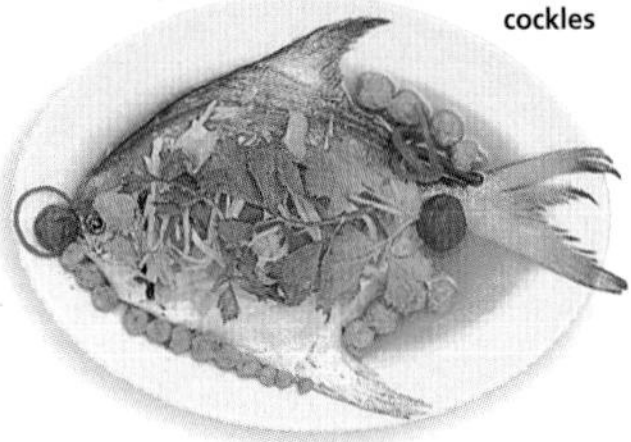

Charamet fish, *prized for its succulent, soft flesh, is cooked here in sweet plum sauce* (neung buay), *accompanied by ginger, lemon grass, and chili peppers.*

BARBECUED SEAFOOD

Barbecued seafood, known as *thale phao*, is popular with both Thais and foreign visitors. Diners make their selection of freshly caught fish and shellfish displayed on banks of crushed ice. Pricing is usually by weight.

Thot man kung (deep fried shrimp cakes) *are served with a sweet sauce dip. This is a favorite dish with those who don't like very spicy food.*

Meuk op sos noei (squid baked in butter sauce) *is decorated with exquisitely carved vegetable "flowers" and "leaves." Garnishes of this type accompany many Thai dishes and are generally not eaten.*

Kung mangkon phat phrik phao (barbecued lobster with chili sauce) *is particularly popular around Phuket, where lobsters abound.*

Phanaeng kung makheuathet *is a creamy, fragrant dish of tomatoes stuffed with a shrimp and coconut milk curry. It is a specialty of Hat Yai and Phuket.*

Pattani ⑫

ปัตตานี

Pattani province. 🏃 74,000. 🚐 🚍
ℹ️ TAT, Narathiwat (0-7352-2411).
🏠 daily. 🎭 Lim Ko Niaw Festival
(Mar).

Founded in the early 1400s,
Pattani was once a semiauto-
nomous Malay-speaking sul-
tanate. Today, it is the heart
of Muslim South Thailand
(75 percent of the province's
population are followers of
Islam). Pattani is one of four
southern provinces that have
seen rising violence by
Islamic extremists against the
minority Buddhist population.

Apart from the **Matsayit
Klang** mosque, there
are few notable sights,
but the town is lively,
particularly around
the harbor with its
brightly colored boats.

Environs
The mosque of **Kru Se**,
7 km (4 miles) east of
town, is unremarkable
in design but has an
interesting story behind
it. In the 1570s, Lim To
Khieng, a Chinese merchant,
married a local woman and

Wat Khuha Phimuk, with its adjacent cave containing a reclining Buddha

converted to Islam. To show
his devotion to his new faith
he started building a mosque.
His sister, Lim Ko Niaw,
sailed from China to
protest about his con-
version, and he swore
he would return to
China as soon as the
mosque was finished.
However, he made sure
that it never was, and
his sister, on her death-
bed, cursed the build-
ing and anyone who
attempted to complete
it. Her shrine and the
still unfinished mosque attract
huge numbers of devotees.

**Muslim women
in Pattani**

KORLAE FISHING BOATS

Along mainly the east coast of the peninsula, from Ko
Samui southward, colorful, painted fishing boats called
korlae have been built and decorated by Muslim fishermen
for hundreds of years. The finest examples of this now de-
clining industry originate in the boatyards of Saiburi district,
Pattani. Originally sailboats, they are now run with engines
by fishermen. Among the characters commonly depicted on
the superbly detailed hull designs are the *singha* lion, the
gagasura horned bird, *payanak* sea serpent, and the *garuda*
bird from Asian mythologies. Artists, however, don't feel
anything is amiss if they add a Swiss Alpine background.

Battling mythical beasts, intricately painted on a *korlae* boat

---

Yala ⑬

ยะลา

Yala province. 🏃 93,000. 🚐 🚍
ℹ️ TAT, Narathiwat (0-7352-2411).
🎭 ASEAN Barred Ground Dove
Festival (1st weekend Mar); Yala City
Pillar Celebrations (end of May).

Yala, often heralded as the
cleanest town in Thailand, is
laid out in an orderly fashion
with a grid pattern of streets
and tree-lined boulevards. It's
a prosperous and rather staid
place, at its most lively during
the annual cooing competition
of the ASEAN Barred Ground
Dove Festival, which attracts
entrants from all over Southeast Asia. Yala's mosque is
the largest in Thailand.

Environs
For many people, the main
reason to visit Yala is **Wat
Khuha Phimuk**, called Wat Na
Tham locally, located 8 km
(5 miles) outside the town. It
is one of the most sacred and
important archaeological sites
in South Thailand. A cave next
to the temple contains a 25-m-
long (82-ft) reclining Buddha.
The statue, which allegedly
once had the head of the
Hindu god Vishnu, dates from
the 8th century, the beginning
of the Srivijaya period.

Among the priceless icons
from that era found here are
votive *stupas* from Northeast
India and 9th-century bronze
standing Buddha images in
the style of South India.

The small museum hall, at
the foot of the *naga* staircase
leading up to the temple cave,
displays a range of Srivijayan
artifacts found in the area.

Betong
เบตง

Yala province. *29,000.* *TAT, Narathiwat (0-7352-2411).* *daily.*

Betong is the southernmost town in Thailand. It sits high in the hills, 5 km (3 miles) from the Malaysian border and 140 km (87 miles) from Yala.

The surrounding countryside is of more interest than the town itself, which has few sights other than the 40-m-high (130-ft) *stupa* in **Wat Phuttha Tiwat**. This was built in the late 1980s in a modified Srivijayan style.

Environs
The winding road from Yala to Betong climbs through remote mountain forests where bands of the Sakai tribe still hunt.

From the 1940s until the 1980s this dense forest was home to an active unit of the Communist Party of Malaya, taking refuge in Thailand. A paved road leads to their former underground guerrilla camp, **Piya Mit**, which has now been converted into a museum. Around 180 Communists lived here undetected in 1 km (1,100 yds) of tunnels, 10 m (33 ft) below the surface.

The end came peacefully in 1989 when "an honorable settlement" was reached with the Malaysian and Thai governments. Most of the former revolutionaries settled in the area, and some now guide visitors through the network of dank tunnels and explain the camp's facilities. The cleverly constructed kitchen area has a flue that would disperse smoke on the other side of the hill, thus concealing the camp's location. It was so successful that the stronghold remained undetected until the end. Other items on display include old shoes, uniforms, knives, and torches used by the fugitive comrades. Simple accommodations are available in modern bungalows.

Piya Mit
Betong province. Off Hwy 410, 19 km (12 miles) N of Betong. ☐ *daily.*

Narathiwat
นราธิวาส

Narathiwat province. *68,000.* *TAT, Narathiwat (0-7352-2411).* *Chao Mae Toe Moe Festival (late Apr or early May), Narathiwat Fair (3rd week Sep).*

The town of Narathiwat is visited by few tourists, but it makes a useful base for exploring the surrounding region. However, caution is advised as the province experiences frequent acts of violence carried out by Islamic extremists. The Muslim fishing village is a good place to see the traditional painted *korlae* boats. There are a number of good beaches near the town – the best is Ao Manao, 6 km (4 miles) to the south.

Immense golden-tiled Buddha on Khao Kong, Narathiwat

Environs
Taksin Palace, south of town, is the summer residence of the King and Queen. It is open to the public when the royal family is not in residence. The gardens have views of the adjacent beach and an aviary with peacocks and cockatoos.

On the road to Rangae is the hill **Khao Kong**, perched upon which is the tallest seated Buddha image in Thailand. The 24-m (79-ft) statue is covered in golden tiles.

Close to the Malaysian border, 34 km (21 miles) south of Narathiwat, is the village of **Tak Bai**. Its main attraction is Wat Chonthara Sing He: an outpost of Thai Buddhism in an almost exclusively Malay-speaking, Muslim area. The *wat* was erected in 1873 by King Chulalongkorn to stake his claim to a region that the British wanted to incorporate into Malaya (Malaysia).

The architecture of the temple mixes Southern Thai with Chinese influences, the latter being particularly evident in the tiered roof. One of the buildings in the large grounds contains a reclining Buddha decorated with Chinese ceramics from the Song dynasty. Another is adorned with fine murals depicting many aspects of local life painted during the reign of King Mongkut.

Taksin Palace
Off Hwy 4084, 8 km (5 miles) S of Narathiwat. ☐ *daily.* ● *usually Aug & Sep.*

A lively scene of daily life from a mural at Wat Chonthara Sing He

TRAVELERS' NEEDS

WHERE TO STAY 392–421

WHERE TO EAT 422–449

SHOPPING IN THAILAND 450–457

ENTERTAINMENT IN THAILAND 458–461

OUTDOOR ACTIVITIES &
SPECIAL INTERESTS 462–471

WHERE TO STAY

Accommodations in Thailand come in all price ranges, although the distribution of hotels is very uneven: massive development in the beach resorts contrasts with basic guesthouses (or no facilities at all) in many rural areas. All major cities have at least one international-class hotel, while Bangkok boasts of some of the best hotels anywhere in the world. These are equipped with swimming pools, gyms, restaurants, business services, and other luxury facilities. Middle-range accommodation is available in most towns

Bellboy at the
Mandarin Oriental

and, although much lacks character, it is uniformly clean, efficient, and friendly. The current trend in Thailand is for luxurious spas, resorts, and pool villas featuring contemporary Thai design and decor. These fabulously chic properties can now be found across the country. Guesthouses provide remarkably cheap accommodations for budget travelers. Other alternatives include, for the hardy, camping or staying in bungalows in the national parks, and, for the ascetic, bedding down in a monastery.

HOTEL GRADING AND FACILITIES

Hotels are not officially graded, although some are registered with the **Thai Hotels Association**. Price is therefore the only indication of what to expect (see p394). Accommodations range from basic to luxury. At the low end of the market cleanliness is not always a priority.

Often the best value is to be found in the once-luxury establishments that have been downgraded since the arrival of international luxury chains. These hotels offer the facilities available in first-class hotels at a fraction of the cost.

LUXURY HOTELS

Thailand's luxury hotels are probably the equal of any in the world – and their number and standards are rising year after year. Expect to be treated like a visiting dignitary in the air-conditioned oases of Bangkok and the other major cities. Rooms are sure to have every conceivable luxury, from a king-size bed and massive television to a well-stocked minibar and perhaps even a marble Jacuzzi. In such world-famous hotels as the Mandarin Oriental and the Shangri-La Bangkok, the magnificent views of the Chao Phraya River are an added privilege.

These first-class hotels offer their guests a huge range of facilities, including business centers, conference rooms,

Hilton Hua Hin Resort & Spa, noted for fine sea views (see p416)

shopping malls, coffee shops, fitness centers, and swimming pools, as well as numerous food outlets. However, the major hotels are facing increasingly stiff competition from small but luxurious boutique hotels that can offer a more personalized service. The Chedi in Chiang

Mai rates as one of the finest design-led hotels in the country, while the Indigo Pearl in Phuket is an outstanding resort with a unique style and striking decor.

All luxury hotels in Thailand provide an extensive range of cuisines, some having as many as ten restaurants; Thai is, of course, standard, and Chinese – often with a regional variant such as Cantonese or Szechuan – is common. Italian and French restaurants are very popular, usually complete with imported European chef.

RESORT HOTELS

Like the urban luxury hotels, the resort hotels of Thailand are unsurpassed in style, comfort, and elegance by the majority of their counterparts elsewhere in the world. They also usually offer stunning views. Such resorts as the

The Conrad Room at the Mandarin Oriental Hotel, Bangkok (see p400)

◁ Fresh watermelons on display at the Damnoen Saduak Floating Market, near Bangkok

Felix River Kwai Resort, Khwae Yai River, Kanchanaburi *(see p403)*

Regent in Chiang Mai, Honeymoon Private Island Resort in Phuket, and the Dusit Resort in Cha-am are luxury designer-built oases of tranquillity and opulence. You should expect – and will usually get – the best of everything. Charming service is provided by traditionally dressed waiting staff. The food is varied and generally of an excellent standard.

Most resorts offer their guests a wide range of entertainments and distractions, such as swimming – for which there might be several pools – outdoor Jacuzzis, saunas, tennis courts, water sports facilities, and even riding or polo. In Chiang Mai, resorts may be able to organize elephant trekking.

GUESTHOUSES

Guesthouses in Thailand, date from the backpacker explosion of the 1970s. Still frequented primarily by Western travelers, they offer a superb value for the money and often have a lot of charm.

In Bangkok, Khao San Road is the primary haunt of budget travelers. Offering low-cost accommodation in an otherwise expensive capital city seems to have taken priority over comfort, and, with few exceptions, Bangkok guesthouses are at best unremarkable.

Outside the capital, however, and especially in Chiang Mai, guesthouses are usually clean, friendly, and astoundingly cheap. Most have rooms with air-conditioning or fans, as well as bathrooms. Some establishments offer swimming pools, restaurants, and good service for around 400 *baht* a

night, just a fraction of the cost of a top resort hotel. Cheap guesthouses may cost as little as 100 *baht*, but for this expect basic facilities, with communal Asian toilets and showers, although the quality of service should still be good.

THAI AND CHINESE HOTELS

Thai and Chinese hotels can be found just about everywhere in Thailand, though relatively few foreign visitors choose to stay in them. They generally offer basic facilities, often without Western-style toilets (they are clean, but you must squat rather than sit), and are cheap, functional, and unexceptional.

Thai hotels are architecturally unexciting, generally being multistory concrete blocks containing numerous identical rooms. As ever in Thailand, however, they are usually clean and the service is

friendly. Most will offer you a choice between air-conditioned rooms *(hong air)* and fan-cooled rooms *(hong patlom)*.

Chinese hotels, by contrast, are readily identifiable by a number of distinctly "Middle Kingdom" features – and not just the serious-looking concierge who usually guards the keys. Wall partitions generally stop a foot short of the ground, and several feet below the ceiling, making privacy distinctly elusive. Mirrors are strategically placed to repel evil spirits, and Chinese decorative features, such as dragons and red-and-gold Chinese characters (for good luck), are much in evidence.

Only a few Thai and Chinese hotels are equipped with restaurants. However, in some remote areas, particularly little-visited areas of the Central Plains and Northeast Thailand, these hotels may well provide the only option for travelers.

STAYING IN MONASTERIES

Monasteries are traditionally places of refuge and contemplation. Whether you are a Buddhist, or want to learn more about Buddhism, it is often possible to stay overnight in a *wat* for a small donation.

Facilities are basic, and early rising is the norm. Mixed-sex accommodation is not available. Clean, tidy dress and an appropriate demeanor are also important. For temple etiquette see page 479.

A charming guesthouse in rural surroundings, in the north of the country

RENTALS

Rental accommodations are widely available throughout Thailand at reasonable rates. However, rental is an option rarely taken up by short-term visitors, mainly because advertisements of apartments for rent are generally aimed solely at Thais.

Serviced apartments are an increasingly popular choice for visitors intending to stay in Thailand for a month or longer. Properties usually occupy prime locations and offer guests the service and convenience of a five-star hotel at significantly lower prices. For more information, visit www.sabaai.com.

STAYING IN NATIONAL PARKS

The majority of national parks allow camping (for a minimal fee), although the facilities provided are invariably extremely basic when compared to those available in Europe and North America. Camping has never taken off in Thailand, as Thais do not understand why anyone would choose to sleep under canvas when there is a cheap hotel

A traditional-style bedroom with mattresses on the floor

nearby. Additionally, campers have to face the perils of the outdoors. Mosquito nets and coils and copious amounts of insect repellent are essential.

In many national parks visitors can also stay in clean, if usually charmless, concrete bungalows. As there are only limited numbers of these, it is advisable to book ahead by phoning the **Forestry Department** in Bangkok.

PRICES

Thailand's extraordinary range of accommodations includes something to suit every visitor's budget. At the top end of the market, which includes such hotels as Bangkok's Mandarin Oriental and Chiang Mai's Regent, the sky is the limit. Celebrities and heads of state may take suites at 40,000 *baht* a night, although for more everyday luxury expect to pay between 10,000 and 15,000 *baht* a night.

Tourist accommodations cost from 1,000 to 5,000 *baht* a night in Bangkok, Chiang Mai, Pattaya, Phuket, or Ko Samui. A comfortable air-conditioned room in a standard provincial hotel goes for between 700 and 1,500 *baht*, depending on the season. Prices everywhere are at their highest in the cool season. In the hot season (March to May) and the rainy season (May to October) rates often fall, except in the capital, which is open for business all year round. A clean but spartan room in a Thai or Chinese hotel in Bangkok will cost around 500 *baht*, falling to 150 to 250 *baht* in the regions.

Local factors should also be taken into consideration. For example, in Surin the hotel prices soar during the Elephant Roundup in November, when rooms in this otherwise moderately priced city are booked up months in advance.

The best deals available are probably the guesthouses of Chiang Mai and other tourism-oriented towns. It is possible to stay in traditional Thai houses, with teak walls and stilts, for between 100 and 500 *baht* a night. This is difficult to beat, and visitors often stay for weeks longer than planned. Beach bungalow accommodations are similarly priced, but less comfortable, and more prone to invasion by insects.

An idyllic setting: tent and bungalows at Ao Phrao on Ko Samet

BOOKING

Advance booking is advisable for luxury hotels and mid-range establishments, especially during national and local festivals. Thai and Chinese hotels and guesthouses are unlikely to take bookings. In popular tourist areas, and at luxury hotels, staff speak English. Elsewhere, making a booking may be difficult unless you speak some Thai. TAT offices are able to make bookings on behalf of tourists.

TAXES

The tax situation in Thailand is rather confusing and apparently anomalous. All hotels should charge seven percent VAT (value added tax), and some luxury hotels will also add a 10 percent service charge on top of their basic rates. Some of the top hotels – such as the Mandarin Oriental, Shangri-La, and others in this category – include tax in the room rates quoted. Less expensive hotels, catering to tourists, may simply add tax to the final bill. Thus, it is important to ask whether it is included in the price when booking or before checking in.

At small hotels outside the main resorts, tax is rarely (if ever) charged, and service is paid for (if at all) by tipping.

BARGAINING

It is always a good idea to ask about "special rates" or the possibility of a reduction in price. The worst that can happen is a polite refusal, and very often, especially outside Bangkok and out of season, such an inquiry can lead to substantial savings. It is not considered impolite to ask, but it is bad manners to press the point. Many hotels give discounts if bookings are low, and if special rates are available, most Thai proprietors will certainly let you know.

TIPPING

Outside the capital and the major destinations of Ko Samui, Phuket, Pattaya, and Chiang Mai, tipping is unusual. Porters will expect a tip, and staff are rewarded for good service. Use your discretion: if you have received particularly good service, then leave a tip if you wish. Thanks, and a smile, are also much appreciated.

There are no hard and fast rules, and the standard British 10 percent – let alone the American 15 percent – would be far too much on a large bill. Between 10 and 50 *baht* is adequate in almost every circumstance. Expensive hotels will automatically include a service charge on the bill.

FACILITIES FOR CHILDREN

Thais love children and are incredibly tolerant of them, especially if they are blond-haired and blue-eyed. Such kids seem as exotic and doll-like to Thais as their own offspring do to the average Westerner. However, very few mid-range hotels have facilities for children or nursing mothers, and supervised play areas are rare. By contrast, the majority of seaside resorts and luxury hotels offer some kind of babysitting services, and children can often stay in their parents' room for free. Paddling pools may be provided, but you must look after your own children.

Khon Kaen Hotel, Northeast Thailand (see p409)

DISABLED TRAVELERS

Even luxury hotels have few facilities for disabled visitors. Wheelchair ramps are beginning to make an appearance in newly commissioned luxury hotels, and nearly every luxury or tourist-class establishment has an elevator. However, that is the limit of facilities in most hotels.

Thailand has a fast developing economy and a booming tourist trade, but it is likely to be many years before a serious awareness of the needs of the disabled develops. Hotels should be carefully chosen, with the help of the Thai Hotels Association, and bookings made well in advance.

DIRECTORY

THAI HOTELS ASSOCIATION

Ratchadamnoen Klang Rd.
Tel 0-2281-9496.

FORESTRY DEPARTMENT

Phahon Yothin Rd, Bangkok.
Tel 0-2562-0760.

MAIN TAT OFFICES

Bangkok
Tel 0-2250-5500 / 1672.
www.tat.or.th

Chiang Mai
Tel 0-5324-8604/07.

Ko Samui
Tel 0-7728-8818, 0-7742-0504.

Pattaya
Tel 0-3842-8750.

Phuket
Tel 0-7621-1036.

Bungalows and coconut palms on Ko Chang

Thailand's Best Luxury Hotels

Thailand boasts a remarkable number of superb, international-class hotels. These tend to be clustered in major cities like Bangkok and Chiang Mai, and around the big resorts such as Pattaya and on Phuket. However, as tourism keeps on increasing in Thailand, fine hotels are appearing in smaller towns and resorts, and few countries in Southeast Asia can boast a similar range and quantity of first-rate accommodation. Many hotels also represent excellent value for the money when compared with similar standard hotels in Europe and the US. Some Thai hotels, such as the renowned Mandarin Oriental in Bangkok and Amanpuri Resort on Phuket have been acclaimed the best in the world. Listed here are the top luxury hotels in each region.

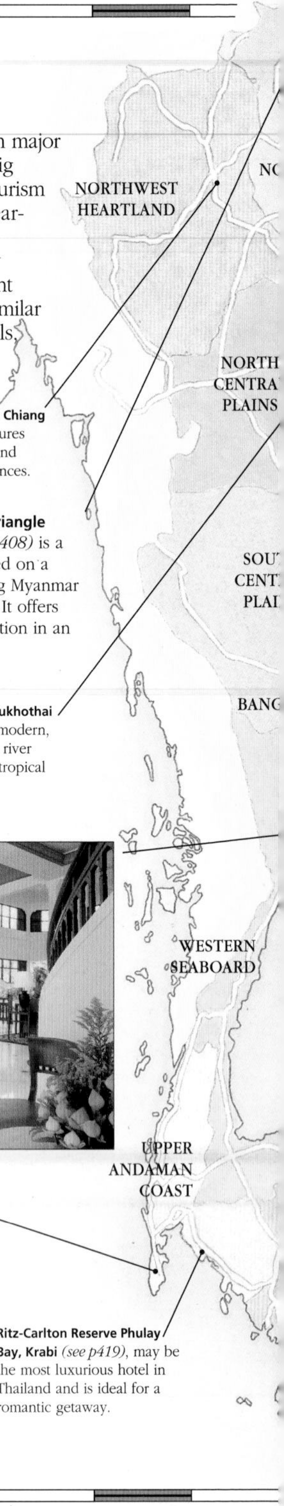

NORTHWEST HEARTLAND

NC

NORTH CENTRA PLAINS

Four Seasons Resort Chiang Mai *(see p406)* features 64 pavilion suites and 16 luxurious residences.

Anantara Golden Triangle Resort & Spa *(see p408)* is a rural retreat perched on a hillside overlooking Myanmar (Burma) and Laos. It offers stylish accommodation in an idyllic setting.

SOU CENT PLAI

Tharaburi Resort, Sukhothai *(see p404)*, offers modern, stylish rooms with river views in peaceful tropical surroundings.

BANG

Sofitel Centara Grand Resort & Villas, Hua Hin *(see p416)*, is one of the finest colonial-style hotels in the region. The hotel wing is complemented by several elegant villas with private pools.

WESTERN SEABOARD

Amanpuri Resort, Phuket (see p420), *is architecturally stunning and offers facilities of unparalleled luxury. Guests stay in spacious individual pavilions within a shady coconut grove.*

UPPER ANDAMAN COAST

Ritz-Carlton Reserve Phulay Bay, Krabi *(see p419)*, may be the most luxurious hotel in Thailand and is ideal for a romantic getaway.

Loei Palace Hotel *(see p411)* is located in the beautiful northeastern province of Loei, in the Mekong River Valley. It offers 156 spacious rooms and suites for leisure and business travelers alike. Facilities include a swimming pool, Jacuzzi, and fitness center.

MEKONG
RIVER
VALLEY

Sima Thani Hotel, Khorat
(see p410), situated out of the center of town, is spacious and attractively decorated. Amenities are first rate and include swimming pool, fitness center, sauna, two restaurants, and two bars. The five-story atrium lounge is particularly striking.

KHORAT
PLATEAU

Krung Sri River Hotel, Ayutthaya *(see p402)*, is housed in a nine-story building on the banks of the Pasak River. It boasts first-class standard rooms with marble bathrooms and luxurious furnishings. Facilities include a traditional Thai spa.

EASTERN
SEABOARD

Mandarin Oriental, Bangkok
(see p400), *has long been recognized as one of the world's great hotels. Its standards of luxury and superlative service make a stay here a memorable experience.*

Sheraton Grande Sukhumvit, Bangkok
(see p400), is renowned for its unparalleled service.

DEEP
SOUTH

Royal Cliff Beach Hotel, Pattaya (see p414), *located near Jomtien beach, is the best family resort in the area. It offers high-quality accommodations, excellent service, and a wide range of sports and leisure facilities. Most rooms have sea views.*

0 kilometers 200
0 miles 100

Choosing a Hotel

Hotels have been selected across a wide price range for facilities, good value, and location. All rooms have private bath, TV, air conditioning, and are wheelchair accessible unless otherwise indicated. Most have Internet access, and in some cases, fitness facilities may be offsite. The hotels are listed by area. For map references, *see pp148–55*.

PRICE CATEGORIES
For a standard double room per night, including tax for luxury hotels.

ⓑ Under 550 *baht*
ⓑⓑ 550–1,000 *baht*
ⓑⓑⓑ 1,000–2,500 *baht*
ⓑⓑⓑⓑ 2,500–4,500 *baht*
ⓑⓑⓑⓑⓑ Over 4,500 *baht*

BANGKOK

CHINATOWN New Empire Hotel   ⓑⓑ
572 Yaowarat Rd, Bangkok, 10100 **Tel** *0-2234-6990* **Fax** *0-2234-6997* **Rooms** *100*   **Map** *6 F2*

Just a short walk to Hua Lampong railway station and the MRT underground, the New Empire Hotel offers standard two-star accommodation in the heart of Bangkok's Chinatown. The sparse, clean, and comfortable rooms are housed in an eight-story no-frills building, but they are good value. Friendly service. **www.newempirehotel.com**

CHINATOWN River View Guesthouse   ⓑⓑ
768 Soi Panurangsri, Songwat Rd, Sanjao Tosuekong, Bangkok, 10100 **Tel** *0-2234-5429* **Rooms** *45*   **Map** *6 F2*

Tucked away in deepest Chinatown, but just five minutes from Hua Lampong railway station, this is a great place to stay if you want to experience the vibrancy of the area. Basic rooms are offset by excellent river views from a nice rooftop restaurant. Hard to find down the maze of alleyways but worth the effort. **www.riverviewbangkok.com**

CHINATOWN Woodlands Inn   ⓑⓑ
1158/5-7 Charoenkrung 32 Rd, Bangrak, Bangkok, 10500 **Tel** *0-2235-3894* **Rooms** *75*   **Map** *6 F4*

You will find clean but basic accommodation at this budget hotel with Southern Indian management. Staff speak English, Hindi, Tamil, and Thai. The restaurant serves excellent Indian food, plus Thai and international dishes. Close to the river and within walking distance of a night market. **www.woodlandsinn.org**

CHINATOWN White Orchid   ⓑⓑⓑ
409-421 Yaowarat Rd, Samphantawong, Bangkok, 10100 **Tel** *0-2226-0026* **Rooms** *199*   **Map** *6 E2*

The no-frills budget-class White Orchid is aimed squarely at tour groups. Deluxe and executive rooms are the best choice, since standard rooms are windowless. However, the location is excellent if you want to immerse yourself in the sights and sounds of Chinatown. Ten minutes from Hua Lampong railway station and underground. **www.whiteorchidbkk.com**

CHINATOWN Grand China Princess Hotel   ⓑⓑⓑⓑ
215 Yaowarat Rd, Samphantawong, Bangkok, 10100 **Tel** *0-2224-9977* **Fax** *0-2224-7999* **Rooms** *155* **Map** *6 E1*

In the heart of Chinatown, surrounded by a maze of streets and shops, this hotel is housed in the Grand China Trade Tower, at the intersection of Ratchawong and Yaowarat roads. The comfortable rooms and suites have full amenities, and there is also a revolving restaurant with panoramic views of the city. **www.grandchina.com**

CHINATOWN Shanghai Mansion   ⓑⓑⓑⓑ
479-481 Yaowarat Rd, Samphantawong, Bangkok, 10100 **Tel** *0-2221-2121* **Rooms** *76*   **Map** *6 E1/2*

Designed with care and attention to detail, this charming four-star hotel celebrates the colors and romance of Chinatown. The decor is outstanding and a showcase for traditional Chinese design. Lavish accommodation and good service. Indulge yourself at the Yin Yang Spa or enjoy a drink in the Tea Room. **www.shanghaimansion.com**

DOWNTOWN Soi 1 Guesthouse   ⓑ
220/12 Soi 1, Sukhumvit Rd, Bangkok, 10110 **Tel** *0-2655-0604* **Rooms** *24*   **Map** *8 F1*

This popular hostel on a quiet, well-lit side street has air-conditioned dormitories, 24-hour access lounge and games room, Wi-Fi, DVD movies, and satellite TV. On the downside, rooms are somewhat cramped, and the ensuite bathrooms have showers only. Toilets are shared. Staff are friendly and knowledgeable. **www.soi1guesthouse.com**

DOWNTOWN A One Inn   ⓑⓑ
25/13-15 Soi Kasasun 1, Rama 1 Rd, Bangkok, 10330 **Tel** *0-2215-3029* **Fax** *0-2216-4771* **Rooms** *25*   **Map** *7 C1*

Tucked away down a quiet side street, the A One Inn is one of the few cheap guesthouses in the city center. It may be a little rough around the edges, but it is hard to beat its price and convenience. Rooms have TV, Internet, hot showers, and air-conditioning. Weekly and monthly rates are available. **www.aoneinn.com**

DOWNTOWN Bangkok Centre Sukhumvit 25   ⓑⓑⓑ
2 Soi 25, Sukhumvit Rd, Wattana, Bangkok, 10110 **Tel** *0-2259-6908* **Rooms** *60*

This upmarket youth hostel has clean dormitories and private rooms with cable TV, air-conditioning, fridges, and private bathrooms. Breakfast is included. The hostel adjoins a large courtyard with a Thai restaurant and an Internet café. Non-members of Hostel International can join on the spot to enjoy discounted rates.

Key to Symbols *see back cover flap*

DOWNTOWN Le Fenix Sukhumvit

 ⓑⓑⓑ

33/33 Soi 11, Sukhumvit Rd, Klong Toey Nua, Wattana, Bangkok, 10110 **Tel** *0-2305-4000* **Rooms** *147*

Le Fenix is aimed at the hip crowds who flock to Bangkok for its nightclub scene. The hotel opts for minimalist design, clean lines, atmospheric lighting, and retro art. Close to the equally cool Q Bar and Bed Supper Club. All rooms have air-conditioning, Wi-Fi and a view over the city. **www.lefenix-sukhumvit.com**

DOWNTOWN S2S Boutique Resort

ⓑⓑⓑ

21/1 Soi Ratchatapan, Ratchaprarop Rd, Makkasan, Bangkok, 10400 **Tel** *0-2642-4646* **Fax** *0-2245-4386* **Rooms** *38*

The rooms at this contemporary hotel with Thai-style interiors and friendly service look out onto a well-tended garden. Amenities include king-size beds, Wi-Fi, TV, and Thai cooking classes. Monthly and daily room rates are available. Located next to a large public park, ideal for a morning walk or jogging. **www.moeleng-bangkok-resort.com**

DOWNTOWN Salil Hotel

ⓑⓑⓑ

50/1 Soi 8, Sukhumvit Rd, Klong Toey, Bangkok, 10110 **Tel** *0-2253-2474* **Fax** *0-2253-2478* **Rooms** *27*

This clean, comfortable hotel in Bangkok's entertainment district offers good service from helpful staff. The small but nicely decorated rooms have good amenities, including LCD TV, DVD player, satellite TV, in-room movies, and Wi-Fi. The restaurant serves Thai and international food. Close to Nana BTS Skytrain station. **www.salilhotel.com**

DOWNTOWN The Davis Bangkok

ⓑⓑⓑⓑ

88 Soi 24, Sukhumvit Rd, Klongton, Klong Toey, Bangkok, 10110 **Tel** *0-2260-8000* **Fax** *0-2260-8100* **Rooms** *247*

A boutique feel and excellent attention to detail are the trademarks at this large but stylish inner-city sanctuary. Exquisite furnishings and themed designs give every room a unique character. The highlight is Baan Davis, a collection of ten stunning traditional Thai pavilions set in a tropical garden. Facilities include a spa. **www.davisbangkok.net**

DOWNTOWN The Dream Hotel

ⓑⓑⓑⓑ

10 Sukhumvit Soi 15, Klong Toey, Bangkok, 10110 **Tel** *0-2254-8500* **Fax** *0-2254-8534* **Rooms** *195*

Billing itself as "hautel couture," the Dream Hotel delivers a five-star experience like no other. Its clientele is young, hip, and wealthy. Rooms offer the ultimate in chic designer style, with cool blue lighting and pre-loaded iPod audio players. Chill out in the Flava Lounge and the Avatar Spa. **www.dreambkk.com**

DOWNTOWN Luxx Hotel

ⓑⓑⓑⓑ

6/11 Decho Rd, Bangrak, Bangkok, 10500 **Tel** *0-2635-8800* **Fax** *0-2635-8088* **Rooms** *13* **Map** *7 B4*

The Luxx is one of Bangkok's smallest hotels. The converted Chinese shop-house has been transformed into sophisticated designer lodgings, with plenty of chrome and wood. Suites feature a wooden bathtub, LCD TV, DVD player, iPod station, and views of the courtyard. Free Wi-Fi throughout. **www.staywithluxx.com**

DOWNTOWN Pullman Bangkok King Power

ⓑⓑⓑⓑ

8/2 Rangnam Rd, Thanon-Phayathai, Bangkok, 10400 **Tel** *0-2680-9999* **Fax** *0-2680-9998* **Rooms** *386* **Map** *4 E4*

The Pullman Bangkok King Power was the first of the established Accor brand to open in Asia. This sleek, chic hotel features contemporary Thai-style decor. Fully IT-wired rooms include a workstation and flat-screen TV. It is close to the Phaya Thai Skytrain station. **www.pullmanbangkokkingpower.com**

DOWNTOWN Swiss Lodge

ⓑⓑⓑⓑ

3 Convent Rd, Silom, Bangrak, Bangkok, 10500 **Tel** *0-2233-5345* **Fax** *0-2236-9425* **Rooms** *46* **Map** *7 C4*

In a quiet enclave of Bangkok's entertainment district, this hotel offers comfortable rooms with the latest technology. Exceptional service ensures many returning guests. The hotel's bijou restaurant, Three-on-Convent, serves Californian cuisine and excellent wines. A short walk from Sala Daeng Skytrain and Silom underground. **www.swisslodge.com**

DOWNTOWN VIE Hotel Bangkok

ⓑⓑⓑⓑ

117–39 Phaya Thai Rd, Ratchathewi, Bangkok, 10400 **Tel** *0-2309-3939* **Fax** *0-2309-3838* **Rooms** *154* **Map** *4 D5*

VIE Hotel Bangkok offers upscale accommodation and excellent service at affordable prices. This sleek hotel provides luxurious rooms and suites, a superb restaurant, a rooftop pool, and a spa. Located steps away from the Ratchathewi Skytrain station and Siam Paragon shopping mall. **www.viehotelbangkok.com**

DOWNTOWN Dusit Thani

ⓑⓑⓑⓑⓑ

946 Rama IV Rd, Bangkok, 10500 **Tel** *0-2200-9000* **Fax** *0-2236-6400* **Rooms** *517* **Map** *8 D4*

At the flagship hotel of Thailand's most respected hotel brand, elegant rooms with Thai decor range from superior to super-elegant Thai Heritage Suites. Facilities include the Devarana Spa, a golf driving range, swimming pool, fitness center, and eight restaurants. Home to the Cordon Bleu Dusit Academy of World Cuisine. **www.dusit.com**

DOWNTOWN The Eugenia

ⓑⓑⓑⓑⓑ

267 Soi 31, Sukhumvit Rd, Wattana, Bangkok, 10110 **Tel** *0-2259-9017* **Fax** *0-2259-9010* **Rooms** *12*

Step back in time at this unique hotel, which offers 12 suites in a late 19th-century colonial-style house. The decor includes antiques, four-poster beds, and large copper bathtubs. The hotel's collection of cars used for airport transfers and exploration of Bangkok include vintage Jaguars and Mercedes Benz. **www.theeugenia.com**

DOWNTOWN Le Méridien Plaza Athénée

ⓑⓑⓑⓑⓑ

10 Wireless Rd, Bangkok, 10330 **Tel** *0-2650-8800* **Fax** *0-2650-8500* **Rooms** *378* **Map** *8 E2*

Located in Bangkok's central business and diplomatic district, the Méridien Plaza Athénée is a short walk from the Skytrain. The hotel is a gleaming glass tower and an icon of the city skyline. Luxurious accommodation, award-winning restaurants, and the finest traditional Thai hospitality await discerning guests. **www.starwoodhotels.com**

DOWNTOWN Mandarin Oriental
48 Oriental Avenue, Bangkok, 10500 **Tel** *0-2659-9000* **Fax** *0-2659-9284* **Rooms** *393*   **Map** *6 F4*

The Mandarin Oriental's timeless elegance and superior level of service have secured its reputation as one of the finest hotels in the world. Located beside the Chao Phraya River, the hotel has been receiving dignitaries and distinguished guests for more than 130 years. Exceptional restaurants and bars complete the experience. **www.mandarinoriental.com**

DOWNTOWN Sheraton Grande Sukhumvit
250 Sukhumvit Rd, Bangkok, 10110 **Tel** *0-2649-8888* **Fax** *0-2649-8000* **Rooms** *420*

The Sheraton Grande Sukhumvit is regarded as one of the finest business hotels in Asia. It includes award-winning restaurants, a jazz lounge, and a chic night venue. Located in the heart of Bangkok, with a direct link from the lobby to Asoke Skytrain station, it provides easy access to the city's main sights. **www.sheratongrandesukhumvit.com**

DOWNTOWN Siam @ Siam Design Hotel & Spa
865 Rama 1 Rd, Wang Mai, Patumwan, Bangkok, 10330 **Tel** *0-2217-3000* **Fax** *0-2217-3030* **Rooms** *203*   **Map** *7 A1*

Dramatic interiors define the Siam @ Siam. Fun and funky, the spacious rooms feature creative decor and the ultimate in comfortable living. As well as a trendy bar, restaurant, and spa, this elegant hotel has easy access to major entertainment areas and shopping centers. Close to the National Stadium Skytrain station. **www.siamatsiam.com**

DOWNTOWN Sofitel Silom
188 Silom Rd, Bangrak, Bangkok, 10500 **Tel** *0-2238-1991* **Fax** *0-2238-1992* **Rooms** *469*   **Map** *7 B4*

Five-star luxury in the heart of Bangkok. Spacious lodgings feature contemporary Thai design, wooden floors, and floor-to-ceiling windows. Enjoy panoramic views and fine dining at the V9 wine bar on the 37th floor *(see p430)*, or unwind in the fitness center or spa. Easy access to the Skytrain and the underground. **www.sofitel.com**

DOWNTOWN The Sukhothai
13/3 South Sathorn Rd, Bangkok, 10120 **Tel** *0-2344-8888* **Fax** *0-2344-8899* **Rooms** *210*   **Map** *8 D4*

Renowned for its style and sophistication, the Sukhothai is one of Bangkok's finest hotels. Rooms are decorated to create a unique Thai ambience, with exquisite furnishings, silk fabrics, antiques, and teakwood floors. Fabulous dining includes Italian and Thai options. Spa, saunas, and squash and tennis courts are available. **www.sukhothai.com**

DOWNTOWN Swissôtel Nai Lert Park
2 Wireless Rd, Pathumwan, Bangkok, 10330 **Tel** *0-2253-0123* **Fax** *0-2253-6509* **Rooms** *338*   **Map** *8 E1*

Understated and elegant interior decor, luxurious rooms, fine dining, and the funky Syn Bar make the five-star Nai Lert a popular choice for discerning travelers. Guests on the Executive Club floor enjoy complimentary breakfast, tea, and cocktails in the Executive Club Lounge. **www.swissotel.com**

DUSIT Bangkok International Youth Hostel
25/14 Phitsanoluk Rd, Dusit, Bangkok, 10300 **Tel** *0-2628-7413* **Fax** *0-2628-7416* **Rooms** *67*   **Map** *2 F2*

The IYH is a standard hostel option for serious budget travelers. It offers double rooms, as well as eight-bed dormitories. A library and café, Internet, and laundry service are also available, as is a travel agency service. Located a short walk from the Chao Phraya River and a host of historic sites. **www.tyha.org**

DUSIT Hotel De' Moc
78 Prajatipatai Rd, Pra-Nakorn, Bangkok, 10200 **Tel** *0-2282-2831* **Fax** *0-2280-1299* **Rooms** *100*   **Map** *2 E4*

Located in the heart of Rattanakosin Island's historic district, the De' Moc offers three-star accommodation and a pleasant atmosphere. Clean, spacious rooms, and facilities such as Wi-Fi, bicycle hire, and a free *tuk-tuk* service to nearby Khao San Road (although the area is only a ten-minute walk away) are available. **www.hoteldemoc.com**

DUSIT New World City Hotel
2 Samsen Rd, Banglamphu, Pranakorn, Bangkok, 10200 **Tel** *0-2281-5596* **Fax** *0-2282-5614* **Rooms** *172*   **Map** *2 D3*

Geared up for both business and leisure travelers, this hotel provides excellent value, tidy rooms, and good facilities in a quiet but convenient location. There are plenty of bars, restaurants, and banks in the area. The Grand Palace and Khao San Road are within easy walking distance. **www.newworldlodge.com**

DUSIT Swana Bangkok Hotel
332 Visuttikasat Rd, Bangkok, 10200 **Tel** *0-2282-8899* **Fax** *0-2281-7816* **Rooms** *55*   **Map** *2 E3*

The Swana is a great choice for visitors exploring the historic district. This boutique-style hotel is nicely furnished and decorated in a contemporary Thai design. The Anda Café serves Thai and international favorites for breakfast, lunch, and dinner. Good security and 24-hour Internet access complete the picture. **www.swanabangkok.com**

OLD CITY D&D Inn
68-70 Khao San Rd, Bangkok, 10200 **Tel** *0-2629-0526* **Fax** *0-2629-0529* **Rooms** *230*   **Map** *2 D4*

This affordable Khao San Road favorite offers good, clean, air-conditioned rooms. It is the largest guesthouse in the area and extremely popular, so booking ahead is advised. There is an adjoining shopping plaza with specialty shops and boutiques on the first floor, and a pool and bar on the top floor. Pleasant garden. **www.khaosanby.com**

OLD CITY New Siam II Guesthouse
50 Trok Rong Mai, Phra Ahtit Rd, Bangkok, 10200 **Tel** *0-2282-2795* **Fax** *0-2629-0303* **Rooms** *130*   **Map** *2 D3*

Close to many of Bangkok's attractions, including the ever-popular Khao San Road, this tidy hotel offers spacious, well-kept rooms with full amenities. Twin rooms, doubles, and triples are available, all with ensuite bathrooms, cable TV, and keycard lock. Excellent value, and one of the best guesthouses in the area. **www.newsiam.net**

Key to Price Guide *see p398* **Key to Symbols** *see back cover flap*

OLD CITY Phra Athit Mansion Inn

22 Phra Athit Rd, Chanasongkram, Bangkok, 10200 **Tel** *0-2280-0744* **Fax** *0-2280-0742* **Rooms** *38*   **Map** *2 D3*

The apartment-style Phra Athit Mansion Inn is close to the Phra Athit Chao Phraya ferry and Bangkok's historic sites. It is the ideal base for exploring the Old City and the waterways, providing better-than-average rooms with air-conditioning, TV, hot water, and minibar. The friendly staff are knowledgeable about the area.

OLD CITY Sawasdee Banglumpoo Inn

162 Khao San Rd, Banglamphu, Bangkok, 10200 **Tel** *0-2282-3748* **Fax** *0-2282-6655* **Rooms** *52*   **Map** *2 D4*

One in a chain of well-managed budget hotels, the Sawasdee is quiet and clean, with friendly staff. It is a good alternative to the usual cheap and cheerless backpacker hotels in the Khao San Road area. Nicely decorated rooms have private bathrooms and cable TV. There is also 24-hour security and room service. **www.sawasdee-hotels.com**

OLD CITY Shanti Lodge

Soi 16, 37 Sri Ayutthaya Rd, Si Sou Tewet, Bangkok, 10300 **Tel** *0-2281-2497* **Rooms** *45*   **Map** *2 E2*

Just behind the National Library and within walking distance of Khao San Road, the popular Shanti Lodge offers nicely furnished, comfortable rooms. On the downside, bathrooms are shared. A bar, a good vegetarian restaurant, and a handicrafts store are located downstairs. Close to an excellent wet market. **www.shantilodge.com**

OLD CITY Baan Chantra

120/1 Samsen Rd, Bangkok, 10200 **Tel** *&* **Fax** *0-2628-6988* **Rooms** *7*   **Map** *2 D3*

Lovingly restored and furnished, this 1930s wooden house comes with lots of character and period decor. Rooms have private bathrooms. The library is well stocked and has complimentary Internet access. Within walking distance of the Temple of the Emerald Buddha, the Grand Palace, and other landmarks. **www.baanchantra.com**

OLD CITY Boonsiri Place

55 Burangsart Rd, Pranakorn, Bangkok, 10200 **Tel** *0-2622-2189* **Fax** *0-2622-1414* **Rooms** *48*   **Map** *2 D4*

This contemporary boutique hotel is making efforts to implement an environmental and social policy. All rooms use low-energy light bulbs, and leftover food is regularly given to stray animals. Each room is decorated with pictures painted by physically challenged artists. **www.boonsiriplace.com**

OLD CITY Trang Hotel

99 Visut-Kasat Rd, Banglampoo, Bangkok, 10200 **Tel** *0-2281-1402* **Fax** *0-2280-3610* **Rooms** *180*   **Map** *2 D4*

A family-run hotel close to Khao San Road and other famous landmarks, including Rattanakosin Island, the Grand Palace, and the Thai National Museum. Rooms have air-conditioning, wall-to-wall carpet, and ensuite bathrooms. There is also a delightful tropical garden, a coffee shop, and a Cantonese restaurant. **www.tranghotelbangkok.com**

OLD CITY Royal Princess

269 Larn Luang, Pomprab, Bangkok, 10100 **Tel** *0-2281-3088* **Fax** *0-2280-1314* **Rooms** *167*   **Map** *2 D4*

Four-star hotel in the historic district of Rattanakosin Island, close to the Grand Palace and the Temple of the Emerald Buddha. All rooms, from the Standard Deluxe up to the Princess Suite, are equipped with Internet connection and private balconies. Japanese, Chinese, Thai, and Italian restaurants. **www.dusit.com**

THON BURI Royal River Hotel

219 Soi Charansanitwong 66/1,Charansanitwong Rd, Bangplad, Bangkok, 10700 **Tel** *0-2422-9222* **Rooms** *436*

Popular with business and leisure travelers, the 21-story Royal River provides sweeping views of the Bangkok skyline. There are four room categories (Superior, Deluxe, Executive Suite, and Deluxe Suite) and a range of good restaurants and bars. The location allows for easy access to the historic area of the city by boat. **www.royalriverhotel.com**

THON BURI Anantara Bangkok Riverside Resort & Spa

257 Charoennakorn Rd, Samrae, Thon Buri, Bangkok, 10600 **Tel** *0-2476-0022* **Fax** *0-2476-1120* **Rooms** *413*

This stunning resort features classic Thai architecture in expansive tropical gardens and great river views. On-site restaurants include Trader Vic's *(see p431)*. A complimentary shuttle boat service to Saphan Taksin Skytrain station and dining river cruises on a rice barge can be arranged at reception. **http://bangkok-riverside.anantara.com**

THON BURI Millenium Hilton Bangkok

123 Charoennakorn Rd, Klongsan, Thon Buri, Bangkok, 10600 **Tel** *0-2442-2000* **Rooms** *543*   **Map** *6 F4*

Each of the five-star suites at the Millennium Hilton has panoramic views, a living room, high-speed Internet, two LCD TVs, Jacuzzi, and rain shower. An infinity pool and beach deck, sauna, gym, and fine dining are also on offer, as is a free shuttle boat to Saphan Taksin Skytrain station every 20 minutes. **www.bangkok.hilton.com**

THON BURI The Peninsula

333 Charoennakorn Rd, Klongsan, Bangkok, 10600 **Tel** *0-2861-2888* **Fax** *0-2861-1112* **Rooms** *370*   **Map** *6 F5*

Regarded as one of Bangkok's finest hotels, the Peninsula has been included in the *Condé Nast Traveler* Gold List; it has been voted Best Bangkok Hotel four times by readers of *Travel + Leisure* magazine. Located on the banks of the Chao Phraya River, it offers splendid views from every room. **www.bangkok.peninsula.com**

FARTHER AFIELD 13 Coins Airport Grand Resort Hotel

37, 37-1-3, Rama 9, Soi 57 Visetsuk 3, Suanluang, Bangkok, 10250 **Tel** *0-2374-9913* **Fax** *0-2374-2986* **Rooms** *80*

Just off the highway between Suvarnabhumi Airport and downtown, 13 Coins offers three-star accommodation complete with swimming pool, fishing pond, and a Thai boxing gym. Ideal for airport stopovers, the hotel offers a special 24-hour deal: check in at 11pm and check out at 11pm the next night. **www.13coinsairportgrandresort.hostel.com**

FARTHER AFIELD Bansabai Lad Phrao

8/137 Moo 3, Soi Sahakon 15, Lad Phrao 71, Lad Phrao Rd, Bangkok, 10230 **Tel** *0-2539-0150* **Rooms** *100*

Superior hostel accommodation, with spacious dorms and rooms with private balconies, not to mention a garden and pool. The Bansabai is a little out of the way but easily accessible by underground. Massage and Thai cookery classes are available. Special deals are offered to one-night airport-stopover travelers. **www.bansabaihostel.com**

FARTHER AFIELD KT Guesthouse

12 Soi Inthamara 4, Suttisarn Rd, Din Daeng, Bangkok, 10400 **Tel** *0-2276-3462* **Fax** *0-2277-0736* **Rooms** *35*

Basic, but clean and well-maintained, accommodation on the outskirts of the city center. The KT has large and airy rooms, a terraced garden, and a good restaurant. Very helpful and friendly staff make this a popular hotel with budget travelers who want to be away from downtown's hustle and bustle. **www.ktguesthouse.com**

FARTHER AFIELD Convenient Resort

9-11 Soi 38 Lat Krabang, Bangkok, 10520 **Tel** *0-2327-4118* **Fax** *0-2327-4004* **Rooms** *100*

This aptly named non-smoking hotel provides comfortable three-star accommodation just five minutes away from Suvarnabhumi International Airport and is a great choice for quick stopovers. Thai massage is offered for weary travelers, and the restaurant/bar is the perfect place to unwind. Countryside views. **www.convenientresort.com**

FARTHER AFIELD Queen's Garden Resort

44 Soi 7 Lat Krabang, Bangkok, 10540 **Tel** *0-2734-4540* **Fax** *0-2734-4542* **Rooms** *129*

An excellent, cheap, and comfortable hotel close to Suvarnabhumi International Airport, this is the ideal place to relax for a few hours between flights. The 24-hour reception is always ready to serve. Guests can enjoy a massage to ease aching muscles before taking their next flight. Wireless Internet is available. **www.queensgardenresort.net**

FARTHER AFIELD Amari Don Muang Airport Hotel

333 Chert Wudthakas Rd, Bangkok, 10210 **Tel** *0-2566-1020* **Fax** *0-2566-1941* **Rooms** *423*

Don Muang Airport remains open for the majority of domestic flights, so this deluxe hotel is still a good choice if you have time to kill between transfers to Suvarnabhumi International Airport. The Amari offers a high standard of accommodation at an affordable price, along with good restaurants and bars. **www.amari.com**

FARTHER AFIELD Novotel Suvarnabhumi Airport Hotel

Moo 1, Nongprue, Bang Phli, Samutprakarn, Bangkok, 10540 **Tel** *0-2131-1111* **Rooms** *612*

Nodding off in the airport lounge only adds to the exhaustion of international travel. Ten minutes' walk from the main terminal, the Novotel Suvarnabhumi Airport Hotel is the perfect place to recharge your batteries. Relax in the luxurious spa, restaurants, and bars, or sleep in comfort in the plush rooms. **www.novotel.com**

SOUTH CENTRAL PLAINS

AYUTTHAYA Prom Tong Mansion

23 Pathon Soi 19, Pathon Rd (Dechawut Rd), T Pratuchai, Ayutthaya **Tel** *08-9165-6297* **Rooms** *18*

This small hotel is one of Ayutthaya's best budget options. The rooms are utilitarian, but the service is top notch. Centrally located near Wat Maha That and the night market, Prom Tong Mansion is an excellent base for exploring Ayutthaya and other historic sites nearby. A 5 percent fee is charged for card payments. **www.promtong.com**

AYUTTHAYA Bann Kun Pra

48 U Thong Rd, Ayutthaya **Tel** *0-3524-1978* **Rooms** *15*

With an excellent location by the river (a few rooms have river views), this attractively decorated teak house represents a stylish option at backpacker prices. A newer building has a few air-conditioned rooms, and there is also a dormitory on the top floor, a restaurant *(see p433)*, Internet access, and bicycle rental. **www.bannkunpra.com**

AYUTTHAYA Kantary Hotel Ayutthaya

168 Moo 1, Rojana Rd, Tambol Tanu, Amphur U-Thai, Ayutthaya **Tel** *0-3533-7177* **Fax** *0-3533-7178* **Rooms** *193*

Centrally located for Ayutthaya's historic sites, this stylish hotel is the most modern in the city. While not to the same standard as Bangkok's luxury hotels, the Kantary offers excellent value and comfort, and is an ideal base for exploring the Southern Plains. **www.kantarycollection.com**

AYUTTHAYA Krung Sri River Hotel

27/2 Moo 11 Rojana Rd, Ayutthaya **Tel** *0-3524-4333* **Fax** *0-3524-3777* **Rooms** *204*

This nine-story hotel, which opened in the mid-1990s and sits on the banks of the Pasak River, makes a comfortable base from which to explore the ancient ruins of Ayutthaya. All rooms have satellite TV, and the hotel operates its own boat for dinner cruises. **www.krungsririver.com**

KANCHANABURI Apple's Guest House

52 Soi Rongheeboay, Kanchanaburi **Tel** *0-3451-2017* **Fax** *0-3451-4958* **Rooms** *20*

Though the rooms here are sparsely furnished, they are immaculately clean, and service is as attentive as one might expect in a top resort. Add to that the popular cookery classes, laundry, and massage service, and it is not surprising this place is often full. It is best to make a booking through the website. **www.applesguesthouse.com**

Key to Price Guide *see p398* **Key to Symbols** *see back cover flap*

KANCHANABURI Baan Suan Fon 🏨🏊🛏 ⓑⓑ

20/3 Moo 8 Tambon Kaengsieng, Amphur Muang, Kanchanaburi **Tel** *0-3462-4587* **Rooms** *100*

This remote and lovely hotel is situated near the River Kwai. Guests can choose from rooms in the main house, cabins, or rafts floating on the river. This is ideal for people who love to be in or near the water for swimming, canoeing, or adventure sports. Excellent views of the mountains and countryside. **www.baansuanfon.com**

KANCHANABURI Sam's House 🏊🏨🛏 ⓑⓑ

14/2 Moo 1, Thamakarm, Kanchanaburi **Tel** *0-3451-5956* **Rooms** *35*

Sam's House offers a great variety of rooms, from airy bamboo huts to wooden or stone bungalows and a floating raft house, set around a lush garden. The most appealing are probably the wooden bungalows, which are set on stilts and have ensuite bathrooms and balconies overlooking the garden. **www.samsguesthouse.com**

KANCHANABURI Royal River Kwai Resort & Spa 🏨🏊🛏🛋🆔 ⓑⓑⓑ

88 Kanchanaburi-Saiyok Rd, Kanchanaburi **Tel** *0-3465-3297* **Rooms** *89*

Probably the prettiest of Kanchanaburi's upmarket resorts, this low-rise place offers smartly furnished rooms. Some have balconies, and all overlook an attractive garden; there's also an inviting pool surrounded by wood decking. The Rantee Spa offers relaxing treatments to guests. **www.royalriverkwairesort.com**

KANCHANABURI Felix River Kwai Resort 📶🏨🏊🛋🛏🛋🆔 ⓑⓑⓑⓑ

9/1 Moo 3, Thamakham, Kanchanaburi **Tel** *0-3455-1000-23* **Rooms** *255*

Located on the banks of the Khwae Yai River, this place is attractively laid out, with landscaped gardens and two pools. The rooms have all the modern comforts; those with views command higher prices. The Felix is only a short walk to the famous railway bridge, but a couple of kilometers to the center of town. **www.felixriverkwai.co.th**

LOPBURI Nett Hotel 🛋🛏 ⓑ

17/1-2 Soi 2, Ratchadamnoen Rd, Lopburi **Tel** *0-3641-1738* **Rooms** *29*

In addition to offering amazingly affordable daily rates, the Nett Hotel is also the best option for those looking for somewhere central in Lopburi from which to explore the ruins. There is a choice of fanned or air-conditioned rooms, and the latter also have TV, hot water, and a fridge, making them excellent value for money.

LOPBURI Lopburi Inn 📶🏨🛏🆔 ⓑⓑ

28/9 Narai Maharat Rd, Lopburi **Tel** *0-3641-2609* **Rooms** *133*

Few tourists stay overnight in Lopburi, so accommodation options are limited here. This hotel is located a few kilometers out of town, but it is the most comfortable place around, promising a good night's rest after walking around Lopburi's sights, which are scattered around the town center. **www.lopburiinnhotel.com**

SANGKHLA BURI P Guest House 🛋🏨🛏 ⓑⓑ

81/2 Moo 1, Nonglu, Sangkhla Buri **Tel** *0-3459-5061* **Rooms** *24*

For adventurous types who want to explore the countryside west of Kanchanaburi, this tranquil lakeside resort in the border town of Sangkhla Buri is a great base. Rustic rooms fashioned from smooth stones are furnished with chunky chairs and beds, and there is an atmospheric restaurant on site. **www.p-guesthouse.com**

NORTH CENTRAL PLAINS

KAMPHAENG PHET Three J Guest House 🛋🏨🛏 ⓑ

79 Rajwithee Rd, Kamphaeng Phet **Tel** *0-5571-3129* **Rooms** *10*

This family-run place is typical of good-value guesthouses in rural Thailand. There are several bungalows, some with fans and others with air-conditioning, all set in a rock garden. The owners will go out of their way to help guests, and bicycle or motorbike hire can be arranged. **www.threejguesthouse.com**

KAMPHAENG PHET Phet Hotel 📶🏨🛏 ⓑⓑ

189 Bumrungrat Rd, Kamphaeng Phet **Tel** *0-5571-2810* **Rooms** *215*

This simple but well-maintained hotel offers excellent value in Kamphaeng Phet. All rooms are a decent size and have air-conditioning; some also have good views over town. There is a small swimming pool and a restaurant on site, plus Internet access and Wi-Fi compatibility. **www.phethotel.com**

MAE SOT Ban Thai Guest House 🛋🛏 ⓑⓑ

740/1 Inthakhiri Rd, Mae Sot **Tel** *0-5553-1590* **Rooms** *18*

It is a pleasant surprise to find such a well-organized guesthouse in such a remote part of the country. The attractively furnished rooms are set in a peaceful garden and have cable TV and free Wi-Fi, so this is a popular home-from-home for locally based NGO workers. There is also bicycle rental and cookery classes. **www.banthaithabo.com**

MAE SOT Centara Mae Sot Hill Hotel 📶🏨🏊🛏🆔 ⓑⓑⓑ

100 Asia Highway, Mae Sot **Tel** *0-5553-2601-8* **Fax** *0-5553-2600* **Rooms** *120*

The best hotel in Mae Sot lies on the highway that bypasses the town, about 10 minutes from the city center. Rooms are a good size, all with air-conditioning, TV, and other amenities. On-site facilities include a pool, tennis courts, a good restaurant, a ballroom, and a disco. **www.centarahotelsresorts.com**

PHITSANULOK Pailyn Hotel

38 Baroma Trailokanart Rd, Phitsanulok **Tel** *0-5525-2411* **Rooms** *247*

This big hotel is a bit impersonal, but the large rooms are good value, all with air-conditioning and ensuite bathrooms. Rooms on the upper floors have balconies and good views of the river. Staff are friendly and helpful, and there are two restaurants and frequent live music in the bar.

PHITSANULOK The Grand Riverside Hotel

59 Praroung Rd, Muang, Phitsanulok **Tel** *0-5524-8333* **Fax** *0-5521-6420* **Rooms** *79*

This hotel offers clean, comfortable rooms and a good location near the center of town. It is an ideal base from which to explore the surrounding historical sites at Kamphaeng Phet and Sukhothai. There is no pool or gym, but guests can use these facilities at the hotel's sister resorts in Phitsanulok. **www.tgrhotel.com**

SUKHOTHAI Cocoon House

86/1 Singhawat Rd, Sukhothai **Tel** *0-5562-2157* **Rooms** *5*

Located in New Sukhothai, this tiny place has just a handful of rooms, but all are attractively decorated and set in a lush garden. There is a choice of fans or air-conditioning, and ensuite or shared bathrooms. Cocoon House sits behind the Dream Café *(see p434)*, probably Sukhothai's best restaurant.

SUKHOTHAI Lotus Village

170 Ratchathani Rd, Sukhothai **Tel** *0-5562-1484* **Rooms** *20*

The main attraction here, as the name suggests, is the beautiful garden with lotus ponds and teak rooms on stilts that blend into the background. There is a variety of rooms, from smallish ones with fans and shared bathrooms to huge, air-conditioned bungalows. An on-site spa is also available. **www.lotus-village.com**

SUKHOTHAI Orchid Hibiscus Guest House

407/2 Route 1272, Sukhothai **Tel** *0-5563-3284* **Rooms** *16*

This, one of Sukhothai's longest-standing guesthouses, is conveniently located near the Old City for sightseeing. It has some well-appointed rooms set around a pool and surrounded by tropical greenery, plus a few big lodgings that are ideal for families. **www.orchidhibiscus-guesthouse.com**

SUKHOTHAI Tharaburi Resort

113 Srisomboon Rd, Sukhothai **Tel** *0-5569-7132* **Rooms** *20*

This swish boutique resort at the edge of the Old City is by far Sukhothai's smartest place to stay, with just a handful of deluxe rooms and suites. Attention to detail is impressive, and facilities include a massage service, cookery classes, and bicycles for exploring the ruins of Sukhothai Historical Park. **www.tharaburiresort.com**

TAK Mae Ping Hotel

231 Mahattai Bamroong, Tak **Tel** *0-5551-1807* **Rooms** *37*

If you want an authentic Thai experience while in Tak, check into this cheap hotel, where there are no frills at all – just basic, small bedrooms, most with fans, none with hot water. The location couldn't be better, though: the Mae Ping is in the heart of town, close to the market and the river, and within walking distance of all of Tak's sights.

TAK Viang Tak Riverside

236 Chompol Rd, Tak **Tel** *0-5551-2507* **Rooms** *144*

The Viang Tak Riverside is the newer and smarter of two hotels in town run by the same company, offering comfortable, carpeted rooms with good river views from its eight floors. There is a pool and Internet access, and in the evening, live bands play in the music hall. **www.viangtakriverside.com**

UMPHANG Umphang Country Hut

Umphang–Palata Rd **Tel** *0-5556-1079* **Rooms** *24*

Most people stay here on their way to and from the splendid Thi Lo Su waterfall, often as part of a package that includes two days' rafting on the river and one night's camping near the falls. The location is pretty enough, and rooms are clean, if a little lacking in character. **www.umphangcountryhut.com**

NORTHWEST HEARTLAND

CHIANG DAO Chiang Dao Hill Resort

28 Moo 6 Chiang Mai-Fang Rd, Tambon Pingkong, Amphur Chiang Dao, 50170 **Tel** *0-5323-2434* **Rooms** *52*

Situated in the Mae Rim Valley, surrounded by tropical jungle, the wooden chalets, cabins, and rooms at this resort may be a bit worn, but the isolated location and beautiful setting are certainly appealing. Activities include fishing, elephant riding, trekking, and organized visits to hill-tribe villages. **www.chiangdaohillresort.com**

CHIANG MAI Daret's Guest House

4/5 Chaiyaphum Rd, Amphur Muang, Chiang Mai, 50300 **Tel** *0-5323-5440* **Fax** *0-5325-2292* **Rooms** *20*

This long-established guesthouse in the central Tha Phae Gate area is a popular backpacker hangout and a good source of information on treks and tours. The downside is that it gets very noisy. The on-site eatery serves up cheap, tasty Thai fare and is renowned for its fresh fruit juices.

Key to Price Guide *see p398* **Key to Symbols** *see back cover flap*

CHIANG MAI Hollanda Montri House ⓑ

365 Charoenrat Rd, Amphur Muang, Chiang Mai, 50000 **Tel** *0-5324-2450* **Rooms** *16*

This guesthouse is a *tuk-tuk* ride from the center, but the spotless rooms with private bathrooms and garden terrace overlooking the Ping River make up for the slightly out-of-the-way location. There is Internet access, and the staff can coordinate treks, tours, and cooking classes. Not all rooms have air-conditioning. **www.hollandamontri.com**

CHIANG MAI Pagoda Inn ⓑ

49 Chang Moi Rd, Chiang Mai, 50100 **Tel** *0-5323-3290* **Rooms** *28*

Next door to the 600-year-old golden temple of Wat Cham Phu, this elegant, intimate guesthouse is one of Chang Mai's hidden gems. Behind the terra-cotta facade are two renovated traditional wooden houses with crimson walls, chic Thai decor, and a shady garden with benches and hammocks. Great value and gay-friendly.

CHIANG MAI Your House ⓑ

8 Soi 2 Ratwithl Rd, Chiang Mai, 50200 **Tel** *0-5321-7492* **Fax** *0-5341-8461* **Rooms** *25*

Handily located in the historic center, this popular guesthouse is spread over two properties: a traditional Thai teak house and a modern building. Rooms have shared bathrooms, and only some have air-conditioning. The helpful staff can organize treks, tours, cooking classes, visas, tickets, and motorcycle hire. **www.yourhouseguesthouse.com**

CHIANG MAI Changmai Gate Hotel & Chatree Guest House ⓑⓑ

11/10 Suriyawongsa Rd, Chiang Mai, 50100 **Tel** *0-5320-3895* **Fax** *0-5327-9085* **Rooms** *124*

Situated outside the Old City, a 20-minute walk from the Night Bazaar, this hotel offers standard rooms in the guesthouse or more elegant, Thai-style rooms in the newer hotel wing. All have satellite television and fridge, while deluxe rooms boast a minibar and terrace. **www.chiangmaigate.com**

CHIANG MAI Lai Thai Guest House ⓑⓑ

111/4-5 Khotchasarn Rd, Chiang Mai, 50100 **Tel** *0-5327-1725* **Fax** *05327-2724* **Rooms** *110*

This modern hotel features traditionally decorated rooms with wooden floors, rattan walls, and carved furniture, set around a garden with a swimming pool. Located near the walled city's moat, it is ideal for viewing the water fights during April's Songkran Festival *(see p48)*. Rooms have complimentary wireless Internet. **www.laithai.com**

CHIANG MAI Baan Jong Come ⓑⓑⓑ

47 Thapae Rd, Soi 4, Chiang Mai, 50100 **Tel** *0-5320-7043* **Rooms** *24*

This central, modern, budget hotel with attractive decorative touches offers spotless rooms with tiled floors. Jazz music can often be heard from the pleasant courtyard, and guests enjoy access to the swimming pool next door, which is perfect for cooling off after a busy day of sightseeing. However, be warned: it is often crowded.

CHIANG MAI Chiang Mai Orchid Hotel ⓑⓑⓑ

23 Huay Kaew Rd, Chiang Mai, 50200 **Tel** *0-5322-2099* **Fax** *0-5322-1625* **Rooms** *266*

Situated in the newer part of town, with scores of cafés, restaurants, and shops on its doorstep, this modern hotel is a short *tuk-tuk* ride to the Old Town and Night Bazaar. While rather old-fashioned and decorated in a bland, international-business style, the rooms are well maintained and very comfortable. **www.chiangmaiorchid.com**

CHIANG MAI Riverview Lodge ⓑⓑⓑ

25 Charoen Prathet Rd, Soi 2, Chiang Mai, 50100 **Tel** *0-5327-1109* **Fax** *0-5327-9019* **Rooms** *36*

The spotless understated rooms at this tranquil riverside hotel have been lovingly decorated with local textiles and wooden carvings; it is worth paying more for one with a balcony over the Ping River. There's a verdant tropical garden with pavilions, terraces, a small pool, and a pleasant café. Friendly and efficient staff. **www.riverviewlodgch.com**

CHIANG MAI Tapae Place Hotel ⓑⓑⓑ

2 Tapae Rd, Soi 3, Chiang Mai, 50100 **Tel** *0-5327-0159* **Fax** *0-5327-1982* **Rooms** *90*

Conveniently situated near Chiang Mai's Old City sights and Night Bazaar, this modern hotel has clean, spacious rooms with attractive Thai decor, private bathrooms, satellite TV, and minibar. There is a decent spa where you can unwind after a long day walking around the temples and specially reduced rates for longer stays. **www.tapaeplacehotel.com**

CHIANG MAI Baan Tazala ⓑⓑⓑⓑ

55/5 Moo 1 Chiang Mai-Sankampaeng Rd, Chiang Mai, 50000 **Tel** *0-5385-0111* **Fax** *0-5385-1211* **Rooms** *8*

This exclusive property 15 minutes from Chiang Mai is ideal for couples seeking privacy. The spacious rooms are decorated in an Oriental style with beautiful bathroom amenities and a complimentary minibar. Hi-tech extras include plasma TV, high-speed Internet, and a PlayStation. The restaurant offers imaginative cuisine. **www.banntazala.co.th**

CHIANG MAI Manathai Village ⓑⓑⓑⓑ

39/3 Soi 3 Tapae Rd, Chiang Mai, 50100 **Tel** *0-5328-1666* **Fax** *0-5320-8385* **Rooms** *29*

This exquisitely decorated hotel combines Zen minimalism with quirky touches and a warmth unexpected in such a sleek, contemporary hotel. The elegant rooms feature polished wooden floors, teak furniture, and all the creature comforts. The central swimming pool and teak bar are simply stunning. **www.manathai.com**

CHIANG MAI The Chedi ⓑⓑⓑⓑⓑ

123 Charoen Prathet Rd, Chiang Mai, 50100 **Tel** *0-5325-3333* **Fax** *0-5325-3352* **Rooms** *84*

Situated on the Ping River, the Chedi has enormous windows, open verandas, and alfresco terraces with breathtaking river views. Other attractions are the clean contemporary lines, striking decor, and water features with which the hotel has become synonymous; stylish lounges, bars, and restaurants will keep you sated. **www.ghmhotels.com**

CHIANG MAI D2

100 Chang Klan Rd, Chiang Mai, 50100 **Tel** *0-5399-9999* **Fax** *0-5399-9900* **Rooms** *131*

This hip hotel oozes style. Adjoining the Night Bazaar, it is ideally located for food-lovers and shopaholics. The funky tangerine-accented rooms come with cool orange extras (umbrellas, yoga mats) and hi-tech amenities (DVD players, plasma TVs, high-speed Internet). The chic lobby bar is a lively venue. **www.dusit.com/d2cm**

CHIANG MAI Mandarin Oriental Dhara Dhevi

51/4 Chiang Mai-Sankampaeng Rd, Moo 1, Chiang Mai, 50000 **Tel** *0-5388-8888* **Rooms** *123*

This palatial resort features generously sized colonial-Thai suites, villas, and residences, all furnished with exotic artifacts. Spread over 60 acres of rice paddies and plantations, it also features a renowned spa and cultural museum dedicated to the Lanna kingdom within the grounds. **www.mandarinoriental.com**

CHIANG MAI Puripann Baby Grand Boutique Hotel

104/1 Charoen Muang Soi 2, Charoen Muang Rd, Chiang Mai, 50100 **Tel** *0-5330-2898* **Rooms** *30*

With an air of grandeur unexpected in such a small hotel, the "Baby Grand Boutique" title is certainly apt. Extremely elegant, with tropical gardens, a beautiful (if small) swimming pool, exquisite attention to detail in the rooms, and excellent service. It is close to riverside bars and restaurants. **www.puripunn.com**

CHIANG MAI Rachamankha

6 Rachamankha 9, Chiang Mai, 50200 **Tel** *0-5390-4111* **Fax** *0-5390-4114* **Rooms** *24*

A splendid boutique hotel with an idiosyncratic sense of style. While the exterior architecture is Lanna, the interior design combines Chinese antiques, Art Deco influences, and contemporary elements. Rooms are stylish; the gardens, lush; the swimming pool is sublime; and the restaurant is one of Chiang Mai's finest. **www.rachamankha.com**

CHIANG MAI Tamarind Village

50/1 Rajdamnoen Rd, Chiang Mai, 50200 **Tel** *0-5341-8896* **Fax** *0-5341-8900* **Rooms** *45*

This is one of Chiang Mai's most sublime hotels. From the dramatic bamboo-forest entrance and garden of tamarind trees, to the elegant, airy, flower-filled lobby with teak furniture and cushions crafted from hill-tribe textiles, Tamarind Village is truly special. The dark-green swimming pool is especially seductive. **www.tamarindvillage.com**

CHIANG MAI Yaang Come Village

90/3 Sridonchai Rd, Chiang Mai, 50100 **Tel** *0-5323-7222* **Fax** *0-5323-7230* **Rooms** *42*

This boutique hotel in the traditional Lanna style is simply magical. The spacious rooms feature beautiful frescoes on the walls and touches such as mosaic-framed mirrors, four-poster beds, and floral-patterned bowls for sinks. There is an enormous aquamarine tiled swimming pool surrounded by tropical gardens. **www.yaangcome.com**

CHIANG MAI (MAE RIM) Imperial Chiang Mai Resort Spa & Sport Club

284 Moo 3 Don Kaew, Chiang Mai-Fang Rd, Mae Rim, 50180 **Tel** *0-5312-1649* **Fax** *0-5312-1646* **Rooms** *48*

Ideal for active families and groups, this sprawling resort 20 minutes from Chiang Mai offers a long list of recreation and sporting facilities, including an Olympic-sized swimming pool, children's pool, tennis, squash, and horse riding. Rooms are decorated in a rustic style, with balconies and views of the countryside. **www.imperialhotels.com/chiangmai/**

CHIANG MAI (MAE RIM) Four Seasons Resort Chiang Mai

Mae Rim-Old Samoeng Rd, Mae Rim, 50180 **Tel** *0-5329-8181* **Fax** *0-5329-8190* **Rooms** *80*

An excellent cookery school, renowned spa, stunning pool, and plush Lanna-style pavilions overlooking rice paddies where buffalo roam make for a memorable stay. Not all rooms have spectacular views, so book ahead. The resort is 20 minutes from Chiang Mai's center; a complimentary shuttle is provided. **www.fourseasons.com/chiangmai/**

LAMPANG Boonma Guesthouse

256 Taladkao Rd, Lampang, 52000 **Rooms** *4*

This delightful, tiny, family-run hotel on the river offers pleasant rooms spread over two buildings: a traditional Thai teak house and a separate (and not as atmospheric) building out back. While the rooms in the first building are more attractively decorated, all lodgings are spotlessly clean and excellent value.

LAMPANG Pin Hotel

8 Suandok Rd, Lampang, 52100 **Tel** *0-5422-1509* **Fax** *0-5432-2286* **Rooms** *58*

This hotel may be a little old-fashioned, with floral bedspreads and padded headboards, but rooms are clean, large, and comfortable. The Evergreen restaurant serves decent Thai, Chinese, and European dishes, and the tour desk can organize local excursions to temples and the Elephant Conservation Center. **www.travelthailand.com/pinhotel**

LAMPANG Riverside Guest House

286 Talad Kao Rd, Lampang, 52000 **Tel** *0-5422-7005* **Fax** *0-5432-2342* **Rooms** *17*

Book ahead for Lampang's most beautiful riverside accommodation, since it is often full. This intimate family-run guesthouse occupies several restored traditional Thai teak buildings, with a gorgeous garden and a relaxing riverside area. The homely atmosphere and midnight curfew do not appeal to everyone. **www.theriverside-lampang.com**

LAMPHUN Gassan Lake City Golf & Resort

88 Moo 7 Ban Thi, Lamphun, 51180 **Tel** *0-5392-1888* **Fax** *0-5392-1802* **Rooms** *74*

This stunning Thai-style resort with pagoda roofs boasts one of the country's best courses. Spectacularly built around a series of lakes, surrounded by rice paddies and majestic mountains, the 18-hole green is maintained by a European PGA greenkeeper. Rooms are plush, and there is an attractive central swimming pool. **www.gassangolf.com**

Key to Price Guide *see p398* **Key to Symbols** *see back cover flap*

MAE HONG SON Piya Guest House

1/1 Khunlumphrapat Soi 3, Mae Hong Son, 58000 **Tel** *0-5361-1260* **Fax** *0-5361-2308* **Rooms** *14*

Spacious, spotlessly clean rooms with air-conditioning and television make this simple, white-walled, A-roofed guesthouse one of the most popular in the region. When you book, be sure to ask for a large room, which will be the same price as a small one. The lush garden is lovely, breakfasts are good, and students get a discount.

MAE HONG SON Golden Pai Resort

285/1 Ban Pangmoo, Mae Hong Son, 58000 **Tel** *0-5362-0653-5* **Fax** *0-5362-0417* **Rooms** *70*

Hire a car to drive to this beautiful resort of pretty teak bungalows situated beneath mist-shrouded mountains 5 km (3 miles) from Mae Hong Son. The simple, individually decorated rooms have polished floorboards or tiles, traditional decor, and spacious patios to relax on. The alfresco restaurant has spectacular river views. **www.goldenpaihotel.com**

MAE HONG SON Sang Tong Huts

250 Moo 11, off Makasanti Rd, Bang Moo, Mae Hong Son, 58000 **Tel** *0-5361-1680* **Rooms** *10*

This unique property of beautiful, individually designed bamboo and wooden houses is just 10 minutes from Mae Hong Son. Its setting in serene countryside against a spectacular mountain backdrop is ideal for those who love the simple life. Days here are lazy, while evenings are for gazing at the stars. **www.sangtonghuts.com**

MAE HONG SON Imperial Tara Mae Hong Son Hotel

149 Moo 8, Tambon Pang Moo, Mae Hong Son, 58000 **Tel** *0-5368-4444* **Fax** *0-5368-4440* **Rooms** *104*

This modern low-rise resort is set in stunning surroundings within a teak forest in the heart of trekking country, on the edge of town. The well-equipped, generous rooms have polished wooden floors and balconies overlooking luxuriant tropical gardens. Reserve a table on the restaurant's wooden deck for dinner. **www.imperialhotels.com**

PAI Pai River Lodge

Moo 3 Wiang Tai Rd, Pai, 58130 **Tel** *no phone* **Rooms** *10*

A longtime backpacker favorite, these bamboo bungalows arranged around a grassy lawn may be primitive, but that is their appeal. The hammocks get plenty of use, and the riverside beach sees guests sharing tales around the campfire late into the night. The open-air restaurant has a small library and a bar.

PAI Baan Tawan Guesthouse

117 Moo 4, Pai, 58130 **Tel** *0-5369-8116* **Rooms** *20*

Take advantage of the tranquil setting here by relaxing in the airy riverside room. The basic teakwood bungalows and traditional teak houses are ideal for those who like the simple life, and they make a great getaway for travelers wanting to unwind after exploring the surrounding countryside. **www.baantawan-pai.com**

PAI Belle Villa Resort

113 Moo 6, Huay Poo-Wiang Nua Rd, Pai, 58130 **Tel** *0-5369-8226* **Rooms** *47*

These beautiful wooden houses on stilts in the splendid countryside outside Pai have been built in traditional Lanna style, with wooden roofs and verandas and modern rustic interiors. Guests make as much use of the hammocks about the place as they do of the organized excursions to hill tribes and local temples. **www.bellevillaresort.com**

FAR NORTH

CHIANG KHONG Ruanthai Sophapan

83 Moo 8 Sai Klang Rd, Chiang Khong, 57140 **Tel** *0-5379-1023* **Fax** *0-5379-1446* **Rooms** *25*

While the Mekong River vistas and views to Laos are the highlight here, the hotel itself is pretty special. Constructed from aged teak, the tall house on stilts has wonderful wide verandas and charming shutters on its windows. The self-service restaurant operates on an honesty system, and breakfast is included.

CHIANG RAI Chat House

3/2 Sangkaew Trirat Rd, Chiang Rai, 57000 **Tel** *0-5371-1481* **Fax** *0-5374-4220* **Rooms** *20*

Rooms are cozy, even homely, at Chat House, one of Chiang Rai's oldest guesthouses, and travelers like them that way. The communal spaces are charming; the gardens, lush; the atmosphere is laid-back; and the staff are helpful and friendly and can organize treks and tours. **www.chatguesthouse.com**

CHIANG RAI Ben Guesthouse

351/10 Sankhong Noi Rd, Soi 4, Chiang Rai, 57000 **Tel** *0-5371-6775* **Rooms** *28*

In a beautiful teak house with traditional decor, this is one of Chiang Rai's most charming and best-value guesthouses. It is popular with both families and backpackers, who like its low-key atmosphere and tranquil surroundings. The Ben is a 20-minute walk to the city center. Staff are always on hand to help guests. **www.benguesthousechiangrai.com**

CHIANG RAI Golden Triangle Inn

590/2 Paholyothin Rd, Chiang Rai, 57000 **Tel** *0-5371-3918* **Fax** *0-5374-0478* **Rooms** *30*

Traditional Thai decor, wide verandas, and a shady tropical garden keep guests returning to this small hotel a short stroll from the city center. The airy colonial-style lobby is an ideal spot for a drink after a day spent on the back of an elephant. The hotel also organizes treks and tours. **www.goldenchiangrai.com**

CHIANG RAI Little Duck
ⒷⒷⒷ

199 Paholyothin Rd, Chiang Rai, 57000 **Tel** *0-5371-5628* **Fax** *0-5371-5639* **Rooms** *330*

Despite its name, this modern hotel is a massive complex with numerous facilities, including gift shops, café, swimming pool, snooker club, beauty salon, massage parlor, and convention center. While the rooms are rather old-fashioned, they are comfortable and generously sized – not to mention great value. **www.littleduck.co.th**

CHIANG RAI Wiang Inn
ⒷⒷⒷ

893 Paholyothin Rd, Chiang Rai, 57000 **Tel** *0-5371-1533* **Fax** *0-5371-1877* **Rooms** *258*

This elegant property has a business-hotel vibe to it and is best suited to those missing big-city creature comforts. Only the traditional Thai touches – silk cushions, wall hangings, and rattan chairs – rescue the rooms from blandness. The retro karaoke bar makes for an entertaining night out. **www.wianginn.com**

CHIANG RAI Dusit Island Resort
ⒷⒷⒷⒷ

1129 Kraisora Sit Rd, Chiang Rai, 57000 **Tel** *0-5371-5777* **Fax** *0-5371-5801* **Rooms** *271*

With a tranquil island setting in the middle of the Mae Kok River, this elegant, albeit slightly dated, five-star resort is a great place to relax. The comfortable rooms are in the classic Dusit style with traditional touches, and there are plenty of bars, restaurants, and cafés to keep you entertained. **www.dusit.com**

CHIANG RAI Rimkok Resort Hotel
ⒷⒷⒷⒷ

6 Moo 4, Chiang Rai-Thatorn Rd, Chiang Rai, 57000 **Tel** *0-5371-6445* **Fax** *0-5371-5859* **Rooms** *256*

The rooms at this enormous resort on the banks of the Mae Kok River are rather characterless in comparison to the breezy, colonial feel of the rest of the property, the atmospheric Heritage Grill in particular. While lacking personality, they are spacious, clean, and comfortable, with rattan furniture and shady balconies. **www.rimkokresort.com**

CHIANG SAEN Chiang Saen River Hill Hotel
ⒷⒷ

714 Moo 3 Tambol Viang, Chiang Saen, 57150 **Tel** *0-5365-0826* **Fax** *0-5365-0830* **Rooms** *63*

Guests can rent bicycles here to pedal the short way into town or to explore the picturesque surroundings. Rooms are in concrete blocks rather than the teakwood buildings popular in these parts, but they are furnished in a whimsical style, with comfortable cushions around low tables under parasols. The colorful café is popular. **www.chiangsaenriverhill.net**

CHIANG SAEN Sanboonma Resort
ⒷⒷⒷ

679 Moo 2 Wiang, Chiang Saen, 57150 **Tel** *0-5365-0124* **Rooms** *8*

Sanboonma is a very pleasant, Lanna-style guesthouse set in a beautiful garden. All the rooms are clean and tidy, and the guesthouse is well managed by a team of friendly staff. Located within the old town wall and a short walk from the Mekong River. **www.sanboonmaresort.com**

GOLDEN TRIANGLE The Imperial Golden Triangle Resort
ⒷⒷⒷⒷ

222 Golden Triangle, Sop Ruak, 57150 **Tel** *0-5378-4001* **Fax** *0-5378-4006* **Rooms** *72*

Golden Triangle and Mekong River views can be enjoyed from your balcony at this grand hotel. The elegant (if old-fashioned) rooms are well appointed, and the restaurant serves up Thai and international cuisine, along with more spectacular views. Ideally situated for trekking and village excursions. **www.imperialhotels.com/goldentriangle/**

GOLDEN TRIANGLE Anantara Golden Triangle Resort & Spa
ⒷⒷⒷⒷⒷ

229 Moo 1, Golden Triangle, Sop Ruak, 57150 **Tel** *0-5378-4084* **Fax** *0-5378-4090* **Rooms** *77*

Consisting of striking traditional Thai-style pavilions and pagodas set in a bamboo jungle overlooking a Mekong tributary to Myanmar, this must be one of Thailand's most enchanting resorts and one of the most exotically sited. The luxurious rooms are beautifully appointed, and the swimming pool and spa are sublime. **www.anantara.com**

GOLDEN TRIANGLE Four Seasons Tented Camp Golden Triangle
ⒷⒷⒷⒷⒷ

Golden Triangle, Sop Ruak, 57150 **Tel** *0-5391-0200* **Fax** *0-5365-2189* **Rooms** *15*

A dramatic arrival by long-tail boat along the Mekong River; awesome views of mist-shrouded Myanmar from the veranda, bed, bath, and rain shower of your luxury tent; and bareback elephant riding make this one of Thailand's must-do experiences. Price is all inclusive; three night minimum stay. **www.fourseasons.com/goldentriangle/**

MAE SAI Mae Sai Riverside Guesthouse
Ⓑ

Riverside Rd, Mae Sai, 57130 **Tel** *0-5373-2630* **Rooms** *12*

While not as atmospheric as the Mae Sai Guesthouse *(see below)*, the Mae Sai Riverside offers friendly service and quaint accommodation in a concrete building (not as bad as it sounds) on the banks of the river. The decent restaurant has views across to Myanmar and is a good spot to meet fellow travelers.

MAE SAI Mae Sai Guesthouse
ⒷⒷ

Riverside Rd, Mae Sai, 57130 **Tel** *0-5373-2021* **Rooms** *14*

This charming family-operated guesthouse on the Sai River offers quaint wooden bungalows with wide verandas right on the water – perfect for relaxing sundowners after a day of traveling. It is so close to Myanmar, you can make out the faces of the women washing clothes and fishing on the riverbank opposite.

MAE SALONG Khum Nai Phol Resort
ⒷⒷ

58 Moo 1, Mae Salong, 57110 **Tel** *0-5376-5001* **Fax** *0-5376-5004* **Rooms** *24*

Enjoy spectacular views from the wide verandas of these wooden bungalows looking out over a tea plantation. There are cheaper hotel rooms near the restaurant and reception, but the bungalows are worth the little trek and extra expense. All accommodations are clean and comfortable. Situated on the outskirts of Mae Salong. **www.khumnaipholresort.com**

Key to Price Guide *see p398* **Key to Symbols** *see back cover flap*

MAE SALONG Phu Chaisai Mountain Resort & Spa

388 Moo 4, Ban, Mae Salong, 57110 **Tel** *0-5391-8636* **Fax** *0-5391-0500* **Rooms** *55*

Expect sublime mountain views and exquisite attention to detail at this chic boutique resort consisting of stylish bamboo huts, romantic airy "love nests," and stunning pool villas sprawled across a hillside. The open-air restaurant has the most dramatic views. There is a lovely spa and a beautiful, if small, swimming pool. **www.phu-chaisai.com**

NAN Nan Fah Hotel

436–440 Sumonthewarat Rd, Nan, 55000 **Tel** & **Fax** *0-5471-0284* **Rooms** *14*

Situated in an atmospheric old wooden building, the Nan Fah may have seen better days, but backpackers love this budget hotel for its big communal veranda, even bigger Western breakfasts, clean rooms, and hot showers. If you are a light sleeper, be sure to ask for a room at the back of the hotel.

NAN Dhevaraj

466 Sumonthewarat Rd, Nan, 55000 **Tel** *0-5471-0078* **Fax** *0-5471-1365* **Rooms** *152*

While looking a little worn around the edges, the Dhevaraj is still the best hotel in Nan, and its clean, spacious, and comfortable rooms make it popular with travelers. The lovely swimming pool is ideal for cooling off after a day of trekking, and the staff speak English, which is unusual in these parts. **www.dhevarajhotel.com**

PHRAE Nakorn Phrae Tower

3 Muanghit Rd, Phrae, 54000 **Tel** *0-5452-1321* **Fax** *0-5452-3503* **Rooms** *139*

This large, modern hotel may be a bit dated, with its quilted bedspreads and fake wood paneling, but the clean, comfortable rooms and amenities keep most guests happy. The Nakorn Phrae Tower is a short stroll to the markets, shops, and cafés in town, and staff can organize tours to nearby tribe villages and craft centers. **www.nakornphraetowerhotel.co.th**

PHRAE Mae Yom Palace

181/6 Yantrakitkosan Rd, Phrae, 54000 **Tel** *0-5452-1029* **Fax** *0-5452-2904* **Rooms** *104*

This big, modern hotel is Phrae's finest, offering large, clean, comfortable rooms and first-class facilities for a town of this size. The well-equipped rooms have a television and minibar, and there is a good pool surrounded by gardens. The friendly staff can organize trips to hill-tribe villages and other excursions.

THA THON Mae Kok River Village Resort

84 Moo 3, Ban Thathon, Tha Thon, 50100 **Tel** *0-5345-9328* **Fax** *0-5345-9329* **Rooms** *36*

In addition to its "Track of the Tiger" treks, this family-friendly resort offers an array of activities, including Thai cooking classes and massage lessons. The "Bamboo Man Adventure Club" is dedicated to rock climbing, mountain biking, canoeing, and hiking, and the clubhouse has a rock-climbing wall. **www.track-of-the-tiger.com**

KHORAT PLATEAU

BAN CHIANG Lakeside Sunrise Guesthouse

West side of lake, Ban Chiang **Tel** *0-4220-8167* **Rooms** *6*

If you are visiting the archaeological site and museum at Ban Chiang, it is worth considering a stay at this basic but cozy guesthouse run by one of the museum's employees. The fanned rooms share bathrooms, and there is a large balcony with views over the lake, plus bicycles for rent.

CHAIYAPHUM Lert Nimit Hotel

447/1 Nivesrat Rd, Chaiyaphum **Tel** *0-4481-1522* **Rooms** *79*

This is probably the best accommodation option in the small town of Chaiyaphum, which is a good base for visiting the Khorat Plateau's silk-weaving villages. There is a stylish lobby but rather ordinary rooms, though some have good views of the nearby mountains.

KHON KAEN Khon Kaen Hotel

43/2 Pimpasute Rd, Khon Kaen **Tel** *0-4333-3222* **Rooms** *130*

One of the best mid-range options in the region, the Khon Kaen offers well-furnished rooms with traditional decor and attached balconies. The hotel is particularly popular among business people, and includes a nightclub, karaoke, and massage facilities. **www.khonkaen-hotel.com**

KHON KAEN Charoen Thani Princess

260 Si Chan Rd, Khon Kaen **Tel** *0-4322-0400* **Rooms** *320*

This swanky hotel, operated by the Dusit group, presents a stiff challenge to the nearby Sofitel *(see below)* with its comfortable rooms, comprehensive facilities, attentive service, and cheaper rates. There is a pool with a good view of the city, several restaurants and bars, and a disco. **www.charoenthani.com**

KHON KAEN Sofitel Raja Orchid

9/9 Prachasamran Rd, Khon Kaen **Tel** *0-4332-2155* **Rooms** *292*

Perhaps the most luxurious hotel in the entire Northeast, this elegant place has bright and spacious rooms that are tastefully furnished and have nice traditional touches. There is a spa and a huge choice of restaurants serving Japanese, Cantonese, Italian, Vietnamese, Thai, and international dishes. **www.sofitel.com**

KHORAT Lamai Homestay and Guesthouse 🖥 🍴 📧   ⓑⓑ
23/1 Moo 3, Ban Khopet, Bua Yai, Khorat **Tel** *08-6258-5894* **Rooms** *4*

Staying at this simple but comfortable guesthouse feels like a visit to a little village with friends. Situated in a small rice-farming town, it offers three rooms in the hosting family's two-story house, while the fourth is in a separate annexe. The friendly owners can arrange trips, and the food is well prepared. **www.thailandhomestay.com**

KHORAT Siri Hotel 🔽 🍴 📧   ⓑⓑ
167-8 Pho Klang Rd, Khorat **Tel** *0-4424-2831* **Rooms** *67*

This place is very popular among budget travelers for its good value, its spacious, air-conditioned rooms, and its convenient location. The staff can also help arrange minibus trips to the Khmer temple at Phimai. On the premises is the Veterans of Foreign Wars Café (*see p440*), which is something of a Khorat institution. **www.sirihotel.com**

KHORAT Sripatana Hotel 🔽 🍴 ≈ 📧 🅱 24   ⓑⓑ
346 Suranari Rd, Khorat **Tel** *0-4425-1652-4* **Rooms** *176*

This smart, centrally located hotel is a good mid-range choice, since its rooms offer all basic comforts, including air-conditioning, TV, and ensuite bathrooms, at very reasonable rates. There is also a beer garden and a nightclub, and an on-site massage service is available to weary travelers. **www.sripatana.com**

KHORAT Dusit Princess Khorat 🔽 🍴 ≈ 🍴 📧 🅱 24   ⓑⓑⓑ
1137 Suranari Rd, Khorat **Tel** *0-4425-6629* **Rooms** *186*

Offering a mixture of superior and deluxe rooms as well as suites, this hotel is nearer the city center than the Sima Thani (*see below*) and has comparable facilities and rates. Guests can dine at the coffee shop by the pool or savor Chinese specialties in the Empress Restaurant. There is also a nightclub on site. **www.dusit.com**

KHORAT Sima Thani Hotel 🔽 🍴 ≈ 🍴 📧 🅱 24   ⓑⓑⓑ
Mittraphap Rd, Khorat **Tel** *0-4421-3100* **Rooms** *265*

This hotel is located a little way from the city center, but its well-equipped rooms and extensive facilities make it worth this inconvenience. There are five restaurants and bars to choose from, serving Thai, Chinese, Japanese, and Western food. The hotel also has a decent-sized swimming pool and fitness center. **www.simathani.com**

PHIMAI Old Phimai Guest House 🖥 📧   ⓑ
214 Moo 1 Chomsudasadet Rd, Phimai **Tel** *0-4447-1918* **Rooms** *6*

This is one of those charming and cheap guesthouses for which Thailand is justifiably famous. Ideally located for exploring the Khmer temple of Phimai, it offers a choice of fanned or air-conditioned rooms in a delightful wooden building. There is also a pleasant roof garden.

ROI ET Petcharat Garden Hotel 🔽 🍴 ≈ 📧 24   ⓑⓑ
404 Chotchaplayuk Rd, Roi Et **Tel** *0-4351-9000* **Rooms** *146*

This hotel is a good mid-range option, with appealing decor, shuttered windows, and high ceilings. The standard rooms are good value, while the deluxe rooms are worth the extra expense for the additional comfort. The staff are very attentive and eager to please. **www.petcharatgardenhotel.com**

ROI ET Roi Et City Hotel 🔽 🍴 📧 🅱 24   ⓑⓑⓑⓑ
78 Ploenchit Rd, Roi Et **Tel** *0-4352-0387* **Rooms** *167*

This large hotel has very friendly and helpful staff and is located on the eastern edge of town. Its large rooms are sumptuously furnished, and the bathrooms are also very stylish. The City Hotel also has a swimming pool, a gym, and a business center. **www.roietcityhotel.com**

SURIN Pirom's House 🖥 🍴   ⓑ
55/326 Soi Arunee, Thungpo Rd, Surin **Tel** *0-4451-5140* **Rooms** *9*

Something of a legend among local guesthouses, this friendly establishment is a kilometer west of the town center. The basic but tasteful wooden rooms share bathrooms and have wonderful views over rice paddies. The owners are a good source of local information and can cook up some tasty food, too.

SURIN Sangthong Hotel 🖥 🔽 📧 24   ⓑ
155–161 Tannasarn Rd, Surin **Tel** *0-4451-2099* **Rooms** *100*

There is nothing fancy about this functional, Chinese-style hotel, but it has a variety of decent-sized rooms – some with fans and others with air-conditioning – that are excellent value. Add its central location and friendly staff to the equation, and the Sangthong represents an appealing budget option.

SURIN Surin Majestic 🔽 🍴 ≈ 🍴 📧 🅱 24   ⓑⓑ
99 Jitbumrung Rd, Surin **Tel** *0-4471-3980* **Rooms** *72*

This impressive-looking hotel set in ample grounds is by far the best accommodation option in Surin. The comfortable rooms include writing desks and Internet connections, while facilities include a swimming pool, conference rooms, and a health center. **www.surinmajestichotel.com**

UDON THANI Charoensri Grand Royal Hotel 🔽 🍴 ≈ 🍴 📧 24   ⓑⓑⓑ
277/1 Prajak Rd, Udon Thani **Tel** *0-4234-3555* **Rooms** *255*

This is Udon's most luxurious hotel, with plush and spacious rooms equipped with TV and minibar. Among the hotel's facilities are a spa and health club, a pool, and several restaurants serving Thai, Chinese, and international dishes. **www.charoensrigrand.com**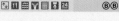

Key to Price Guide *see p398* **Key to Symbols** *see back cover flap*

MEKONG RIVER VALLEY

CHIANG KHAN Loogmai Guest House   ⬚   ⓑ
112 Chai Khong Rd, Chiang Khan **Tel** *0-4210-0447* **Rooms** *5*

Located by the riverside in Chiang Khan, this lovely colonial-style villa is decorated with modern and minimalist art. The Loogmai has just a few tastefully furnished rooms for rent, which makes the atmosphere cozy and familiar, and there is also a terrace overlooking the Mekong River where guests can relax.

CHIANG KHAN Chiang Khan Hill Resort   🍴🛏📋   ⓑⓑⓑ
Kaeng Khut Ku, Chiang Khan **Tel** *0-4282-1285* **Rooms** *50*

This upmarket resort takes full advantage of the picturesque scenery on the banks of the Mekong River, about 6 km (4 miles) east of Chiang Khan. It features a variety of smartly furnished rooms in wooden buildings that are surrounded by greenery. There is a swimming pool, too. **www.chiangkhanhill.com**

LOEI Sugar Guest House   ⬚📋   ⓑ
4/1 Soi 2, Wisuttitep Rd, Loei **Tel** *0-4281-2982* **Rooms** *8*

If you are looking for good-value budget accommodation in Loei, then this is the place for you. The Sugar Guest House is located about a 10-minute walk north of the town center and has both fanned rooms with shared bathrooms and air-conditioned quarters with ensuite bathrooms and cable TV.

LOEI Loei Palace Hotel   📶🍴🛏📋🛗24   ⓑⓑⓑⓑ
167/4 Charoenrat Rd, Loei **Tel** *0-4281-5668-74* **Rooms** *156*

Part of the Amari chain, this is easily Loei's most luxurious hotel. Rooms are large, bright, and comfortably furnished, and facilities include a big pool, business center, and a choice of restaurants. The Loei Palace is a good place to recover after climbing the nearby Phu Kradung (Bell Mountain). **www.amari.com/loeipalace**

MUKDAHAN Hua Nam Hotel   ⬚🍴📋   ⓑ
36 Samut Sakdarak Rd, Mukdahan **Tel** *0-4261-1197* **Rooms** *30*

This is the best budget option in Mukdahan, located near the Mekong River, with fanned rooms sharing bathrooms and air-conditioned lodgings that have attached bathrooms, TVs, and fridges. It is a quiet and airy compound, and there is also a café that serves good breakfasts, plus bicycle rental.

MUKDAHAN Mukdahan Grand   📶🍴📋🛗24   ⓑⓑ
78 Songnang Sathit Rd, Mukdahan **Tel** *0-4263-0959* **Rooms** *199*

Before the Ploy Palace *(see below)* opened, this used to be Mukdahan's best hotel, and it still offers a good upmarket option. Most of the comfortably furnished rooms have views across the Mekong River to Suwannakhet in Laos, and the staff are extremely helpful. **www.mukdahangrand.com**

MUKDAHAN Ploy Palace   📶🍴🛏📋🛗24   ⓑⓑⓑ
40 Phitak Phanom Khet Rd, Mukdahan **Tel** *0-4263-1111* **Rooms** *154*

All the rooms in this smart business hotel have views of the park, the mountains, or the river, and they are comfortably equipped, with some stylish touches to the decor. Some rooms have beehives on their balconies, which are believed to bring good luck, but be careful you don't get stung! **www.ploypalace.com**

NAKHON PHANOM View Kong Hotel   📶🍴📋🛗24   ⓑⓑ
527 Sunthorn Wichit Rd, Nakhon Phanom **Tel** *0-4251-3564* **Rooms** *112*

As the name implies, there are some great views to be enjoyed from the well-appointed rooms at this friendly hotel located just south of Nakhon Phanom, beside the Mekong River. The spacious balconies allow guests to make the most of their stay. **www.viewkonghotel.com**

NONG KHAI Mut Mee Guest House   ⬚🍴📋   ⓑⓑ
1111/4 Kaew Worawut Rd, Nong Khai **Tel** *0-4246-0717* **Rooms** *28*

Set among a mango orchard on the banks of the Mekong River, this is Nong Khai's best guesthouse, with a wide range of rooms ranging from basic to quite plush. The owners are a good source of local information, and there are bicycles for rent. **www.mutmee.com**

NONG KHAI Pantawee Hotel   🍴🛏📋🛗24   ⓑⓑ
1049 Haisoke Rd, Nong Khai **Tel** *0-4241-1568-9* **Rooms** *95*

This is a good mid-range option in Nong Khai, offering a range of rooms from small singles to spacious family lodgings. All rooms have TVs and DVD players, and the hotel has a good library of movies to select from. It is also wired for Wi-Fi. There is even a spa and pool. **www.pantawee.com**

NONG KHAI Nong Khai Grand Hotel   📶🍴🛏📋🛗24   ⓑⓑⓑ
589 Nong Khai-Poanpisai Rd, Nong Khai **Tel** *0-4242-0033* **Rooms** *130*

This is one of Nong Khai's best upmarket options, a business hotel with stylish decor and elegant furnishings in the rooms and suites. Though the latter are more expensive, there are big discounts off-season, allowing guests to treat themselves to a taste of luxury. **www.nongkhaigrandhotel.net**

PHU KRADUNG Phu Kradung National Park Bungalows   ℬℬ

Phu Kradung National Park **Tel** *0-2562-0760* **Rooms** *40*

There are several basic wooden bungalows for rent on the summit of Phu Kradung, and a few others at the base of the mountain. Most of them are huge and can accommodate large groups. Advance booking is advisable, and you should also be aware that the national park is closed from July to November. **www.dnp.go.th**

THAT PHANOM Niyana Guest House   ℬ

Rimkhong Rd Soi 33, That Phanom **Tel** *0-4254-0880* **Rooms** *3*

Not many visitors stay overnight in That Phanom, but for those who do, this small, family-run place makes a good advertisement for Thai hospitality. Facilities are basic, and bathrooms are shared, but the owners' enthusiasm more than makes up for these minor shortcomings.

THAT PHANOM Kritsada Rimkhong Resort   ℬℬ

90-93 Rimkhong Rd, That Phanom **Tel** *0-4254-0088* **Rooms** *18*

For those who need comforts such as air-conditioning in That Phanom, this is the place to head for. There is a mix of concrete and wooden rooms, some of which are very big and have separate living rooms, but they do not have much in the way of character. **www.kritsaderesort.com**

UBON RATCHATHANI Sri Isan   ℬℬ

62 Phadaeng Rd, Ubon Ratchathani **Tel** *0-4526-1011* **Rooms** *32*

Describing itself as a boutique hotel, this attractive place by the Mun River has clean, air-conditioned rooms with cable TV and fridges. They are set around an open-roofed atrium that gives the place real character, and there is a restaurant serving Thai, Chinese, and Vietnamese dishes. **www.sriisanhotel.com**

UBON RATCHATHANI Pathumrat   ℬℬℬ

337 Chayangkun Rd, Ubon Ratchathani **Tel** *0-4524-1501* **Rooms** *169*

Dating from the days of the Vietnam War, the Pathumrat is beginning to show its age, but it still has a kind of funky feel to it. Rooms are well equipped, and the hotel is conveniently located just north of the town center, making it a good choice as a base from which to explore Ubon's *wats*.

UBON RATCHATHANI Toh Sang Hotel   ℬℬℬℬ

251 Phalochai Rd, Ubon Ratchathani **Tel** *0-4524-5531* **Rooms** *76*

The huge and classy rooms at this swish, modern hotel are the best that you can get in Ubon Ratchathani. Set in 10 acres of tropical grounds just to the west of the city center, the Toh Sang has a wonderfully relaxing atmosphere and extremely attentive staff. **www.tohsang.com**

EASTERN SEABOARD

CHANTHABURI River Guest House   ℬ

3/5-8 Sri Chan Rd, Chanthaburi **Tel** *0-3932-8211* **Rooms** *29*

This welcoming guesthouse is conveniently located beside both the Chanthaburi River and the gem-dealing district. There is a choice of fanned or air-conditioned rooms; the former are situated at the back of the building and are the quietest. There is also Internet access.

CHANTHABURI Kasemsarn Hotel   ℬℬℬ

98/1 Benchamarachutit Rd, Chanthaburi **Tel** *0-3931-1100* **Rooms** *60*

The Kasemsarn has been not so much renovated as reborn, and has transformed from what was once a dowdy budget alternative to boutique-style Asian-chic lodgings. Located just north of the town center, it represents the best mid-range option in town.

CHANTHABURI KP Grand   ℬℬℬ

35/200-201 Trirat Rd, Chanthaburi **Tel** *0-3932-3201* **Rooms** *202*

This spacious and swanky hotel is located just across the bridge to the south of town. Rooms are carpeted and well equipped, with cable TV and minibars. Facilities include a big pool, fitness center, sauna, and massage service. The hotel's meeting and seminar rooms make it popular for business conventions. **www.kpgrandhotel.com**

KO CHANG White Sand Beach Resort   ℬℬℬ

Hat Sai Khao, Ko Chang **Tel** *08-6310-5553* **Rooms** *99*

Hat Sai Khao (White Sand Beach) is the island's longest and most beautiful sandy stretch, though it gets rather crowded near the south end. This place is located farther north, making it quieter. It offers a range of rooms, some with air-conditioning and others with fan, and some with superb beach views. **www.whitesandbeachresort.info**

KO CHANG Ko Chang Lagoon   ℬℬℬℬ

Hat Sai Khao, Ko Chang **Tel** *0-3955-1201* **Rooms** *82*

Located in the middle of White Sand Beach, this two-story mid-range resort has attractively landscaped gardens and a range of well-equipped rooms. Some are in the main building and others in detached bungalows on the seafront. There is also Internet access and barbecues on the beach each evening. **www.kohchanglagoonresort.com**

Key to Price Guide *see p398* **Key to Symbols** *see back cover flap*

KO CHANG Sea View Resort and Spa

Hat Kaibae, Ko Chang **Tel** *0-3955-2888* **Rooms** *126*

Set in a shady garden, all of the rooms at this resort, from standard cottages to suite spas, are beautifully designed and luxuriously furnished. Facilities include a spa, pool, fitness center, terrace restaurant, and a number of bars by the pool and on the beach. **www.seaviewkohchang.com**

KO CHANG Siam Beach Resort

Hat Tha Nam, Ko Chang **Tel** *08-9161-6664* **Rooms** *72*

Located at the northern end of Hat Tha Nam (Lonely Beach), the southernmost beach on the west coast of Ko Chang, this place has comfortable air-conditioned bungalows scattered on a hillside, plus some air-conditioned rooms with balconies on the beach. **www.siambeachresort.in.th**

KO CHANG Aana

Hat Klong Phrao, Ko Chang **Tel** *0-3955-1539* **Rooms** *71*

This resort is typical of the upmarket trend on Ko Chang, and it certainly seems to have everything, including two pools, a private beach, a spa, an Internet bungalow, kayak service, mini gym, and beach club. All the luxurious rooms have big balconies, and some have their own Jacuzzi. **www.aanaresort.com**

KO SAMET Naga

Ao Hin Kok, Ko Samet **Tel** *0-3864-4168* **Rooms** *35*

Something of a legend among budget travelers, Naga still offers simple, clean bungalows perched on a hillside at reasonable rates, while the rest of the island is unstoppably moving upmarket. There is also a library, a gym, a Thai boxing ring, and a good restaurant with homemade bread and cakes.

KO SAMET Jep's Bungalow

Ao Hin Kok, Ko Samet **Tel** *0-3864-4112* **Rooms** *40*

One of Ko Samet's best-value places, Jep's offers a choice of fanned or air-conditioned rooms in concrete or wooden bungalows spread across a hill. The air-conditioned rooms also have cable TV. The nearby beach is one of the best on the island for swimming and is popular among budget travelers.

KO SAMET Sai Kaew Villa

Hat Sai Kaew, Ko Samet **Tel** *0-3864-4144* **Rooms** *100*

This place occupies a large compound on Ko Samet's most popular beach and offers some of the cheapest rates available (for a fanned room with garden view), though the air-conditioned bungalows with a beach view cost a lot more. Discounts are possible if you are staying several nights. **www.saikaew.com**

KO SAMET Sang Thian Beach Resort

Ao Thian, Ko Samet **Tel** *0-3864-4255* **Rooms** *32*

The days when Ao Thian (Candlelit Beach) had no electricity have long gone, and now this resort has comfortable lodgings in attractive wooden bungalows on a hill, including some large ones for families or groups. Though developed, this beach is definitely quieter than those farther north on the east coast. **www.sangthianbeachresort.com**

KO SAMET Tub Tim Resort

Ao Tub Tim, Ko Samet **Tel** *0-3864-4025* **Rooms** *100*

This is one of Ko Samet's longest-running establishments, having opened in the early 1980s. The Tub Tim is set at the southern end of a pretty bay on the east coast and offers comfortable facilities in its concrete and wooden rooms. It also has one of the island's best restaurants *(see p442)*. **www.tubtimresort.com**

KO SAMET Vongdeuan Resort

Ao Vong Deuan, Ko Samet **Tel** *0-3864-4171-4* **Rooms** *49*

Ao Vong Deuan was one of the first of Ko Samet's beaches to go upmarket, and it is certainly one of the prettiest, with a lovely, crescent-shaped bay. This resort has attractive cottages and Thai houses that are comfortably equipped, and there is a decent restaurant, too. **www.vongdeuan.com**

KO SAMET Samed Villa

Ao Phai, Ko Samet **Tel** *0-3864-4094* **Rooms** *45*

Located at the southern end of what has become known as Ko Samet's "party beach," this place has some big and comfortable bungalows, including some family bungalows for four people. Under Swiss management, Samed Villa also has a decent restaurant. Staff can organize snorkeling trips. **www.samedvilla.com**

KO SAMET Moo Ban Talay

Ao Noi Na, Ko Samet **Tel** *0-3864-4251* **Rooms** *21*

Spacious bungalows in a gorgeous setting make Moo Ban Talay one of the best of Ko Samet's many stylish resorts. Located on a private beach at the north end of the island, the place radiates exclusivity. All rooms have platform beds and garden bathrooms, and some also have huge decks. **www.moobantalay.com**

KO SAMET Paradee Resort and Spa

Ao Kiu Na Nok, Ko Samet **Tel** *0-2438-9771-2* **Rooms** *45*

This expensive and luxurious resort may be the shape of things to come on Ko Samet, even though the island is part of a marine national park. The Paradee has spectacular villas with private Jacuzzi, spa, and butler, plus two private beaches. It is promoted as a couples' resort, so it is not suitable for young children. **www.kohsametparadee.com**

KO SAMET Sai Kaew Beach Resort

Hat Sai Kaew, Ko Samet **Tel** *0-3864-4195* **Rooms** *87*

Located at the northern end of Hat Sai Kaew (Diamond Beach), this is one of the island's fanciest resorts, with a choice of expensive, deluxe bungalows located on a quiet stretch, or slightly cheaper superior cottages on a busier part of the beach. The decor is very stylish, plus there is a pool and restaurant. **www.samedresorts.com**

KO SICHANG Sichang Palace

81 Atsadang Rd, Ko Sichang **Tel** *0-3821-6276-9* **Rooms** *56*

This is the smartest place to stay on Ko Sichang, which has some interesting historic sites but no great beaches. The price of the rooms varies according to the view, but all rooms are equipped with air-conditioning and TV, and there is a pool as well. The Sichang Palace is a good spot to escape the tourist hordes. **www.sichangpalace.com**

PATTAYA Ice Inn

528/2-3 Second Rd, Pattaya **Tel** *0-3872-0671* **Rooms** *32*

With its central location and well-maintained rooms, this place is one of Pattaya's best budget options. Rooms come with air-conditioning or fans, and some have a TV and fridge too. There is a handy Internet café on the ground floor, and the beach is only a few steps away.

PATTAYA Diana Inn

216/6-20 Between Soi 11-12, Second Rd, Pattaya **Tel** *0-3842-1623-4* **Rooms** *141*

This place has some of the best-value rooms available in Pattaya, considering it also has a large pool for guests' use. Room rates include an all-you-can-eat buffet breakfast, though the rooms themselves are rather plain. The central location makes it popular with long-stay visitors for whom discounts are available.

PATTAYA Garden Lodge Pattaya Beach Resort

170 Moo 5 Naklua Rd Soi 12, Pattaya **Tel** *0-3842-9109* **Rooms** *78*

For anyone who wants to find restful accommodation in bustling Pattaya, this mid-range option located to the north of town might be of interest. The Garden Lodge features an appropriately gorgeous outside area, a delightful pool, a welcoming restaurant, and well-furnished rooms. **www.gardenlodgepattaya.net**

PATTAYA Jomtien Boathouse

380/5-6 Jomtien Beach Rd, Pattaya **Tel** *0-3875-6143* **Rooms** *24*

This low-rise place offers luxury accommodation at mid-range prices, and therefore represents a very good deal. Rooms are nicely furnished and contain all amenities, and some also have private balconies. There is no pool, but the beach in front is good for swimming. **www.jomtien-boathouse.com**

PATTAYA Lek Hotel

284/5 Soi 13, Second Rd, Pattaya **Tel** *0-3842-5552* **Rooms** *158*

If you are looking for somewhere with budget rates but a few classy touches, the Lek might be just the place. Rooms here are rather small and basic, but there is a pool, a snooker room, and a roof terrace to make up for it. The hotel is centrally located, which means it is only a few steps from Pattaya's beach and shops. **http://lekhotel.tripod.com**

PATTAYA Siam Bayview

310/2 Moo 10, Beach Rd, Pattaya **Tel** *0-3842-3871-7* **Rooms** *260*

One of Pattaya's most conveniently located hotels, the Siam Bayview sits right in the center of Pattaya Bay, and the rooms near the top of the nine-story main building enjoy excellent sea views. Facilities include tennis courts, swimming pools, restaurants, a business center, and massage pavilion. **www.siamhotels.com**

PATTAYA Woodlands Resort

164/1 Moo 5, Pattaya–Naklua Rd, Pattaya **Tel** *0-3842-1707* **Rooms** *133*

This attractive colonial-style resort is set in a quiet area to the north of Pattaya and is ideal for families. The bright and spacious rooms are comfortably furnished, and the stylish restaurant serves good Thai and international food. A spa and cookery classes are also available. **www.woodland-resort.com**

PATTAYA Pattaya Marriott
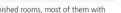

218 Moo 10, Beach Rd, Pattaya **Tel** *0-3841-2120* **Rooms** *295*

Located in the center of Pattaya Bay, this beautiful resort hotel has elegantly furnished rooms, most of them with beach views, and a range of activities for guests. These include golf, horse riding, rock climbing, diving, and flying. Large pool, plus several restaurants and bars. Discount options available. **www.marriotthotels.com/pyxmc**

PATTAYA Royal Cliff Beach Hotel
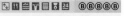

353 Moo 12 Pratumnak Rd, Pattaya **Tel** *0-3825-0421* **Rooms** *544*

Something of a legend among Pattaya hotels, this award-winning five-star facility set in 64 acres of grounds between Pattaya and Jomtien satisfies every wish. With several restaurants and bars, two health spas, five swimming pools, tennis courts, a jogging trail, and a putting green, guests need never leave the premises. **www.royalcliff.com**

PATTAYA Sheraton Pattaya Resort

437 Pratumnak Rd, Pattaya **Tel** *0-3825-9888* **Rooms** *156*

Nestled on a picturesque headland south of Pattaya, this luxurious resort has a tiny private beach and three swimming pools set in lush gardens, with sweeping views from the hillside rooms. Facilities are as one would expect from this respected chain, and staff at the Amburaya Spa are waiting to pamper you. **www.starwoodhotels.com**

Key to Price Guide *see p398* **Key to Symbols** *see back cover flap*

PATTAYA Sugar Hut

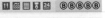

391/18 Moo 10, Thapraya Rd, Pattaya **Tel** *0-3825-1686* **Rooms** *28*

If it is atmosphere and privacy you are looking for, then consider this gem of a place. The traditional Thai villas with curving roofs are set in a rambling garden populated by peacocks and rabbits. Rooms are tastefully furnished, with low beds and mosquito nets, and the restaurant *(see p443)* serves top-notch cuisine. **www.sugar-hut.com**

RAYONG Hinsuay-Namsai Resort Hotel

250 Moo 2 Klang, Rayong **Tel** *0-3863-8260–5* **Rooms** *174*

This smart resort offers excellent facilities, while its own private beach provides a tempting alternative to the crowded bays of Ko Samet. All of the air-conditioned rooms with cable TV have sea views, and there are several sports on offer, including tennis, squash, badminton, and table tennis. **www.hinsuaynamsaihotel.com**

RAYONG Star Hotel

109 Rayong Trade Centre Rd, Rayong **Tel** *0-3861-4901* **Rooms** *576*

This big place geared to business conventions is the fanciest place in Rayong, and offers huge, well-equipped rooms. Facilities include an elegant restaurant, a 24-hour coffee shop, two swimming pools, a karaoke lounge, and a bowling center. **www.starhotel.th.com**

RAYONG Purimas Beach Hotel

4/5 Moo 3 Pae Klag Kam Rd, Rayong **Tel** *0-3863-0382* **Rooms** *79*

This stylish and relaxing resort has its own private beach, superb facilities, and attentive service. All the spacious and airy suites have private balconies, as well as minibars, TVs, and comfortable furnishings. The Purimas Beach also has a spa and two excellent restaurants. **www.purimas.com**

TRAT Ban Jaidee

67 Chaimongkon Rd, Trat **Tel** *0-3952-0678* **Rooms** *8*

If you need to stop over in Trat on your way to Ko Chang, consider this friendly budget option. A handful of simple but clean rooms are split between an old building and a newer extension; bathrooms are shared between guests. The Ban Jaidee also has a comfortable communal area downstairs.

WESTERN SEABOARD

CHA-AM Nana House

208/3 Ruamchit Rd, Cha-am, 76120 **Tel** *0-3243-3632* **Rooms** *27*

Behind this little hotel's purple street front, its ever-present English-speaking owner Nana keeps busy ensuring that her brightly painted, tile-floored rooms are kept spotlessly clean. While the beach is within splashing distance, if you take the rooftop suite, you will be reluctant to leave its private patio with sea views. **www.nanahousechaam.com**

CHA-AM Regent Chalet Regent Beach Cha-am

849/21 Phetkasem Rd, Cha-am, 76120 **Tel** *0-3245-1240* **Fax** *0-3247-1492* **Rooms** *560*

This sprawling property on Cha-am beach is popular with families and groups of friends, who like the spacious and comfortable chalets, bungalows, and suites; the long list of sport and recreational facilities (squash, tennis, golfing, cycling, horseback riding, etc); the casual seaside dining; and the vicinity to the beach. **www.regent-chaam.com**

CHA-AM Dusit Resort Hua Hin

1349 Phetkasem Rd, Cha-am, 76120 **Tel** *0-3252-0009* **Fax** *0-3252-0296* **Rooms** *300*

The five-star Dusit Resort Hua Hin is actually at Cha-am, not Hua Hin, but the latter's attractions are only 10 minutes away. This stunning resort features plush rooms with all the creature comforts you would expect and balconies with sea views. There are two sublime swimming pools, a Devarana spa, and superb recreation facilities. **www.dusit.com**

CHA-AM The Hotel Cha-am

115 Moo 7, Tambon Bangkao Rd, Cha-am, 76120 **Tel** *0-3270-9555* **Fax** *0-3247-3190* **Rooms** *79*

The Hotel Cha-am offers the ultimate in chic, contemporary style. Every detail of this luxurious beachfront resort has been carefully considered. Spacious rooms come with floor-to-ceiling windows, flatscreen TVs, and Wi-Fi. Rooftop pools, private courtyards, and a hip nightclub make this property stand out from the rest. **www.hotel-cha-am.com**

CHA-AM Sheraton Hua Hin Resort & Spa

1573 Phetkasem Rd, Cha-am, 76120 **Tel** *0-3270-8000* **Fax** *0-3270-8088* **Rooms** *240*

Set within a tropical garden, this contemporary beachfront resort offers stylish rooms and suites, 56 of which have direct access to the 200-m (650-ft) lagoon pool. Spacious rooms provide five-star comfort, chic decor, and great views. Guests can enjoy pampering in the spa or an exotic cocktail at the beach bar. **www.starwoodhotels.com**

CHUMPHON Chumphon Cabana Resort & Diving Centre

69 Moo 8, Hat Thung Wua Laen, 86000 **Tel** *0-7756-0246* **Fax** *0-7756-0245* **Rooms** *139*

Located on a beautiful stretch of pristine white-sand beach with crystal-clear azure waters, this modern resort has bright standard rooms and private bungalows, and a breezy restaurant right on the beach. A specialized diving and snorkeling center on site offers PADI-approved diving courses and trips to the best sites. **www.cabana.co.th**

HUA HIN K Place

116 Naresdamri Rd, Hua Hin, 77100 **Tel** *0-3251-1396* **Fax** *0-3251-4506* **Rooms** *12*

In a resort town not known for its budget hotels, K Place is a surprising bargain, with big, simple rooms that are spotlessly clean, all equipped with fridge and television. Behind a supermarket off Naresdamri Road near the Hilton, it is close to the action and only a short stroll to the beach and Night Bazaar.

HUA HIN Leng Hotel

113/14 Phetkasem Rd, Hua Hin, 77100 **Tel** *0-3251-3546* **Fax** *0-3253-2095* **Rooms** *18*

This popular guesthouse is close to Hua Hin beach and the lively Night Bazaar. The simple, homely rooms are spotlessly clean and come with fridge, cable television, and wireless Internet. There is a good-sized swimming pool, a decent café, and friendly staff to help with transfers and excursions. Book ahead. **www.lenghotel.com**

HUA HIN Araya Residence

15/1 Chomsin Rd, Hua Hin, 77100 **Tel** *0-3253-1130* **Rooms** *12*

Centrally located, this intimate boutique hotel has an Asian Zen minimalist style about it, with teak furniture and contemporary Thai decor. The attractive rooms are comfortable, with cable TV, minibar, and complimentary Wi-Fi, and the rooftop rooms have sun beds and sea views. **www.araya-residence.com**

HUA HIN Sirin Hotel

6/3 Damnoenkasem Rd, Hua Hin, 77100 **Tel** *0-3251-1150* **Fax** *0-3251-3571* **Rooms** *25*

Centrally located in the thick of Hua Hin's shopping and eating action, this is a great mid-range option. While it won't win any design awards, the pleasant, clean and well-maintained rooms come with satellite television, minibar, and balcony. There is a small shady swimming pool and a casual restaurant, too. **www.sirinhuahin.com**

HUA HIN Thipurai Beach Hotel & Annexe

113/27 Phetkasem Rd, Hua Hin, 77100 **Tel** *0-3253-2731* **Fax** *0-3251-2210* **Rooms** *59*

A short walk from Hua Hin beach, this hotel offers clean, bright rooms with balconies, minibars, and cable television. The hotel rooms are smarter, while the cheaper rooms at the annexe are more homely, with floral bedspreads and curtains. There is a small swimming pool and a casual eatery serving Thai and European food. **www.thipurai.com**

HUA HIN Aleenta Resort & Spa

183 Moo 4 Paknampran, Pranburi, 77220 **Tel** *0-2514-8112* **Rooms** *20*

This sleek minimalist property on a pretty beach south of Hua Hin makes for an ideal seaside escape. With just 21 luxury suites, bungalows, and a beach house, all with sea views, guests are assured peace and privacy. Thoughtful touches include iPod docks, complimentary wireless Internet, and daily gourmet treats. **www.aleenta.com**

HUA HIN Anantara Resort & Spa

45/1 Phetkasem Rd, Hua Hin, 77100 **Tel** *0-3252-0250* **Fax** *0-3252-0259* **Rooms** *187*

This enchanting resort – with its luxuriant fragrant gardens, exotic architecture, and excellent restaurants – is wonderful. While the rooms with sea views are hard to resist, the plush lagoon rooms with waterside verandas come with access to a private swimming pool. The spa is one of Thailand's best. **www.anantara.com**

HUA HIN Chiva Som Health Resort

73/4 Petchkasem Rd, Hua Hin, 77100 **Tel** *0-3253-6536* **Fax** *0-3251-1154* **Rooms** *57*

In tranquil gardens with lily ponds and Buddha statues, this seaside destination spa and health resort is dedicated to revitalizing the body and mind. Guests receive a consultation on arrival, and all meals and a wide array of spa treatments, fitness classes, and activities are included; minimum three-night stay required. **www.chivasom.com**

HUA HIN Evason Hua Hin Resort/Evason Hideaway & Six Senses Spas

9 Moo 3 Paknampran Beach, Pranburi, 77220 **Tel** *0-3263-2111* **Fax** *0-3263-2112* **Rooms** *185*

On a beautiful palm-lined beach south of Hua Hin town, these adjacent eco-friendly resorts are ideal retreats. The Hideaway, with its luxurious villas, is more exclusive, but both share superb facilities, excellent restaurants and bars, a sublime swimming pool, and several spas, including the extraordinary Earth Spa. **www.evasonresorts.com**

HUA HIN Hilton Hua Hin Resort & Spa

33 Naresdamri Rd, Hua Hin, 77100 **Tel** *0-3253-8999* **Fax** *0-3253-8990* **Rooms** *296*

This high-rise resort on the main beach has stylish, comfortable rooms with balconies and ocean views. The swimming pool is enormous, but be sure to get there early to get a sun bed. While this promotes itself as a family hotel, the wet bar can get pretty rowdy. The buffet breakfast is excellent. **www.huahin.hilton.com**

HUA HIN Sofitel Centara Grand Resort & Villas

1 Damnernkasem Rd, Hua Hin, 77100 **Tel** *0-3251-2021* **Fax** *0-3251-1014* **Rooms** *249*

This classic hotel is consistently voted one of the top ten in Asia, and it is easy to see why. The grand colonial-style building, expansive manicured grounds, and beachfront location are simply fabulous. Superior service and fine-dining opportunities make for an exceptional experience. The private-pool villas are truly luxurious. **www.sofitel.com**

KO PHA NGAN Island View Cabana

106 Moo 7, Mae Haad Beach, Ko Pha Ngan, 84280 **Tel** *0-7737-4173* **Rooms** *25*

Backpackers love these cheap, beachfront bungalows with balconies and views of tiny Ko Ma offshore. The bamboo walls are paper-thin, and there is the occasional leak when it rains, but the beach and sea views are what's important for most guests here. There is a relaxed bar and a restaurant serving fresh seafood.

KO PHA NGAN Thongtapan Resort

22 Moo 5, Baantai, Ko Pha Ngan, 84280 **Tel** *0-7723-8538* **Fax** *0-7744-5068* **Rooms** *32*

Located on the beautiful Thong Nai Pan Noi beach, this tranquil resort is made up of bungalows built from natural stone and wood that blend in well with the surroundings. Facilities include a restaurant and café, Internet access, security boxes, and numerous accommodation choices. Ideal for long- or short-stay guests. **www.thongtapan.com**

KO PHA NGAN Green Papaya Resort

64/8 Moo 8, Salad Beach, Ko Pha Ngan, 84280 **Tel** *0-7734-9278* **Fax** *0-7737-4230* **Rooms** *20*

In a fragrant, coconut palm-filled garden by the beach, these beautiful bungalows with polished wooden floors and art on the walls are probably the most stylish you will find on the island. The boat-shaped restaurant and beach bar offer spectacular sunset views, and the curvy swimming pool is something special. **www.greenpapayaresort.com**

KO SAMUI Golden Sand Resort

124/2 Lamai Beach, Ko Samui, 84320 **Tel** *0-7745-8111* **Fax** *0-7742-4430* **Rooms** *63*

While most guests rarely seem to leave the sun beds by the beautiful beachfront swimming pool, the pristine white sands of Lamai beach are just a few steps away. Accommodation is in comfortable hotel rooms or bungalows, all surrounded by tropical gardens. There's also a Jacuzzi and a kids' pool. **www.goldensand-resort.com**

KO SAMUI Coral Cove Chalet

210 Moo 4, Coral Cove Beach, Tong Takian Beach, Ko Samui, 84320 **Tel** *0-7742-2260* **Fax** *0-7742-2496* **Rooms** *81*

These attractive chalets are nestled on a palm-covered hillside overlooking a pretty cove and private white-sand beach with crystal-clear waters. The spacious rooms are painted in pretty pastel colors with big beds covered in mosquito nets. It is possible to snorkel and scuba dive the coral reefs offshore. **www.coralcovechalet.com**

KO SAMUI Anantara

99/9 Moo 1, Bo Phut Bay, Ko Samui, 84320 **Tel** *0-7742-8300* **Fax** *0-7742-8310* **Rooms** *106*

With its exotic Thai architecture, Zen minimalist rooms, and tranquil tropical gardens replete with palms, lily ponds, lotus flowers, frogs, and pretty Thai pavilions, the Anantara is simply sublime. If they weren't reasons enough to stay, there is an infinity pool, an exotic spa, and a superb restaurant, Full Moon *(see p445)*. **www.anantara.com**

KO SAMUI Blue Lagoon Hotel

99 Moo 2, Chaweng Beach, Ko Samui, 84320 **Tel** *0-7742-2037* **Fax** *0-7742-2401* **Rooms** *74*

Beautiful Thai-style architecture and a location on an attractive stretch of Chaweng beach make this resort a popular choice. Families love the swimming pools and long list of water sports, including kayaking, snorkeling, sailing, and waterskiing. The Kantara restaurant is excellent. Half- and full-board available. **www.bluelagoonhotel.com**

KO SAMUI Centara Villas Samui

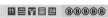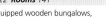

38/2 Moo 3, Natien Beach, Ko Samui, 84320 **Tel** *0-7723-2474* **Rooms** *204*

Situated on the pretty, palm-lined Natien beach in southern Samui, this property boasts a wide stretch of gorgeous white-sand beach. The light-filled Thai-style villas feature colorful, contemporary decor, and some come with private Jacuzzis or plunge pools. The beachside Reef Café is popular. **www.centarahotelsresorts.com**

KO SAMUI Chaweng Regent Beach Resort

155/4 Moo 3, Chaweng Beach, Ko Samui, 84320 **Tel** *0-7742-2008* **Fax** *0-7742-2222* **Rooms** *141*

Situated on Chaweng beach, this beautiful Thai-style resort offers a range of well-equipped wooden bungalows, rooms, and suites. All have parquet floors, wooden or bamboo furniture, traditional Thai touches, and shady patios or verandas. The breezy beachfront restaurant is excellent. **www.chawengregent.com**

KO SAMUI Coral Bay Resort & Spa

9 Moo 2, Tambon Bophut, Ko Samui, 84320 **Tel** *0-7723-4555* **Fax** *0-7723-4558* **Rooms** *42*

At the northern end of Chaweng beach, this eco-friendly beachfront resort is set amid lush tropical gardens. The bungalows have thatched roofs, big verandas, and sea views, and they are beautifully decorated inside with coconut-wood furniture. There is a spa on site, and guests can go snorkeling, diving, and fishing. **www.coralbay.net**

KO SAMUI Four Seasons Koh Samui

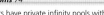

219 Moo 5, Angthong, Ko Samui, 84140 **Tel** *0-7724-3000* **Fax** *0-7724-3002* **Rooms** *74*

Sprawled across palm-covered hills, overlooking a cove, these luxurious villas on stilts have private infinity pools with spectacular sea views. There are two superb restaurants serving Thai, Italian, and seafood dishes; a beachside lounge bar; and a sublime spa set amid the jungle. Samui's best resort by far. **www.fourseasons.com/kohsamui**

KO SAMUI The Library

14/1 Moo 2, Chaweng Beach, Ko Samui, 84320 **Tel** *0-7742-2767* **Fax** *0-7742-2344* **Rooms** *26*

This chic design hotel was developed around the idea that, when on holiday, people spend many pleasurable hours reading. The Library has a sleek floor-to-ceiling glass room crammed with books, magazines, and CDs for guests to use – right beside the red-tiled swimming pool. The minimalist white rooms are striking. **www.thelibrary.co.th**

KO SAMUI Muang Kulaypan Hotel

100 Moo 2, Chaweng Beach, Ko Samui, 84320 **Tel** *0-7723-0850* **Rooms** *42*

This hip hotel attracts a funky crowd to its boho-chic rooms with tie-dye bed covers, big black bathrooms, and art on the walls. There is an arty vibe with sculptures around the property and a stunning black-tiled swimming pool. From the casual beach bar you can survey the action on Chaweng beach. **www.kulaypan.com**

KO SAMUI Poppies Samui Seaside Cottages   Ⅱ❖☰   ⒷⒷⒷⒷⒷ

21/8 Moo 3, Chaweng Beach, Ko Samui, 84320 **Tel** *0-7742-2419* **Fax** *0-7742-2420* **Rooms** *24*

At the southern end of Chaweng beach, Poppies is a lovely village of Thai-style cottages set amid tropical gardens. While the decor has dated somewhat, the rooms are nevertheless comfortable and well appointed. The big attraction here is the white-sand beach; Poppies also offers a wide selection of water sports. **www.poppiessamui.com**

KO SAMUI Punpreeda Hip Resort   Ⅱ❖Ⅶ🖬   ⒷⒷⒷⒷⒷ

32 Moo 4, Bang Rak Beach, Ko Samui, 84320 **Tel** *0-7724-6154* **Fax** *0-7724-6155* **Rooms** *13*

Natural wood, warm glowing lamps, beaded curtains, and hand-dyed fabrics create a boho-chic vibe in the rooms and villas at this stylish beachfront resort with a gorgeous, deep-green pool. *Punpreeda* means "sharing happiness from the heart," and if you are not happy here, you probably won't be happy anywhere. **www.punnpreeda.com**

KO TAO Nangyuan Island Dive Resort   Ⅱ☰   ⒷⒷⒷ

Ko Nang Yuan, near Ko Tao, Surat Thani, 84280 **Tel** *0-7745-6088-93* **Fax** *0-7745-6088* **Rooms** *55*

This private island in a small three-island archipelago offers beautiful bungalows set among big boulders around a gorgeous azure-colored cove. Guests come for the excellent diving among superb marine life on the coral reef encircling the island. Depending on the tide, you will walk or swim to the resort café. **www.nangyuan.com/**

PHETCHABURI Fisherman's Resort   Ⅱ❖Ⅶ☰   ⒷⒷⒷⒷⒷ

170 Moo 1, Haad Chao Samran, Phetchaburi, 76100 **Tel** *0-3244-1370* **Fax** *0-3244-1380* **Rooms** *35*

This stylish boutique resort of luxury villas on the beautiful beachfront of Haad Chao Samran, a traditional fishing village in rural Phetchaburi, has an alluring swimming pool, a lovely spa, and an array of activities, including fishing, water sports, hiking, biking, and birdwatching. **www.thefishermansresort.com**

PRACHUAP KHIRI KHAN Hadthong Hotel   🖥Ⅱ❖☰   ⒷⒷⒷ

21 Suseuk Rd, Prachuap Khiri Khan, 77000 **Tel** *0-3260-1050* **Fax** *0-3260-1057* **Rooms** *140*

This first-class international hotel offers the only quality accommodation in the area. Its spacious, comfortable, but rather bland rooms have stunning views of the Gulf of Thailand and the nearby mountains from their balconies. The hotel restaurant may be rather drab, but it serves excellent seafood. **www.hadthong.com**

SURAT THANI Grand Saowaluk Hotel   🖥Ⅱ❖Ⅶ☰🖬24   ⒷⒷⒷ

99 Karnjanawitee Rd, Bangkung, Surat Thani, 84000 **Tel** *0-7721-3700* **Rooms** *175*

One of the best hotels in town, the Grand Saowaluk offers a good range of modern facilities. The accommodation comprises superior, deluxe, and junior suite rooms all of which are spacious and well-equipped. Thai and international cuisine is served in the restaurant and there is live music nightly. **www.sawadee.com**

UPPER ANDAMAN COAST

KO LANTA Kaw Kwang Beach Resort   Ⅱ❖☰   ⒷⒷⒷ

16 Moo 1, Saladan, Ko Lanta Yai, 81150 **Tel** *0-7566-8260* **Fax** *0-7566-8259* **Rooms** *60*

These little wooden cottages would not win any design awards, but they are good value. There is a wide choice – from standards without views to deluxe with sea vistas. All are spacious, comfortable, and set in lush grounds, but the highlights are the big, round swimming pool and lovely beachside location. **www.lanta-kawkwangresort.com**

KO LANTA Costa Lanta Resort   Ⅱ❖   ⒷⒷⒷⒷ

212 Moo 1, Saladan, Ko Lanta, 81150 **Tel** *0-7566-8186* **Fax** *0-2325-0926* **Rooms** *22*

This sleek one-of-a-kind beach resort, with its contemporary, minimalist architecture and low-key vibe, attracts a hip young crowd. The open-sided polished-concrete rooms will not suit those who value their privacy, but style-seekers love them. The large restaurant and bar has a wonderfully relaxed vibe. **www.costalantaresort.com**

KO LANTA Narima Bungalow Resort   Ⅱ❖☰   ⒷⒷⒷⒷ

98 Moo 5, Klong Nin, Ko Lanta, 81150 **Tel** *0-7566-2668* **Fax** *0-7566-2669* **Rooms** *32*

This eco-friendly designer bungalow resort (and dive school) is beautiful, and its verandas and hammocks are positioned to take full advantage of the tropical garden and sea views. There is an excellent restaurant and jazz bar, but what really makes the resort special is the warmth of its Thai owners. **www.narima-lanta.com**

KO LANTA Pimalai Resort & Spa   Ⅱ❖Ⅶ🖬24   ⒷⒷⒷⒷⒷ

99 Moo 5, Ba Kan Tiang Beach, Ko Lanta, 81150 **Tel** *0-2320-5500* **Fax** *0-2320-5503* **Rooms** *121*

This award-winning resort with luxurious pavilion suites and villas has superb cafés, bars, and restaurants, including the beachside Rak Talay, where you can dine with your toes in the sand. There are two infinity pools, complimentary bikes, water sports, island excursions, and sunset cruises. **www.pimalai.com**

KO LANTA Sri Lanta   Ⅱ❖Ⅶ☰   ⒷⒷⒷⒷⒷ

111 Moo 6 Klongnin Beach, Ko Lanta, 81150 **Tel** *0-7566-2688* **Fax** *0-7566-2687* **Rooms** *49*

This stunning boutique beach resort set on 12 acres of tropical hillside successfully mixes a chic sense of style with a rustic warmth rarely found in contemporary design hotels. The black-tiled beachside swimming pool is enticing, the Sri Spa sublime, and the beach bar and café are relaxed. Service is excellent. **www.srilanta.com**

Key to Price Guide *see p398* **Key to Symbols** *see back cover flap*

KO PHI PHI Ao Toh Ko Bungalows

Ao Toh Ko Beach, Ko Phi Phi, 81000 **Tel** *081-537-0528* **Rooms** *32*

The beautiful, deserted, white-sand beach and great snorkeling are the big attractions here, and while these no-frills bungalows are basic, they do have decent-sized balconies and stunning beach and sea views. The owner and staff are friendly, and there is a good little restaurant and hillside bar with sea views.

KO PHI PHI Phi Phi Island Village Beach Resort & Spa

49 Moo 8, T Aonang, Ko Phi Phi, 81000 **Tel** *0-7621-5014* **Fax** *0-7622-2784* **Rooms** *112*

Spectacularly situated on one of Thailand's best beaches, in lush vegetation thick with coconut palms, this is as close to paradise as resorts get. There are plenty of accommodation choices (from hillside pool villas to beachfront bungalows), restaurants and bars, swimming pools, water sports, and a PADI dive center. **www.ppisland.com**

KO PHI PHI Zeavola

11 Moo 8 Laem Tong, Ko Phi Phi, 81000 **Tel** *0-7562-7000 or 0-7562-7024* **Fax** *0-7562-7023* **Rooms** *52*

These charming teak villas with country Thai decor featuring hill-tribe textiles should be more suited to rural Thailand than a Southern Thai beach resort, but the owner's aim was to create a luxurious rural Thai village on the beach – and he succeeded. One of Thailand's must-do experiences. **www.zeavola.com**

KRABI Krabi Resort

232 Moo 2 Tambon Ao Nang, Krabi, 81000 **Tel** *0-7563-7030* **Fax** *0-7563-7051* **Rooms** *170*

This picturesque resort is better known for its range of activities – excursions, canoeing, fishing, rock climbing, sailing, scuba diving, snorkeling, cycling, horse riding, and elephant trekking – than for its uninspiring if comfortable and well-appointed rooms, villas, and bungalows scattered throughout a verdant garden. **www.krabiresort.net**

KRABI Pakasai Resort

88 Moo 3, T Ao Nang, Krabi, 81000 **Tel** *0-7563-7777* **Fax** *0-7563-7637* **Rooms** *104*

The views from the big infinity pool across tropical gardens out to the azure Andaman Sea are gorgeous, and the location adjoining Nopparat Thara National Marine Park is special. The rooms are not nearly as exotic, with simple rattan furniture and conservative decor, but the rustic spa makes up for any shortcomings. **www.pakasai.com**

KRABI Railei Beach Club

Railay Beach West, Krabi, 81000 **Tel** *08-6685-9359* **Fax** *0-7581-9445* **Rooms** *24*

Ideal for families and groups, these comfortable, traditional Thai teak houses are situated on a lush private estate on a beautiful beach that's accessible only by boat. Houses have big verandas, gardens, and great views. There is also a clubhouse with rooms. Activities include diving, snorkeling, fishing, and birdwatching. **www.raileibeachclub.com**

KRABI Phra Nang Inn

119 Moo 2, Ao Nang Beach, Krabi, 81000 **Tel** *0-7563-7130* **Fax** *0-7563-7134* **Rooms** *69*

With its charming, rustic architecture (the resort is constructed from pine and coconut palms), tropical gardens, and rather whimsical decor of mismatched furniture, the Phra Nang Inn has lots of character. It is also centrally located, has great views over Ao Nang beach, a terrific restaurant, and a decent-sized pool. **www.vacationvillage.co.th/**

KRABI Ritz-Carlton Reserve Phulay Bay

111 Moo 3 Nongthalay, Muang, Krabi, 81000 **Tel** *0-7562-8111 ext. 1800* **Fax** *0-7562-8123* **Rooms** *54*

If you are seeking once-in-a-lifetime, break-the-budget luxury, look no farther. This artfully created resort is ideal for a romantic retreat but also manages to be family-friendly. Every room has a private outdoor space, and attention to detail and customer service are second to none. **http://reserve.ritzcarlton.com/phulay_bay/home.aspx**

PHANGNGA Aleenta Resort & Spa

33 Moo 5 T Khokkloy, Phangnga, 82140 **Tel** *0-7658-0333* **Fax** *0-7658-0350* **Rooms** *50*

This chic resort set on a deserted stretch of beach 20 minutes north of Phuket airport, makes for an accessible secluded escape. The sleek, white, minimalist suites have stunning sea views, iPods, yoga mats, and plunge pools. There is a sublime beach bar and an excellent restaurant on site. **www.aleenta.com**

PHUKET Square One

241/34 Ratuthit Rd, Patong Beach, Phuket, 83150 **Tel** *0-7634-9909* **Fax** *0-7634-9908* **Rooms** *14*

This budget hotel offers great value. The rooms are simply decorated, but spotlessly clean, with satellite TVs and fridges. Long-stay guests should upgrade to a suite, which is considerably more comfortable. There is wireless Internet and a small swimming pool, but with little room to sunbathe you will probably head to the beach. **www.square1.biz**

PHUKET Summer Breeze Inn Hotel

85/130 Iravadee Village Moo 6, Soi 2, Phuket Town, Phuket, 83000 **Tel** *08-1893-7651* **Fax** *0-7652-6686* **Rooms** *5*

This family-run, no-frills guesthouse is situated on a quiet side street in a village center, close to a bus station and 15 minutes from the pier. The rooms are clean, well appointed, and complete with air-conditioning and TVs. The friendly owners do all they can for their guests. **www.summerbreezeinn.com**

PHUKET Kamala Dreams

74/1 Moo 3 Tambon Kamala, Katu, 83120 **Tel** *0-7627-9131* **Fax** *0-7627-9132* **Rooms** *18*

Situated on lovely, low-key Kamala beach, not far from colorful Patong and 15 minutes from Phuket Airport, Kamala Dreams consists of comfortable studios with sea views set around a decent-sized pool. Rooms have kitchenettes with fridges and microwaves. There is a small garden and a footbridge leading to the beach. **www.kamaladreams.net**

PHUKET Manathai

121 Srisuntorn Rd, Surin Beach, Phuket, 83000 **Tel** *0-7627-0900* **Fax** *0-7627-0909* **Rooms** *52*

This chic boutique resort features spacious, stylish rooms with contemporary teak furnishings, Thai textiles, Oriental antiques, and hi-tech extras (CD/DVD players, Wi-Fi). The public spaces include a pool (enchantingly lit at night), welcoming lounge areas (wonderful for cocktails), and the superb Weaves restaurant. **www.manathai.com**

PHUKET Amanpuri Resort

118 Moo 3, Sri Santhorn Rd, Pansea Beach, Phuket, 83110 **Tel** *0-7632-4333* **Fax** *0-7632-4100* **Rooms** *40*

Amanpuri's name, Sanskrit for "place of peace," aptly reflects the tranquillity of this luxurious pavilion and villa complex, nestled within coconut groves, overlooking a white-sand beach. The infinity pools with spectacular sea views are alluring, there is a library, and the restaurants are superb (and romantic at night). **www.amanresorts.com**

PHUKET Banyan Tree Resort

33, 33/27 Moo 4, Srisoonthorn Rd, Cherngtalay, Phuket, 83110 **Tel** *0-7632-4374* **Fax** *0-7632-4375* **Rooms** *150*

Overlooking a tranquil lagoon, with an open lobby surrounded by water courts, this luxurious resort exudes serenity. The watery theme continues throughout, from the public pools to the lavishly appointed villas with private plunge pools and the Spa Pool Villa, where a glass-encased bedroom appears to float on water. **www.banyantree.com**

PHUKET Diamond Cliff Resort & Spa

284 Pra Baramee Rd, Kalim, Patong, Phuket, 83150 **Tel** *0-7634-0501* **Fax** *0-7634-0507* **Rooms** *333*

While the architecture and interiors look dated, this big resort keeps families and groups entertained with eight restaurants and cafés, themed nights, and myriad activities, including cooking classes, vegetable carving, batik painting, glass painting, and massage, tennis, and golf lessons. **www.diamondcliff.com**

PHUKET Evason Six Senses Spa Resort

100 Vised Rd, Moo 2, Tambol Rawai, Phuket, 83100 **Tel** *0-7638-1010* **Fax** *0-7638-1018* **Rooms** *260*

Sprawled across a tropical garden, this eco-friendly resort has something for everyone, from pool suites for couples seeking privacy to family-size villas; all are superbly appointed. There is a children's pool and kids' club if parents want to retreat to the sublime adults-only infinity pool. **www.sixsenses.com/evason-phuket**

PHUKET Indigo-Pearl

Nai Yang Beach, adjoining Nai Yang National Park, 83110 **Tel** *0-7632-7006* **Fax** *0-7632-7015* **Rooms** *277*

The striking design at this hotel evokes the area's tin-mining history while incorporating recycled objects found post-tsunami and the owner's family heirlooms. While it is a large resort, clever architecture and landscaping succeed in making it feel more intimate. The pools are stunning, and the village nearby is charming. **www.indigo-pearl.com**

PHUKET Laguna Beach Club

323 Sri Sunthorn Rd, Cherngtalay, Phuket, 83110 **Tel** *0-7632-4352* **Fax** *0-7632-4353* **Rooms** *252*

Set around a tropical lagoon, this large resort may not be luxurious, but it is super-comfortable. Rooms are spacious, with contemporary Thai decor and lagoon views. There are several alfresco eating places and an array of sports activities to keep the family entertained, including a waterpark and a supervised kids' club. **www.lagunabeach-resort.com**

PHUKET Sawasdee Village

38 Katekwan Rd, Kata Beach, 83100 **Tel** *0-7633-0979* **Fax** *0-7633-0905* **Rooms** *54*

Sawasdee Village is a superb boutique resort set in tropical gardens next to Kata Beach. The hotel boasts beautifully appointed rooms and its luxurious Baray Spa, where guests can indulge in ancient Thai treatments, is considered to be the best on the island. The elegant Sawasdee Thai Cuisine offers authentic Thai fare. **www.phuketsawasdee.com**

PHUKET Thara Patong Beach Resort

81 Thaweewongse Rd, Patong, Phuket, 83150 **Tel** *0-7634-0135* **Fax** *0-7634-0446* **Rooms** *172*

The smart lobby and friendly faces give way to an attractive seaside resort with myriad restaurants, bars, and cafés, two free-form swimming pools, Jacuzzi, tennis courts, and sauna. There is a pool for the kids and an excellent seafood restaurant. Ask about the promotional packages, far cheaper than the full rates. **www.tharapatong.com**

DEEP SOUTH

HAT YAI Louise Guesthouse

21-23 Thamnoonvitti Rd, Hat Yai, 90110 **Tel** *0-7422-0966* **Rooms** *22*

Backpackers love this simple guesthouse, definitely the best deal in town. Staff are warm and friendly and can give reliable travel advice (essential in this region), and the hotel is close to transport connections and the bustling eating and shopping scene. While rooms may be spartan, they are reasonably well maintained and clean.

HAT YAI Lee Gardens Plaza Hotel

29 Prachatipat Rd, Hat Yai, 90110 **Tel** *0-7426-1111* **Fax** *0-7435-3555* **Rooms** *405*

This modern high-rise resort attached to a shopping mall has clean, comfortable (if characterless) rooms. There is a pleasant rooftop pool and a good fitness center. The Sky View Buffet restaurant has spectacular views of the city, although regular business guests rave about the Tian Chwu Chinese restaurant, also on site. **www.leeplaza.com**

Key to Price Guide *see p398* **Key to Symbols** *see back cover flap*

HAT YAI Sakura Grand View

186 Niphat Uthit 3 Rd, Hat Yay, 90110 **Tel** *0-7435-5700* **Fax** *0-7435-5720* **Rooms** *230*

Although it looks a little dated, this high-rise hotel has clean, comfortable rooms with television and fridge. Catering primarily to business travelers, it also has a karaoke club, billiard room, and massage parlor. The hotel boasts that their security system is the best – an important consideration in this region. **www.sakuragrandviewhotel.com**

HAT YAI Novotel Centara Hat Yai

3 Sanehanusorn Rd, Hat Yay, 90110 **Tel** *0-7435-2222* **Fax** *0-7435-2223* **Rooms** *245*

Aimed at business travelers, this high-rise hotel in the center of Hat Yay is very comfortable, with well-appointed rooms with pay-movies and Internet access (only dial-up). It is a rather stylish hotel with several good restaurants and bars (Ginger is recommended) and a fantastic rooftop swimming pool. **www.centarahotelsresorts.com**

KO TARUTAO National Park Bungalows

Ko Tarutao and Adang National Marine Park **Tel** *0-7478-3485* **Rooms** *16*

While these national-park bungalows are basic, the beach setting is incredibly beautiful – a true delight for nature lovers. There are toilets and showers, an information center, a mini-supermarket, and even a restaurant serving cheap tasty food and beer all day. Note that the nearest ATM is at La Ngu.

NAKHON SI THAMMARAT Thaksin Hotel

1584/23 Sriprad Rd, Nakhon Si Thammarat, 80000 **Tel** *0-7534-2790* **Fax** *0-7534-2794* **Rooms** *115*

Most of Nakhon Si Thammarat's hotels are rather characterless, and this is no exception; however, this big business hotel is great value. It boasts spacious, clean rooms with fridge and television, and a decent restaurant serving Thai and Chinese food that turns into a karaoke bar at night. Staff are friendly. **www.thaksinhotel.com**

NAKHON SI THAMMARAT Twin Lotus Hotel

97/8 Pattanakarn-Kukwang Rd, Nakhon Si Thammarat, 80000 **Tel** *0-7532-3777* **Fax** *0-7532-3821* **Rooms** *400*

This is a very opulent-looking hotel for a three star, with padded leather sofas, grand columns, enormous flower arrangements, and a starry ceiling in the lobby. The rooms are not as flash, with rather dated furnishings that could do with an upgrade. There is a good Chinese restaurant and a big swimming pool. **www.twinlotushotel.net**

NAKHON SI THAMMARAT Racha Kiri Resort & Spa

99 Naiplao-Thong Yee Rd, Nai Plad Beach, 80210 **Tel** *0-7530-0245* **Fax** *0-7530-0295* **Rooms** *33*

This stylish boutique resort is spectacularly situated above a white-sand beach on beautiful Nai-Plou peninsula, not far from the Ko Samui ferry pier. The chic rooms sport contemporary four-poster beds with silk cushions and mosquito nets. The alfresco restaurant and swimming pool have stunning sea views. **www.rachakiri.com**

NARATHIWAT Tanyong Hotel

16/1 Sophapisai Rd, Narathiwat, 96000 **Tel** *0-7351-1477* **Fax** *0-7351-1834* **Rooms** *84*

Situated in town, not too far from the beach, this high-rise business hotel has comfortable, clean, no-frills rooms with television; there are sea views from the rooms on the higher floors. Facilities include a decent 24-hour restaurant, a popular disco, a rather rowdy karaoke bar, a snooker club, and a massage parlor. **www.tanyonghotel.com**

PATTANI CS Pattani

299 Moo 4 Nongjik Rd, Pattani, 94000 **Tel** *0-7333-5093* **Fax** *0-7333-1620* **Rooms** *125*

This modern hotel may be out of town, but it is the best in the area, and staff will help you organize transport. The generously sized rooms are good value. Try the hotel's home-grown specialty of bird's-nest soup. There are two swimming pools that are ideal for cooling down after a hard day's traveling. **www.cspattanihotel.com**

TRANG Coco Cottage

109/77 Moo 9, Tambol Koke-Lor, Trang, 92000 **Tel** *08-7898-6522* **Fax** *08-6478-2522* **Rooms** *76*

This low-key eco-friendly resort on the paradise-like island of Ko Ngai makes for an ideal beach getaway. Travel around the tranquil car-free Ko Ngai is by foot or boat. The thatched-roof log cottages are simply decorated, and there are "longhouses" for families. The Thai owners are very hospitable. **www.coco-cottage.com**

TRANG Thumrin Thana Hotel

69/8 Trang Thana Rd, Trang, 92000 **Tel** *0-7521-1211* **Fax** *0-7522-3288* **Rooms** *289*

This swish high-rise hotel in central Trang has plush, comfortable rooms with good views of the city and thoughtful extras that include complimentary minibar, daily newspapers, and free airport transfers. There is a good Japanese restaurant, an even better bakery, and a popular pub and karaoke bar with VIP rooms. **www.thumrin.co.th**

TRANG Anantara Si Kao Resort & Spa

Pak Meng-Chang Lang Rd, Chang Lang Beach, Trang, 92150 **Tel** *0-7520-5888* **Fax** *0-7520-5899* **Rooms** *138*

Trang's limestone peaks, pristine sandy beaches, tropical forest, and beautiful waterfalls and caves see few foreign tourists, and for many this is their main attraction. The elegant design of the luxurious Anantara takes advantage of the spectacular surroundings, with sea-facing rooms and alfresco dining. **www.anantara.com**

TRANG Koh Mook Sivalai Beach Resort

211/1 Moo 2, Ko Mook, Trang, 92110 **Tel** *0-8765-0999* **Fax** *0-7521-4685* **Rooms** *31*

For many, these beautiful, thatched-roof bungalows, nestled under coconut palms and within splashing distance of the sea, are simply paradise. Their glass doors open onto the beach, with the water just steps away. Also available are a good restaurant, a big swimming pool, and a good range of water sports. **www.komooksivalai.com**

The Flavors of Thailand

Thai food is popular worldwide for its aromatic and spicy qualities. Chili peppers were first imported to Thailand from the New World in the 16th century by European traders. They were adopted into Thai cuisine (especially the small, fiery ones) with great enthusiasm, but mildly spiced dishes are also widely available. Although influences from China and India can be detected in stir-fries and curries, Thai inventiveness has resulted in a dizzying range of dishes unique to the country. The cuisine is full of distinctive flavors and complementary textures, nutritionally balanced and delightfully presented.

Nam pla phrik

Fish for sale on a local market stall in Chiang Rai

RICE AND NOODLES

In common with those of all its Southeast Asian neighbours, the Thai diet is based on the staples of rice and noodles. The most popular type of rice is the long-grained *khao hom mali*, or fragrant jasmine rice, which is usually steamed. However, in the north and northeast, locals prefer *khao niaw*, or

sticky rice, which is eaten with the fingers, rolled into little balls, and dipped in sauces. Rice porridge *(jok)* is a typical breakfast dish, often with egg, chilies, and rice vinegar stirred in.

Noodles, made of rice *(kuaytiaw)*, wheat and egg *(bami)* or mung beans *(wun sen)*, are usually served fried or in a soup. The most well-known Thai noodle dish among foreigners is *phad thai* (literally "Thai fry").

An irresistible mix of noodles fried with fresh or dried shrimp, egg, beancurd (tofu), and beansprouts, it vies with *tom yam* for the title of Thai national dish.

THE FOUR FLAVORS

All Thai dishes strike a balance between the "four flavors" – sweet, sour, salty, and hot – although the balance varies from dish to dish. While Thai cuisine has

Lemongrass **Ginger** **Shallots** **Thai basil** **Galangal** **Chilies**
Kaffir lime leaves **Turmeric**

Selection of typical Thai herbs, spices and flavourings

REGIONAL DISHES AND SPECIALITIES

Central Thai food is strongly influenced by Chinese cuisine and accounts for most dishes on menus nationwide, including the country's signature dish *tom yam kung*. Northern Thai cuisine takes much of its inspiration from Burma and Yunnan province in China. Examples include *khao soi*, a delicious dish of boiled and crispy noodles in a mild curry broth, and *kaeng hang le*. North-eastern Thais like their food with a kick, and one of their best-known imports from nearby Laos is tangy, crunchy *som tam* salad. Southern food is the fieriest of the lot, with creamy coconut, vibrant turmeric, and sharp tamarind featuring in such typical dishes as sour and spicy *kaeng luang pla*.

Pea eggplants (aubergines)

Tom Yam Kung *uses lemongrass, galangal, kaffir lime, and chili to flavor the hot and sour shrimp broth.*

Traders selling fruit and vegetables at Damnoen Saduak floating market

a reputation for being liberal with its use of chilies, it also features a wide range of subtly flavoured dishes that make use of aromatic herbs and spices such as galangal, lemon grass, kaffir lime leaves, basil, and coriander (cilantro) to enhance aroma and taste. Pastes using these ingredients are pounded by hand in a mortar to ensure the freshest flavor. However, the real key to Thai cuisine is fish sauce *(nam pla)*, which adds its piquancy to the vast majority of dishes. Mixed with chilies, garlic, and lemon it becomes the popular condiment *nam pla phrik*.

THE THAI MEAL

A typical Thai meal consists of a soup, a curry, a stir-fry and a spicy Thai salad, as well as side dishes of raw or steamed vegetables, served with a big bowl of rice. The meal is rarely divided into formal courses. Westerners who do not realize this often order a soup or a salad as a starter whereas, in fact, the spiciness of these dishes is

Melon, expertly carved in the Thai style, as a table decoration

intended to be toned down by eating them with rice. However, Thai restaurant staff are very likely to serve all dishes ordered at the same time anyway. The only concession that Thais make to courses is with dessert, which is usually a plate of mixed fruit intended to clear the palate after the savory dishes. Many foreign visitors also like to indulge in a national favorite – *khao niaw mamuang*, or mango with sticky coconut rice.

WHAT TO DRINK

Fruit juices Thailand's wealth of luscious fruits, such as watermelon, mango, lychee, and papaya, are blended into juices, shakes and smoothies. Chilled coconut juice, drunk through a straw straight from the nut, is perfect for slaking a thirst on the beach.

Beers There is a good range of beers available. Popular choices are the full-bodied local Singha and Chang.

Wines and spirits As well as locally made rice wine, wines from Europe and the New World are widely available, and Thai vineyards are also starting to produce acceptable varieties. The local spirits, Mekong and Sang Som, are very palatable when mixed with ice and soda.

Coffee and tea While not traditional Thai drinks, excellent varieties of both are now grown in the northern hills.

Kaeng Hang Le, *a dry, mild curry of pork with ginger, peanuts, and garlic, is served with rice and Chinese greens.*

Som Tam *is shredded unripe papaya and other vegetables, with lime juice, chili, fish sauce, and dried shrimps.*

Kaeng Lueng Pla *is a spicy fish soup with bamboo shoots, flavored with tamarind, chili, garlic, and palm sugar.*

A Glossary of Typical Thai Dishes

*Khanom khrok –
coconut puddings*

Thai cuisine is famously creative and varied *(see pp38–9)*. Even street vendors delight in their culinary skills, and it is not uncommon to see food being encased in a banana leaf as delicately as if it were being gift wrapped. Such artful presentations and the sheer range of dishes can be bewildering to newcomers: it may not even be obvious what is savory or sweet. This glossary covers typical dishes; phonetic guidance for food words is on page 527.

A street vendor cooking over charcoal on a road-side stall

CHOOSING DISHES

Restaurant menus in tourist areas may include descriptions in English, and sometimes other languages. The Thai names of dishes often derive simply from the main elements – for instance, the dish *khao mu daeng* translates literally as "rice, pork, red." Thus, the basic components of any dish can often be worked out with only a little knowledge of Thai. If there is no menu, the dishes of the day will be on display. If you don't recognize the dish, pointing and saying *"nee arai na?"* ("what's this?") should elicit a list of ingredients.

Vegetarians should find it easy to order food without meat *(mai ao nua)*, but ought to be aware that fish sauce is used in many dishes. Dairy products feature only rarely in Thai cuisine, so vegans should not fare worse than vegetarians.

Thais are accustomed to foreigners asking if a dish is spicy *(phed mai?)*, or requesting a non-spicy meal *(mai ao phet na)*. To enliven any dish, diners can use the ubiquitous condiments of chilies in vinegar, chili flakes, sugar (for savory dishes), and fish sauce usually found on tables.

SNACKS

Chicken satay

Thais love to snack. Almost every street corner has a selection of food stalls selling raw and freshly cooked snacks.

Bami mu daeng
บะหมี่หมูแดง
Egg noodles with red pork.
Khai ping
ไข่ปิ้ง
Charcoal-roasted eggs.
Kai yang
ไก่ย่าง
Charcoal-grilled chicken.
Khanom beuang
ขนมเบื้อง
Filled, sweet, crisp pancakes.

Khanom khrok
ขนมครก
Coconut puddings.
Khao tom mud
ข้าวต้มมัด
Sticky rice served in banana leaves.
Kluay ping
กล้วยปิ้ง
Charcoal-grilled bananas.
Look chin ping
ลูกชิ้นปิ้ง
Meatballs with a chili sauce.
Po pia tod
ปอเปี๊ยะ
Deep-fried spring rolls.
Sai krok
ไส้กรอก
Thai beef or pork sausages.

Satay
สะเต๊ะ
Slivers of beef, pork, or chicken grilled on a stick, served with peanut sauce and cucumber.
Tua thod
ถั่วทอด
Roasted cashews or peanuts.

NOODLES

Rice noodles come as *sen yai* (broad), *sen lek* (medium), and *sen mi* (thin). *Bami* are egg noodles. *Woon sen* are thin, transparent soy noodles.

Bami nam
บะหมี่น้ำ
Egg noodles in a broth with vegetables and meat or fish.
Kuaytiaw haeng
ก๋วยเตี๋ยวแห้ง
Rice noodles served "dry" with vegetables and meat or fish.
Kuaytiaw nam
ก๋วยเตี๋ยวน้ำ
Rice noodles in a broth with vegetables and meat or fish.
Kuaytiaw look chin pla
ลูกชิ้นปลา
Fishballs with noodles.
Phad thai
ผัดไทย
Rice noodles fried with bean-curd, egg, dried shrimp, peanuts, bean sprouts, and chili.

Street sellers and their customers in a Bangkok market

RICE DISHES

Rice is the staple food. A familiar Thai greeting, equivalent to "how are you?" is *kin khao mai?*, literally "have you eaten rice?"

Khao man kai
ข้าวมันไก่
Chinese-style chicken with rice cooked in chicken stock.

Khao mok kai
ข้าวหมกไก่
Thai-style chicken biriyani.

Khao mu daeng
ข้าวหมูแดง
Chinese-style red pork served on a bed of fragrant rice.

Khao na ped
ข้าวหน้าเป็ด
Roast duck served on a bed of fragrant rice.

Khao phad mu/kung
ข้าวผัดหมูหรือกุ้ง
Fried rice with pork or shrimp.

SOUPS

Soups are diverse and inventive. Some, such as *jok*, are eaten for breakfast. The word *"sup"* is widely recognized.

Jok
โจ๊ก
Ground rice porridge with minced pork and ginger.

Khao tom
ข้าวต้ม
Rice soup with a selection of meat and vegetable side dishes.

Tom jeud tao hu
ต้มจืดเต้าหู้
Mild broth with beancurd and minced pork.

Tom kha kai
ต้มข่าไก่
Chicken soup with galingale, coconut milk, and lemon grass.

Tom yam kung
ต้มยำกุ้ง
Shrimp, mushrooms, lemon grass, galingale, and coriander.

CURRIES

Curries are served either *rat khao* (on a plate of rice) or in a bowl as an accompaniment to a central bowl of rice.

Kaeng kari kai
แกงกะหรี่ไก่
Indian-style chicken and potato.

Kaeng khiaw wan
แกงเขียวหวาน
Slightly sweet green curry.

Fragrant green leaves make a perfect wrapping for sticky rice

Kaeng matsaman
แกงมัสมั่น
A mild curry from the Muslim South with chicken, peanuts, potatoes, and coconut milk.

Kaeng phanaeng
แกงแพนง
Southern-style "dry" curry with coconut and basil.

Kaeng phed
แกงเผ็ด
A hot curry with red chilies, lemon grass, and coriander.

Kaeng som
แกงส้ม
Hot and sour curry, often with fish.

SEAFOOD

An amazing variety of seafood is available at reasonable prices, particularly in the South.

Hoi malaeng pu op
หอยแมลงภู่อบ
Steamed green mussels.

Hoi thod
หอยทอด
Oysters fried in batter with egg on a bed of beansprouts.

Hu chalam
หูฉลาม
Shark's fin soup.

Southern seafood, including crab

Kung mangkon phao
กุ้งมังกรเผา
Grilled lobster.

Pla meuk yang
ปลาหมึกย่าง
Roasted sliced squid.

Pla nung khing
ปลานึ่งขิง
Steamed fish with ginger, chili, and mushrooms.

Pla thod
ปลาทอด
Deep fried fish.

Pu neung
ปูนึ่ง
Steamed crab.

REGIONAL DISHES

Kaeng hang le
แกงฮังเล
Pork, peanut, and ginger curry from Chiang Mai.

Khao soi
ข้าวซอย
Chicken or beef curry served with wheat noodles, fresh lime, and pickled cabbage. A Northern specialty.

Larb ped
ลาบเป็ด
Northern spicy minced duck.

Som tam
ส้มตำ
Green papaya salad with peanuts, from the Northeast.

Yam thalay
ยำทะเล
Southern spicy seafood salad.

DESSERTS

Known as *khong wan* or "sweet things," these are mostly coconut or fruit based.

Foy thong
ฝอยทอง
Sweet, shredded egg yolk.

Khao niaw mamuang
ข้าวเหนียวมะม่วง
Fresh mango served with sticky rice and coconut milk.

Kluay buat chi
กล้วยบวดชี
Bananas in coconut milk.

Mo kaeng
หม้อแกง
Thai-style egg custard.

DRINKS

Bia
เบียร์
Beer. Usually served in bottles.

Cha ron
ชาร้อน
Tea with condensed milk.

Kafae
กาแฟ
Coffee, often instant.

Nam cha
น้ำชา
Chinese-style tea without milk.

Nam kuad
น้ำขวด
Bottled water.

Coconut seller on the Floating Market

Choosing a Restaurant

The restaurants in this guide have been selected across a wide range for their good value, exceptional food, or interesting location. These listings highlight some of the factors that may influence your choice, such as whether you can eat outdoors or if the venue offers live music. Entries are alphabetical within each price category.

PRICE CATEGORIES
For an evening meal for one, including service, but not alcohol.

Ⓑ Under 120 *baht*
ⒷⒷ 120–250 *baht*
ⒷⒷⒷ 250–500 *baht*
ⒷⒷⒷⒷ 500–800 *baht*
ⒷⒷⒷⒷⒷ Over 800 *baht*

BANGKOK

CHINATOWN/OLD TOWN Kor Panich

Ⓑ

431-3 Tanao Rd, Saochingcha, Bangkok, 10200 **Tel** *0-2221-3554*

Map 2 D5

Kor Panich has been in the business of serving sweet sticky rice for more than 80 years. This fabulous dessert is a real treat and must be sampled when in Thailand. At Kor Panich you can try the classic sticky rice and mango, or the delicious alternative, durian in coconut-milk sauce. *Sangkhaya*, a type of Thai egg custard, is also available.

CHINATOWN/OLD TOWN Phad Thai Loong Pha

Ⓑ

315 Mahachai Rd, Somranrat, Bangkok, 10200 **Tel** *0-2621-0082*

Map 6 D1

Phad thai is one of the country's most famous dishes. In the West, it is served in fancy Thai restaurants, but here in Thailand, it is a budget one-pot wonder. Devotees of this tasty noodle dish swear by Pad Thai Loong Pha. This unassuming shop-house restaurant serves up phad thai and other specialty noodle dishes at rock-bottom prices.

CHINATOWN/OLD TOWN Punjab Sweets

Ⓑ

436/5 Chakraphet Rd, Phahurat, Bangkok, 10200 **Tel** *0-8186-9381-5*

Map 6 D1

Vegetarian restaurants are few and far between in Bangkok, but there are a few tucked away in the Indian district of Phahurat, on the border of Chinatown. The small and basic restaurant serves up authentic Indian cuisine, including dosa, puri, samosa, and of course, Indian sweets. This is one of two Punjab Sweets in the Chakraphet Road area.

CHINATOWN/OLD TOWN Roti Mataba

Ⓑ

136 Pra Ahtit Rd, Chansasongkarm, Bangkok, 10220 **Tel** *0-2282-2119*

Map 1 C3

This small Thai-Muslim eatery has become a travelers' favorite. Roti Mataba is an inexpensive place to enjoy a classic Indian/Malay roti, a delicious fried flatbread served with a small bowl of dahl or curry sauce for dipping. This satisfying dish is traditionally served as a breakfast meal. The restaurant, however, is open throughout the day.

CHINATOWN/OLD TOWN Fisherman's Seafood Restaurant

ⒷⒷⒷⒷ

1/12 Soi Mahathat, Maharaj Rd, Bangkok, 10200 **Tel** *08-4457-8800*

Map 1 C5

Located on the banks of the Chao Phraya River and enjoying views of the Royal Palace, this well-known restaurant has been given a modern makeover and is one of the most enjoyable places to discover Thai and Western seafood. The grilled seafood satay and the steamed blue swimming crab with ginger sauce come highly recommended.

DOWNTOWN Long Table

Ⓑ

25th Floor, 48 Column Building, Sukhumvit Soi 16, Bangkok, 10110 **Tel** *0-2302-2557*

This fabulous restaurant serves great drinks and tasty, Thai-inspired contemporary fine dining to an attractive client base. The building dates from 2006 and is decorated in a suitably modern style. The terrace offers stunning views across the city. This is a popular restaurant, so be sure to make a reservation in advance.

DOWNTOWN Hai Somtam

ⒷⒷ

2/4–5 Convent Rd, Silom, Bangkok, 10500 **Tel** *0-2631-0216*

Map 7 C4

Devotees of Northeastern Thai food, known as *aharn Issan*, flock to Hai Somtam. This unassuming, open-fronted restaurant is packed at lunchtimes and early evenings with locals eating spicy *som tam* (papaya salad), grilled chicken, sun-dried pork, sticky rice, and other Issan favorites. Ideal for an authentic taste of the Northeast in Bangkok.

DOWNTOWN Suda

ⒷⒷ

6-6/1 Sukhumvit Soi 14, Bangkok, 10110 **Tel** *0-2229-4664*

Suda has become a favorite evening haunt of the expatriate community in the Sukhumvit area thanks to its inexpensive and delicious cuisine. The open-sided dining room is conveniently located close to Asoke Skytrain station. Popular menu choices include tuna with chilies and cashews, and green curry.

DOWNTOWN Basilico

ⒷⒷⒷ

8 Soi 33, Sukhumvit Rd, Bangkok, 10110 **Tel** *0-2662-2323*

Despite the popularity of Italian food in Bangkok, good pizza is hard to find. Enter Basilico. Since the day its doors opened, this restaurant has been packed. At the heart of the atrium is an enormous wood-fired oven delivering delicious thin-crust pizzas every few minutes. Pasta, fresh seafood, and good wine are also available.

Key to Symbols *see back cover flap*

DOWNTOWN Bua
📋🗺️💲V   ⑧⑧⑧

1/4 Convent Rd, Silom, Bangkok, 10500 **Tel** *0-2237-6640*   **Map 7 C4**

The popular Bua is frequented by both locals and foreigners drawn by its extensive menu of delicious Thai dishes at reasonable prices. The food includes appetizers, salads, soups, and seafood from four of Thailand's main culinary regions. Dishes like *pla neung manaow*, steamed sea bass in lime juice, have sealed the restaurant's reputation.

DOWNTOWN Cabbages & Condoms
⑧⑧⑧

6 Sukhumvit Soi 12, Klong Toey, Bangkok, 10110 **Tel** *0-2229-4611*

Cabbages & Condoms is run by Thailand's Population & Community Development Association (PDA), whose founder, former Thai senator Mechai Viravaidya, believes "birth control should be as cheap as vegetables." The menu includes Thai classics, seafood, and regional dishes. Profits support family planning and AIDS-preventions projects in Thailand.

DOWNTOWN Little Hanoi
⑧⑧⑧

New Food Hall 5F, Emporium Shopping Center, Sukhumvit Soi 24, Bangkok, 10110 **Tel** *no phone*

This modern, casual restaurant is run by Tamarind Café and serves delicious Vietnamese cuisine. Options include beef *pho* noodles, crispy prawns on lemongrass, and fresh spring rolls. Tamarind Café also runs a vegetarian-only outlet called Tamarind Express, in the food hall of the Mahboonkrong (MBK) shopping mall in Patumwan.

DOWNTOWN Oam Thong
⑧⑧⑧

7/4-5 Soi 33, Sukhumvit Rd, Bangkok, 10110 **Tel** *0-2279-5958*

Exquisite food and contemporary Thai decor define Oam Thong. The ambience and traditional music make this the place for a romantic dinner or a special evening with friends. Try coconut-milk soup with chicken and galangal, wing bean salad with minced pork and shrimps, or a sizzling seafood hot plate. Sister restaurant Naj is on Convent Road.

DOWNTOWN Somboon Seafood
⑧⑧⑧

169 Suriwong Rd, Bangrak, Bangkok, 10500 **Tel** *0-2233-3104*   **Map 7 B4**

Thais love nothing more than to sit down to a dinner of fresh seafood. Somboon Seafood is one of the best places to delve into a bewildering array of squid, fish, clam, shrimp, crab, and lobster dishes. Somboon is regularly fully booked, so make a reservation. Also, don't confuse this eatery with other similarly named ones.

DOWNTOWN Coyote Bar & Grill
⑧⑧⑧⑧

575–579 Sukhumvit Rd, Klong Toey Nua, Wattana, Bangkok, 10110 **Tel** *0-2662-3838*   **Map 7 C4**

Voted the number-one place to be seen, Coyote Bar & Grill is Bangkok's best Mexican eatery. This bright, funky restaurant and bar on Sukhumvit Road also has a sister outlet on Convent Road. Tuck into quesadillas, burritos, enchiladas, and racks of pork ribs, and choose from more than 75 different types of margaritas.

DOWNTOWN Indus
⑧⑧⑧⑧

71 Soi 26, Sukhumvit Rd, Bangkok, 10110 **Tel** *0-2258-4900*

This flagship restaurant of Kashmiri chef and food writer Sonya Sapru brings modern Indian cuisine to Bangkok. Light, simple dishes place the emphasis on health without sacrificing flavor. The dining-room decor draws on northern India's cultural heritage, with stunning results. A bar and café add to this fabulous restaurant's ambience.

DOWNTOWN Le Dalat Indochine
⑧⑧⑧⑧

57 Soi Prasarnmitr Sukhumvit 23, Bangkok, 10110 **Tel** *0-2664-0670*

Run by Madame Doan-Hoa-Ly, the head of a well-to-do French-Vietnamese family, Le Dalat Indochine is renowned for the culinary blend of her two cultures. Appetizers include *hue flute* (crabmeat and herbs rolled in rice paper and gently fried). A signature dish is *cua reng mee* (pan-fried crab with tamarind sauce, spring onions, and garlic).

DOWNTOWN Witch's Oyster Bar
⑧⑧⑧⑧

20/20 Ruamrudee Village, Ploenchit Rd, Bangkok, 10330 **Tel** *0-2255-5354*   **Map 8 F2**

Bangkok's only oyster bar is located in the heart of the central business district and attracts a lively after-work crowd. The extensive menu features imported oysters, fresh seafood, grilled meat dishes, tapas, pastas, and risottos. In addition to the fine food, Witch's Oyster Bar is noted for an excellent selection of wines, malt whiskies, and beers.

DOWNTOWN BarSu
⑧⑧⑧⑧⑧

Sheraton Grande Sukhumvit, 250 Sukhumvit Rd, Klong Toey, Bangkok, 10110 **Tel** *0-2649-8358*

BarSu, in the Sheraton Grande Sukhumvit *(see p400)*, is a chic night venue serving cutting-edge cuisine. With a menu created by Michelin-starred chef Yves Mattagne, BarSu presents culinary delights designed for sharing, including sushi, tempura, fresh oysters, seared fish, grilled meats, tapas, and sweet treats. Impressive wine list and signature cocktails.

DOWNTOWN basil
⑧⑧⑧⑧⑧

250 Sukhumvit Rd, Bangkok, 10110 **Tel** *0-2649-8888*

Emerging as the benchmark of contemporary Thai dining in Bangkok, this restaurant has a well-deserved reputation for serving high-quality cuisine in a sophisticated environment. With a repertoire of more than 100 dishes, basil offers traditional Thai food presented with modern flair and artistry. A la carte and set menus are available.

DOWNTOWN China House
⑧⑧⑧⑧⑧

Oriental Hotel, 48 Oriental Avenue, Bangkok, 10150 **Tel** *0-2659-9000*   **Map 6 F5**

Inspired by the Art Deco period of 1930s Shanghai, China House at the Oriental Hotel *(see p400)* is an avant-garde restaurant serving classic cuisine with a contemporary twist. Guests can enjoy exquisite dishes such as roasted Peking duck with traditional condiments, and hand-pulled noodles with shredded abalone and shark's fin in a golden broth.

DOWNTOWN Drinking Tea, Eating Rice

Conrad Bangkok, 87 Wireless Rd, Bangkok, 10330 **Tel** *0-2690-9999*   **Map** *8 E2*

Drinking Tea, Eating Rice is a stylish Japanese restaurant with a sophisticated menu. Discover the artistry and subtle flavors of beautifully presented sashimi, sushi, and flame-charred meats. The signature dish is the Kobe beef sirloin teppanyaki with stir-fried vegetables and a trio of sauces. Private dining rooms are available.

DOWNTOWN Koi

26 Sukhumvit Soi 20, Klong Toey, Bangkok, 10110 **Tel** *0-2258-1590*

Koi, an ultra-trendy Japanese restaurant, is a stunning addition to Bangkok's increasingly eclectic dining scene. Although it has branches in Los Angeles and New York, this is the first one in Asia. The interior design is fabulous, and the restaurant attracts the stars of Bangkok, who come for sushi and sashimi presented with a Californian flair.

DOWNTOWN Le Normandie

Mandarin Oriental Hotel, 48 Oriental Avenue, Bangkok, 10500 **Tel** *0-2237-0041*   **Map** *6 F5*

Said to be the finest French restaurant in Asia, Le Normandie offers an elegant setting in the Mandarin Oriental's Garden Wing *(see p400)*, impeccable service, an exceptional wine list, and à la carte seafood and meat dishes. Thai celebrities, politicians, and royalty often dine here. Highlights include breast of Bresse pigeon with foie gras.

DOWNTOWN Reflexions

Le Méridien Plaza Athénée, 10 Wireless Rd, Bangkok, 10330 **Tel** *0-2650-8800*   **Map** *8 E2*

On the third floor of the Plaza Athénée hotel *(see p399)*, Reflexions is a sophisticated restaurant offering modern French fare. Chef Thibault Chiumenti's inspired cuisine won the place a spot on *Thailand Tatler*'s Best Restaurants list three years running. Dishes are made using the finest seasonal ingredients and served with style and creativity.

DOWNTOWN Sala Rim Nahm

Mandarin Oriental Hotel, 48 Oriental Avenue, Bangkok, 10500 **Tel** *0-2659-9000*   **Map** *6 F5*

This is the signature Thai restaurant of the Mandarin Oriental Hotel *(see p400)*. Lunch consists of a lavish buffet, while evening diners are treated to a set gourmet dinner menu and a performance of traditional Thai dance. The refined cuisine is complemented by a selection of Thai wines. An open-air pavilion overlooks the Chao Phraya River.

DOWNTOWN Sirocco

1055 State Tower, Silom Rd, Bangkok, 10500 **Tel** *0-2624-9555*

Sirocco takes dining to new heights, with a spectacular open-air rooftop restaurant occupying the 63rd floor of one of Bangkok's tallest buildings. Diners can enjoy Mediterranean cuisine and breathtaking views of Bangkok's night skyline. The cocktail bar is one of the city's most popular drinking spots. Reservations are recommended.

DOWNTOWN V9

Sofitel Silom, 188 Silom Rd, Bangkok, 10500 **Tel** *0-2238-1991*   **Map** *7 B4*

V9 is a sophisticated French restaurant and wine bar on the 37th floor of the Sofitel Silom *(see p400)*. Diners can sample dishes from a choice of tasting menus, which, with six small themed dishes, are ideal for sharing. An exquisite set menu of French food and one of the best selections of wine in Bangkok make V9 an essential dining experience.

DOWNTOWN Vertigo Grill and Moon Bar

Banyan Tree Hotel, 21/100 South Sathorn Rd, Bangkok, 10120 **Tel** *0-2679-1200*   **Map** *8 D4*

Voted one of the best bars in the world, this fabulous open-air restaurant is on the 60th floor of the Banyan Tree Hotel. The view is breathtaking, and a meal or evening cocktail here is a must for all visitors. Barbecued dishes include red mullet en papillote with thyme, and grilled scallops with coriander butter. In bad weather, check it is open beforehand.

DUSIT May Kaidee's Vegetarian Restaurant II

33 Soi 1, Samsen Rd, Bangkok, 10300 **Tel** *0-2281-7137*   **Map** *2 D3*

May Kaidee has developed a considerable reputation among vegetarians. With the original branch on Bangkok's Tanao Road and another in Chiang Mai, her eateries are firmly on the meat-free diner's map. Spring rolls, green curry with tofu, and phad thai feature on the extensive menu. The chef also offers cooking classes and runs a guesthouse.

DUSIT Kaloang Home Kitchen

2 Soi Wat Tevarakunchorn, Bangkok, 10300 **Tel** *0-2281-9228*   **Map** *2 E2*

Although a little hard to find, Kaloang Home Kitchen is worth visiting. Tucked away behind the National Library, this plain and simple alfresco riverside venue serves excellent and inexpensive Thai cuisine. Must-try dishes include the fried cotton fish with a raw mango salad, seafood *tom yam* (spicy soup), and stir-fried crab with curry powder.

DUSIT TaraTara Thai

131/4 Kao Rd, Samsen, Dusit, Bangkok, 10300 **Tel** *0-2241-7900*   **Map** *2 E1*

At this riverside restaurant with an expansive terrace, you can watch as your food is prepared over an open grill. The menu includes salads, curries, and stir-fried vegetables. Try *goong ob wun sen*, baked noodles with river prawns. A dining boat leaves every evening at 7:30pm for a two-hour cruise. The lunchtime buffet is exceptional value.

DUSIT Spice & Rice Thai Restaurant

Siam City Hotel, 477 Si Ayuthaya Rd, Phayathai, Bangkok, 10400 **Tel** *0-2247-0123*

Spice & Rice serves Royal and regional Thai cuisine in the elegant surroundings of the Garden Pavilion. Try the *tom som pla chon*, deep-fried fish in a spicy and sour soup with tamarind and ginger, or the stir-fried barbecued duck in a sweet chili paste. After the meal, retire to the Red Elephant Bar for a cocktail.

Key to Price Guide *see p428* **Key to Symbols** *see back cover flap*

THON BURI Brio

Anantara Bangkok Riverside Resort & Spa, 257 Chareonnakorn Rd, Bangkok, 10600 Tel 0-2476-0022 Map 6 E5

One of several dining options in the Anantara Bangkok Riverside *(see p401)*, Brio offers a casual setting in which to enjoy authentic Italian cuisine. The interior is designed in the style of a Tuscan villa and diners can choose from a menu of pastas, risottos, and wood-fired pizzas. The restaurant boasts views of the Chao Phraya River.

THON BURI Prime

Millennium Hilton Hotel, 123 Chareonnakorn Rd, Bangkok, 10600 Tel 0-2442-2000 Map 6 F5

Regarded as one of the best steakhouses in Bangkok, Prime serves the finest imported beef, fresh lobster, and oysters. Watch as your Caesar salad is skilfully prepared tableside, savor fine wines, or tuck into a shellfish platter. Contemporary chic decor and sweeping river views add to the ambience of this top-notch steakhouse.

THON BURI Supatra River House

266 Soi Wat Rakhang, Arun Amarin Rd, Bangkok, 10700 Tel 0-2411-0305 Map 5 B1

Dining beside the Chao Phraya River is an essential part of any visit to Bangkok. With a view of the Wat Arun temple lit up against the night sky, Supatra River House is perfect for a memorable evening feasting on Thai seafood. Try fried soft-shell crab with garlic and pepper sauce or charcoal-grilled mixed seafood. Set menus are also available.

THON BURI Trader Vic's

Anantara Bangkok Riverside Resort & Spa, 257 Chareonnakorn Rd, Bangkok, 10600 Tel 0-2476-0022 Map 6 E5

Trader Vic's offers diners a unique experience: a Polynesian ambience and fine food and cocktails on the riverside deck. The highlight of the week for many in Bangkok is the spectacular Sunday Mai Tai Jazz Brunch here. The fabulous spread of gourmet international cuisine is one of the best in the city and excellent value.

FARTHER AFIELD Hsien Jong Vegetarian Restaurant

1146/4-5 Thanon Chan, by Thanon Chan Soi 39, Bangkok, 10120 Tel no phone

This cheap and cheerful Chinese vegetarian restaurant with an open-fronted dining area serves a wide variety of tasty dishes. Don't worry about not understanding the menu: everything is displayed on stainless-steel trays, and you simply point at what you want. The nearest Skytrain station is Surasak. Take a taxi from there.

FARTHER AFIELD Somtam Nua

4/20 Kaset-Nawamin Rd, Ladprao, Bangkok, 10230 Tel 0-2570-0067

If there is a dish that Thais can't live without, it is *som tam*, the classic Northeastern spicy papaya salad. Somtam Nua is a spacious upscale Issan restaurant and a haven for lovers of dishes such as *som tam*, *larb moo* (pork salad), and *kai yang* (charcoal-grilled chicken). Live acoustic music from 7pm. Somtam Nua also has a branch at Siam Square Soi 1.

FARTHER AFIELD Thip Samai

313 Mahachai Rd, Samranrat, Pranakorn, Bangkok, 10200 Tel 0-2221-6280 Map 6 D1

The Thai clientele regard Thip Samai as the best place in the city to eat phad thai. In business for more than 40 years, this restaurant serves seven different variations of the dish. Try the original, with egg and dried shrimp, or phad thai *song-kreung*, made with glass noodles, shrimp roe, prawn, egg, crab, cuttlefish, and mango.

FARTHER AFIELD Anotai Vegetarian Restaurant and Bakery

976/17 Soi Rama 9 Hospital Rimklong, Samsen Rd, Bangkapi, Bangkok, 10320 Tel 0-2641-5366

Anotai is one of the finest vegetarian restaurants in Bangkok. Named after the owner, a Cordon Bleu-trained chef, Anotai's green credentials extend beyond meat-free meals: the vegetables served here are grown on a certified organic farm in Ratchaburi. The menu has an impressive selection of Thai and Western dishes and delicious pastries.

FARTHER AFIELD Good View

2525 Charoenkrung Rd, Bang Kho Laem, Bangkok, 10120 Tel 0-2689-1393

Big, brash, and bold, Good View offers an eclectic selection of great food, live music, and a superb riverside location. If you are looking for a fun-filled night out with friends, this is the place to eat, drink, and party. Excellent Thai, Western, and Japanese food, plus a cocktail menu. Good-quality Thai bands play all night.

FARTHER AFIELD Indy Trees

44/4 Chuaplerng Rd, Chongnonsi Yannawa, Bangkok, 10120 Tel 0-2249-0222

Indy Trees is a cool, out-of-the-way bar and restaurant with live music and unpretentious Thai food. The converted house features retro-style decor, indoor dining, and an atmospheric garden. The extensive menu serves delicious bar food like squid frittos with sweet plum sauce, and fried *som tam* (papaya salad). Fast, friendly service.

FARTHER AFIELD Pola Pola

150/7 Soi 55, Sukhumvit Rd, Bangkok, 10110 Tel 0-2381-3237

Pola Pola is a popular restaurant serving authentic Thai and Italian dishes. The traditional thin-crust pizza pulled from a brick oven is a favorite of the visiting clientele. Salads, pasta dishes, and special set menus are also available. Children can enjoy drawing with crayons on the white-paper tablecloths. Pola Pola has four branches in Bangkok.

FARTHER AFIELD Royal Dragon Restaurant

35/222 M.4 Bangna-Trad Rd, Bangna, Bangkok, 10260 Tel 0-2398-0037

The Royal Dragon is listed in the *Guinness Book of Records* as the largest restaurant in the world. Dining here is a true spectacle, with the 1,000-strong waiting staff speed-skating around the restaurant and flying through the air on cables. The Royal Dragon specializes in Thai and Chinese seafood dishes. There are also Thai music and dance shows.

FARTHER AFIELD Spring and Summer ⓑⓑⓑ

*199 Soi Promsi 2, Soi 39, Sukhumvit Rd, Bangkok, 10110 **Tel** 0-2392-2757*

If you are looking for a glamorous place to dine, Spring and Summer fits the bill. Owned by a Thai actor and housed in two converted 1950s building, the restaurant promotes a new culinary concept. While Spring serves up classic Thai dishes in its modern interior, neighbouring Summer is the perfect place to retreat for home-made cakes and desserts.

FARTHER AFIELD Suan Kularb ⓑⓑⓑ

*162 Rama 6 Rd, Soi Ruamrudee 30, Bangkok **Tel** 0-2617-0425*

Suan Kularb is popular with office staff at the nearby Ministry of Finance. Spacious, clean, and with contemporary Thai decor, the restaurant serves an extensive menu with some interesting dishes such as stir-fried ostrich. At lunchtime, good-value dim sum pulls in the crowds, especially on Sundays. Ample parking space is available.

FARTHER AFIELD Tawandang German Brewery ⓑⓑⓑ

*462/61 Rama 3 Rd, Chongnonsi, Yanawa, Bangkok, 10120 **Tel** 0-2678-1114*

Tawandang was Bangkok's first microbrewery and restaurant. The massive hall, complete with a domed beer-barrel roof, gets packed with locals who come for the live entertainment, great food, and the three excellent draft beers made on site. The menu features Thai and German delicacies. An excellent choice for a party of friends.

FARTHER AFIELD Vientiane Kitchen ⓑⓑⓑ

*8 Soi 36, Sukhumvit Rd, Klong Toey, Bangkok, 10110 **Tel** 0-2258-6171*

The cuisine at Vientiane Kitchen is rustic Northeastern Thai food and Lao. The more usual and tasty dishes on the menu include vegetable curry with ant eggs, fried snakehead fish with aromatic herbs, jackfruit salad, and sundried beef. Diners can also enjoy spectacular performances of Thai classical dance and Issan music.

FARTHER AFIELD Buri Tara Bar & Restaurant ⓑⓑⓑⓑ

*762/2 Rama 3 Rd, Chatuchak Rama 2, Bangkok, 10900 **Tel** 0-2682-9457*

Buri Tara is a large stylish venue located on a quiet stretch of the Chao Phraya River. It offers modern decor, river views, and live jazz every evening from 9pm. Try the deep-fried fish with lemongrass, and end your meal with a sweet treat of mango and sticky rice with coconut ice cream. It is quite tricky to find, so call for directions.

FARTHER AFIELD Watermark Italian Restaurant ⓑⓑⓑⓑ

*131 Soi Sukhumvit 53 (Paidee-Madee), Sukhumvit Rd, Wattana, Bangkok, 10110 **Tel** 0-2712-9991*

For several years now, the area of Thonglor has been at the center of Bangkok's burgeoning creativity. Watermark brings a touch of Milan chic to Bangkok. The restaurant has a reputation among discerning diners for beautifully executed classic Italian dishes. A bar, a family room, and two private rooms also feature at this delightful restaurant.

FARTHER AFIELD L'Opera ⓑⓑⓑⓑⓑ

*53 Soi 39 Sukhumvit Rd, Wattana, Bangkok, 10110 **Tel** 0-2258-5606*

L'Opera is Bangkok's most highly regarded Italian restaurant. The warm welcome, rustic atmosphere, and delicious cuisine make it a favorite among the expatriate community. Try the thinly sliced Chianina veal from Tuscany served with grilled vegetables, and, for a devilish dessert, the classic tiramisu. Excellent selection of wines.

SOUTH CENTRAL PLAINS

AYUTTHAYA Moon Café B80 ⓑ

*Soi Thor Kor Sor **Tel** no phone*

There is not much nightlife in Ayutthaya, but several bars and cafés have opened in the budget-accommodation quarter. This is one of the best among them. It is small but stylish and offers both Thai and Western dishes on its short menu. There is regular live music and the chance to swap travelers' tales with other customers.

AYUTTHAYA Chainam ⓑⓑ

*36/2 U Thong Rd **Tel** 0-3525-2013*

In a lovely setting on the west bank of the Pasak River, this restaurant is particularly popular among foreigners for its extensive menu of Thai and Western dishes, though Thai food tends to be toned down for Western tastes. Chainam also offers a good range of breakfasts, ideal for building up energy before exploring the city's ruins.

AYUTTHAYA Malakor ⓑⓑ

*Chikun Rd, opposite Wat Ratchaburana **Tel** no phone*

A delightful local restaurant serving a wide range of Thai food. Malakor occupies a traditional-style, two-story wooden building where diners can sit on the balcony and enjoy the spicy cuisine and views of Wat Ratchaburana. This is a particularly nice venue to dine in the evenings when the temple is lit up.

AYUTTHAYA Sombat Chao Phraya ⓑⓑ

*U Thong Rd **Tel** no phone*

Competing with other riverside restaurants in Ayutthaya, this one is located on the north bank of the Chao Phraya River and offers the choice of dining on the breezy terrace or on a moored boat. There's a good view of the *chedi* at Wat Phutthaisawan, and options on the menu include several seafood specials.

AYUTTHAYA Bann Kun Pra

48 U Thong Rd **Tel** 0-3524-1978

This atmospheric restaurant, attached to the guesthouse of the same name *(see p402)*, enjoys a romantic riverside location of which its terrace makes maximum benefit. There are lots of tempting items on the menu, including some appealing snacks, but the house specialty is seafood, particularly prawns.

KANCHANABURI Apple's Guest House

52 Soi Rongheabaow **Tel** 0-3451-2017

If you are not sure where to eat in Kanchanaburi, you could do worse than head for Apple's Guest House *(see p402)*, which also runs the best cookery school in town. You may have to wait a while, but it is worth it for the delicious curries and aromatic stir-fries. There are also set dinners for those who find it tough to choose from the extensive menu.

KANCHANABURI Nitas Raft House

271/1 Pak Praek Rd **Tel** 0-3451-4521

If you don't sleep on a raft on the river in Kanchanaburi, it can be a novel experience to dine on one, sitting Thai-style on floor cushions and eating from low tables. Traditional Thai dishes are the thing to go for here, like a fiery *tom yam kung*, Thailand's trademark hot and sour soup with prawns.

KANCHANABURI Schluck

Maenam Kwai Rd **Tel** 0-3462-4599

Westerners looking for comfort food make a beeline for this German-run place. Get stuck into a steak, a pizza, a salad, or even a spicy Thai salad at this air-conditioned venue located in the center of town. Schluck also has attractive decor and a few tables out on the street.

LOPBURI Thai Sawang

11/8 Surasak Rd **Tel** no phone

Conveniently located near King Narai's Palace, this small, air-conditioned eatery is one of the few restaurants in Lopburi that offers an English menu, as well as Western breakfasts and an appealing range of Thai and Vietnamese dishes. It is popular among locals, but it closes before 9pm, so do not leave it too late for dinner.

LOPBURI White House Garden

18 Tambon Tha Hin **Tel** no phone

If you are looking for a touch of class in non-touristy Lopburi, this is your spot. Located in the town center, White House Garden serves up excellent seafood dishes at very reasonable prices in an open-air setting. Most establishments tend to close early in Lopburi, and this is no exception – the kitchen is closed by 10pm.

NORTH CENTRAL PLAINS

KAMPHAENG PHET Phae Rim Ping

120 Soi 1, Thesa 2 Rd **Tel** no phone

For an atmospheric meal while staying in Kamphaeng Phet, check out this floating restaurant just north of the bridge over the Ping River. Phae Rim Ping has a wide-ranging menu of Thai dishes, including lots of seafood options. Try the *miang sawoei*, small packets of ginger, peanuts, and spicy sauce wrapped in leaves.

MAE SOT Kung's

668/3 Intharakhiri Rd **Tel** no phone

Though there is no English sign outside, Kung's still manages to attract a crowd of local expats, who come here to taste exotic Thai dishes like snakehead curry and morning-glory tempura. This is as much a bar as a restaurant, with a pool table for use of customers and a good range of cocktails on offer.

MAE SOT Krua Canadian

3 Sri Phanit Rd **Tel** 0-5553-4659

This place has become very popular among NGO workers and visitors for its welcoming atmosphere and big portions of Thai and Western food at reasonable prices. For something different, try the bird curry or the catfish salad. There is also good coffee here and DVD screenings some evenings.

MAE SOT Bai Fern

660/2 Inthakhiri Rd **Tel** 0-5553-3343

The restaurant attached to a guesthouse offers a relaxing atmosphere and a tempting variety of Western and Thai dishes. The steaks are very popular here, as are the pasta dishes and authentic Thai curries. Try to save room for some of their delicious apple pie.

PHITSANULOK Ban Khun Por

4–4/1 Chaophraya Phitsanulok Rd **Tel** no phone

The biggest problem in this atmospheric restaurant with antique decor is deciding what to choose from the extensive menu. First, you need to decide between Western, Japanese, or Thai food, and then narrow down your choice. If you still cannot make up your mind, go for the crunchy and tangy winged bean salad.

PHITSANULOK Rim Nam Food Market

Phuttha Bucha Rd **Tel** *no phone*

There are plenty of stalls selling seafood dishes like fried mussels here, but the dish to order is *phak bung loy fa*, or "floating morning glory." This iron-rich vegetable is stir-fried with garlic and soy beans, then launched through the air from the cook to the waiter, who tries to catch it on a plate.

SI SATCHANALAI Wang Yom Resort

500 m southeast of entrance to Historical Park **Tel** *0-5561-1179*

This is the best option for eating near Si Satchanalai Historical Park. Big wooden chairs and tables sit under the resort's main house, and the kitchen can rustle up a wide selection of tasty Thai dishes. Service can be slow, however, so be sure to order well before you are starving hungry.

SUKHOTHAI Khun Tanode

Charodvithitong Rd **Tel** *no phone*

Located on the west side of the bridge over the Yom River, this simple restaurant is not particularly tourist-oriented but is very popular among the local community for its crispy chicken and steamed mussels, among other dishes, and for its very reasonable prices.

SUKHOTHAI Naa's

40/4 Charodvithitong Rd **Tel** *no phone*

The owner of this restaurant also runs a guesthouse and teaches cookery classes, so she's a busy lady. She is from the south of the country and specializes in hot and sour curries, though some are toned down for Western tastes. There are also many vegetarian options on the menu.

SUKHOTHAI Night Market

Charodvithitong Rd **Tel** *no phone*

Many Thai towns have a night market with stalls selling skewered snacks, plus a huge variety of noodle and rice dishes. Sukhothai's Night Market is no exception, but many of the stalls here also have an English-language menu to tempt tourists to sample Thai food as eaten by most Thais every day.

SUKHOTHAI Poo's

24/3 Charodvithitong Rd **Tel** *no phone*

This bright and clean establishment is a welcome addition to the Sukhothai dining scene. It offers big Western breakfasts, tasty sandwiches, and well-prepared Thai dishes. Watch out for the chocolate specials (the owner is Belgian). Poo's also offers motorbike rental.

SUKHOTHAI Dream Café

86/1 Singhawat Rd **Tel** *0-5561-2081*

This is Sukhothai's culinary highlight. On the menu are excellent pasta and steak dishes, as well as classic Thai offerings such as *tom yam kung* (hot and sour soup with prawns). The classy decor includes antique cabinets and curios. Dream Café also serves a huge range of ice creams and fortifying herbal concoctions.

UMPHANG Phu Doi

294 Moo 1 Prawet Wan Rd **Tel** *0-5556-1049*

There are not too many eating options in Umphang, which is little more than a village, but this camp base for tours to Thi Lor Su falls is probably your best bet. It serves up a tongue-tingling *tom yam kung* (hot and sour soup with prawns) and lip-smacking curries, with cold beers to wash them down.

TAK Chom Ping

Viang Tak Riverside Hotel, 236 Chompol Rd **Tel** *0-5551-2507*

Chom Ping serves up the best food in Tak in an attractive riverside setting. There is a choice of continental or American breakfasts, set Thai and Western lunch and dinner menus, and à la carte offerings. Try the fried chicken in red-wine sauce and the spicy chili dip with steamed vegetables.

NORTHWEST HEARTLAND

CHIANG MAI Galare Food Centre

89/2 Chang Khlan Rd, 50100 **Tel** *0-5327-2067*

Handily located near the buzzing Night Market, this brightly lit mix of outdoor food stalls offers a wide range of Northern and Central Thai dishes, as well as dedicated seafood and Indian food stalls. Traditional Thai dancing shows provide the entertainment – if watching your dishes being cooked isn't engaging enough. Open evenings only.

CHIANG MAI New Lamduan Faham Khao Soi

352/22 Charoen Rat Rd, North of Rama IX Bridge, 50100 **Tel** *0-5324-3519*

This unassuming restaurant stays perpetually busy serving up delicious local specialties, including a highly regarded *kao soi* (chicken and noodles in a spicy broth). This signature dish has become legendary in Chiang Mai and has the distinction of attracting royal patronage. Do not leave the region without sampling it. Closes at 9pm.

Key to Price Guide *see p428* **Key to Symbols** *see back cover flap*

CHIANG MAI Kalare Night Bazaar Food Court

Thanon Chang Khlan, 50100 **Tel** *no phone*

A little more upmarket than the Galare Food Centre *(see p434)*, this food market behind the Night Market offers a good selection of Northern and Central Thai, Indian, and vegetarian stalls. With a bar and live entertainment, it makes for a welcome break from shopping. The stalls use a coupon system.

CHIANG MAI Noi's Kitchen

227 Tha Phae Rd, 50100 **Tel** *0-5327-2244*

Popular with local university students and backpackers alike, Noi's Kitchen is a casual Thai restaurant with wooden tables and garden bench-style seating in a leafy courtyard. It makes for a refreshing pit stop on a steamy day, but it is also lovely in the evenings, and it is open until late. The tangy, crunchy papaya salad is excellent.

CHIANG MAI Art Café

291 Thapae Rd, 50100 **Tel** *0-5320-6365*

On a busy corner across from Tha Pae Gate, this agreeable café serves a wide-ranging international menu in modern surroundings. Italian and Mexican specialties feature heavily on the eclectic menu, along with soups and salads, all competently prepared, making it an excellent option for those looking for Western solace.

CHIANG MAI The Gallery

25–29 Charoen Rat Rd, 50100 **Tel** *0-5324-8601*

Located in a century-old local teak house on the banks of the Mae Ping River, this beautiful restaurant takes full advantage of its riverside terraces. The Gallery specializes in Northern Thai cuisine; stick to local favorites such as *nam prik ong* (spicy tomato and minced pork served with fresh vegetables). The restaurant often features local artists.

CHIANG MAI Heun Phen

112 Ratchamanka Rd, 50200 **Tel** *0-5381-4548*

For excellent northern Thai food, head to Heun Phen. This rather basic-looking restaurant gets packed with locals and Bangkok Thais keen to sample classic northern dishes such as *nam prik num* (chili paste and rice), *kaeng hang le* (pork and ginger curry), and *kaeng kai* (chicken curry). The northern-style sausage, *si oua*, is excellent. Closes at 4pm.

CHIANG MAI Vieng Joom On

53 Chareonrat Rd, T. Watgate, 50100 **Tel** *0-5330-3113*

This serene pink-hued tea house on the Ping River is filled with the enticing aromas of a substantial selection of teas, lined in quaint canisters along the walls. Delicious cakes and sandwiches complement your brew or contribute to a filling high tea for a more substantial snack. Tea and tea accessories are available for purchase. Closes at 7pm.

CHIANG MAI Whole Earth

88 Si Don Chai Rd, 50100 **Tel** *0-5328-2463*

Located in a lovely Lanna house near the Night Market, this restaurant has a menu that features Indian and Thai dishes and a satisfying number of vegetarian options, as well as fish and seafood. An elegant dining room is the setting, with verandas overlooking landscaped gardens and occasional live music to entertain diners. Book ahead.

CHIANG MAI Giorgio

2/6 Prachasamphan Rd, 50000 **Tel** *0-5381-8236*

An authentic, casual slice of Venice close to the Night Market, Giorgio's is a standout among Chiang Mai's myriad Italian restaurants. From *carpaccio di manzo* (raw, thinly sliced beef) and some Venetian favorites (such as *minestrone veneto*) to some fine pizzas, there is barely a false note played by the open-plan kitchen. Good Italian wine list.

CHIANG MAI The House

199 Moon Muang Rd, 50100 **Tel** *0-5341-9011*

Refined but cozy, this notable restaurant housed in a colonial-style building is one of the best in town and run by a local Thai chef with extensive overseas training. The Pacific Rim menu features starters such as scallops on pea purée and mains such as hoisin-marinated duck on pumpkin risotto. Bar and tapas bar. Reserve for dinner.

CHIANG MAI Mi Casa

60/2 Moo Soi Wat Padaeng, 14 Suthep Rd, 50100 **Tel** *0-5381-0088*

Spanish chef Kike Garcia brings Mediterranean sunshine to this pleasant restaurant with both indoor and outdoor seating. From classic tapas to heavier main courses such as duck confit or paella (order 24 hours ahead), Kike prepares everything with a fine touch. The house sangria is a hit. The sweet-toothed should try the dessert sampler.

CHIANG MAI Piccola Roma Palace

144 Charoen Prathet Rd, 50100 **Tel** *0-5327-1256*

In a charming, elegant room, chef/owner Angelo presents authentic Italian cuisine – fresh and flavorful. Classic antipasti, such as Parma ham with melon, are recommended, and the spaghetti with mixed seafood is delicious – as are any of the seafood dishes on offer. The wine list is comprehensive and Italian-focused.

CHIANG MAI The Rachamankha

6 Rachamankha 9, T. Phra Singh, 50200 **Tel** *0-5390-4111*

A beautifully decorated restaurant in the hotel of the same name *(see p406)*, featuring 19th-century paintings and large Lanna lanterns. The modern-meets-traditional ambience complements the eclectic cuisine, which combines flavors from Thailand with influences of Japan, Vietnam, China, and Myanmar. The result is pretty and flavorsome.

CHIANG MAI Tabeya Japanese Café

2Br Office Center Sirimuangklajan Rd, Soi 11, 50100 **Tel** *0-5322-1484*

At this small Japanese restaurant decorated in a contemporary Japanese style, the emphasis is on fresh fish and seafood, both featured on an ever-changing menu. While there are some fusion dishes on the menu, the sushi, along with some sake or rice wine, is the best choice, along with their tasty starters.

CHIANG MAI Weaves

Manathai Village, 39/3 Soi 3 Thapae Rd, 50100 **Tel** *0-5328-1666*

Located at the Manathai *(see p405)*, Weaves is set in a 140-year-old teak house, with plenty of Lanna touches. The cuisine mixes modern pan-Thai cooking with some Western- and Asian-influenced plates. Candlelit tables are set by the pool at night; inside, a modish soundtrack matches the contemporary cuisine.

CHIANG MAI Akaligo

Mandarin Oriental Dhara Dhevi Resort, 51/4 Moo 1, Chiang Mai-Sankampaeng Rd, 5060 **Tel** *0-5388-8621*

This restaurant is located in the heart of the Mandarin Oriental Dhara Dhevi Resort. On offer is good Mediterranean cuisine in a lovely setting with views of landscaped gardens. The restaurant also hosts a Sunday Jazz Brunch with a gourmet buffet, live food stations, and a jazz band.

CHIANG MAI Fujian

Mandarin Oriental Dhara Dhevi, 51/4 Moo 1, Chiang Mai-Sankampaeng Rd, 50100 **Tel** *0-5388-8888*

This elegant 1930s Shanghai-style restaurant is set over two small, richly decorated floors. While lunchtimes are busy with a range of dim-sum steamers, the evening menu offers a refined journey through the Chinese provinces featuring contemporary touches and first-class seafood. Outstanding wine list and notable tea selections.

CHIANG MAI Le Coq d'Or

68/1 Koh Klang Rd, 50100 **Tel** *0-5314-1555*

Chiang Mai's best French restaurant is housed in a romantic residence that once belonged to the first British consul. Expect premium ingredients such as foie gras, truffles, caviar, and lobster, all presented with flair. The service is outstanding, and the fascinating wine list is one of the best in Northern Thailand. Reservations recommended.

CHIANG MAI Moxie

D2 Hotel, 100 Changklan Rd, 50100 **Tel** *0-5399-9999*

The restaurant of the hip D2 hotel *(see p406)* has both style and substance. With an eclectic menu running from Thailand to Tuscany, the dishes are fascinating and beautifully presented. Start with the signature appetizer platter, try the spaghetti with Chiang Mai sausage or *khao soi* (chicken curry), and do not miss the sublime trio of crème brûlée.

CHIANG MAI The Restaurant

The Chedi Chiang Mai, 123 Charoen Prathet Rd, 50100 **Tel** *0-5325-3333*

At the slick and stylish Chedi hotel *(see p405)*, The Restaurant is in a freestanding split-level colonial-style building that was once the British consulate. It has won plaudits for its Northern Thai, Pacific Rim, and Asian (Indian) specialties on an extensive menu. It is also open for afternoon tea. Reservations are recommended. Closes at 9pm.

CHIANG MAI Sala Mae Rim

Four Seasons Chiang Mai, Mae Rim-Samoeng Old Rd, Mae Rim, 50180 **Tel** *0-5329-8181*

Overlooking the rice paddies at the sumptuous Four Seasons *(see p406)*, this elegant restaurant provides an uplifting setting for exemplary Northern Thai cuisine. Feel the heat with the Lanna-style appetizers (with delicious Chiang Mai sausage) and follow with the local *kaeng hang le moo* (dry-spiced pork curry). Exceptional service and wine list.

LAMPANG Baan Rim Nam

328 Tipchang Rd, 52000 **Tel** *0-5422-1861*

A perennially popular eatery located right on the Yom River. The cuisine here (both Thai and Western) is excellent. Sample outstanding Thai dishes such as *phat kari pu* (crabmeat in yellow curry sauce), and be sure to visit at night, when live local folk music is played.

LAMPANG Khrua Tai Rim Nam

Pamai Rd, Amphur Wiang Neua, 52000 **Tel** *no phone*

Superbly located on the banks of the Wang River, in a classic, old, large teak house, Khrua Tai Rim Nam is easily the best restaurant in the old Wiang Neua part of the city. On the excellent Thai menu, one must-do is the *tot man kung* – delicious fried shrimp cakes served with a sweet tamarind sauce.

LAMPANG Suki Bhami Coca

138/72-74 Paholyothin Rd, 52000 **Tel** *0-5431-6440*

This popular restaurant is notable for its Thai-style *suki* cuisine, where diners cook their own food at the table on hot plates. Only remotely reminiscent of Japanese sukiyaki, it is actually similar to *shabu shabu*, or Chinese hot-pot cooking – and just as much fun. An enduring hit with the locals. Open evenings only.

LAMPHUN Ba-Mii Kwangtung

On the corner of Rot Kaew and Inthayongyot rds, 52000 **Tel** *no phone*

The excellent selection of fresh noodle dishes makes this daytime noodle shop one of the best places to eat in Lamphun. Like most of the eateries in the town, there is no English sign outside, but since all the cooking is done right by the entrance, you will have no difficulty locating it.

Key to Price Guide *see p428* **Key to Symbols** *see back cover flap*

MAE HONG SON Good Luck Restaurant

Khunlum Phraphat Rd, 58000 **Tel** *no phone*

While this place might be small, it manages to turn out a bewildering array of cuisines from disparate corners of the globe – perfect if you are looking for something a little different. Thai, Greek, Turkish, Jewish, Arab, and vegetarian dishes all feature on the extensive menu, and they are all produced to a surprisingly high standard.

MAE HONG SON Khai Muk

71 Khunlum Prapas Rd, 58000 **Tel** *0-5361-2092*

Simple yet attractive surroundings are the setting for this very popular restaurant featuring an extensive Thai and Chinese menu. While both cuisines are well represented, the *kai phat met mamuang* (fried chicken with cashew nuts) is highly recommended. Khai Muk is very popular with both locals and small tour groups.

MAE HONG SON Golden Teak

Imperial Tara Hotel, 149 Moo 8, Tambon Pang Moo, 58000 **Tel** *0-5368-4444-9*

This resort hotel (*see p407*), 3 km (2 miles) out of town, is worth the trek for its delicious Thai food. The outside tables are easily the best choice (weather permitting), since they overlook a lush terraced valley. While Chinese and Western dishes are available, the local specialties are the best picks. Golden Teak has the best wine list in town.

MAE SARIANG Inthira Restaurant

Wiang Mai Rd, 58000 **Tel** *0-5368-1529*

While it may be a simple restaurant, Inthira is deservedly popular for serving the best Thai and Chinese food in remote Sariang. The restaurant is renowned for its lunchtime *kop krob* (batter-fried frogs), as well as its huge portions and excellent value, making it popular with both locals and visitors. Closes at 9pm.

PAI Na's Kitchen

Ratchadamrong Rd, 58130 **Tel** *no phone*

This unpretentious local favorite dishes up some delicious Thai staples, such as flavorsome phad thai noodles and tangy salads. Look for Na's Kitchen among a row of casual restaurants and bars at the intersection of Ratchadamrong and Rungsiyanon roads; if you are still having trouble finding it, just ask the locals.

PAI Own Home Restaurant

Ratchadamrong Rd, 58130 **Tel** *no phone*

A surprising mix of cuisines awaits visitors to this out-of-the-way spot. Middle Eastern fare is the first surprise on the menu, with falafel and hummus alongside Indian favorites such as samosas. Mexican burritos are another revelation, as well as the fact that they sit alongside a decent selection of vegetarian Thai dishes.

PAI Tai Yai Restaurant

Ratchadamrong Rd, 58130 **Tel** *no phone*

For those craving a decent Western breakfast, Tai Yai provides home-baked white bread, muesli, and, to get your day really started, fragrant, locally grown coffee. This is not just a breakfast stop, though. While the majority of Pai's restaurants are shut by 10pm, this eating place stays open late into the night.

PAI Laan Taung

Rungsiyanon Rd, 58130 **Tel** *no phone*

This is another longtime local favorite, although the word has also spread among travelers now. Pai's finest restaurant specializes in refined Royal Thai cuisine, and meets expectations with rich, complex flavors and pretty presentation. Aim for a table on one of the terraces if the weather is good, and try the specials of the day.

FAR NORTH

CHIANG KHONG Fai Ngeun

Nam Khong Hotel, Sai Klang Rd, 57140 **Tel** *0-5379-1796*

Grab a table on the veranda overlooking the river at Nam Khong Riverside, the town's finest restaurant. While you will see Thai standards on the menu, as well as some local favorites (that means anything with fried pork), there are also some Western dishes (pasta and burgers, mainly).

CHIANG RAI Baan Chivit Mae Bakery

172 Thanon Prasop Sook, 57000 **Tel** *0-5371-2357*

This Scandinavian bakery opposite the bus station does delicious breads, croissants, cakes, and sandwiches, and serves great coffee and tea in air-conditioned comfort. Operated by a Swedish NGO, it trains the young hill-tribe women who work here and supports HIV-positive adolescents and drug-addicts around Chiang Rai. Closes at 9pm.

CHIANG RAI Night Market

Paholyothin Rd, 57000 **Tel** *no phone*

At around 6pm every night, Chiang Rai's dozens of food vendors start setting up their stalls at the bustling Night Market, and by 7pm the tiny tables are already crammed with locals and tourists alike slurping up spicy soups and curries and munching into crispy fried Thai treats. Surprisingly, you will also find a stall selling Italian pizza.

CHIANG RAI Aye's Restaurant

879/4-5 Paholyothin Rd, 57000 **Tel** *0-5375-2534*

This low-key restaurant serves up tasty, authentic Thai food. It is all pretty spicy, so be sure to let them know in advance if you want it otherwise. There is also a wide range of Western dishes. The outdoor seating is especially popular, and if you eat early, you will be able to watch stallholders get ready for the night market across the road.

CHIANG RAI Mae Oui Kiaw

106/9 Ngam Muang Rd, 57000 **Tel** *no phone*

An exceptional venue for Northern Thai cuisine, Mae Oui Kiaw is a great place to taste all the favorite local dishes, including *nam phrik ong* (a very spicy dip of tomato and minced pork served with raw vegetables) and *kaeng hang le* (a fragrant pork and ginger curry).

CHIANG RAI Raan Abaan Islam
142 Itsaraphap Rd, 57000 **Tel** *no phone*

One of the town's top establishments, serving food that is halal (meeting Islamic dietary standards for the Muslim community). This daytime eatery's specialties include *khao mok kai* (chicken biryani) and *khao soi* (a local specialty of wheat noodles and coconut milk curry served with beef or chicken).

CHIANG RAI Cabbages & Condoms
620/25 Thanalai Rd Amphoe Mueang, 57000 **Tel** *0-5371-9167 ext 111*

Located below the Hill Tribe Museum, this restaurant run by the Population & Community Development Association (PDA) aims to promote safe sex; proceeds are used to fund PDA social development programs. Noble aims aside, it is worth visiting Cabbages & Condoms for the delightful Thai food, which includes some local specialties.

CHIANG RAI Chinatown
Dusit Island Resort, 1129 Kraisorasit Rd, 57000 **Tel** *0-5371-5777*

This elegant Chinese restaurant has river views and an extensive Chinese menu with an emphasis on Cantonese fare. The delicious dim sum is a perennial lunchtime favorite, while the classic Peking duck (presented and served as it should be) is a notable dish offered in the evenings, when an elegant ambience prevails. Open evenings only.

CHIANG RAI Golden Triangle International Café
590 Paholyothin Rd, 57000 **Tel** *0-5371-1339 or 0-5371-5487*

Serving Central Thai food made for Western tastes, and with plenty of helpful suggestions on the menu for Thai-cuisine novices, the Golden Triangle International Café won't make your dishes too hot – unless requested. If Thai does not take your fancy, there are Western dishes on the menu, too, including filling breakfasts. Closes at 9pm.

CHIANG RAI Yunnan
2211/9 Khwae Wai Rd, 57000 **Tel** *0-5371-3263*

Boats from the Yunnan province in China unload goods in this region every day, so it is not surprising to find that the food from the southwest of China has such a presence here. This restaurant showcases specialties such as the delicately salty Yunnanese ham, as well as Kunming-style (the capital of Yunnan) fried milk.

DOI MAE SALONG (SANTIKHIREE) Morning Market
Mae Salong Rd, 57110 **Tel** *no phone*

Wake up at dawn to breakfast (and buy hill-tribe handicrafts) at the bustling roadside Morning Market on Doi Mae Salong's main street, near Shin Sane Guest House: all the stalls pack up by 7am. There are few, if any, signs in English, so just watch the locals and try some of the tasty fried treats and locally produced hill-tribe coffee.

FANG Parichat Rd
Rawp Wiang Rd, 57150 **Tel** *no phone*

This small, clean, and unassuming Thai restaurant stays busy serving up plenty of noodle dishes to locals and travelers alike. Be sure to try the excellent Northern Thai specialty *khao soi* – a bowl of wheat noodles served in a chicken or beef curry broth, sprinkled liberally with chili and fresh lime juice.

GOLDEN TRIANGLE/CHIANG SAEN Chiang Saen Market
Phaholyothin Rd, 57150 **Tel** *no phone*

Apart from the fine restaurants at the Four Seasons and Anantara resorts, there is little in the way of quality dining in the Golden Triangle-Chiang Saen area. Your best bet is the sleepy daily Chiang Saen market, where, among the bamboo worms, frogs, and eels, you'll find some delicious curries, sticky rice, and fried Thai snacks.

GOLDEN TRIANGLE/CHIANG SAEN Baan Dahlia
Anantara Resort & Spa Golden Triangle, 229 Moo 1, Chiang Saen, 57150 **Tel** *0-5378-4084*

Gastronomes shouldn't miss out on a meal on the terrace of the Anantara's Baan Dahlia. Enjoy sublime Mekong Valley views accompanied by some of the most refined and authentic Italian cuisine you will experience in Northern Thailand, complemented by some of the best wines from around the globe.

GOLDEN TRIANGLE/CHIANG SAEN Nong Yao
Four Seasons Tented Camp Golden Triangle, Chiang Saen, 57130 **Tel** *0-5391-0200*

Dining at this atmospheric restaurant is only possible if you are staying at the Tented Camp *(see p408)*, and, since all meals are included in the package, it is worth checking in just to eat here. The daily changing menu features Lao, Myanmar, Thai, and Western-fusion specialties. Open 24 hours.

Key to Price Guide *see p428* **Key to Symbols** *see back cover flap*

MAE SAI Rabieng Kaew

356/1 Nu 1, Paholyothin Rd, opposite Krung Thai Bank, 57130 **Tel** *0-5373-1172*

Expats who do visa runs across the bridge to Myanmar swear that this is this border town's best eatery. This bustling spot serves up excellent Central and Northern Thai food, as well as some unexpected Asian specialties, such as melt-in-your-mouth Korean barbecued beef. Northern Thai music sometimes plays in the evenings. Closes at 8:30pm.

NAN Riverside restaurants

Under the bridge on the riverside, 55000 **Tel** *no phone*

Nan has myriad little no-name restaurants and bars on the banks of the Nan River that dish up some delicious Northern Thai specialties in addition to the usual Thai soups, noodles, and curries. Look for the places that are popular with the locals. The riverside is a wonderful spot for a late afternoon lunch, sunset drink, or evening meal.

PHRAE Night Market

Pratuchai intersection, 54000 **Tel** *no phone*

As in most Thai towns, you will find the tastiest local food in Phrae at the Night Market. There, a collection of food stalls serves up inexpensive spicy Central Thai and Thai-Chinese food. Each vendor specializes in a different dish or style of cuisine, either freshly cooked in a wok or simmering in big hot pots.

PHRAE Ran Jay Jay Noi

52/9-10 Thung Tom Rd, Ni Wieng, 54000 **Tel** *no phone*

You will find few decent eating options in Phrae, a town that sees few travelers linger for a meal. However, this big vegetarian eatery is one of the most interesting dining establishments. There are mostly Thai and Chinese dishes on the menu, and while the food is really vegan, they will add eggs if you ask nicely.

PHRAE Ban Fai

Phrae-Den Chai Rd, 54000 **Tel** *no phone*

This big, breezy, barn-like eatery on the edge of town is considered to be Phrae's best dining experience. While it is no fancier than any of the other no-frills, no-name restaurants in town, locals swear by its delicious food, especially Northern Lanna specialties such as spicy pork sausages (*nem* in Thai) and tasty dry pork curries.

PHRAE Malakaw

Ratsadamnoen Rd, 54000 **Tel** *no phone*

While it is slightly more expensive than the stalls at the Night Market, Malakaw is justifiably popular for serving up spicy Thai soups, salads, noodles, and rice dishes. You will see more expats and travelers eating at this bustling, rustic eatery than you will at the market, not least because here they have a menu in English.

KHORAT PLATEAU

BURIRAM Bamboo Bar and Restaurant

14/13 Romburi Rd **Tel** *0-4462-5577*

A firm favorite with resident expats and foreign visitors, the Bamboo Bar and Restaurant offers steaks, schnitzels, and pasta dishes, in addition to several Thai staples. It is centrally located and also rents out motorbikes for those who would like to explore the local area. Open evenings only.

KHON KAEN Huaan Lao

39 Pimpasoot Rd **Tel** *no phone*

There is no English sign outside Huaan Lao, but it is worth tracking down this restaurant to enjoy the sophisticated ambience of the modern wooden house decorated with antiques and local crafts. The menu features many classic Thai dishes and a few specialties from Laos as well.

KHON KAEN Lighthouse Pub & Restaurant

Charoen Thani Princess, 260 Si Chan Rd **Tel** *no phone*

Set in the car park of the Charoen Thani Princess hotel (see p409), the Lighthouse offers a choice of sitting outdoors or in the air-conditioned interior. It is equally popular among Thais and foreigners for its wide-ranging menu, which includes American breakfasts, as well as many noodle and rice dishes.

KHON KAEN Bua Luang

Rop Bueng Kaen Nakhon Rd **Tel** *0-4322-2504*

This popular place with its terrace jutting out over a tranquil lake offers diners a great, relaxing ambience. The peaceful setting is matched by the excellent Thai and Chinese specialties on offer, among which the seafood is highly recommended.

KHORAT Suan Sin

163 Watcharasarit Rd **Tel** *no phone*

This no-frills place on the south side of the city keeps customers coming back with its delicious Issan specialties: *kai yang* (grilled chicken), *som tam* (green papaya salad), and *khao niaw* (sticky rice). Most foreigners enjoy all three, but watch out for the chilies and crunchy crabs in the *som tam*.

KHORAT VFW (Veterans of Foreign Wars) Café (B)

167-8 Phok Klang Rd **Tel** *0-4425-3432*

Khorat used to be a base for US planes during the Vietnam War, and some of the GIs stayed on, with this classic American diner as their legacy. The VFW Café is centrally located and serves decent breakfasts as well as burgers and a handful of Thai dishes. Closes at 9pm.

KHORAT Cabbages & Condoms (B)(B)

86/1 Seup Siri Rd **Tel** *0-4425-3760*

This quirky restaurant chain now has outposts in most major Thai cities, and consistently high standards of food preparation and service keep them all popular with diners. Cabbages & Condoms is run by the Population & Community Development Association (PDA) and helps to fund their socially aware projects.

KHORAT Chez Andy (B)(B)(B)

5–7 Manat Rd **Tel** *0-4428-9556*

Chez Andy is the second branch of a Swiss-run restaurant first established on the island of Ko Samui, and it caters to the expat crowd with steaks, fondues, and schnitzels. There are also several Thai dishes on the menu, which seems to have something for everyone. Reservations can be made in advance.

PHIMAI Bai Teiy (B)(B)

Phimai-Chompaung Rd **Tel** *0-4428-7103*

Located to the south of Phimai's town center, this is definitely the place to eat while visiting the Khmer temple here. The garden is scattered with reproductions of sandstone carvings, and specialties on the menu include fish from the local Mun River. Bai Teiy is also a good source of local information.

ROI ET White Elephant (B)(B)(B)

Robmung Dannok Rd **Tel** *0-4351-4778*

Located beside the old moat around Roi Et, the White Elephant is a German-run restaurant that serves several typical German dishes, such as sausage, sauerkraut, and schnitzels, in addition to popular Thai dishes. It has an attractive outdoor terrace and an air-conditioned dining room.

SURIN Larn Chang (B)(B)

199 Siphathai Saman Rd **Tel** *0-4451-2869*

Located in an atmospheric wooden house beside a remnant of the old city moat, Larn Chang serves classic Thai fare and Issan favorites such as *larb*, a tangy dish that includes ground roasted rice and fiery chilies. There is also a rooftop patio for alfresco eating. Closes around 9pm.

UDON THANI Rabiang Phatchanee (B)(B)

53 Suphakit Janya Rd **Tel** *0-4224-1515*

Choose between outdoor seating on a deck overlooking the Nong Prajak Lake and the air-conditioned interior rooms at this stylish restaurant. There is a wide range of Thai dishes on the menu, as well as Issan specialties that are particularly popular among the locals.

MEKONG RIVER VALLEY

CHIANG KHAN Rabiang (B)(B)

299 Chai Khong Rd **Tel** *0-4282-1532*

As Chiang Khan is a little way off the tourist trail, there are no fancy restaurants in town. There is no English sign outside this riverside place, but the lovely river views and laid-back mood make it a fine spot to enjoy one or more of the many classic Northeastern Thai dishes on offer.

LOEI Loei-Danang (B)(B)(B)

22/58-60 Soi Pia, Chumsai Rd **Tel** *0-4283-0413*

Rural Thailand seems full of surprises when it comes to culinary treats, and this spot is a good example. Top-notch Vietnamese and Issan food is served up here along with a good range of Thai dishes and ice creams. There is even a picture menu to help you order if you are not familiar with the language.

MUKDAHAN Night Market (B)

Song Nang Sathit Rd **Tel** *no phone*

If you have made it as far as Mukdahan without trying the perfect combination of Issan food – grilled chicken, *som tam* (papaya salad), and sticky rice – this is the perfect place to do so. Another delightful treat here is Vietnamese spring rolls, which come either fresh or fried.

MUKDAHAN Riverside (B)(B)

103/4 Samran Chai Khong Rd **Tel** *0-4261-1705*

Sometimes it appears that all the successful eating establishments in Thailand are called "Riverside," and Mukdahan's most popular restaurant is no exception. Fish from the Mekong River is the big attraction here, enjoyed on a breezy terrace with views across the river to Laos. This eatery is a particular favorite of Westerners.

MUKDAHAN Wine Wild Why?

11 Samran Chai Khong Rd **Tel** *0-4263-3122*

As the unusual name suggests, this quirky place with a distinctive character is quite different to most other places in town. Located in a lovely wooden house by the river, it serves excellent Thai food, especially spicy salads, but do not expect too much in the way of wine.

NAKHON PHANOM Satang

Sunthorn Wichit Rd **Tel** *no phone*

Located a short distance south of the town center, beside the river, this unpretentious eatery is a great place to sit down and enjoy some unusual Thai dishes. Try the *hor mok talae*, a spicy soufflé with chunks of seafood steamed in a banana leaf.

NAKHON PHANOM View Kong Hotel

527 Sunthorn Wichit Rd **Tel** *0-4251-3564*

This is where the locals usually go when they want something a bit special, and the breezy terrace is definitely a great place to enjoy Thai classics such as *tom yam kung*, a spicy and sour shrimp soup, or *kaeng kiaw wan*, a coconut-based green curry. Closes at 9pm.

NONG KHAI Mut Mee Guest House

1111/4 Kaew Worawut Rd **Tel** *0-4246-0717*

Some guesthouses get a name for their kitchen as much as for their rooms; such is the case at this riverside favorite *(see p411)*. There's a good range of Western dishes on offer, as well as plenty of traditional Thai options. Vegetarians are also well catered for.

NONG KHAI Nobbi's

997 Rimkhong Rd **Tel** *no phone*

This is yet another restaurant that takes advantage of the expansive views across the Mekong River to Laos. It provides a special treat for lovers of home-made sausages and smoked hams, which are prepared by the German owner. There is German beer on tap as well.

NONG KHAI Daeng Namnuang

526 Rimkhong Rd **Tel** *0-4241-1961*

It may seem strange to recommend a Vietnamese restaurant in a rural Thai town, but Daeng Namnuang has earned its reputation by producing consistently tasty dishes such as deep-fried prawns on sugarcane skewers, and *namnuang*, pork spring rolls.

THAT PHANOM That Phanom Pochana

31 Phanom Phanarak Rd **Tel** *0-4254-1189*

This no-frills place located just north of the Victory Arch in town is a good place to recharge your batteries with a tasty phad thai, the traditional dish of fried noodles with beansprouts, egg, and prawns or meat, or a *khao phad*, fried rice with your choice of meat or prawns. There are also plenty of Issan specialties on the menu. Closes at 9pm.

UBON RATCHATHANI Chiokee

307-317 Kheuan Thani Rd **Tel** *0-4525-4017*

This friendly café has an extensive menu of both Thai and Western dishes and is conveniently located in the center of town. It is particularly popular for breakfast, when you can choose between bacon and eggs or *khao tom* (rice soup), the classic Thai breakfast. Closes at 4pm.

UBON RATCHATHANI Kai Yang Wat Jaeng

228 Suriyat Rd **Tel** *0-4526-3596*

There is nothing fancy about this place, which specializes in *kai yang* (grilled chicken) and a few other Issan specialties like *som tam* (papaya salad). Kai Yang Wat Jaeng's fame among the local community keeps it frantically busy until the food runs out at about 3pm each day.

EASTERN SEABOARD

CHANTHABURI PunJim Restaurant Latte Coffee Cha Cha Hut

Maharat Bridge, Maharat Rd **Tel** *0-3933-2270*

This café and restaurant is centrally located and offers good inexpensive cuisine. The menu specializes in local dishes such as *som tam* (shredded green papaya salad with chili, lime juice, and fish sauce), salted fried chicken, and many other Northeastern Thai favorites.

CHANTHABURI Faa Sai Resort & Spa Restaurant

Kung Wiman Beach, 26/1 Moo 7, Sanam Chai **Tel** *0-3941-7404*

Popular eco resort Faa Sai lives up to its promises in its highly recommended restaurant, serving regional and "forest" cuisine. The latter features innovative dishes made from local herbs and flowers. It is advisable to book in advance. Closes around 8pm.

KO CHANG The Bay   ⊞ Ⅴ   ⓑⓑ

Pier, Ban Bang Bao **Tel** *no phone*

One of several seafood restaurants located on the pier in this picturesque fishing village at the southern end of the island, this particular place has a sophisticated atmosphere and a good range of cocktails. The Bay is popular among divers who leave from and return to Ko Chang.

KO CHANG Oodie's Place   ⊞ 🎵 Ⅴ   ⓑⓑ

Hat Sai Khao **Tel** *no phone*

This lively place on pretty White Sand Beach is run by a local musician who entertains his guests by playing covers of rock classics most nights from around 10pm. Diners can choose from a reliable menu full of Thai dishes and French specialties, then sit back, relax, and sing along.

KO CHANG Tonsai   ⊠ ⊞ 🍷 Ⅴ   ⓑⓑ

Klong Prao **Tel** *08-9895-7229*

This treehouse restaurant is set in and around a big banyan tree. Tonsai just oozes atmosphere and is the ideal spot for an afternoon drink or an evening dinner on White Sand Beach. Its menu offers both Thai and international dishes and is very vegetarian-friendly.

KO CHANG Sabay Bar   ⊞ 🎵 🍽 Ⅴ   ⓑⓑⓑ

Hat Sai Khao **Tel** *0-3955-1097*

For the past few years, this has been one of the most popular spots to spend an evening on White Sand Beach. Sabay Bar's successful formula involves the choice between a fancy air-conditioned interior where a live band plays nightly, and mats and cushions on the sand for stargazing alfresco.

KO SAMET Ploy Talay   ⊞ Ⅴ   ⓑ

Hat Sai Kaew **Tel** *0-3864-4212*

There are several seafood restaurants that set out mats and cushions for diners on Ko Samet's most popular beach each evening. Mostly, they all charge very high prices by Thai standards. At least at Ploy Talay the standard of cooking is reliably good, so customers do not feel cheated.

KO SAMET Tub Tim Resort   ⊠ ⊞ 🍷 Ⅴ   ⓑ

Ao Tub Tim **Tel** *0-3864-4025*

Even if you do not stay at the Tub Tim Resort *(see p413)*, it is worth dropping by to sample the excellent food on offer while enjoying stunning views of the bay. Everything is good here, but if you find it difficult to decide, try the *hor mok talae*, a spicy soufflé with seafood steamed in a banana leaf.

KO SAMET Jep's   ⊞ 🍷 Ⅴ   ⓑⓑ

Ao Hin Kok **Tel** *0-3864-4112*

Wriggle your toes in the soft sand as you ponder countless choices of Thai, Western, Indian, and Mexican dishes in this inviting spot. As with most restaurants on Ko Samet, seafood is the most popular item on the menu, and there is a wide variety of cocktails, too.

KO SAMET Ao Prao Resort   ⊞ 🍷 Ⅴ   ⓑⓑⓑⓑⓑ

Ao Prao **Tel** *0-3864-4101*

Although formal dress is not officially required, you might like to dress smart/casual at this stylish restaurant on the west coast of the island. Watch the sun sink into the sea as you enjoy a selection of elegantly served Thai or international dishes and sip on a glass of wine.

KO SICHANG Pan and David   ⊞ 🍷 Ⅴ   ⓑⓑ

Moo 3 Makhaam Thaew Rd **Tel** *0-3821-6629*

This sophisticated restaurant comes as a surprise on this non-touristy island. The American/Thai couple who run it serve up an impressive range of classic Thai specialties, pasta dishes, steaks, and vegetarian options. There is also a range of ice creams and a choice of wines.

PATTAYA Food Wave   ⊠ 🍽 Ⅴ   ⓑ

Top Floor, Royal Garden Plaza, Beach Rd **Tel** *no phone*

It can be difficult in this tourist town to find anything to eat that is both tasty and cheap. Fortunately, this food court offers a wide range of choices, including Thai, Vietnamese, Indian, Japanese, and Western dishes, all at reasonable prices. The good views of the bay round up the pleasant experience.

PATTAYA Lobster Pot   ⊞ 🍷   ⓑ

228 Beach Rd **Tel** *0-3842-6083*

Most visitors to Pattaya like to indulge in a seafood splurge, and there is nowhere better to do it than at this place, which is atmospherically perched on a pier in South Pattaya. Go for the lobster thermidor or grilled tiger prawns, and wash it all down with a chilled glass of wine.

PATTAYA Ali Baba   🍽 🍷 Ⅴ   ⓑⓑ

1/13-14 Central Pattaya Rd **Tel** *0-3836-1620*

If you are hankering for an Indian curry, then head on down to Ali Baba. Interestingly, typically North Indian food, such as tandoori dishes and naan breads, is served inside; while outside the menu focuses on South Indian specialties, including spicy vegetable curries and dahl.

Key to Price Guide *see p428* **Key to Symbols** *see back cover flap*

PATTAYA The Grill House

Rabbit Resort, Dongtan Beach, Jomtien **Tel** *0-3825-1730-2*

Probably the most romantic restaurant in Jomtien, the Grill House serves a wide range of Thai and Western dishes, from a massive buffet breakfast to steaks and seafood skewers from the Charcoal Beach Grill in the evening. For maximum effect, try to arrive just before sunset.

PATTAYA Kitchen

10 Soi 5, Second Rd **Tel** *0-3842-8387*

Traditional Thai food is served in a compound of traditional teak houses with low tables and floor cushions, making for a memorable evening. Kitchen also has a few private dining rooms, a jazz bar upstairs, and occasional performances of classical Thai dancing.

PATTAYA Sugar Hut

391/18 Tappaya Rd **Tel** *0-3825-1686*

Even if you cannot afford to stay at this atmospheric resort *(see p415)*, which consists of an exclusive shady compound of Thai teak houses, you should consider splashing out on a meal at this restaurant. On the menu you will find delicious Central Thai food, all beautifully presented and delicately served.

PATTAYA Siam Elephant

Siam Bayshore Hotel, 599 Moo 10, Beach Rd **Tel** *0-3842-8678-81*

One of Pattaya's most elegant locations for dining is this tastefully furnished restaurant with open-air bar. Siam Elephant is located near the beginning of the city's Walking Street. Fine Thai cuisine is the focus here, and great taste, superb presentation, and attentive service are main features.

PATTAYA Brasseria La Luna

3/333 Moo 6, 3rd Rd, North Pattaya **Tel** *0-3837-1322*

This superb Italian restaurant offers candlelit fine dining. Sit outside by the poolside or savor the gourmet delights in the air-conditioned restaurant. All ingredients are fresh and sourced daily from the local market. Pizzas from the authentic wood-fired oven are always delicious and the wine list is sophisticated and varied. Closed Tue.

PATTAYA Mantra

Amari Orchid Resort, 240 Moo 5, Beach Rd **Tel** *0-3842-9591*

If you consider yourself dynamic, stylish, and seriously cool, then you should be seen at Mantra, tucking into a piping-hot Szechuan seafood soup or the tandoori lamb chops, and browsing the list of 140 wines. To blend with the decor, try to dress in red and black.

SI RACHA Chua Li

46/22 Sukhumvit Rd **Tel** *0-3831-1244*

The small town of Si Racha is famed for its spicy sauce and its seafood restaurants. Those traveling between Bangkok and Pattaya should stop off at this popular place, order up a lobster or grilled prawns, douse them in the delicious local sauce, breathe the salty sea air, and enjoy.

SI RACHA Grand Seaside

Soi 18, Chermchophon Rd **Tel** *0-3831-2537*

For a seafood dinner with a touch of class, visit this place. The Grand Seaside is located near the pier for ferries to Ko Sichang. Lap up the sea views and stylish decor while devouring a seafood rice claypot or a crab with chili, and wash it all down with an iced coffee.

TRAT Cool Corner

Thoncharoen Rd **Tel** *no phone*

If you have time to kill in Trat, check out this neat place in the middle of town. It is simply but tastefully furnished and features travelers' favorites, such as homemade bread and pancakes, in addition to tasty Thai curries. There are also books of travelers' comments and tips on nearby Ko Chang.

WESTERN SEABOARD

CHA-AM Beachside seafood stands

Ruamchit Rd, 76120 **Tel** *no phone*

Cha-am is where many Thais go on vacation. Some of the best fare here is the freshly caught fish sold raw and cooked to order at the simple beachside seafood stands each evening. Hardly a night market, most stands consist of buckets of fish swimming in salt water and a wok to cook them to your liking.

CHA-AM Rabiang-lay

Veranda Resort & Spa, 737/12 Mung Talay Rd, Cha Am, 76120 **Tel** *0-3270-9000*

A funky, white, open-air sala (pavilion) right on the beach at Cha Am is the setting for this relaxed Thai fusion restaurant. The menu has a strong emphasis on seafood (oysters are excellent if in season), so dishes such as *tom yam kung* (a deliciously spicy and sour shrimp soup) and stir-fried soft-shell crab are standouts.

HUA HIN Coustiero
*AKA Resort, 152 Moo 7, Baan Nhong Hiang, 77100 **Tel** 0-3261-8900*

With its delightful setting, Coustiero will charm you even before you order from the refined French-influenced menu. The plates that arrive are just as pretty as the locale, and the flavors are fabulous. The menu is seasonal, but dishes involving foie gras, scallops, or seafood are superb.

HUA HIN Let's Sea
*83/155 Soi Talay 12, Khao Takiab Rd, 77100 **Tel** 0-3253-6888*

In a resort that bills itself as an alfresco one, it is not surprising to see that their restaurant's emphasis is on seafood and sea views. The food is Thai with an international twist and works well with the setting, so try dishes such as fish cakes wrapped in mini croutons and lobster cappuccino.

HUA HIN Moon Smile & Platoo
*Poon Suk Rd, 77110 **Tel** 0-3251-1664*

Despite its unassuming exterior, the small and characterful Moon Smile & Platoo, close to Hua Hin railway station, serves top-quality, authentic local specialties at low prices. Such is the restaurant's reputation that you must arrive early in order to get a seat. Feel free to bring your own wine, too.

HUA HIN Som Moo Joom
*51/6 Dechanuchit Rd, 77100 **Tel** no phone*

There might not be any English signs for this unassuming seafood eatery with indoor and outdoor seating, but it is worth the effort to find it – especially once you taste their seafood soup with noodles, the blockbuster hit of the menu. There's other freshly cooked seafood on offer, and it is all amazingly inexpensive and, most importantly, fresh.

HUA HIN White Lotus
*Hilton Hua Hin Resort & Spa, 33 Naresdamri Rd, 77100 **Tel** 0-3253-8999*

The seating at this stylish restaurant at the top of the huge Hilton resort *(see p416)* is positioned to take advantage of the stunning views of the town and coastline. The menu of contemporary Chinese fare focuses on the cuisine of the Szechuan and Canton provinces, with a couple of degustation menus. Well-drilled service and a notable wine list.

HUA HIN Tapas Café
*62 Naresdamri Rd, 77100 **Tel** 08-0080-6811*

It is best to book in advance for the very popular Tapas Café in central Hua Hin. The restaurant offers a wide range of delicious authentic Spanish dishes in an atmospheric and beautiful old wooden Thai house, which is finished with elegant Vietnamese furnishings.

HUA HIN Chao Lay Seafood
*15 Naresdamri Rd, 77100 **Tel** 0-3251-3436*

This large outdoor restaurant on a wooden pier is a favorite with visitors and local families alike. The proximity to the ocean hints at the focus of the menu – seafood. With a high turnover of tables, the produce is always fresh here, so it is a great place to enjoy some Thai seafood specialties. Service can be haphazard, though.

HUA HIN Hagi
*Sofitel Centara Grand Resort & Villas, 1 Damnernkasem Rd, 77100 **Tel** 0-3251-2021*

Hagi is a stylish restaurant serving a varied and excellent selection of contemporary and traditional Japanese dishes, each one beautifully executed and presented with artistic flair. A 16-seat teppanyaki kitchen turns cooking into theater for a dramatic dining experience. Guests can watch as their meal is cooked in front of them.

HUA HIN McFarland House
*Hyatt Regency Hua Hin, 91 Hua Hin Takiab Rd, 77100 **Tel** 0-3252-1234*

Set within the secluded compound of the Barai spa villas at the Hyatt Regency, McFarland House is among the best casual restaurants in Hua Hin. Try the blue crab and corn cakes with chile and coriander salsa, shredded duck and cucumber rolls, or succulent grilled Angus beef, mushroom, and zucchini skewers. Excellent Sunday lunches.

HUA HIN Museum Tea Corner
*Sofitel Centara Grand Resort & Villas, 1 Damnoen Kasem Rd, 77100 **Tel** 0-3251-2021*

High tea must have been invented to take advantage of the wonderful colonial-style ambience of the original lobby of this historic hotel *(see p416)*. In addition to the excellent selection of coffees and teas, there are some tempting chocolate cakes and, of course, an excellent afternoon tea medley of sweet and savory delights.

HUA HIN Palm Seafood Pavilion & Palm Terrace
*Sofitel Centara Grand Resort & Villas, 1 Damnernkasem Rd, 77100 **Tel** 0-3251-2021*

A seafood bisque or panfried scallops make a great starter at this elegant restaurant, and the seafood platter is a popular main course. There is also plenty of tableside preparation of dishes such as the Caesar salad and flambé specials. Exhaustive wine list of Old and New World wines and attentive service complete the experience.

HUA HIN Sala Thai at the Sofitel Centara Grand Resort & Villas
*107/1 Phetkasem Beach Rd, 77100 **Tel** 0-3251-1881*

As the name implies, this excellent Thai restaurant is set in a *sala* (pavilion), but it also features outdoor seating right on the beach, with an atmospheric soundtrack of lapping waves. The menu is pan-Thai, with all the top hits, and the chefs are well accustomed to adjusting the heat for palates not quite in tune with local spiciness levels.

HUA HIN Supatra by the Sea

122/63 Soi Moo Baan Takiab, Nong Gae, 77100 **Tel** *0-3253-6561*

Supatra enjoys one of the best settings in Hua Hin, with pavilions offering panoramic sea views in front of a terraced tropical garden. The menu leans toward a mix of contemporary and traditional Thai, with an emphasis on fresh seafood – no surprise, given the location. Try the crab and minced pork, and the deep-fried fish.

KO PHA NGAN The Beach Club Bar & Grill

Baan Panburi Village, Thong Nai Pan Yai Beach, 84280 **Tel** *0-7744-5075*

This is one of the island's most popular spots – and with good reason: you get to eat succulent seafood grilled at live cooking stations, watch the skilful chef work the flames, and get to rub your toes in the squeaky sand while you dine – the bamboo chairs and tables are within splashing distance of the sea. Very romantic.

KO SAMUI The Pier

Fisherman's Village, Bo Phut Beach, 84320 **Tel** *0-7743-0681*

Right on Bo Phut beach, in Fisherman's Village, this chic restaurant serves up an eclectic menu of Thai, international, and, of course, seafood dishes. There is everything on offer, from samosas to herbal ribs to fajitas, but the pick of the menu is the lobster, cooked and served in several variations. Good bar and hip soundtrack.

KO SAMUI Prego

Amari Palm Reef Resort & Spa, Chaweng Beach Rd, Chaweng Beach, 84320 **Tel** *0-7742-2015*

Milanese chef Marco Boscaini's restaurant is one of the most striking on Chaweng Beach Rd, with both indoor and outdoor seating. The vast Italian menu includes antipasti, soups (try the pumpkin), risottos, fresh pastas, and pizzas from the prominent wood-fired oven. A signature tiramisu headlines the desserts.

KO SAMUI La Brasserie

Beachcomber Hotel, 3/5 Moo 2, Chaweng Beach, 84320 **Tel** *0-7742-2041*

La Brasserie offers a satisfying beachfront dining experience where the sound of lapping waves is accompanied by separate Italian (clearly the specialty) and Thai menus, with myriad seafood creations (such as king prawns and rock lobster). A romantic evening venue, so be sure to reserve for dinner.

KO SAMUI Full Moon

Anantara, 99/9 Moo 1, Bophut Bay, 84320 **Tel** *0-7742-8300*

With a tranquil pond on one side and an infinity pool giving way to the sea on the other, Full Moon certainly has an arresting setting. Equally engaging is the cuisine by chef Donald Lawson, who elegantly mixes Italian classics with dishes featuring tempting extravagances such as truffles and incredibly tender Wagyu beef. Well-chosen wine list.

KO SAMUI Ocean 11

23 Moo 4, Bangrak, Bophut, 84320 **Tel** *0-7724-5134*

One of the top independent dining establishments on Samui, Ocean 11 is popular with locals and visitors alike. Situated on a peaceful stretch of beach, it offers top-notch Thai and international dishes, including fresh seafood, in a beautiful setting, without the sting of five-star prices.

KO SAMUI Tamarind

91/2-3 Moo 3, Chaweng Noi Beach, 84320 **Tel** *0-7742-2011*

Elegant Tamarind does "East meets West" to stunning effect. The most popular item on the menu is the seafood basket for two people, consisting of everything from rock lobster to snapper satay. However, the crispy-skinned snapper fillet with plantains and coconut curry sauce is a deliciously mouthwatering main course.

KO SAMUI The Three Monkeys

Chaweng Beach Rd, Chaweng Beach, 84320 **Tel** *08-1821-9388*

This bar-restaurant is one of the best family bets in town. In a classic Thai pub atmosphere, the children can enjoy dishes such as Mrs Crab (a crab burger) and Panda Fried Rice, while the grown-ups will enjoy the Mango Monkeys (marinated king prawns topped with mango sauce), as well as the laid-back atmosphere.

KO SAMUI The Beach Club

Buri Rasa Village, Chaweng Beach, 84320 **Tel** *0-7723-0222*

The Beach Club claims to offer the island's only Mediterranean-Asian cuisine. The airy feel of the open dining room, combined with the contemporary soundtrack, leads one to the lighter dishes on the menu, such as the warm seafood salad or the open lobster ravioli, followed by snapper with bok choy. Good cocktails, too.

KO SAMUI Budsaba

Muang Kulaypan Hotel, 100 Moo 2, Chaweng Beach, 84320 **Tel** *0-7723-0850*

The most intimate restaurant along busy Chaweng beach, Budsaba consists of a contemporary dining room and 14 private *salas* (open wooden huts), generously spaced for privacy, outside. The Royal Thai cuisine on offer is fittingly indulgent, and the traditional music and dancing (most nights) add another dimension to the enchanting atmosphere.

KO SAMUI Chef Chom's

84 Moo 5, Bophut Beach, 84320 **Tel** *0-7724-5480*

With breathtaking ocean views, this spacious and airy restaurant is the perfect venue to try some seriously spicy Royal Thai cuisine and let the sea breezes cool you off. The sophisticated Central Thai dishes, such as their salads (try the *tongsai thai* salad, with seafood) and delicate curries are exemplary. Live Thai music and dance on Fridays.

KO SAMUI The Cliff Bar & Grill

On the cliff between Chaweng and Lamai, 84320 **Tel** *0-7741-4266*

Stylish but relaxed, this first-rate bar and grill would be a standout even without the stunning views of the bay. The Mediterranean menu emphasizes the freshness of the produce, and the uncomplicated presentation shows faith in the ingredients. The seafood platter and steaks are outstanding. Great for a sundowner. Dinner reservations advised.

KO SAMUI Dining on the Rocks

Evason Hideaway, 9/10 Moo 5, Baan Plai Lam, Bophut, 84320 **Tel** *0-7724-5678*

The magnificent views from the terrace of the signature restaurant of the Sila Evason Hideaway are matched by some of the island's best cuisine and an astounding wine selection. The Asian-inspired à la carte menu is overwhelming, so enjoy the views and order one of the five- or ten-course set menus. Reservations recommended.

KO SAMUI Eat Sense

11 Moo 2, Tambon Bo Phut, 84320 **Tel** *0-7741-4242*

Eat Sense has become one of the most popular beachfront restaurants on the Chaweng strip. It is classic Samui dining, with palm trees swaying, waves lapping, the stars twinkling, and scores of seafood dishes. Soft-shell crab, deep-fried whole fish, and lobster – an Eat Sense favorite – are all highly recommended.

KO SAMUI The Five Islands Restaurant

348 Moo 3, Taling Ngam, 84320 **Tel** *0-7741-5359*

The Five Islands is housed in an open *sala* (pavilion), designed in a Balinese-Thai style, overlooking the beach. The location is perfect for a romantic dinner. The starter set (*kantoke*) is a must-do, and the rest of the menu, a roll call of pan-Thai favorites (with excellent seafood choices), is also handled with great assurance.

KO SAMUI Padma

80/32 Moo 5, Bo Phut Beach, 84320 **Tel** *0-7723-4500*

With gorgeous ocean views, the Padma experience gets off to a wonderful start. The contemporary Thai menu, supplemented with a fresh market menu, is enticing, while dishes such as *yam pla* salmon (crispy salmon with green mango, dried shrimp, mint, and sweet fish sauce) complete the picture. Do not miss the slow-braised crispy duck.

KO SAMUI The Page

The Library, 14/1 Moo 2, Bo Phut, 84320 **Tel** *0-7742-2767*

The beachfront restaurant of the Library resort (*see p417*) is a stylish affair, especially compared to the other restaurants along this strip. Dining next to a red-tiled pool, you would expect something outlandish, but the menu offers simply solid Thai and Mediterranean food with an Asian twist and a decent wine list.

KO SAMUI Rice

167/7 Moo 2, Chaweng Beach, 84320 **Tel** *0-7723-1934*

Rice stands apart from the other Italian restaurants along the Chaweng Beach Road by being the hippest. With an open plan, split-level design, and an accompanying DJ, you would half expect the food to be an afterthought. However, with homemade pasta and pizzas straight from a wood-fired oven, Rice proves it has both style and substance.

KO TAO Ko Tao Resort

19/1 Chalok Ban Khao Beach, 84280 **Tel** *0-7745-6133*

Repeat visitors to Ko Tao swear that this is one of the tiny island's best restaurants, pleasantly isolated from the main center of activity at Ban Hat Sairee. Not surprisingly, the menu features freshly caught seafood, as well as Thai staples and a sprinkling of Western dishes, all served up in a low-key setting where the focus is firmly on the food.

PHETCHABURI Ban Khanom Thai

130 Petchkasem Rd, 76100 **Tel** *0-3242-8011*

Phetchaburi is justifiably famous for its delicious Thai sweets, and the name of this trusty establishment translates as "house of Thai sweets." One sweet thing definitely worth sampling is the *khanom mo kaen*, a firm custard of mung beans, egg, coconut, and sugar. It is a market staple and goes wonderfully with the local coffee.

PRACHUAP KHIRI KHAN Phloen Samut

44 Beach Rd, 77000 **Tel** *0-3260-1866*

Perennially popular with both locals and visitors to Prachuap Khiri Khan, Phloen Samut is a good place to try the local specialty (and a favourite in Bangkok), *pla samli taet diaw*, which is flash-fried, sundried cotton fish, served with a fresh mango salad. Other Thai dishes featuring seafood come highly recommended as well.

UPPER ANDAMAN COAST

KO LANTA Funky Fish

Ao Phra-Ae (Long Beach), near Somewhere Else bungalow resort, 81150 **Tel** *no phone*

This funky little joint's reputation may be built on its ability to pump up the music and pour out the (lethal) cocktails to an easily excitable and enthusiastic young backpacking crowd, but it also produces some tasty bar food, including deliciously simple cheesy pizzas, aimed at soaking up the alcohol.

Key to Price Guide *see p428* **Key to Symbols** *see back cover flap*

KO LANTA Sayang Beach Resort

Sayang Beach Resort, Ao Phra-Ae (Long Beach), 81150 **Tel** *0-7568-4156*

There are few more romantic dining experiences on the island than eating barefoot at tables set on the beach, under trees strung with fairy lights. This casual restaurant serves up freshly caught seafood and deliciously authentic Indian specialties – the best choices being from the tandoori oven – along with Thai and Western dishes.

KO PHI PHI Papaya

Laem Hin promontory, Ton Sai, 81000 **Tel** *no phone*

One of the first restaurants to reopen after the tsunami, Papaya keeps hungry local divers sated (always a good sign) and travelers happy with authentic, fiery Thai food – ask them to tone it down if you do not like it hot. Beside the curries, there is an excellent phad thai (rice noodles) and fried-rice dishes.

KO PHI PHI Tacada

Zeavola, 11 Moo 8 Laem Tong, 81000 **Tel** *0-7562-7000*

Dine under the stars on mats and cushions on the sand, or at slightly more comfortable but less interesting director's chairs and tables, on the beautiful white-sand beach at chic Zeavola *(see p419)*. The Thai and international fare, ranging from tapas-like snacks to full meals, are delicious, but people really come here for the atmosphere.

KRABI Baie Toey

Kongka Rd, next to Thara Guesthouse, 81000 **Tel** *0-7561-1509*

Baie Toey has a wonderful location right on the Krabi River, so be sure to get there early for lunch or dinner to grab the tables with the best views. The extensive Thai menu covers all the bases: soups, salads, curries, and stir-fries. Try their local seafood specials, or just order what the locals are having.

KRABI Ruan Tip

Maharat Rd, Krabi Town, 81000 **Tel** *0-7561-1635*

One of the best Thai restaurants in town, Ruan Tip gives Ruan Mai *(see below)* a run for its money. The traditional Thai menu is excellent, and the house specialties, such as the Ruan Tip salad of lansa fruit *(longkong)*, cashew nuts, and delicious crispy dried sea perch, are worth sampling. Live music and attentive service.

KRABI Ruen Mai

Maharat Rd, Krabi Town, 81000 **Tel** *0-7563-1797*

Long-standing Ruen Mai, set around a lovely outdoor garden, continues to be arguably the best Thai restaurant in Krabi. The extensive menu includes many Southern Thai specialties, but it is the outstanding quality of everything that goes in (the freshest ingredients) and comes out of the kitchen that really sets it apart.

PHANGNGA Duang

122 Phetkasem Rd, Phangnga, 82140 **Tel** *0-7641-2216*

Both Chinese and Southern Thai cuisine are featured on this restaurant's tasty menu. The seafood is particularly excellent, with delicious and spicy dishes such as tom yam thalay (spicy seafood stew) and kung phao (grilled shrimp) being favorites, as well as excellent dried shrimp and papaya salad, and a tasty glass-noodle salad.

PHUKET Somjit Noodles

214/6 Phuket Rd, Phuket Town, 83000 **Tel** *0-7625-6701*

This small, clean, unassuming daytime noodle shop has a strong following thanks to its excellent range of Thai and Hokkien noodle dishes. This is a great place to try the island's best-known dish, khanom chin nam ya phuket (Chinese noodles in a curried fish sauce) – after all, they have had more than 50 years to perfect it.

PHUKET China Inn Café

20 Thalang Rd, Phuket Old Town **Tel** *0-7635-6239*

In a restored Sino-Portuguese building, the China Inn Café resembles a tasteful, eclectic antique shop. The outdoor seating offers diners a relaxed ambience in which to peruse the exhaustive Thai and Western menus. The spring rolls and the duck curry are particularly good here, and there is a decent breakfast on offer as well.

PHUKET Watermark

Phuket Boat Lagoon, 22/1 Moo 2 Thepkasattri Rd, Koh Kaew, 83110 **Tel** *0-7623-9730*

In a very San Francisco setting on a marina, this modern, open restaurant is one of Phuket's most vibrant. The cuisine is essentially Pacific Rim, with flavors from Vietnam and Japan as well as Thailand, and features dishes such as grilled tuna on avocado and heavier Western dishes such as duck confit – all handled with a deft touch.

PHUKET Joe's Downstairs

223/3 Prabaramee Rd, Patong Beach, 83150 **Tel** *0-7634-4254*

Joe's Downstairs offers a lounge, bar, and deck to enjoy the stunning views of Kalim Bay. Good for a light lunch or a sundowner, Joe's increases in volume as the night heats up. The menu features eclectic international fare, with both first-rate tapas for a light snack and filling burgers, steaks, and salads. Try the lychee Martini.

PHUKET L'Orfeo

Baan Sai Yuan Rd, Rawai Beach, 83110 **Tel** *0-7628-8935*

A relaxed, casual, and slightly Arabian atmosphere is the setting for this quirky restaurant and bar. The soundtrack spans several genres, and so does the international menu. The standouts are the home-made gnocchi with pine nuts and parsley butter sauce, and the Angus beef tartare with tomato chutney. Reserve for dinner. Closed on Sundays.

PHUKET Ratri Jazztaurant

 ®®®®

Patak Rd, Kata **Tel** *0-7633-3538*

Ignore the unfortunate name: this is a hip two-story space perfect for sunset views. In addition to an oyster bar, it features Thai and other Asian delights in the dining pavilion, and cool jazz from the live band. Menu highlights are the sirloin salad and salmon sashimi for starters, and *kaeng matsaman nuah* or *kai* (beef or chicken Muslim curry).

PHUKET Sala Bua

®®®®

Impiana Phuket Cabana Resort & Spa, 41 Taweewong Rd, Patong Beach, 83110 **Tel** *0-7634-0138*

A romantic and discreet beachfront pavilion is the setting for this award-winning restaurant. Filipino chef Ronnie Macuja is one of the best-known chefs on the island, and his East-meets-West creations are inventive and show solid technique. Try his celebrated pan-seared New Zealand beef tenderloin, which comes with a surprising kiwi fruit relish.

PHUKET Silk

®®®®

15 Moo 6, Kamala Beach, Kathu 83150 **Tel** *0-7633-8777*

In a beautifully low-lit space, Silk exudes style. The menu is full of pan-Thai classics such as *tom kha gai* (chicken in coconut broth) and *goong saroong* (deep-fried prawns in noodles), and the presentation and flavors by chef Supreeda Khemkhang are very impressive. Great bar, atmosphere, and a notable range of New World wines.

PHUKET Taste Surin Beach

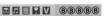 ®®®®

Surin Beach **Tel** *0-7627-0090*

On offer at Taste Surin Beach is fine dining, with a focus on seafood served in a variety of styles, bringing in influences from Thai, French, and Mediterranean cuisines. This restaurant is consistently highly rated, and its beach location and beautiful contemporary interior only add to the whole experience.

PHUKET Baan Rim Pa

®®®®®

100/7 Kalim Beach Rd, Patong Beach, 83150 **Tel** *0-7634-0789*

A long-standing Phuket favorite, set on the cliff at the northern end of Patong Beach. Dining here is a visual feast. The Royal Thai cuisine on offer is always a sure bet, and while the long menu, fine views, and live jazz are a distraction, there are well-chosen set menus and a superior wine list.

PHUKET Black Ginger

®®®®®

Indigo-Pearl, Nai Yang Beach and National Park, 83110 **Tel** *0-7632-7006*

While the tin-mining design of the Indigo-Pearl *(see p420)* is contentious, Black Ginger avoids the controversy by being located in a stand-alone Thai house on a lake, the only concession to the quirkiness of the resort being the black interior. The food on offer is classic Thai – executed particularly well. Try the Phuket noodles.

PHUKET Boathouse

®®®®®

Kata Beach, 83110 **Tel** *0-7633-0015*

It is hard to go wrong with a location right on Kata beach, and the elegant Boathouse does not disappoint. Both the Thai and French menus are heavy on seafood, and they will make for a difficult choice, as they are both handled with aplomb. Try the degustation menus with matching wines. Outstanding wine list and good by-the-glass selection.

PHUKET Da Maurizio

®®®®®

223/2 Prabaramee Rd, Patong Beach, 83150 **Tel** *0-7634-4079*

This well-run restaurant has one of the most romantic locations in town – right on the boulder-lined beach. The contemporary Italian menu covers all the bases, with plenty of seafood starters, wood-fired pizzas, handmade pasta dishes (try the rock lobster ravioli), and tempting mains – if you get that far. Interesting wine list and attentive service.

PHUKET Into the Sea

®®®®®

Evason Six Senses Spa Resort, 100 Vised Rd, Moo 2, Rawai Beach, 83110 **Tel** *0-7638-1010*

The signature restaurant of this resort *(see p420)* takes advantage of the superb views and is a favorite romantic destination. Given its proximity to the sea, the emphasis is on fresh seafood, as their seafood platter and shellfish risotto testify. Meat lovers should opt for the sumac-spiced lamb. Excellent wine list and informed staff.

PHUKET La Gaetana

®®®®®

352 Phuket Rd, Phuket Town, 83110 **Tel** *0-7625-0523*

Located in the heart of Phuket town, in an old heritage building, this rustic and homely Italian restaurant is authentic right down to the daily specials' blackboard menu. Start with the excellent sea scallops before a fresh home-made pasta dish or one of the heavier specialties, such as the ossobuco or lamb cutlets. Good Italian wine list.

PHUKET Oriental Spoon

®®®®®

Twin Palms, 106/46 Moo 3, Surin Beach Rd, Cherngtalay, 83110 **Tel** *0-7631-6577*

A very hip space serves as the signature restaurant of the Twin Palms resort, with the dining room opening onto a small pond. The menu is modern Thai, with a few non-Thai extravagances thrown in (such as fresh oysters and a seafood platter). The signature dishes are worth sampling, as is the extensive wine list.

PHUKET La Trattoria

 ®®®®®

Dusit Thani Laguna Resort, 390 Sri Sunthorn Rd, Cherngtalay, 83110 **Tel** *0-7632-4324*

Quality Italian food is served in this open-air setting (be sure to book for a terrace table). The decor is as classic as the menu, with white linen and crockery reflecting the simplicity that Italian food expresses. All the classics are here: tomato and mozzarella salad, spaghetti with clams, ossobuco, and tiramisu – all handled in a fuss-free manner.

PHUKET Saffron

Banyan Tree Resort, 393 Moo 2, Cherngtalay, 83110 **Tel** *0-7632-4374*

In a beautifully detailed room, with a candlelit feature wall and high-back chairs, Saffron impresses with a creative approach to Thai cuisine and fantastic presentation, matched by sublime flavors. The signature dishes, such as the duo of crabmeat and mixed pork, the deep-fried crispy squid, and the roasted banana crème brûlée, are taste sensations.

PHUKET Siam Indigo

8 Phang Nga Rd, Talad Yai, 83110 **Tel** *0-7625-6697*

Housed in an elegant triple-fronted historical building in the heritage area, this bar and restaurant places its culinary emphasis on fresh, organic ingredients, with a mix of Thai and international dishes. On the Thai side of the ledger, the duck salad is notable, while the grills (both meat and seafood) are the hit of the international offerings.

RANONG Thanon Ruangrat Night Market

Thanon Ruangrat **Tel** *no phone*

This bustling Night Market is a typical Thai night market in its lively atmosphere and sights and smells. However, the difference here is that the number of Muslim foodstalls is far greater, reflecting the population of Thailand's South. Try the delicious byrianis. There are also some stalls selling Chinese pastries.

RANONG Sophon's Hideaway

Thanon Ruangrat **Tel** *no phone*

This casual Thai eatery is a local favorite, with a lounge, billiard table, and television set. The place is popular with Thais and expats alike for its tasty Thai food. Favorites include the deliciously finger-licking fried pork ribs and the spicy seafood curries. The beers are icy cold and inexpensive.

DEEP SOUTH

HAT YAI Boo Bar

213 Seangchan Rd, Songkhla, 90110 **Tel** *08-0541-2058*

British visitors will feel at home in this relaxed bar and café serving such traditional English fare as Cumberland sausage with mash, fish and chips, and all-day English breakfasts. Roast dinner with lamb, pork, chicken, or beef is available every Sunday. Sandwiches and baguettes as well as Thai options such as Tom Yam soups are also on the menu.

NAKHON SI THAMMARAT Hao Coffee

Bovorn Bazaar, Ratchadamnoen Rd, 80000 **Tel** *no phone*

This pleasant daytime coffee shop is attractively and endearingly decorated with Thai antiques. It serves up tasty Thai snacks, hearty Western meals (the breakfasts are excellent), cakes, teas, and, of course, a range of quality international coffees, none really matching the local filter coffee (for which it is famous) or the excellent iced coffees.

NAKHON SI THAMMARAT Krua Nakhon

Bovorn Bazaar, Ratchadamnoen Rd, Thawang Intersection **Tel** *no phone*

Located within the Bovorn Bazaar, this canteen-style restaurarant has been a staple for several years. The Southern Thai specialties, such as khao yam pak tai, are basic but offer good value. The decor is pleasant, and the ingredients and hygiene are of a high standard. Closes at 3pm.

NARATHIWAT Rim Nam

Narathiwat-Tak Bai Rd, 96000 **Tel** *0-7351-1559*

Narathiwat's best restaurant is about a couple of kilometers (one mile) from the town center, and worth the short stroll or *tuk-tuk* ride. The place serves up excellent Thai and Malay seafood and curries, such as the local specialty, *kaeng matsaman* (a curry of beef, peanuts, potatoes, and coconut milk).

TRANG Khao Tom Phui

11 Talat Rd **Tel** *0-7521-0127*

With its house specialty rice soup, from which it takes its name, being among the best in the area, Khao Tom Phui has become a local institution and is often very busy, especially in the morning. Simple cafeteria-style tables and chairs, and great-value soups, rice dishes, and other local fare make this place a cheap and delicious favorite.

TRANG Ruen Thai Dimsum

Ploen Pitak Rd **Tel** *no phone*

Conveniently situated close to the bus station, this canteen-style eatery is a perennial favorite with locals. From dawn onward, it is packed with people coming for the steamed dumplings from which the restaurant takes its name and for which it is rightly renowned.

TRANG Wunderbar

22–26 Sathani Rd, 92000 **Tel** *0-7521-8122*

This laid-back bar-cum-eatery adjacent to the Sri-Tang Hotel caters primarily to expats and travelers passing through Trang on their way to the islands. In addition to tucking into a hearty pasta dish, big burger, or tasty Thai noodles, followed by a cheap beer, you can also organize transport and book a hotel, as they also serve as a travel agent.

SHOPPING IN THAILAND

Thailand is well known as a country that offers good shopping. The high quality, wide variety, and low prices of many Thai goods are a major attraction for tourists. Arts and crafts are probably the most tempting buys. These range from inexpensive wicker rice steamers to valuable antiques, and include many typically Thai items such as triangular cushions, colorful hill-tribe artifacts, and finely crafted silver jewelry. Many are available from specialty crafts centers. Thai silk has an international reputation and comes in a huge variety of designs, both traditional and modern. Tailors, particularly in Bangkok, can make clothes in silk or any other fabric to high standards for low prices. The country is also known for its rich supply of gems, and the capital is a major gem trading center. With the appearance of huge, luxurious shopping malls in Bangkok alongside vibrant, chaotic markets and street stands, Thailand offers shoppers a mix of the contemporary and the traditional.

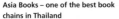
Market stall selling herbs

Asia Books – one of the best book chains in Thailand

OPENING HOURS

Most small stores open from about 8am to 8pm or 9pm, while department stores, shopping malls, and tourist shops typically open from 10:30am until 9pm or 10pm in busy areas. Business days are normally Monday to Saturday, but most shops in Bangkok, tourist areas, and resorts also open on Sundays and public holidays. During the Chinese and Thai new years (in February and April) many shops shut for several days. Market hours are usually dawn to mid-afternoon for fresh produce, or late afternoon to midnight or even later for tourist markets.

HOW TO PAY

The Thai *baht*, linked to the US dollar, has been a stable currency since the mid-1980s. *Baht* will always be accepted throughout the country (and in Laos). Credit cards can be used in many stores in Bangkok and resorts, and increasingly so in provincial towns. VISA and American Express are probably the most widely accepted, followed by MasterCard. Upscale places usually take all major cards. Be warned, though, that many shops will add on a surcharge of up to five percent if you pay by credit card.

RIGHTS AND REFUNDS

When buying expensive items, ask for a written receipt (*bai set*) with the shop's address and tax number. For goods on which you want to reclaim the seven percent sales tax, shops should fill out a form for you to present to customs at the airport. However, the hassle and handling fees involved mean that this is rarely worth the trouble.

If you are arranging to have goods shipped home make sure you confirm all the costs involved with the supplier in advance, including insurance, tax, and shipping charges.

Refunds are almost unheard of, but exchange of faulty or poorly fitting non-sale goods from reputable stores should be possible, if sometimes complicated. In small shops you may succeed through charm.

BARGAINING

The trend in cities, especially Bangkok, is toward chain stores with fixed prices and endless discount sales. However, the Thai love of bargaining means you can still often negotiate at small shops, specialty retailers, and, of course, market stands. There are a few tips for successful bargaining. Be aware of the going rate for items so as not to offer embarrassingly low sums. Talking in Thai numbers may restrain the vendor's initial bid. You can try faking disinterest if the seller's bids remain high. This is a better policy than enthusiastically bargaining, then deciding not to buy when the vendor agrees on your price.

Jewelry stall on Khao San Road, Bangkok

The huge Siam Paragon shopping complex in downtown Bangkok

DEPARTMENT STORES AND MALLS

International-style department stores are a mainstay of Bangkok shopping. However, Thai market habits die hard, and many stores fill their aisles with bargain stands.

The two main Thai chains are **Robinson's**, with a branch on Sukhumvit road; and the upscale **Central** at the Silom Complex, farther down Silom Road, Chidlom, and Lad Phrao.

The scale of the change in Thai shopping habits is remarkable. Residents of Bangkok already have countless downtown malls, such as **Peninsula Plaza**, to choose from, as well as luxury shopping complexes like **Emporium**, **Central World Plaza** and **Siam Paragon**. But the trend is for vast malls out of the center of the city – such as **Fashion Island** on Ramindra Road. These are the focus for growing suburbs and resemble self-contained, air-conditioned towns, selling not only fashion and domestic items, but even houses and cars. They incorporate huge food courts, water parks, movie theaters, concert halls, skating rinks, bowling alleys and entertainment theme parks.

Two of the world's five biggest shopping malls are in outer Bangkok. **Seacon Square** on Srinakharin Road, southeast of the city, contains a fun fair and stretches for more than 1 km (1,100 yds). The rest of Thailand has yet to experience such excesses,

but a few modern malls are now appearing in the larger towns and resorts. Examples include **Kad Suan Kaew** in Chiang Mai and the **Mike Shopping Mall** and **Central Pattaya Festival Beach Shopping** in Pattaya.

ENGLISH-LANGUAGE BOOKSTORES

Thailand has three English-language book and magazine chains: **Asia Books**, **Kinokuniya**, and **Bookazine**. All have several branches in Bangkok; there are two DK outlets in Chiang Mai, and a Bookazine in Pattaya. DK's Seacon Square branch is Southeast Asia's largest bookstore.

MARKETS AND STREET VENDORS

There is a market at the heart of every Thai town. Even the smallest will offer a good range of fresh produce, and the larger markets often sell everything from arts and crafts to fruit and vegetables and household items. The most notable are Chatuchak Market *(see p135)*, the Chiang Mai Night Bazaar *(see p226)*, the Pattaya Floating Market, and the night market in Chiang Rai. For markets in central Bangkok, see pages 140–41.

Impromptu roadside stands are also found all over the country. Some sell devotional items such as jasmine rings *(see p31)*, and others are good for souvenirs (though many of the goods are of dubious legality). Chiang Mai, Pattaya, and Patong in Phuket have many such stands. In Bangkok they are found on Silom and Sukhumvit roads, and in Banglampu and Patpong districts.

FACTORIES AND CRAFT CENTERS

Tours of factory outlets and craft centers are popular, particularly in the North and Northeast. No bargaining is required as prices are fixed, but be aware that guides take commissions.

FAKE GOODS

Thailand's trade in fakes is so notorious that many people seek out the most kitsch items as souvenirs. Most prized are goods with a deliberately fake quality, using famous logos on products they'd never normally grace, such as Louis Vuitton fanny packs or Chanel T-shirts. Conversely, identical copies with spoof labels like Live's Jeans are even becoming collectors' items. Original manufacturers are understandably outraged by the piracy. Although it could be argued that aping an original is a way for a developing country to gain skill on which to build new industries, it is still illegal. In fact, a growing copyright clampdown has shrunk the trade in fakes and even led to some forgers becoming official import agents. Be warned that customs officers may confiscate fakes.

Street stall in Pattaya selling fake versions of expensive watches

THAI SILK

The ancient art of Thai silk-weaving (see pp266–7) was revived by American Jim Thompson (see pp118–19) after World War II and is now a booming export business. Silk can be plain, patterned, or in the subtle *mut mee* style made from pre-tie-dyed *(ikat)* thread. Aside from Thai designs, this heavy, bright, and slightly rough cloth is now imaginatively used for ties, dresses, shirts, skirts, and other Western fashion items, plus cushions, hangings, and sundry ornaments. Many shops will tailor clothes to your measurements, even to your own designs.

Most silk comes from the Northeast and the North, but some is woven in and around Bangkok. For range and quality, Surawong Road in Bangkok is reliable, particularly **Jim Thompson's**, as well as **Shinawatra** on Sukhumvit Road. Chiang Mai's San Kamphaeng Road is renowned for its silk, the most famous producer being **T. Shinawatra Thai Silk**.

The Thai Silk Fair is held annually in Khon Kaen in late November or early December, when the town is packed with vendors and their bolts of cloth. If you miss the fair, **Prathamakant** sells a superb selection of silk all year round.

A dazzling selection of swatches of colorful Thai silk

CLOTHES

Thai tailors can make suits and dresses to order for low prices. Resist the rip-off 24-hour package deals including a "free gift." You get better service by seriously assessing

Made-to-measure suits are a specialty of many tailors in Thailand

the designs, fabric, and cut, and insisting on one or two intermediate fittings. In Bangkok, countless Chinese and Indian tailors advertise in tourist magazines and outside their shops along Sukhumvit, Charoen Krung, and Khao San Roads. Designs are usually copied, often with considerable skill, from magazines or catalogues of famous brands such as Armani and Hugo Boss. The quality of workmanship can vary considerably. Ask around for recommendations.

Other popular items of Thai clothing include baggy fishermen's pants; batik sarongs (especially in the South, such as at Ko Yo, Songkhla); vests and trousers made from hill-tribe fabrics; Thai silk and other Northeastern fabrics.

ARTS AND CRAFTS

Most Thai handicrafts are produced in the North and Northeast, and Chiang Mai is undoubtedly where visitors will find the widest choice of goods. The vibrant, diverse Night Bazaar sells everything from lacquerware to teak furniture, and you will need several hours if you want to peruse the often overpriced shops on San Kamphaeng Road (Highway 1006).

Prathamakant in Khon Kaen stocks a fine selection of Northeastern items such as the colorful triangular pillows.

Ayutthaya is a good source of crafts and antiques, particularly around Wat Phra Si Sanphet and on Si Sanphet Road,

where you can find unique stone carvings at **Kim Jeng**. Nearby **Bang Sai Folk Arts and Crafts Center** is the focus of Queen Sirikit's SUPPORT Foundation, which enables villagers to make a living from preserving their traditions (see p105). The fine pieces they produce are also sold at the dozen **Chitrlada** shops around Thailand. High-quality ethnic crafts at fixed prices are available from boutiques in most top hotels, **Silom Village**, **River City**, and the less expensive **Narayana-phand** department store in Bangkok. In the South, **Thai Village and Orchid Farm** in Phuket town is a good bet.

HILL-TRIBE ARTIFACTS

The costumes and artifacts of the hill tribes make fascinating anthropological souvenirs. Items might include Akha coin headdresses, Lahu geometric blankets and cushion covers, Hmong red-ruffled black jackets, brightly colored Lisu tunics, wooden cattle bells, almond-shaped bamboo boxes, wooden boxes with carvings, and woven rattan.

Some of the best outlets in Chiang Mai are the **Hill Tribe Products Foundation**, **Thai Tribal Crafts**, and the **Old Chiang Mai Cultural Center**. The **Chiang Rai Handicraft Center** also has a large range. In Bangkok, the best selection is found at Chatuchak Market (see p135). Buying from the shop at **Cabbages and Condoms** will ensure that your money goes to the tribes.

Lisu tribeswoman, selling tribal goods at a Chiang Rai bazaar

Roadside basket seller in Northern Thailand

WOOD, BAMBOO, AND RATTAN

Bamboo, rattan, and wooden items are very cheap and can be shipped home. Carved wooden friezes, screens, headboards, doors, and lintels are readily available. Chiang Mai is the best source – **Pen Phong** is good for rattan/bamboo. Woodcarving is a specialty of Mae Tha and Ban Luk near Lampang, as well as the Bo Hang district of Chiang Mai. Hang Dong and Saraphi, south of Chiang Mai, are known for their intricate basketware.

Be aware that if you buy wooden items, you may be contributing to Thailand's already disastrous deforestation problem.

Attractive celadon and blue and white ceramics in Bangkok

CERAMICS

Delicate Bencharong pottery was historically made in China and sent to Thailand to be decorated with intricate floral patterns using five colors. Today the entire process occurs in Thailand. You can buy complete dinner services in Bencharong, and myriad designs, including the more typical spherical pots. In Bangkok,

Chatuchak Market is cheaper and offers a wider choice than the downtown shops. The heavy celadon pottery style is distinguished by its etched designs under a thick, translucent green, blue, or brown glaze with a cracked patina. It's best bought direct from the potteries in Chiang Mai, where the top producer is **Mengrai Kilns**, but is also available in Bangkok from **Thai Celadon House** and many craft shops including those on Silom and Charoen Krung roads.

Lampang is notable for its fine blue and white ceramics, produced by companies such as **Indra Ceramics**.

LACQUERWARE

Lacquerware is a Northern Thai specialty. It usually has floral, flame, or portrait designs in black and gold on bamboo and wood. More common is the Burmese style of red ocher on bamboo and rattan with pictorial scenes or floral designs. Traditional items include boxes for food and jewelry. Lacquerware is plentiful in the craft shops of Chiang Mai and Bangkok.

NIELLOWARE AND PEWTERWARE

Nielloware, the intricate process of silver (or, more rarely, gold) inlay in a black metal amalgam in floral and flame patterns, makes for beautiful items like cufflinks, pill boxes, and jewelry. Some of the finest is from Nakhon Si Thammarat.

Southern Thailand has significant tin deposits, so pewterware has become a major craft. Typical items include tankards, plates, vases, and boxes. Department stores in Bangkok and stores in Phuket town stock good selections.

KALAGA TAPESTRIES

The weaving of *kalaga* tapestries involves metallic and multicolored threads, beads, patches, and sequins sewn onto a padded black background. It is a 200-year-old Burmese art but has only now been revived, so antique examples are rare and very expensive. The ubiquitous modern embroideries are often gaudy and sloppily made, but the more carefully constructed (and more expensive) simple traditional designs can make attractive cushions, hangings, bags, and even caps. Towns near to the Burmese border such as Mae Sot and Mae Sai are usually the best sources.

MUSICAL INSTRUMENTS, MASKS AND PUPPETS

Musical instruments including *khaens* (Northeastern "pan pipes"), *piphat* ensemble gongs, and drums make impressive souvenirs. They are available at Chiang Mai's Night Bazaar and at Silom Village, Narayanaphand, Chatuchak, and Nakorn Kasem markets in Bangkok. These places are also good sources of *khon* masks and theatrical items such as intricate *hoon krabok* puppets and *nang taloong* and *nang yai* shadow puppets.

In the South, Nakhon Si Thammarat is the place for shadow puppets. They can be bought from the **Shadow Puppet Theater**, and, if you phone in advance, the master puppet-maker will show you how the puppets are made.

Narayanaphand department store in Bangkok

ANTIQUES

The delicacy and charm of Thai antiques are so appealing to shoppers that the few antiques remaining in the country are very expensive, fakes, or illegally obtained. Thailand is, in fact, one of the principal outlets for antiques from all over Southeast Asia. Some shops resemble museums, jumbled with tapestries, statues, cabinets, bells, puppets, ceramics, baskets, lacquerware, and temple artifacts. They're enchanting even if you're not buying.

Bargains are rare, although prices are lower than in Hong Kong or Singapore. Chiang Mai's Tha Phae and Loi Khro Roads are a bit cheaper than the main sources in Bangkok: Charoen Krung Road, River City, Chatuchak Market, and in Chinatown at Wang Burapha and Nakorn Kasem Market. There are antique auctions at River City on the first Saturday of each month. The excellent copies available are a cheaper, more culturally responsible alternative.

Recommended shops include **Amaravadee Antiques** and **Borisoothi Antiques** in Chiang Mai, and Bangkok's **The Fine Arts** and **NeOld**.

Export permits are required for antiques and all Buddha images from the Fine Arts Department via the **National Museum** and take at least a week to obtain *(see p475)*. Not surprisingly, given that so much of their cultural heritage has left the country, Thai customs officers are vigilant in enforcing this regulation.

Shoppers admiring gold jewelry in Bangkok's Chinatown

JEWELRY

Thai jewelry tends to be large and expressive, often with superb detailing. The country has a long history of silverwork, particularly in the North and Northeast and among the hill tribes. The Wualai Road shops in Chiang Mai offer a good selection.

Necklaces, bracelets, earrings, and Lao-style belts are typical in employing silver thread and filigree detail, often incorporating silver beads and large, plate-like pendants. Contemporary and international styles are increasingly preferred in cities and resorts. More affordable modern costume jewelry sells well in Siam Square and Chatuchak Market in Bangkok, where you can buy inexpensive ethnic wares and jewelry imaginatively created from such diverse materials as nuts, seeds, shells, and beans.

Intricate bejeweled silver pendant

Some of Thailand's best jewelry is found in Bangkok's **Peninsula Plaza** shopping mall as well as hotels such as the Dusit Thani. Some shops will work to your own specifications, notably **Uthai's Gems** in Bangkok and **Shiraz** in Chiang Mai. Richard Brown designs personalized Vedic astrological jewelry at **Astral Gemstone Talismans**.

Gold is a popular, age-old form of portable wealth, and the most common type is the very yellow, Chinese-style gold. There are Chinese-owned gold shops in most sizable towns.

Be warned that amulets are not classed as jewelry and the trade in these sacred items is widely disapproved of, not least by the Buddhist authorities who believe it exploits and encourages superstition. You need a licence to export them.

GEMS

Bangkok is possibly the world's biggest gem-trading center. The local stones are rubies, red and blue spinels, orange and white zircons, and yellow and blue sapphires *(see pp310–11)*. Markets operate around Chanthaburi, Kanchanaburi, Mae Sai, and in Mae Sot on the Burmese border, where gems are cheaper than in Bangkok. However, you'll need an expert eye to pick out the bargains and should be wary of illegally smuggled gems. Phuket is Thailand's only good source of high quality pearls (try **Pearl Center** in Phuket town).

Gem scams are notorious in Bangkok and Chiang Mai, so run a mile if someone friendly says it's a public holiday so there's a government suspension of tax. Countless people have fallen for this ruse before being coaxed into parting with large sums of money by clever salesmanship and even, sometimes, drugged drinks.

It is possible to learn gemology and have stones authenticated and graded (but not valued) at the **Asian Institute of Gemological Sciences** in Bangkok.

Antiques in one of Bangkok's more exclusive shops

DIRECTORY

DEPARTMENT STORES AND MALLS

Central Department Store
Silom Complex, 191 Silom Rd, Bangkok. **Map** 7 A4. *Tel 0-2231-3333.*

Central Pattaya Festival Beach Shopping
Beach Rd & 2nd Rd, Pattaya. *Tel 0-3836-1443-5.*

Central World Plaza
Ratchadamri Rd, Bangkok. **Map** 8 D1. *Tel 0-2635-1111.*

Emporium
Sukhumvit Rd, Prompong, Bangkok. **Map** 8 F1. *Tel 0-2269-1000.*

Fashion Island
5/5 Ramindra Rd, Bangkok. *Tel 0-2947-5000.*

Kad Suan Kaew
99/4 Mu 2, Huai Kaew Rd, Chiang Mai. *Tel 0-5322-4444.*

Mike Shopping Mall
262 Mu 10, Pattaya Beach Rd, Pattaya. *Tel 0-3841-2000.*

Peninsula Plaza
153 Ratchadamri Rd, Bangkok. **Map** 8 D1. *Tel 0-2253-9762.*

Robinson's
259 Sukhumvit Rd, North Klong Toey, Bangkok. *Tel 0-2252-5121.*

Seacon Square
904 Srinakharin Rd, Bangkok. *Tel 0-2721-8888.*

Siam Paragon
Rama I Rd, Bangkok. **Map** 7 C1. *Tel 0-2690-1000.*

ENGLISH-LANGUAGE BOOKSTORES

Asia Books
221 Sukhumvit Rd, Bangkok. *Tel 0-2651-0428.*

Bookazine
Floor 1, CP Tower, 313 Silom Rd, Bangkok. **Map** 7 C4. *Tel 0-2231-0016.*

Kinokuniya
Floor 6, Isetan, Ratchadamri Rd, Bangkok. **Map** 8 D1. *Tel 0-2255-9834.*

THAI SILK

Jim Thompson's
9 Surawong Rd, Bangkok. **Map** 7 C3. *Tel 0-2235-8931.*

Prathamakant
79/2–3 Ruenrom Rd, Khon Kaen. *Tel 0-4322-4080.*

Shinawatra
94 Sukhumvit Rd, Soi 23, Bangkok. *Tel 0-2258-0295.*

T. Shinawatra Thai Silk
145/1–2 Chiang Mai-San Kamphaeng Rd, Chiang Mai. *Tel 0-5333-1187.*

ARTS AND CRAFTS

Bang Sai Folk Arts and Crafts Center
Tambon, Bang Sai, Ayutthaya province. *Tel 0-3536-6092.*

Chitrlada Shop
Chitrlada Palace, Bangkok. **Map** 3 B2. *Tel 0-2229-4611.*

Kim Jeng
12 Mu 2, Kamang, Ayutthaya.

Narayanaphand Department Store
127 Ratchadamri Rd, Bangkok. **Map** 8 D1. *Tel 0-2252-4670.*

River City
23 Trok Rongnamkaeng, Yotha Rd, Bangkok. **Map** 6 F3. *Tel 0-2237-0077.*

Silom Village
286 Silom Rd, Bangkok. **Map** 7 A4. *Tel 0-2233-9447.*

Thai Village and Orchid Farm
52/11 Thepkasattri Rd, Muang Phuket. *Tel 0-7621-4860.*

HILL-TRIBE ARTIFACTS

Cabbages and Condoms
10 Sukhumvit, Soi 12, Bangkok. **Map** 8 F1. *Tel 0-2229-4611.*

Chiang Rai Handicrafts Center
732 Mu 5 Rimkok, Phahon Yothin Rd, Chiang Rai. *Tel 0-5371-3355.*

Hill Tribe Products Foundation
21/17 Suthep Rd, Chiang Mai. *Tel 0-5327-7743.*

Old Chiang Mai Cultural Center
185 Wualai Rd, Chiang Mai. *Tel 0-5320-2993.*

Thai Tribal Crafts
208 Bamrung Rad Rd, Chiang Mai. *Tel 0-5324-1043.*

WOOD, BAMBOO, AND RATTAN

Pen Phong
189/25 Nongkaew Rd, Hangdong, Chiang Mai. *Tel 0-5343-3745.*

CERAMICS

Indra Ceramics
382 Lampang–Denchai Rd, Lampang. *Tel 0-5422-1189.*

Mengrai Kilns
79/2 Araks Rd, Chiang Mai. *Tel 0-5327-2063.*

Thai Celadon House
8/3–8/5 Ratchadapisek Rd, Sukhumvit, Bangkok. *Tel 0-2229-4383.*

PUPPETS

Shadow Puppet Theater
10/18 Si Thammasok Soi 3, Nakhon Si Thammarat. *Tel 0-7534-6394.*

ANTIQUES

Amaravadee Antiques
141 Chiang Mai–Hot Rd, Chiang Mai. *Tel 0-5344-1628.*

Borisoothi Antiques
15/2 Chiangmai-San Kamphaeng Rd, Chiang Mai. *Tel 0-5333-8460.*

National Museum
Fine Arts Department, 1 Na Phra That Rd, Bangkok. **Map** 1 C4. *Tel 0-2224-1370.*

NeOld
149/2–3 Surawong Rd, Bangkok. **Map** 7 B4. *Tel 0-2235-8352.*

The Fine Arts
3/F Room 354 River City, Bangkok. **Map** 6 F3. *Tel 0-2237-0077 ext.354.*

JEWELRY

Astral Gemstone Talismans
Sri Hrisikesh Plaza, C3 Building, Joe Louis Theater, Lumpini Night Bazaar, Bangkok. *Tel 0-2252-1230.*

Shiraz
170 Thapae Rd, Chiang Mai. *Tel 0-5325-2382.*

Thai Lapidary
1009–11 Silom Rd, Bangkok. **Map** 7 C4. *Tel 0-2236-2134.*

Uthai's Gems
28/7 Soi Ruam Rudi, Phloen Chit Rd, Bangkok. **Map** 8 F2. *Tel 0-2253-8582.*

GEMS

Asian Institute of Gemological Sciences
33rd Floor, Jewellery Trade Center, 919/1 Silom Rd, Bangkok. **Map** 7 A4. *Tel 0-2267-4315.*

Pearl Center
83 Ranong Rd, Soi Phutorn, Phuket town. *Tel 0-7621-1707.*

What to Buy in Thailand

Toy
tuk-tuk

Thai market stalls, craft centers, and specialty shops offer a wide and tempting range of souvenirs and gifts. Handicrafts are particularly good buys, and there are few regions of the country without their own specialty. In the south you can find delicately worked niello-ware, pewter, and shadow puppets; colorful hill-tribe artifacts, lacquerware, and silver jewelry are made in the North; the Northeast is famed for its silk and cushions. The widest selection is available in major cities such as Bangkok and Chiang Mai.

Nang taloong **puppet**

TRADITIONAL MASKS AND PUPPETS

Thailand has a rich tradition of masked dance and puppetry, and although performances are becoming increasingly rare, masks and puppets make evocative souvenirs. Most depict characters from the Ramakien *(see pp40–41)* and include huge leather *nang yai* figures, smaller *nang taloong* shadow puppets, *hoon krabok* marionettes, and the smaller *hoon lek (see pp42–3)*. Puppets can be bought in the South as well as at markets such as Chatuchak in Bangkok.

Figure of a Thai musician

Khon **mask of a demon**

Rattan and wickerwork *come in many guises, from simple rice steamers to attractive and durable sets of rattan furniture. Trays, boxes, and bags are popular and can be found for sale in many Thai markets, particularly in Bangkok and Chiang Mai. Reputable shops can arrange for large items to be shipped overseas.*

Nielloware *is an ancient craft that has been practiced in the South of Thailand for several centuries. Nakhon Si Thammarat province is the center of Thai nielloware production today. The process involves the decorative etching of silver and gold items that are then rubbed with a black metal alloy. Jewelry and small boxes are the most afford- able items.*

Wood-carving *is a highly skilled profession, and visitors can buy everything from tiny carved bowls and pill boxes to huge screens, cabinets, and beds. However, be aware that some hardwood items may be made from illegally felled trees.*

Lacquerware *items include jewelry boxes, bangles, bowls, and trays. The process of coating split bamboo or wood with lacquer and then adding delicate hand-paintings is a specialty of the north. The two most common styles of decoration are gold on black lacquer and the Burmese style of yellow and green on red. Chiang Mai is the best source.*

Hill-tribe artifacts *are sold in towns and villages all over Northern Thailand, although Chiang Mai undoubtedly has the widest range of handicrafts. Among the most attractive items are patchwork bags, brightly colored blankets, delicately wrought silver jewelry, and hand-embroidered jackets and hats. If you go on a trek it is likely that you will visit at least one hill-tribe village, enabling you to buy the local handicrafts direct from the producers and, sometimes, see them being made.*

Ceramics *have been produced in Thailand for hundreds of years. Although many styles show a pronounced Chinese influence, there are also several types of ceramics that are given a distinctive Thai stamp. One is the colorfully enameled Bencharong pottery that is most commonly found as small pots and vases. Celadon is another example. It is recognizable by its characteristic crazed surface on a typically light green glaze.*

Blue and white dinner service

Bencharong pot

Celadon vase

Silverware *is another traditional Northern Thai craft. Beaten silver bowls, vases, and boxes, often with expertly worked relief patterns, are popular buys, particularly in Chiang Mai. Delicate silver jewelry in traditional and modern designs is also widely available throughout the North and in Bangkok.*

Silver bird

Orchid jewelry

Yellow and blue sapphire ring

A selection of sapphires

Silver bowl

Hanuman on silver box lid

Jewelry and gems *are particularly tempting purchases in Thailand. Not only is the country one of the world's major sources of rubies and sapphires, but it is also well known for skillfully crafted jewelry. Jewelers who display their work in the shops within the top hotels usually offer good quality at fair prices, but it is unwise to buy gems with the intention of reselling at a profit unless you are an expert.*

THAI FABRICS

Silk is without doubt the best known Thai fabric and probably the number-one buy for visitors *(see p452)*. It comes in an enormous range of styles, weights, and designs, both ancient and modern, including tie-dyed *mud mee*. Thai cotton goods are also excellent – *pha sin* skirts and triangular *mawn sam liam* cushions often feature complex patterns. The hill tribes are known for their bold, geometric fabric designs. In the South, batik sarongs and baggy fishermen's trousers are widely available.

Colorful silk hanging

Mawn sam liam cushion

Patterned silk tie

Scarf of raw Thai silk

Traditional cotton fishermen's trousers

Cotton *pha sin* skirt

ENTERTAINMENT IN THAILAND

Modern Thailand may have adopted many foreign pursuits, from Hollywood movies to karaoke, but traditional entertainments still flourish. Although the graceful movements of classical *khon* dance-dramas survive mainly as tourist shows, the grassroots following of such typically Thai obsessions as *muay thai* boxing remains as strong

Thai dancers at the Rose Garden, Bangkok

as ever. High-spirited *sanuk* (fun) is an all-embracing activity, even on the most serious of occasions such as religious festivals. Indulging in the local passions is essential to understanding life in Thailand, whether it be a song-filled night out at a bar or folk music club, a colorful temple fair, a classical concert, a *takraw* game, or watching the latest Thai movie.

The Thailand Cultural Center, the country's premier concert venue

INFORMATION SOURCES

Details of the major events and festivals throughout Thailand are provided in a booklet available from TAT offices. *Big Chilli*, Thailand's leading English-language news magazine, is a useful source for what's going on in the capital as well as in the rest of the country. It is also worthwhile consulting the English-language newspapers, the *Bangkok Post* and the *Nation*, and the many free tourist magazines. Good hotels should also be able to provide information.

Bangkok's listings magazine

BOOKING TICKETS

Major hotels and travel agencies can book tickets for cultural shows and sports events. Alternatively, you can buy tickets direct from venues or, for major events, from Thai TicketMajor counters at Central Department Store *(see p455)*. To book by phone call 0-2262-3456, or visit www.thaiticketmajor.com.

TRADITIONAL THEATER AND DANCE

Watching the stylized royal all-male masked dance *khon* is like seeing the murals of Wat Phra Kaeo come to life. Sadly, popular interest in the mostly Ramakien-based dance-dramas is waning, and performances of *khon*, and of the equally elaborate but less formal *lakhon*, are becoming increasingly rare. In even greater danger of extinction are the *hoon lek* marionette shows *(see pp42–3)*.

The most atmospheric place to watch traditional dance is at Sanam Luang on the evening of royal ceremonies such as the king's birthday or a funeral. At such times dozens of stages provide entertainment long into the night. Complete performances can last days, so abridged scenes are chosen for shows at the **National Theater** (indoors on the last Saturday and Sunday of the month; outdoors every Saturday and Sunday from December to May) and the hi-tech **Royal Chalermkrung Theater** in Bangkok and at the **Old Chiang Mai Cultural Center**.

Countless tourist dinner shows in the major cities and resorts offer bills of dances from all over the country. Chiang Mai's famous *khantoke* dinners *(see p38)*, including dancing, can be experienced

at the **Khantoke Palace** and **Khum Kaew Khantoke Palace**. Reliable venues in Bangkok include the **Rose Garden** and **Silom Village**, while the Oriental's **Sala Rim Nam** restaurant presents authentic *khon*. *Lakhon* can also be witnessed at Bangkok's Lak Muang shrine near Sanam Luang, and the Erawan Shrine. Traditional Thai puppetry can be seen at the **Joe Louis Theater**.

The most widespread dance-drama is *likay*, a regular feature of temple fairs, festivals, and TV. Its bawdy, slapstick, and satirical elements have allowed it to retain a popular contemporary following. The ancient equivalent from the South of Thailand is *manora*.

Still widespread in Malaysia and Indonesia, *nang talung* shadow puppet shows survive only in the Deep South at Phatthalung and Nakhon Si Thammarat *(see p383)*. Performances of *nang talung* at local festivals can run all night, but an hour or two is usually enough for most tourists. Even rarer are performances of *nang yai*, in which enormous, flat leather puppets are manipulated by a team of puppeteers.

A traditional *khon* performance

CONCERTS, EXHIBITIONS, AND MODERN THEATER

Thailand's major concert and exhibition halls are located in Bangkok. The state-of-the-art **Thailand Cultural Center** has excellent performance facilities and attracts popular international names. The German **Goethe-Institut** and the **Alliance Française** host first-rate exhibitions and concerts. Top stars frequently perform in the ballrooms of hotels such as the **Dusit Thani** (see p399).

Bangkok Playhouse often stages plays in English and it also houses the **Art Corner** gallery, though **Art Republic** is the best place to go and see contemporary Thai art. The **Patravadi Theatre** puts on superb, highly visual musicals based on classical stories, which are easily understandable to non-Thais.

A musical performance at the Patravadi Theatre

MOVIES

Thais are avid movie-goers. Bangkok now has a number of huge multiplexes, but there are still 2,000 mobile units in the country that offer impromptu open-air screenings in villages.

The film industry in Thailand has a long, erratic history. Despite socially aware classics like *Luk Isan* (1978), it has mostly produced formulaic melodramas, comedies, and violent action films. Hong

BANGKOK INTERNATIONAL FILM FESTIVAL 2007 19-29 JULY

Promoting the Bangkok Film Festival

Kong action movies have long been popular, but, since the early 1990s, Hollywood movies have dominated the Thai market. However, Thai cinema has been enjoying a renaissance and it is now regarded as one of the most creative in Southeast Asia. The capital also hosts the increasingly prestigious annual Bangkok International Film Festival.

Some of the theaters in Bangkok (such as **The Lido** and **Siam Cinema**), Chiang Mai, Pattaya, Phuket, and Hat Yai show movies with their original soundtracks.

DISCOS, BARS, COMEDY, MUSIC, AND FOLK CLUBS

Challenged by international rock and sugary Thai pop, folk music has retained its popularity. It can be heard on the radio and TV, in bars, at festivals, and impromptu gatherings, particularly outside the capital, although concerts are rarely publicized in English. It is also played in the unsalubrious cafés staging *talok* (comedy), which do not welcome tourists.

The main styles include the exuberant, rhythmic *rum wong*, which is often accompanied by a jocular dance; *look thung* ("country music"), combining big band music, costumed dance troupes, and singing; and the schmaltzy, ballad-based *look krung*. Favored by bus and taxi drivers, the faster Northeastern *mo'lam* sound is distinguished by *khaen* pipes and rap-like vocals. The Khmer-style *kantrum* music of the southern region of the Northeast can be heard in Surin's **Petchkasem Hotel** on weekends. The plaintive,

radical *phleng phua chiwit* ("songs for life") emerged during the student protests of the 1970s and has a few dedicated spots, such as **Raintree**, in Bangkok.

Emerging rock bands often play at **O'Reilly's Irish Pub**, while hotels host classier venues: **Spasso** (Grand Hyatt Erawan), **Angelini** (Shangri-La), and the Oriental's **Lord Jim's** and jazzy **Bamboo Bar**.

Friends sharing food and whisky while listening to live music is the nightlife formula throughout Thailand, although karaoke, discos, and themed bars are gaining ground. In Bangkok, fashionable districts come and go at great speed, though Sarasin remains an enduring strip. The original trendy hangout, Silom Soi 4, is still packed with young "glitterati," while the gay scene is centered on Silom Soi 2 and the multipurpose center **Utopia**. The most impressive internet café is **Cyberia**. In Chiang Mai, **The Riverside** leads a string of venues beside the Ping River.

Discos can be found throughout all of the major resorts in Thailand. The many large Bangkok nightclubs include the ever-popular **Narcissus**.

The flesh-trade districts – such as Patpong (see p116), Nana Entertainment Plaza (Sukhumvit Soi 3), and Soi Cowboy (off Soi Asoke) in Bangkok, plus Pattaya and Patong in Phuket – are notorious for their bizarre gynecological "entertainments." Rip-offs are common, although the King's Group's bars are among the most "reputable." One of Thailand's most infamous and popular attractions on stage and TV is its cross-dressing *katoeys*, or "lady-boys." Tourists flock to their sanitized transvestite shows at **Calypso Cabaret** in Bangkok, **Blue Moon Cabaret** in Chiang Mai, **Simon Cabaret** in Patong, and **Alcazar** in Pattaya, which boasts the best performers.

"Adult" entertainment from the King's Group

TEMPLE FAIRS AND FESTIVALS

The Thai calendar is packed with national holidays and local festivals *(see pp46–51)*. These festivals may be religious or in honor of a local hero, to promote seasonal produce, or dedicated to other activities like boat racing and kite flying.

As well as often hosting other events, most *wats* stage temple fairs. But apart from scheduled major fairs such as the Golden Mount Temple Fair in Bangkok at Loy Krathong *(see p50)*, it's usually a matter of chance whether you encounter one. The sideshows are often as entertaining as the ceremonies with vendors selling food and trinkets, colorful characters like the cross-dressing *katoeys*, folk music such as *likay* and *lam wong*, beauty contests, and who-can-eat-the-hottest-*som-tam* competitions. Other activities might include cock fighting or Siamese fighting fish contests.

Staged spectaculars aimed at tourists include the sound-and-light, fireworks, and other festivities at the Sukhothai ruins during Loy Krathong in November and during the Khwae River Bridge Week at Kanchanaburi *(see p50)*.

Parade during the Loy Krathong festival in Lampang

MUAY THAI AND KRABI-KRABONG

Thai kick boxing, *muay thai*, is a national passion *(see pp44–5)*. Most provinces have a boxing arena, but the nation's top two venues are in the capital. **Lumphini Stadium** has bouts on Tuesdays, Fridays, and Saturdays, and boxing can be seen at

Muay thai **boxing – passionately followed all over Thailand**

Ratchadamnoen Boxing Stadium on Mondays, Wednesdays, Thursdays, and Sundays.

If you are interested in learning, rather than simply watching, the skills involved in *muay thai*, then contact the **International Amateur Muay Thai Federation**, who should be able to recommend suitable gyms and instructors.

Another revered, long-established Thai martial art is *krabi-krabong*, named "sword-staff" after some of the hand weaponry used. The techniques are taught to ancient standards, although skill and stamina rather than injuries inflicted are now the measures of an accomplished fighter. Demonstrations are often included in tourist cultural shows.

TAKRAW

The acrobatic Southeast Asian sport of *takraw* is played by young males at seemingly any clear patch of ground in Thailand. The idea is to keep a woven rattan ball in the air using any part of your body except your hands. The players' extraordinary agility, balletic leaps, and speed of reactions are a revelation to visitors reared on more ponderous sports.

There are elaborate versions emphasizing individual skill, but the classic original style has a team trying to get the ball into a basketball-like net more times in a set period than their rivals. Despite the competitive version, *sepak*

takraw, which resembles volleyball, now being incorporated into the Olympics and Asian Games, professional games are played surprisingly rarely.

The remarkably acrobatic *takraw*

SOCCER, RUGBY, AND SNOOKER

Thais have developed a feverish enthusiasm for soccer. In 1996 a professional soccer league was introduced. Rugby has also sparked remarkable interest, with established clubs competing in a league and the Hong Kong Sevens. Games are mostly held in Bangkok at the **Pathumwan Stadium**, **Hua Mark Stadiums**, **Army Stadium**, and **Royal Bangkok Sports Club**.

Thailand is the most successful non-Anglophone country to adopt snooker, which has become hugely popular. Its dangerous association with underground gambling makes it hard for players to emulate champions like James Wattana, though there are some safe clubs around. Thailand hosts world ranking tournaments in March and September.

DIRECTORY

TRADITIONAL THEATER AND DANCE

Joe Louis Theater
1875 Rama IV Rd,
Bangkok.
Tel 0-2252-9683.

Khantoke Palace
288/19 Chang Khlan Rd,
Chiang Mai.
Tel 0-5327-2757.

Khum Kaew Khantoke Palace
252 Phra Pok Klao Rd,
Chiang Mai.
Tel 0-5321-0663.

National Theater
1 Na Phra That Rd,
Bangkok. **Map** 1 C4.
Tel 0-2224-1342.

Old Chiang Mai Cultural Center
185/3 Wualai Rd,
Chiang Mai.
Tel 0-5327-5097.

Rose Garden
Off Hwy 4, 32 km
(20 miles) W of Bangkok.
Tel 0-2295-3261.

Royal Chalerm-krung Theater
66 Charoen Krung Rd,
Bangkok. **Map** 6 D1.
Tel 0-2222-0434.

Sala Rim Nam
Oriental Hotel,
48 Oriental Ave, Bangkok.
Map 6 F4.
Tel 0-2236-0400.

Silom Village
286 Silom Rd, Bangkok.
Map 7 A4.
Tel 0-2635-6810.

CONCERTS, EXHIBITIONS, AND MODERN THEATER

Alliance Française
29 Sathorn Tai Rd,
Yannawa, Bangkok.
Map 8 D4.
Tel 0-2670-4200.
www.alliancefr.org

Art Republic
Peninsula Plaza, 3rd Floor,
Ratchadamri Rd, Bangkok.
Map 8 D1.
Tel 0-2652-1801.
www.artrepublicbkk.com

Bangkok Play-house/Art Corner
2884/2 New Phetchaburi
Rd, Bangkok.
Tel 0-2718-0600.

Goethe-Institut
18/1 Soi Atthakan Prasit,
Sathorn Tai Rd, Bangkok.
Map 8 E4.
Tel 0-2287-0942.
www.goethe.de/
bangkok

Patravadi Theatre
69/1 Soi Wat Rakhang,
Arun Amarin Rd, Thon
Buri, Bangkok. **Map** 1 B5.
Tel 0-2412-7287.
www.patravadi
theatre.com

Thailand Cultural Center
Ratchadaphisek Rd,
Bangkok.
Tel 0-2247-0028.

MOVIES

The Lido
256 Rama I Rd,
Siam Square, Bangkok.
Map 7 C1.
Tel 0-2252-6498.

Siam Cinema
Siam Square, Rama I Rd,
Bangkok. **Map** 7 C1.
Tel 0-2251-1735.

DISCOS, BARS, COMEDY, MUSIC, AND FOLK CLUBS

Alcazar
Pattaya Second Rd,
Pattaya.
Tel 0-3841-0224-5.

Angelini
Shangri-La Hotel,
89 Soi Wat Suan Phu,
Bangkok. **Map** 6 F5.
Tel 0-2236-7777.

Bamboo Bar
Oriental Hotel,
48 Oriental Ave, Bangkok.
Map 6 F4.
Tel 0-2236-0400.

Blue Moon Cabaret
5/3 Mun Muang Rd,
Chiang Mai.
Tel 0-5327-8818.

Calypso Cabaret
Asia Hotel,
296 Phayathai Rd,
Bangkok.
Tel 0-2216-8937.

Cyberia
654/8 Sukhumvit Rd,
crn Soi 24, Bangkok.
Map 8 F1.
Tel 0-2259-3356.

Lord Jim's
Oriental Hotel,
48 Oriental Ave, Bangkok.
Map 6 F4.
Tel 0-2236-0400.

Narcissus
112 Sukhumvit Soi 23,
Bangkok.
Tel 0-2258-4805.
www.narcissusclub
bangkok.com

O'Reilly's Irish Pub
62 Silom Rd, Bangkok.
Map 8 C4.
Tel 0-2632-7515.

Petchkasem Hotel
104 Chitbumrung Rd,
Surin.
Tel 0-4451-1274.

Raintree
116/64 Soi Rang Nam,
off Phaya Thai Rd,
Bangkok.
Tel 0-2245-7230.

The Riverside
9–11 Charoenraj Rd,
Chiang Mai.
Tel 0-5324-3239.

Simon Cabaret
100/6–8 Mu 4,
Karon Rd, Patong,
Phuket.
Tel 0-7634-2011.

Spasso
Grand Hyatt Erawan Hotel,
494 Ratchadamri Rd,
Bangkok.
Map 8 D1.
Tel 0-2254-1234.

Utopia Centre
Soi Sukhumvit 23, jnct
Soi Sawatdee, Bangkok.
Map 8 F1.
Tel 0-2259-9619.

MUAY THAI AND KRABI-KRABONG

International Amateur Muay Thai Federation
Pathumwan Stadium,
154 Rama I Rd,
Bangkok.
Map 7 B1.
Tel 0-2215-6212-4.

Lumphini Stadium
Rama IV Rd,
Bangkok.
Map 8 E4.
Tel 0-2252-8765.

Ratchadamnoen Boxing Stadium
1 Ratchadamnoen
Nok Rd, Bangkok.
Map 2 F4.
Tel 0-2281-4205.

SOCCER, RUGBY, AND SNOOKER

Army Stadium
Wiphawadirangsit Rd,
Bangkok.
Tel 0-2278-5095.

Hua Mark Indoor and Outdoor Stadiums
2088 Ramkhamhaeng Rd,
Bangkok.
Tel 0-2318-0946.

Pathumwan Stadium
154 Rama I Rd,
Bangkok.
Map 7 B1.
Tel 0-2214-0120.

Royal Bangkok Sports Club
1 Henri Dunant Rd,
Pathumwan, Bangkok.
Map 8 D2.
Tel 0-2652-5000.
www.rbsc.org

OUTDOOR ACTIVITIES
& SPECIAL INTERESTS

Thailand offers an impressive range of outdoor activities and special interests. The coastline in the south is ideal for aquatic fun, from sailing, waterskiing, and windsurfing to big-game fishing and diving to see some spectacular coral reefs. Northern Thailand's mountainous forests are famous for their waterfalls, caves, and wildlife, including rare birds, gibbons, elephants, and tigers. Trekking in this beautiful region to see hill tribes is a controversial activity, and there are claims that constant visits from outsiders are eroding

Traveling by long-tail boat

traditional culture, so be sure to choose a responsible trekking company with knowledgeable guides. Thailand also has an extensive network of national parks. Exciting ways to explore the country's natural wilderness include sea canoeing, bamboo rafting, white-water rafting, elephant riding, and rock climbing.

Some visitors take advantage of the growing number of excellent golf courses. Others come to learn cultural skills such as Buddhist meditation, traditional massage, and Thai cooking techniques, which include delicate vegetable carving.

DIVING AND SNORKELING

Abundant coral reefs thronging with aquatic life – serviced by countless diving operations – make Thailand one of the world's most accessible and rewarding destinations for underwater exploration. In particular, the Andaman coast and islands have some stunning reefs, ocean drop-offs, and submerged pinnacles – not to mention visibility often exceeding 30 m (100 ft). A rich variety of marine life can be spotted in these waters, such as whale sharks off the Burma Banks.

Much of the best diving is to be found in the national marine parks containing the Surin, Similan, and Tarutao archipelagos in the Andaman

Sea; Ko Tao in the western Gulf of Thailand; and Ko Chang in the eastern Gulf. The once-magnificent Ko Phi Phi has not been protected by this preserve status, and has been heartbreakingly damaged by careless anchoring and snorkelers breaking the coral. Reckless fishing with dragnets, harpoons, and explosives has also killed some reefs, while siltation and pollution pose growing threats. Though the devastating tsunami of 2004 caused a tragic loss of lives, its effect on the coral reefs of the Andaman Sea was fortunately minimal.

Because of rough weather brought on by monsoons *(see pp26–7)*, the Andaman sites are accessible from November to April; the shallower waters of the western Gulf are best

Spectacular diving around the reefs off Thailand's coasts and islands

visited between January and October. The Eastern Seaboard is accessible all year round.

Diving trips vary in length from one to several days, and many tours accommodate snorkelers, too. Selected dive companies are listed in the directory *(see pp468–9)*, and fuller listings and details of dive sites appear in the books *Asian Diver Scuba Guide: Thailand* (Asian Diver) and *Diving in Thailand* (Asia Books).

PADI- and NAUI-approved diving courses are widely available in Thailand. The main centers offering courses are Phuket, Pattaya, Khao Lak, Ko Tao, Ko Samui, Ko Phi Phi, and Krabi.

Basic diving rules include: inspect your equipment and get the right fit; don't dive unless you are confident

Snorkeling with the marine life off the upper Andaman coast

in your instructor and have been well trained; make sure there's a buddy system; check that your group is small enough for the dive masters to monitor; and never touch the coral.

For people who do not want to spend the time or money on the training necessary to become a certified diver, snorkeling is an excellent alternative, since all you need is the ability to swim. Most hotels and guesthouses located near reefs can rent out equipment, but to make the most of the experience, it's best to buy your own. While the beautiful patterns of the corals and brilliant colors of the fish that live among them can be mesmerizing, it's important to be constantly aware of your position and not to venture too far from the shore.

SAILING

Thailand's dramatic coastline is popular with the yachting fraternity, who come to Phuket every December for the King's Cup Regatta. Chartering a yacht – with or without a skipper – is possible, though daily rates for this very exclusive sport are not cheap. **Gulf Charters Thailand** operates on the Eastern Seaboard, where sea breezes are often ideal, but the widest choice of sailing companies is found on Phuket. Some of the best are **Phuket Sailing**, **Yachtpro**, and **South East Asia Liveaboards**.

WATER SPORTS

Water sports are hugely popular at many Thai beach resorts, but the disturbance they cause to holidaymakers is of concern, and in places such as Krabi they are banned. However, at most other seaside towns it is possible to rent windsurfing boards, and jet skis and banana-boat rides are becoming commonplace even in national marine parks such as Ko Samet.

For the best range of water sports, including paragliding, waterskiing, and motorboat rental, head for Jomtien

Jet-skiing: an ever-popular but increasingly controversial activity

beach at Pattaya; Hua Hin and Cha-am; and Patong and Karon beaches on Phuket.

Anglers can make use of the excellent facilities for big-game fishing at Pattaya and Phuket. This can be a thrilling way to pass a day, but be prepared to pay in excess of 10,000 *baht* for boat rental.

See the directory *(pp468–9)* for details of service providers.

CANOEING

Sea canoeing is not just the most peaceful way to enjoy the unusual karst islets of Phangnga Bay and the Angthong archipelago, but also the only way to explore their collapsed sea caves. Ringed by forest and often containing tiny beaches, many of these spectacular *hong* (literally "rooms") were first discovered by **Sea Canoe Thailand**, which runs the most responsible tours to these fragile "lost worlds." Another reliable outfit that operates

tours around Phangnga Bay, Ko Tarutao National Marine Park, and the huge reservoir in Khao Sok National Park is **Paddle Asia**.

WHITE-WATER RAFTING AND KAYAKING

Sedate bamboo rafting is a popular tourist pastime, particularly on the rivers in the north. More exciting, though, is white-water rafting on hardy inflatables. No experience is necessary apart from the ability to swim, since instruction is given to paddlers before setting out, and each raft has a capable crew to deal with any emergency. The upper reaches of the Pai and Moei rivers in the north are ideal for this thrilling sport, and Umphang's Mae Klong district near Mae Sot is particularly notable for world-class rafting. **Thai Adventure Rafting**, **Siam Rivers**, and **The Wild Lodge** are a few of the best trip organizers.

For athletic types looking for a challenge, white-water kayaking offers plenty of thrills and spills. Siam Rivers offers day courses for beginners on the Mae Taeng River, just north of Chiang Mai, and tougher, five-day trips on the Nam Wa River in Nan Province.

The season for white-water rafting and kayaking in Thailand lasts from July to December: this is when water levels are high enough to ensure an exciting ride.

Canoeing is a peaceful way to explore the splendid Thai coastline

GOLF

With green and caddie fees cheaper than in the West, it's easy to see why so many visitors include a round of golf on their itinerary. Golf is very popular in Thailand, and the country has hosted several international competitions at its growing number of courses, many designed by the game's top names. The greens around Bangkok are mostly flat and uninteresting, but there are some beautiful backdrops at golfing resorts in Phuket, Khao Yai, and Chiang Mai.

Exclusivity is a feature of some clubs, though many are open to non-members, and golfing vacation packages are particularly popular at places such as Pattaya, Phuket, and Hua Hin. Visit www.golf thailand.net for an idea of what is on offer. The best printed guides to courses are the *Thailand Golf Map* and *Thailand Golf Guide*; TAT also publishes a free directory of the country's top 75 courses. For improving your handicap, there's a David Leadbetter Academy of Golf at the **Thana City Golf and Country Club**.

See the directory *(pp468–9)* for additional golf clubs.

ELEPHANT RIDING

After the mechanization of logging, and then its supposed ban in 1989, working elephants found

An elephant ride through the forest

themselves unemployed, and their *mahouts* were reduced to begging on city streets for a living. Offering elephant rides is a positive move toward securing the survival of this national symbol, since their lowland forest habitat has been largely destroyed.

Most of the elephant camps in the north of the country put on elaborate shows in which the elephants play musical instruments, paint pictures, and generally amuse the audience before offering treks through the forest. During the elephant ride, participants will be able to take photos as they lurch through forests, and they will likely be sprayed by the animal's trunk.

Most of the elephant camps are clustered around Chiang Mai and include the **Elephant Training Center** *(see p220)* near Chiang Dao, the **Mae**

Sa Elephant Camp, and the **Thai Elephant Conservation Center**. Bangkok's **Dusit Zoo** *(see p105)* and **Safari World** *(see p136)* also offer rides.

These days it is possible to get even more intimate with elephants by taking a *mahout* training course, in which participants learn how to ride bareback and give basic commands, as well as join in the fun at bath time. Such courses are available at the **Thai Elephant Conservation Center**, and, in considerably more style, at the **Four Seasons Tented Camp** *(see p471)* and the **Anantara Resort**, both in the Golden Triangle.

TREKKING

Thailand has some ideal terrain for hiking, from the precipitous karst forests of Krabi and Khao Sok in the south to the undulating mountains around Mae Hong Son and Loei in the north.

Aside from the country's outstanding natural beauty, it is the opportunity to visit hill tribes that has caused the trekking business to boom. The novelty of encountering hill tribespeople in elaborate costumes undeniably adds cultural interest to a trek. However, over time, traditional tribal values cannot but be eroded by continued exposure to tourists. Many villages close to Chiang Mai, Chiang Rai, Pai, and Mae Hong Son are depressingly exploited. Additionally, there is the issue of trekkers feeling like voyeurs, especially at cynical shows such as the long-necked Padaung *(see p216)*. Try to establish a rapport with tribespeople and always ask their permission before taking photos.

Be wary of Burmese border areas, especially around Mae Sariang, where there is a chance of skirmishes between the Burmese military and ethnic armies fighting for independence. Malaria is also a risk around these parts, as it is in Kanchanaburi. In general, the health risks increase the farther you travel away from the towns.

Lining up a putt at one of Thailand's growing number of golf courses. As well as the sport, visitors can enjoy the beautiful settings of the courses

Trekking through Thailand's beautiful and varied forests

For nature-based treks, head for **Khao Yai National Park** *(see pp184–5)*. Many treks also include an elephant ride and, if the rivers are high enough, poling on a bamboo raft. Treks can last a week, but most take place over two to three nights and include visits to several villages. Be aware that scams are commonplace; to avoid being swindled, ask TAT for the list of companies recognized by the Professional Association of Guide Chiang Mai or the Jungle Tour Club of Northern Thailand, of which **Eagle House** and **Mae Ping Riverside Tours** are both members.

All treks should be led by at least two competent guides (who should speak the tribal languages and be aware of local customs). Check that the group doesn't exceed about eight trekkers, that the trek is registered with the police, and that transportation is not by public buses. Useful tips include lining backpacks with plastic bags to keep damp out; sleeping in dry clothes (even if it means wearing wet clothes by day); wearing a sun hat and cream, long trousers to protect against leeches, insect repellent, and worn-in hiking boots or at least supportive athletic shoes. Nights are cold in the mountains, so take warm layers – thermal tops and leggings, and silk sleeping bags. The best times to trek are November to February and early in the wet season, in June and July. For eco-friendly visitors, **Siam Safari**, **The Trekking Collective**, **The Wild Lodge** *(see White-water Rafting and Kayaking)*, and **Phuket Trekking Club** have a good reputation, and **Friends of Nature** organizes genuinely ecological treks.

WILDLIFE WATCHING

Animal on a trail at Khao Yai National Park

Unfortunately, Thailand's wildlife has been hunted almost to extinction, so there is little point in spending a few days in a hide in the hope of seeing a wild tiger or a bear. However, the country has a wide network of national parks, where some effort has been made to protect pockets of natural beauty. Here, visitors might well see rare and colorful birds, huge butterflies, and foot-long centipedes. The entrance fee to national parks for foreigners has been doubled to 400 *baht*, and while this may be justified for a stay of a few days, it is hardly worth paying for a brief visit. Some parks have camp sites, and most have log-cabin-style accommodation that can be reserved through the **National Park, Wildlife, and Plant Conservation Department**. The more popular parks, such as Khao Yai *(see pp184–5)*, Khao Sok *(see p356)*, Phu Kradung *(see pp286–7)*, and Doi Inthanon *(see pp230–31)*, have well-marked trails, but in less popular parks, visitors should ask park rangers to lead them to interesting features.

BOAT TRIPS

Before the arrival of the motor car, boats were the only form of transportation in Thailand apart from walking. Low-lying areas of the country, such as the Central Plains, were criss-crossed by canals that enabled locals to visit friends and do their shopping. These days, floating markets are strictly for tourists, where visitors can enjoy the colorful spectacle and bustle of boats at places like Damnoen Saduak *(see p132)*.

Apart from the floating markets, there are several other locations around the country where visitors can go sightseeing by boat. In Bangkok, **Chao Phraya Express Boats** offers short tours with commentary on the main riverside sights, such as the Grand Palace and Wat Arun. In the south, companies like **Sayan Tour** organize half-day and day trips in long-tail boats around the limestone stacks in Phang Nga Bay, with the option of canoeing for an hour. In the north, one of the most popular trips is along the Mae Kok River from Tha Ton to Chiang Rai, either on bamboo rafts that take a couple of days or on long-tail boats that roar downriver in a few hours. Some of these tours, which can be arranged at the jetty in Tha Ton, include a stop at the Karen village of Ruammit for visitors to take a quick elephant ride.

The traditional long-tail boat, now popular for tourist excursions

CYCLING

With cycling growing in popularity worldwide, it is no surprise that more and more people consider touring Thailand by bike, on a model either brought from home or rented locally. Not only is cycling healthy and environmentally sound, it also guarantees meaningful encounters with local people along the way. Though traffic on main roads can be dangerous to negotiate, it is possible to put a bike on a bus or train and head for quieter rural areas. Mostly the terrain is cyclist-friendly, and several companies organize guided rides along country lanes.

Anyone considering a cycling holiday would be advised to consult www.thai cycling.com and www.mr pumpy.net for information on possible itineraries. One of the most popular routes in the country follows the flow of the Mekong River from Chiang Khan to Nong Khai, or even right round to Mukdahan.

The best time to cycle in Thailand is from November to February, when temperatures are cooler, particularly in the north; the worst is between March and May, when pedalers are guaranteed to end each day dripping with sweat. Cycling in the rainy season (June–October) is worth considering, since there is frequently cloud cover, tropical storms tend to pass over quickly, and the landscapes are at their most lush at this time.

See the directory (pp468–9) for cycling tour operators.

ROCK CLIMBING

Those looking for an activity that gets the adrenalin flowing will find that rock climbing is hard to beat. Providing dramatic views from limestone peaks at the end of a climb, Thailand is one of the world's most popular destinations for this sport.

The epicenter of rock climbing in Thailand is around Krabi, especially at Railay beach, where several companies offer half-day to three-day courses for beginners and rent out equipment to experienced climbers; the more reliable operators here include **Phuket Cliffshanger**, **King Climbers**, and **Hot Rock**. More than 700 bolted routes in the region offer climbs ranging from 5a to 8c in terms of difficulty, graded according to the French system. For more details of rock climbing and other activities in this area, visit www.railay.com.

Ko Phi Phi has a similar limestone terrain, and a few local companies, like **Cat's Climbing Shop**, offer instruction for beginners at Ton Sai Tower or Hin Taek.

Rock climbing is also getting a foothold in the north, where **The Peak Adventure** runs climbs on more than 100 bolted routes at Crazy Horse Buttress, near San Kamphaeng, about 40 km (25 miles) east of Chiang Mai. These routes range in difficulty from easy to extremely challenging.

The large cave system of Tham Lot, which dates back 1,700 years

CAVING

Though Thailand's limestone landscapes are peppered with caves, few are set up for visitors to explore, so caving remains an activity largely for specialists. However, one cave that has been popularized is **Tham Lot** (see p219), near Soppong, in the northwest of the country. It contains some coffins that date back 1,700 years, and each evening there is a spectacular sight when hundreds of thousands of swifts return to nest in the cave. **Cave Lodge** is an ideal base from which to explore Tham Lot, and they can even arrange kayaking trips that pass right through the cave.

BUNGEE JUMPING

Visitors who fancy having their feet bound and being thrown off a platform 50 m (165 ft) above the ground should head to **Jungle Bungy Jump**, a successful company operating in popular tourist locations such as Phuket, Pattaya, and Chiang Mai. A certificate is issued on completion of the jump.

Thailand's best rock climbing, at Railay beach, near Krabi

HORSE RACING AND RIDING

Plenty of people enjoy a day at the races in their homeland, so why not try your luck in tropical Thailand? It may be difficult to decipher the form card, but a keen eye on the runners in the paddock might just land a winner. As one of the few forms of gambling allowed in Thailand, horse racing attracts a strong local following, and the atmosphere is always vibrant. Races are held on weekends in Bangkok at the **Royal Bangkok Sports Club** *(see p117)* and the **Royal Turf Club**.

For a more hands-on experience, check out the activities on offer at the **International Riding School** near Pattaya, the **Phuket Riding Club**, and **Chiang Mai Horse Riding**.

AIR SPORTS

As if visitors to Chiang Mai didn't have enough activities to keep them busy, a couple more options, depending on weather conditions, are microlighting and hot-air ballooning. Both **Chiang Mai Sky Adventure** and **Oriental Balloon Flights** have regular take-offs from bases just northeast of Chiang Mai during the cool season, giving the chance for a bird's-eye view of the Ping Valley and some spectacular photos.

Parasailing over the heads of sun-worshippers at Chiang Mai

CULTURAL STUDY

Courses in meditation can give a valuable insight into Thai culture and, if followed diligently, also provide an invaluable skill to help cope with stress in the modern world. Participants are required to dress in white and adhere to the fundamental vows of Buddhism, which include refraining from killing, stealing, lying, and eating after midday. Practitioners are also expected to be up before dawn and to plan their day around sessions of walking and sitting meditation, as well as abstaining from entertainment (for example, no watching TV or listening to music) and idle chat (no mobile phones). Since the Dharma (literally, "Way of the Higher Truths," or code of conduct) is given for free, most places suggest that students make a donation to cover their lodging and food.

Delicately carved vegetables

For meditation sessions in English and longer, disciplined retreats, contact the **World Fellowship of Buddhists** or visit www.dhammathai.org. Visitors are welcome to join the 10-day course that is run by the **International Dhamma Hermitage** at the beginning of each month at Wat Suan Mokkh, near Chaiya in the south. Other options include the **Northern Insight Meditation Center**'s month-long retreats at Wat Ram Peong in Chiang Mai, **Wat Mahathat** in Bangkok, **Wat Kow Tahm** on Ko Pha Ngan, and the **Dhammakaya Foundation**'s retreats and Sunday sessions. Some locations have facilities for women to study, while others are male only.

Visitors also come to Thailand to study traditional

Learning to cook Thai food the Thai way

Thai massage, a vigorous combination of yoga, reflexology, and acupressure. Courses typically last between a week and two weeks and consist of theory, demonstration, and practice, leading to certification of competence. Popular training in English is conducted at **Wat Pho** *(see pp92–3)* in Bangkok and in Chiang Mai's subtler style at centers including the **Old Medicine Hospital** and the **Thai Massage School of Chiang Mai**.

The techniques of preparing Thai food – including fruit and vegetable carving – can be learned at the cooking schools in the Dusit Thani and Oriental hotels *(see p399 and p400)*, the **Blue Elephant** restaurant and cooking school, and **Baipai Thai Cooking School** in Bangkok. Reliable schools in the north include the **Chiang Mai Thai Cookery School** and **Baan Thai Cookery School**. Students can sign up for either a day or several days, and a typical day's "study" includes a shopping trip to the market, a demonstration of how to prepare a few dishes, followed by practice, then the best part – homework – in which students get to taste their own creations.

DIRECTORY

DIVING AND SNORKELING

Dive Asia
24 Karon Rd,
Kata Beach,
Phuket.
Tel 0-7633-0598.
www.diveasia.com

Dive Info
Chuancheun Village,
Pattanakarn 57, Bangkok.
Tel 0-8182-5960-7.
www.diveinfo.net

Phi Phi Scuba
Ton Sai Bay, Ko Phi Phi.
Tel 0-7561-2665.
www.ppscuba.com

Private Dive Phuket
168/12 Nanai Road,
Patong, Phuket.
Tel 0-8197-9747-3.
www.privatedive.net

Samui International Diving School
Chaweng Beach,
Ko Samui.
Tel 0-7724-2386.
www.samui-diving.com

Santana Diving & Canoeing
49 Thaweewong Rd,
Patong Beach, Phuket.
Tel 0-7629-4220.
www.santanaphuket.com

Sea Dragon Dive Center
5/51 Moo 7, T Khuk
Khak, Khao Lak.
Tel 0-7648-5418.
www.seadragondive
center.com

SAILING

Gulf Charters Thailand
Ocean Marina,
167/5 Sukhumvit Rd,
Sattahip.
Tel 0-3823-7752.
www.gulfcharters
thailand.com

Phuket Sailing
20/28 Soi Suksan, Moo 4,
Tambon Rawai, Phuket.
*Tel 0-8990-9695-9 or
0-8189-5182-6.*
www.phuket-sailing.com

South East Asia Liveaboards
P.O. Box 381, Phuket
Town. *Tel 0-7652-2807.*
www.seal-asia.com

Yachtpro
Adjacent to Yacht Haven
Marina, Phuket.
Tel 0-7634-8117.
www.sailing-thailand.com

WATER SPORTS

Barracuda Bar
157/132–133 Moo 5,
Pattaya-Naklua Rd,
Chonburi.
Tel 0-8434-5717-7.
www.barracudabar-
pattaya.com

Pattaya Fishing
SEAduction Dive Centre,
Bali Hai Pier, 551/2 Moo
10, Tambon Nongprue,
Banglamung, Chonburi.
Tel 0-3871-0029.
www.pattayafishing.com

Phuket Deep Sea Fishing
Chalong Bay, Phuket.
Tel 0-8690-05341.
www.phuketdeepsea
fishing.com

Phuket Fishing
Chalong Bay, Phuket.
Tel 0-7638-3581.
www.phuket-fishing.com

CANOEING

Paddle Asia
9/71 Rasdanusorn Rd,
Phuket. *Tel 0-7624-0952.*
www.paddleasia.com

Sea Canoe Thailand
125/461 Moo 5, Baan
Sapan Rd, Muang Phuket.

Tel 0-7652-8839/40.
www.seacanoe.net

WHITE-WATER RAFTING AND KAYAKING

Siam Rivers
17 Ratchawithi Rd,
Chiang Mai.
Tel 0-8951-5191-7.
www.siamrivers.com

Thai Adventure Rafting
420/3 Changklaan Rd,
Chiang Mai.
Tel 0-5320-4664/5.
www.activethailand.com

The Wild Lodge
666 Sukhumvit 24,
Bangkok.
Tel 0-2261-4412.
www.thewildlodge.com

GOLF

Blue Canyon Country Club
165 Moo 1, Thepkasattri
Rd, Thalang, Phuket.
Tel 0-7632-8088.
www.bluecanyonclub.com

Laem Chabang International Country Club
106/8 Moo 4, Beung,
Siracha, near Pattaya.
Tel 0-3837-2273.
www.laemchabanggolf.
com

Lanna Golf Club
Chotana Rd,
Chiang Mai.
Tel 0-5322-1911.

Thana City Golf and Country Club
100-100/1 Moo 4,
Bang Na Trat Rd,
off Hwy 34, km 14,
near Bangkok.
Tel 0-2336-0568/74.

ELEPHANT RIDING

Anantara Resort
Golden Triangle.
Tel 0-5378-4084.
www.goldentriangle.
anantara.com

Mae Sa Elephant Camp
119/9 Tapae Rd, Muang
Chiang Mai.
Tel 0-5320-6248.
www.maesaelephant
camp.com

Thai Elephant Conservation Center
Thung Kwian, 37 km (23
miles) NW of Lampang.
Tel 0-5422-9042.

TREKKING

Eagle House
16 Chang Moi Kao,
Chiang Mai.
Tel 0-5323-5387.
www.eaglehouse.com

Friends of Nature
133/21 Ratchaprarop Rd,
Bangkok.
Map 4 E4–5.
Tel 0-2642-4426.
www.friendsofnature93.
com

Mae Ping Riverside Tours
101 Chiang Mai-Lamphun
Rd, Chiang Mai.
Tel 0-5330-2121.
www.tours-chiangmai.
com

Phuket Trekking Club
55/779–780 Villa
Daowroong Village,
East Chaofah Rd,
Tambon Vichit, Phuket.
Tel 0-7637-7344.
www.phukettrekking
club.com

DIRECTORY

Siam Safari
45 Chao Far Rd, Chalong,
Phuket.
Tel 0-7628-0116.
www.siamsafari.com

**The Trekking
Collective**
3/5 Loy Kroh Road Soi 1,
Chiang Mai.
Tel 0-5320-8340.
www.trekkingcollective.
com

WILDLIFE WATCHING

**National Park,
Wildlife, and Plant
Conservation
Department**
61 Phaholyothin Rd,
Chatuchak, Bangkok.
Tel 0-2562-0760.
www.dnp.go.th

BOAT TRIPS

**Chao Phraya
Express Boats**
78/24–29 Maharaj Rd,
Phra Nakhorn, Bangkok.
Tel 0-2623-6001.
www.chaophrayaboat.
co.th

Sayan Tour
209 Phangnga Bus
Terminal, Phangnga.
Tel 0-7643-0348.
www.sayantour.com

CYCLING

Bike & Travel
Prathum Thani.
Tel 0-2990-0274.
www.cyclingthailand.com

Click and Travel
158/42 Chiang Mai-Hod
Rd, Chiang Mai.
Tel 0-5328-1553.
www.clickandtravel
online.com

Spice Roads
14/1-B Soi Promsri 2,
Sukhumvit Soi 39,
Bangkok.
Tel 0-2712-5305.
www.spiceroads.com

ROCK CLIMBING

Cat's Climbing Shop
Ton Sai Vilage, Ko Phi Phi.
Tel 0-8178-75101.

Hot Rock
Railay Beach, near Krabi.
Tel 0-7562-1771. **www**.
railayadventure.com

King Climber
Railay Beach, near Krabi.
Tel 0-7562-2096.

Phuket Cliffshanger
6/6 Chaloemphakiet Rd,
(Soi Eden) Patong Beach.
Tel 0-7634-5815.

The Peak Adventure
302/4 Chiang Mai-
Lamphun Rd, Chiang Mai.
Tel 0-5380-0567.
www.thepeakadventure.
com

CAVING

Cave Lodge
15 Moo 1, Pang Mapha,
near Mae Hong Son.
Tel 0-5361-7203.
www.cavelodge.com

BUNGEE JUMPING

Jungle Bungy Jump
Tel 0-5329-7700.
www.junglebungy.com

HORSE RACING AND RIDING

**Chiang Mai Horse
Riding**
Travel Shoppe, 2/2
Chaiyaphum Rd, Chiang
Mai. *Tel* 0-5387-4091.
www.horseriding.
chiangmaiinfo.com

**International Riding
School**
100 Moo 9, Tambon Pong,
Amphur Banglamung,
Chonburi. *Tel* 0-3824-
8026. **www**.riding
schoolasia.com

Phuket Riding Club
Chalong, Phuket.
Tel 0-7628-8213.

Royal Turf Club
Phitsanulok Rd, Dusit,
Bangkok.
Tel 0-2628-1810.
www.rtcot.com

AIR SPORTS

**Chiang Mai Sky
Adventure**
Doi Saket, Chiang Mai.
Tel 0-5386-8460.
www.skyadventures.info

**Oriental Balloon
Flights**
Doi Saket, Chiang Mai.
Tel 0-8461-1412-8.
www.orientalballoon
flights.com

CULTURAL STUDY

**Baan Thai Cookery
School**
11 Rachadamnern Rd,
Soi 5, Chiang Mai.
Tel 0-5335-7339.
www.cookinthai.com

**Baipai Thai Cooking
School**
150/12 Soi Naksuwan,
Nonsee Rd, Chongnonsee,
Yannawa, Bangkok.
Tel 0-2294-9029.
www.baipai.com

Blue Elephant
233 South Sathorn Rd,
Bangkok. *Tel* 0-2673-
9353. **www**.blueelephant.
co.th

**Chiang Mai Thai
Cookery School**
47/2 Moon Muang Rd
Chiang Mai.

Tel 0-5320-6388.
www.thaicookeryschool.
com

**Dhammakaya
Foundation**
40 Moo 8, Khlong Song,
Khlong Luang, Pathum
Thani.
Tel 0-2831-1000.
www.dhammakaya.org

**International
Dhamma Hermitage**
Wat Suan Mokkh,
Chaiya, Surat Thani.
Tel 0-7743-1552.
www.suanmokkh-idh.org

**Northern Insight
Meditation Center**
Wat Ram Poeng,
Canal Rd, Chiang Mai.
Tel 0-5327-8620.
www.palikanon.com/
vipassana/tapotaram/
tapotaram.htm

**Old Medicine
Hospital**
238/8 Wualai Rd, Chiang
Mai. *Tel* 0-5320-1663.
www.thaimassageschool.
ac.th

**Thai Massage School
of Chiang Mai**
203/6 Mae Jo Rd,
Chiang Mai.
Tel 0-5385-4330.
www.tmcschool.com

Wat Kow Tahm
Near Ban Tai,
Ko Pha Ngan.
www.watkowtahm.org

**Wat Mahathat
(Section Five)**
Maharat Rd, Bangkok.
Tel 0-2222-6011.

**World Fellowship
of Buddhists**
616 Benjasiri Park, Soi
Medhinivet, off Sukhumvit
24, Bangkok.
Tel 0-2661-1284.
www.wfb-hq.org

Spa Breaks in Thailand

Thai spas offer a wide variety of treatments

Thailand has thousands of spas offering every kind of treatment possible, and its sultry temperatures, idyllic landscapes, and sense of tranquility make it an ideal destination for a spa break. Traditional Thai architecture, serene Zen-minimalist decor, and enchanting gardens blend with the Thai people's gentle and giving nature to make a truly memorable spa experience. Massage has been practiced in Thailand for some 2,500 years, and while it's possible to have a cheap shoulder rub in simple backstreet shop fronts, nothing beats some serious pampering at a luxury resort or an indulgent afternoon at a day spa.

Relaxing in the peaceful garden environment of the Anantara Resort & Spa

HOTEL & RESORT SPAS

Travelers tend to visit a hotel or resort spa as part of a wider holiday, with the main focus being a beach or cultural experience. However, Thailand's luxury five-star hotels and resorts are home to some of the world's very best spas, offering a wide range of professional, unique, and blissful treatments.

The greatest concentration of spas is on the islands of Phuket and Ko Samui, in the beach resort towns of Hua Hin and Cha-am, and in the northern Chiang Mai area.

The country's foremost spa resorts include the **Four Seasons Resort Koh Samui**, the **Banyan Tree Spa Phuket**, the **Evason Phuket Resort & Six Senses Spa**, and the **Anantara Resort & Spa** in Hua Hin and Ko Samui.

Spa treatments are generally an added extra, but many resorts are now increasingly offering all-inclusive packages. The Anantara resorts offer three-day and seven-day programs that include between four and ten treatments.

SPA RETREATS

Thailand has a number of luxury resorts situated in truly breathtaking settings. Visitors looking for an intimate getaway on a deserted white-sand beach skirted by palm trees should head to the **Six Senses Hideaway Hua Hin**, south of Hua Hin, or the **Aleenta Resort & Spa Phang Nga**. Those who like the sound of a plush villa with a private infinity pool set among tropical jungle overlooking lush rice fields – or, more dramatically, the Mekong River across to Burma – should book at the **Four Seasons Chiang Mai** or the **Four Seasons Tented Camp at the Golden Triangle**. The aim of staying here is to experience the local culture and lush environment as much as it is to have a spa experience. The fact that these resorts are often set in remote locations and may be accessible only by speedboat (such as the **Rayavadee Spa** near Krabi) or traditional long-tail boat (the Four Seasons Tented Camp at the Golden Triangle) adds to the allure. The spas at these resorts offer longer programs of daily treatments for those who really want to unwind.

DESTINATION SPAS

Revitalizing the mind, body, and spirit is the central purpose of destination spas, with guests rarely leaving the resort after checking in. Thailand's first and best, the **Chiva-Som International Health Resort**, offers more than 150 treatments focused on relaxation and rejuvenation, stress relief, detoxification, and weight loss. Guests undergo an extensive health consultation upon arrival, and a program is created to match their goals. There is a three-night minimum stay, though most guests stay a week or more, and nutritious spa cuisine, activities, and treatments are included in the rate. Another famous destination spa is the **Kamalaya Wellness Sanctuary & Holistic Spa** in Ko Samui.

Because spa resorts tend to provide an array of non-spa activities – from elephant and water-buffalo riding to mountain climbing – signature

A poultice massage at Banyan Tree Spa Phuket, a popular spa resort

treatments at destination spas cater for travelers who may be suffering some after-effects. The signature treatment at the Four Seasons Tented Camp, for instance, is a Mahout Recovery Treatment, where poultices filled with camphor, lime, and lemongrass are used to massage the body and inner thighs – the perfect antidote for sore muscles from elephant riding.

Working out stress through yoga at Chiva-Som International Health Resort

DAY SPAS

All over Thailand, travelers can find day spas – stand-alone operations not attached to resorts or hotels – and many hotels also offer treatments to non-guests on a per-session basis. Most day spas are in Bangkok and include the stylish **Being Spa** and **Pirom Spa**, the **Harnn Heritage Spa**, and **Spa of Qinera**. Chiang Mai also has an excellent repuation for day spas.

SPA TREATMENTS

Despite Thailand's long history of therapeutic massage and natural healing – including Thai massage,

medicinal herbs, and natural springs – the country is at the cutting edge of spa offerings. Expect to see anything and everything on a spa menu, from Tropical Sprinkles and Tranquility Mists at the Banyan Tree Spa Phuket, to their famous four-hand Harmony Banyan treatment, where two therapists work on you at once. Other spas, such as the Six Senses Spa and Anantara Spas, also offer versions of this indulgent treatment. While some

treatments are indigenous to Thailand – traditional Thai massage, for example – others, such as hydrotherapy, thalassotherapy, aromatherapy, and Ayurvedic treatments, can be found all over the world. Many spas have also developed their own signature treatments. The Four Seasons Spas have an array of sensual offerings connected to the cycles of the moon, with treatments that should be experienced only during certain lunar phases.

DIRECTORY

HOTEL & RESORT SPAS

Anantara Resort & Spa Hua Hin
Phetkasem Beach Rd, Hua Hin.
Tel 0-3252-0250.
www.anantara.com

Anantara Resort & Spa Koh Samui
99/9 Moo 1, Bo Phut Bay, Ko Samui.
Tel 0-7742-8340.
www.anantara.com

Banyan Tree Spa Phuket
33 Moo 4, Srisoonthorn Rd, Cherngtalay, Phuket.
Tel 0-7632-4374.
www.banyantreespa.com

Evason Phuket Resort & Six Senses Spa
100 Vised Rd, Moo 2 Tambol Rawai, Phuket.
Tel 0-7638-1010.

www.sixsenses.com/evason-phuket

Four Seasons Resort Koh Samui
219 Moo 5, Angthong, Ko Samui.
Tel 0-7724-3000.
www.fourseasons

SPA RETREATS

Aleenta Resort & Spa Phang Nga
33 Moo 5, T Khokkloy, Phang Nga.
Tel 0-7658-0333.
www.aleenta.com

Six Senses Hideaway Hua Hin
9/22 Moo 5, Paknampran Beach, Pranburi.
Tel 0-3261-8200.
www.sixsenses.com/hideaway-huahin

Four Seasons Chiang Mai
Mae Rim-Old Samoeng Rd, Mae Rim, Chiang Mai.
Tel 0-5329-8181.
www.fourseasons.com

Four Seasons Tented Camp at the Golden Triangle
Off Chaeng Saen Rd, Chaeng Saen.
Tel 0-5391-0200.
www.fourseasons.com

Rayavadee Spa
214 Moo 2, Tambol Ao-Nang, Amphur Muang, Krabi. *Tel* 0-7562-0740-3.
www.rayavadee.com

DESTINATION SPAS

Chiva-Som International Health Resort
Petchkasem Rd, Hua Hin.
Tel 0-3253-6536.
www.chivasom

Kamalaya Wellness Sanctuary & Holistic Spa
102/9 Moo 3, Laem Set Rd, Na-Muang, Ko Samui.
Tel 0-7742-9800.
www.kamalaya.com

DAY SPAS

Being Spa
88 Soi Sukhumvit, 51 Klongton Nua, Bangkok.
Tel 0-2662-6171.

Harnn Heritage Spa
Siam Paragon, 4th Floor, Bangkok. *Tel* 0-2610-9715.

Pirom Spa
87 Nai Lert Building, Sukhimvit Rd, Bangkok.
Tel 0-2655-4177.
www.piromspa.com

Spa of Qinera
172/1 Soi Pipat 2, Chong Nonsi, Bangkok.
Tel 0-2636-8306.
www.qineraspa.com

SURVIVAL GUIDE

PRACTICAL INFORMATION 474–489

TRAVEL INFORMATION 490–497

PRACTICAL INFORMATION

Thailand caters well to its growing number of tourists. The 12 million people who visit each year find one of the biggest and best-organized tourist industries in Asia. The headquarters of the helpful Tourism Authority of Thailand (TAT) is in Bangkok, and there are offices across the country and several overseas branches. The relevant address and telephone number is given for each town and sight throughout this guide. The tourist industry has developed so rapidly that the

Changing of the Royal Guard, Bangkok

adventurous traveler is no longer restricted to organized tours or major tourist destinations such as Bangkok and Phuket – the whole country is accessible to independent travelers. There are many reputable travel agencies all over Thailand. They offer advice, book flights and accommodations, and organize sightseeing tours. Some pre-travel planning is necessary to avoid the worst of the rainy season and holiday periods such as the Chinese New Year (see pp48–51).

WHEN TO GO

Thailand's weather can be tempestuous, with year-round humidity, rocketing temperatures, and rains of biblical proportions. However, the optimum time to visit the country is during the cooler, drier months from November to February. It is no coincidence that this is the peak tourist season, when sights may get crowded. The hot season, from March to May, can be unbearable, while the rainy season, which generally lasts from June to October, is the least predictable of the three periods. Climate and rainfall charts can be found on pages 48–51.

Tourists relaxing in the sun at Patong beach, Phuket

ADVANCE BOOKING

Bangkok is a popular launching point for other Southeast Asian destinations, so it is necessary to book airline tickets well in advance. This is especially true during Thailand's peak tourist season, November to February, when flights and hotels are heavily booked. If you plan to travel during this period, it is wise to make arrangements at least three to six months prior to departure.

VISAS AND PASSPORTS

Many nationalities, including the citizens of most European countries, Australia, and the US, can enter Thailand for up to 30 days without a pre-arranged visa. Proof of

adequate funds for the duration of a visitor's stay (10,000 *baht* per person or 20,000 *baht* per family) can be requested upon arrival – a credit card is sufficient proof of this. Also be aware that certain visas have minimum fund requirements – check with your local Thai embassy before traveling for current information. Proof of a confirmed return flight or other on-going travel arrangements might also be required, although this is rare. The 30-day period is extendible for a maximum of 10 days. Nationals of several smaller European countries must obtain a visa before traveling. For those wishing to stay longer, a 60-day tourist visa can be arranged from a Thai embassy or consulate prior to arrival in Thailand. This usually takes two to three working days to process, but may take longer during busy periods.

A 90-day nonimmigrant visa must be applied for in your home country and requires a letter of verification from a Thai source giving a valid reason, such as business or study, for spending three months in Thailand. This visa is slightly more expensive than the 60-day tourist visa.

With all visas, entry into Thailand must occur within 90 days of issue. Visa extensions are at the discretion of the **Immigration Department** in Bangkok or any other immigration office in Thailand. Overstaying a visa carries a fine of 200 *baht* per day and can result in serious penalties. Single and multiple re-entry visas can be obtained relatively easily, allowing the visitor to leave the country and return within 60 days. These can be applied for at the Immigration Department in Bangkok. Strictly speaking,

◁ **A row of *samlors* at the market in Lop Buri**

travelers entering Thailand should have at least six months left on their passport. It is best to confirm all such details with a Thai embassy or consulate before traveling.

Crossing the border into neighboring countries generally depends on the current political situation, *(see p480)* so it is wise to check prior to travel. A four-week tourist visa for Myanmar (Burma) can be obtained from the Myanmar Embassy in Bangkok (there will be a small charge). The quickest way to obtain a 30-day tourist visa for Laos is to apply for it at a travel agency in major cities such as Bangkok or Chiang Mai. Visitors to Cambodia can obtain a 30-day tourist visa free of charge upon arrival at Phnom Penh airport.

CUSTOMS INFORMATION

Customs regulations in Thailand are standard. During an inbound flight you will be given a customs form that must be filled in and handed over at the customs desk after claiming your baggage.

Thai customs restrictions for goods carried into the country are 200 cigarettes and/or one liter of wine or spirits. For complete details about export declarations, duty payments, and VAT refunds visit www.customs.go.th

A car or motorbike can be brought into the country for touring purposes for up to six months, but this requires prior arrangement through the Thai embassy in your home country. The carrying of drugs *(see p480)*, firearms, or pornography is strictly prohibited. There are no restrictions on the maximum amount of money an individual may bring into the country, however there are sometimes

minimum requirements *(see Visas and Passports)*. It is illegal to leave Thailand with more than 50,000 *baht* without the correct authorization.

Antiques and Buddha images are not allowed out of Thailand without authorization. If you wish to export such items you must first contact the **Fine Arts Department** of the National Museum in Bangkok at least five days before the date of shipment and fill in a form accompanied by two frontal photographs of the object being purchased (no more than five pieces to be shown in any one photograph). Contemporary "works of art," such as paintings bought in markets, can be taken out of the country without permission.

TOURIST INFORMATION

The many branches of the **Tourism Authority of Thailand (TAT)** are very helpful, offering plenty of practical and background information on sights and festivals, as well as maps, brochures, miniguides, and posters. They also have a useful list of reputable travel agents and hotels.

Logo of TAT

There is a small information booth in Suvarnabhumi airport. Many of the provincial capitals in Thailand have a TAT office (listed throughout this guide), as do some

Local travel agency offering tourist information

overseas countries. The TAT website is also a useful source of information.

ADMISSION PRICES

Admission charges to sights in Thailand are usually nominal, ranging between 10 and 50 *baht* for government-run establishments. National parks, however, charge either 200 or 400 *baht* per person (children are usually admitted at half price). Private museums are generally either free or charge up to 200 *baht*. Occasionally, foreigners may be charged a higher admission price than locals on the assumption that they earn more than most Thais. Under Thai law this is not totally legal, but to prevent embarrassment it is usually best to pay the extra amount. A few major tourist *wats* charge a set fee; in others there is usually a box for donations.

OPENING HOURS

Most sights can be visited throughout the year, though access to some of the southern islands may be limited in the rainy season. In general, major tourist attractions open at 8am or 9am and close any time between 3:30pm and 6pm. A few also shut for lunch between noon and 1pm. Most major sights are open daily, but some national museums close for public holidays and on Mondays and Tuesdays.

Typical entrance tickets to major historical sites

Department stores are usually open daily, 10am–9pm, and smaller shops are open 8am–9pm. Commercial offices open 8am–noon and 1–5pm Monday to Friday. Government offices are open 8:30am–noon and 1–4:30pm Monday to Friday. During the Chinese New Year, many businesses close, especially in the south. For banking hours, *see page 484*.

WHAT TO TAKE

As the climate in Thailand is generally hot and humid, it is advisable to dress in cool, nonrestricting clothes made from natural fibers. A sweater may be needed in northern and northeastern regions during the cool season. The rainy season brings sudden downpours when a light rain-coat is handy. If visiting temples, appropriate dress is required *(see p479)*, as is easily removable footwear. A first-aid kit is also useful *(see p482)*.

TRAVELERS WITH SPECIAL NEEDS

There are few facilities for disabled travelers in Thailand. Sidewalks can be uneven and pedestrian bridges are often accessed only by steep steps. Wheelchair access is limited to the top-class hotels. The easiest way to travel is to book an organized tour *(see p491)* or to contact the **Association of Physically Handicapped People** for further information.

TRAVELING WITH CHILDREN

Children are always welcome in Thailand. The larger hotels have baby-sitting services, and TAT offers advice on attractions for kids. Hats and sunblock are a must for children out in the sun. There are plenty of fast-food outlets and adaptable chefs who will gladly provide a choice of suitable alternatives to spicy meals.

SENIOR TRAVELERS

Older citizens of Thailand are treated with great respect, as are senior citizens from other countries. Unfortunately, this higher status does not translate into any discounts or savings.

GAY AND LESBIAN TRAVELERS

On the whole Thai society takes a fairly relaxed attitude to homosexuality. A number of bars, clubs, and other venues cater exclusively to a gay and lesbian crowd. However, at heart, Thai society is still quite conservative, and public displays of affection by both homosexuals and heterosexuals are frowned upon.

Prominent gay and lesbian scenes can be found in Bangkok, Pattaya, and Phuket, and to a lesser extent in Chiang Mai. General information for gay and lesbian visitors is available online at **Dragoncastle**, and both this website and **Utopia** are excellent for details of gay and lesbian related activities and events in Thailand.

CENTERS OF WORSHIP FOR VISITORS

There are many facilities for visitors to undertake Buddhist studies *(see p467)*. The **International Buddhist Meditation Center** has details of English-language courses at *wats* in and around Bangkok. Most other religious denominations are represented in Thailand – listed below are religious centers in Bangkok offering services in English. **Christ Church** holds Anglican and Episcopalian services. The **International Church** has services on Sundays, as does the **Holy Redeemer Catholic Church**. The Jewish Association of Thailand has occasional services at the **Jewish Community Center**. The **Haroon Mosque** has services for Muslims.

LANGUAGE

It is always useful to learn a few Thai phrases *(see pp524–8)*. Many local people in tourist towns speak some English, as do most hotel receptionists. Sight and road names in these areas are transliterated, and menus are often in English as well as in Thai. Prices and road numbers are generally in Arabic numerals. Transliterated spellings vary in different maps and guides, and on signs. Note that "j" and "ch" are interchangeable, as are "d" and "t." The letters "ph" (e.g. as in Phuket) are pronounced "p," never "f." Likewise, the "h" in "th" is always silent (e.g. Thailand).

THAI TIME SYSTEMS AND CALENDAR

Bangkok time is seven hours ahead of Greenwich Mean Time (GMT), 12 hours ahead

Transliterated road sign

of Eastern Standard Time, and 15 hours ahead of Pacific Standard Time (6, 11, and 14 hours ahead, respectively, during Daylight Saving Hours). Although the standard clock and 24-hour clock are used and widely understood, Thailand also has its own unique system. Thais divide the day into four segments of six hours each. For example, 7am for us is 1am for Thais.

Two calendars are used in Thailand: the Gregorian (Western) and the Buddhist calendars. The Buddhist Era (BE) starts 543 years before the Gregorian era. To convert from the Gregorian calendar to the Buddhist calendar, add 543 years. For example, AD 1957 is the equivalent of 2500 BE.

CONVERSION CHART

US Standard to Metric
1 inch = 2.54 centimeters
1 foot = 30 centimeters
1 mile = 1.6 kilometers
1 ounce = 28 grams
1 pound = 454 grams
1 US quart = 0.947 liter
1 US gallon = 3.6 liters

Metric to US Standard
1 centimeter = 0.4 inch
1 meter = 3 feet 3 inches
1 kilometer = 0.6 mile
1 gram = 0.04 ounce
1 kilogram = 2.2 pounds
1 liter = 1.1 US quarts

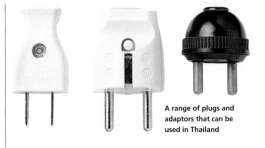

A range of plugs and adaptors that can be used in Thailand

ELECTRICITY

The electric current throughout Thailand is 220 volts AC, 50 cycles. Dual-prong rounded plugs as well as flat-pin plugs can be used. Major hotels also have 110-volt outlets for electric razors. Adaptors and power-surge cables (for laptops) are sold in department stores and electrical stores.

In smaller towns, especially during the rainy season, there can be power failures and flashlights can be useful.

RESPONSIBLE TRAVEL

Attitudes towards environmental issues are slowly beginning to change in Thailand. The authorities are actively promoting awareness of the need for conservation, from prohibiting locals fishing with dynamite and drag-netting coral reefs, to encouraging tourists to "leave nothing but your footprints". Ecologically

aware dive companies forbid visitors to take anything away, even a seashell, and the use of plastic bags and plastic water bottles in national parks, where they might be abandoned, is increasingly discouraged.

Open World, an ecological tour operator, conducts culture, nature, and conservation tours throughout Thailand, which include a tiger conservation program, flora and fauna and birdwatching tours. The **Thailand Environment Institute** website has information about environmental projects and the conservation of natural resources in Thailand.

Set against all this good work, visitors should be aware that in some areas there are still environmentally destructive shrimp farms, the clearing of natural forest for palm oil plantations, and the farming of tigers in captivity for their body parts under the guise of "tiger zoos".

DIRECTORY

TRAVELERS WITH SPECIAL NEEDS

Association of Physically Handicapped People
73/7-8 Tivanond Rd, Talad Kwan, Nonthaburi.
Tel 0-2951-0445.

GAY AND LESBIAN TRAVELERS

Dragoncastle
www.dragoncastle.net

Utopia
www.utopia-asia.com

CENTERS OF WORSHIP

Christ Church
11 Covent Rd, Bangkok.
Tel 0-2234-3634.
www.christchurch bangkok.org

Haroon Mosque
25 Charoen Krung 36 Rd, Chinatown, Bangkok.
Tel 0-2630-9435.

Holy Redeemer Catholic Church
123/19 Soi Ruam Rudi, 5 Witthayu (Wireless) Rd, Bangkok. *Tel* 0-2256-6305. www.holyredeemer bangkok.net

International Buddhist Meditation Center
Wat Mahathat, 3 Maharaj Rd, Bangkok.
Tel 0-2623-6326.

International Church
61/2 Soi Saen Sabai, Sukhumvit 36, Bangkok.
Tel 0-2258-5821.
www.icbangkok.org

Jewish Community Center
121 Soi Sainamtip 2, Soi 22 Sukhumvit Rd, Bangkok. *Tel* 0-2663-0244. www.jewish thailand.com

RESPONSIBLE TRAVEL

Open World International Travel Service
89/14-15 Phahonyothin 54/1, Saimai, Bangkok.
Tel 0-2974-3867.
www.openworld thailand.com

Thailand Environment Institute
16/151 Muang Thong Thani, Bond Rd, Pakkred, Nonthaburi. *Tel* 0-2503-3333. www.tei.or.th

Etiquette

It is not by accident that Thailand is often referred to as "the land of smiles." The Thais are exceptionally friendly and helpful people, and getting along with them is easy – simply smile wide and laugh a lot. Being Buddhists, they are an amazingly tolerant people. Avoiding offensive behavior can generally be achieved through simple courtesy and common sense. A few taboos do exist, though, mostly with regard to the monarchy and Buddhism. Visitors should be particularly careful to behave respectfully at *wats* and in front of any Buddha image. Confrontation is also considered extremely rude, and Thais will bend over backward to avoid arguments of any sort. Losing your temper or shouting, whatever the situation, is seen as an embarrassing loss of face.

King Bhumibol and Queen Sirikit

ROYALTY

The royal family is the most revered institution in Thailand. Criticizing or defaming it in any way can be considered *lèse-majesté*. Not only could this mean a jail sentence, but Thai people will nearly always be deeply offended. Coins, bills, and stamps bear the images of kings and therefore should not be treated lightly. Similarly, you cannot photograph certain sacred sights connected to royalty, such as the *bot* of Wat Phra Kaeo, which houses the highly revered Emerald Buddha image.

THE NATIONAL ANTHEM

The national anthem is played twice a day, at 8am and 6pm, on the radio and through tannoys in small towns and some public parks and buildings such as Lumphini Park and Hua Lampong Station in Bangkok. At these times it is polite to stop whatever you are doing and stand still. In

Two Thais addressing each other with a *wai*, the traditional greeting

GREETING PEOPLE

The Thai greeting is known as the *wai* and consists of the palms being pressed together and lifted towards the chin. The *wai* evolved from an ancient greeting used to show that neither party was carrying weapons. The *wai* is layered with intricacies of class, gender, and age: each of these dictates a certain height at which the two hands must be held. The inferior party initiates the *wai* and holds it higher and for longer than the superior, who returns it according to his or her social standing. Non-Thais are not expected to be familiar with these complexities, and the easiest method is simply to mirror whatever greeting you receive. As a general rule of thumb, however, you should not *wai* children or workers such as waiters, waitresses, and street vendors.

Thais use first names to address people, even in formal situations. The polite form of address is the gender-neutral title Khun, followed by the first name or nickname. Every Thai person has a nickname, usually a one- or two-syllable name with a simple meaning, such as Moo (pig) or Koong (shrimp).

BODY LANGUAGE

The head is considered a sacred part of the body by Thais. Never touch someone's head, not even that of a child. The feet are seen as the lowliest part of the body and to point your feet toward someone or rest them on a table is considered rude. When sitting on the floor, especially inside a temple, tuck your legs away behind you or to the side and try not to step over people sitting around you; allow them time to move out of your way.

Devotees kneeling before a Buddha, their feet facing away from the image

A man offering food to a line of monks on the daily alms round

theaters the national anthem is played before all performances. When it is playing the audience stands in silent respect to a portrait of the king on the screen.

MONKS

The monkhood *(sangha)* is a respected institution that comes just below royalty in the social hierarchy. Most taboos in dealing with monks concern women: it is prohibited for a monk to touch a woman or for him to receive anything directly from her. Therefore, when traveling by public transportation, women should avoid sitting near or next to a monk. If she has to offer anything to a monk she should either use a middleman or place the item nearby for him to pick up. These rules are confined to monks and do not apply to nuns.

It is not forbidden for people to talk to monks – many are eager to try out their English. However, monks never return *wais*.

ETIQUETTE AT WATS

"No shoes" sign outside Wat Phra Kaeo, Bangkok

As in churches and other houses of worship, a certain decorum should be observed when entering the grounds of any *wat*. Temples are calm, quiet places, so try to avoid disturbing the peace. Dress should be clean, respectable, and unrevealing

(strictly speaking, the upper arms and legs down to mid-calf should be covered). Shoes should be removed when entering any temple building. Step over, not on, the thresholds of *wat* buildings as Thais believe that one of the nine spirits that inhabit buildings lives in the threshold.

All Buddha images are sacred no matter how small, ruined, or neglected, and you must never sit with your feet pointing toward them.

Some areas of a temple may be off limits for women – there is usually a sign indicating such areas.

SUITABLE DRESS

Because the Thais are a modest people, clothing should be kept respectable whether you are in the city or in the country. Women especially should take care not to wear revealing skirts, shorts, or skimpy tops. In formal settings and restaurants you will rarely see Thai women with bare shoulders; sleeveless dresses or tops are considered too revealing for such situations. Topless sunbathing is frowned upon greatly – regardless of whether others are doing it – even in resorts dominated by Western tourists. Most Thais find the practice embarrassing and many of them find it offensive.

COMMUNICATING

Bargaining is common throughout Thailand (*see p450*). Though everyone develops a personal technique – whether it involves smiling or remaining poker-faced – it is important not to get too tough or too mean. Likewise, be patient with receptionists, waitresses, and others whom you may deal with. In general, you should avoid raising your voice or becoming obviously irritable – Thais learn in childhood always to speak softly and avoid direct conflict. Foreigners who may be used to getting results if they show impatience are likely to find Thais ignoring them rather than attempting to continue communicating with them.

Tourists bargaining with vendors on the platform of Hua Hin Station

TIPPING

Traditionally, tipping is not common practice in Thailand, though in Westernized establishments it is fast becoming so. Taxi drivers expect tips – as a rule you should round up the fare to the nearest ten *baht*. Porters, hairdressers, and barbers also often expect tips. A service charge of ten percent is common on up-scale restaurant and hotel bills, even if they also charge government tax (*see p395 and p423*).

SMOKING

Smoking is prohibited in all public areas such as theaters, department stores, government buildings, and on all public transport systems. It is also banned in restaurants (except on terraces), nightclubs, and pubs. Fines for smoking in public places can be hefty, usually 2,000 *baht*.

Personal Security and Health

Thailand is a fairly safe country, and simple health and safety precautions keep the vast majority of travelers out of trouble. For instance, ignore hustlers, keep away from troubled border areas, take care of valuables, and avoid staying or eating in unsanitary conditions. The infrastructure of emergency services for both health and crime is efficient throughout Bangkok and provincial capitals. As a rule of thumb, the more remote the area, the higher the health risk and the less support available in the event of any mishap. The main hospitals in Bangkok, Chiang Mai, the main resorts, and other large cities have modern equipment and well-trained doctors, many of whom speak some English.

Tourist policeman wearing a beret, and an ordinary officer

IN AN EMERGENCY

There are no national emergency telephone lines except for ambulances, and operators do not speak English. For English-speaking help, call the Tourist Assistance Center, which will contact the appropriate service for you. Lines are open from 8am to midnight, after which you will have to rely on English-speaking hotel staff. During office hours, TAT *(see p475)* may also be able to help. The Metropolitan Mobile Police cover general emergencies in Bangkok. All Bangkok's hospitals have 24-hour accident and emergency departments.

Fire engine

Ambulance

Police car

GENERAL PRECAUTIONS

Despite its size, Bangkok is relatively safe. Crime and violence do exist, but most travelers are untouched by it. Discretion and sobriety are the best means of avoiding problems. Be alert at tourist sights and bus and train stations, where hustlers and pickpockets occasionally operate: scam artists outside the Grand Palace *(see pp80–81)* direct tourists to pricier, less impressive sights. Do not flash large amounts of cash or leave your luggage unattended. If you are leaving valuables in a hotel safe, make sure to get a receipt, and do not let credit cards out of your sight when paying for shopping.

The drugging, then robbing, of tourists on long-distance trains and buses has occurred, so politely decline food or drink from strangers. Thailand is an excellent place to buy gems *(see p454)*, but do not be tempted into buying large quantities to sell back at home unless you are familiar with the market and its pitfalls. Extra care is necessary in more remote areas of the country where locals are less accustomed to tourists and you are more likely to stand out. Care should also be taken in poorer parts of cities, particularly at night, or if traveling alone.

DRUGS

Thai law prohibits the sale or purchase of opium, heroin, or marijuana. Charges for possession, smuggling, or dealing drugs can lead to a 2–15 year jail sentence or, in extreme cases, the death sentence. Border areas in the north attract drug runners. Be wary of strangers in these areas, and do not leave baggage unattended, or offer to check in a "friendly" stranger's suitcase at airports.

DANGER SPOTS

Border areas are sometimes precarious places. Changing political conditions, tribal skirmishes, and the haziness of border lines have made a few areas of Thailand dangerous.

There are sporadic clashes on the Myanmar (Burmese) and Cambodian borders, so it is best to avoid traveling alone on remote roads in those areas. In the three Deep South provinces of Narathiwat, Pattani, and Yala, the militant Malay-Muslim group, PULO (Pattani United Liberation Organization) represents a real danger, and has made travel in this region extremely difficult. Again, common sense should prevail and it is wise to stay away from the most remote border areas.

WOMEN TRAVELERS

Female travelers are unlikely to be harassed in Thailand. Bangkok itself is not dangerous for women; hotels are safe, and taxis are readily available. If traveling alone it is a good idea to keep in touch with someone in Bangkok and let them know where you are going and for how long. Note that Thais perceive lone travelers as people to be pitied, and may offer to accompany you without any ulterior motive.

TOURIST POLICE

There are tourist police stations in the main tourist cities. Tourist police officers all speak some English and are attached to TAT offices. Set up in 1982 to deal with tourist-related crime, they are happy to help with anything from credit card scams to ludicrous bar surcharges. They are also helpful in emergencies, and can act as an English-speaking liaison. The Bangkok branch of the tourist police is located in front of the southwest entrance to Lumphini Park. The Tourist Assistance Center is also helpful in emergencies, and is experienced in dealing with complaints such as fraudulent business charges.

LEGAL ASSISTANCE

Some insurance policies cover legal costs, for example, after an accident. If involved in an accident when driving a rental car, it may be wise to go to the nearest telephone and call the tourist police or the Tourist Assistance Center, then return to the scene of the accident. In Thailand there are no legal bodies specifically representing foreigners.

In an emergency, contact your embassy *(see p475)*. At night there is an answering service, giving the number of the duty officer. If you are not insured for legal proceedings, then you should contact your nearest consulate for advice.

Logo of the Thai Red Cross Society, part of Chulalongkorn University

MEDICAL FACILITIES

Medical insurance is advisable when traveling in Thailand. Some policies pay bills direct, while others refund you later. Hospitals in Bangkok, both public and private, are modern, clean, and efficient, although waiting times are longer at public ones. Some doctors are Western-trained and speak good English.

Badge identifying the tourist police

Outside the capital the best facilities are in the large towns: Khon Kaen in the northeast, Chiang Mai in the north, or Phuket in the south. Emergency care is available from military hospitals, which treat tourists in emergency cases. For dental or eye care, it is best to seek treatment in Bangkok. The Thai Red Cross on Rama IV Road does not offer medical treatment, but is able to deal with vaccinations and snake bites.

PHARMACIES

There is no shortage of well-stocked pharmacies in Bangkok – there will be several on every main street and shopping mall, and supermarkets will have drugstore kiosks. They are all supplied with up-to-date medications and can dispense antibiotics over the counter without a prescription.

Most pharmacies are open from 8am to 9pm. In the central areas of Bangkok, around Silom and Sukhumvit Roads, a few stay open until 10pm or 11pm. Pharmacy signs are the same all over the country. In small towns pharmacies are less prolific and have fewer supplies. For instance, disposable diapers and tampons can be hard to find in remote areas.

Pharmacy sign found throughout Thailand

DIRECTORY

EMERGENCY NUMBERS

Tourist Assistance Center
Tel 1155 (Bangkok).

Metropolitan Mobile Police
Tel 191 (Bangkok).

TOURIST POLICE

Bangkok
Tel 0-2356-0582/3/4 or 1155.

Chiang Mai
Tel 0-5324-7317-8 or 1155.

Ko Samui
Tel 0-7743-0016 or 1155.

Pattaya
Tel 0-3842-9371 or 1155.

Phuket
Tel 0-7622-3891/2 or 1155.

Surat Thani
Tel 0-7740-5575 or 1155.

Trat
Tel 0-3955-7382/3 or 1155.

HOSPITALS

Bangkok
Bangkok General Hospital, Soi Soonvijai, New Petchaburi Rd. *Tel 0-2310-3000 or 1719.* **www**.bangkokhospital.com
Bumrungrad Hospital, Sukhumvit, Soi 3. *Tel 0-2667-1000.* **www**.bumrungrad.com

Chiang Mai
McCormick Hospital, Kaew Nawarat Rd. *Tel 0-5392-1777.* **www**.mccormick.in.th

Phuket
Phuket International Hospital, 44 Chalermprakiat Ror 9 Rd. *Tel 0-7624-9400.* **www**.phuketinternational hospital.com

AMBULANCE

Tel 1554 (whole country).

PUBLIC TOILETS

All hotels and many guest-houses have Western-style flush toilets. In some restaurants and at many major sights, you will encounter the Asian squat toilet. Nearby will be a bucket of water, used to sluice out the toilet after use. Paper is disposed of in a bin.

IMMUNIZATION

There are no legal immunization requirements unless you are traveling from a country known to be infected with yellow fever. It is recommended that everyone be immunized against polio, tetanus, typhoid, and hepatitis A. In addition, for those travelers going to remote or rural areas, or who are staying more than two to three weeks, BCG (tuberculosis), hepatitis B, rabies, diphtheria, and Japanese encephalitis vaccinations are advised. For the most up-to-date advice, contact your doctor, who will also be able to advise on the current guidelines for malaria prevention, as the drug recommendations change fairly often.

Some vaccines need to be given separately or in stages. Some malaria tablets, meanwhile, are started a week before traveling and continued for several weeks after returning. Therefore, it is advisable to contact your doctor at least eight weeks before departure.

COPING WITH THE HEAT

Acclimatization to the sometimes oppressive humidity and heat of Thailand can often take longer than expected. In the first few days it is not advisable to exert yourself. Make sure you drink plenty of fluids, take plenty of rest in the shade, and avoid being out and about in the midday sun. Once you are acclimatized, dehydration and salt deficiency can still be a problem – always keep up a high intake of fluids, especially bottled water, or special electrolyte drinks. Minor fungal infections can occur due to the heat, especially if tight clothing or shoes are worn. Perspiration trapped beneath the skin can cause the itchy rash

Treatment for prickly heat

A fan to beat the heat

called prickly heat. The local remedy and prophylactic for this is a talcum powder that contains a tingling cooling agent. Clothing should be loose and light – 100 percent cotton is best.

The sun, especially at midday and on the islands, is very powerful; sunscreen and a wide-brimmed hat are indispensable.

FIRST-AID KIT

Although most first-aid items can be obtained from any pharmacy in main towns, when traveling to rural areas or quiet islands it is advisable to carry a basic first-aid kit. This should include the following: any personal medication; aspirin or paracetamol for fevers and minor aches and pains; an antiseptic for minor cuts and bites; a digestive preparation to soothe upset stomachs; insect repellent; bandages; scissors, tweezers, and a thermometer. Tiger Balm, available at any pharmacy, is Asia's miracle cure-all, relieving headaches, muscle pains, and insect bites.

MINOR STOMACH UPSETS

If you should contract diarrhea, eat plain foods for a few days and drink plenty of fluids. It is never wise to drink tap water – bottled water is readily available throughout the country. Ice should be fine in main hotels and restaurants, but avoid crushed iced drinks from street vendors. Eating in hotels and restaurants is generally safe. It is when you venture into the street vendors' moveable feasts that the danger of "Bangkok belly" can arise. Choose food stalls that are popular with locals, and watch how the dishes are prepared. It can take time for visitors' stomachs to adjust to new foods. If your constitution is delicate, stick to unpeeled fruits and well-cooked foods, and make sure you eat dishes while they are still hot.

Drugs such as Lomotil and Imodium can bring relief to diarrhea, but rehydrating solutions are usually the best remedy. For immediate relief, a single 500 mg dose of the prescription called Ciprofloxacin is effective and safe.

Tiger Balm – provides relief from aches, pains, bites, and strains

CUTS AND BITES

Always take precautions in rural areas: wear boots and long trousers when walking through grassland or forested areas to protect against snake bites and leeches (in the rainy season). Few snake bites are dangerous. If you are bitten, apply an elastic bandage firmly to the bite, keep the limb immobile, and seek immediate medical help.

Jellyfish stings are painful – vinegar will soothe the wound. Coral cuts are slow to heal as coral contains a mild poison. Cuts should be treated with an antiseptic to prevent infection. Bandages keep wounds wet so should be used only sparingly.

INSECT-BORNE DISEASES

Seven of Thailand's 410 mosquito species carry malaria. Symptoms of the disease include headache, fever, and violent chills. If you experience such symptoms, seek medical

Spicy curries from food stalls – best avoided if your stomach is delicate

advice immediately. Pollution in the main towns and resorts keeps them largely free of malarial mosquitoes. The areas of greatest risk are the Myanmar (Burmese) and Cambodian border regions and some rural areas north of Chiang Mai. However, malarial zones are continually changing. For up-to-date information and advice on the most suitable prophylactic drug, visit your doctor or contact a specialist travel clinic.

Mosquitoes have become resistant to certain malaria tablets. Prevention is by far the best defense against the disease. Malarial mosquitoes are active from sundown till sunrise, during which time you should spray on plenty of repellent, wear long-sleeved clothing in light colors (dark attracts mosquitoes), and use mosquito nets and coils.

Dengue fever, another mosquito-borne disease, is a risk during the daytime. However, few mosquitoes are infected with the virus, and the symptoms, though intense and unpleasant, are rarely fatal. These include fever, headache, severe joint and muscle pains, and a rash. No preventive treatment or vaccination is available.

In Northern Thailand and some rural areas there is a risk of contracting Japanese encephalitis, which is spread by night-biting mosquitoes and ticks. The symptoms are headache, fever, chills, and vomiting. Vaccination is advisable if your plans include traveling to rural areas (particularly during the rainy season), or trekking. Should any of the above symptoms occur seek immediate medical help.

PEOPLE- AND ANIMAL-BORNE DISEASES

Acquired immune deficiency syndrome (AIDS) is passed through bodily fluids. Blood transfusion methods in Thailand are not always reliable – it is safest to seek treatment in the main hospitals. The same goes for inoculations – make sure needles are new or bring your own supply. Be wary of all procedures involving needles, including ear-piercing, dentistry, and tattooing.

The high turnover of clients in Thailand's pervasive sex industry means that unprotected sex carries a serious risk (see p116). Not only AIDS, but other sexually transmitted diseases are commonplace.

Hepatitis B is also transmitted through bodily fluids. Symptoms include fever, nausea, fatigue, and jaundice, and it can lead to severe liver damage. A prophylactic vaccine is available.

Rabies is carried in the saliva of infected animals and can be passed on by a bite or lick to a wound or scratch. Any bite from a dog, cat, or monkey should be cleaned immediately and checked by a doctor. Treatment involves a long series of inoculations.

Tetanus is a potentially lethal disease transmitted through infected cuts and animal bites. The first symptoms are difficulty in swallowing (tetanus is also known as lockjaw) and muscle stiffness in the neck area, which can lead to convulsions. As with rabies, all wounds should be speedily cleaned and examined by a doctor. Effective vaccinations are available.

Bilharzia is contracted from tiny worms that infect some types of freshwater snail. They burrow into the skin and cause a general feeling of sickness and abdominal pain. Avoid swimming in untested rivers and lakes.

FOOD- AND WATER-BORNE DISEASES

Dysentery, a severe form of food or water poisoning, is rare in Thailand, but not unknown. Bacillary dysentery – characterized by stomach pains, vomiting, and fever – is highly contagious but rarely lasts longer than a week. Amebic dysentery has similar symptoms but takes longer to develop. It can recur and cause chronic health problems. Medical help should be sought without delay if you think you have either type.

Hepatitis A is passed on in conditions of poor sanitation (contaminated water or food) and can be prevented with a vaccine. Symptoms include fatigue, aching, fever, chills, and jaundice. Little can be done to treat it beyond rest.

Typhoid is transmitted through contaminated water or food, and fluid replacement is the most important treatment. Symptoms are similar to those of flu but quickly accelerate to fever, weight loss, and severe dehydration. Medical attention is essential as complications such as pneumonia can easily occur. Although a vaccination is available, it is not always reliable.

Bottled water

Banking and Local Currency

Siam Commercial Bank credit card logo

Throughout Bangkok and the main provincial towns, banking facilities and exchange services are plentiful, well-run, and easy to access. In the major centers, tellers often speak some English. Exchange booths are usually located in the central parts of towns, and mobile exchange units are stationed near larger tourist attractions. Automatic Teller Machines (ATMs) can be found in all cities. Smaller towns are less likely to have exchange facilities, but most have banks or ATMs. Rural villages, unless they are tourist destinations, probably will not have banking or currency exchange services.

HSBC, an international bank operating in Bangkok

BANKS AND BANKING HOURS

The four main banks are the **Bangkok Bank**, the **Kasikorn Bank**, the **Siam Commercial Bank**, and the **Krung Thai Bank**. The **Bank of Ayudhya** and **CIMB Thai** also have branches throughout the country. Foreign-owned banks offering full banking services include the **Bank of America**, **Citibank**, **Deutsche Bank**, **Hongkong and Shanghai Bank (HSBC)** and **Standard Chartered Bank**.

Banking hours are generally 8:30am–3:30pm, Monday to Friday. Some banks have branches in department stores which are open 10am–8pm. Exchange booths are open daily, until late. Major banks can arrange international money transfers.

ATM SERVICES

Most ATMs provide instructions in both Thai and English. Any ATM displaying the VISA or MasterCard sign will accept these cards and dispense cash

Automatic Teller Machines, found in Bangkok and many Thai towns

in *baht* using your PIN. There are surcharges for such trans-actions. If you are planning an extended stay in Thailand, it might be worth opening an account at a Thai bank. This allows access to all ATMs, free of exchange rates or charges.

CHANGING MONEY

Banks offer the best exchange rates, and rates differ little between them. Hotels usually offer the worst rates, while those at exchange booths can vary. US dollars are widely accepted when buying *baht*, although sterling and euro are also taken. In Bangkok, hole-in-the-wall exchange booths can be found in large department stores and shop-ping malls and on major roads. Mobile exchange units are located near tourist attractions and market areas and are open daily between 7am and 9pm. Exchange rates are published daily in the *Bangkok Post* and the *Nation*.

DIRECTORY

THAI BANKS

Bangkok Bank
333 Silom Rd, Bangkok.
Tel 0-2231-4333.
www.bangkokbank.com

Bank of Ayudhya
1222 Rama 3, Bangkok.
Tel 0-2296-2000.
www.krungsri.com

CIMB Thai
44 Langsuan Rd, Bangkok.
Tel 0-2626-7000.
www.cimbthai.com

Kasikorn Bank
1 Kasikornthai Lane,
Ratburana Rd, Bangkok.
Tel 0-2888-8888.
www.kasikornbank.com

Krung Thai Bank
35 Sukhumvit Rd,
Bangkok.
Tel 0-2255-9391/2/3.
www.ktb.co.th

Siam Commercial Bank
9 Rachadaphisak Rd,
Bangkok. *Tel 0-2544-1000.* **www**.scb.co.th

FOREIGN BANKS

Bank of America
All Seasons Place,
CRC Tower, 33rd Floor,
87/2 Wireless Rd, Bangkok.
Tel 0-2305-2900. **www.**
bankofamerica.com/th

Citibank
399 Sukhumvit Rd,
Bangkok.
Tel 1588 or 0-2788-2000.
www.citibank.co.th

Deutsche Bank
Athenee Tower,
Levels 27–29,
63 Wireless Rd,
Bangkok.
Tel 0-2646-5000.
www.db.com/thailand

HSBC
HSBC Building,
968 Rama IV Rd,
Bangkok.
Tel 0-2614-4000.
www.hsbc.co.th

Standard Chartered Bank
90 Fl. 16A Building 3, North Sathorn Rd, Bangkok.
Tel 0-2724-4777. **www.**
standardchartered.co.th

CARDS

American Express
*Tel 0-2273-5544,
0-2273-5522.*

Diners Club
Tel 0-2655-7246.

MasterCard
Tel 001-800-11-887-0663.

VISA
Tel 001-800-441-3485.

CREDIT AND DEBIT CARDS

Credit cards are accepted in department stores, major hotels, and upscale shops and restaurants. They can also be used at banks (and some exchange kiosks) for cash advances. A surcharge will be applied. **VISA** and **MasterCard** are the most widely accepted cards; the use of **Diners Club** and **American Express** is more limited.

MasterCard debit cards can be used to withdraw cash at most foreign exchange booths, and at Bangkok Bank and Siam Commercial Bank. VISA debit cards can do the same at the Kasikorn Bank. Debit cards can also be used at ATMs, but a surcharge will be levied.

As the popularity of plastic money increases, so too does the incidence of credit-card fraud. Visitors should always carefully check what they sign.

TRAVELERS' CHECKS

Travelers' checks are the safest method of carrying money. Banks, main hotels, and most exchange booths cash them, with banks providing the lowest surcharge. Banks charge a fee per check cashed, so using large-denomination checks works out cheapest.

CURRENCY

The Thai unit of currency is the *baht*, usually seen abbreviated to "B." There are 100 *satang* in a *baht*, but the *satang* represents such a small sum today that it is scarcely

Bangkok Bank
The Asian International Bank

Logo for one of Thailand's long-established banks

used. You may hear 25 *satang* referred to as a *saleung*. However, inflation is rendering this colloquial term redundant.

Banknotes come in the following denominations: 20 *baht*, 50 *baht*, 100 *baht*, 500 *baht*, and 1,000 *baht*. Changing large denomination notes in rural areas may prove difficult.

The coin denominations are 25 *satang* (1 *saleung*), 50 *satang*, 1 *baht*, 2 *baht*, 5 *baht*, 10 *baht*. The gold 2 *baht* coin is slightly bigger than the silver 1 *baht* coin. The silver

5 *baht* coin has a copper rim and the 10 *baht* coin has a bronze center surrounded by a silver outer ring. Old coins feature Thai numerals only, while newer coins have both Thai and Arabic numerals.

VAT

Thailand imposes a 7 percent Value Added Tax (VAT) on goods and services, generally levied only in upscale hotels, restaurants, and shops. There is a VAT refund scheme for tourists who are in the country for less than 180 days. Look out for shops displaying a "VAT Refund For Tourists" sign.

20 *baht*

50 *baht*

100 *baht*

500 *baht*

1,000 *baht*

Coins come in the following denominations:

25 *satang*

50 *satang*

1 *baht*

2 *baht*

5 *baht*

10 *baht*

Communications and Media

A domestic phone booth

Thailand's communication network is becoming increasingly sophisticated. The telephone system is run by the Telephone Organization of Thailand (TOT) under the umbrella of the Communications Authority of Thailand (CAT). It is possible to make international calls and send faxes from all business centers and main hotels. Public phones can be found on all main roads and many minor ones. The postal system, however, can be erratic; if you are sending valuables it is advisable to use courier services. Many major international newspapers and magazines can be easily obtained. Locally published English-language newspapers and magazines can be bought in almost every hotel and bookstore, and at many curbside news stands.

A green card-phone for local and long-distance domestic calls

INTERNATIONAL CALLS

All major hotels and most guesthouses offer international dialing services. Business centers and Internet cafés in small towns will usually provide phone, fax, and printing services.

Bangkok's Central Post Office on Charoen Krung New Road and some major post offices around the country have a CAT center that can arrange collect and credit card calls. In Bangkok these are open from 7am until midnight, with reduced hours in the provinces.

To dial directly from a hotel room, either contact the reception, or dial 001 (for an international line) followed by the country code and telephone number. It is also possible to use 007, 008, or 009 to prefix your number – these offer cheaper rates. Alternatively, dial the international operator at 100.

Blue and yellow international pay phones can be found on the street, in shopping malls, and in airports. The blue phones take some credit cards. The yellow phones accept Lenso phonecards, which are sold in the post office and by agents displaying the Lenso logo.

LOCAL CALLS

Local calls can be made from any public pay phone other than the blue-and-yellow international pay phones.

Domestic calls can be made from blue-and-silver coin phones or green card-phones. Coin-operated phones accept one-, five-, and ten-*baht* coins. Calls within the same area code cost one *baht* for three minutes.

Cards for green and orange card-phones can be bought at most post offices, bookstores, and hotels and come in several denominations: 25 *baht*, 50 *baht*, 100 *baht*, and 240 *baht*.

The long-distance domestic service also covers Malaysia and Laos, as well as regional Thai calls.

CELL PHONES

There are four main GSM (Global System for Mobile Communications) frequencies in use around the world, so if you want to guarantee that your phone will work, make sure you have a quad-band phone. Contact your service provider for clarification. Cell phones are extremely cheap in Thailand. There are several operating companies, including AIS, True, and DTAC. SIM cards can be bought from cell phone shops. Customers can pay monthly or buy the popular scratch cards with a dial-in code to top up their credits. Cards are available from all 7-Eleven stores around the country and range from 50 to 500 *baht* in value.

INTERNET AND EMAIL

Internet access is available in Internet cafés, hotels, and guesthouses all over Thailand. Charges range from 20 *baht* per hour in a local Internet café to 250 *baht* per hour in a five-star hotel. In some places, Wi-Fi hotspots are available for free (ask staff for the code). However, in airports and upmarket hotels there can be a charge of as much as 600 *baht* per day.

Connections in Bangkok and some of the larger provincial centers are usually fast, but generally speaking the further you move away from urban centers, the slower the connection. Even the most remote islands now have reasonable, if slow, Internet connections.

One of Thailand's many Internet cafés

POSTAL SERVICES

Thailand has a reliable postal system. Letters and postcards usually take at least one week to reach Europe and North America. Stamps are available at all post offices and at many hotels. Packages should be sent by registered mail or via International Express Mail

Service (EMS), which can be a cheaper alternative to international shipping companies.

General delivery facilities are available at all main post offices. Letters will normally be held for up to three months. To claim mail from general delivery, you must show your passport and sometimes pay a small fee. Letters should be addressed to you (last name written in capitals and underlined), poste restante, GPO, address, town, Thailand. Thus for Bangkok's main GPO, correspondents should send mail care of GPO, Charoen Krung Road, Bangkok.

Post offices are usually open 8:30am–4:30pm Monday to Friday and 9am–noon on Saturdays. The main international courier companies, such as **DHL**, **FedEx**, and **UPS**, operate in Thailand.

Thai mail box

TELEVISION AND RADIO

Thailand has numerous television channels; programs are mostly in Thai, though in Bangkok some are broadcast with an English simulcast on FM radio. Most international English-language satellite and cable networks such as the BBC, CNN, Al Jazeera, and CNBC are readily available.

Many hotels provide satellite and cable television as well as an in-house video channel. Check the *Bangkok Post* and *The Nation* for details.

English-language radio stations are listed in the *Outlook* section of the *Bangkok Post*. The national public radio station, Radio Thailand, broadcasts English-language programs on 107 and 105 FM 24 hours a day, and listings for short-wave frequencies are found in the *Bangkok Post* and *The Nation*.

NEWSPAPERS AND MAGAZINES

The main English-language newspapers are the *Bangkok Post* and *The Nation*. Both provide reliable local, regional, and international coverage. Their daily inserts include features on lifestyle and travel, as well as listings for food, films, concerts, and exhibitions in Bangkok. Both are sold in news kiosks and shops throughout Bangkok.

The *International Herald Tribune* and the *Asian Wall Street Journal* are sold in hotels and bookstores such as Asia Books and Bookazine, which also stock international magazines. News weeklies *The Economist*, *Time*, and *Newsweek* are widely available.

DIRECTORY

DIRECTORY ASSISTANCE

Greater Bangkok Metropolitan Area
Tel 1133.

Provincial Areas
Tel 1133.

OPERATOR

International Service or Auto Long Distance Service from Thailand to Malaysia, Myanmar, Cambodia, and Laos
Tel 007 or 008.

COURIER COMPANIES

DHL
209 K Tower A, 12th Floor, 21 Sukhumvit Rd, Bangkok.
Tel 0-2345-5000.
www. dhl.co.th

FedEx
Green Tower, 3656/22 Rama IV, Bangkok. *Tel* 1782.
www.fedex.com.th

UPS
16/1 Soi 44/1 Sukhumvit Rd, Bangkok.
Tel 0-2762-3300.
www.ups.com

Among the local English-language monthly publications is the useful listings guide *Big Chilli*. In addition to this, helpful free guides that are widely available, including in restaurants, bars, and bookstores, are *BK Magazine*, *Absolute Lifestyle*, and *Thaiways*.

Newspaper seller on the beach

USEFUL DIALING CODES

- Whether calling from within or outside the province, you need to dial a 9-digit number for Bangkok and all other provinces.
- For international calls, dial 001, 007, 008, or 009, followed by the country code.
- Country codes are: UK 44; Ireland 353; France 33; US & Canada 1; Australia 61; New Zealand 64. It may be necessary to omit the first digit of the destination area code. This will also apply when calling international mobile numbers.

- For directory assistance dial 1133 from anywhere in the country.
- To put a call through the international operator, or to report technical problems, dial 101.
- To speak to the domestic operator, dial 101.
- To make a reverse charge (collect) call dial 101 for the international operator.
- Note that the speaking clock and similar telephone services such as directory assistance are all in Thai.
- For a wake-up call, contact your hotel switchboard or front desk.

TRAVEL INFORMATION

For most visitors, flying is the most convenient way of getting to Thailand. Other routes include ferry, road, and rail via Malaysia; ferry and road via Cambodia; and limited but rapidly improving road links via Laos. Domestic flights within Thailand are easy and cut journey times considerably, with provincial airports dotted generously around the country. Flights to surrounding countries are cheaper if booked within

Thailand. Regular rail services run between Bangkok and Singapore, via Kuala Lumpur, Butterworth (for Penang), and some Southern Thai towns. Rail travel is efficient, clean, and comfortable, but there is a limited number of lines. Long-distance and provincial buses of varying quality run to all towns and to most villages. At a local level there is a variety of taxis, *songthaews*, and *tuk-tuks* with which to get around.

Thai Airways logo

GREEN TRAVEL

Travel around Thailand is easy, convenient, and cheap, but not really very green. Most people will travel by train, long-distance coach, or car hire – the latter being the most flexible and user-friendly, as the kingdom's roads are uniformly good and well-maintained (though driving can be hazardous at times). The only possibility for green travel in terms of fuel is the use of Liquid Petroleum Gas (LPG). This less-polluting fuel has been introduced in an attempt to combat increasing exhaust pollution in large cities and rising oil prices. However, vehicles using LPG are still relatively few, so the best that can reasonably be hoped for is the use of Gasohol, which combines ordinary benzene with fuel derived from sugar cane.

Some of Bangkok's newer local buses now use LPG and the city authorities are slowly replacing the old polluting buses, but this will take time. Both LPG and Gasohol are,

A Boeing 747 in the traditional livery of Thai Airways

to some extent, subsidized by the government in an attempt to encourage their use.

Bangkok's Skytrain and MRT underground have made a huge difference to the city's once clogged arteries, providing transport for thousands of commuters who would previously have used their cars.

ARRIVING BY AIR

Thailand is served by numerous airlines from all over the world. Direct flights are available from North America, Europe, Australasia, and Asia. **Thai Airways** operates direct flights from Los Angeles to Bangkok, and **British Airways**, **United Airlines**, and **Delta** have a connecting service from New York. **Qantas** has direct flights to Bangkok from Sydney, Melbourne, and London and **Singapore Airlines** flies from Australia to Bangkok via Singapore. International flights also land at U-Tapao Airport, located 45

Gasohol service station

minutes from Pattaya. Flights from Asian countries may land at Phuket, Chiang Mai, Hat Yai, Krabi, or Ko Samui.

AIR FARES

The cost of flying to and from Thailand varies according to the destination, the airline, and the time of year. In the northern hemisphere low fares are available from September to April, and in the southern hemisphere from March to November. Bangkok is one of the cheapest cities in the world to fly out of due to loose government restrictions on air fares and fierce competition between the airlines and Bangkok's travel agencies.

SUVARNABHUMI INTERNATIONAL AIRPORT

Opened in 2006, this huge modern airport is located in Racha Thewa in Bang Phli district, Samut Prakan Province, 30 km (18 miles) east of the capital. One of the busiest airports in Asia, Suvarnabhumi is used for all international as well as most domestic flights.

Named by King Bhumibol, *Suvarnabhumi* means "Golden Land." The airport's futuristic design makes it a striking architectural feat as well as a functional airport. In total Suvarnabhumi stretches over 11 miles, and boasts the world's tallest air traffic control tower. The large roof trellis structure is sized for the future growth of the airport, which at present operates 76 flights per hour and can accommodate 45 million passengers a year. This number will potentially increase to a staggering 100 million passengers once the airport is fully expanded. This massive project commenced less than one month after the airport's official opening, and is expected to be finished between 2015 and 2020.

Arriving passengers enter the terminal on the second floor of the concourse buildings. After passing through passport control checkpoints and customs, they can proceed to the arrivals hall, where they will find transportation and accommodation counters, and a tourist information center. A meeting point can be found on the third floor.

Suvarnabhumi International Airport

AIRPORT SHOPPING

With more than 100 duty free shops, Suvarnabhumi Airport is a shopper's paradise. Tourists should, however, refrain from touching or moving merchandise that they do not intend to buy. Such actions might give the impression of shoplifting, and this may result in detention and questioning by the police.

GETTING TO AND FROM SUVARNABHUMI INTERNATIONAL AIRPORT

Metered taxis are available outside the first floor. There is a surcharge of 50 *baht* in addition to the meter fare. A trip into the city will cost roughly 400 *baht*, including expressway charges, and take around 45 minutes, depending on traffic. Passengers can also take a shuttle bus or the rail link.

People traveling to the airport by road are strongly advised to allow at least one hour for travel time and to take the expressway. Check-ins, particularly at the Thai Airways counter, are often subject to delays. The walk from the passport checkpoint to the flight departure lounge is also a considerable distance.

A direct airport rail link runs every 40 minutes from Bangkok City Airport Terminal at Makkasan Station in the center of Bangkok to Suvarnabhumi Airport. The non-stop journey takes 15 minutes, while the stopping service takes about 30 minutes. Both services have considerably cut the journey time between the airport and the center of Bangkok.

Travelers wishing to go to Suvarnabhumi Airport from outside Bangkok should allow plenty of time – at least two hours per 100 km (60 miles) of the journey. It is advisable to shop around for taxis as fares can vary greatly. Many tourist areas now have air-conditioned regular minibus services at a fraction of the cost of private taxis (130 *baht* from Pattaya for example).

Planes on the tarmac at Suvarnabhumi Airport

AIRPORT	TEL INFORMATION	DISTANCE TO TOWN OR RESORT	AVERAGE TAXI FARE	AVERAGE JOURNEY TIME
Bangkok: Don Muang	0-2535-1111 0-2535-1253	City center 25 km (16 miles)	300 *baht*	Rail: 50 minutes Road: 1–2 hours
Bangkok: Suvarnabhumi	0-2132-1888	City center 30 km (18 miles)	400 *baht*	Rail link: 15 mins Road: 45–60 mins
Chiang Mai	0-5327-0222	City center 4 km (2.5 miles)	100 *baht*	Road: 20 minutes
Phuket	0-7632-7230-7	Patong 32 km (20 miles)	550 *baht*	Road: 45 minutes
Ko Samui	0-7742-8500	Chaweng 26 km (16 miles)	300 *baht*	Road: 30 minutes
Hat Yai	0-7422-7000	City center 12 km (7.5 miles)	200 *baht*	Road: 30 minutes

DOMESTIC FLIGHTS

While most domestic flights from Bangkok leave from Suvarnabhumi, some fly from Don Muang Airport. Located on Bangkok's Vibhavadi Rangsit Road, Don Muang serves all the domestic flights of local budget carriers **Nok Air** and **Solar Air**.

Local carriers **Thai Airways** and **Bangkok Airways** fly to all major destinations, such as Chiang Mai, Hat Yai, Ko Samui, Phuket, and Sukhothai. They also serve towns such as Krabi, Mae Hong Son, and Chiang Rai. Other local airlines include **Thai Air Asia** and **SGA Airlines**. Tickets can be bought through travel agents and hotels, or booked directly through the airlines – in this case passengers will need to pick up their ticket at the airport at least one hour before flying.

On public holidays *(see p51)* and on weekends, when there are more people traveling, it can be difficult to get a flight, so book tickets well in advance or travel during the week.

ARRIVING VIA LAND OR WATER

Thailand shares land borders with four countries – Myanmar (Burma), Laos, Cambodia, and Malaysia. Presently there are six border crossings with Myanmar, seven with Laos, six with Cambodia, and seven with Malaysia.

Myanmar is the most difficult country to enter Thailand from, with the authorities regularly closing border points and causing many other problems for independent travelers. It is not recommended to enter Thailand from Myanmar via any of the land routes.

The crossings from Laos are Huay Xai to Chiang Khong; Nam Hong to Nakasing; Tha Na Leng to Nong Khai via the Friendship Bridge; Paksan to Beung Khan; Tha Khaek to Nakhon Phanom; Savannakhet to Mukdahan; and Vang Tao to Chong Mek. The Friendship Bridge is the most popular entry point as it is close to the capital, Vientiane.

Entry from Cambodia is relatively easy. Crossings include Poipet to Aranya Prathet; Cham Yeam to Hat Lek; O'Smach to Chong Jom; Anlong Veng to Chong Sa-Ngam; Phsa Prom Pailin to Ban Pakard; and Daun Lem to Ban Laem.

Entry from Malaysia has in the past been a formality, but with ongoing troubles in the three southernmost, mainly Muslim provinces, Narathiwat, Pattani, and Yala, many Western governments may advise against crossing the border in these areas.

Currently there are two crossings in Satun Province which are perfectly safe: Wang Prajan next to the Thale Ban National Park and Kuala Perlis to Satun town. The Butterworth to Bangkok express train uses the Padang Besar to Sadao crossing and this is also a safe point for crossing.

Bus from Don Muang Airport to Bangkok center

DIRECTORY

AIRLINES

Bangkok Airways
Tel 1771.
www.bangkok.air.com

British Airways
Tel 0-2627-1701.
Tel (0844) 493 0787 (UK).
www.britishairways.com

Delta
Tel 0-2660-6900.
Tel (800) 221 1212 (US).
www.delta.com

Nok Air
Tel 1318.
www.nokair.com

Qantas
Tel 0-2236-2800.
Tel (0845) 774 7767 (UK).
www.qantas.com.au

SGA Airlines
Tel 0-2641-4190.
www.sga.co.th

Singapore Airlines
Tel 0-2353-6000.
Tel (800) 742-3333 (US).
www.singaporeair.com

Solar Air
Tel 0-2535-2455.
www.solarair.co.th

Thai Air Asia
Tel 0-2515-9999.
www.airasia.com

Thai Airways
Tel 0-2356-1111.
Tel (800) 426-5204 (US).
www.thaiair.com

United Airlines
Tel 0-2353-3939.
Tel (800) 538-2929 (US).

Entrance to the Friendship Bridge, the border crossing to Thailand from Laos

Organized Tours

Hundreds of tour companies are based in Bangkok, Chiang Mai, and major resorts such as Phuket, and most hotels throughout the country offer tours of one sort or another. Typical excursions available range from one-day city tours covering the main sights to more comprehensive itineraries taking in several towns and locations over several days. Costs are naturally higher than taking public transit, but in some cases – for instance many sights in the Greater Bangkok region – much time and effort simply in getting to the destination may be saved. The drawback of most organized tours is, of course, that there is rarely time to linger.

as are jeeps for gaining access to remote areas. Most vehicles are well maintained and safe.

Boat tours are popular in many resorts, though the majority of operators follow the same routes. Day trips to islands, including opportunities for water sports, are common. Transfers to and from hotels are often part of the deal. Trips to remote islands, usually offering diving facilities on board (see p462), can span several days, and accommodation may be provided on the boat itself.

BOOKING A TOUR

It should be possible to book a tour of Thailand from your home country that will include all travel and accommodations. Such all-inclusive tours typically last between one and two weeks and include a few nights in Bangkok followed by excursions to Chiang Mai and other Northern locations, or to a beach resort. Other packages are more specialized, concentrating, say, on trekking in the North (see p464), and may vary from a few days to several weeks in duration. Based in Bangkok, **Diethelm Travel** and **Thai Overlander Travel & Tour** are major operators.

Most regional hotels and many guesthouses offer tours of the surrounding area, or are in close contact with local tour companies. The local TAT office will also be able to recommend reputable tour companies. Day trips to the most popular sights can usually be booked just one day in advance. Tours to

more distant sights should include arrangements for accommodations, and usually have at least one departure day each week. In most cases, the tour company will pick you up direct from your hotel or guesthouse.

TOUR BUSES AND BOATS

Many tour companies use luxury, or "VIP," coaches, with reclining seats, on-board refreshments, air-conditioning, and a toilet. Air-conditioned minibuses are also common,

GUIDED TOURS

Bilingual guides accompany many tours, especially to popular cultural sights such as Ayutthaya. In Northern Thailand a knowledgeable guide is essential for safety reasons when trekking through the jungle and visiting hill-tribe villages. The quality of guides varies considerably: a listing of reputable ones is published by the Professional Guide Association and available from TAT (see p475).

Elephant trekking, a popular tour option in Northern Thailand

DIRECTORY

MAJOR TOUR COMPANIES

Arlymear Travel
6th Floor, CCT Building,
109 Surawong Rd,
Bangkok. *Tel 0-2236-9317*. www.arlymear.com

Diethelm Travel
12th Fl.Kian
Gwan Building II,
140 Wireless Rd, Bangkok.
Tel 0-2660-7000.
www.diethelmtravel.com

NS Travel & Tours
133/48 Ratchaprarop 12,
Makkasan Ratchathewee,
Bangkok.
Tel 0-2640-1440.
www.nstravel.com

P&O Regale Travel
191/1-2 Soi
Suksaviddhaya,
North Sathorn Rd,
Bangkok.
Tel 0-2635-2450.
www.regaleintl.com

STA Travel
14th Floor,
Wall Street Tower Building,
33/70 Surawong Rd,
Bangkok.
Tel 0-2236-0262 ext 211.
www.statravel.co.th

Thai Orchid Service
PO Box 54, Talat Kamtieng
Post Office, Chiang Mai.
Tel 0-5322-2945.
www.thaiorchidservice.
com

Thai Overlander Travel & Tour
407 Sukhumvit Rd,
Bangkok.
Tel 0-2258 4778/80.

World Travel Service Ltd
1053 Charoen Krung Rd,
Bangkok.
Tel 0-2233-5900.
www.wts-thailand.com

Traveling Around by Train, Bus, and Boat

Thailand has an efficient railroad system known as the SRT (State Railway of Thailand), with four major lines connecting Bangkok with the North, Northeast, East, and South. Though trains are comfortable and safe, trip times are similar, sometimes even longer, than by bus, and the number of towns on the network is limited. Phuket and Chiang Rai, for instance, do not have train stations. By contrast, comfortable, well maintained, long-distance buses connect all major cities to Bangkok, and provincial buses serve all smaller towns as well as many villages. The main islands are accessible via regular scheduled ferry services.

RAILROAD NETWORK

The main station in Bangkok is **Hua Lampong**, which serves all four major lines. The first line runs to **Chiang Mai** via the Central Plains. A second, which later divides in two, runs to Nong Khai and Ubon Ratchathani in Northeast Thailand. A third connects Bangkok to the Eastern Seaboard and Cambodia, and a fourth runs down the peninsula to Malaysia. **Thon Buri Station** in Bangkok Noi is the principal departure point for trains to Kanchanaburi and the Khwae River Bridge.

TRAINS

Train services in Thailand are labeled Special Express (the fastest), Express, Rapid (slower than Express), and Ordinary. Travel times, even on Express trains, can be longer than by road. The trip from Bangkok to Chiang Mai, for instance, takes between 11 and 13 hours.

First-class coaches (available on Express and Special Express trains) consist of individual cabins with air-conditioning. Second-class coaches have reclining seats and a choice of fans or air-conditioning. Sleepers in this class have individual seats that are converted into curtained-off beds at night. Toilets (there should be at least one Western toilet) and washing facilities are at the end of coaches. Most tourists find that second class is comfortable enough for long distances and far more relaxing than a bus journey.

Third-class coaches have wooden benches, each seating two or three passengers: these coaches are cheap but are not recommended for long distances. Seats cannot be booked in advance.

Most trains are clean and well maintained. Uniformed vendors stroll up and down the aisles with refreshments, and buffet cars are attached to trains on long-distance routes.

TRAIN TICKETS AND FARES

A train timetable in English is available from Hua Lampong Station in Bangkok. Be aware that trains at peak periods (weekends and holidays) can be sold out days in advance. Hua Lampong has an advance booking office with English-speaking staff. Some travel agents will also book tickets.

Fares depend on the speed of the train and the class of the carriage. A second-class ticket between Bangkok and Chiang Mai is about 431 *baht*. Shorter trips, such as from Bangkok to Ayutthaya, cost anything between 15–120 *baht*. Tourists can also buy 20-day rail passes which cost 1,500–3,000 *baht*. Information about these is available from Hua Lampong Station.

LONG-DISTANCE BUSES

Long-distance buses run from the **Eastern (Ekamai)**, **Northern (Morchit)**, and **Southern (Pin Klao)** bus terminals in Bangkok. Most provincial capitals can be reached direct from Bangkok. Large cities such as **Chiang Mai**, Phitsanulok, Khorat, and **Surat Thani** also act as transit hubs, with both long-distance and local connections. Buses can be faster than trains: Bangkok to Chiang Mai takes about ten hours. Vehicles are air-conditioned, with a toilet, reclining seats, and plenty of leg room. "VIP" buses have the best facilities, including free refreshments served by a stewardess. Overnight services can get rather chilly – blankets should be provided.

BUS TICKETS AND FARES

Fares for long-distance bus trips are similar in price to second-class train tickets. "VIP" buses are at the top of the price range. Book well in advance through a travel agent or at the bus station if traveling on the weekend or during a public holiday. Otherwise, just turn up at the coach station at least half an hour before departure. Tickets are always bought as one-way.

Fountain in front of Hua Lampong Station, Bangkok

EASTERN & ORIENTAL EXPRESS

The world-renowned Eastern & Oriental Express operates between Bangkok and Singapore. The journey takes three days and two nights, including stops at Butterworth (Penang) and Kuala Lumpur in Malaysia. The 22 carriages are bedecked with fabrics and fittings evocative of 1930s rail travel. Double and single cabins come in private and presidential classes, and there are two restaurants, a saloon car, a bar, and an observation deck. Such luxuries are, of course, reflected in the price.

Dining car on the Eastern & Oriental Express

PROVINCIAL BUSES

The government bus company is called *Bor Kor Sor* (BKS). Its buses are frequent, relatively reliable, and the cheapest form of transportation in Thailand. Booking is rarely necessary. On many buses simply pay the driver or conductor. Almost every town will have a terminal. The non air-conditioned *(rot thamadaa)* buses are the cheapest and slowest, and they stop almost everywhere along the way. Air-conditioned *(rot aer)* local buses do not necessarily provide blankets, so take a jacket or sweater, especially when traveling at night.

Traveling on provincial buses is a good way to meet local people and reach many villages and sights. Beware, though, that refreshment and toilet stops may be infrequent, buses may be in a poor state of repair, and the road skills of drivers will vary. Local services are nearly always slow and crowded. Back seats are reserved for monks, so be prepared to move or stand. Women should avoid sitting next to monks *(see p479)*.

BOATS TO THE ISLANDS

Scheduled ferries are always erratic, since their service is dependent on the weather conditions. Regular services are available to Ko Samui, Ko Pha Ngan, and Ko Tao from Chumphon and Surat Thani. Ko Phi Phi is served by ferries from Phuket and Krabi. A regular daily service ferries cars and passengers between Laem Ngop and Ko Chang. Smaller islands have less regular services – sometimes just a makeshift ferry run by local fishermen. Travel agents will be able to give you rough timetables, but these will vary. Many services stop in the rainy season. Some companies offer deals on train and boat tickets combining Bangkok and the islands of Ko Samui, Ko Pha Ngan, and Ko Tao. Reliable operators include **Lomprayah**, **Seatran** and **Songserm**.

Small island ferry service

DIRECTORY

TRAIN INFORMATION

Chiang Mai Station
Charoen Muang Rd, Chiang Mai. **Tel** 0-5324-7462 or 0-5324-4795.

Eastern & Oriental Express
Tel (020) 7921 4010 (UK). **Tel** (800) 524-2420 or (843) 937-9068 (US). **Tel** 0-2255-9150 (Bangkok). **Tel** (65) 392 3500 (Singapore). **www**.orient-express.com

Hua Lampong Station, Bangkok
Rama IV, Bangkok. **Tel** 1690. **www**.railway.co.th/English Advance booking office open 7am–4pm daily.

Surat Thani Station
14 km (9 miles) west of Surat Thani in Kha Tham town. **Tel** 0-7731-1963 or 0-7731-1213.

Thon Buri/Bangkok Noi Station
Arun Amarin Rd, Bangkok Noi. **Tel** 0-2411-3102.

BUS TERMINALS

Chiang Mai
Chiang Mai Arcade, Kaew Nawarat Rd, Chiang Mai. **Tel** 0-5324-2664.

Eastern/Ekamai Bus Terminal, Bangkok
Sukhumvit Rd, Bangkok. **Tel** 0-2391-8097 (Ekamai).

Northern and Northeastern/Morchit Bus Terminal, Bangkok
Kampheng Phet Rd, Morchit, Bangkok. **Tel** 0-2936-3388.

Southern/Pin Klao Bus Terminal, Bangkok
Boromratchonnee Rd, Phra Pin Klao, Bangkok. **Tel** 0-2793-8111 (dial 2 for operator).

Surat Thani
Talat Kaset Bus Terminal, Tha Thong Rd, Surat Thani. **Tel** 0-7720-0032.

FERRY INFORMATION

Lomprayah
Ko Samui Office. **Tel** 0-7742-7765/6. **www**.lomprayah.com

Seatran Discovery Ferry
Bangkok Office. **Tel** 0-2240-2582. Ko Samui Office. **Tel** 0-7724-6086. **www**.seatrandiscovery.

Songserm Express Boat
Khao San Road Office, Bangkok. **Tel** 0-2280-8076. Chumphon Office. **Tel** 0-7750-6205. **www**.songserm-expressboat.com

Renting a Car, Moped, or Bicycle

Kilometer marker

Driving in Thailand is not for the faint-hearted. Hazards come in the form of pot-holed roads, confusing intersections, poorly maintained vehicles, and dangerous driving. For many visitors wanting to explore away from the usual tour routes, hiring a car with a driver who is used to the roads is by far the best option. International car rental firms operate in Bangkok and provincial capitals. The standard of local rental companies varies enormously. In the resorts, mopeds and jeeps are popular with tourists.

Sign for a local car rental company: check if insurance is included

RENTING A CAR

A valid international driver's license is a necessity for most visitors, while those from ASEAN countries (Association of Southeast Asian Nations) need only have a license from their home countries. International rental agencies offer safe cars and the most extensive insurance and backup services. **Avis**, **Budget**, and **Hertz** have desks at some airports and in major cities. Charges range from about 1,800 *baht* for a day to 35,000 *baht* for a month.

With other car rental companies, you should check the small print on the contract for liabilities. Insurance may not be included. Obtain a copy of the vehicle registration and carry it around with you. You should also have with you your passport and driving license, or at the very least good copies of these.

HIRING A CHAUFFEUR-DRIVEN CAR

Hiring an experienced driver with a car is gaining popularity in Thailand. The cost can be surprisingly low – often less than 50 percent extra on top of the normal price of car rental. Some drivers are knowledgeable about sights and will suggest interesting itineraries. Most car rental firms can arrange drivers. **Siam Express** offers packages including a chauffeur, car, and accommodation in a wide range of hotels.

RENTING A MOPED

Mopeds and motorcycles are widely available for rent in the resorts, provincial capitals, and other large towns. If you have never driven a motorbike before it's best to rent one of the small automatic gear 80cc bikes. Driver's licenses are rarely requested, and few firms bother with insurance. Costs are low: 200–400 *baht* is average for a day's rental. Safety precautions are essential. Check tires, oil, and brakes before you set out. Wear a helmet (compulsory in Thailand) and proper shoes. Long sleeves and trousers will minimize cuts and grazes in a minor accident. Take care on dirt roads and avoid driving alone in rural areas.

Mopeds and motorcycles for rent

GASOLINE AND SERVICING

Gas stations in Thailand are well manned and are located on main roads in towns and along highways. They are modern and most provide unleaded gas. Attendants will fill your tank, wash your windows, and pump up your tires. Some garages have a resident mechanic, or will at least be able to recommend one. Most of them have a small general shop, and all have Asian toilet facilities. Many garages open 24 hours, while others close at 8pm.

Logo of PTT, a gasoline company with stations throughout Thailand

PARKING

Multistory parking lots in Bangkok are generally attached to major hotels and department stores. Parking is usually free for hotel guests, and for visitors for up to two or three hours. A ticket is issued on entry and should be stamped by a cashier; pay on the way out. Apart from these arrangements, parking can be difficult in Bangkok.

Throughout Thailand, pavements painted with red and white stripes indicate a no-parking zone. In provincial cities, many hotels and large guesthouses provide free parking facilities for guests. In quieter towns you can generally park anywhere that is not obstructive.

ROADS

Multilane national highways exist mostly in and around Bangkok. A toll is charged to travel on some of these expressways, including the one to Bangkok airport. The fee is indicated above the booth – the exact change is required at manually operated booths. Toll fees vary between 15 and 45 *baht* for ordinary vehicles. The expressways are

Traffic policeman waving vehicles through at a Bangkok intersection

less congested than other Bangkok roads, but they are still prone to traffic jams. Many roads in Bangkok are one-way, though a lane may be reserved for buses traveling in the opposite direction.

National highways (in some places also known as routes), such as Highway 1 through the Central Plains, are fast but can be congested in places. Provincial highways are paved and vary in quality. Smaller roads linking villages are sometimes no more than dirt tracks. Main roads in towns are called *thanons*; numbered lanes leading off these are called *sois* and *trawks*. In the rainy season, all roads can become flooded.

Destinations are often given in Roman as well as Thai script. Arabic numerals are always used for distances, and kilometer markers are placed along all main roads.

RULES OF THE ROAD

Driving is on the left. The speed limit is 60 kph (35 mph) within city limits, unless signed otherwise, and 80 kph (50 mph) on open roads. On expressways and major highways the speed limit is 110 kph (70 mph). The standard international road rules apply, but are of little interest to Thais. The only consistent rule of thumb is "size wins."

The eccentric use of indicators and headlights can be unnerving. A left signal can

indicate to another driver that it is alright to pass, while a right signal can indicate hazardous oncoming traffic, and a flash of the headlights means: "I'm coming through."

Horns are not used enough as Thais tend to see them as impolite. When they are used it is often as a warning of presence rather than obvious danger. Drivers think nothing of straddling lanes and passing on curves and up hill. Yield to larger vehicles at unmarked intersections. It is legal to turn left at red lights if there is a blue sign with a white left arrow, or occasionally if you are in the left lane. On minor roads, beware of animals.

Traffic fines are most commonly imposed for illegal turns. If you get a ticket and your license is taken, go to the local police station, the address of which will be on the ticket, and pay the fine. Drive slowly through army checkpoints in border areas, and be prepared to stop.

ROAD MAPS

Tourist maps are widely available but cover major roads only. Some provincial, foldout maps produced by the Prannok Witthaya Map Center are excellent, showing all roads and reliefs. The *Thailand Highways Map* by the Auto Guide Company and the *Thailand Highway Map* by the Roads Association are the best atlases, and are written in Thai and Roman scripts.

Typical road scene with several lanes of one-way traffic

RENTING A BICYCLE

In the cool season, cycling in quiet areas is a pleasant way to get around. Guesthouses and small agencies often have

bicycles for rent for 20–100 *baht* a day, though the bikes may be rickety. New mountain bikes may be available, but, perhaps surprisingly, costs may exceed those of mopeds. Taking plenty of water is essential and, of course, great care is always necessary on the roads.

Local Transportation

Transportation in the provinces is certainly less frenetic than in Bangkok: bicycle rickshas *(samlors)* and colorful *tuk-tuks* run alongside services such as *songthaews,* and bargaining for the fare on *samlors* is part of the Thai experience. Do not climb on before agreeing a price, or you may be taken for a ride in more ways than one. The one city outside of Bangkok to run its own bus service is Chiang Mai and this has only been in operation a few years, so the most convenient form of transportation in most towns and resorts is the ubiquitous *songthaew.*

Bangkok tuk-tuk

A *songthaew* – uncomfortable, but cheaper and safer than a *tuk-tuk*

TAXIS

Meter taxis operate in Bangkok, Chiang Mai, and Hat Yai, and are distinguishable by the "Taxi-Meter" sign on the roof. Drivers tend to know only the names and locations of the major hotels and sights. In nonmeter taxis, mainly found in Ko Samui and Phuket, you need to bargain for the fare before getting in.

Motorcycle taxis operate in some towns. Drivers tend to congregate near markets and long *sois* (streets) and can be identified by their colorful numbered vests. Prices are negotiated. Although motorcycle taxis are sometimes the quickest way to get between two points think twice about using them as they are not the safest form of transportation. They are also not practical if you are hauling a suitcase.

Shared taxis are not too common except in the Deep South where it's possible to share a taxi between Hat Yai and the Malaysian border and beyond. Drivers wait for cars to fill up, usually with a maximum of six people, before departing.

SONGTHAEWS

Songthaews (literally translated as "two rows") are vans with two rows of seats in the back. They are more common than city buses outside Bangkok and run popular routes for set fares, typically between 20 and 40 *baht.* Drivers may wait until they are at least half full before starting out. Routes are sometimes written in English on the sides of the vans. On the whole they don't usually have a terminus, but do tend to cluster around large markets and shopping centers. *Songthaews* can be hailed anywhere along a route and will stop just about anywhere. To let the driver know you need to get off, press one of the buzzers located along the inner side of the roof. *Songthaews* can be rented like taxis, but are far less comfortable.

TAXI-METER

Roof sign of a metered taxi

SAMLORS AND TUK-TUKS

Samlors are three-wheeled vehicles that can transport one or two people up to a few kilometers. Motorized samlors are known as tuk-tuks – their two-stroke engines, introduced by the Japanese during World War II, are notoriously noisy. In heavy traffic or during the rainy season, *tuk-tuks* can be uncomfortable and unstable, but are always popular with tourists. Nonmotorized *samlors* are often in the form of bicycle rickshas. You need to negotiate a price before climbing into either type: 30–60 *baht* is reasonable for short hops.

LONG-TAIL BOATS

Thailand is a country of waterways, especially in the central region around Bangkok, and where there's a waterway there's a long-tail boat waiting to take passengers. Other areas of the country, such as Krabi, also play host to a variety of long-tail boats. The greatest drawback of these elegant boats is the extremely noisy diesel engines clamped to the back. A maximum of twenty passengers is the norm and costs vary depending on whether the boat has been privately hired. Expect to pay around 200 *baht* an hour to rent a boat privately *(see p74).*

Three-wheeled bicycle ricksha, or *samlor*, in a seaside resort

Getting Around Bangkok

Following years of chronic traffic congestion, Bangkok launched the mass-transit BTS Skytrain in 1999 and the underground MRT in 2004. These fast, clean, relatively cheap services, in conjunction with the Chao Phraya Express riverboats, have revolutionized travel in the city. (For a map of the MRT and Skytrain network, see the back endpaper.) Unfortunately, these services don't cover the whole city and a huge fleet of sometimes dirty, noisy buses fill in the gaps. Older, smoke-belching buses have mostly been replaced over the last few years by new, cleaner ones, but there is a long way to go before Bangkok's streets are pollution free.

Bangkok's mass-transit BTS Skytrain

BTS SKYTRAIN

Downtown, the efficient, fast **BTS Skytrain** has two lines: the Sukhumvit route from Morchit Station in the north to Onnut Station in the east, and the Silom route from the National Stadium to Wongwian Yai in Thonburi, with an interchange between the two routes at the Siam Center. The Sukhumvit line is being extended to Baering in the Bang Na District of eastern Bangkok.

The airport rail link has an express service from the Phaya Thai and Makkasan stations. The City line makes eight stops along the same route, serving areas east of downtown.

Trains run daily every 3 to 6 minutes from 6:30am to midnight. Fares are calculated by distance and magnetic fare cards are sold at all stations in values from 15 to 40 baht. Several passes are available, but of most interest to the visitor is the One-Day Pass costing 120 baht and offering limitless use of the Skytrain.

MRT

The **MRT** (Mass Rapid Transit) underground runs 20 km (12 miles) from Hua Lampong Station to Bang Sue in the north of Bangkok. There are at present 18 stations with more planned for the future. Silom and Sukhumvit stations connect with the BTS Skytrain network. Trains run daily every 4 to 10 minutes from 6am to midnight. Fares range from 16 to 41 baht with black tokens issued for a single journey. Unlimited 1-, 3-, and 30-day passes cost 120, 230, and 1,200 baht respectively.

WATERWAYS

Chao Phraya Express boats serve popular piers on the Chao Phraya River. The company runs different lines recognizable by the colour of flag each is flying. Tickets are purchased on board and range from 10 to 29 baht depending on the flag. The orange flag boats are the most useful as they stop at all piers

Chao Phraya Express

and are also the most frequent (they have a set fare of 14 baht). Ferries also link east and west banks.

BUSES

The *Tourist Map Bangkok City* and *Tour 'n' Guide Map Bangkok* show bus routes. Blue air-conditioned buses ("AC" in the transport details for each Bangkok sight), and white metrobuses (indicated by "M") are comfortable and cover the popular routes. Ordinary (non air-conditioned) buses are cheap, cover all of Bangkok, and run all night.

TAXIS

Metered taxis operate all over Bangkok. The minimum fare is 35 baht for the first kilometer and then 5 baht per kilometer for the second to the 12th kilometer. Some taxi drivers will attempt not to use the meter and try to charge a fixed fare, it is always best to insist on the meter.

ON FOOT

Bangkok is not much of a place for exploring on foot. Walking areas that might be considered include the Ratan-akosin District around the Grand Palace and Wat Pho, and parts of Chinatown between Sampeng Lane and Yaowarat Road. Other than this it's best to take local transport between sights.

DIRECTORY

TRANSPORTATION IN BANGKOK

Airport Rail Link
Tel 1690.
www.bangkokairporttrain.com

BTS Skytrain
1000 Phahonyothin Rd.
Tel 0-2617-6000 (Hotline).
www.bts.co.th

Chao Phraya Express
Tel 0-2623-6143.
www.chaophrayaboat.co.th

MRT
189 Rama IX Rd.
Tel 0-2354-2000.

General Index

Page numbers in **bold** refer to main entries

A

Abhisek Dusit Throne Hall (Bangkok) 103, 105
Acclimatization 482
Accommodation see Hotels
Achutarat, King of Chiang Saen 243
Adaptors 477
Admission prices 475
AIDS 116, 483
Air sports **467**, 469
Air travel 488–90
advance booking 474
airports **488–9**
Air-conditioned buses see Buses
Airport rail link 489, 497
Akha tribespeople **206–7**, 239
arts and crafts 208
Mae Salong 243
Mae Saruai 252
Saam Yekh Akha 246
Wiang Pa Pao 252
Alcohol, customs allowances 475
Aleenta Resort & Spa Phang Nga 470, 471
Alliance Française (Bangkok) 459, 461
Amanpuri Resort (Phuket) 396, **420**
Amaravadee Antiques (Chiang Mai) 454, 455
Amarin Plaza (Bangkok) 138, 139
Ambulances 480, 481
Amebic dysentery 483
American Express 484
Amulets 41, **79**, 454
Ananda Mahidol (Rama VIII), King 68, 85
Ananta Samakhom Throne Hall (Bangkok) 91, 105, 107
Anantara Golden Triangle Resort & Spa 396, **408**, 464, 468
Anantara Ko Samui **417**, 470, 471
Anantara Resort & Spa Hua Hin **416**, 470, 471
Ancient City (Bangkok) **137**
Ancient Cloth and Silk Museum (Bangkok) 102
Andaman Sea
coral reefs 348
dugongs 381
sea gypsies 363

Andaman sea (cont.)
Trang's Andaman islands **380**
Upper Andaman Coast **353–73**
Ang Thong **172**
Angkhan Kalyanaphong 287
Angkor Wat 264, 265
Anglican Christ Church (Bangkok) 115
Angling 463, 468
Angthong National Marine Park 13, 306, **340–41**
map 340
Animal-borne diseases 483
Animals see Wildlife
Animism 207
Antiques
customs information 475
shops 139, 454, 455
Anuwong, Prince of Vientiane 275
Ao Bang Bao 322
Ao Cho 318
Ao Kui 318
Ao Nang **370**
Ao Nuan 318
Ao Phai 318
Ao Phrao 319
Ao Wong Duan 318
Apsonsi 81
Arabs 346
Aranyik Ruins (Kamphaeng Phet) 193
Architecture
Bangkok's modern architecture 119
Chaiya's role 332
religious architecture **34–5**
Srivijayan architecture 347
traditional Thai houses **36–7**
Area codes 487
Arlymear Travel (Bangkok) 491
Army Stadium (Bangkok) 460, 461
Art 25
arts and crafts shops 139, 452, 455
gestures of the Buddha 173
Sukhothai art 160–61
see also Museums and galleries
Art of Thai food **38–9**
Art Republic (Bangkok) 459, 461
Aruna 126
Asanha Bucha 49
ASEAN (Association of Southeast Asian Nations) 21, 69
map 68
ASEAN Barred Ground Dove Fair (Yala) 48, 388
Asia Books (Bangkok) 139, 451, 455
Asian Institute of Gemological Sciences (Bangkok) 454, 455
Association of Physically Handicapped People (Nonthaburi) 476, 477

Association of Southeast Asian Nations see ASEAN
Assumption Cathedral (Bangkok) 113, **114**
Assumption College (Bangkok) 114
Astral Gemstone Talismans (Bangkok) 454, 455
Athitayarai, King of Haripunchai 229
Automatic Teller Machines (ATMs) 484
Avis (car hire) 494, 495
Ayodhya 40
see also Ayutthaya
Ayutthaya 10, 159, **176–81**
foreigners in 162–3
hotels 402
maps 53, 162–3, 177
in the Ramakien 40
religious architecture 35
restaurants 432–3
Wat Phra Si Sanphet 35, **178–9**
see also Ayutthaya Kingdom
Ayutthaya Historical Study Center 178
Ayutthaya Kingdom 53, **60–61**
Lop Buri 174
Mekong River Valley 283
Ubon Ratchathani 302

B

Bacillary dysentery 483
Bai semas (boundary stones) 160
Baiyoke Tower I (Bangkok) 119
Baiyoke Tower II (Bangkok) 119
"Ballad of Phu Kradung" 287
Ballooning 467, 469
Bamboo 453, 455
Bamrung Muang Road (Bangkok) **90**
Ban Bat (Bangkok) 90
Ban Chiang 12, **54–5, 272**, 299
hotels 409
pottery 54–5
Ban Chiang National Museum 55, **272**
Ban Kao 54, 55, 170
Ban Ko Noi, Sukhothai-era kilns 161
Ban Kok see Thon Buri
Ban Muang, King 58
Ban Na Di 55
Ban Phe 317
Ban Phitsanulok (Bangkok) 106
Ban Prathup Chai (Phrae) 259
Ban Sao Nak (Lampang) 236, 237
Ban Ta Klang **279**
Ban Winai 290
Ban Yipun (Ayutthaya) 181
Bang Niew Temple (Phuket town) 360
Bang Pa-in **181**
Bang Phli, festivals 47, 50
Bang Phra Reservoir 316

Bang Sai Folk Arts and Crafts Center
452, 455
Bangkok 10, **70–155**
  airport *see* Don Muang Airport;
  Suvarnabhumi International Airport
  bus terminals 493
    BTS Skytrain 497
  car rental 495
  Chinatown 95–9
  Don Muang Airport 490
  Downtown Bangkok 111–21
  Dusit 101–7
  early Chakri dynasty 65
  entertainment 142–3
  Farther Afield 131–7
  festivals 46, 48–51
  foundation of 53
  hospitals 481
  hotels 398–402
  local transportation 496–7
  map: Bangkok City Center *see* Back
  Endpaper
  map: Bangkok and Environs 16
  map: Street Finder 144–55
  markets 140–41
  Mass Rapid Transit 497
  modern architecture 119
  Old City 77–93
  railroad stations 492, 493
  restaurants 428–32
  river view of 74–5
  shopping 138–9
  Suvarnabhumi International Airport
  489
  taxis 497
  Thon Buri 123–9
  tourist police 480–81
  Western writers in 115
Bangkok Airways 490
Aruna 126
Bangkok Art and Culture Center
118
"Bangkok belly" 482
Bangkok Bicentennial (1982) 68
Bangkok Planetarium 136
Bangkok Playhouse/Art Corner 459,
461
Banglamphu Market (Bangkok) 140
Bangpra Golf Course (Pattaya) 308
Bangrak 337
Bangrak Market (Bangkok) 115, 141
Bank of America (Bangkok) 484
Bank of Ayudhya (Bangkok) 484
Bank notes 485
Banking **484–5**
Banthat Mountains 381, 386
Banyan Tree Spa Phuket 470, 471
Banyan Valley cave 54

Bargaining 479
  in hotels 395
  in shops 138, 450
Barges *see* Royal barges
Barot, Prince 295
Bars 143, 459, 461
Bayinnaung, King of Burma 180
BCG 482
Beaches
  Cha-am 330–31
  Gulf of Thailand 308–9
  Hua Hin 331
  Ko Chang 322
  Ko Pha Ngan 339
  Ko Samui 336–8
  Pattaya 317
  Phuket 358, 362
  Rayong 317
  Upper Andaman Coast 354
Benjasiri Park (Bangkok) 136
Betel-chewing 209
Betong **389**
Bhirasi, Silpa 87, 128
Bhumibol Adulyadej (Rama IX), King
24, 478
  becomes king 68
  Chitrlada Palace (Bangkok) 106
  Coronation Day 48
  ends military coup (1992) 69
  Grand Palace (Bangkok) 85
  His Majesty the King's Birthday 51
  Khao Kho 201
  as a monk **30**, 86
  and the opium trade **233**
  Phra That Naphamataneedon (Doi
  Inthanon) 230
  royal barges 124
  Trooping of the Colors 46, 107
  Wat Bowonniwet (Bangkok) 86
Bhumibol Reservoir 232
Bicycles, renting 495
Bilharzia 483
Birds
  Bang Phra Reservoir 316
  Khao Phanom Bencha National
  Park 370
  Khao Sam Roi Yot National Park
  332
  Northern Thailand **210–11**
  Thale Noi Waterfowl Park 383
  tips for bird-watching 211
  see also Wildlife
Bird's-nest soup 341
Bites
  animal 483
  snake 482
Blood transfusions 483
Bo Be Market (Bangkok) 140

Bo Rai **321**
Bo Sang 212, **228**
  crafts 208
  festivals 46, 51
Boat trips **465,** 469
Boats
  Chao Phraya Express Boats 465,
  469, 496–7
  island ferries 493
  long-tail 496
  korlae fishing boats 345, 388
  organized tours 491
  riverboats on the Chao Phraya
  River 74, 496
  Royal Barge Museum (Bangkok)
  124-5
  sailing **463,** 468
  sea canoeing **463,** 468
  traditional boat races in Nan 50, 255
  whitewater rafting **463,** 468
Bodhi trees 32, 173
Body language 478
Boisselier, Jean 265
Bond, James 125, 366, 367
Bookazine (Bangkok) 139, 451, 455
Booking
  airline tickets 474
  entertainment tickets 142, 458
  hotels 395
Bookstores 139, 451, 455
Bophut 337
Bor Kor Sor (BKS) 493
Borisoothi Antiques (Chiang Mai)
454, 455
Borommakot, King
  Wat Phu Khao Thong (Ayutthaya)
  180
  Wat Phu Phra Men (Ayutthaya) 180
Borommaracha I, King 176
Borommaracha II, King 60
  Wat Maheyong (Ayutthaya) 181
  Wat Ratchaburana (Ayutthaya) 176
Borommaracha III, King 179
Borommaracha IV, King 178
Borommatrailokanat, King 60
  Wang Luang (Ayutthaya) 176
  Wat Chulamani 201
  Wat Phra Ram (Ayutthaya) 177
  Wat Phra Si Rattana Mahathat
  (Phitsanulok) 201
  Wat Phra Si Sanphet (Ayutthaya)
  178, 179
Boromphiman Mansion 85
Bots 33
Bovorn Bazaar (Nakhon Si
Thammarat) 379
Bowring, Sir John 64, 85
Bowring Treaty (1855) 64, 65

Boxing, Thai *see Muay thai*
Bridge over the Khwae Yai River 10, 171
British Airways 488, 490
Bronze Age **54–5**
  Phayao 252
BTS Skytrain 497
Buddha
  "Buddha's shadow" 172
  Emerald Buddha 83
  Enlightenment 31, 173
  festivals 46, 49, 50
  Footprints of the Buddha 172
  gestures of **173**
  Golden Buddha 98
  Ho Phra Buddha Sing Shrine 379
  Luang Pho Phra Sai Buddha 292
  Nak Buddha 83
  Phitsanulok Buddha 160-61
  Phra Buddha Chinarat 201
  relics of 33, 83, 104, 243, 295, 297
  "Walking" Buddha 59, 160
  Wat Indrawihan (Bangkok) 104
  see also Emerald Buddha
Buddha Foundry (Phitsanulok) 201
Buddhadhasa Bhikkhu 333
Buddhaisawan Chapel
  (Bangkok) 74, 88
Buddhism 21, **30–31**
  and the arts 25
  cultural study courses 467, **467,**
  469, 476
  elephants in 253
  festivals 49
  King Bhumibol Adulyadej (Rama
  IX) as a monk 30, 86
  Mahayana Buddhism 30
  meditation 31, 467, 469
  monkhood 24, 30
  naga figures 228
  Phi Ta Khon Festival 47, 289
  popular Buddhist rituals 129
  Sri Lankan influence 198
  staying in monasteries 393
  Thammayut sect 303
  Theravada Buddhism **30–31**
  wats 32–3
Buddhist Rains Retreat 49, 50
Budget (car hire) 494, 495
Bun Bang Fai (Rocket Festival)
  (Yasothon) 47, 48
Bung Phlan Chai 269
Bungee jumping **466,** 469
Buriram, restaurants 439
Burma *see* Myanmar
Burma-Siam Railroad 168
  bridge over the Khwae Yai River
  10, **171**

Burma-Siam Railroad (cont.)
  Burma-Siam Railroad Memorial
  Trail 169
  Kanchanaburi 170
Burmese Kingdom 62–3
Burney Treaty (1826) 65
Buses
  local transport 497
  long-distance buses 492
  organized tours 491
  provincial buses 493
Business facilities *see*
  Communications
Butterflies 232
Butterfly Garden and Insect World,
  Phuket 359, 361

C

Cabbages and Condoms (Bangkok)
  452, 455
Calendar 476–7
Calypso Cabaret (Bangkok) 142, 143,
  461
Cambodia
  Embassy 475
  Prasat Khao Phra Wihan 302
  visas 475
Camping 394
Canadian Embassy 475
Candle Festival (Ubon Ratchathani)
  47, 49
Canoeing **463,** 468
Carmelite Convent (Bangkok) 115
Cars
  chauffeur-driven cars 494
  customs information 475
  gas and servicing 494
  parking 494
  renting **494–5**
  road signs 494
  rules of the road 495
  see also Tours by car
Cartland, Barbara 115
Cathedrals
  Assumption Cathedral (Bangkok)
  113, **114**
  Church of the Immaculate
  Conception (Chanthaburi) 320-21
Cats 275
Cave paintings 55
  Upper Andaman Coast 373
Caves
  Khao Ngu 132
  Khao Wong 319
  Phangnga Bay 364, 367
  Phu Phrabat Historical Park 55, **295**
  Sai Yok National Park 169
  Tam Muang On 229

Caves (cont.)
  Tham Chang Hai 381
  Tham Chiang Dao 220
  Tham Khao Luang 330
  Tham Lot 219
  Tham Luang 246
  Tham Morakhot (Ko Muk) 380
  Tham Pha Tup Forest Reserve 255
  Tham Phraya Nakon 332
  Tham Pla (Chiang Rai province) 246
  Tham Pla (Mae Hong Son
  province) 218
  Tham Pum 246
  Tham Sai 332
  Tham Tup Tao 220
  Tham Wang Badan 169
  Wat Tham Sua (Krabi) 371
Caving **466,** 469
Cemeteries
  Chong Kai Cemetery 170, 171
  Kanchanaburi War Cemetery 170,
  171
  POW Cemetery (Kanchanaburi)
  166
Central Department Store (Bangkok)
  139, 451, 455
Central Pattaya Festival Beach
  Shopping 451, 455
Central Plains 22, **157–201**
  festivals 46
  hotels 402–4
  map 158–9
  North Central Plains 187–201
  restaurants 432–4
  South Central Plains 165–85
  traditional Thai houses 36–7
Central World Plaza (Bangkok) 138,
  139, 451, 455
Ceramics
  Ban Chiang 54–5
  Sangkhalok 59, 160, 161, 200
  shops **453,** 455
  Sukhothai-era kilns 161
  What to Buy in Thailand 457
Cha-am 13, 308, **330–31**
  beach 308
  hotels 415
  restaurants 443
Chaem River Valley 232
Chaiya 332, **333,** 346
Chaiya National Museum 333
Chaiyaphum, hotels 409
Chakri Day 48
Chakri dynasty 40, 53
  Bangkok Bicentennial (1982) 68
  early Chakri dynasty **64–5**
  Grand Palace and Wat Phra Kaeo
  (Bangkok) 80–85

Chakri dynasty (cont.)
  Rank and Portrait Museum
  (Bangkok) 102
Chalieng *see* Si Satchanalai-Chalieng
  Historical Park
Chaloem Rattanakosin National Park
  171
Chaloklam 339
Chamadevi of Lop Buri 56
Chan and In (Siamese twins) 125
Chan Kasem Palace (Ayutthaya) 176
Chanthaburi 12, **320–21**
  gemstones 310–11
  hotels 412
  restaurants 441
Chanthara Phisan Hall (Lop Buri) 167
Chao Fa Mung Muang shrine
  (Mukdahan) 298
Chao Pho Kut Pong (Loei) 289
Chao Phraya Chakri (Rama I), King
  64, 123
  Chakri Day 48
  Chiang Saen 248
  and Chinatown 95
  Giant Swing (Bangkok) 91
  Grand Palace (Bangkok) 84, 85
  Luang Pho Phra Sai Buddha 292
  Phra Buddha Sihing 88
  royal barges 124
  Wat Pho 92
  Wat Phra Kaeo 82, 83
  Wat Rakhang (Bangkok) 125
  Wat Saket (Bangkok) 87
  Wat Suthat (Bangkok) 90
  Wat Suwan Dararam (Ayutthaya) 178
  Wat Suwannaram (Bangkok) 124
Chao Phraya Express Boats 465, 469
  map *see* Back Endpaper
Chao Phraya River 22, 53, 165
  Paknam Incident (1893) 67
  river view of Bangkok 74–5
Chao Sam Phraya National Museum
  (Ayutthaya) 178
Charoen Krung Road (Bangkok) **114–5**
Chatuchak Market **135**
Chauffeur-driven cars 494
Chaumont, Chevalier de 162
Chaweng beach 326, 336, 338
Chedis 33
Cheng Weng, Princess 296
Chiang Dao
  Doi Chiang Dao **220**
  hotels 404
  trekking around 221
Chiang Khan **290**
  hotels 411
  Mekong villages tour 290
  restaurants 440

Chiang Khong **249**
  Golden Triangle driving tour 247
  hotels 407
  restaurants 437
Chiang Mai 11, 204, **224–7**
  airport 489
  bus terminal 493
  car rental 494
  festivals 46, 48, 51
  history 62–3
  hospital 481
  hotels 404-6
  map 17, 227
  restaurants 434-6
  Songkran festivities in the North
  236
  Street-by-Street map 224–5
  tourist police 481
  train station 493
  wats 225
Chiang Mai National Museum 227
Chiang Rai 11, 205, **250–51**
  hotels 407–8
  map 251
  restaurants 437–8
Chiang Rai Handicraft Center 452, 455
Chiang Saen 11, **248–9**
  Golden Triangle driving tour 247
  hotels 408
  restaurants 438
Chiang Saen National Museum 249
Children 476
  in hotels 395
China House (Bangkok) 113
Chinatown (Bangkok) **95–9**
  area map 95
  hotels 398
  restaurants 428
  Street-by-Street map 96–7
Chinese hotels 393
Chinese Mansions (Phuket town) 360
Chinese Nationalist Army *see*
  Kuomintang
Chinese New Year 51
Chinese in Thailand 22, 99
Chitrlada Palace (Bangkok) 80, **106**
Chitrlada Shop (Bangkok) 452, 455
Chiva-Som International Health
  Resort (Hua Hin) 470, 471
Cho fas 33
Choeng Mon 337
Cholera 483
Chom Thong 232
Chompupan 40
Chong Kai Cemetery 170, 171
Chong Kham Lake (Mae Hong Son)
  217
Chong Mek **299**

Christ Church (Bangkok) 476, 477
Christianity 175
  Dusit's Christian Churches
  (Bangkok) 104
  see also Churches
Chui Tui Temple (Phuket town) 361
Chulachakrabongse, Prince 331
Chulalongkorn (Rama V), King 53, **65**
  Bang Pa-in Palace 181
  becomes king 65
  Chanthaburi 321
  Chulalongkorn University
  (Bangkok) 117
  cremation of 66–7
  Dusit 101
  Dusit Park (Bangkok) 102
  Dusit Zoo 105
  festivals 50
  Golden Mount (Bangkok) **87**
  Grand Palace and Wat Phra Kaeo
  (Bangkok) 80, 84, 85
  Hua Lamphong Station (Bangkok)
  98
  Khao Sabap National Park 321
  and kite-flying 79
  Phra Pathom Chedi (Nakhon
  Pathom) 134
  Phuket town 360
  reign of 66–7
  statues of 115
  Summer Palace (Ko Sichang)
  316–17
  Tak Bai 389
  Tansadet waterfall 339
  Vimanmek Mansion (Bangkok)
  104-5
  Wang Luang (Ayutthaya) 176
  Wat Benchamabophit (Bangkok)
  106–7
  Wat Phra Kaeo 82
  Wat Phra Si Rattana Mahathat
  (Phitsanulok) 201
  Wat Rachabophit (Bangkok) 91
Chulalongkorn Day (Bangkok)
  50
Chulalongkorn University (Bangkok)
  117
Chumbhot, Prince and Princess 119
Chumphon **332**
  hotels 415
Chumphon, Prince 332
Churches
  Assumption Cathedral (Bangkok)
  113, 114
  Church of the Immaculate
  Conception (Bangkok) 104
  Church of the Immaculate
  Conception (Chanthaburi) 320–21

Churches (cont.)
  Church of Santa Cruz (Bangkok) 128
  Dusit's Christian Churches (Bangkok) 104
  Holy Redeemer Catholic Church (Bangkok) 476, 477
  International Church (Bangkok) 477
  St. Francis Xavier Church (Bangkok) 104
  St. Joseph's Church (Ayutthaya) 162, 180
Cigarettes
  customs allowances 475
  see also Smoking
CIMB Thai (Bangkok) 484
Cinema 25, 142, 143, 459, 461
Citibank (Bangkok) 484
Climate **48-51**
  coping with the heat 482
  monsoon 26–7
  when to go 474
Climbing see Rock-climbing
Clothes
  coping with the heat 482
  shops 139, 452, 455
  suitable dress 479
  What to Buy in Thailand 457
  what to take 476
  see also Fabrics
Coastal forest 29
Coedès, George 265
Coffee shops 422
Comedy shows 459, 461
Commercial Co. of Siam (Bangkok) 113
Commonwealth War Graves Commission 170
Communicating 479
Communications **486–7**
Communications Authority of Thailand (CAT) 486
Communists
  Chiang Khong 249
  Communist Party of Malaya 389
  Communist Party of Thailand (CPT) 69, 288
  Doi Phu Kha 254
  and Kuomintang 242
  Phu Hin Rong Kla 288
  and the Vietnam War 68
Concerts 459, 461
Confucianism, Leng Noi Yee Temple (Bangkok) 97, 99
Congdon Museum of Anatomy (Bangkok) 125

Conrad, Joseph 115
"Conservatives" 66
Conversion chart 477
Cookery schools **467,** 469
Cool season 50–51
Coral reefs **348–9**
  coral cuts 482
  diving and snorkeling 462
Coronation Day 48
Cotton, shopping for 138, 139
Courier services 487
Coward, Noël 115
CPT see Communist Party of Thailand
Crafts
  crafts centers 451, 455
  Hill Tribe Education Center (Chiang Rai) 251
  Northern Arts and Crafts 208–9
  shops 139, **452,** 455
  SUPPORT Museum (Bangkok) 105
Crawfurd, John 85
Credit cards 485
  safety 480
  in shops 138, 450
Cremation ceremonies 31
Crime 480–81
Crocodile Farm (Bangkok) **137**
Cultural study **467,** 469
Currency 485
Currency exchange 484–5
Curries 427
Customs information 475
Cuts and bites 482
Cycling **466,** 469, 495

D

Dam, Sirindhorn 299
Damnoen Saduak Floating Market 23, 130, **132**
Dan Kwian **275**
Dan Sai
  festivals 12, 47, 49
  Phi Ta Khon Festival 289
Dan Sun Kingdom 55
Dance
  dance-drama see Khon
  Lakhon, Likay traditional dance 142, 143, 458, 461
Danger spots 480
Day spas 471
Day trips 491
Debit cards 485
Deep South 13, **375–89**
  hotels 420–21
  map 376–7
  restaurants 449

Dehydration 482
Delaporte, Louis 265
Delta 490
Democracy Monument (Bangkok) 68, **87,** 107
Dengue fever 483
Department stores **451,** 455
  opening hours 476
Desserts 427
Destination spas 470–71
Deutsche Bank (Bangkok) 484
Devawongse, Prince 66
Dhammakaya Foundation (Thani) 467, 469
DHL 487
Diarrhea 482
Diethelm Travel (Bangkok) 491
Diners Club 484
Diphtheria 482
Disabled travelers 476
  in hotels 395
Discos 459, 461
Diseases
  food- and water-borne 483
  insect-borne 482–3
  people- and animal-borne 483
Diving 309, **462–3,** 468
  Chumphon 332
  Ko Surin and Ko Similan 357
  Ko Tao 341
  scuba diving 349
  Tarutao National Marine Park 386
Doctors 481
Doi Ang Khang 242
Doi Chiang Dao **220**
Doi Inthanon National Park 11, 204, **230–31**
Doi Mae Salong 243
  Golden Triangle driving tour 246
  see also Mae Salong
Doi Phu Kha National Park **254**
Doi Saket **228**
Doi Suthep **222–3**
Doi Suthep-Doi Pui National Park 222
Doi Tung 205, **243**
  Golden Triangle driving tour 247
Doi Tung Royal Villa 243
Don Chedi 172
Don Chedi Memorial Fair 51
Don Muang Airport (Bangkok) 490
Don Tha Phet, prehistoric artifacts 54, 55
Dong Sak Ngan Forest 252
Dong Son 346
Dong Son people 378
Dongrek Mountains 302

Downtown Bangkok **111–21**
    area map 111
    hotels 398–400
    Jim Thompson's House 120–21
    Old Farang Quarter 112–13
    restaurants 428–30
Dragoncastle 477
Drinks **425**
    glossary **427**
    water 482
    see also Food and drink
Driver's licenses 494
Drugs 480
    Doi Tung area 243
    Fang area 242
    Golden Triangle 246
    heroin 480
    history of opium in Thailand 233
    pharmacies 481
Dugongs **381**
Dusit (Bangkok) **101–7**
    area map 101
    Christian Churches **104**
    hotels 400
    restaurants 430
Dusit Park (Bangkok) **102–3**
Dusit Thani Hotel (Bangkok) **399,** 459
Dusit Zoo (Bangkok) **105,** 464
Dutch East India Company 163, 347
Dvaravati Kingdom 53, 56
    architecture 35
Dysentery 483

E

East Asiatic Company (Bangkok) 113
East India Companies 163
Eastern & Orient Express 493
Eastern Asia Flyway 210
Eastern Seaboard 12, **313–23**
    hotels 412–15
    map 314–15
    restaurants 441–3
Eating habits 423
Economy 22–3
Electricity 477
Elephants **253**
    Ban Ta Klang 279
    Elephant Kraal
    (Ayutthaya) 180
    Elephant Nature Park (Mae Taeng Valley) 221
    Elephant Training Center Chiang Dao 220, 464
    Phuket FantaSea 262
    riding **464,** 468
    royal howdahs 208–9
    royal white elephants **106**

Elephants (cont.)
    Samphran Elephant Ground and Zoo 134
    Surin Elephant Roundup 12, 50, 271, **278,** 279
    Thai Elephant Conservation Center 215, 237, 464, 468
    White Elephant Monument (Doi Suthep) 222
Embassies 475
    emergencies 481
Emerald Buddha **83**
    in Chiang Rai 250
    Haw Pha Kaew (Vientiane) 294
    in Lampang 236
    Wat Arun (Bangkok) 126–7
    Wat Phra Kaeo 75, 80, 82
Emergencies 480, 481
Emporium (Bangkok) 138, 139, 451, 455
Encephalitis *see* Japanese encephalitis
Endangered wildlife 219
English East India Company 163
English-language bookstores 139, 451, 455
Enlightenment of the Buddha 31, 173
Entertainment **458–61**
    bars 143, 459, 461
    booking tickets 458
    cinemas 142, 143, 459, 461
    comedy 459, 461
    concerts 459, 461
    discos 459, 461
    exhibitions 459, 461
    folk clubs 459, 461
    information sources 458
    krabi-krabong 460, 461
    modern theater 459, 461
    muay thai 142, 143, 460, 461
    music clubs 459, 461
    nightclubs 143, 459, 461
    puppet shows 142, 143, 458
    rugby 460, 461
    snooker 460, 461
    soccer 460, 461
    takraw 460, 461
    temple fairs and festivals 460
    traditional theater and dance 142, 143, 458, 461
    see also Khon; Lakhon; Likay
Environment 23
Erawan falls 169
Erawan Museum (Bangkok) 131, **137**
Erawan National Park 10, **169**
Erawan Shrine (Bangkok) **118**
Erewan (Bangkok) 138, 139
ethnic groups 22
    see also individual ethnic groups

Etiquette 24, **478–9**
    eating habits 423
Evason Hideaway & The Earth Spa by Six Senses (Pranburi) 470, 471
Evason Phuket Resort & Six Senses Spa 470, 471
Exchange rates 484–5
Exhibitions 459, 461
Exposition, as a gesture of the Buddha 173
Expressways 495

F

Fabrics
    Ancient Cloth and Silk Museum (Bangkok) 102
    kalaga tapestries **453,** 455
    Northern Thailand 209
    Thai silk 138, 139, 266-7, **452,** 455
    What to Buy in Thailand 457
    see also Clothes
Factory outlets 451
Fake goods 451
Fang **242**
    restaurants 438
Far North 11, **239–59**
    Golden Triangle driving tour 246
    hotels 407–9
    map 240–41
    restaurants 437–9
Far South *see* Deep South
Farming 22
    rice 26–7
Fashion Island (Bangkok) 451, 455
Federal Express 487
Ferries, island 493
Festivals **46–51**
    hill tribes 206–7
    Loy Krathong at Sukhothai 195
    Maytime fruit festivals 321
    Phi Ta Khon Festival 47, **289**
    Songkran festivities in the North 236
    temple fairs and festivals 460
    Vegetarian Festival (Phuket town) 360
Film *see* Cinema
Fine Arts Department (Bangkok) 178, 475
Fine Arts, The (Bangkok) **454,** 455
Fire services 480
First aid *see* Health
First states 56–7
First-aid kit 482
Fish
    coral reefs 348–9
    seafood of the South 387

Fisheries Department (Si Chiangmai) 291

Fishing 463, 468
  korlae fishing boats 345, 388

Flag, Thai 21

Flowers
  Festival (Chiang Mai) 51
  landscape of Thailand **28–9**
  orchids 220
  Pak Khlong Market (Bangkok) 98
  Rafflesia kerri 357

Folk clubs 459, 461

Folklore Museum (Ko Yo) 385

Food and drink
  art of Thai food **38–9**
  bird's-nest soup 341
  carving 38
  coffee shops 422
  drinks 425
  Flavours of Thailand 424–5
  food-borne diseases 483
  glossary of dishes **426–7**
  roadside and market food stands 422–3
  safety 482
  seafood of the South 387
  Thai fruits and vegetables 133
  see also Markets; Restaurants

Food and Fruits Fair (Nakhon Pathom) 50

Footprints of the Buddha 172

Foreigners in Ayutthaya **162–3**

Forestry Department 394, 395

Forests
  Khao Phra Taew Forest Park 363
  landscape of Thailand **28–9**
  mangrove forests 350–51
  Thailand's teak industry 249
  Tham Pha Tup Forest Preserve 255
  see also National Parks

Forgeries *see* Fake goods

Fortune tellers, Sanam Luang (Bangkok) 79

Four Seasons Resort Chiang Mai 396, **406**, 470, 471

Four Seasons Resort Koh Samui 417, 470, **471**

Four Seasons Tented Camp at the Golden Triangle 464, 470, 471

France 162–3

Franco-Siamese Crisis (1893) 67

French Embassy (Bangkok) 112

Frescoes
  Ayutthayan 60
  see also Murals

Fresh Produce Market (Phuket town) 360

Friday Mosque (Nakhon Si Thammarat) 376

Friendship Bridge (Nong Khai) 292, 293

Front Palace Crisis (1875) 66

Fruits 133
  carving 38
  Maytime fruit festivals 321

Funan 55

Fungal infections 482

G

Galleries *see* Museums and galleries

Ganesh 115, 253, 384

Garages 494

Gardens *see* Parks and gardens

Gas stations 494

Gay and Lesbian Travelers 476

Gaysorn Plaza (Bangkok) 138, 139

Gemstones **310–11**
  Bo Rai 321
  Chanthaburi 321
  shops 139, 454, 455
  What to Buy in Thailand 457

General delivery 486–7

General Post Office (Bangkok) 114

Gestures of the Buddha 173

Geysers
  San Kamphaeng Hot Springs 229
  see also Springs

Giant Swing (Bangkok) **90–91**

Gibbon Rehabilitation Center (Phuket) 359, 363

Gibbon, white-handed 219

Glass Sand Beach (Hat Sai Kaeo) 308

Goethe-Institut (Bangkok) 459, 461

Gold 454

Gold leaf 30

Golden Buddha 98

Golden Mount (Bangkok) 87

Golden Mount Fair (Bangkok) 46, 50

Golden Triangle 11, 239
  Golden Triangle Apex (Sop Ruak) **248**
  Golden Triangle driving tour **246–7**
  history of opium in Thailand 233
  hotels 408
  restaurants 438

Golf 463

Government House (Bangkok) 106

Governor's Palace (Phatthalung) 382

Grand Palace (Bangkok) 10, 25, **84–5**
  Aphonphimok Pavilion 84
  Audience Chamber 85
  Boromphiman Mansion 85

Grand Palace (cont.)
  Chakri Throne Hall 84
  Dusit Throne Hall 84
  Inner Palace 85
  Phra Maha Monthien Buildings 84–5
  plan 80–81
  scams 480
  Siwalai Gardens 85
  see also Wat Phra Kaeo

Green Travel 488

Greene, Graham 115

Greeting people 478

Guesthouses 393
  see also Hotels

Guided tours 491

Guided treks *see* Trekking

Gulf of Thailand **305–41**
  beaches 308–9
  Eastern Seaboard 313–23
  festivals 47
  map 306–7
  Thai gemstones 310–11
  Western Seaboard 325–41

Gupta art 57

Gypsies *see* Sea gypsies

H

Haeo Suwat waterfall 184

Hanuman 40–41

Haripunchai Empire **56**, 62
  Lampang 236
  Lamphun 229

Harmonique restaurant (Bangkok) 112

Haroon Mosque (Bangkok) 112, 476, 477

Hat Chao Mai National Park **380**

Hat Karon 362

Hat Kata 362

Hat Khlong Phrao 322

Hat Lek 323

Hat Patong 362

Hat Phra Nang 370

Hat Rin 339

Hat Sai Kaeo (Glass Sand Beach) 308, 318

Hat Sai Khao (White Sand Beach) 308, 316, 322

Hat Sai Tai Muang 296

Hat Samila 384

Hat Tham 316

Hat Yai 376, **385**
  hotels 420–21
  restaurants 449

Haw Pha Kaew (Vientiane) 294

Health **480–83**

Heat 482

"Hellfire Pass" 169
"Hell's banknotes" 99
Hepatitis A 482, 483
Hepatitis B 482, 483
Her Majesty the Queen's Birthday 49
Heroin 480
  Golden Triangle 246
  history of opium in Thailand 233
Heroines' Monument (Phuket)
  359
Hertz (car hire) 494, 495
Hia Kui Market (Damnoen Saduak)
  132
Highways 495
Hiking **464–5,** 468–9
  see also Trekking
Hill Tribe Education Center (Chiang
  Rai) 251
Hill Tribe Products Foundation
  (Chiang Mai) 452, 455
Hill tribes 22, **206–7**
  artifacts 452, 455, 456
  trekking 464
  see also Akha; Hmong; Karen;
    Lahu; Lisu; Mien; Padaung
Hinduism **30**
  elephants in 253
  Maha Uma Devi Temple (Bangkok)
    115
His Majesty the King's Birthday 51,
  107
History **53–69**
Hmong tribespeople **206–7**
  Ban Winai 290
  Doi Inthanon National Park 231
  Doi Phu Kha National Park 254
  Fang 242
  Khao Kho 201
  Mae Teng Valley 221
  Mae Wong National Park 192
  Nan National Museum 255
  Phrao 220
HMS Chumphon 332
Ho Chi Minh 295
Ho Chi Minh City 294
Ho Phra Buddha Sing Shrine
  (Nakhon Si Thammarat) 379
Ho Phra I-suan (Shiva) Shrine
  (Nakhon Si Thammarat) 379
Ho Phra Narai Shrine (Nakhon Si
  Thammarat) 379
Ho rakangs 33
Ho trais 32
Hok Sai waterfall 319
Hokkien Chinese 356
Holidays, public 51
Holy Redeemer Catholic Church
  (Bangkok) 476, 477

Hongkong Shanghai Bank (Bangkok)
  484
Hongsa 124
Horse racing **467,** 469
  Royal Bangkok Sports Club
    (Bangkok) 117, 467, 469
Horse riding **467,** 469
Hospitals
  McCormick Hospital (Chiang Mai)
    227
  medical emergencies 480, 481
  Old Medicine Hospital (Chiang
    Mai) 467, 469
  Overbrook Hospital (Chiang Rai)
    251
  Phuket International Hospital 481
Hot 232
Hot season 48–9
Hot springs see Springs
Hot-air balloons 467, 469
Hotels **392–421**
  Bangkok 398–402
  bargaining 395
  booking 395
  Deep South 420–21
  disabled travelers 395
  Eastern Seaboard 412–15
  facilities for children 395
  Far North 407–9
  grading and facilities 392
  guesthouses 393
  Khorat Plateau 409–10
  luxury hotels 392, **396–7**
  Mekong River Valley 411–12
  North Central Plains 403–4
  Northwest Heartland 404–7
  prices 394
  resort hotels 392–3
  South Central Plains 402–3
  spas 470–71
  staying in monasteries 393
  tax 395
  Thai and Chinese hotels 393
  tipping 395, 479
  Upper Andaman Coast 418–20
  Western Seaboard 415–18
House of Gems (Bangkok) 112
House of Opium Museum (Sop Ruak)
  233, 248
Houses
  khlongs 125
  traditional Thai houses **36–7**
Htin tribespeople, Doi Phu Kha
  National Park 254
Hua Hin 13, **331**
  beach 308
  hotels 416
  restaurants 444–5

Hua Lampong Station (Bangkok)
  98, 492, 493
Hua Mark Stadiums (Bangkok) 460,
  461
Huai Kha Khaeng 168–9
Huai Khamin falls 169
Huay Sadeh waterfall 370
Huay To waterfall 370
Huay Xai 249
Hun krabok puppets 40, 43

I

I Chinga 332
Ice 482
Illuminated Boat Procession (Nakhon
  Phanom) 47, 50
Imaging Technology Museum
  (Bangkok) 117
Immigration, Chinese 99
Immigration Department (Bangkok)
  474, 475
Immunization 482
Indochina 249, 294
Indochina Market (Nong Khai) 292
Indra 257, 286
Indra Ceramics (Lampang) 453, 455
Indravarman II, King 57
Insect-borne diseases 482-3
Insect World 361
Institute of Massage (Bangkok) 92
Insurance
  cars 494
  medical 481
International Amateur Muay Thai
  Federation (Bangkok) 460, 461
International Buddhist Meditation
  Center (Bangkok) 476, 477
International Church (Bangkok) 477
International Dhamma Hermitage
  (Surat Thrani) 467, 469
Internet and Email 486
Intharacha I, King 60, 176
Intharacha II, King 180
Isan see Northeast Thailand
Islam **346**
  Deep South 375
  Haroon Mosque (Bangkok) 112,
    476
  Nurul Islam Mosque (Mae Sot) 190
  Pattani 388
Island ferries 493
Islands see under Ko

J

"James Bond Island" 366
Japan Bridge Company 171
Japanese encephalitis 483

Jataka tales **30**
Hokkien Chinese
    and naga figures 228
    in theater and music 42-3
Jayavarman VII, King 57, 170
    Prasat Ta Muen Tot 278
    Si Satchanalai-Chalieng Historical
    Park 198
JEATH War Museum (Kanchanaburi)
    170–71
Jellyfish stings 482
Jesuits 162-3
Jet skis 463
Jewelry
    gemstones 310–11
    shops 139, 454, 455
    What to Buy in Thailand 457
Jewish Community Center (Bangkok)
    476, 477
Jim Thompson's House (Bangkok)
    120–21
Jim Thompson's Silk Shop (Bangkok)
    138, 139, 452, 455
Joe Louis Theater (Bangkok) 142,
    143, 458, 461
Jomtien beach 308, 317

K

Kad Suan Kaew (Chiang Mai) 451,
    455
Kaeng Krachan National Park 13, **330**
Kaeng Krachan Reservoir 330
Kaeng Kut Khu rapids 290
Kalaga tapestries 453, 455
Kamalaya Wellness Sanctuary &
    Holistic Spa (Ko Samui) 470–71
Kamphaeng Phet 11, 158, **192–3**
    hotels 403
    map 193
    restaurants 433
Kamphaeng Phet National Museum
    192
Kanap Nam twin limestone peaks 371
Kanchanaburi 10–11, 158, **170–71**
    festivals 46, 50
    hotels 402–3
    restaurants 433
Kanchanaburi War Cemetery 170, 171
Kao Market (Bangkok) 96, 141
Karen tribespeople **206–7**
    Fang 242
    Mae Hong Son 216
    Mae Sariang 232
    Ruamit 251
    Sangkhla Buri 168
    Thailand-Burma border refugees
    191
    Umphang **191**

Karon, Hat 362
Kasikorn Bank 484
Kata, Hat 362
Kawila of Lampang 63
Kayaking **463**, 468
Kayan tribespeople 216
Kedah 67
Kelantan 67
Khaen 273
Khaen Nakhon Lake 273
Kham Fu, King 225
Khantoke dinners 423, 458
Khantoke Palace (Chiang Mai) 458,
    461
Khao Chamao waterfall 319
Khao Chamao-Khao Wong National
    Park 313, **319**
Khao Chong Nature and Study Center
    381
Khao Hua Taek 382
Khao Khieo Open Zoo **316**
Khao Kho 201
Khao Kitchakut National Park **320**
Khao Kong 389
Khao Lak 354
Khao Lak Coast **356**
Khao Lak/Lam Ru National Park 356
Khao Ngu 132
Khao Noi (Songkhla) 384
Khao Ok Talu 382
Khao Phanom Bencha National Park
    13, **370**
Khao Phansa 47, 49
Khao Phra Taew Forest Park 363
Khao Sam Roi Yot National Park 13,
    327, 332
Khao San Road Market (Bangkok)
    140
Khao Seng 384
Khao Soi Dao Wildlife Sanctuary 320
Khao Sok National Park 13, 355, **356**
Khao Tung Kuan 384
Khao Wong caves 319
Khao Yai National Park 10, 159,
    184–5, 465
Khatta Kumara 256, 257
Khaw Sim Bee Na-Ranong 360,
    380–81
Khlong Lamchan 381
Khlong Lan National Park **192**
Khlong Phlu waterfall 323
Khlong Thom **371**
Khlong Yai **323**
Khlong Yaw Market (Bo Rai) 321
Khlongs 125
Khmer Empire 53, **56-7**
    Kamphaeng Phet 192
    Lop Buri 174

Khmer Empire (cont.)
    Mekong River Valley 283
    Prasat Hin Khao Phnom Rung
    280–81
    Prasat Hin Phimai 276–7
    Prasat Khao Phra Wihan 302
    Prasat Muang Sing 170
    Prasat Prang Ku 302
    Prasat Ta Muen and Prasat Ta
    Muen Tot 278
    religious architecture 34
    Si Satchanalai-Chalieng Historical
    Park 198, 199
    temples 264–5
    Ubon Ratchathani 302
Khmer Rouge 279
Khon (dance-drama) 25, 42–3
Khon Kaen **272–3**
    hotels 409
    restaurants 439
Khon Kaen National Museum
    273
Khong Chiam **299**
Khorat 12, **274–5**
    hotels 410
    map 274
    restaurants 439–40
Khorat cats 275
Khorat Plateau 12, 22, **269–81**
    hotels 409–10
    map 270–71
    restaurants 439–40
Khrua In Khong 86
Khrubaa Siwichai 229
Khumlum Phraphat Road (Mae Hong
    Son) 217
Khun Kaew Khantoke Palace (Chiang
    Mai) 458, 461
Khun Patpongpanit 116
Khun Phitak Market (Damnoen
    Saduak) 132
Khun Sa 242, 248
Khunying Mo 275
Khwae Noi River 168
Khwae River Bridge Week
    (Kanchanaburi) 46, 50
Khwae Yai Bridge 10, 165, **171**
Kick boxing *see Muay thai*
Kilns, Sukhothai-era 161
Kim Jeng (Ayutthaya) 452, 455
King Bhumibol's Photographic
    Museums (Bangkok) 102
The King and I 115
King Narai's Palace (Lop Buri) 174
King Ramkamhaeng Monument
    (Sukhothai Historical Park) 195
King's Royal Park (Bangkok) 136
Kinokuniya 139, 451, 455

Kite-flying 51
   at Sanam Luang (Bangkok) 79
Kitti Thonglongya 169
Kiu Wong In 361
Klai Klangwon (Hua Hin) 331
Klong River 132
KMT *see* Kuomintang
Ko Adang 386
Ko Chang 12, 307, 312, 313, 315, **322–3**
   beaches 308, 309
   hotels 412–13
   restaurants 442
Ko Hai 380
Ko Hong 366, 370
Ko Hua Khwan 370
Ko Khai 386
Ko Khao Phing Kan 366, 367
Ko Kra 386
Ko Kradan 13, **380**
Ko Kradat 323
Ko Kut 323
Ko Lanta **373**
   hotels 418
   restaurants 446–7
Ko Lanta Yai 373
Ko Libong 380
Ko Lipey 386
Ko Loi 316
Ko Mae Ko 341
Ko Mak 323
Ko Man Klang 317
Ko Man Nok 317
Ko Mattra 332
Ko Muk 13, **380**
Ko Nang Yuan 341
Ko Ngai *see* Ko Hai
Ko Ngam Noi 332
Ko Ngam Yai 332
Ko Pha Ngan 13, **339**
   hotels 416–17
   map 339
   restaurants 445
Ko Phanak 366
Ko Phi Phi 13, 354, **372–3**
   hotels 419
   map 372
   restaurants 447
Ko Phuket *see* Phuket
Ko Poda 355, 370
Ko Rang 323
Ko Rawi 386
Ko Saket 317
Ko Sam Sao 340
Ko Samet 12, 307, **318–19**, 332
   beaches 308, 314
   hotels 413–14
   map 318
   restaurants 442

Ko Samui 13, 28, 306, 326, **336–8**
   airport 489
   hotels 417–18
   map 336–7
   restaurants 445-6
   tourist police 481
Ko Sichang **316–17**
   hotels 414
   restaurants 442
Ko Similan 13, 354, **357**
Ko Surin 13, 354, **357**
Ko Tao 13, **341**
   hotels 418
   restaurants 446
Ko Tapu 366, 367
Ko Tarutao 376, 386
   hotels 421
Ko Wai 323
Ko Wua Talab 340, **341**
Ko Yang 386
Ko Yo 385
Kok River 242, 251
Korlae fishing boats 345, 388
Kra, Isthmus of 22, 346
Krabi 13, 354, **371**
   hotels 419
   restaurants 447
   rock-climbing **371,** 466
Krabi-Krabong 460, 461
Krailasa, Mount 280
Krathin 50
Krathin waterfall 320
Kru Se 388
Krua Khonpae 124
Krung Sri River Hotel (Ayutthaya)
   397, **402**
Krung Thai Bank (Bangkok) 484
Krung Thep *see* Bangkok
Ku Na, King 62
Kuang River 229
Kuomintang (KMT) 233
   Chiang Khong 249
   Mae Aw 218
   Mae Salong 242

L

Lacquerware 453, 455
   What to Buy in Thailand 456
Lahu tribespeople **206–7**
   Fang 242
Lak Muang (Mukdahan) 298
Lakeside Pavilion, Dusit Park
   (Bangkok) 103
Lakhon (dance-drama) 25, 42
Lakshman 40–41, 276
Lam Pam 382
Lam Takhong River 184, 185, 275
Lamai 338

Lampang 204, **236**
   hotels 406
   restaurants 436
Lamphun **229**
   hotels 406
   restaurants 436
Lamphun National Museum 229
Lan Sang National Park 191
Lan Xang Kingdom 294, 295
Landscape of Thailand **28–9**
Laneau, Father Louis 104
Language
   phrase book 524-8
   Thai 476
Lanna Kingdom 53, **62–3**
   Chiang Rai 250
   religious architecture 35
Lanna Museum (Lampang) 236, 237
Lanna School, Emerald Buddha 82
Lao Patriotic Front 295
Lao Revolutionary Museum
   (Vientiane) 294
Laos
   Chong Mek 299
   Friendship Bridge 292, 293
   Golden Triangle 246
   Huay Xai 249
   Pathet Lao 295
   Vientiane 12, **294–5**
   visas 249, **475**
Lean, David 171
Lee, Christopher 367
Leeches 482
Legal assistance 481
Legend of the Emerald Buddha **83**
Leonowens, Anna 115
Li Thi Miew (Bangkok) 97
Libraries
   National Library (Bangkok) 104
   Neilson-Hays Library (Bangkok)
   115
   see also Ho trais
Likay (dance-drama) 43
Lim Ko Niaw 388
Lim To Khieng 388
Limestone, Phangnga Bay 364–5
Lisu tribespeople 24, **206–7**, 238, 240
   Doi Chiang Dao 220
   Fang 242
   Mae Taeng Valley 221
   Pai 219
   Phrao 220
   Wiang Pa Pao 252
Literature 25
   Poetry of Sunthorn Phu 319
   Western writers in Bangkok 115
Lo Thai, King 59
Local transport 496

Loei 12, **289**
  festivals 47, 49, 284
  hotels 411
  restaurants 440
Loei Palace Hotel 397, **411**
Loei River 289
Lomprayah (ferry information) 493
Long-distance buses 492
"Long-neck women" see Padaung
  women
Longka 40
Lop Buri 10, 57, 159, **174–5**
  hotels 403
  restaurants 433
  Street-by-Street map 174–5
Lost Khmer temples 264–5
Louis XIV, King of France 162, 163,
  175
Loy Krathong 20, 46, **50**
  at Sukhothai 195
Luang Pho Phra Sai Buddha 292
Luang Pho Somchai 319
Luang Pu Bunleua Surirat 293
Luang Vichit Chetsada 124
Lue people see Thai Lue people
Lue Thai, King 196
Lumphini Park (Bangkok) **117**
Lumphini Stadium (Bangkok) 460,
  461
Luxury hotels 392, **396–7**

M

McCormick Hospital (Chiang Mai)
  227
Mae Aw **218**
Mae Chaem 232
Mae Hong Son 204, **216–17**
  festivals 46–7, 48
  hotels 407
  restaurants 437
  Street-by-Street map 216–17
Mae Khongkha 46, 50
Mae Sa Elephant Camp (Chiang Mai)
  464, 468
Mae Sai 11, **246**
  Golden Triangle driving
  tour 247
  hotels 408
Mae Salong (Santikhiree) **242–3**
  hotels 408–9
  restaurants 438
Mae Sam Laep 232
Mae Sariang **232**
  restaurants 437
Mae Saruai **252**
Mae Sot 11, **190**
  hotels 403
  restaurants 433

Mae Surin National Park **218**
Mae Taeng Valley **221**
Mae Wong National Park 192
Mae Ya waterfall 231
Mae Yom National Park 252
Maenam 336–7
Magazines 487
  entertainment listings 142, 458
Mahboonkrong Center (Bangkok) 118
Maha Thammaracha I, King 59, 176
Maha Uma Devi Temple (Bangkok)
  115
Maha Uparaja Bovornvijaya Jarn 102
Maha Weerawong National Museum
  (Khorat) 275
Mahanikai monastic sect 86
Mahayana Buddhism 30
Mahboonkrong (Bangkok) 138, 139
Mai Market (Bangkok) 97
Makha Bucha 51
Malacca, Straits of 346–7
Malaria 482
Malaysian Embassy 475
Malls, shopping 138, 139, 451, 455
Mandarin Oriental Hotel (Bangkok)
  112, **114**, 397, 400
Manfredi, Hercules 106–7
Mangrove forests **350–51**
  Phangnga Bay 364, 367
Mao Zedong 242
Maps
  Angthong National Marine Park 340
  ASEAN in 2008 68
  Ayutthaya 53, 162–3, 177
  Ayutthaya in 1540 60
  Bangkok 16, 72–3
  Bangkok: Central Chinatown 96–7
  Bangkok: Chinatown 95
  Bangkok: City Centre see Back
    Endpaper
  Bangkok: Downtown Bangkok 111
  Bangkok: Dusit 101
  Bangkok: Dusit Park 102–3
  Bangkok: Farther Afield 131
  Bangkok: Old City 77
  Bangkok: Old Farang Quarter 112–3
  Bangkok: Around Sanam Luang
    78–9
  Bangkok: Street Finder 144–55
  Bangkok's Markets 140–41
  Central Plains 158–9
  Chao Phraya Express Boats see
    Back Endpaper
  Chiang Mai 17, 224–5, 227
  Chiang Rai 251
  city maps 494
  Deep South 376–7
  Eastern Seaboard 314–15

Maps (cont.)
  Far North 240–41
  Golden Triangle driving tour 246–7
  Greater Bangkok 73
  Gulf of Thailand 306–7
  Gulf of Thailand Beaches 308–9
  Kamphaeng Phet 193
  Khao Yai National Park 184–5
  Khmer Empire 264
  Khmer Empire in AD 960 56
  Khorat 274
  Khorat Plateau 270–71
  Ko Chang 322
  Ko Pha Ngan 339
  Ko Phi Phi 372
  Ko Samet 318
  Ko Samui 336–7
  Lanna in 1540 62
  Lop Buri 174–5
  Mae Hong Son 216–17
  Mekong River Valley 284–5
  Mekong villages tour 290–91
  Nakhon Si Thammarat 379
  Nong Khai 293
  North Central Plains 188–9
  Northeast Thailand 262–3
  Northern Thailand 16–17, 204–5
  Northwest Heartland 214–15
  Phetchaburi 328–9
  Phrae 258–9
  Phu Kradung National Park 286–7
  Phuket 358–9
  Phuket town 361
  prehistoric sites 54
  road maps 495
  ruby and sapphire mining 310
  Si Satchanalai-Chalieng Historical
    Park 199
  Siam in 1809 64
  Siam in 1909 66
  Songkhla 384
  South Central Plains 166–7
  Southeast Asia 15
  Southern Thailand 18–19,
    344–5
  Sukhothai in 1300 58
  Sukhothai Historical Park 194
  Thailand 14–15
  Thailand's Best Luxury Hotels
    396–7
  Thon Buri 123
  trade routes and the Peninsula
    346–7
  trekking around Chiang Dao 221
  Ubon Ratchathani 303
  Upper Andaman Coast 354–5
  Vientiane 294
  Western Seaboard 326–7

Mara 173
Marble Temple *see* Wat Benchamabophit
Mareukathayawan Palace **331**
Marijuana 480
Marine Research Center (Phuket) 359, 363
Markets 138, 451
  Bangkok's Markets 140–41
  Banglamphu Market (Bangkok) 140
  Bangrak Market (Bangkok) 115, 141
  Bo Be Market (Bangkok) 140
  Bovorn Bazaar (Nakhon Si Thammarat) 379
  Chatuchak Market 135
  Damnoen Saduak Floating Market 130, **132**
  food stands 422–3
  Fresh Produce Market (Phuket town) 360
  Indochina Market (Nong Khai) 292
  Kao Market (Bangkok) 96, 141
  Khao San Road Market (Bangkok) 140
  Khlong Yaw Market (Bo Rai) 321
  Mae Hong Son 216
  Mai Market (Bangkok) 97
  Nakorn Kasem (Bangkok) 98, 141
  Night Bazaar (Chiang Mai) 226
  Night Market (Khorat) 275
  Pak Khlong Market (Bangkok) 98, 140
  Patpong/Silom Market (Bangkok) 141
  Phahurat Market (Bangkok) **98,** 138, 139, 140
  Pratunam Market (Bangkok) **118–19,** 141
  Sampeng Lane Market (Bangkok) 141
  Saphan Han Market (Bangkok) 98
  Siam Square (Bangkok) 118
  Stamp Market (Bangkok) 141
  Thewet Flower Market (Bangkok) **104,** 140
  Thung Kwian Forest Market 237
  Warorot Market (Chiang Mai) 226
Martial arts 460, 461
Marzotto (Bangkok) 139
Masks
  shops 453, 455
  What to Buy in Thailand 456
Massage **93,** 467
  Institute of Massage (Bangkok) 92
  Thai Massage School of (Chiang Mai) 467, 469

Mass Rapid Transit 497
Matsayit Klang mosque (Pattani) 388
Maugham, Somerset 114, 115
Maya, Queen 106
Maytime fruit festivals **321**
MBK Center (Bangkok) 118
Medical facilities 481
  see also Hospitals
Meditation 31, 467, 469
  as a posture of the Buddha 173
Mekong River valley 12, 22, **283–303**
  festivals 50
  Golden Triangle Apex (Sop Ruak) 248
  hotels 411–12
  map 284–5
  Mekong villages tour **290–91**
  restaurants 440–41
Memorial Bridge (Bangkok) 75
Mengrai, King **62**
  Chiang Mai 224
  Chiang Rai 250
  death of 226
  Fang 242
  Wat Chiang Man (Chiang Mai) 226
Mengrai Kilns (Chiang Mai) 453, 455
Menus 426
  see also Food and drink
Merit-making 30, 129
Meru, Mount **126–7,** 198
Metric system 477
Metropolitan Mobile Police 481
Microlighting 467, 469
Mien tribespeople **206–7,** 239
  Doi Phu Kha National Park 254
  Fang 242
  Mae Salong 243
  Nan National Museum 255
  Pha Dua 246
Mike Shopping Mall (Pattaya) 451, 455
Mileage chart 19
Missionaries 162–3
Mon people 56
  Dan Kwian 275
  Sangkhla Buri 168
Monarchy 24
Monasteries *see* Wats
Mondops 32
Money
  banking and local currency **484–5**
  customs information 475
  in shops 138, 450
Mongkut (Rama IV), King **53**
  Bang Pa-in Palace 181
  Chan Kasem Palace (Ayutthaya) 176

Mongkut (Rama IV), King (cont.)
  death of 65
  Grand Palace (Bangkok) 84, 85
  The King and I 115
  modernization of Thailand 64, **65**
  Phra Nakhon Khiri Historical Park (Phetchaburi) 329, 330
  Phra Pathom Chedi (Nakhon Pathom) 134
  Phuket town 360
  Pisai Sayalak Tower (Ayutthaya) 176
  portrait of 65
  Ratchadamnoen Avenue (Bangkok) 107
  Tak Bai 389
  Wat Arun (Bangkok) 126–7
  Wat Bowonniwet (Bangkok) 86
  Wat Chalerm Phrakiet (Nonthaburi) 135
  Wat Indrawihan (Bangkok) 104
  Wat Phra Kaeo (Bangkok) 82, 83
  Wat Rachapradit (Bangkok) 91
  Wat Supattanaram Worawihan (Ubon Ratchathani) 303
Monkhood 24, 30
  during the Buddhist Rains Retreat 49, 50
  and etiquette 479
  and popular Buddhist rituals **129**
Monk's Bowl Village (Ban Bat, Bangkok) **90**
Monsoon **26–7,** 48
Montane tropical forest 28
Moore, Roger 125, 367
Mopeds, hiring 494
Mosques
  Haroon Mosque (Bangkok) 112, 476
  Nurul Islam Mosque (Mae Sot) 190
Mosquitoes 482–3
Motorcycles
  renting 494
  taxis 496
Mouhot, Henri 178, 265
Movies *see* Cinema
MRT (Mass Rapid Transit) 497
Muang Tam *see* Prasat Hin Muang Tam
Muay thai **44–5,** 142, 143, 460, 461
Mukdahan **298**
  hotels 411
  restaurants 440–41
Mun River 299
Murals
  Wat Nong Bua 254
  Wat Phumin (Nan) 256–7
  see also Frescoes

Museums and galleries
admission prices 475
opening hours 476
Ancient Cloth and Silk Museum
(Bangkok) 102
Art Gallery (Chulalongkorn
University, Bangkok) 117
Art Republic (Bangkok) 459,
461
Ban Chiang National Museum 55,
272
Bangkok Art and Culture Center
118
Ban Kao Museum 170
Ban Sao Nak (Lampang) 236, 237
Chaiya National Museum 333
Chao Sam Phraya National
Museum (Ayutthaya) 178
Chiang Mai National Museum 227
Chiang Saen National
Museum 249
Congdon Museum of Anatomy
(Bangkok) 125
Erawan Museum (Bangkok) 137
Folklore Museum (Ko Yo) 385
Hill Tribe Education Center (Chiang
Rai) 251
House of Gems (Bangkok) 112
House of Opium Museum (Sop
Ruak) 233, 248
Imaging Technology Museum
(Bangkok) 117
JEATH War Museum
(Kanchanaburi) 170–71
Jim Thompson's House (Bangkok)
120–21
Kamphaeng Phet National Museum
192
Khon Kaen National Museum 273
King Bhumibol's Photographic
Museums (Bangkok) 102
Lamphun National Museum 229
Lanna Museum (Lampang) 236, 237
Lao Revolutionary Museum
(Vientiane) 294
Maha Weerawong National
Museum (Khorat) 275
Museum of Ecology
(Chulalongkorn University,
Bangkok) 117
Museum of Forensic Medicine
(Bangkok) 125
Museum of Siam (Bangkok) 91
Museums at the Siriraj Hospital
(Bangkok) 125
Nakhon Si Thammarat National
Museum 378
Nan National Museum 254–5

Museums and galleries (cont.)
National Gallery (Bangkok) 86
National Museum (Bangkok) 79,
88-9, 454, 455
Old Clock Museum (Bangkok) 103
Patrsee Museum (Songkhla) 384
Phra Nakhon Khiri Historical Park
(Phetchaburi) 329, **330**
Phra Pathom Chedi National
Museum (Nakhon Pathom) 134
Prasart Museum (Bangkok) 137
Ramkamhaeng National
Museum (Sukhothai Historical
Park) 194–5
Rank and Portrait Museum
(Bangkok) 102
Ratchaburi National Museum 132
Royal Barge Museum (Bangkok)
124–5
Sawankha Woranayok National
Museum (Sawankhalok) 200
Sergeant Major Thawee's Folk
Museum (Phitsanulok) 201
Somdej Phra Narai National
Museum (Lop Buri) 174
Songkhla National Museum 345,
384, 385
Suan Pakkad Palace (Bangkok)
119
SUPPORT Museum (Bangkok) 100,
103, **105**
Surin Museum (Surin) 279
Thai Human Imagery Museum 134
Thailand-Burma Railroad Center
(Kanchanaburi) 170
Thalang National Museum (Phuket)
363
Thavorn Hotel Lobby Exhibition
(Phuket town) 360
Tribal Research Institute (Chiang
Mai) 227
U Thong National Museum 172
Ubon National Museum (Ubon
Ratchathani) 302–3
Wat Mae Phrae Museum (Bangkok)
104
Music **42–3,** 459, 461
concerts 459, 461
khaen 273
piphat 44
shops 453, 455
Muslims *see* Islam
Myanmar (Burma)
besieges Ayutthaya 61
Burmese Kingdom **62–3**
Golden Triangle 246
Myanmar Embassy 475
Tachilek 246

Myanmar (Burma) (cont.)
Thailand-Myanmar border refugees
191
Victoria Point 356
visas 246, **475**

N

Na Dan 318
Naga figures 228
Naga Pearl Farm 363
Nai Khanom Dtom 44
Nak Buddha 83
Nakhon Pathom 134
festivals 50
Nakhon Phanom 283, **296**
festivals 47, 50
hotels 411
restaurants 441
Nakhon Ratchasima *see* Khorat
Nakhon Sawan 74
Nakhon Si Thammarat 13, 345, 346,
375, **378–9**
hotels 421
map 379
restaurants 449
Nakhon Si Thammarat National
Museum 378
Naklua Bay 317
Nakorn Kasem (Bangkok) **98,** 141
Namtok Phlio National Park 321
Namuang waterfall 338
Nan 11, 205, 254–5
hotels 409
traditional boat races in Nan 50,
255
Wat Phumin 256-7
Nan National Museum **254–5**
Nan River 74, 201, 254, 259
Nandakwang 139
Nandin the bull 281
Nang talung shadow puppets 383
Nang yai shadow plays 41
Narai, King 61
Bang Pa-in Palace 181
and foreigners in Ayutthaya 163
Khorat 275
King Narai's Palace (Lop Buri) 174
Lop Buri 174
Phaulkon Residence (Lop Buri) 175
Wat Phra Thong Thong (Lop Buri)
174
Narathiwat **389**
hotels 421
restaurants 449
Narathiwat Fair 47, 50
Narathiwat province 376, 377
Narayanaphand (Bangkok) 139,
452, 455

Naresuan, King of Ayutthaya 61
  Battle of Nong Sarai **62–3**, 172
  Chan Kasem Palace (Ayutthaya)
    176
  Don Chedi Memorial Fair (Suphan
    Buri province) 51
  Surin Elephant Roundup 278
  Wat Yai Chai Mongkhon
    (Ayutthaya) 181
Naris, Prince 106–7
Nat spirits 120
Nathon 336
National anthem 478–9
National Gallery (Bangkok) **86**
National Library (Bangkok) 104
National Marine Parks
  Angthong 13, **340–41**
  Ko Lanta 373
  Phi Phi-Hat Nopparat Thara **370**,
    372
  Tarutao 13, 345, 375, 376, **386**
National Museum (Bangkok) 79,
    88–9
  export permits 454, 455, 475
National Parks
  accommodation in 394
  Chaloem Rattanakosin 171
  Doi Inthanon 11, 204, **230–31**
  Doi Phu Kha 254
  Doi Suthep-Doi Pui 222
  Erawan 10, **169**
  Hat Chao Mai 380
  Kaeng Krachan 13, **330**
  Khao Chamao-Khao Wong 313, 319
  Khao Kitchakut 320
  Khao Lak/Lam Ru 356
  Khao Phanom Bencha 13, **370**
  Khao Sam Roi Yot 13, **332**
  Khao Sok 13, 355, **356**
  Khao Yai 10, 159, **184–5**, 465
  Khlong Lan 192
  Lan Sang 191
  Mae Surin 218
  Mae Wong 192
  Mae Yom 252
  Namtok Phlio 321
  Phu Hin Rong Kla 288
  Phu Kradung 262, **286–7**
  Phu Rua 288
  Ramkamhaeng 197
  Sai Yok 169
  Si Nakharin 169
  Si Satchanalai 200
  Taksin Maharat 191
  Tanboke Koranee 367
  Thale Ban 386
  Thung Salaeng Luang 201
National Stadium (Bangkok) 118

National Theater (Bangkok) 142, 143,
    458, 461
Neilson-Hays, Jennie **115**
Neilson-Hays Library (Bangkok) 115
NeOld (Bangkok) 454, 455
New Road (Bangkok) *see* Charoen
    Krung Road
New Year
  Chinese New Year 51
  Songkran festivities in the North
    236
Newspapers 487
Ngao **252**
Ngua Nam Thom, King 59
Nielloware **453**, 455
  What to Buy in Thailand 456
Night Bazaar (Chiang Mai) 226
Nightclubs 143, 459, 461
Nok Air 490
Nong Bua **254**
Nong Khai 12, 263, **292–3**
  hotels 411
  map 293
  restaurants 441
Nong Prachak Park (Udon Thani)
    272
Nong Sarai, Battle of (1693) 61, 62–3,
    172
Nonthaburi **135**
Noodles 426
  see also Food and drink
North Central Plains 11, **187–201**
  hotels 403–4
  map 188–9
  restaurants 433–4
North Gate (Nakhon Si Thammarat)
    379
Northeast Thailand (Isan) 22,
    261–303
  festivals 47
  Khmer temples 264–5
  Khorat Plateau 269–81
  map 262–3
  Mekong River Valley 283–303
  silk production 266–7
Northern Insight Meditation Center
    (Chiang Mai) 467, 469
Northern Thailand 22, **203–59**
  arts and crafts 208–9
  birds 210–11
  festivals 46–7
  hill tribes 206–7
  map 16–17, 204–5
  traditional houses 36
Northwest Heartland **213–37**
  hotels 404–7
  map 214–15
  restaurants 434–7

NS Travel & Tours (Bangkok) 491
Nurul Islam Mosque (Mae Sot) 190

O

Ok Phansa 47, 50
Old Chiang Mai Cultural Center 452,
    455, 458, 461
Old City (Bangkok) **77–93**
  area map 77
  hotels 400–401
  National Museum 88–9
  restaurants 428
  Sanam Luang 78–9
  Wat Pho 92–3
Old Clock Museum (Bangkok) 103
Old Customs House (Bangkok) 112
Old Farang Quarter (Bangkok),
    Street-by-Street map 112–13
Old Medicine Hospital (Chiang Mai)
    467, 469
Old Sukhothai *see* Sukhothai
Open forest 28
Opening hours 476
  banks 484
  restaurants 422
  shops 138, 450
Open World International Travel
    Service 477
Opera, Chinese 99
Opium **233**, 480
  Doi Tung area 243
  Golden Triangle 246
Orchids **220**
  Thai Village and Orchid Garden
    (Phuket) 359, **361**
Organized tours 491
  see also Guided tours
Oriental Plaza (Bangkok) 139, 454
Outdoor activities **462–9**
Overbrook Hospital (Chiang Rai) 251

P

P & O Regale Travel 491
"Pack of Cards Bridge" 169
Paddy fields 26–7
Paduang women 216
Pai **219**
  hotels 407
  restaurants 437
Pak Chom **290**
  Mekong villages tour 290
Pak Khlong Market (Bangkok) **98**,
    140
Paknam Incident (1893) 67
Palaces
  Bang Pa–in Palace 181
  Chan Kasem Palace (Ayutthaya)
    176

Palaces (cont.)
    Chitrlada Palace (Bangkok) 80, 106
    Governor's Palace (Phatthalung)
      382
    King Narai's Palace (Lop Buri) 174
    Klai Klangwon (Hua Hin) 331
    Mareukathayawan Palace 331
    Phra Nakhon Khiri Historical Park
      (Phetchaburi) 329, 330
    Sanam Chan Palace (Nakhon
      Pathom) 134
    Suan Pakkad Palace (Bangkok) 119
    Summer Palace (Ko Sichang)
      316–17
    Taksin Palace (Narathiwat) 389
    Vimanmek Mansion (Bangkok)
      103, 104–5
Pali canon 30
Pallegoix, Bishop 128
Pantip Plaza (Bangkok) 139
Panyi Fishing Village 366
Parking 494
Parks and gardens
    Ancient City (Bangkok) 137
    Benjasiri Park (Bangkok) 136
    Doi Tung Royal Villa 243
    Dusit Park (Bangkok) 102–3
    Dusit Zoo (Bangkok) 105
    Fisheries Department (Si
      Chiangmai) 291
    Khao Noi (Songkhla) 384
    King's Royal Park (Bangkok) 136
    Lumphini Park (Bangkok) 117
    Nong Prachak Park (Udon Thani)
      272
    Phrae public park 259
    Queen's Park (Bangkok) 136
    Rose Garden (Bangkok) 134
    Siam Park (Bangkok) 136–7
    Siwalai Gardens (Bangkok) 85
    Taksin Park (Chanthaburi) 320
    Thai Village and Orchid Garden
      (Phuket) 359, **361**
    see also National Parks
Parmentier, Henri 265
Pasang 229
Passports 474–5
Pathet Lao 288, 290, 293, **295**
Pathumwan Stadium (Bangkok) 460,
    461
Patong, Hat 362
Patpong (Bangkok) **116**
Patpong/Silom Market (Bangkok) 141
Patravadi Theater (Bangkok) 142,
    143, 459, 461
Patsee Museum (Songkhla) 384
Pattani 347, **388**
    hotels 421

Pattani province 376
Pattaya 12, 307, **317**
    beaches 308, 309, 317
    festivals 47, 48
    hotels 414–15
    restaurants 442–3
Pattaya Festival 48
Pearls
    Naga Pearl Farm 363
    Pearl Center (Phuket town) 454,
      455
Pen Phong (Chiang Mai) 453, 455
Peninsula, history of **346–7**
Peninsula Plaza (Bangkok) 139, 451,
    454, 455
Personal security **480–81**
Pewterware 453, 455
Pha Baen 290
Pha Charoen falls 190
Pha Dua 246
Pha Lom Sak (Phu Kradung National
    Park) 286
Pha Nok An (Phu Kradung National
    Park) 287
Pha Taem 54, 55, **298–9**
Pha That Luang (Vientiane) 295
Phahurat Market (Bangkok) **98,** 138,
    139, 140
Phangnga Bay 13, 344, **364–9**
    hotels 419
    mangrove forests 350
    prehistoric paintings 346
    restaurants 447
Pharmacies 481
Phatthalung **382**
Phaulkon, Constantine 163, 175
Phaulkon Residence (Lop Buri) 175
Phayao **252**
Phea Muang Phi 259
Phet River 326, 330
Phetchaburi 13, 306, 326, **328–30**
    hotels 418
    restaurants 446
    Street-by-Street map 328–9
Phi Phi Don 372
    see also Ko Phi Phi
Phi Phi Ley 373
    see also Ko Phi Phi
Phi Phi-Hat Nopparat Thara National
    Marine Park **370,** 372
Phi Ta Khon Festival (Loei) 12, 47,
    49, 284, **289**
Phibun Songkram 22, 53, 68
Phichit Boat Races (Nan) 50
Phimai see Prasat Hin Phimai
Phitsanulok 11, **201**
    hotels 404
    restaurants 433–4

Phitsanulok Buddha 160–61
Phitsanulok Road (Bangkok) **106**
Phliu waterfall 321
Phnom Penh 294
Phnom Rung see Prasat Hin Khao
    Phnom Rung
Phone Kingphet 44, 287
Phone Phop waterfall 287
Phonecards 486
Photography
    Imaging Technology Museum
      (Bangkok) 117
    King Bhumibol's Photographic
      Museums (Bangkok) 102
Phra Anon 274
Phra Boromathat Chaiya (Chaiya) 57,
    333
Phra Buddha Chinarat 201
Phra Buddha Sihing 88
Phra Chaiya Wiwat 333
Phra Nakhon Khiri Historical Park
    (Phetchaburi) 329, **330**
Phra Nang, Princess 370
Phra Pathom Chedi (Nakhon Pathom)
    134
    festivals 50
Phra Pathom Chedi National Museum
    (Nakhon Pathom) 134
Phra Phutthabat **172**
Phra Phutthabat Fair (Saraburi) 46, 48
Phra Phutthachai 172
Phra Song Road (Phetchaburi) 328
Phra That Chaw Hae Fair 48
Phra That Naphamataneedon (Doi
    Inthanon) 230
Phra That Nong Khai (Nong Khai)
    293
Phra That Renu (Renu Nakhon) 296
Phra Wanawatwichit 125
Phrae **258–9**
    hotels 409
Phrao **220**
Phraya Aniruttheva, Major General
    106
Phraya Surin Phakdi Si Narong Wang
    279
Phu Hin Rong Kla National Park **288**
Phu Kradung National Park 12, 262,
    286–7
    hotels 412
Phu Man Khao 288
Phu Manorom 298
Phu Phrabat Histocial Park 55, **295**
Phu Rua National Park **288**
Phuket 13, 344, 352, 353, **358–63**
    airport 489
    car rental 494
    festivals 47, 50, 360

Phuket (cont.)
history 347
hotels 419–20
map 358–9
restaurants 447–9
tourist police 481
see also Phuket town
Phuket Butterfly Garden and Insect
World 359, 361
Phuket FantaSea 262
Phuket province, festivals 50
Phuket town 359, **360–61**
map 361
Vegetarian Festival 360
Phum Duang River 333
Phumintharacha, King 180
Pillars
Phrae Muang Phi 259
Sao Din 255
Ping River Valley 74, **232**
Kamphaeng Phet 192
Tak 191
Piphat bands 44
Piphek 40
Pisai Sayalak Tower (Ayutthaya) 176
Piya Mit 389
Places of worship *see* Religion
Plan Architecture 119
Planetariums, Bangkok Planetarium
136
Plants
landscape of Thailand 28–9
orchids 220
poppies 233
Rafflesia kerri 357
Poetry of Sunthorn Phu **319**
Poi Sang Long Festival (Mae Hong
Son) 46–7, 48
Police
highway police 495
tourist police 480, 481
Polio 482
Politics 23–5
Population and Community
Development Association (PDA)
251
Postal system 486–7
Pottery *see* Ceramics
POW Cemetery (Kanchanaburi) 166
Prachuap Khiri Khan 325, **332**
hotels 418
restaurants 446
Prajadhipok (Rama VII), King 68
Chitrlada Palace (Dusit) 80
Grand Palace (Bangkok) 85
Wat Suwan Dararam (Ayutthaya)
178
Prajak Road (Nong Khai) 292

Prang Khaek (Lop Buri) 175
Prang Sam Yot (Lop Buri) 175
Prap Ho Monument (Nong Khai) 292
Prasart Museum (Bangkok) **137**
Prasart Vongsakul 137
Prasat Hin Khao Phnom Rung 12, 34,
56–7, 262, **280–81**
Fair 48
Prasat Hin Muang Tam 268, **278–9**
Prasat Hin Phimai 12, 57, 262, 264,
270, **276–7**
hotels 410
restaurants 440
Prasat Khao Phra Wihan 263, **302**
Prasat Muang Sing **170**
Prasat Prang Ku **302**
Prasat Ta Muen **278**
Prasat Ta Muen Tot **278**
Prasat Thong, King 61
Bang Pa-in Palace 181
Wat Chai Watthanaram (Ayutthaya)
180
Wat Na Phra Men (Ayutthaya) 180
Prathamakant (Khon Kaen) 452, 455
Pratunam (Bangkok) **119**
Pratunam Market (Bangkok) **118–19,**
141
Prayun Bunnag 128
Prehistoric Thailand **54–5**
Ban Kao 170
Pha Taem 299
Phangnga Bay 346
Upper Andaman Coast 373
Prem Tinsulanond bridge 385
Prickly heat 482
Pridi Phanomyong 68
Prince of Lampang's Palace 37
Princess Mother 118
Promthep, Cape 358, 362, 363
Prostitution 116
Provincial buses 493
Public holidays 51
Public toilets 481
PULO (Pattani United Liberation
Organization) 480
Puppets 142, 143, 458
hun krabok 40, 43
nang talung shadow puppets 383
nang yai 41
Phatthalung 382
Shadow Puppet Theater (Nakhon
Si Thammarat) 378, 453, 455
shops 453, 455
What to Buy in Thailand 456

Q

Quantas Airways 490
Queen's Park (Bangkok) 136

R

Rabies 483
Rachabrapha Dam 356
Racing, horse *see* Horse racing
Radio 487
Rafflesia kerri 357
Rafting, whitewater rafting **463,** 468
Rahu 293
Railay–Phra Nang headland **370,** 371,
466
Railroads *see* Trains
Rainfall 50
Rainy season 49–50
Raja's Fashions (Bangkok) 139
Rama
Prasat Hin Phimai 276, 277
Ramakien 40–41
Rama I, King *see* Chao Phraya Chakri
Rama II, King **64**
Grand Palace and Wat Phra Kaeo
(Bangkok) 80, 85
and the poetry of Sunthorn Phu
319
Wat Arun (Bangkok) 126
Wat Phra Kaeo (Bangkok) 83
Wat Suthat (Bangkok) 91
Rama III, King **64,** 65
and gestures of the Buddha 173
Golden Mount (Bangkok) 87
Grand Palace (Bangkok) 85
Phatthalung 382
and the poetry of Sunthorn Phu 319
Wat Arun (Bangkok) 126
Wat Bowonniwet (Bangkok) 86
Wat Chalerm Phrakiet (Nonthaburi)
135
Wat Kalayanimit (Bangkok) 128
Wat Pho (Bangkok) 92
Wat Phra Kaeo (Bangkok) 82, 83
Wat Prayun (Bangkok) 128
Wat Suthat (Bangkok) 90
Wat Suwannaram (Bangkok) 124
Wat Thung Si Muang (Ubon
Ratchathani) 303
Rama IV, King *see* Mongkut
Rama V, King *see* Chulalongkorn
Rama VI, King *see* Vajiravudh
Rama VII, King *see* Prajadhipok
Rama VIII, King *see* Ananda Mahidol
Rama IX, King *see* Bhumibol
Adulyadej
Ramakien 25, **40–41,** 64
Grand Palace and Wat Phra Kaeo
(Bangkok) 80, 83
khon (dance-drama) 42
Ramathibodi I, King 60
Ayutthaya 176
Wat Phra Ram (Ayutthaya) 177

Ramathibodi II, King 60
   Wat Phra Si Sanphet (Ayutthaya)
   178
Ramayana 265
Ramesuan, King 60
   Wat Mahathat (Ayutthaya) 176
   Wat Phra Ram (Ayutthaya) 177
Ramkamhaeng, King 53, 422
   King Ramkamhaeng Monument
   (Sukhothai Historical Park) 195
   Old Sukhothai 58–9, 194
   royal white elephants 106
   Tak 190–91
   Wat Chang Lom 200
Ramkamhaeng National Museum
   (Sukhothai Historical Park) 194–5
Ramkamhaeng National Park 197
Ramkamhaeng Stone 88
Rang Hill (Phuket town) 360
Ranong **356**
   restaurants 449
Ratchaburi **132**
Ratchaburi National Museum
   132
Ratchadamnoen Avenue (Bangkok)
   107
Ratchadamnoen Boxing Stadium
   (Bangkok) 107, 142, 143, 460,
   461
Rattan **453,** 455
   What to Buy in Thailand 456
Rattanakosin style 90
   religious architecture 35
   Wat Suwannaram (Bangkok)
   124
Rayavadee Spa 470, 471
Rayong **317**
   hotels 415
Reassurance, as a gesture of the
   Buddha 173
Receiving of the Lotus Festival
   (Bang Phli) 47, 50
Reclining posture of the Buddha
   173
Red House 37
Reefs, coral see Coral reefs
Refugees, Thailand-Burma
   border 191
Refunds in shops 138, 450
Religion
   hill tribes 207
   religious architecture 34–5
   religious organizations 476, 477
   see also Buddhism
Rental accommodations 394
Renting cars, mopeds and bicycles
   494–5
Renu Nakhon **296**

Reservoirs
   Bhumibol 232
   Kaeng Krachan 330
   Sirikit 259
Resort hotels 392–3
Responsible travel 477
Restaurants **422–49**
   Bangkok 428–32
   coffee shops 422
   Deep South 449
   drinks 425
   Eastern Seaboard 441–3
   eating habits 423
   Far North 437–9
   Flavours of Thailand 424–5
   glossary of dishes 426–7
   khantoke dining 423
   Khorat Plateau 439–40
   Mekong River Valley 440–41
   North Central Plains 433–4
   Northwest Heartland 434–7
   prices 423
   South Central Plains 432–3
   tipping 423, 479
   Upper Andaman Coast 446–9
   Western Seaboard 443–6
   see also Food and drink
Restraining the waters as a gesture of
   the Buddha 173
Riboud, Marc 265
Rice
   and the monsoon 26–7
   and religion 39
   rice dishes 427
Rickshas 494
Riding elephants **464,** 468
Rights, in shops 138, 450
Ritz-Carlton Reserve Phulay Bay
   (Krabi) 396, 419
River City (Bangkok) 139, 452,
   455
River houses 37
River view of Bangkok 74–5
Riverboats
   Bangkok 497
   Chao Phraya Express 465, 469
   Chao Phraya River 74
Road maps 495
Road signs 494–5
Roads 494
Roadside food stands 422–3
Robinson's (Bangkok) 451, 455
Robot Building (Bangkok)
   69, 119
Rock-climbing **466,** 469
   Krabi 371
Rocket Festival (Yasothon) 12, 47, 48,
   271, 274

Roi Et 269, **273**
   hotels 410
   restaurants 440
Roman Catholic Church 163, 180
   Church of the Immaculate
   Conception (Chanthaburi) 320–21
Rose Garden (Bangkok) **134,** 458,
   461
Royal Bangkok Sports Club **117,** 460,
   461
Royal barges 60–61
   Royal Barge Museum (Bangkok)
   124–5
Royal Cliff Beach Hotel (Pattaya) 397,
   414
Royal houses 37
Royal Paraphernalia Museum
   (Bangkok) 102
Royal Plowing Ceremony (Bangkok)
   46, 48
Royal Thai cuisine 38
Royal Turf Club (Bangkok) 106
Royal white elephants 106
Royalty, etiquette 478
Ruamit 251
Rubber plantations
   Phanagnga Bay 367
   Trang province 381
Rubies 310–11
Rugby 460, 461
Rules of the road 495

S

Sa Anodat pond 287
Sa Phra Nang 370
Saam Yekh Akha 246
Saenphu 248
Safari World (Bangkok) **136**
Safety see Personal security
Sai River 246
Sai Yok National Park **169**
Saigon 294
Sailing **463,** 468
St. Francis Xavier Church (Bangkok)
   104
St. Joseph's Church (Ayutthaya) 162,
   180
Sairung falls 381
Sakai tribespeople 381, 389
Sakhon Nakhon **296**
Sala Chalermkrung Theater
   (Bangkok) 142, 143, 458, 461
Sala Rim Nam (Bangkok) 142, 143,
   458, 461
Salawin River 232
Salt deficiency 482
Samai pattana 68
Samet see Ko Samet

Samlors 496

Sampeng Lane Market (Bangkok) 141

Samphran Elephant Ground and Zoo 134

San Kamphaeng **228–9**

San Kamphaeng Hot Springs 229

San Somdej Prachao Taksin (Chanthaburi) 320

Sanam Chan Palace (Nakhon Pathom) 134

Sanam Luang (Bangkok) 75, 107
festivals 46
Street-by-Street map 78–9

Sanchao Dtai Hong Kong (Bangkok) 97

Sanchao Kun Oo (Bangkok) 96

Sangaroon Ratagasikorn 136

Sangkhalok pottery 59, 160, 161, 200

Sangkhla Buri 37, **168**
hotels 403

Sangkhom 291
Mekong villages tour **291**

Sanphet Maha Prasat 84

Santikhiree see Mae Salong

Sao Din 255

Saowapha Phongsi, Queen 91

Saphan Han Market (Bangkok) 98

Sapphires 310–11

Saraburi, festivals 48

Sarit Thanarat 68

Sathing Phra 346, 385

Satun 386

Sawankha Woranayok National Museum (Sawankhalok) 200

Sawankhalok 200

Scuba diving 349

Sea gypsies **363**
Ko Lanta 373
Ko Lipey 386
Ko Phi Phi 372

Seacon Square (Bangkok) 451, 455

Seafood 427
seafood of the South 387

Seatran Discovery Ferry 493

SEAWrite Award 115

Senior Travelers 476

Sergeant Major Thawee's Folk Museum (Phitsanulok) 201

Serpents, naga figures 228

Sex workers 116
AIDS risk 483
sexually transmitted diseases 483

SGA Airlines 490

Shadow Puppet Theater (Nakhon Si Thammarat) 378, 453, 455

Shadow puppets see Puppets

Shan (Tai Yai) tribespeople
festivals 47
Mae Hong Son **216**
Pai 219
Tham Chiang Dao 220

Shan United Army 233

Sheraton Grande Sukhumvit (Bangkok) 397, **400**

Shinawatra (Bangkok) 452, 455

T. Shinawatra Thai Silk (Chiang Mai) 452, 455

Shiraz (Chiang Mai) 454, 455

Shiva 115, 296
Giant Swing (Bangkok) 91
Ho Phra I-suan Shrine (Nakhon Si Thammarat) 379
Prasat Hin Khao Phnom Rung 280, 281
Prasat Hin Phimai 276
Prasat Khao Phra Wihan 302

Shivalinga 265

Shop-houses, Chinese 99

Shopping **450–57**
antiques 139, 454, 455
airport 488
arts and crafts 139, 452, 455
Bangkok 138–9
Bangkok's markets 140–41
bargaining 138, 450
bookstores 139, 455
ceramics 453, 455
clothes 139, 452, 455
craft centers 139, 451, 455
department stores and malls 138, 139, 451, 455
electronic goods 139
factories 451
fake goods 451
gems 139, 454, 455
hill-tribe artifacts 452, 455
jewelry 139, 454, 455
kalaga tapestries 453, 455
lacquerware 453, 455
markets and street vendors 138, 451
masks 453, 455
musical instruments 453, 455
nielloware 453, 455
opening hours 138, 450, 476
paying 138, 450
pewterware 453, 455
puppets 453, 455
rights and refunds 138, 450
Thai silk 452, 455
What to Buy in Thailand 456–7
wood, bamboo and rattan 453, 455

Si Chiangmai **291**
Mekong villages tour 291

Si Intharathit, King of Sukhothai 58
Wat Mahathat (Sukhothai) 196
Wat Phra Boromathat (Kamphaeng Phet) 193

Si Nakharin National Park 169

Si Racha **316**
restaurants 443

Si Satchanalai
reconstruction of 58–9
religious architecture 34
restaurants 434

Si Satchanalai National Park 200

Si Satchanalai-Chalieng Historical Park 11, 158, **198–9**
map 199

Si-oui 125

Siam, name changed to Thailand 22, 68

Siam Center/Siam Discovery (Bangkok) 138, 139

Siam Commercial Bank (Bangkok) 484

Siam Express 494, 495

Siam Niramit (Bangkok) 142, 143

Siam Paragon (Bangkok) 138, 139, 451, 455

Siam Park (Bangkok) **136–7**

Siam Society 136

Siam Square (Bangkok) **118**

Siamese twins 125

Siddhartha Gautama see Buddha

Silk 138, 139, **452,** 455
and Jim Thompson 120–21
San Kamphaeng 229
silk production **266–7**
What to Buy in Thailand 457

Silom Complex (Bangkok) 138, 139, 451

Silom Road (Bangkok) **115**

Silom Village (Bangkok) 139, 142, 143, 452, 455, 458, 461

Silpakorn University of Fine Arts (Bangkok) 78

Silverware, What to Buy in Thailand 457

Sima Thani Hotel (Khorat) 397, **410**

Similan islands see Ko Similan

Singapore, as a destination on the Eastern & Oriental Express 493

Singapore Airlines 490

Sirikit, Queen
Her Majesty the Queen's Birthday 49
SUPPORT Museum (Bangkok) 105
Vimanmek Mansion (Bangkok) 105

Sirikit Reservoir **259**

Sirindhorn Dam **299**
Siriraj Hospital (Bangkok) 125
Sita 40–41
Siwali Gardens (Bangkok) 85
Skytrain (Bangkok) 497
Smoking 479
Snacks 426
Snake bites 482
Snake Farm (Bangkok) **116**
Snooker 460, 461
Snorkeling 348, **462–3**, 468
Soccer 460, 461
Society 23–5
Sofitel Centara Grand Resort & Villas
  (Hua Hin) 308, **331**, 396, 416
Solar Air 490
Somdej Phra Narai National Museum
  (Lop Buri) 174
Song Tham, King of Ayutthaya 172
Songkhla 13, **384–5**
  map 384
Songkhla National Museum 345, **384,**
  385
Songkran (Thai New Year) 46, **48**
  in the North 236
Songserm Express Boat 493
Songthaews 496
Songwat Road (Bangkok) 96
Sop Ruak 11, **248**
  Golden Triangle driving tour 247
  see also Golden Triangle
Soppong **218–19**
Soups 427
  bird's-nest soup 341
South Central Plains 10–11, **165–85**
  hotels 402–3
  map 166–7
  restaurants 432–3
Southeast Asia, map 15
Southern Thailand 22, **343–89**
  coral reefs 348–9
  Deep South 375–89
  festivals 47
  history 346–7
  mangrove forests 350–51
  maps 18–19, 344–5
  Upper Andaman Coast 353–73
Spas **470–71**
Special interest holidays **462–9**
Special interest tours 495
Speed limits 495
Spirit Cave 54
Spirit houses 37
Spiritual beliefs
  hill tribes 207
  see also Religion
Sports **25**
  air sports **467,** 469

Sports (cont.)
  bungee jumping **466,** 469
  canoeing **463,** 468
  caving **466,** 469
  cycling **466,** 469
  diving and snorkeling **462,** 468
  golf **464,** 468
  horse riding **467,** 469
  kayaking **463,** 468
  krabi-krabong 460, 461
  muay thai 460, 461
  rock climbing **466,** 469
  rugby 460, 461
  sailing **463,** 468
  soccer 460, 461
  takraw 460, 461
  Thai boxing 44–5
  water sports **463,** 468
  white-water rafting **463,** 468
Springs
  Fang area 242
  Khlong Thom 371
  Ranong 356
  San Kamphaeng Hot Springs 229
Sri Lanka, influence of 198
Srivijaya Empire 53, 56, **56–7**, 346
  architecture 347
  Chaiya's role 332
  Nakhon Si Thammarat 378
SRT (State Railroad of Thailand) 492
STA Travel (Bangkok) 491
Stamp Market (Bangkok) 141
Standard Chartered Bank
  (Bangkok) 484
Standard Chartered Bank (Phuket
  town) 360
Stilt houses 125
Stings, jellyfish 482
Stomach upsets 482
Stonework, Davaravati 56
Street names *see* Addresses
Street vendors 451
Suan Dok Gate (Chiang Mai) 226
Suan Pakkad Palace (Bangkok) 119,
  119
Suan Son 317
Suay tribespeople
  Ban Ta Klang 279
  Surin 279
Suchart House (Nakhon Si
  Thammarat) 378
Sukhothai 11, **194–7**
  festivals 20, 46, 50
  hotels 404
  Loy Krathong 195
  religious architecture 34
  restaurants 434
  Wat Mahathat 196–7

Sukhothai Historical Park 11, 159,
  194–5
  map 194
Sukhothai Kingdom 20, 53, **58–9**
  art 160–61
  Kamphaeng Phet 192
  music 42
  Nan 254
  Wat Chang Lom 200
Sukhothai School 160
Sukhumvit Road (Bangkok) **136**
Sukrip 40
Sumet Jumsai 69
Sunantha, Queen 321
Sunbathing 479
  safety 482
Sunshine 49
Sunthorn Phu 25, **319**
  statues of 317, 318, 319
Suphran Buri **172**
  festivals 51
SUPPORT Museum (Bangkok) 100,
  103, **105**
Surat Thani **333**
  bus terminal 493
  hotels 418
  restaurants 446
  tourist police 481
Surin 12, **279**
  Elephant Roundup 12, 271, **278,**
  279
  festivals 50
  hotels 410
  restaurants 440
Surin island *see* Ko Surin
Surin Museum (Surin) 279
Suryavarman I, King 276
Suryavarman II, King 57
Suvarnabhumi International Airport
  (Bangkok) 489
Suwan Kuha Cave (Wat Tan) 366
Suwannakhet 298
Swimming
  diving and snorkeling 462–3
  see also Beaches
Swing, Giant (Bangkok) *see* Giant
  Swing

T

Tachilek 246
Taeng River 221
Tai people 21, 53, 56–7, 254
Tai Yai *see* Shan
Tak 59, **190–91**
  hotels 404
  restaurants 434
Tak Bai 389
Takraw 460, 461

Taksin, King 63, 64
　Chanthaburi 320
　statue of 191
　Taksin Monument (Bangkok) 128
　Uttaradit 237
　Wat Arun (Bangkok) 126
Taksin Maharat National Park 191
Taksin Monument (Bangkok) **128**
Taksin Palace (Narathiwat) 389
Taksin Park (Chanthaburi) 320
Takua Pa 346
Tam Munag On 229
Tambralinga 378
Tamils, Maha Uma Devi Temple
　(Bangkok) 115
Tanboke Koranee National Park 367
Tang To Kang Gold Shop (Bangkok)
　96
Tansadet waterfall 339
Tantrism 30
Taoism, Leng Noi Yee Temple
　(Bangkok) 97, 99
Tapestries, *kalaga* 453, 455
Tapi River 333
Tarutao National Marine Park 13, 345,
　375, 376, **386**
TAT *see* Tourism Authority of
　Thailand
Tattoos 31
Taxes
　hotels 395
　refunds 138, 450
　VAT 485
Taxis **496**
　Suvarnabhumi International Airport
　489
　tipping 479
Teak 249
　Lampang 236
　teak houses (Phrae) 259
Telephone Organization of Thailand
　(TOT) 486
Telephones **486–7**
　cell phones 486
　international calls 486
　local calls 486
　phonecards 486
Television 487
Temperatures 51
　coping with the heat 482
Temple of the Holy Footprint, festival
　at 46
Temples
　fairs and festivals 460
　Khmer 34, 264–5
　Maha Uma Devi Temple (Bangkok)
　115
　see also Prasat; Wat

Tenasserim Mountains 325, 354
　Phangnga Bay 364
Terengganu 67
Tetanus 483
Textiles *see* Fabrics
Tha Bon 316
Tha Chang Road (Nakhon Si
　Thammarat) 379
Tha Phae Gaet (Chiang Mai) 226
Tha Ton **242**, 246, 251
　hotels 409
Thai Air Asia 490
Thai Airways 488, 490
Thai Celadon House (Bangkok) 453,
　455
Thai Elephant Conservation Center
　(Lampang) 215, **237**, 464, 468
Thai food, Art of **38–9**
　see also Food and drink
Thai hotels 393
Thai Hotels Association 392, 395
Thai Human Imagery Museum 134
Thai Lapidary (Bangkok) 454, 455
Thai Lue people 239
　Chiang Khong 249
　Doi Phu Kha National Park 254
　Nong Bua **254**
Thai Massage School of Chiang Mai
　467, 469
"Thai Modernism" 119
Thai Orchid Service (Chiang Mai) 491
Thai Overlander Travel & Tour
　(Bangkok) 491
Thai Red Cross 116
Thai Silk Company 121
Thai TicketMajor 458
Thai Tribal Crafts (Chiang Mai) 452,
　455
Thai Village and Orchid Farm
　(Phuket town) 359, **361**, 452, 455
Thailand Cultural Center (Bangkok)
　459, 461
Thailand Environment Institute 477
Thailand-Burma border refugees 191
Thailand-Burma Railroad Center
　(Kanchanaburi) 170
Thaksin Shinawatra 69
Thalang **363**
Thalang, Battle of (1785) 359,
　363
Thalang National Museum (Phuket)
　363
Thale Ban National Park **386**
Thale Noi Waterfowl Park **383**
Tham Chang Hai 381
Tham Chiang Dao 220
Tham Hua Gralok 367
Tham Khao Luang 330

Tham Lot 219, 366
Tham Luang 246
Tham Morakhot (Ko Muk) 380
Tham Pha Tup Forest 255
Tham Phra Nang Nok 370
Tham Phraya Nakon 332
Tham Pla (Chiang Rai province) 246
Tham Pla (Mae Hong Son province)
　218
Tham Pum 246
Tham Sai 332
Tham Tup Tao 220
Thammasat University (Bangkok) 79
Thammayut sect 303
Than Mayom waterfall 322–3
Than Thip Falls 291
Thana City Golf and Country Club
　(Bangkok) 464, 468
Thao Suranari Monument (Khorat)
　275
That Phanom
　hotels 412
　restaurants 441
Thavorn Hotel Lobby Exhibition
　(Phuket town) 360
Theater **42–3**
　modern 459, 461
　traditional 142, 143, 458, 461
　see also Khon; Lakhon; Likay
Theme parks, Ancient City (Bangkok)
　137
Theravada Buddhism *see* Buddhism
Thewet Flower Market (Bangkok)
　104, 140
Thi Lo Su falls 191
Thieves' Market (Bangkok) *see*
　Nakorn Kasem
Thip, General 63
Thompson, Jim 120, **121**
　Jim Thompson's House (Bangkok)
　120–21
　Jim Thompson's Silk Shop
　(Bangkok) 138, 139, 452, 455
　silk production 138, 266, 452
Thon Buri (Bangkok) 61, 65, **123–9**
　area map 123
　hotels 401
　restaurants 431
　Wat Arun 126–7
Thon Buri Station (Bangkok)
　493
Thong Son 337
Three Pagodas Pass 11, **168**
Thung Kwian Forest Market
　237
Thung Salaeng Luang National Park
　201

Thung Setthi Fort (Kamphaeng Phet) 193
Thung Yai Naresuan **168–9**
Tickets
  airline 474
  entertainment 142, 458
"Tiger economies" 22, 68
Tigers 219
Tilok, King 62, 224
Time system 476–7
Tip Chang 234
Tipping 479
  in hotels 395
  in restaurants 423
Toilets, public 481
Ton Khem Market (Damnoen Saduak) 132
Ton Nga Chang waterfall 385
Ton Tay falls 381
Tong Nai Pan 339
Tong Sala 339
Tosakan 40–41, 277
Touching the Earth, as a gesture of the Buddha 173
Tourism 23
Tourism Authority of Thailand (TAT) 23, 475
  headquarters (Bangkok) 477
  logo 126
  TAT offices 395, 475
Tourist Assistance Center (Bangkok) 481
Tourist information 475
Tourist police 480, **481**
Tours by car
  Golden Triangle driving tour 246–7
  Mekong villages tour 290–91
Trade routes, historic, Straits of Malacca 346–7
Traditional Thai houses 36–7
Trains 492, 493
  Eastern & Oriental Express 493
  Suvarnabhumi International Airport 489
Trang 13, **380–81**
  festivals 50
  hotels 421
  restaurants 449
  Trang coast 376
  Trang's Andaman Islands **380**
Trat **323**
  hotels 415
  restaurants 443
Travel **488–97**
  air 488–90
  bicycles 495
  cars 494
  Deep South 377

Travel (cont.)
  Eastern & Oriental Express 493
  Eastern Seaboard 315
  Far North 241
  Khorat Plateau 271
  local transport 496
  long-distance buses 492
  Mekong River Valley 285
  mopeds 494
  North Central Plains 189
  Northwest Heartland 215
  organized tours 491
  provincial buses 493
  samlors 496
  Songthaews 496
  South Central Plains 167
  taxis 496
  trains 492, 493
  tuk-tuks 496
  Upper Andaman Coast 355
  Western Seaboard 326
Travelers' checks 485
Treatments, spa 471
Trekking **464–5**, 468–9
  Chiang Dao 221
Tribal Research Institute (Chiang Mai) 227
Tribespeople *see* Hill tribes
Trooping of the Colors (Bangkok) 46, 51, 107
Tropic of Cancer 28
Tsunami (2004) 69
Tuberculosis 483
Tuk-tuks 496
Tung Tieo forest trail 371
Twins, Siamese 125
Typhoid 483

U

U Thong National Museum 172
Ubon National Museum (Ubon Ratchathani) 302–3
Ubon Ratchathani **302–3**
  festivals 47, 49
  hotels 412
  map 303
  restaurants 441
Udayadityavarman 57
Udon Thani **272**
  hotels 410
  restaurants 440
Umbrellas
  Bo Sang 228
  Umbrella Fair (Bo Sang) 46, 51
Umphang **191**
  hotels 404
  restaurants 434
Umphang Wildlife Sanctuary 11, **191**

UNESCO World Heritage Sites
  Kamphaeng Phet 193
  Old Sukhothai 194
  Thung Yai Naresuan and Huai Kha Khaeng 168
United Airlines 491
United Kingdom Embassy 475
United States Embassy 475
Upper Andaman Coast 13, **353–73**
  cave paintings 373
  hotels 418–20
  map 354–5
  restaurants 446–9
UPS 487
Ussa, Princess 295
Uthai's Gems (Bangkok) 454, 455
Utopia 477
Uttaradit **237**

V

Vaccinations 482
Vachirathan waterfall 214
Vajiravudh (Rama VI), King 67, **68**
  archaeological interests of 161
  Ban Phitsanulok (Bangkok) 106
  Grand Palace (Bangkok) 85
  Mareukathayawan Palace 331
  Siam Society 136
  statue of 117
  Ubon Ratchathani 303
Van Heekeren 170
VAT 485
Vegetables 133
  carving 38
Vegetarian Festival (Phuket) 47, 50, 360
Vessandorn, Prince 49, 289
Vessantara, Prince 120
Victoria, Queen of England 66, 84
Victoria Point 356
Vidal, Gore 115
Vientiane 12, **294–5**
  map 294
Vietnam War **68**, 242
  Khorat 275
  Pathet Lao 295
  Pattaya 309, 317
  Ubon Ratchathani 302
  Udon Thani 272
Viking Cave (Phi Phi Ley) 373
Vimanmek Mansion (Bangkok) 103, **104–5**
VISA/MasterCard 484
Visakha Bucha 46, 49
Visas 474–5
Vishnu 31, 115, 296, 388
  Prasat Hin Phimai 277
  Prasat Prang Ku 302

Vishnu (cont.)
statues of 55, 275, 378
Sukhothai art 160
VOC (Dutch East India Company) 163

W

Wai (greeting) 24, 478
Walking, trekking **464–5**, 468–9
"Walking" Buddha 59, 160
Wang Luang (Ayutthaya) 176
Wang River 236
Warorot Market (Chiang Mai) 226
Wats 25
accommodation at 393
and etiquette 479
and popular Buddhist rituals 129
Wat complex **32–3**
Wat Arun (Bangkok) 75, **126–7**
Wat Atsadangnimit (Ko Sichang) 317
Wat Benchamabophit (Bangkok) 35,
43, **106–7**
Wat Bot Mani Sibunruang (Tak) 190,
191
Wat Bowonniwet (Bangkok) 86
Wat Bun Thawi (Phetchaburi) 330
Wat Bupharam (Trat) 323
Wat Buraphaphiram (Roi Et) 273
Wat Chai Mongkhon (Songkhla) 384
Wat Chai Watthanaram (Ayutthaya)
61, 180
Wat Chaiyo Wora Wihan (Ang Thong
province) 172
Wat Chalerm Phrakiet (Nonthaburi)
135
Wat Chama Thewi
(Lamohun) 229
Wat Chan Khao Manirat (Huay Xai)
249
Wat Chang Kham Wora Wihan (Nan)
255
Wat Chang Lom (Si Satchanalai-
Chalieng Historical Park) 198, **200**
Wat Chang Rop (Aranyik) 193
Wat Chao Chan (Si Satchanalai-
Chalieng Historical Park) 199
Wat Chedi Chet Thaeo (Si
Satchanalai-Chalieng Historical
Park) 198
Wat Chedi Luang (Chiang Mai) 225,
226
Wat Chedi Luang (Chiang
Saen) 228
Wat Chedi Si Hong (Sukhothai) 197
Wat Cheng (Ubon Ratchathani) 303
Wat Chet Yot (Chiang Mai) 227
Wat Chet Yot (Chiang Rai) 250
Wat Chetuphon (Bangkok)
see Wat Pho

Wat Chiang Man (Chiang Mai) 35,
215, 226
Wat Chom Sawan (Phrae) 259
Wat Chong Kham (Mae Hong Son)
217
Wat Chong Klang (Mae Hong Son)
217
Wat Chong Kra Chok (Prachuap Khiri
Khan) 332
Wat Chong Sung (Mae Sariang) 232
Wat Chulamani (Phitsanulok
province) 201
Wat Chumphon Khiri (Mae Sot) 188,
190
Wat Doi Kong Mu (Mae Hong Son)
217
Wat Dok Ban (Ngao) 252
Wat Hai Sok (Vientiane) 295
Wat Haisoke (Nong Khai) 293
Wat Hat Yai Nai (Hat Yai) 385
Wat Hin Mak Peng 291
Wat Hua Khon (Si Satchanalai-
Chalieng Historical Park) 199
Wat Hua Wiang (Mae Hong Son) 216
Wat Indrawihan (Bangkok) **104**
Wat Jong Paen (Fang) 242
Wat Kalayanimit (Bangkok) **128**
Wat Kalothai (Kamphaeng
Phet) 193
Wat Kamphaeng Laeng (Phetchaburi)
329
Wat Khaek (Nong Khai) 293
Wat Khao Chan Ngam (Khorat) 275
Wat Khao Lad (Hua Hin) 331
Wat Khao Phnom Phloeng (Si
Satchanalai-Chalieng Historical
Park) 199
Wat Khao Sukim (Chanthaburi
province) 315, **319**
Wat Khao Yai Bon (Si Satchanalai-
Chalieng Historical Park) 199
Wat Khian (Nonthaburi) 135
Wat Khlong Thom (Khlong Thom)
371
Wat Khong Chiam (Khong Chiam)
299
Wat Khuha Phimuk (Yala) 388
Wat Khun In Pramun (Ang Thong
province) 172
Wat Klang (Pai) 219
Wat Kow Tahm (Ko Pha Ngan) 467,
469
Wat Kuha Sawan (Phatthalung) 382
Wat Kuti Dao (Ayutthaya) 180
Wat Kuti Rai (Si Satchanalai-Chalieng
Historical Park) 199
Wat Lak Muang (Si Satchanalai-
Chalieng Historical Park) 199

Wat Lamduan (Nong Khai) 293
Wat Lokaya Sutharam (Ayutthaya) 177
Wat Luang (Chiang Khong) 249
Wat Luang (Phrae) 258
Wat Mae Phrae Museum (Bangkok)
104
Wat Maha Wanaram (Ubon
Ratchathani) 303
Wat Mahathat, cultural studies
(Bangkok) 467, 469
Wat Mahathat (Ayutthaya) 164, 176
Wat Mahathat (Bangkok) 78, **86**
Wat Mahathat (Phetchaburi)
324, 328
Wat Mahathat (Sukhothai Historical
Park) 34, 195, **196–7**
Wat Mahathat Yasothon (Yasothon)
274
Wat Maheyong (Ayutthaya) 181
Wat Mixai (Vientiane) 295
Wat Mongkol Nimit (Phuket town)
361
Wat Muen Ngon Kong (Chiang Mai)
224
Wat Mungmuang (Chiang Rai) 250
Wat Na Phra Men (Ayutthaya) 35, **180**
Wat Nang Phaya (Si Satchanalai-
Chalieng Historical Park) 198
Wat Nong Bua (Nong Bua) 241, 254
Wat Ong Theu (Vientiane) 295
Wat Pa Daet (Mae Chaem) 232
Wat Pa Mamuang (Sukhothai) 197
Wat Pa Mok (Ang Thong province)
172
Wat Pa Sak (Chiang Saen) 249
Wat Pan Tao (Chiang Mai) 35
Wat Pathum Wanaram (Bangkok) **118**
Wat Pha Kho (Sathing Phra) 374
Wat Pha Non (Phrae) 258
Wat Phan Tao (Chiang Mai) 225
Wat Phan Waen (Chiang Mai) 224
Wat Phanan Choeng (Ayutthaya) 181
Wat Pho (Bangkok) 75, **92–3**
cultural studies 467, 469
Wat Pho Chai (Nong Khai) 292
Wat Pho Si Nai (Ban Chiang) 272
Wat Phra Bat (Phrae) 241, 258
Wat Phra Boromathat (Kamphaeng
Phet) 193
Wat Phra Boromathat (Uttaradit) 237
Wat Phra Kaeo (Bangkok) 10, 75,
80–83
bot and peripheral buildings 82
festivals 48
northern terrace 83
prangs 83
Ramakien Gallery 83
Ramakien murals 40–41

Wat Phra Kaeo (cont.)
upper terrace 82–3
yakshas 83

Wat Phra Kaeo (Chiang Rai) 250

Wat Phra Kaeo Don Tao (Lampang) 236

Wat Phra Kaeo (Kamphaeng Phet) 186, 192–3

Wat Phra Mahathat (Nakhon Si Thammarat) 13, 375, **378**

Wat Phra Narai Maharat (Khorat) 275

Wat Phra Phai Luang (Sukhothai) 160

Wat Phra Ram (Ayutthaya) 177

Wat Phra Ruang (Phrae) 258

Wat Phra Si Rattana Mahathat (Lop Buri) 175

Wat Phra Si Rattana Mahathat (Phitsanulok) 189, 201
Phitsanulok Buddha 160–61

Wat Phra Si Rattana Mahathat (Si Satchanalai-Chalieng Historical Park) 199

Wat Phra Si Sanphet (Ayutthaya) 35, **178–9**

Wat Phra Sing (Chiang Mai) 35, 63, 225, **226**

Wat Phra Sing (Chiang Rai) 250

Wat Phra That Chedi Luang (Chiang Saen) 248

Wat Phra That (Kamphaeng Phet) 193

Wat Phra That Chae Haeng (Nan) 255

Wat Phra That Chaw Hae (Phrae) 259

Wat Phra That Choeng Chum (Sakhon Nakhon) 285, **296**

Wat Phra That Chom Kitti (Chiang Saen) 249

Wat Phra That Doi Suthep (Chiang Mai province) 11, **222–3**

Wat Phra That Doi Thong (Chiang Rai) 250

Wat Phra That Doi Tung (Chiang Rai province) 243

Wat Phra That Doi Wao (Mae Sai) 246

Wat Phra That Haripunchai (Lamphun) 229

Wat Phra That Lampang Luang (Lampang) 11, 62, 213, **234–5**, 236

Wat Phra That Mae Yen (Pai) 219

Wat Phra That Narai Cheng Weng (Sakhon Nakhon) 296

Wat Phra That Nong Bua (Ubon Ratchathani) 303

Wat Phra That Pha Ngao (Chiang Saen) 249

Wat Phra That Phanom (That Phanom) 12, 263, **297**

Wat Phra That Si Chom Thong (Chom Thong) 232

Wat Phra Tong (Phuket) 358

Wat Phraphutthabat Bok (Phu Phrabat Historical Park) 295

Wat Phu Khao Thong (Ayutthaya) 180

Wat Phumin (Nan) 11, 254, **256–7**

Wat Phuttha Tiwat (Betong) 389

Wat Phutthaisawan (Ayutthaya) 180

Wat Pongsanuk Tai (Lampang) 236–7

Wat Pradu Songtham (Ayutthaya) 181

Wat Prayun (Bangkok) **128**

Wat Rachabophit (Bangkok) 66, 67, **91**

Wat Rachanadda (Bangkok) **87**

Wat Rachapradit (Bangkok) **91**

Wat Rakhang (Bangkok) 33, 74, **125**

Wat Ram Poeng (Chiang Mai) 227

Wat Ratchaburana (Ayutthaya) 35, 176

Wat Ratchaburana (Phitsanulok) 201

Wat Sa Si (Sukhothai Historical Park) 59

Wat Saket (Bangkok) 34, **87**

Wat Sala Loi (Khorat) 275

Wat Sao Thong Thong (Lop Buri) 174

Wat Sao Thong Tong (Nakhon Si Thammarat) 379

Wat Saphan Hin (Sukhothai) 197

Wat Si Bunruang (Mai Sariang) 232

Wat Si Chum (Lampang) 237

Wat Si Chum (Phrae) 259

Wat Si Chum (Sukhothai) 34, 59

Wat Si Khun Muang (Nong Khai) 293

Wat Si Komkam (Phayao) 252

Wat Si Mongkol Thai (Mukdahan) 298

Wat Si Muang (Nong Khai) 292

Wat Si Muang (Vientiane) 295

Wat Si Sumang (Nong Khai) 293

Wat Si Suthawat (Wiang Pa Pao) 252

Wat Si Ubon Rattanaram (Ubon Ratchathani) 303

Wat Sisaket (Vientiane) 294

Wat Sok Pa Luang (Vientiane) 295

Wat Sorasak (Sukhothai) 160

Wat Suan Dok (Chiang Mai) 227

Wat Suan Mok (Chaiya) 333

Wat Suan Phu (Bangkok) 113

Wat Suan Tan (Nan) 255

Wat Supattanaram Worawihan (Ubon Ratchathani) 303

Wat Suthat (Bangkok) 35, 65, **90–91**

Wat Suwan Dararam (Ayutthaya) 178

Wat Suwan Khiri (Si Satchanalai-Chalieng Historical Patk) 199

Wat Suwannaram (Bangkok) **124**

Wat Tapotaram (Ranong) 356

Wat Tha Khaek (Chiang Khan) 290

Wat Tha Thanon (Uttaradit) 237

Wat Tha Ton (Tha Ton) 242

Wat Thai Watthanaram (Tak province) 190

Wat Tham Chiang Dao (Doi Chiang Dao) 220

Wat Tham Khao Pun (Kanchanaburi) 170

Wat Tham Sua (Krabi) 371

Wat Thammikarat (Ayutthaya) 176

Wat Thamyaiprig (Ko Sichang) 317

Wat Thep Phitak Punnaram (Khorat) 275

Wat Thung Sawang (Yasothon) 274

Wat Thung Si Muang (Ubon Ratchathani) 303

Wat Traimit (Bangkok) **98**

Wat Traphang Thong (Sukhothai) 188, 194

Wat U Mong (Chiang Mai) 227

Wat Wang (Phatthalung) 382

Wat Wangwiwekaram (Sangkhla Buri) 168

Wat Yai Chai Mongkhon (Ayutthaya) 167, **181**

Wat Yai Suwannaram (Phetchaburi) 329

Wat Yot Kaew Siwachai (Mukdahan) 298

Water
drinking water 482
water-borne diseases 483

Water sports **463**, 468

Waterfalls
Erawan falls 169
Haeo Suwat waterfall 184
Hok Sai waterfall 319
Huai Khamin falls 169
Huay Sadeh waterfall 370
Huay To waterfall 370
Khao Chamao waterfall 319
Khao Phra Taew Forest Park 363
Khlong Phlu waterfall 323
Krathin waterfall 320
Mae Ya waterfall 231
Namuang waterfall 338
Pha Charoen falls 190
Phliu waterfall 321
Phone Phop waterfall 287
Phu Kradung National Park 287
Sairung falls 381
Tansadet waterfall 339
Than Mayom waterfall 322–3
Than Thip falls 291
Thi Lo Su falls 191
Ton Nga Chang waterfall 385
Ton Tay falls 381

Waterskiing 463
Waterways 497
Weather **48–51**
  coping with the heat 482
  monsoon seasons 26–7
  when to go 474
Weaving
  kalaga tapestries 453, 455
  silk 267
Western Seaboard 13, **325–41**
  hotels 415–18
  map 326–7
  restaurants 443–6
Western writers in
  Bangkok 115
Wetlands 29
Wheelchair access
  see Disabled travelers
White Elephant Monument (Doi
  Suthep) 222
White Sand Beach (Hat Sai Khao)
  308
Whitewater rafting **463,** 468
Wiang Pa Pao **252**
Wichai Prasit Fortress (Bangkok) 128
Wickerwork, What to Buy in
  Thailand 456
Wihan Lai Kham (Chiang Mai) 225,
  226
Wihan Phra Mongkhon (Ayutthaya)
  177
Wihans 33
Wild Tigers 68
Wildlife 23, **28–9**
  Angthong National Marine
  Park 340
  Bang Phra Reservoir 316
  Banthat Mountains 381
  Birds of Northern Thailand 210–11
  coral reefs 348–9
  Crocodile Farm (Bangkok) 137
  Doi Inthanon National Park 230–31
  dugongs 381
  Elephant Nature Park (Mae Taeng
  Valley) 221
  Elephant Training Center Taeng
  Dao 220, 464
  Gibbon Rehabilitation Center
  (Phuket) 359, 363

Wildlife (cont.)
  Huai Kha Khaeng 168–9
  Kaeng Krachen National
  Park 330
  Khao Chong Nature and Study
  Center 381
  Khao Phanom Bencha National
  Park 370
  Khao Sam Roi Yot National Park
  332
  Khao Soi Dao Wildlife Sanctuary
  320
  Khao Sok National Park 356
  Khao Yai National Park 184–5
  Khlong Lan National Park 192
  Ko Chang 322
  Ko Surin and Ko Similan 357
  Mae Wong National Park 192
  Mae Yom National Park 252
  mangrove forests 350–51
  Marine Research Center (Phuket)
  363
  Namtok Phlio National Park 321
  orchids 220
  Phu Hin Rong Kla National Park
  288
  Phu Kradung National Park
  286–7
  Phu Rua National Park 288
  Phuket Butterfly Garden and Insect
  World 359, 361
  Phuket FantaSea 262
  Rafflesia kerri 357
  Samphran Elephant Ground and
  Zoo 134
  Snake Farm (Bangkok) 116
  Surin Elephant Roundup 271, **278,**
  279
  Tarutao National Marine Park
  386
  Thai Elephant Conservation Center
  (Lampang) 237
  Thailand's endangered wildlife **219**
  Thale Ban National Park 386
  Thale Noi Waterfowl Park 383
  Thung Yai Naresuan 168–9
  tips for bird-watching 211
  Umphang Wildlife Sanctuary 11, **191**
  Wat Doi Suthep 222–3

Wildlife (cont.)
  wildlife watching **465,** 469
  see also Zoos
Windsurfing 463
Wine, customs allowances 475
Women travelers 480–81
Wood, Thailand's teak industry 249
Wood-carving **453,** 455
  What to Buy in Thailand 456
World Bank 299
World Fellowship of Buddhists
  (Bangkok) 467, 469
World Travel Service Ltd (Bangkok) 491
World War II 68
  Bridge over the Khwae Yai River 171
  Burma-Thailand Railroad Memorial
  Trail 169
  JEATH War Museum
  (Kanchanaburi) 170–71
  Kanchanaburi 170

Y

Yala 376, **388**
  festivals 48
Yaowarat Road (Bangkok) 97
Yasothon **274**
  Rocket Festival 12, 47, 48, 271, 274
Yawi language 375
Yellow fever 482
Yom River 58
  Mae Yom National Park 252
  Phrae 258
  Si Satchanalai 198, 199
Yot Fa, King 180
Young Elephant Training Center **237**
Yuam River 232

Z

Zoos
  Dusit Zoo (Bangkok) 105, 464
  Khao Khieo Zoo 316
  Safari World (Bangkok) 136
  Samphran Elephant Ground and
  Zoo 134
  see also Wildlife

Acknowledgments

Dorling Kindersley would like to thank the following people whose contributions and assistance have made the preparation of this book possible.

Main Contributor
Philip Cornwel-Smith is a journalist focusing on entertainment, lifestyle and topical issues. After working on guides to London, in 1994 he moved to Thailand and was founding editor of the Bangkok listings magazine *Metro*.

Andrew Forbes has studied Thai history and culture for more than 20 years and has lived in the country on and off since 1984. He writes for the *Asian Wall Street Journal* and *Far Eastern Economic Review* among other publications.

Tim Forsyth is a writer and lecturer at the London School of Economics. He has travelled extensively throughout Northern Thailand and other parts of Southeast Asia.

Rachel Harrison has lectured at the School of Oriental and African Studies in London and contributed to Thai phrase books. She has a special interest in Northeast Thailand.

David Henley is director of Crescent Press Agency's Thailand Bureau and has lived in Thailand for more than a decade. An authority on Thai cuisine, he contributes regularly to the *Bangkok Post* and *The Australian*.

John Hoskin has been based in Bangkok since 1980. He is the author of several books on travel, art and culture in Thailand and Indochina, including *The Mekong: A River and Its People*.

Gavin Pattison is a London-based writer who has contributed to the *Blue Guide to Thailand* among other titles. He has travelled extensively in Thailand, Indonesia, and other parts of Southeast Asia.

Picture Research
Vicky Peel, Ellen Root.

Additional Illustrations
Robert Ashby, Graham Bell, Peter Bull, Joanna Cameron, Chris Forsey, Paul Guest, Stephen Gyapay, Ruth Lindsay, Maltings Partnership, Mel Pickering, Robbie Polley, Sally Anne Reisen, Mike Taylor, Pat Thorne, Paul Weston.

Additional Photography
Alberto Cassio, Peter Chadwick, CPA Media, Philip Dowell, Neil Fletcher, Allen Hopkins, Dave King, James Marshall, Alan Newnham, Ian O'Leary, Alex Robinson, Rough Guides/Karen Trist; Mick Shippen, Harry Taylor.

Additional Cartography
Christine Purcell and Gary Bowes (ERA-Maptec Ltd).

Design and Editorial Assistance
Alexander Allan, Emma Anacootee, Gillian Allan, Douglas Amrine, Vicky Barber, Tessa Bindloss, Vivien Crump, Catherine Day, Lara Dunston, Ron Emmons, Emer FitzGerald, Fay Franklin, Silvia Gaillard, Victoria Heyworth-Dunne, Paul Hines, Leanne Hogbin, Laura Jones, Nancy Jones, Priya Kukadia, Esther Labi, James Marshall, Victor Matthews, Sonal Modha, Catherine Palmi, Helen Partington, Sudarat Ponpangpa, Rada Radojicic, Mani Ramaswamy, Lee Redmond, Natalie Revie, Sands Publishing Solutions, Julian Sheather, Ellie Smith, Veronica Wood.

Additional Research
Parita Boonyoo, Debbie Guthrie Haer, Sathorn Leelakachornjit, Elizabeth Lu, James Mahon, Pharadee Narkkarphunchiwan, Warangkana Nibhatsukit, Larry O'Sullivan, Mick Shippen, Pimalaporn Wongchinsri, Wanee Tipchindachaikul, Somchai Worasart.

Proofreader
Denise Heywood.

Index
Helen Peters.

Special Assistance
Dorling Kindersley would like to thank all the regional branches of the Tourism Authority of Thailand (TAT). Particular thanks also to: the Ayutthaya Historical Studies Centre (Thailand), Dr Peter Barrett (Medical Advisory Service for Travellers Abroad, London), William Booth (Jim Thompson's House, Bangkok), Alberto Cassio (Photobank, Bangkok), Crescent Press Agency (Chiang Mai),Gerald Cubitt, John Dransfield (Kew Gardens Herbarium, London), Michael Freeman, Helen Goldie (Durham University), Philip Harris (Bahn Thai Restaurant, London), Kietisak Itchayanan (National Culture Commission, Bangkok), Elizabeth Moore (London School of Oriental and African Studies), Tony Moore (British Thai Boxing Council), Phra Maha Pradit Panyatulo (Wat Buddhapadipa, London), Paisarn Piammattawat, Rattika Rhienpanish (Mai Thai Restaurant, London), Vidhisha Nayanthara Samarasekara, Philip Stott (London School of Oriental and African Studies), Dusadee Swangviboonpong (London School of Oriental and African Studies), Thai Airways (London), William Warren (Bangkok), Terri S Yamaka (TAT, London).

Photography Permissions
Dorling Kindersley would like to thank the following for their assistance and kind permission to photograph at their establishments: Ancient City, Ayutthaya Historical Park, Ban Chiang National Museum, Ban Phin (House of Opium), Chakra Bongse House, Chan Kasem National Museum, Chao Sam Phraya National Museum, Chiang Mai National Museum, In Buri National Museum, Jim Thompson's Thai Silk Shop, Kamphaeng Phet Historical Park, Khon Kaen National Museum, Khorat (Nakhon Ratchasima) National Museum, Lampang National Museum, Lamphun National Museum, Lop Buri National Museum, Muang Tam Historical Park, Nakhon Pathom National Museum, Nakhon Si Thammarat National Museum, Nan National Museum, Narai Ratchaniwet Palace, National Gallery, National Museum (Bangkok), Oriental Hotel, Pha Taem, Phimai National Museum, Phnom Rung Historical Park, Prasart Museum, Ramkamhaeng National Museum, Ratchaburi National Museum, Royal Barge Museum, Sawankha Woranayok National Museum, Siriraj Hospital, Si Satchanalai-Chalieng Historical Park, Songkhla National Museum, Sukhothai Historical Park, Surin National Museum, Ubon Ratchathani National Museum, U Thong National Museum. Also all the other temples, museums, hotels, restaurants, shops, galleries and sights too numerous to thank individually.

Picture Credits
a = above; b = below/bottom; c = centre; f = far; l = left; r = right; t = top.

The publisher would like to thank the following individuals, companies and picture libraries for kind permission to reproduce their photographs.

4CORNERS IMAGES: SIME/Mehlig Manfred 304 main c.

ALAMY IMAGES: AA World Travel Library 142br; Piti Anchaleesahakorn 138 cb; Roger Arnold 12tr; Asia 425tl; Jack Barker 12bl; Simone van den Berg 424cla; Tibor Bognar 13tr; Ian Buswell 10br; William Casey 138cl; Cassidy Images/Anthony Cassady 11tl; Emilio Ereza 425c; Philip Game 487 br; Henry Westheim Photography 465tl; Zach Holmes 465br; Norma Joseph 138cr; Simon Reddy 110; Royalty Free/Barry Mason 13bl; Fredrik Renander 486 crb; Anders Ryman 466cra; Nat Sumanatemeya 462bl; The Photolibrary Wales 11br, 466bl; Daan Toner 10cl, 106c; Topcris 143cra; Terry Whittaker 490bl; Andrew Woodley 463tc; AMAN RESORTS: 470cl; AMARI HOTEL AND RESORTS: 39tr; ARDEA LONDON: Francois Gohier 211tl; Wardene Weisser 211lb; ASIA ACCESS: Jeffrey Alford 380t; Naomi Duguid 238, 380b; ASIA IMAGES: © 1988 42–43c, 46b; © 1993 Matthew Burns 47cr, 267br, 352, 491crb; © 1995 Matthew Burns 38br; © 1990 Allen W Hopkins 283b, 308tr; © 1991 Allen W Hopkins 464bl; © 1995 Allen W Hopkins 87br; AUSCAPES INTERNATIONAL: Kevin Deacon 349ca; AXIOM: © 1995 Jim Holmes 302c/b.

BAN PHIN (HOUSE OF OPIUM): 233cb, 248b; BANYAN TREE SPAS: 470br; BED SUPPERCLUB 143tl; BFI STILLS POSTERS & DESIGNS: © 1974 Danjaq, LLC and United Artists Corporation Inc. All Rights Reserved 367br; THE BOWERS MUSEUM OF CULTURAL ART: 54cl/clb; ASHLEY J BOYD: 317c, 323c, 341cl/cr, 345b, 348tl/ca/cb/bl/br, 349c/br/bc/bl, 357cr, 359b, 386c/bl; BY PERMISSION OF THE BRITISH LIBRARY: Manuscript Or 14025: 30–31c; BRITISH THAI BOXING COUNCIL: Tony Moore 44tl DEMETRIO CARRASCO: 23br, 32cla, 46tl, 47bl, 284, 300–1;

CHAO PHRAYA EXPRESS BOAT CO.: 497bc; JEAN-LOUP CHARMET 233cra, 264–5c, 265br; CHIVA-SOM INTERNATIONAL HEALTH RESORTS: 471ltr; BRUCE COLEMAN LTD: © Werner Layer 211c; © J Zwaenepoel 211tr; CORBIS: John Van Hasselt 142cla; Kevin R. Morris 462t; Anders Ryman 467tr; Luca Tettoni 114br; JAI/Russell Young 10tc; CPA MEDIA: 393tl; Joe Cummings 295b; Ron Emmons 309c; David Henley 23c, 26tr, 30tr, 38tl, 40bl/br, 41bra/br, 44clb, 51t, 53b, 61br, 63cla, 64tl/cbr, 65t/ca/b, 66tl/ca, 67t, 68b, 75bl, 81cr, 91b, 99t/bra, 120tl/cb, 121ca/br, 125t, 133t/cra/cr/clb/cb/cl/ cbc/crb/bl/ bc/bra/br, 134b, 162tl, 163tl/br, 175t, 206tl/tr/cb/br, 207tl/br, 208tr, 224tl, 225b, 226t/b, 253t, 254t, 275b, 282, 347tl/br/bl, 376c, 377tr, 391c, 392c, 452br, 460cr, 473 inset; John Hobday 28bla, 219cr; Daniel Kestenholz 102ca; Rainer Krack 30tl, 355b, 365cr, 396bl, 423t; 474cr; GERALD CUBITT: 24tc, 28 all except bla, 29 all except crb/bl, 55tl, 81tl, 83t, 105br, 131t, 133cla, 159t/cb, 184tl/tr/ bl, 185t all, 191t, 205b, 207bl, 210t/c/cb, 214b, 219cl/bl, 221t, 223bl, 230tl/cb/b, 231tl/ca/cb, 233bl, 249bl, 254c, 255t, 256bc, 280ca, 286cb, 289t, 297cla, 306ca/cb, 307br, 310–11c, 312, 315b, 323b, 326c, 327, 346t, 349tl, 350tl/ca/ cb/bl/bc, 351tl/tr/c, 354bl, 355t, 356c, 370c/b, 373clb, 381t/cl, 385c, 395b, 453tl, 454bl, 483tl; MICHAEL CUTHBERT: 370t, 371c, 376br.

JAMES DAVIS TRAVEL PHOTOGRAPHY: 159b, 308ca, 344c; JEAN-LEO DUGAST: 30cl.

JOHN EVERINGHAM: 4t, 5t, 26bl, 27tl, 30br, 38cl, 39tc, 40–41c, 41cra/cr/crb/bl, 45cra, 48b, 79bl, 132tl, 220b, 221cr, 240b, 267cb, 309b, 336b, 337t/b, 338bl, 348tr, 351b, 354cl, 358cl, 362tr, 363t, 364cl, 366ca, 460tr.

FEATURE MAGAZINE: 321t, 381br; MICHAEL FREEMAN: 23tl, 26tl, 38tr, 42cla/crac, 49ca, 56–7c, 57tl, 58c/clb, 61t/ca/crb, 63t/bl, 64bl, 69t, 83b, 84b, 85b, 105t, 107b, 120bc, 136b, 136bl, 160ca/cb/br/brb, 161crb/bl, 178t, 179tr, 180tl, 187b, 191b, 200b, 204t, 206ca, 207tr/ca, 208b, 209t/bl/brb, 212, 213b, 225ca, 260–1, 263br, 264c, 265tl, 270b, 310ca, 311c, 330t, 331b, 357tl, 423c, 454c, 457clc; TIM FORSYTH: 207cr, 256bl; FOUR SEASONS HOTELS AND RESORTS: 470tl.

GETTY IMAGES: Chumsak Kanoknan 478tr; The Image Bank/Angelo Cavalli 489tr; image.net 459tc; GRAMMY ENTERTAINMENT PUBLIC COMPANY LTD: 459cl.

ROBERT HARDING PICTURE LIBRARY: 48t, 72cbl, 74c, 82c, 236b, 266tr, 267tl, 289cr/br, 349tr, 460clb; © Alain Evrard 20, 26cb, 47t, 49cb, 116bl; © Robert McCleod 49b; © Luca Tettoni 271t, 278b; © Ken Wilson 181b; CHRISTINE HEMMET: 31bl, 383bra; THE HUTCHISON LIBRARY: 3c, © Robert Francis 496tl; Jeremy Horner 205c.

THE IMAGE BANK: 15tr; © Peter Hendrie 80tr; © Andrea Pistolesi 130.

JEWELRY REALTY LTD, BANGKOK: 310tl, 311tr. DR OY KANCHAVANIT: 357bc; SUTHEP KRITSANAVARIN: 129cl.

FRANK LANE PICTURE AGENCY: © D Fleetham/Silvestris 29cb; © T & P Garner 350br; © David Hosking 168b; © E & D Hosking 184cb, 210b, 363c; © L Lee Rue 29bl; © T Whittaker 286tr; © De Zylva 341bl; LEONARDO MEDIABANK: 396crb; 396cl. MAGNUM: © Marc Riboud 265bl; MANDARIN ORIENTAL: 397cr; STUART MILLER: 371b.

THE NATIONAL MUSEUM (BANGKOK): 54tl, 55cl, tc, 62tl, 62–63c, 79cr, 88tl, tr, cl, 89tcb, cr, crb.

ONASIA: 68–69; Peter Charlesworth 136tr; Vinai Dithajohn 116tl; 488bl; Thierry Falise 119cb; THE ORIENTAL BANG-KOK: 112br.

PATRAVADI THEATRE: 459clb; PHOTOBANK (BANG-KOK): 1, 8–9, 24c, 25t, 26–7c, 27tr/cra, 31tl/cra, 38–9c, 39bl, 40tr/cl, 41t, 42tl/tr/clb/br, 43 all, 46c, 53t, 54ca/cr, 55ca/bla/bra, 56tl,/ca/c, 57ca/cb, 58cla, 59crb, 60clb, 62c/b, 64cla, 66–7c, 67cb, 69cr, 72tr, 75tc, 80b, 88bl, 89tl, 99c/bl/br, 129cra/crb/b, 140cla, 141c, 156–7, 158t/b, 159ca, 160–61c, 161ca, 162ca, 163c, 165b, 170b, 176tl, 182–3, 184cl, 195b, 204cl, 216b, 230ca, 233br, 249br, 255b, 263c, 264b, 294c, 307b, 308tl, 309t, 310b, 317b, 324, 325b, 328c, 330b, 332bl/ br, 346bl/br, 350tr, 359tl, 360b, 365t, 367tl/tr, 372b, 373tl/tr/b, 384c, 422c, 423b, 426tr/bl, 457cra, 458t/cla/br, 462cr, 489clb; PHOTOBANK (SINGAPORE): 22t, 30bl, 39cr, 42bl, 43cra/bra, 44ca, 44–5c, 45tc, 52, 54–5c, 55ca/cbr, 56cbc, 58tl, 59tc/cla, 60cla/cra, 63bca, 64ca/cra, 64–5c, 65cbr, 66cb/bc, 68cr, 73ca/b, 85t, 86b, 92ca, 95t, 106b, 120tr/cl, 121t/cr, 124b, 125b, 161tl/crb, 162l, 162–3c, 164, 178b, 179tl, 180c, 186, 206bl, 206–7c, 208cla, 208–9c, 209tr/ca/cb/bra, 224ca, 225t, 226c, 241t, 253 all except t, 256tr, 257 all, 262clb/bc, 265c, 267bl/bc, 268, 347c, 383bl, 454tr; PHOTO EFFEO: 265tr; PHOTOLI-BRARY: Halaska Jacob 464tc; Montgomery Jock 463br; JTB Photo 467bl; PHOTOSHOT/NHPA: Gerald Cubbitt 465c; PICTOR INTERNATIONAL: 2–3, 4b, 51b, 70–71, 204br, 344b, 353b, 366bl, 368–9; PICTURES COLOUR LIBRARY: 69crb, 247tr, 306b; Picture Finders 139ca; POP-PERFOTO: 115b; PTT PUBLIC COMPANY LIMITED: 496crb.

REUTERS: Ho New 69br; Sukree Sukplang 69cla; RIVER BOOKS (BANGKOK): 31crb, 68cl, 102clb, 161tr. SEACO PICTURE LIBRARY: 479cr, 493t; WWW.SIAMPARAGON. CO.TH: 451tl; SCIENCE PHOTO LIBRARY: CNE, 1988 Distribution Spot Image 14bl; SHERATON GRANDE SUKHUMVIT: 397bl; TONY STONE IMAGES: Glen Allison 48c, 334–5; David Hanson 22b; Hideo Kurihara 108–09; Ed Pritchard 497b; SUPERSTOCK LTD: 126cl, 338t.

THAI AIRWAYS INTERNATIONAL PUBLIC COMPANY LTD: 488t/cr; JIM THOMPSON'S THAI SILK COMPANY: 266cl/cr/b; TOURISM AUTHORITY OF THAILAND: 25cr, 50b, 273cr/bl; TRAVEL INK: Alan Hartley 72ca, 127t, 307t, 308cb, 314b, 326b, Pauline Thornton 21ca, 126bl.

WELLCOME INSTITUTE LIBRARY (LONDON): 233cla.

Front endpaper: All special photography except Asia Access/ Naomi Duguid tlc; Asia Images © 1993 Matthew Burns bl; CRESCENT PRESS AGENCY: Photo David Henley tr; GERALD CUBITT crc; JAMES DAVIS TRAVEL PHOTOGRAPHY blc; MICHAEL FREEMAN tl; PHOTOBANK BANGKOK cr; PHOTOBANK (SINGAPORE) cl, clc, trc. Back endpapers: ALAMY IMAGES: Simon Reddy cr. JACKET - Front: GETTY IMAGES: Paul Photography. Back: AWL IMAGES: Travel Pix Collection tl; DORLING KINDERSLEY: David Henley cla; David Reed bl; Kim Sayer clb. Spine: GETTY IMAGES: Paul Photography t

All other pictures © Dorling Kindersley. See www.dkimages.com for more information.

SPECIAL EDITIONS OF DK TRAVEL GUIDES

Phrase Book

Thai is a tonal language and regarded by most linguists as head of a distinct language group, though it incorporates many Sanskrit words from ancient India, and some of modern English ones, too. There are five tones: mid, high, low, rising, and falling. The particular tone, or pitch, at which each syllable is pronounced determines its meaning. For instance "mâi" (falling tone) means "not," but "măi" (rising

tone) is "silk." The Thai script, meanwhile, is one of the most elaborate in the world, running left to right and using over 80 letters. In the third column of this phrase book is a phonetic transliteration for English speakers, including guidance for tones in the form of accents. This differs from the system used elsewhere in the guide, which follows the Thai Royal Institute's recommended romanization of common names.

GUIDELINES FOR PRONUNCIATION

When reading the phonetics, pronounce syllables as if they form English words. For instance:

a	as in "ago"
e	as in "hen"
i	as in "thin"
o	as in "on"
u	as in "gun"
ah	as in "rather"
ai	as in "Thai"
air	as in "pair"
ao	as in "Mao Zedong"
ay	as in "day"
er	as in "enter"
ew	as in "few"
oh	as in "go"
oo	as in "boot"
OO	as in "book"
oy	as in "toy"
g	as in "give"
ng	as in "sing"

These sounds have no close equivalents in English:

eu	can be likened to a sound of disgust – the sound could be written as "errgh"
bp	a single sound between a "b" and a "p"
dt	a single sound between a "d" and a "t"

Note that when "p," "t," and "k" occur at the end of Thai words, the sound is "swallowed." Also note that many Thais use an "l" instead of an "r" sound.

THE FIVE TONES

Accents indicate the tone of each syllable.

no mark	The **mid tone** is voiced at the speaker's normal, even pitch.
á é í ó ú	The **high tone** is pitched slightly higher than the mid tone.
à è ì ò ù	The **low tone** is pitched slightly lower than the mid tone.
ă ĕ ĭ ŏ ŭ	The **rising tone** sounds like a questioning pitch, starting low and rising.
â ê î ô û	The **falling tone** sounds similar to an English speaker stressing a one-syllable word for emphasis.

MALE AND FEMALE POLITE FORMS

In polite speech, Thai men add the particle "**krúp**" at the end of each sentence; women add "**ká**" at the end of questions and "**kâ**" at the end of statements. These particles have been omitted from all but the most essential polite terms in this phrase book, but they should be used as much as possible. The polite forms of the word "I" are, for men, "**pŏm**" and, for women, "**dee-chún**."

In an Emergency

Help!	ช่วยด้วย	chôo-ay dôo-ay!
Fire!	ไฟไหม้	fai mâi!
Where is the nearest hospital?	แถวนี้มีโรงพยาบาล อยู่ที่ไหน	tăir-o née mee rohng pa-yah-bahn yòo têe-năi?
Call an ambulance!	เรียกรถพยาบาล ให้หน่อย	rêe-uk rót pa-yah-bahn hâi nòy!
Call the police!	เรียกตำรวจให้หน่อย	rêe-uk dtum ròo-ut hâi nòy!
Call a doctor!	เรียกหมอให้หน่อย	rêe-uk mŏr hâi nòy!

Communication Essentials

Yes.	ใช่ or ครับ/ค่ะ	châi or krúp/kâ
No.	ไม่ใช่ or ไม่ครับ/ไม่ค่ะ	mâi châi or mâi krúp/ mâi kâ
May I have ...?	ขอ ...	kŏr ...
Please can you ...?	ช่วย ...	chôo-ay ...
Thank you.	ขอบคุณ	kòrp-kOOn
No, thank you.	ไม่เอา ขอบคุณ	mâi ao kòrp-kOOn
Excuse me/sorry.	ขอโทษ (ครับ/ค่ะ)	kŏr-tôht (krúp/kâ)
Never mind.	ไม่เป็นไร	mâi bpen rai
Hello.	สวัสดี (ครับ/ค่ะ)	sa-wùt dee (krúp/kâ)
Goodbye.	ลาก่อนนะ	lah gòrn ná
Here.	ที่นี่	têe-nêe
There.	ที่โน่น	têe-nûn
What?	อะไร	a-rai?
Why?	ทำไม	tum-mai?
Where?	ที่ไหน	têe năi?
How?	ยังไง	yung ngai?

Useful Phrases

How are you?	คุณสบายดีหรือ (ครับ/คะ)	kOOn sa-bai dee reu (krúp/kâ)?
Very well, thank you – and you?	สบายดี (ครับ/ค่ะ) แล้วคุณล่ะ	sa-bai dee (krúp/kâ) – láir-o kOOn lâ?
What is your name?	คุณชื่ออะไร (ครับ/คะ)	kOOn chêu a-rai (krúp/kâ)?
My name is ...	(ผม/ดิฉัน) ชื่อ ...	(pŏm/dee-chún) chêu ....
Where is/are ...?	... อยู่ที่ไหน	.... yòo têe-năi?
How do I get to ...?	... ไปยังไง	.... bpai yung- ngai?
Do you speak English?	คุณพูดภาษาอังกฤษ เป็นไหม	kOOn pôot pah-săh ung-grìt bpen mái?
I understand.	เข้าใจ	kâo-jai
I don't understand.	ไม่เข้าใจ	mâi kâo-jai
Could you speak slowly?	ช่วยพูดช้าๆหน่อย ได้ไหม	chôo-ay pôot cháh cháh nòy dâi mái?
I can't speak Thai.	พูดภาษาไทย ไม่เป็น	pôot pah-săh tai mâi bpen
I don't know.	ไม่ทราบ or ไม่รู้	mâi sâhp or mâi róo

Useful Words

wife	ภรรยา	pun-ra-yah
husband	สามี	săh-mee
daughter(s)	ลูกสาว	lôok săo
son(s)	ลูกชาย	lôok chai
woman/women	ผู้หญิง	pôo-yĭng
man/men	ผู้ชาย	pôo-chai
child/children	เด็ก	dèk
big	ใหญ่	yài
small	เล็ก	lék
hot	ร้อน	rórn
cold	เย็น or หนาว	yen or năo
good	ดี	dee
bad	ไม่ดี	mâi dee
enough	พอ	por
well	สบายดี	sa-bai dee
open	เปิด	bpèrt
closed	ปิด	bpìt
left	ซ้าย	sái
right	ขวา	kwăh
straight ahead	อยู่ตรงหน้า	yòo dtrong nâh
between	ระหว่าง	ra-wàhng
on the corner of	ตรงหัวมุม	dtrong hŏo-a mOOm
near	ใกล้	glâi
far	ไกล	glai
up	ขึ้น	kêun
down	ลง	long
early	เช้า	cháo
late	ช้า or สาย	cháh or săi
entrance	ทางเข้า	tahng kâo
exit	ทางออก	tahng òrk
toilet	ห้องน้ำ	hôrng náhm
free/no charge	ฟรี	free

Telephoning

Where is the nearest public telephone?	แถวนี้มีโทรศัพท์อยู่ที่ไหน	tăir-o née mee toh-ra-sùp yòo têe-năi?
Can I call abroad from here?	จะโทรศัพท์ไปต่างประเทศจากที่นี่ได้ไหม	ja toh bpai dtàhng bpra-tâyt jàhk têe nêe dâi mái?
I'd like to reverse the charges.	ขอให้เก็บเงินปลายทาง	kŏr hâi gèp ngern bplai tahng
Hello, this is … speaking.	ฮันโล (ผม/ดิฉัน) … พูด (ครับ/ค่ะ)	hello (pŏm/dee-chún) … pôot (krúp/kâ)
I would like to speak to …	ขอพูดกับคุณ … หน่อย (ครับ/ค่ะ)	kŏr pôot gùp khun … nòy (krúp/kâ)
May I leave a message?	ขอฝากสั่งอะไรหน่อยได้ไหม	kŏr fàhk sùng a-rai nòy dâi mái?
Could you speak up a little, please?	ช่วยพูดดังๆหน่อยได้ไหม	chôo-ay pôot dung nòy dâi mái?
Hold on.	รอสักครู่	ror sùk krôo
I'll call back later.	เดี๋ยวจะโทรมาใหม่	dĕe-o ja toh mah mài
local call	โทรศัพท์ภายในท้องถิ่น	toh-ra-sùp pai nai tórng tìn
phone booth/kiosk	ตู้โทรศัพท์	dtôo toh-ra-sùp
phone card	บัตรโทรศัพท์	but toh-ra-sùp

Shopping

How much does this cost?	นี่ราคาเท่าไร	nêe rah-kah tâo-rài?
I would like …	ต้องการ …	dtôrng-gahn …
Do you have …?	มี … ไหม	mee … mái?
I am just looking.	ชมดูเท่านั้น	chom doo tâo-nún
Do you take credit cards/travelers' checks?	รับบัตรเครดิต/เช็คเดินทางไหม	rub but cray-dit/ chék dern tang mái?
What time do you open/close?	เปิด/ปิดกี่โมง	bpèrt/bpìt gèe mohng?
Can you ship this overseas?	ส่งของนี้ไปต่างประเทศได้ไหม	sòng kŏhng nee bpai dtàhng bpra-tâyt dâi mái?
Does it come in other colors?	มีสีอื่นอีกไหม	mee sĕe èun èek mái?
black	สีดำ	sĕe dum
blue	สีน้ำเงิน	sĕe núm ngern
green	สีเขียว	sĕe kĕe-o
red	สีแดง	sĕe dairng
white	สีขาว	sĕe kăo
yellow	สีเหลือง	sĕe lĕu-ung
cheap	ถูก	tòok
expensive	แพง	pairng
gold	ทอง	torng
hill-tribe handicrafts	หัตถกรรมชาวเขา	hùt-ta-gum chao kăo
ladies' wear	เสื้อผ้าสตรี	sêu-pâh sa-dtree
silver	เงิน	ngern
Thai silk	ผ้าไหมไทย	pâh-măi tai
bookstore	ร้านขายหนังสือ	ráhn kăi núng-sĕu
department store	ห้าง	hâhng
market	ตลาด	dta-làht
newsstand	ร้านขายหนังสือพิมพ์	ráhn kăi núng-sĕu pim
pharmacy	ร้านขายยา	ráhn kăi yah
shoe shop	ร้านขายรองเท้า	ráhn kăi rorng táo
supermarket	ซุปเปอร์มาเก็ต	sOOp-bpèr-mah-gèt
tailor	ร้านตัดเสื้อ	ráhn dtùt sêu-a

Sightseeing

travel agent	บริษัทนำเที่ยว	bor-ri-sùt num têe-o
tourist office	สำนักงานการท่องเที่ยว	sŭm-núk ngahn gahn tôrng têe-o
tourist police	ตำรวจท่องเที่ยว	dtum-ròo-ut tôrng têe-o
closed on public holidays	ปิดวันหยุดราชการ	bpìt wun yOOt râht-cha-gahn
beach	หาด or ชายหาด	hàht or chai-hàht
cave	ถ้ำ	thûm
cliff	หน้าผา	nâh păh
coral	หินปะการัง	hĭn bpa-gah-rung
elephant camp	ค่ายช้าง	kâi cháhng
festival	งานออกร้าน	ngahn òrk ráhn
hill/mountain	เขา	kăo
hill-tribe village	หมู่บ้านชาวเขา	mòo bâhn chao kăo
historical park	อุทยานประวัติศาสตร์	ÒO-ta-yahn bpra wùt sàht
island (ko)	เกาะ	gòr

lake	ทะเลสาบ	ta-lay sàhp
temple (wat)	วัด	wút
museum	พิพิธภัณฑ์	pí-pít-ta-pun
national park	อุทยานแห่งชาติ	ÒO-ta yahn hàirng cháht
old town	เมืองเก่า	meu-ung gòw
palace	วัง	wang
park/garden	สวน	sŏo-un
river	แม่น้ำ	mâir náhm
ruins	โบราณสถาน	boh-rahn sa-tǎhn
Thai boxing	มวยไทย	moo-ay tai
Thai massage	นวด	nôo-ut
trekking	การเดินทางเท้า	gahn dern tahng táo
waterfall	น้ำตก	náhm dtòk
zoo	สวนสัตว์	sŏo-un sàt

Transportation

When does the train for … leave?	รถไฟไป … ออกเมื่อไร	rót fai bpai … òrk meu-rài?
How long does it take to get to …?	ใช้เวลานาน เท่าไรไปถึงที่ …	chái way-lah nahn tâo-rài bpai těung têe …?
A ticket to … please.	ขอตั๋วไป … หน่อย (ครับ/ค่ะ)	kŏr dtŏo-a bpai … nòy (krúp/kâ)
Do I have to change?	ต้องเปลี่ยนรถ หรือเปล่า	dtôrng bplèe-un rót réu bplào?
I'd like to reserve a seat, please.	ขอจองที่นั่ง	kŏr jorng têe nûng
Which platform for the … train?	รถไฟไป … อยู่ ชานชาลาไหน	rót fai bpai … yòo chahn cha-lah nǎi?
What station is this?	ที่นี่สถานีอะไร	têe nêe sa-tǎhn-nee a-rai?
Where is the bus stop?	ป้ายรถเมล์อยู่ที่ไหน	bpâi rót may yòo têe-nǎi?
Where is the bus station?	สถานีรถเมล์อยู่ที่ไหน	sa-tǎhn-nee rót may yòo têe-nǎi?
Which buses go to …?	รถเมล์สายไหนไป …	rót may sǎi nǎi bpai …?
What time does the bus for … leave?	รถเมล์ไป … ออกกี่โมง	rót may bpai … òrk gèe mohng?
Would you tell me when we get to …?	ถึง … แล้ว ช่วยบอกด้วย	těung … láir-o chôo-ay bòrk dôo-ay?
Do you know … Road?	รู้จักถนน … ไหม	róo-jùk ta-nǒn … mái?
Is it far?	ไกลไหม	glai mái?
Turn left.	เลี้ยวซ้าย	lée-o sái
Turn right.	เลี้ยวขวา	lée-o kwǎh
Go straight.	เลยไปอีก	ler-ee bpai èek
Park over there.	จอดที่โน่น	jòrt têe-nôhn
Park right here.	จอดตรงนี้	jòrt dtrong née
air-conditioned bus	รถปรับอากาศ	rót bprùp ah-gàht
arrivals	ถึง	těung
booking office	ที่จองตั๋ว	têe jorng dtŏo-a
bus station	สถานีรถเมล์	sa-tǎhn-nee rót may
departures	ออก	òrk
baggage room	ที่ฝากของ	têe fàhk kŏrng
ordinary bus	รถธรรมดา	rót tum-ma-dah
tour bus	รถทัวร์	rót too-a

ticket	ตั๋ว	dtŏo-a
ferry	เรือข้ามฟาก	reu-a kâhm fâhk
train	รถไฟ	rót fai
railroad station	สถานีรถไฟ	sa-tǎhn-nee rót fai
moped	รถมอเตอร์ไซค์	rót mor-dter-sai
bicycle	รถจักรยานต์	rót jùk-gra-yahn
taxi	แท็กซี่	táirk-sêe
airport	สนามบิน	sa-nǎhm bin

Bargaining

How much is this?	นี่ราคาเท่าไร	nêe rah-kah tâo-rai?
How much to go to …?	ไป … เท่าไร	bpai … tâo-rài?
That's a little expensive.	แพงไปหน่อย	pairng bpai nòy
Could you lower the price a bit?	ลดราคาหน่อยได้ไหม	lót rah-kah nòy dâi mái?
How about … baht?	… บาทได้ไหม	… bàht dâi mái?
Will you go for … baht?	… บาทไปไหม	… bàht bpai mái?
I'll settle for … baht.	… บาทแล้วกัน	… bàht gôr láir-o gun

Staying in a Hotel

Do you have a vacant room?	มีห้องว่างไหม	mee hôrng wâhng mái?
double/twin room	ห้องคู่	hôrng kôo
single room	ห้องเดี่ยว	hôrng dèe-o
air-conditioned room	ห้องแอร์	hôrng air
I have a reservation.	จองห้องไว้แล้ว	jorng hôrng wái láir-o
I'd like a room for one night/three nights.	(ผม/ดิฉัน) จะพักอยู่ คืนหนึ่ง/สามคืน	(pŏm/dee-chún) ja púk yòo keun nèung / sǎhm keun
What is the charge per night?	ค่าห้องวันละเท่าไร	kâh hôrng wun la tâo-rài?
I don't know yet how long I'll stay.	ไม่ทราบว่าจะอยู่นาน เท่าไร	mâi sâhp wâh ja yòo nahn tâo-rài
May I see the room first please?	ขอดูห้องก่อนได้ไหม	kŏr doo hôrng gòrn dâi mái?
May I leave some things in the safe?	ขอฝากของไว้ในตู้เซฟ ได้ไหม	kŏr fàhk kŏrng wái nai dtôo sáyf dâi mái?
Will you spray some mosquito repellent, please?	ช่วยฉีดยากันยุงให้ หน่อยได้ไหม	chôo-ay chèet yah gun yOOng hâi nòy dâi mái?
air conditioner	เครื่องปรับอากาศ	krêu-ung bprùp ah-gàht
bedroom	ห้องนอน	hôrng norn
bill	บิล	bin
fan	พัดลม	pùt lom
hotel	โรงแรม	rohng-rairm
key	กุญแจ	gOOn-jair
manager	ผู้จัดการ	pôo-jùt-gahn
mosquito screen	มุ้งลวด	mÓOng lôo-ut
shower	ฝักบัว	fùk boo-a
swimming pool	สระว่ายน้ำ	sà wâi náhm
toilet/bathroom	ห้องน้ำ	hôrng náhm

Eating Out

A table for two please.	ขอโต๊ะสำหรับสองคน	kŏr dtó sŭm-rùp sŏrng kon
May I see the menu?	ขอดูเมนูหน่อย	kŏr doo may-noo nòy
Do you have ...?	มี ... ไหม	mee ... mái?
I'd like ...	ขอ	kŏr ...
Not too spicy, ok?	ไม่เอาเผ็ดมากนะ	mâi ao pèt mâhk na
Is it spicy?	เผ็ดไหม	pèt mái?
I can eat Thai food.	ทานอาหารไทยเป็น	tahn ah-hăhn tai bpen
May I have a glass of water, please.	ขอน้ำเข็งเปล่า แก้วหนึ่ง	kŏr núm kăirng bplào gâir-o nèung
I didn't order this.	นี่ผมไม่ได้สั่ง (ครับ/คะ)	nêe mâi dâi sùng (krúp/kâ)
Waiter/waitress!	คุณ (ครับ/คะ)	kOOn (krúp/kâ)
That was an excellent meal.	อร่อยมาก (ครับ/ค่ะ)	a-ròy mâhk (krúp/kâ)
The check, please.	ขอบิลหน่อย (ครับ/ค่ะ)	kŏr bin nòy (krúp/kâ)
ashtray	ที่เขี่ยบุหรี่	têe-kèe-a bOO-rèe
bamboo shoots	หน่อไม้	nòr mái
banana	กล้วย	glôo-ay
beef	เนื้อวัว	néu-a woo-a
beer	เบียร์	bee-a
boiled	ต้ม	dtôm
bottle	ขวด	kòo-ut
bowl	ชาม	chahm
char-grilled	ย่าง	yâhng
chicken	ไก่	gài
chili	พริก	prík
chili paste	น้ำพริก	núm prík
chopsticks	ตะเกียบ	dta-gèe-up
coconut	มะพร้าว	ma-práo
coffee	กาแฟ	gah-fair
crab	ปู	bpoo
crispy noodles	หมี่กรอบ	mèe gròrp
custard apple	น้อยหน่า	nóy-nàh
deep fried	ทอด	tôrt
drink(s)	เครื่องดื่ม	krêu-ung dèum
dry noodles	ก๋วยเตี๋ยวแห้ง	gŏo-ay dtĕe-o hâirng
duck	เป็ด	bpèt
durian	ทุเรียน	tÓO-ree-un
egg	ไข่	kài
egg noodles	บะหมี่	ba-mèe
fish	ปลา	bplah
fish sauce	น้ำปลา	núm bplah
fork	ส้อม	sôrm
fruit	ผลไม้	pŏn-la-mái
fruit juice	น้ำผลไม้	núm pŏn-la-mái
ginger	ขิง	kĭng
glass	แก้ว	gâir-o
iced coffee	กาแฟเย็น	ga-fair yen
iced water	น้ำเข็งเปล่า	núm kăirng bplào
jackfruit	ขนุน	ka-nÓOn
mango	มะม่วง	ma-môo-ung
Mekong whisky	แม่โขง	mâir-kŏhng
menu	เมนู	may-noo
morning glory	ผักบุ้ง	pùk bÔOng
mushroom	เห็ด	hèt
noodle soup	ก๋วยเตี๋ยวน้ำ	gŏo-ay dtĕe-o náhm
oven-cooked	อบ	òp
papaya	มะละกอ	ma-la-gor
pineapple	สับปะรด	sùp-bpa-rót
plate	จาน	jahn
pomelo	ส้มโอ	sôm oh
pork	เนื้อหมู	néu-a mŏo
rambutan	เงาะ	ngór
restaurant	ร้านอาหาร	ráhn ah-hăhn
rice	ข้าว	kâo
rice noodles	ก๋วยเตี๋ยว	gŏo-ay dtĕe-o
shrimp	กุ้ง	gÔOng
soy sauce	อาหารว่าง	ah-hăhn wâhng
snack	น้ำซีอิ๊ว	núm see éw
spoon	ช้อน	chórn
spring greens	ผักคะน้า	pùk ka-náh
squid	ปลาหมึก	bplah-mèuk
sticky rice	ข้าวเหนียว	kâo-nĕe-o
stir-fried	ผัด	pùt
sweet corn	ข้าวโพด	kâo pôht
tea	น้ำชา	núm chah
vegetables	ผัก	pùk
vinegar	น้ำส้ม	núm sôm
waiter	คนเสริฟ	kon sèrp
waitress	คนเสริฟหญิง	kon sèrp yĭng
water	น้ำ	náhm

Health

I do not feel well.	รู้สึกไม่สบาย	róo-sèuk mâi sa-bai
I have a pain in ...	เจ็บที่	jèp têe ...
It hurts here.	เจ็บตรงนี้	jèp dtrong née
It hurts all the time.	เจ็บตลอดเวลา	jèp dta-lòrt way-lah
It hurts only now and then.	เจ็บเป็นบางครั้ง บางคราว	jèp bpen bahng krúng bahng krao
I have a fever.	ตัวร้อนเป็นไข้	dtoo-a rórn bpen kâi
I'm allergic to ...	(ผม/ดิฉัน) แพ้ ...	(pŏm/dee-chún) páir ...
How many tablets do I take?	ต้องกินยากี่เม็ด ต่อครั้ง	dtôrng gin yah gèe mét dtòr krúng
accident	อุบัติเหตุ	OO-bùt-dti-hàyt
acupuncture	ฝังเข็ม	fŭng kĕm
ambulance	รถพยาบาล	rót pa-yah-bahn
aspirin	แอสไพริน or ยาแก้ไข้	air-sa-bprin or yah-gâir-kâi
asthma	โรคหืด	rôhk hèut
bite (by dog)	หมากัด	măh gùt
bite (by insect)	แมลงกัด	ma-lairng gùt
blood	เลือด	lêu-ut
burn	ไหม้	mâi
cholera	อหิวาต์	a-hi-wah
cough	ไอ	ai
dentist	ทันตแพทย์ or หมอฟัน	tun-dta-pâirt or mŏr fun
diabetes	โรคเบาหวาน	rôhk bao wăhn
diarrhea	ท้องเสีย	tórng sĕe-a
dizzy	เวียนหัว	wee-un hŏo-a
doctor	หมอ	mŏr
dysentery	โรคบิด	rôhk bìt

English	Thai	Romanization
earache	ปวดหู	bpòo-ut hŏo
fever	ไข้	kâi
filling	อุดฟัน	òOt fun
hayfever	ไข้จาม	kâi jahm
headache	ปวดหัว	bpòo-ut hŏo-a
heart attack	หัวใจวาย	hŏo-a jai wai
hepatitis	ตับอักเสบ	dtùp ùk-sàyp
hospital	โรงพยาบาล	rohng pa-yah-bahn
injection	ฉีดยา	chèet yah
malaria	มาเลเวีย	mah-lay-ree-a
medicine	ยา	yah
penicillin	ยาเพนนิซิลลิน	yah pen-ní-seen-lin
prescription	ใบสั่งยา	bai sùng yah
prickly heat	ผด	pòt
rabies	โรคสุนัขบ้า	rôhk sÒO-nùk bâh
sore throat	เจ็บคอ	jèp kor
stomach ache	ปวดท้อง	bpòo-ut tórng
temperature	ตัวร้อน	dtoo-ah rórn
toothache	ปวดฟัน	boo-ut fun
traditional medicine	ยาแผนโบราณ	yah păirn boh-rahn
vomit	อาเจียน	ah-jee-un

Numbers

0	๐ or ศูนย์	sŏon
1	๑ or หนึ่ง	nèung
2	๒ or สอง	sŏrng
3	๓ or สาม	sähm
4	๔ or สี่	sèe
5	๕ or ห้า	hâh
6	๖ or หก	hòk
7	๗ or เจ็ด	jèt
8	๘ or แปด	bpàirt
9	๙ or เก้า	gâo
10	๑๐ or สิบ	sìp
11	๑๑ or สิบเอ็ด	sìp-èt
12	๑๒ or สิบสอง	sìp-sŏrng
13	๑๓ or สิบสาม	sìp-sähm
14	๑๔ or สิบสี่	sìp-sèe
15	๑๕ or สิบห้า	sìp-hâh
16	๑๖ or สิบหก	sìp-hòk
17	๑๗ or สิบเจ็ด	sìp-jèt
18	๑๘ or สิบแปด	sìp-bpàirt
19	๑๙ or สิบเก้า	sìp-gâo
20	๒๐ or ยี่สิบ	yêe-sìp
21	๒๑ or ยี่สิบเอ็ด	yêe-sìp-èt
22	๒๒ or ยี่สิบสอง	yêe-sìp-sŏrng
30	๓๐ or สามสิบ	sähm-sìp
40	๔๐ or สี่สิบ	sèe-sìp
50	๕๐ or ห้าสิบ	hâh-sìp
60	๖๐ or หกสิบ	hòk-sìp
70	๗๐ or เจ็ดสิบ	jèt-sìp
80	๘๐ or แปดสิบ	bpàirt-sìp
90	๙๐ or เก้าสิบ	gâo-sìp
100	๑๐๐ or หนึ่งร้อย	nèung róy
101	๑๐๑ or ร้อยเอ็ด	róy-èt
200	๒๐๐ or สองร้อย	sŏrng róy
1,000	๑๐๐๐ or หนึ่งพัน	nèung pun
1,001	๑๐๐๑ or หนึ่งพันหนึ่ง	nèung pun nèung
10,000	๑๐,๐๐๐ or หนึ่งหมื่น	nèung mèun
100,000	๑๐๐,๐๐๐ or หนึ่งแสน	nèung säirn

Time and Seasons

one minute	หนึ่งนาที	nèung nah-tee
one hour	หนึ่งชั่วโมง	nèung chôo-a mohng
half an hour	ครึ่งชั่วโมง	krêung chôo-a mohng
quarter of an hour	สิบห้านาที	sìp-hâh nah-tee
midnight	เที่ยงคืน	têe-ung keun
1am	ตีหนึ่ง	dtee nèung
2am	ตีสอง	dtee sŏrng
3am	ตีสาม	dtee sähm
4am	ตีสี่	dtee sèe
5am	ตีห้า	dtee hâh
6am	หกโมงเช้า	hòk mohng cháo
7am	เจ็ดโมงเช้า or โมงเช้า	jèt mohng cháo or mohng cháo
8am	สองโมงเช้า	sŏrng mohng cháo
9am	สามโมงเช้า	sähm mohng cháo
10am	สี่โมงเช้า	sèe mohng cháo
11am	ห้าโมงเช้า	hâh mohng cháo
noon	เที่ยงวัน	têe-ung wun
1pm	บ่ายโมง	bài mohng
2pm	บ่ายสองโมง	bài sŏrng mohng
3pm	บ่ายสามโมง	bài sähm mohng
4pm	บ่ายสี่โมง	bài sèe mohng
5pm	ห้าโมงเย็น	hâh mohng yen
6pm	หกโมงเย็น	hòk mohng yen
7pm	ทุ่มหนึ่ง	tÔOm nèung
8pm	สองทุ่ม	sŏrng tÔOm
9pm	สามทุ่ม	sähm tÔOm
10pm	สี่ทุ่ม	sèe tÔOm
11pm	ห้าทุ่ม	hâh tÔOm
half past one (pm)	บ่ายโมงครึ่ง	bài mohng krêung
quarter past one (pm)	บ่ายโมงสิบห้านาที	bài mohng sìp-hâh nah-tee
quarter to two (pm)	อีกสิบห้านาทีบ่ายสองโมง	èek sìp-hâh nah-tee bài sŏrng mohng
a day	หนึ่งวัน	neung wun
a weekend	สุดสัปดาห์	sÒOt sùp-dah
a week	หนึ่งอาทิตย์	nèung ah-tít
a month	หนึ่งเดือน	nèung deu-un
a year	หนึ่งปี	nèung bpee
Monday	วันจันทร์	wun jun
Tuesday	วันอังคาร	wun ung-kahn
Wednesday	วันพุธ	wun pÓOt
Thursday	วันพฤหัส	wun pa-réu-hùt
Friday	วันศุกร์	wun sÒOk
Saturday	วันเสาร์	wun säo
Sunday	วันอาทิตย์	wun ah-tít
cool season	หน้าหนาว	nâh näo
hot season	หน้าร้อน	nâh rórn
rainy season	หน้าฝน	nâh fön
vacation	วันหยุด	wun yÒOt
public holiday	วันหยุดประจำปี	wun yÒOt bpra-jum-bpee
Christmas	คริสต์มาส	krít-sa-maht
New Year	ปีใหม่	bpee mài
Thai New Year	สงกรานต์	sŏng-grahn
Chinese New Year	ตรุษจีน	dtrÒOt jeen

Bangkok City Center

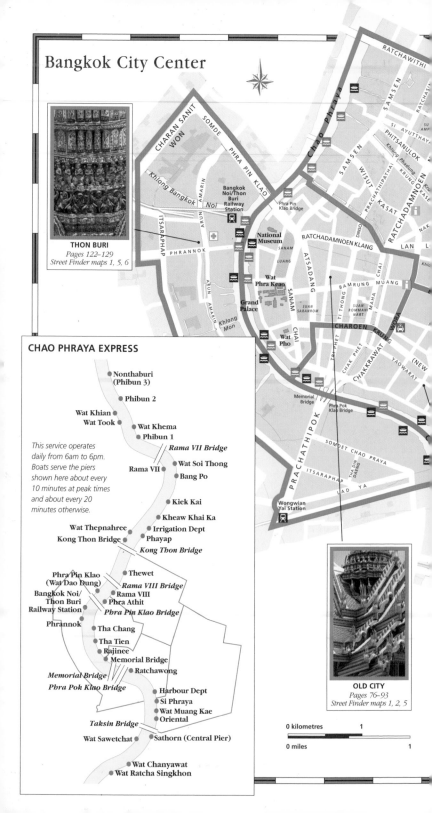

THON BURI
Pages 122–129
Street Finder maps 1, 5, 6

RATCHAWITHI

Chao Phraya

SAMSEN

SI AYUTTHAYA

SU
AMP

PHITSANULOK

Khlong Phadung Kru

KRUNG KASE

PRACHATHIPATHAI

WISUT KASAT

SAMSEN

CHARAN SANIT
WON

SOMDE
PHRA PIN KLAO

Khlong Bangkok

Noi

AMARIN

ARUN

ITSARAPHAP

PHRANNOK

Bangkok
Noi/Thon
Buri
Railway
Station

Phra Pin
Klao Bridge

National
Museum

SANAM
LUANG

RATCHADAMNOEN KLANG

ATSADANG

RATCHADAMNOEN

LAN

NAK

L

Khic

BAMRUNG MUANG

ARUN
AMARIN

Wat
Phra Keao

Grand
Palace

SUAN
SARANROM

SANAM
CHAI

SUAN
ROMMANI
NART

TI THONG

MAHA
CHAI

CHAROEN KRUNG

YORA

Khlong
Mon

Wat
Pho

CHAI

TRI PHET

CHAK PHET

CHAKKRAWAT

YAOWARAT

(NEW

Memorial
Bridge

Phra Pok
Klao Bridge

PRACHATHIPOK

SOMDET CHAO PHRAYA

ITSARAPHAP

THA DIN
DAENG

LAD YA

Wongwian
Yai Station

CHAO PHRAYA EXPRESS

- Nonthaburi (Phibun 3)
- Phibun 2
- Wat Khian
- Wat Took
  - Wat Khema
  - Phibun 1
  - *Rama VII Bridge*

*This service operates
daily from 6am to 6pm.
Boats serve the piers
shown here about every
10 minutes at peak times
and about every 20
minutes otherwise.*

- Wat Soi Thong
- Rama VII
- Bang Po
- Kiek Kai
- Kheaw Khai Ka
- Wat Thepnahree
- Irrigation Dept
- Kong Thon Bridge
- Phayap
- *Kong Thon Bridge*
- Thewet
- Phra Pin Klao (Wat Dao Dung)
- *Rama VIII Bridge*
- Bangkok Noi/ Thon Buri Railway Station
- Rama VIII
- Phra Athit
- *Phra Pin Klao Bridge*
- Phrannok
- Tha Chang
- Tha Tien
- Rajinee
- Memorial Bridge
- *Memorial Bridge*
- Ratchawong
- *Phra Pok Klao Bridge*
- Harbour Dept
- Si Phraya
- Wat Muang Kae
- Oriental
- *Taksin Bridge*
- Wat Sawetchat
- Sathorn (Central Pier)
- Wat Chanyawat
- Wat Ratcha Singkhon

OLD CITY
Pages 76–93
Street Finder maps 1, 2, 5

0 kilometres   1

0 miles   1